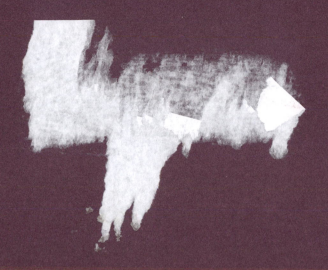

HISTORY
OF FURNITURE
A GLOBAL VIEW

MARK HINCHMAN

UNIVERSITY OF NEBRASKA, LINCOLN

FAIRCHILD BOOKS

NEW YORK

Executive Editor: Olga T. Kontzias
Acquisitions Editor: Joseph Miranda
Senior Development Editor: Jennifer Crane
Development Editor: Michelle Levy
Production Director: Ginger Hillman
Associate Production Editor: Andrew Fargnoli
Associate Art Director: Erin Fitzsimmons
Photo Research: Matthew and Ellen Dudley/
Candlepants, Inc., and J. Karsten Moran
Copyeditor: Peter Grennen
Cover Design: Erin Fitzsimmons
Text Design: Fearn de Vicq
Illustrations: Steve Stankiewicz

Library of Congress Catalog Card Number:
2008931459
ISBN: 978-1-56367-544-7
GST R 133004424
Printed in China
TP15

CONTENTS

EXTENDED TABLE OF CONTENTS

PREFACE

A road makes for a powerful visual metaphor, beloved by artists, writers, and commencement speakers. The journey down a road centers on a perambulating individual, following a path, and with a corresponding progression of time and place. It might seem odd to start a book on furniture, design, and designed objects with a discussion of a road that runs parallel to a river, although a road, too, is a designed object.

A river is nature's pathway, cutting through the landscape in the journey from Point A to Point B, and they existed long before humans created their own roadways. A consistent quality of rivers is that they rarely run a straight course. For precisely that reason, a meandering river can be a metaphor for the history of design that played out over millennia. Rivers run fast, they run dry, they overflow their banks; there are rapids, waterfalls, eddies, shallows and depths; then there are sharp bends, loopy curves, and gentle changes in direction. Life follows a similar course. Consider the river as the billions of people over time, and everything they have done, experienced, and produced. From the stone ages to the twenty-first century (the time period covered by this book), humanity has run a path, sometimes focused, more often disorganized, with exceptions and setbacks, revolutions, evolutions, and stability, the only constant being the relentless march of time forward.

The path is a metaphor for history, the collective journey that humanity has taken through time. It is an apt comparison for the journey through life, through college, or any educational or intellectual endeavor. It therefore also serves as metaphor of what a reader encounters when embarking on the journey of reading this book, over the course of a semester or two.

CHRONOLOGY

This book employs the typical chronological sequence of many history books in the modern Western world, yet tweaks it to include artworks from across the globe, in all chapters.

Chapter 1 starts with caves and the Paleolithic and Neolithic periods. Chapters 2 and 3 present Egypt and Mesopotamia, then Greece and Rome, only from a global perspective, with attention to Nubia and Greek and Roman activities in North Africa and the Middle East. Time marches onward in Chapters, 4, 5, and 6, from Early Christian and Byzantine, to Romanesque and Islamic, and Gothic. Romanesque and Islamic are considered as two sides of a coin, with the Crusades, the religious expeditions of the twelfth and thirteenth centuries, as the mechanism by which Europe incorporated Islamic forms, and the Islamic world incorporated European forms. Chapter 5 can therefore be considered as a look around the world in the year 1100.

Chapters 7, 8, and 9 are a look around the world in the year 1500. Chapter 7 examines some of the pre-Columbian American traditions. The year 1500 is significant because it falls within the period of the Spanish Conquest, when the American indigenous groups were violently incorporated into the Spanish colonial project. The circumstances for the year 1500 are happier in China, covered in Chapter 8. During the Ming dynasty, the development of classic hardwood furniture was at its height. In Europe, Italy was reinventing itself with the help of Renaissance artists, architects, and designers (Chapter 9).

Chapters 9, 10, and 11 present the logical sequence of Renaissance, Baroque, and Rococo, three periods in which artists were reacting to the artistic traditions they inherited. These periods are best understood when studied in succession.

Chapter 12 covers the same time period as the previous chapters, only it examines the artistic production of the British Isles. Chapter 13 looks at the phenomenon of colonialism around the world, including English colonialism, and therefore the United States.

One of the ways that design histories differ from art and architectural histories is that the time period from the eighteenth century to the present is more relevant, and therefore requires more scholarly attention. "Relevant" here means that unlike architecture and art, eighteenth- and nineteenth-century furniture types are still in production, and still being specified. Antiques from those periods are not all in museums, but in people's homes and sold in auction

houses. Chapters 14 through 20 address the nineteenth century and its various design permutations, starting with Neoclassicism and ending with the movements that foreshadowed modernism.

Chapter 21 tackles twentieth-century modernism—not modernism as defined by the field of architectural history, but as it relates to design. Chapters 22 and 23 also constitute a look around the world in the twentieth century.

Regarding dates, the standard scenario is that the years of a person's life follow their name, e.g., Emile Jacques Ruhlmann (1879–1933). There are a few variations on the schema: Zaha Hadid (b. 1950) gives the date of birth for a living person; George Hepplewhite (d. 1786) gives the year of death for a person whose birth year is unknown; Ahuitzotl (r. 1486–1503) gives the years of a ruler's reign. Many cultures only recorded their rulers' reigning years.

OBJECTS OF SCRUTINY

On this journey down the path called history, what do we pick up and marvel at, and what do we leave lying in the gravel, buried in the sandbank, unexamined? This book mostly covers what previously was known as the history of interiors and decorative arts, fleshed-out with pertinent examples of art and architecture. A debt is owed to many books with a traditional focus on interiors and furnishings, from which much of the information here was drawn.

Histories of art and architecture are valuable references. In significant ways, the historians who worked in those arenas set the parameters for how furniture should be covered (Renaissance is followed by Baroque, and so forth). For a long time, those who wrote about the objects that constitute the decorative arts—dishes, vases, candelabra, miniature portraits, salt-and-pepper shakers, beer steins, howdahs, hookahs, spittoons, braziers, commodes, mirrors, brooches and cigarette cases—grudgingly accepted their second-class status, behind their up-scale cousins, art and architectural historians.

Generalizing about how design history is taught, the emphasis is now on context. The practice of examining history with the framework of period styles has been largely (although not completely) abandoned by art history. There has been a general move away from object analysis and individual designers' biographies to an examination of social context. The shift to a focus on the consumer has had many implications.

Recently, the academic side of interior design became a bridge between disciplines. Most historians of design see their field as related to art and architectural history, and the history of decorative arts. The infusion of the field with interdisciplinary spirit has brought new perspectives to design historians. These come from material culture, crafts, archaeology, anthropology, and others. This opening allowed for new approaches, including feminist analysis.

The 1960s saw a shift in the political realm that can be called the politics of inclusion, including the women's rights movement, the civil rights movement, and de-colonization. Under gender came women's studies, and an examination of the intersection of space and sexuality. The design world quickly responded to these changes and this resulted in a shift in how the history of design is taught.

After the epoch of the *ancien régime* (eighteenth-century France), historians of design typically see their field as related to minimal state intervention, a move from seeing objects as instruments of state power to instruments of empowerment or even resistance. These new approaches often result in high-minded discussions rooted in everyday mundane objects. The objects one is surrounded by, and the personal articulation of interior space, can relate to concepts, or constructions, or identity. And the construction of identity can be construed as a member of an ethnic group, a gender, a nation, a family, or an individual. This led to the conclusion that per-

sonal choice, regarding the material world, can become a site of protest. Design, rather than being the instrument of political power, as it was in the reign of Louis XIV, could become a field that mediates between politics and citizen. Design could support or resist the status quo, and become the avant-garde. Looking at any American teenager's bedroom makes clear that personal design choice can be a sign of allegiance and a site of resistance.

The relevance of historical study to studio education remains open for debate. In periods directly concerned about history, including neo-classicism, nineteenth-century revivals, and more recently, post-modernism, the value of history to contemporary design was obvious. This was often accompanied by a renewed appreciation of hand-drawing and rendering techniques. In artistic movements related to modernism, the importance of history was less clear because the individuals involved sought to deny history's importance.

The institutional base for the design professions started in the eighteenth century with the importance of guilds, and the development of professional organizations and educational programs in the nineteenth century.

Recognition of the importance of designed objects, foremost furniture, started to change in the second half of the nineteenth century, when a trio of movements corralled the efforts of some well-meaning object crusaders. This group argued that the objects of daily life were worthy of design attention, and therefore also scholarly attention. Members of this group became active in the artistic movement Arts and Crafts, and also Art Nouveau, and the Vienna Secession (Chapters 16, 19, and 20).

Come the 1910s and 1920s, Bauhaus designers in Germany took on the task of rehabilitating the status of the common object; for them it was a call to arms, absolutely central to their design activities.

Along the way, Africans, Asians, and Native Americans joined the fracas, stating that the division between fine art and craftwork had never done justice to the objects they produced, and they were therefore all too happy to toss the concept of "fine art" aside.

In the mid-twentieth century, Raymond Loewy was one of the innovators of the field now known as industrial design. He expanded the repertoire of what could be considered a designed object to include cigarette packages, buses, and rockets. He had little use for the category of the decorative arts, and instead promoted a paradigm shift. Industrial design was a better category, to Loewy's mind, as it took the non-elitist approach that began with Arts and Crafts, and gave it an American commercial application. Loewy's definition of designed objects included those made by people involved in traditional craftsmanship—artisans, potters, and basketmakers. But he was mostly concerned with commercial products produced by industrial processes.

Marcel Duchamp ran with this idea, took it in a different direction, and in his inimitable way, created (or found) a class of objects that he termed ready-made art. He attached a bicycle wheel to a stool, called it a sculpture, and people have been scratching their heads ever since.

This ever-increasing list of what can be considered a designed object might lead one to think that anything is worthy of inclusion here, such as landscapes and the human body. Not so (for the most part). What is consistent is a steady focus on design. Pencils and toothbrushes are wonderful examples of designed objects whose utility has stood the test of time, but they have no place here. Cars are designed objects with a clear aesthetic bent. But that is a history better left for another place. Almost any object in the right context can pique the interest of archeologists and anthropologists, but we focus here on the items that have made a contribution to the history of interior design, elite or modest, intentional or accidental.

The core of the book is formed around significant examples of interiors and the objects they contained. The legacy of the decorative arts is obvious, as there are lots of pieces of furniture. When examples from other arts, such as painting, fashion, or graphics, are used, it is usually to make a specific point that is particularly clear in that medium. In the Rococo period, the topic of verisimilitude is addressed by looking at portraits, artworks that directly engage the issue of resemblance.

The book's title is *History of Furniture: A Global View*. Global is meant in two ways: One is the sense of a world-wide look. The other regards context; this book considers furniture as objects operating within a socio-cultural context. Thus, each chapter starts with an examination of architectural and design context, looking at the domestic sphere when possible. Furniture and interiors are considered in terms of their political, economic, historic, cultural, social, and personal meanings.

Speaking of furniture, making the selections for furniture is not a simple process. This book mostly focuses on pieces made from wood and metal, but there were also pieces that could be called furniture that were made from bamboo and ceramics. The category of furniture might seem clear, but actually, categorization poses challenges. When crossing cultural lines, it is not always clear what is furniture and what is not. The boundaries vary, according to the purposes of the discussion. In cultures where tall chairs had a limited or non-existent role, should we instead look at mats and cushions? Isn't the topic, then, how people sit, so shouldn't we look at ways of sitting, even if they do not involve objects? Some of the chapters address these questions.

This book attempts to be fair to all cultures, yet also fit the need of its readers, and be reasonable when it comes to periods, cultures, and styles. Reference books typically have a structure, and readers and students come to rely upon that structure. Yet in a cross-cultural endeavor such as this one, readers should expect that with every chapter, the rules change. Sometimes we know the names of artists, sometimes we do not. Sometimes we look at paintings to reinforce ideas that were also being explored in interiors, but not always. Sometimes precise dating is possible; sometimes the best we can do is guess at a century. This book has a major interest in furniture, yet when that is not a viable topic, the design field is explored through other art forms. The forms to be examined are also dictated by what is available.

With the objects selected here, I have a specific and explicit goal: to include the contributions of women, and of those across the globe who have been overlooked too often in histories such as this one. The exploration of non-Western design is achieved in two ways. There are entire chapters devoted to non-Western design on China, Africa, and pre-Columbian America. Chapters that cover material typically presented from a myopic western perspective, art nouveau, art deco, and modernism, are here presented with examples from all continents. And whenever possible, I include the contributions of women, as designers, patrons, or the subject of artworks. I am telling the "master narrative" of design on the one hand; Egypt, Greece, and Rome are all here, yet I am also trying to overturn it by including those who have been ill served by standard histories.

There is no attempt to judge one time period or group as more advanced or artistically gifted than another. Chinese furniture, Chicago skyscrapers, Cambodian sculptures, Italian paintings, and African masks are all superior achievements. For certain times and places, the circumstances do not arise that allow for certain arts to flower: nomadic groups have little need or desire to create monumental architecture. Hence the Tuaregs of Mali employ their design skills crafting small and exquisite tea services, locks, and leather cushions.

One of the oddities of writing a book like this is that, while seeking to be comprehensive, it has to ignore and leave out many wonderful examples. It must be selective. Most of the examples are representative selections of major trends. But, to return to the road and river metaphor, there are also occasional side-trips, detours from the Autobahn, moments to linger along the riverbank, and see what has washed ashore; that is, I've included judiciously selected examples of minor trends.

STYLES

One of the ways historians attempted to tell the story of large swaths of history, thousands of years, is by noticing formal similarities between groups of artifacts, say paintings in Italy in the period 1400-1600, and calling them "Renaissance." Then they articulate the formal qualities those objects seem to share, the humanism, the idealization, and the shared inspiration of ancient Rome. So far so good.

Just when it seems that the problem of classification has been solved, two other problems take its place. Problem one: the historian, the art dealer, or the teacher, is then in the position of defining what the era 1400-1600 in Italy was, effectively giving the requirements for membership in the club "Renaissance art." What then to do with oddballs like Giordano Bruno, or other artistically active people active in the time period under discussion, who clearly don't fit the mold?

Problem two: the stylistic approach encourages the scholar to write about the era as though it were a person, to treat a time period as a biographical entity—as in "the Rococo did such and such." Art historian of the eighteenth century, Matthew Craske, is vexed by the method of investing a style with an autobiographical identity, and then subjecting that creation to a "character assassination" (Craske 1997, p. 8). The criticism of this approach arises from those who logically point out that of course there was no such thing as "the Ming period." Individual artists and artisans were working away, responding to their clients' needs, relying upon their training, responding to the tastes and mores of the time, and trying to make a living while producing the best works they knew how. No structure called "the Ming" dictated their every move.

Yet for certain periods, this lapse into personification is understandable, and sometimes unavoidable. For the Gothic period, for example, little information exists on the thoughts of individuals involved; often we do not even know their names. Hence the tendency to write about "the Gothic" as a collective endeavor.

The concept of style is problematic for historians, and I do not pretend to put the issue to rest. In fact, the task of art and design historians is to endlessly debate questions such as the role of style, and the importance of the individual in history. All I can do is articulate the pragmatic stance of this book, which freely employs stylistic nomenclature for the structure of chapters. There are admirable books that take pains to discuss eighteenth-century France without using the words Rococo and Neoclassical but this seems, to me, to cause as many problems as it solves. To study furniture without using stylistic monikers such as Louis XIV, Louis XV, and Louis XVI seems pointless, particular when that is how many of those designed objects are known. Therefore, many major movements are discussed within the context of style and their major historical monuments; for example, it would seem ludicrous to discuss Hagia Sophia without making reference to Byzantine art. But I also want seek to give a sampling of the rich variety of things that defy categories.

Utilizing the vocabulary of styles need not lead to oversimplification. A healthy approach is to seek to understand how various communities use design vocabulary. These communities include designers, historians, people in sales, and the general public. Words do not have limiting and precise definitions. One motto is that the less precise the definition, the truer it can be.

Where most histories exemplify periods or movements with "perfect" examples (e.g., The Parthenon), I also include modest or imperfect examples (The Temple of Apollo at Bassae). Exceptions to the rule and slightly awkward pieces are valuable as one sees design in the process of being worked through, with the solution not yet at hand. This book therefore includes counter-movements and side measures. Example: Chapter 21 looks at classical modernism (the Bauhaus and French modernism, Le Corbusier, etc.) and the conclusions offered are in keeping with what most researchers have to say. Yet the next two chapters (Chapter 22 and Chapter 23) complicate the issue, and look at alternative design strategies.

As with many survey history books, this book tells the narrative of the history of furniture and interiors over time, and looks at the history of changes and the meanings of why those changes came about. Where it is different than other history books is that it also looks at exceptions.

MEANINGS

The path metaphor also applies to the experience of reading a book. It takes time, the reader sees a lot along the way, and arrives at a different place, a little tired, a little exhilarated, perhaps in need of a shower, thirsty, but no doubt with some new knowledge. The knowledge contained within this book's covers constitutes the core of what most people think an educated person involved in the design world should know. So other than looking at a parade of objects and designed spaces that aesthetically-minded people should be familiar with, what is the purpose for delving so deeply into all this? The equally important goal is to understand the meanings that lie "behind" the art forms: the subtext of designed objects, or, what these things *mean*.

Histories of objects, curiously, are always histories of people, so another way of looking at this book is that it is a history of designed spaces, and the people who created them and the people who lived in them. As Martindale writes, "Every major work of art is an expression of some aspect of the people and society that produced it." (Martindale, p. 13). Buildings, rooms, and objects are cultural expressions of beliefs and values. The exterior and interior spaces we inhabit and the artifacts we use are mirrors of ourselves and how we experience the world around us. Designed spaces and objects also demonstrate our ability to change the world. As a form of communication, manipulated materials add shape and significance by providing a physical framework for events and rituals.

Design historian Clive Dilnot wrote two state-of-the-field essays in 1984 that are still current in many respects, and frequently cited. He wrote: "The most significant aspect about design is that it is produced, received, and used within an emphatically social context. The social is not external to the activity, but internal to it and determining of its essential features" (Part II, p. 14). Designed places and objects reflect the world and also act upon it.

To engage in a scholarly inquiry into the disciplines of furniture and interior design is to embark on an adventure that requires breadth and depth. A broad investigation is required to develop penetrating critical abilities and concise analytical skills. The knowledge gleaned from searching outward from designed spaces and objects and across other disciplines permits, among other things, the precise identification of a context—its historical, institutional, and material dimensions. Designed projects sit at the interface between thinking and making, and incorporate knowledge of materials, artifacts, the processes that produce them, and the environments in which they are placed. This specialized knowledge

is extracted by delving into the act of building as well, using the theories and methods of the social sciences, and the humanities. Scholarly research at the highest level yields skills, abilities, and knowledge required to interpret the past and shape the future.

CONCLUSION

The metaphor of a journey down a path has many applications. It relates to the unfolding of history over time, and the journey of a reader reading a book. I use the metaphor of two different paths, the river and the road, running parallel, in order to explain the aim of this book. One is the direct route, the other the meandering path. The former emphasizes the destination, and its chief attribute is clarity, the other the journey itself, characterized by richness and variety.

As for a reader embarking on a historical project, just as a road guides a traveler to a geographic destination, it can also guide a devotee to a spiritual destination. Here's another way to state this project's central focus: this book is about buildings, rooms, and the people and things in them. It glories in the properties and powers of designed spaces and pieces of furniture.

Sources

Craske, Matthew. *Art in Europe: 1700–1830*. Oxford: Oxford University Press, 1997.

Dilnot, Clive. "The State of Design History, Part I: Mapping the Field". *Design Issues* 1, no. 1 (Spring 1984): p. 4–23.

Dilnot, Clive. "The State of Design History, Part II: Problems and Possibilities". *Design Issues* 1, no. 2 (Autumn 1984): p. 3–20.

Martindale, Andrew. *Gothic Art: From the Twelfth to Fifteenth Centuries*. New York: Praeger, 1967.

ACKNOWLEDGMENTS

Writing this book, I relied on both primary and secondary materials. To the authors whose books are outlined in each chapter's sources, I thank them for their valuable research. By necessity, this work summarizes a great deal of material. I encourage interested readers to consult the works whose richness this text only hints at. For several years I have taught using the textbooks of William Curtis, Spiro Kostof, and John Pile. If I were to acknowledge every time my knowledge of a project has benefited from their insights, they would be cited on every page.

To those who suggested a resource, read a draft, provided encouragement, acted as a sounding board, answered a question, raised an eyebrow, or otherwise pointed me in the right direction, I am grateful. This list includes Mohammed Alajmi, Kwanchai Athikomrungsarit, Nnamdi Elleh, Betsy Gabb, Rumiko Handa, Mark Hoistad, Xiao Hu, Helen Jessup, Hilary Jones, Hyun-Tae Jung, Zeynep Kezer, Elizabeth Liebman, Tekki Lomnicki, Christin Mamiya, Patricia Morgado, Suzanne Noruschat, Michael Schreffler, and Rebecca Zorach. Thanks to Craig Hanson and Carole Levin for sharing their manuscripts with me before publication. For his company on trips that included Luxor, Angkor Wat, and Mexico City—and for sharing airline miles—thanks to Clyde Whitaker.

Over the past several years I have benefited from student research assistants funded by the University of Nebraska's UCARE program, under the capable direction of Laura Damuth. The students who assisted me on this project are Audrey Fisher, Matthew Fulton, Lynette Klein, Meghan McCluskey, John Ogomo, David Orrick, Kate Saroka, and especially valuable this past year, Stephanie Shepard. Amber Ellett bravely assisted with the glossary. At the University of Nebraska, I thank my friends and colleagues in the Architecture and Interior Design programs, the Art History Department, and the History Department.

Four outside readers dutifully waded through the entire manuscript in draft form. Their insightful comments improved the text immeasurably and constitute an act of intellectual generosity for which I am eternally grateful. They are: Lily Robinson of the Design Institute of San Diego; JoEllen Weingart of the Illinois Institute of Art-Schaumberg; Jon

D. Vredevoogd of Michigan State University; and Marilyn Castro of the School of Architecture & Design at Virginia Tech University.

A work of this scope is a testament to the vital role that libraries continue to play in disseminating knowledge. At the University of Nebraska, Love Library, the Interlibrary Loan department literally delivered hundreds of books to my hands. The visual resources coordinator, Judy Winkler, helped me on this project, as she helps me on every project. My thanks to the Northwestern University Library—in any library, I am always amazed at how often the book I'm looking for is the one next to the one I went after. David Easterbrook at the Melville J. Herskovits Library of African Studies is always helpful. Additional research was carried out under the dome of the Burnham Library of the Art Institute of Chicago.

I relied on numerous reference works, including *The Dictionary of Art*, *Encyclopedia Britannica*, and the Getty Research Institute's online sources. Having visited the Victoria and Albert Museum innumerable times, it is a pleasure to work with their collections and resources long distance.

For encouraging the project in its infancy, thanks to Kathy Ankerson, Amber Mohr, Jeremy Hall, and at Fairchild Books/Condé Nast, Joe Miranda and Olga Kontzias. For their work in a particularly frantic time, I bow to Erin Fitzsimmons for her keen eye, Matthew Dudley for his digital sleuthing, and Tina Henderson and Chris Fortunato for their oversight, intelligence, and simple hard work. A special thanks to my editor Michelle Levy for her persistence, attention to detail, and commitment to this project.

PREHISTORY

2,500,000–9000 B.C.E.	9000–2000 B.C.E.	4000–1000 B.C.E.
Paleolithic	**Neolithic**	**Bronze Age**

The oldest known artifact dates back two and a half million years, yet most of what we consider as art, architecture, and craftworks are more recent. The more recent the time period, the more remains we have. Yet it certainly seems plausible that the earliest inhabitants made do with existing natural items that, with relatively little modification, met their needs, such as sitting on stones and logs, and taking advantage of caves. Caves are an example of ready-made structures. Cave interiors had symbolic meaning and provided what is still considered the most basic, if limited, definition of architecture: providing shelter to protect inhabitants from the hazardous world of outdoors, including bad weather and dangerous animals.

Additionally, there is the variety of ways that the human figure has of sitting on the ground, kneeling, crossing the legs, and so on. What Stone Age preferences were, we do not know. The natural world was inescapable, and humans saw utility and meaning in nature. Some natural forms, plant and animal and landscape, were benevolent, some menacing. The term Stone Age does not mean that inhabitants created everything out of stone. Stone being so difficult to work, it is more likely that there

was considerable work with wood, hides, and reeds, almost nothing of which, from the earliest periods, remains.

This chapter addresses two stone ages, the Paleolithic and the Neolithic. It ends with the Bronze Age. Two and a half million years ago, people started making stone tools. One and a half million years ago, there was a humanoid species, *Homo ergaster,* who looked like modern beings, and this *Homo ergaster* started creating hand axes. It is likely that the hand ax is the first example of a designed object (Figure 1.1).

Looking at a hand ax prompts many questions. In attempting to craft a piece of stone into a useful implement, was anything going on in the mind of the person doing the crafting that can be called design? It does not take long to deduce that the person seems to be doing something above and beyond the call of duty if the only purpose were to create a useful object. Surely a jagged edge, with an asymmetrical line, would have served as well?

Looking at the hand ax raises many questions about the person who made it. Had they previous experience with crafting these kinds of objects? Did they have a mental image of what they wanted the

Figure 1.1 Ironstone hand ax, c. 600,000 B.C.E. South Africa.

judging other people. It turns out that it is not pure taste as to why so many people consider Denzel Washington to be handsome; it just so happens that he is quite symmetrical. Making a jump from Thornhill's thesis, from people to objects, we could conclude that Neolithic people responded well to symmetry in humans, and perhaps in objects as well. There is the probability that symmetrical objects were prized, such as whole seashells and perfect flowers. For prehistoric people, symmetrical bodies meant health. It was difficult to maintain symmetry. A humped back, a broken wrist, a droopy shoulder, a cataractal eye, a missing tooth—all were injuries that rendered the human figure asymmetrical. It is likely that the ancients admired beauty in humans and in objects, and that when they made objects they attempted to imbue the objects they crafted with their concept of beauty. A careful human, chipping away with diligence, could eventually achieve symmetry, and therefore designed beauty, in an object.

This exercise, of trying to understand the mind of a historical person by way of the designed object they have left as their only trace, is emblematic of what this book is about. It is tempting to think that we are hardwired in some respects the same way that the ancients were. That is one of the pleasures of looking at historical materials, of making a connection across centuries or millennia with people long gone, using objects as the vehicle of mental transport. But just as significantly, there are many instances when this method does not work, and we need contextual information from other sources to understand people temporally distant from us, who, in many respects, seem very strange indeed.

final product to look like that guided their efforts? Was symmetry a goal? It does seem as though the person crafting this wanted to create a symmetrical object, with the thought that somehow a symmetrical object had a pleasing form.

Of course, we cannot know for certain what a person thought over a temporal distance of hundreds of thousands of years. Yet, just as it seems probable that the person who made this had experience making similar objects—that what lies in front of us is the product of practice and skill—we can make reasonable conjecture about the possible motivation of a person who sought to craft a symmetrical object.

This line of inquiry therefore involves the scientific discussion of the purpose of beauty. Randy Thornhill, a professor at the University of New Mexico, studies why people prefer symmetry when

LASCAUX

The Paleolithic caves at Lascaux, 17,000 B.C.E., date from before the time of permanent architecture (Figure 1.2). There are other caves in southern France and northern Spain that are older, that date

Figure 1.2 McGregor Museum, Kimberly, South Africa.

from between 32,000 and 10,000 B.C.E. The population at the time was sparse, with only approximately 5,000 people in the area that is today France.

Lascaux was not a site of habitation; it is therefore likely that it was a site of ritual activity. There are some 1,500 engravings and approximately 600 painted animals and signs.

A mainstay of anthropological inquiry is the foundation myth, stories that explain the beginnings of a particular group. Myth, in this sense, is not the opposite of factual but rather the traditional telling of historical events of how a group came into being, and which underpins their worldview, beliefs, and practices. Foundation myths are most frequently discussed in terms of ethnic groups or nationalities, such as the biblical foundation myth of Adam and Eve. Foundation myths of the United States involve Captain John Smith and the pilgrims, and explorers

like Christopher Columbus; these are examples of foundation myths involving people moving across a body of water to inhabit a new land.

Foundation myths satisfy the quest of those studying beginnings, including art historians interested in the earliest pieces of art, such as the female figure from Austria, the Venus of Willendorf, and the cave paintings of Lascaux. We can never separate ancient meanings from their importance to modern periods; thus, the modern country of France takes great pleasure in the fact that the earliest examples of art, the cave paintings of Lascaux, are found there.

Many have sought, in interpreting the cave paintings of Lascaux, to see in them some sort of spiritual or ritual belief, a protoreligion. At the most basic level, what seems clear is that the people represented animals because animals were important to them and played significant roles in their lives.

The cave paintings of Lascaux constitute a decorative program, an ancient example of creating meaning in a space by decoration. Little to none of the cave was changed architecturally. In fact, one of the qualities of the caves is that the art responds to the existing configuration. The figures are representational, fairly accurate renditions of natural phenomena, not overtly abstract. Historians of art and design prefer the word "representational" to indicate art that more or less looks like the object portrayed—this is, to distinguish it from the nineteenth-century art movement Realism. There is a relationship between the caves and natural materials; of necessity, natural materials were used for the pigments.

Remains of grasses have been found in the soil in the caves, and Gregory Curtis has posited that the painters sat on grass pillows while working (Curtis, p. 105). This is a beguiling hint of a whole material world, the world of things made from reeds and woods and hides, of which we know next to nothing. Ladders and scaffolding must have been used to create the paintings, so the people who worked in Lascaux had woodworking abilities as well.

The images of Lascaux would have been seen exclusively by firelight. It is a worthwhile exercise to imagine the effect on people who had previously seen little; they were accustomed to the real world, not the represented world. French poet and critic Paul Valéry (1951) contrasted twentieth-century people with those of history. About modern man he wrote: "Your senses have to absorb without a day's respite as much of music, painting, drugs, strange drinks, shows, journeys, rapid changes of attitude and temperature, political and economic anxieties, as in the old days all mankind could absorb in the course of three hundred years" (Valéry, p. 135). He was, by extension, also writing about people at the other end of the chronological scale. The polar opposite of the postmodern being would be cave men and women, who had little to no familiarity with the world of created images. One of our suppositions is that those who saw and experienced few things in their lives knew them well and were greatly impacted by them.

A frequent observation about twenty-first-century viewers is that people across the globe are bombarded with images—many of them advertisements—via print media, television, film, and the Internet. There was no Paleolithic equivalent. People had acute visual powers; their lives often depended on their sight, so we assume that when they looked, they looked with attention, focus, and interest. One effect of seeing painted images of bison, horses, and gazelles by flickering firelight is that they may have appeared to move.

NEOLITHIC

Neolithic is a loose chronologic indicator, roughly 9000–2000 B.C.E., and it also refers to the principal material used for construction and fashioning objects: stone. Stonehenge and Skara Brae are among the latest episodes of the European Neolithic story. *Lithic* means that buildings, and a great number of objects, were crafted from stone. A Neolithic person had other materials on hand—hides, grasses, reeds, wood, sod, bone, and feathers among them, but few of their efforts with those materials survive.

Menhirs and Dolmens

Early examples of Neolithic objects are menhirs, giant stones lifted upright and made into monuments (Figure 1.3). The result is a built form that has meaning by virtue of human intervention. A menhir is a directional focus, and it creates space by virtue of its being a focal point. Yet the human handiwork does not reshape the objects; it simply changes their orientation.

More benign climates—Mesopotamia, Anatolia, the Indus River Valley (Chapter 2 and following)—

Figure 1.3 Menhir, Carnac, France. ca. 6500–4600 B.C.E.

allowed for permanent or semipermanent settlements, where people could begin agricultural food production and animal husbandry, as opposed to hunting and gathering. A Neolithic legacy is, as Spiro Kostof terms it, "a fixed place under the sky" (Kostof 1995, p. 26). Fixity allowed for the construction of furniture to accommodate a more settled and habitual lifestyle and enhance the permanent home.

A later stage was to create monuments, to configure architectural entities to have specific meanings, and to arrange naturally occurring items—tree trunks, stones, and hides—to respond to and encourage certain social interactions.

Megalithic construction was a further step in the development of architecture and designed space. A way to create meaning was to pile stones on top of one another (Figure 1.4). Megalithic architecture is characterized by timbers stuck in the ground, stones piled on top of one another, and mud applied to the gaps.

A dolmen creates an interior space, relying on post-and-lintel construction. There was likely a furniture version of this process: a horizontal piece, stone or wood, on top of two vertical supports, spanned between them, and which resulted in something like a bench. A dolmen was a predecessor to

Figure 1.4 Nicolas Brodu. Dolmen between Limoges and Poitiers. France.

wall and ceiling, made of vertical and horizontal elements, and structurally indicative of future door frame construction.

Stonehenge

There are many henges in England and Scotland, of which Stonehenge, 3200–1600 B.C.E., is the most impressive (Castleden 1987, p. 53). A **henge** is a Neolithic monument in a circular form, created with banks, ditches, and upright stones. The stone construction of Stonehenge was preceded by earthworks and timber constructions. The translation of the site into a construction made of permanent materials, blue stone and sandstone, resulted in one of the most important examples of early monumental European architecture.

Stonehenge was a place for ritual. It consists of two concentric circles, with their openings astrologically positioned according to the lunar and solar paths. Many of the stones weighed tons, and in the final construction stage they were transported eighteen miles. Stonehenge relies on **post-and-lintel,** or **trabeated,** construction (Figure 1.5). It is a structural system using (vertical) columns or posts, and (horizontal) beams or lintels.

One step in this period was from nomadic to permanent settlements. Another was from single dwellings to multiple-unit housing. This constituted the beginning of civic life, and one of the earlier examples is in Scotland. Materials from Neolithic sites include spears; axes; vessels made from pottery, stone, and wood; and some assorted personal items, including gold ornaments.

Skara Brae

Skara Brae is a small Neolithic village in Scotland dating to 3100–2500 B.C.E. (Castleden 1987, p. 33). It can be considered the residential complement to

Figure 1.5 Inner megalithic circle. Stonehenge, Salisbury Plain, England, 2250–1600 B.C.E.

ritual centers such as Stonehenge and Avenbury. Curvilinear houses were built of stone, without mortar, in a group of six to ten structures. There are several examples of built-in furniture. Archaeologist Rodney Castleden (1987) writes: "The high quality of the interior finish of a Skara Brae house really has to be seen to be appreciated. The close-fitting **corbelled** masonry flows in soft curves round the walls. Small beehive cupboards are let into the thickness of the walls and tiny keeping-places like stoups were used for storing personal belongings such as beads and charms" (p. 34).

The most prominent example of built-in furniture is a pair of large shelves, strategically located directly opposite the door (Figure 1.6). Castleden (1987) calls it a "dresser" (p. 34). The central hearth was midway between the low entrance and the dresser, whose scale and location suggest that it had a display purpose in addition to a functional purpose. Sleeping platforms lined the hearth, and some structures at Skara Brae have benches. There was limited decoration on the walls, and some items, such as pins and beads, have been found.

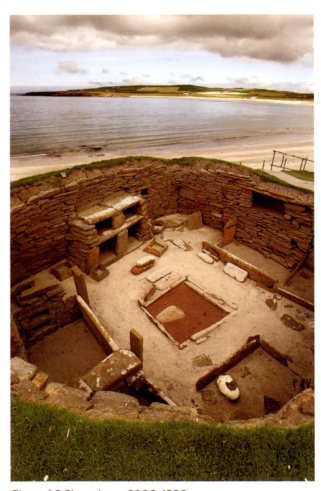

Figure 1.6 Skara-brae, 2000–1500 B.C.E.

Çatal Hüyük

Çatal Hüyük is a Middle Eastern Neolithic site in Anatolia (modern Turkey) dating to 6700–5650 B.C.E. With a population of 5,000–7,000, it was the largest town in the region. The rectilinear houses were made of mud brick coated with plaster. Although few trees grew in the immediate area, houses were outfitted with wooden posts, beams, and ladders.

The houses had a central rectangular hearth; built-in platforms lined the perimeter and were used for sitting, sleeping, and working (Figure 1.7). Some of the platforms and posts were painted red. The walls were white plaster, painted with red figures of humans, animals, or geometric shapes.

Houses had shrines, but there were also buildings used exclusively for ritual purposes. Their form and layout were similar to that of houses. The platforms in ritual buildings were used for the burial of human remains.

James Mellaart, the author of the most comprehensive book on the site, although it is decades old (1967), characterized the material culture of this early urban center: "At Çatal Hüyük it is clear that the crafts of the weaver and the woodworker were much more highly esteemed than those of the potter or the bone-carver" (p. 210).

Çatal Hüyük is chronologically a Neolithic site, although with little stone available, their stone-working activities were limited to crafting human figurines. They had woven textiles, and woven mats—fine and coarse—covered the floors and the adjacent platforms. Tools were made from obsidian and other stones, and highly polished obsidian discs functioned as mirrors. Wooden bowls and coiled baskets existed in large quantities. Preceding the activities of the Bronze Age, artisans in Çatal Hüyük produced beads and pendants out of copper and lead (Mellaart 1967, p. 217).

THE BRONZE AGE

The Neolithic period is followed by the Bronze Age. *The Encyclopedia Britannica* (2007) straightforwardly describes the Bronze Age as "the third phase in the development of material culture among the ancient peoples of Europe, Asia, and the Middle East, following the Paleolithic and Neolithic ages" (p. 548). Looking across the globe, Europe was still in the Neolithic period when parts of the Middle East and Asia had entered the Bronze Age.

The term *Bronze Age* indicates that people were no longer primarily crafting buildings and objects out of stone, although stone was still used. They were increasingly making objects out of metal—copper and bronze—for weapons, jewelry, and tools (Mellaart 1978, p. 18). In making material choices, availability was as important as technological progress or aesthetic decision. The Stone Age people of the British Isles continued to fashion items from stone because they had it in abundance. The people of the Indus River Valley learned to fire mud bricks because they did not.

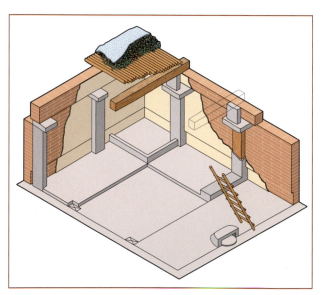

Figure 1.7 Rectangular mud-brick house, with sleeping and sitting platforms. Çatalhüyük, Turkey. 6700–5650 B.C.E.

Mohenjo-Daro

Gregory Possehl (2005) calls Mohenjo-Daro "the premier city of the Indus, or Harappan Civilization" (p. 68). The Indus or Harappan Civilization developed because of the agricultural possibilities afforded by the Indus River in the area that is today Pakistan and Northwest India. Mohenjo-Daro, on the Indus River, at its height supported a population of 20,000–30,000 people. Harappa is another city whose name is used to indicate the entire region. The region existed as a cohesive trading area from 2600 to 1900 B.C.E.

The Harappan Civilization is important for the history of human settlement and the development of a civic infrastructure. The civic amenities in Mohenjo-Daro included brick-lined wells, a street drainage system (Figure 1.8), a grand public bath, and a collective granary or warehouse. Interestingly, no palace or temple has been found. The Great Bath featured a sunken brick-lined pool with platforms and stairways.

Figure 1.8 Street view of rectangular blocks and courtyard houses, Mohenjo-Daro. Indus River Valley, Pakistan. 2600–1900 B.C.E.

The city was laid out on a grid, and most houses had an individual bathing area. The bathing platform was made of tightly joined fired bricks, with a drain issuing out to the street and a raised lip at the platform's edge (Possehl 2005, p. 75). In addition to architectural remains, pottery, beads, and examples of metalworking have been found.

CONCLUSIONS

Studying Paleolithic and Neolithic remains is not for everyone. While Stonehenge's grandeur impresses the hordes of tourists who visit it, most Stone Age remains are incomplete and small in scale. Recovering their meaning takes effort. The Irish and French countrysides are filled with dolmens and menhirs, carefully delineated with fences and historic markers. Yet their unmowed and untrampled grass indicates that they attract few visitors. Approached with patience, and with the imagination that those interested in design are blessed with in abundance, the earliest years of human design activity can be inspiring and evocative.

Though having left the Stone Age, this book is not through with looking at buildings and things in stone. A means of crossing the line from temporary building to enduring monument was to build in stone. This practice was perfected by the Egyptians, Greeks, Khmer, Chinese, Aztec, and Inca.

For this scholarly endeavor, the Bronze Age has just begun. Chapter 2 starts with a region that, with little native stone, created buildings and civic centers on an unprecedented scale, using the humble brick. The first half of Chapter 3 completes the examination of the Bronze Age with the world that was ancient to ancient Greece, the civilizations of Minoan and Mycenaean Greece.

Sources

Castleden, Rodney. *Stonehenge People: An Exploration of Life in Neolithic Britain, 4700–2000 B.C.E.* London: Routledge, 1987.

Curtis, Gregory. *The Cave Painters.* New York: Anchor Books, 2006.

Dales, George. *Excavations at Mohenjo Daro, Pakistan: The Pottery.* Philadelphia: University Museum, University of Pennsylvania, 1986.

Encyclopaedia Britannica. *The New Encyclopaedia Britannica,* vol. 2. Chicago: 2007, p. 548.

Kostof, Spiro. *A History of Architecture: Settings and Rituals.* New York: Oxford University Press, 1995.

Mellaart, James. *The Archaeology of Ancient Turkey.* London: Bodley Head, 1978.

Mellaart, James. *Çatal Hüyük: A Neolithic Town in Anatolia.* New York: McGraw-Hill, 1967.

Possehl, Gregory. "Mohenjo-Daro: The Symbolic Landscape of an Ancient City." In Tony Atkin and Joseph Rykwert, eds. *Structure and Meaning in Human Settlements.* Philadelphia: University of Pennsylvania Museum of Archaeology and Anthropology, 2005, pp. 67–83.

Valéry, Paul. *Reflections on the World Today.* London: Thames and Hudson, 1951.

DISCUSSION AND REVIEW QUESTIONS

1. What is post-and-lintel construction? What is another name for it?
2. How many images, of any kind, do you see in a day, even if peripherally?
3. Think of examples of natural landscapes, untouched by humans, that come to have meanings not related to nature.

4. Think of landscape examples that have been modified by humans, but are not architecture; that is, landscapes that lie somewhere between nature and human artifact.
5. How is value added to a naturally occurring material?
6. What are the qualities of a naturally occurring material that cause them to be prized?
7. Are the Caves at Lascaux Paleolithic or Neolithic?
8. Name a Neolithic site.
9. Name a Bronze Age site.

CHAPTER 2

ANCIENT CIVILIZATIONS

5,000–2,000 B.C.E.			911–612 B.C.E.
MESOPOTAMIA			
SUMER			NEO-ASSYRIAN EMPIRE

2650–2134 B.C.E.	2040–1640 B.C.E.	1570–1070 B.C.E.	752–656 B.C.E.
EGYPT			**NUBIA**
OLD KINGDOM	MIDDLE KINGDOM	NEW KINGDOM	TWENTY-FIFTH DYNASTY

In the ancient world of the Middle East, three civilizations stand out: Mesopotamia, Egypt, and Nubia. Interrelated yet individual entities, each was in contact with the others. Sometimes the nature of the contact was military, sometimes commercial, and there were always cultural implications. These civilizations were not alike in either their importance then or what is known about them now. Egypt produced awe-inspiring monuments that have piqued the world's imagination for millennia. Mesopotamia, home to the world's first urban centers, saw considerable strides in mathematics, writing, and astrology. Nubia, on the southernmost reaches of the Nile, is the least studied of the three. Nubia, also known as Kush, was the African civilization that continually influenced Egypt and that for a brief period ruled it. All three of these regions depended on rivers for their lifeblood: the Nile for Egypt and Nubia, the Tigris and Euphrates for Mesopotamia.

MESOPOTAMIA

Mesopotamia is a geographic designation that includes the fertile plain fed by the Tigris and Euphrates Rivers. It is roughly contiguous with modern-day Iraq. It is generally believed that this region had something approaching agriculture in the period 8000 B.C.E. By 4000 B.C.E., this area had a network of villages that served one of the most productive grain-producing regions of the world. The granary of the Near East, it was cooler and greener than it is today. It is difficult to look at the ancient cultures in this region and not think of the present day, a region so troubled during the twentieth and twenty-first centuries.

Mesopotamia then, as now, was a crossroads, with Anatolia to the north, Egypt and Nubia to the west, and Persia and the Indus River Valley to the east. Circa 3500 B.C.E., Mesopotamia and Egypt were two strong competing economic forces with developed traditions of art and architecture. There is a vitality and ambition to their art. Creating many representations of humans and animals, the ancient Middle Eastern people made great strides in furthering the endowment of matter with symbolic significance.

They were at the forefront of writing, mathematics, time, urban civilization, the sail, and astronomy. The people of the Tigris River Valley had the wheel and, equally important, a system of standardized weights and record keeping. Some of the earliest examples of writing are preserved on their clay tablets. These tools formed part of a commercial and public archival system. The citizens of these cities had a capacity for organization that allowed them to develop the world's first large-scale urban centers. A highly productive agrarian economy was served by an active mercantile economy.

Initially, homes in this region were made of mud, timber, and reeds. The standard building material of **Assyrian** structures, grand and modest, was a mud brick, so in order to build monumental architecture, and to differentiate royal quarters from servants' quarters and less remarkable buildings, an elaborate taxonomy of applied finishes was utilized. Stone and wood, while available, were scarce and expensive and hence used sparingly.

Cities

Mesopotamian urban centers were the sites of ritual cult activities and also functioned as the nucleus of organized agricultural and proto-industrial production. Mesopotamian construction workers built bridges, tunnels, moats, and walled cities with ceremonial gates. Glazed blue bricks used on exteriors highlighted the cities' entryways. These gates were prominent points, nodes where roadways originating in the countryside dove into the dense urban fabric. The urban thresholds signaled entrance, but they were also a means of control. The walled cities themselves were defensive. The most famous example is the Ishtar Gate. These urban features are evident in a reconstruction drawing of Khorsabad (Figure 2.1).

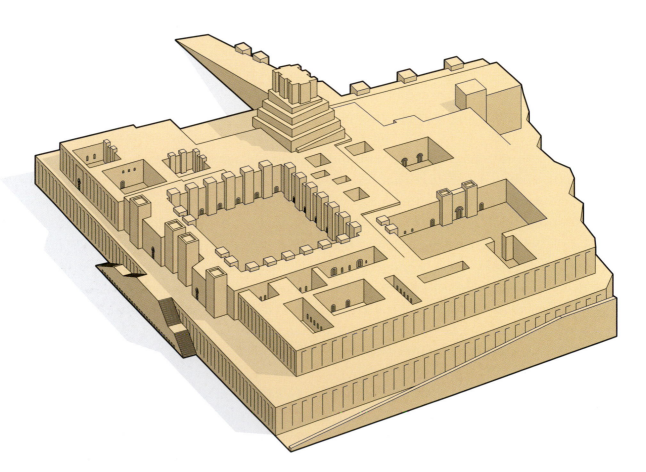

Figure 2.1 Reconstruction of the citadel with royal palace and ziggurat. Khorsabad. 721–705 B.C.E.

Significant architectural monuments are the highlight of early periods, such as the White Temple at Warka, 3500–3000 B.C.E., and the Ziggurat at Ur, 2113–2006 B.C.E. Much of the extant sculpture, and hence our knowledge of furniture, dates from later periods. Mesopotamian cities were subjected to continual pressure and intrusion by the Kassites, Murrians, and Mitannians. The period 746–609 B.C.E., known as the Neo-Assyrian Empire, represents a return to power from the valley, and significant rulers include Ashurnasirpal (reigned 884–859 B.C.E.) and Ashurbanipal (reigned 668–627 B.C.E.). This period produced some of the finest sculptural reliefs and examples of Assyrian architecture. Ashurnasirpal's reign comes toward the end of 3,000 years of Mesopotamian prominence, yet it marks the beginning of the late Assyrian period.

Palaces

The plan of the Palace of Nimrud demonstrates that Assyrian palaces were largely accumulative affairs (Figure 2.2). Individual rooms of the palace were not extraordinarily different from those of modest structures with regard to both size and materials. The largest spaces in the plan were exterior courtyards. What made the palace extraordinary was the quantity of rooms, in the hundreds, and the quality of the artwork. The length of available timbers dictated room width. Assyrian builders could expand a room longitudinally; hence the grandest room is the throne room. The complex had been called Calah, where Ashurnasirpal II built his palace, and today it is called Nimrud.

While the overall complex is impressive in size, the principal rooms are surprisingly narrow. The reliance upon rooms that face a courtyard is a standard layout of residential architecture in a hot climate. With their use of local materials and construction methods, the royal palaces were extensions of vernacular traditions.

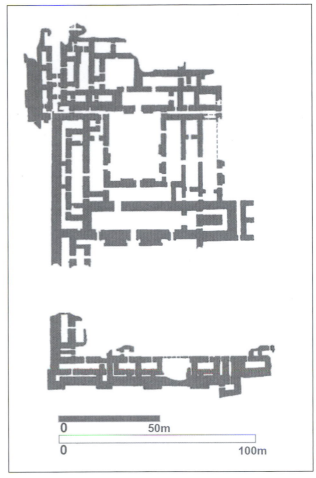

Figure 2.2 Plan of the Northwest Palace, reign of Ashurnasirpal, Nimrud, 883–859 B.C.E.

There were a variety of methods for signaling the importance of rooms and buildings. Mud brick walls could be skim-coated with an additional layer of mud or plaster. For building interiors, walls could be painted. Most exceptionally, important rooms were lined with reliefs carved into alabaster panels and massive three-dimensional sculptures marked the entrances, a technique increasingly important in the neo-Assyrian period.

Sculpture

The most famous artworks from these palaces are the colossal gateway figures that stood guard at entries. They dominate the reconstruction as they originally dominated the throne rooms. With human

Figure 2.3 Reconstruction of an idealized Assyrian throne-room.

heads placed atop muscular winged lions and bulls, these imposing monolithic statues stood 15 feet tall (Figure 2.3). The sphinxes are initially experienced frontally, defining the entrance that they guard as a pair. They also function as directional devices. Carved on two adjacent sides (front and one side), they encourage visitors to perambulate around them, to enter the room, and then to turn the corner. The sculptures are impressive at a distance and also up close. From far away, their size, form, and material impress. At close distance, it is the quantity and quality of the incised details that carefully delineate the contours of flesh and musculature. Part of what makes them monumental is their size and material, but so too is the obvious point that their finely incised details are the product of hundreds of hours

of painstaking work. The Western and Asian penchant for flanking public buildings with recumbent lions has a precedent in the Assyrian palaces.

Reliefs

The sphinxes were but the largest element in an elaborate composition that covered all the walls of the throne room. The sculptural program of a public room was a means of proclaiming the wealth of king and kingdom, and it also served as a sophisticated means of visual communication that played to public audiences, both local and foreign. The state rooms of palaces featured decorative programs that featured scenes of hunting, celebration, worship, processions of courtiers bearing tribute, natural landscapes, and scenes of military technology and organization.

The vitality of the public spaces came from the processions of figures in horizontal motion. Most of the scenes involve movement, which makes the overall decorative program dynamic. Chariots, horses, lions, rows of soldiers, penitents, and dignitaries are all represented in motion, fast or slow. Flowing rivers are populated with fish, all in horizontal motion. Susanna Hare describes the reliefs as showing "figures in endless parade" (Hare 1946, p. 15). They appear as if pressed from a roller. The figures "repeated themselves along the walls in much the same way as the design of a Mesopotamian cylinder seal, rolled across clay, could be repeated almost indefinitely" (Reade 1995, p. 42). These linear compositions were carved in low relief, in comparison to the sphinxes.

While some scenes record natural landscapes or lines of dignitaries paying tribute to the king, the overall theme is intimidation. The reliefs are at once beautiful and horrifying. They reassured the home audience, enforced a sense of decorum, and no doubt terrified non-Assyrians with their forthright expression of Assyrian might. J. E. Reade writes that this decorative program was designed "to impress, astonish, intimidate" (Reade 1995, p. 40).

Ashurnasirpal's own words corroborate the unrelenting pictorial violence: "I captured the city; six hundred of their warriors I put to the sword; three thousand captives I burned with fire; I did not leave a single one among them alive to serve as a hostage. Hulai, their governor, I captured alive. Their corpses I formed into pillars; their young men and maidens I burned in the fire. Hulai, their governor, I flayed, his skin I spread upon the wall of the city of Damdamnsa; the city I destroyed, I devastated, I burned with fire" (Hare 1946, p. 12).

In addition to convincing its readers of Ashurnasirpal's might, the Standard Inscription of Ashurnasirpal II provides a list of materials that were prestigious: "A palace of cedar, cypress, juniper, boxwood, mulberry, pistachio-wood, and tamarisk, for my royal dwelling and for my lordly pleasure for all time I founded therein. Beasts of the mountain and of the seas of white limestone and alabaster I fashioned, and set them up in its gates, I adorned it, I made it glorious, and put copper knobs all around it. Door leaves of cedar, cypress, juniper and mulberry I hung in the gates thereof; and silver, gold, lead, copper, and iron, the spoils of my hand from the lands which I had brought under my sway, in great quantities I took and placed therein" (Hare 1946, p. 7).

Typical relief subjects related to warfare include scenes of laying siege to cities; hunting scenes; battle scenes with chariots. What they have in common is that they rely upon a horizontal composition (Figure 2.4). The scenes frequently juxtapose Assyrians with their neighbors, and these "foreigners" would have been readily recognized by anyone visiting the rooms, identified by their ethnically specific clothing and headwear. The Assyrians are consistently represented as physically and militarily superior. They stand tall and erect, in perfect posture, while non-Assyrians are smaller in scale, broken, crumpled, and trampled upon by horses and chariots, attacked by lions, their bodies ridden with arrows and spears. No Assyrians die. Megan Cifarelli writes, "These images, then, communicated highly organized and specific messages about the nature and goals of Assyrian power" (p. 211). For Assyrians, the reliefs showed that in return for the considerable cost of maintaining a centralized government and their ruler's opulent lifestyle, economically and in labor, there was the benefit of security and knowing that the King was in control and kept enemies at bay.

For non-Assyrians, the decorative program was a dire warning of the consequences of confronting Assyrians. For citizen and visitor alike, these reliefs acted as a visual etiquette, a visual means of com-

Figure 2.4 The Battle of Til-Tuba, showing the Assyrians defeating the Elamites of southern Iran. Carved for Ashurbanipal but installed in Sennacherib's palace. Relief in limestone. 660–650 B.C.E. Ninevah, SW Palace, Room XXXIII, British Museum.

municating to a nonliterate audience. Lines of polite dignitaries respectfully approach kings and priests, with both hands visible. This showed the proper way to act in the throne room; it also made clear the consequences, a violent death, of failing to heed this advice. Lest there be any doubt about the leader's might, the standard Inscription of Ashurnasirpal II (883–859 B.C.E.) describes him as the king "who tramples on the neck of his foes" (p. 6).

To modern viewers this seems extreme; yet it is worth pointing out that across cultures, many government buildings show artworks that document historical scenes, and often these are noble scenes of battle. The passage of time has lessened the impact of viewing the carnage, but battles such as Carthage, Waterloo, and Iwo Jima were certainly bloody in their day.

A fanciful reconstruction makes several points clear that the austere stone remains do not. Published in 1849, it is still useful as it demonstrates that the rooms, even if covered with stone reliefs, were polychromatic. Paint, used as outline and background, blended together elements of stone, plaster, wood, and mud, making them into a consistent and powerful decorative program.

If the ceilings were made of timber beams and joists, and this is a point of some conjecture, the latitudinal width of the throne room was determined by the length of timbers available.

Furniture

Assyrian furniture has not survived to the extent that Egyptian furniture has, but our knowledge of it comes from inscriptions and representations on reliefs. Ashurnasirpal's list of booty also provides valuable information about furniture; it includes "chairs of maple and boxwood, tables of ivory with inlay, silver, gold, lead, copper, iron."

The most famous relief with detailed views of furniture involves King Ashurbanipal and the Queen dining in a garden (Figure 2.5). This relief,

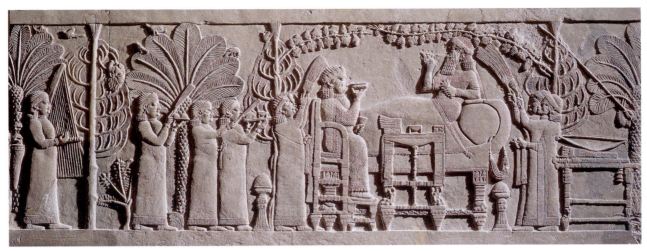

Figure 2.5 Relief of Ashurbanipal and the Queen dining in a garden. 645 B.C.E.

dated to 645 B.C.E., is from their palace at Ninevah. Their suite of furniture is consistent with other representations of furniture. The Assyrian furniture was made of wood. The King reclines on a **couch,** while the Queen sits on a throne with a back; her feet rest on a footrest. There are two high tables. The King and Queen are dining in the fashion most often associated with Rome, in which they lie recumbent on a couch or settee, with food placed on tall tables that stand within arm's reach.

The Ashurbanipal relief shows the kind of furnishings known as the Assyrian Empire style. Chairs, beds, and tables alike rest on conical feet whose forms derive from either inverted pinecones or date **spathes.** Crossbars stabilize the pieces and are decorated with opposed **volutes.** Atlas-like figures, males with upraised arms, are one of the decorative motifs. Although not shown here, there were also backless thrones, some of which had lion's paw feet. Most pieces were made of wood, sometimes adorned with bronze plates attached with small nails. A stone table was found at Khorsabad.

The King and Queen dine outdoors, indicating that furniture used indoors was occasionally relocated for outdoor use. Servants or slaves fan them. The king's couch is furnished with a bolster that fits underneath the curved end, on top of which there are several coverings. Similarly, a blanket or pad is thrown over the Queen's vertical backrest. The wood elements appear to be carved and turned. The table has a tablecloth and stands on three legs (similar to the Greek and Roman trident table). This relief, sometimes called "The Garden Party," is a rare representation of a seemingly tranquil domestic scene that exceptionally also shows the Queen. Yet Ashurbanipal remains his intrepid self. The head of one of his defeated enemies, Teumann, King of Elam, hangs from a tree.

The Assyrians developed a system of decoration in which sculpture and wall decoration in the public rooms of governmental buildings were meant to impress, intimidate, and instill a sense of decorum in visitors, citizens, and foreigners alike. Babylon was the last great Mesopotamian city, whose ruler was the equally renowned Nebuchadnezzar (605–562 B.C.E.). The arrival of Alexander the Great signaled an end to Assyrian hegemony in the region and its absorption into the larger Greco-Roman world.

EGYPT

Egyptian history has a parade of colorful characters and impressive monuments. Ancient Egyptians used a chronology based on dynasties and pharaohs, although modern historians selectively rely upon a simplified system that divides the period into the Old Kingdom, the Middle Kingdom, and the New Kingdom.

Egypt was centered on the Nile. Huge workforces of slaves and laborers worked in fields and crafted buildings of an unprecedented scale. Egyptians had a lot of stone, something that causes Egyptian monumental architecture to be different from Mesopotamian. Their monuments and artistic achievements would only be possible because Egypt was a strong centralized power. Some two millennia before the establishment of the royal dynasties, circa 5200 B.C.E., Egyptians started practicing agriculture. They established small villages where flint blades, grain storage pits, and animal bones were discovered. In Egypt, the knowledge of farming likely came from Mesopotamia via the Red Sea. The earliest settlements did not have permanent architecture.

Monuments

The Old Kingdom

Egyptian religion was focused on death, or better, the afterlife, with architecture and material culture mediating between the ruling elite and gods, Earth, and heaven. The Old Kingdom, 2649–2150 B.C.E., is the age of the pyramids, when Zoser (2686–2613 B.C.E.) built his famous pyramid at Saqqâra and when the great pyramids at Giza were built.

The earliest step in the progression of building pyramids was the Mortuary Complex of Zoser, located west of Memphis and north of Saqqâra. The name of the architect who worked for Zoser is known as Imhotep. (No architects' names have survived from ancient Mesopotamia.) Their collaboration is a watershed moment in Egyptian history, as it involves the first monumental use of stone and monumentally scaled columns. Stone columns from buildings that postdate Saqqâra were based on nat-

Figure 2.6 Mortuary Temple of Tuthmosis, III, 1504–1450, B.C.E. Capital detail from main court. Thebes, Egypt.

Figure 2.7 Great Temple of Amun, Karnak, Egypt, 1530–323 B.C.E. Great Court with Taharka Column, 950 B.C.E.

ural forms, such as bundles of reeds and open lotus blossoms (Figures 2.6 and 2.7).

This period is also important because the elite practiced the custom of entombing the dead masterfully, when the ruler's body was laid to eternal rest. Because of the practice of entombing the ruler's body along with items to serve in the afterlife, we have the oldest surviving pieces of furniture, including, miraculously, wooden furniture.

Because their attention was focused almost exclusively on monuments, tombs, cenotaphs, and temples, we know little about the daily life of Egyptians. Much of what we know about their daily life comes from the art and artifacts of tombs.

The sprawling necropolis at Saqqâra was not just for the pharaoh, but also for members of the royal family and officials who shared in the use of a sumptuously prepared afterlife. Adjacent to the famous mortuary complex lies the entrance to another

tomb that is unlike any other, the twin tomb of two male manicurists, Niankhkhnum and Khnumhotep (Figure 2.8). They were, as the tomb tells us, overseers of manicurists to the king. The paintings inside this otherwise unremarkable tomb are unprecedented in Egyptian art, because they show two men in what appears to be an embrace, a representation of a position that otherwise is only seen in male-female couples. Both Niankhkhnum and Khnumhotep were married and had children, who are also represented in the tomb, although smaller in scale. There are several representations of the two men throughout the tomb that show them intertwined, holding hands, or with Khnumhotep's hand on Niankhkhnum's shoulder. One interpretation is that they were a couple, with royal sanction.

A competing interpretation is that they are Siamese twins. If they were Siamese twins, it is unlikely that artists would have documented the deformity

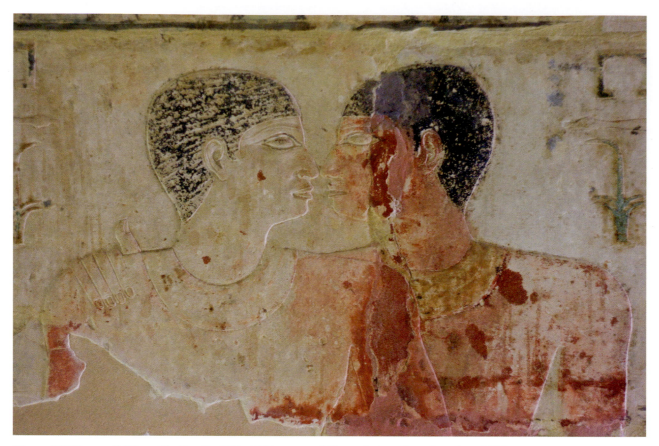

Figure 2.8 Stone relief from the Tomb of Niankhkhnum and Khnumhotep, Saqqâra, circa 2400 B.C.E.

with attention to unflattering and embarrassing details. They are portrayed in the full bloom of youthful vigor.

Egyptian art was highly stylized, conventional, and conservative, meaning that changes came about slowly, over the course of centuries. Within an individual artist's lifetime, changes in style and technique were incremental. Artists worked within existing conventions; they were beholden to relying upon standard methods of representation. Regarding the human figure, the stylistics of Egyptian art show the body in a pose that no flesh-and-blood person can strike. The legs and feet, up to the hips and carefully delineated abdominal muscles, are shown in strict profile, while the upper chest and shoulders face the viewer. Each body part is shown in the way that flatters it and shows it best. Thus, the full chest and broad shoulders face forward. The head, however, appears in almost perfect pro-

file; the nose is therefore in profile; the eyes, however, are shown frontally.

This beguiling image underscores the interpretation of history as an ongoing endeavor and not all historians agree. Our knowledge of history increases and changes over time. Also, contemporary issues, such as race and gender, have an impact on what archaeologists and historians study. So while the precise meaning of the tomb of Khnumhotep and Niankhkhnum eludes us, we are not at a total impasse. Physical proximity in representation clearly represents physical proximity in life and some sort of emotional involvement that they wished to represent eternally, and in that, they have succeeded.

An intermediate step in the development of the pyramids, which the pyramids of Giza are the highest expression of, was during the reign of the Pharaoh Snefru (2613–2589 B.C.E.). He built several pyramids, among them the Bent Pyramid of Snefru in the town of Dahshur. It is noteworthy because it started out ambitiously, initially envisioned to be higher. Then, because of signs of structural failure in the course of construction, the angle of the pyramid was changed.

The most famous pyramids are those of Giza, made by Snefru's son. The pyramid named for him, Khufu (Cheops), is the biggest and was built first. The pyramid of Khafre (Chephren) followed.

Queen Hetepheres was Snefru's wife and Khufu's mother. Snefru reigned from 2575 to 2551 B.C.E. The oldest extant pieces of Egyptian furniture come from her tomb and its funerary furnishings. She was buried in a **mastaba** that is part of the layout of the Great Pyramid. A mastaba is an oblong tomb with sloped walls that covers a vault.

A draped pavilion protected Hetephere's furniture. Thin columns with capitals held up a framework from which light-weight textiles flowed. This shelter maximized air flow, while shielding its users from sunlight and pests.

The resemblance that Egyptian beds bear to modern beds is misleading (Figure 2.9). What looks like the headboard of Hetephere's bed is the footrest. A wooden framework supports a caned platform for the resting body. The wood has been gilded. A separate piece is the headrest. This is one of those items that underscore how very different the Egyptians were regarding conceptions of comfort. The legs have feet that all face the same direction.

Hetephere's armchair reveals the designer's reliance on geometry, cubic massing, and a grid. Seat, back, and armrests are all squares. The cubic composition contrasts with the armrest supports that represent three flowers, bound together, two of which languidly droop. In the conception of its form, this chair differs significantly from the pieces made some 1,000 years later in Egypt.

Figure 2.9 Queen Hetephere's bed, reconstruction. c. 2500 B.C.E.

Middle Kingdom

During the Middle Kingdom (2030–1640 B.C.E.), the hold of pyramids as the principal type of royal monument decreased, and the pharaohs increasingly turned their attention to building and outfitting the great pylon temples.

New Kingdom

Although some pyramids continue to be built during this period, 1550–1070 B.C.E., this is the classic age of Egyptian art and architecture, an age of prosperity and considerable architectural achievement. The state machine was in full operation. In this period, Egypt controlled the southern region of Nubia.

Egypt was a political and cultural entity with an intricate and efficient organization and administration; the rulers also possessed a capable and effective military. This was the age of Thebes and Memphis. Two of the most significant works of architecture are the Mortuary Temple of Queen Hatshepsut, c. 1520 B.C.E., and the Temple of Amun-Re at Karnak, 1490 B.C.E. This period also sees some fascinating characters, such as Akhenaten, Hatshepsut, and Tutankhamen.

Artistically, the reign of Akhenaten is significant because he introduced several new art forms, including a unique style of portraiture and intimate family portrayals. He is responsible for having shifted Egyptian religious practices in the direction of monotheism, an achievement that was reversed upon his death. His unusual representations have prompted theories that he actually had feline or feminine features, and that possibly he was diseased.

There was a zenith in the splendor of the arts, particularly architecture, in the reign of Ramesses II, who was the most active builder in Egyptian history. His structures include the Ramesseum, also in the Valley of Thebes, 1301 B.C.E. It is a **pylon** temple with a **hypostyle hall**. His greatest structure is the Temple of Abu-Simbel, 1301 B.C.E., which is a rock-hewn structure. The imposing façade consists of four monumental seated statues of Ramesses himself, over 65 feet high.

Tutankhamen

Tutankhamen was a minor sovereign who died young and therefore had few political accomplishments to his credit. His greatest legacy is that he is the only pharaoh whose royal tomb was discovered intact. Discovered in 1922, it included among its treasures a wealth of furnishings. Among them was a remarkable folding bed made of wood with rush matting for support (Figure 2.10). Many Egyptian pieces, as with Assyrian pieces, were collapsible, the obvious reason being that furniture pieces were rare and used in travel. The reason for the rush matting is that it would "give," thereby also providing comfort. The bed has animal feet, all facing in the same direction; it is built with a frame structure. Because it folds, this obviously indicates that it was moved about. The Egyptian climate is ideal for preserving artifacts for long periods of time. This, in conjunction with the Egyptian penchant for entombing ar-

Figure 2.10 Folding bed.

ticles of daily life for the afterlife, means that there are an astonishing number of extant pieces of Egyptian wood furniture.

Noted Egyptologist Cyril Aldred (1984) writes that Egyptian art reflects a boxlike conception of the world. The Nile flows south to north and the sun crosses it perpendicularly, thus putting Egypt into a grid. Egyptian art reflects an idealized view of nature. Ground plans and elevations often reflect a strict mathematical order based on a grid and the important "sacred" right angle. Large drawings were created by a drawing being done in one scale then overlain with a grid, which was then transferred to a larger scale.

Pieces of furniture operate under two systems: the importance of the simple geometry, and a sensitivity to the shape of the human figure. In many

Figure 2.12 Chair from Tutankhamun's tomb; cedar wood with golf leaf; c. 1323 B.C.E.

reliefs, chairs are represented as cubes at a right angle, with stretchers occurring at either thirds or quarters.

A child's chair from the tomb of Tutankhamen displays the characteristic Egyptian curved seat (Figure 2.11). The overall composition shows an initial reliance on a grid. The seat and legs form an approximate square. The legs are more or less straight. But then the seat and arms are curved. The back is a cube, lengthened into a rectangle with additional bands of decoration. This piece shows the high level of craft, in all respects, achieved by Egyptian furniture makers. The curves employed in Egyptian furniture were complicated geometrically. The chair has carved legs. It is structurally stabilized with stretchers that look like architectural trusses, with metal inlays. Its overall form is aesthetically pleasing but not over-the-top in its decoration. For its time period, it was comfortable.

Figure 2.11 Child's chair, Tutankhamun's tomb, c. 1350 B.C.E.

Also from the tomb is a wooden chair with no arms (Figure 2.12). Some of the detailing is similar to what one sees in architecture. It shows the God Heh kneeling on the symbol for gold. Conceptually, one can see that the design started out as a square, with the seat and legs forming a cube; the addition of a square decorative panel serving as the backrest doubled the height. Stretchers occur halfway up the legs; midway between the legs, an additional vertical support provides further structural stability.

While these chairs represent the absolute highest level of craft possible by Egyptian furniture makers, it is also possible to imagine that their forms were imitated, in less luxurious ways, in simpler pieces. In fact, representations of furniture on reliefs confirm this.

Figure 2.13 Chest on high legs for storing linens; red cedar wood with bronze hinges and gilding. From Tutankhamun's tomb, c. 1350 B.C.E.

The full chest of drawers would not make its European debut until the Renaissance and does not become common until the eighteenth century. Yet the drawer makes an unheralded appearance in ancient Egypt (Figure 2.13). A small chest on high legs from Tutankhamen's tomb sports a single drawer as a storage device. Drawers were not the primary means of storage for either large-scale items or large quantities of items. Rather, drawers held small objects and precious items, such as fine linens, cosmetics, jewelry, and games. This chest is square in plan, with a frame construction. The decoration includes an **ankh**, a looped cross that is a symbol of the regenerative quality of life.

Aside from the artifacts themselves, surviving images are equally important because they show furniture in use (Figure 2.14). Drawings and carved reliefs also document the existence of modest pieces that have not survived, helping us learn about bygone lifestyles. A relief from Sobekhotep's tomb shows a jewelry worker making an elaborate necklace. The workers sit on two types of stools, one with curved legs and seat, another with straight legs, reinforced with stretchers. They use tables, one with legs, another cubelike. This gives an idea of what straightforward stools were like, in which the sitters sit relatively low to the ground; two of them perform their arts with outstretched legs.

A folding stool from Tutankhamen's tomb has duckbill supports, consistent with Egyptian artistic practices that make constant reference to the natural world (Figure 2.15). The seat curves in a manner characteristic of many pieces of Egyptian furniture, an ancient version of ergonomics—the science of crafting furniture pieces to comfortably support the human form, as a means of increasing the health and efficiency of workers.

The seat shown in Figure 2.16 has a complicated curve that extends in two directions. This is a reproduction of an original chair. Remarkably, a hide has

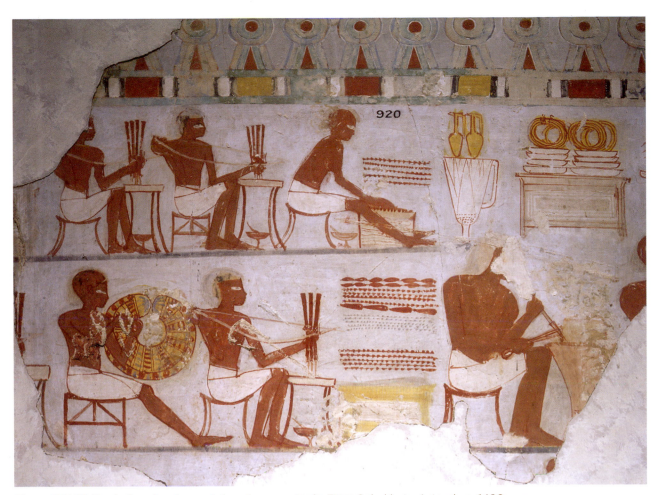

Figure 2.14 Wall painting showing metal workers on stools. From Sobekhotep's tomb, c. 1400 B.C.E.

Figure 2.15 Folding stool, military commander's type, with goose-head legs; probably used with an animal hide, c. 1350 B.C.E.

Figure 2.16 Reconstruction of stool from Tutankhamun's tomb; wood with inlaid ivory and gold mounts to imitate animal skin; goose-head supports; non-folding, c. 1350 B.C.E.

Figure 2.17 White painted stool from Tutankhamun's tomb; with lion's feel and open lattice work, c. 1350 B.C.E.

been transformed to another material. A wooden seat and apron employ the Egyptian artistic stance of transforming forms and decoration originally made in one material to another, here leather to wood.

Stools were not only the purview of workers and slaves (Figure 2.17). Chairs with backs were exceptional, and many nobles are shown sitting on stools. This elaborate stool is painted white, with lion's feet and some gilding.

In Egypt, artists introduced many conceptual approaches to working with materials that would influence later periods. One is that items are initially made in one material; for example, a bunch of reeds or grasses are bundled together and used as a support, such as a column. The form then takes hold in the imagination, and even when a different material is used, such as limestone, the form remains. The result is that Egyptian buildings make constant reference to the material world and organic materials. Structures made of limestone are at home on the banks of the Nile, whose waters nourished lotus blossoms and papyrus reeds.

As with Mesopotamia, the existence of Egyptian art as an autonomous entity starts to unravel with the growing influence of Greece and Rome. A significant date for this is the ascendancy of Alexander the Great, 332 B.C.E.

NUBIA

Nubia, the Mesopotamian kingdoms, and Egypt were coeval; they traded and intermittently fought with one another. Trade, politics, and military maneuvers were complicated mechanisms that resulted in cultural intermingling that had profound religious and social implications. Certainly, one of the interesting aspects of looking at historic styles and their development over time is to understand why change comes about; one of the driving forces of artistic change is exposure to and influence by others.

Nubia is the land to the south of Egypt, below what Egyptians called Upper Egypt (upriver on the Nile). It occupied the area that today lies in Sudan and Ethiopia. Egypt itself is on the continent of Africa. Nubians remain a prominent ethnic group

Figure 2.18 Nubian pyramids.

in Egypt today, and there are both white and black Nubians. Nubia is an African-influenced Egyptian culture, although also a melting pot of African indigenous, Egyptian, and later Roman influence.

Continual Egyptian incursions into Nubia, Libya, and northern Mesopotamia meant that the subjugated peoples took on Egyptian ways in architecture, religion, sculpture, and dress. The most valued of Nubia's natural resources were metals. Nubia helped satiate the Egyptian thirst for gold, and Egyptians relied upon Nubians for their considerable knowledge of iron metallurgy.

Nubia was also known as Kush, and Greeks and Romans referred to the land as "Aethiopia," which means "land of burnt faces." For Greeks and Romans, Ethiopia did not mean the area that is today Ethiopia, or even Nubia, but was used to refer to the entire African continent. Around 3100 B.C.E., Nubia united into a central powerful kingdom.

Egypt, one of the most heavily researched areas of the ancient world, lies next door to one of the least. This is because Egyptian monuments are spectacular, and Egypt has had a political stability that the area of Sudan sadly lacks. Uncovering the riches of Nubian architecture, interiors, and material culture is an ongoing endeavor.

The 25th Dynasty

For most of its history, Nubia was ruled by Egypt. Nubians served as mercenaries in the Egyptian army, and as slaves. Egyptian wall paintings and sculpture have many references to their neighbors to the south.

The 25th Dynasty sees a dramatic turn of events as Nubian pharaohs ruled Egypt. Piankhy (747–716 B.C.E.) ushered in a period when control was centered on the Nubian capital, Napata. The height of Nubia's political and military strength was made possible by the demise of the Egyptian New Kingdom. Nubian control included lower Egypt and extended all the way to the Nile delta. Piankhy's reign was one component of the Kushite rule of Egypt, which occurred in 760–656 B.C.E., a period of less than one hundred years.

Nubian rulers made sure that Napata was architecturally worthy to rule Egypt. Beginning in 730 B.C.E., they built an Egyptian-style pylon temple, the Temple of Amun at Jebel Barkal. There are a significant number of other Kushite monuments and tombs in the area. Nubian pyramids are smaller in scale than their Egyptian counterparts and are characterized by a steep rake. In front of the steep pyramids is a pylon porch (Figure 2.18).

These tombs, with pyramidal form and pylon entrances carved in low relief, underscore the considerable Egyptian influence on Nubian religion and artistic practices. Low-relief carving means the depth of the carving is shallow, placing the art form between sculpture and painting. Nubians worshipped Egyptian gods and built Egyptian-influenced temples and tombs.

Piankhy's successor, Shabaka, ruled from 716 to 701 B.C.E. As most of the 25th Dynasty Nubian rulers did, he ruled from within Egypt, using Thebes as his capital. Part of Shabaka's foreign affairs included dealing with the Assyrians, and for this he turned to his nephew, Taharka. Taharka himself would one day rule Egypt, from 690 to 664 B.C.E., with his center of operations based in Memphis and Thebes. In 690 B.C.E., Taharka was coronated at Memphis. Taharka did not ignore his Nubian homeland, and he added on to the temple of Jebel Barkal. Taharka had continual battles with the Assyrians, who would ultimately be his downfall. He is generally considered to be the greatest of the Nubian kings and one of Africa's greatest rulers. Ashurbanipal defeated Taharka, who returned to Nubia for his final days.

Senkamanisken ruled from 643 to 623 B.C.E. He does not have the hallowed place in African history that Taharka does, although this is not obvious in a grand statue of him (Figure 2.19). The bodies of Nubian statues typically display a more robust physique than their Egyptian counterparts, which have a slimmer profile. The statue of Senkamanisken shows him with broad shoulders and a full muscu-

Figure 2.19 Statue of King Senkamanisken, 643–623 B.C.E.

Figure 2.20 Folding stool from tomb, Meroe, Sudan. sixth to fourth centuries B.C.E.

lar chest. The statue relies upon the Egyptian artistic approach to sculpture in the round; the left leg steps forward and the hands are clenched.

Over the period of Nubian ancient history, there were three capitals, Kerma, Napata, and Meroë. In response to military pressure from the Assyrians, the Kushite rulers moved deeper into the African continent and established their final capital at Meroë. Meroë served as the Kushite capital following the 25th Dynasty, when Nubia no longer ruled Egypt. Nubians continued to trade far and wide, with Alexander and the Persians.

Because fewer excavations have been carried out in Nubia, it is difficult to construct a full picture of Nubian material culture, including furniture. The Nubians, like the Egyptians, buried their nobles with furnishings to serve in the afterlife. A folding stool from a tomb is utilitarian, yet it exhibits a modest concern for aesthetics with regard to form and decoration (Figure 2.20). Its design is consistent with both Egyptian and Roman examples of the period.

When making grand public gestures, such as temples, mortuary tombs, and sculpture of rulers, Nubians looked to Egypt for inspiration, yet to round out our picture of material culture, we should make note that more common objects continued to rely on local traditions, such as baskets, mats, simple pieces of furniture, and certainly ceramics.

Pottery began in Africa as early as the seventh millennium B.C.E. The Neolithic revolution was the period in which the tail end of the Neolithic period morphed into what we consider "history." This involved a move away from hunter-gatherers to agrarian life and included the introduction of pottery to Nubia. Anthropologist Nigel Barley (1994) writes that for the history of Africa, ceramics play an important role: "Pots have a particular place in the grammar of African objects. Pots are naturally used for the storage and cooking of liquids but have a much wider role than the Western saucepan and African clay is almost as versatile as plastic in the West. This is clear from the way that pottery is often used to produce skeuomorphs (representations of objects usually made in one material executed in another) so that pottery designs overlap with those of wood, basketry and leather."

A piece of Nubian pottery has a geometric decoration in which rows of triangles are painted on with a glaze. This is a pattern that is common in baskets and textiles (Figure 2.21).

Figure 2.21 Clay bowl with geometric decoration. Third millenium B.C.E.

Nubian influence on Egypt occurred throughout Egyptian history, and is not limited to the 25th Dynasty. Many have even posited that Thutmose III's mother was Nubian.

CONCLUSION

Wooden furniture from Egypt exists in quantity. Many of the pieces are of high quality in terms of construction, materials, and decoration. The decorative motifs of Egyptian furniture are consistent with those that adorn other art forms, such as buildings and wall paintings. The latter also inform us that most people sat on stools. Egyptian furniture makers ingeniously combined two compositional systems: a hard-edged grid and a curvilinear anthropomorphism.

The Egyptians, like their neighbors to the east, responded to the natural environment by representing it and emulating it. The logic behind taking a form such as a lotus blossom and carving it in stone was not functional but spiritual and aesthetic.

The legacy of the Mesopotamian civilizations includes large-scale cities, mathematics, record keeping, written laws, and the novel. A feature of public buildings around the world also derives from their use of sculpture as a complement to architecture. The important entryways of Assyrian palaces were delineated with a pair of animals carved in stone. These sentries marked the entrance, underscored the seriousness of the place, and guarded the public domain.

Nubia, next door to the all-powerful Egypt, is an ancient example of cultural intermingling. When Nubian rulers were in power, they honored Egyptian prowess by emulating her temples, sculpture, religion, and dress. Yet Nubian art forms also subtly affirm that Nubia was an entity different from Egypt; it was African.

The legacies of these three regions include stone columns, monumental sculpture, and the use of fantastic animals in decorative programs. Recovering the heritage of Nubia is an ongoing project, in large part due to the interest of twentieth- and twenty-first-century African-American scholars such as Harvard's Henry Louis Gates (2001). Interest in ancient Nubia, Egypt, and Mesopotamia is driven in large part by what these civilizations mean to people today.

Sources

Assyria

Budge, Wallis, ed. *Assyrian Sculptures in the British Museum*. London: British Museum, 1914.

Cifarelli, Megan. "Gesture and Alterity in the Art of Ashurnasirpal II of Assyria," *The Art Bulletin* 80 (June 1998): 210–228.

Hare, Susanna, et al. *The Great King: King of Assyria: Assyrian Reliefs in the Metropolitan Museum of Art*. New York: Metropolitan Museum of Art, 1946.

Reade, J. E. and Curtis, J. E. *Art and Empire: Treasures from Assyria in the British Museum*. London: British Museum Press, 1995.

Stearns, John. *Reliefs from the Palace of Ashurnasirpal II*. Graz: Archiv für Orientforschung, 1961.

Egypt

Aldred, Cyril. *The Egyptians*. London: Thames and Hudson, 1984.

Amenta, Alessia. *The Treasures of Tutankhamen and the Egyptian Museum of Cairo*. Vercelli: White Star, 2005.

Badawy, Alexander. *A History of Egyptian Architecture*. Berkeley: University of California Press, 1966.

Edwards, I. E. S. *The Treasures of Tutankhamun*. New York: Viking, 1972.

Smith, W. S. *The Art and Architecture of Ancient Egypt*. New Haven: Yale University Press, 1998.

Svarth, Dan. *Egyptian Furniture-Making in the Age of the Pharaohs*. Skarup: Skippershoved, 1998.

Nubia

Barley, Nigel. *Smashing Pots: Works of Clay From Africa*. Washington, DC: Smithsonian Institution Press, 1994.

Gates, Henry Louis. *Wonders of the African World*. New York: Knopf, 2001.

DISCUSSION AND REVIEW QUESTIONS

1. What are some examples of forms created out of one material that are then crafted out of a new material?
2. How would you characterize the Egyptian approach to crafting monumental architecture?
3. How would you characterize the Mesopotamian approach to crafting monumental architecture?

CLASSICAL CIVILIZATIONS

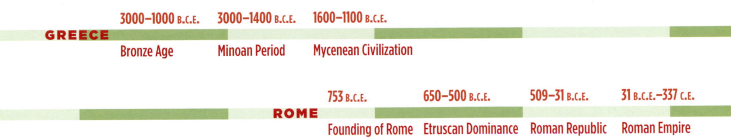

GREECE	3000–1000 B.C.E.	3000–1400 B.C.E.	1600–1100 B.C.E.			
	Bronze Age	Minoan Period	Mycenean Civilization			

		753 B.C.E.	650–500 B.C.E.	509–31 B.C.E.	31 B.C.E.–337 C.E.
ROME		Founding of Rome	Etruscan Dominance	Roman Republic	Roman Empire

GREECE: MINOAN AND MYCENAEAN

The Mycenaeans and the Minoans were ancient to ancient Greece. The Mycenaeans inhabited mainland Greece, where they built citadels that capped mountaintops, including Tiryns, Pylos, and Mycenae. The Minoans had a vibrant seafaring economy, centered on the island of Crete. For their urban centers, Minoans chose inland valleys, preferring to look at mountains from a distance.

Minoan Crete

Neolithic communities existed on Crete from about 6000 B.C.E., but the mature era of the Minoan period is dated to 2000–1400 B.C.E. As with Mycenaean towns, the most important structure was the palace and, significantly, not a temple. Mount Ida is the tallest mountain on the rocky island of Crete, yet Minoan towns did not crown high outcroppings of rock, but took advantage of plains. Minoan cities were not fortified, for the island itself acted as a means of protection from invaders.

The major Minoan historical figures, on whom much of later Greek mythology is based, include Minos, Daedalus, Icarus, Theseus, and Ariadne. The civilization is named for King Minos, the monarch and builder of the largest palace, Knossos. It is worth remembering that in ancient Greece, the line between history and myth is blurry. Daedalus was an architect, inventor, and designer. He invented wings, and his son Icarus met an untimely death because he ignored his father's warnings not to fly too high. Icarus soared higher and higher, the sun melted the wax that bound the feathers together, and he fell to his death. The story of his downfall is a metaphor for ambition and the perils of reaching too high. It is also a familiar familial story in which a son rebels against parental authority. Daedalus created the labyrinth, the prison that held the Minotaur, a creature half bull and half man. Theseus killed the Minotaur, but could only find his way in the labyrinth with the help of Ariadne and her thread, a mythical example of a way-finding device.

Palace

The most important structure on Crete is the Palace of Knossos, and it is likely that the story of the labyrinth derives from those who saw the palace's ruins as a confusing pile of rubble. The palace itself was constructed by an additive design process, its grandeur arising not from huge individual rooms but from the presence of hundreds of them. It is organized around a central courtyard. The palace looked inward toward the court; elaborate exterior façades are not a feature of Minoan architecture.

A central sequence of rooms includes a stairway and a throne room. The vertical connection is formed with broad flights of stairs, clearly ceremonial because of their scale, symmetry, and prominent location. The walls of important rooms were painted. The color palette relied heavily on white, red, and black—attractive colors because of the availability and stability of natural pigments. Blues and greens were rare and expensive and reserved for the most important rooms.

The palace was the center of a town of some 40,000 inhabitants and had ceremonial, administrative, residential, and religious functions. There were no doubt rooms devoted to religious practices, but no separate temples. Houses, like the palace, were two or three stories high, with the ground floor devoted to storerooms; upper floors boasted windows.

The courtyard was an open place, the center of this proto-urban entity, and thus can be considered the predecessor to the agora and the forum. Most streets were paved. On the perimeter of the urban space stood buildings that were distinguished by the unique Minoan cornice and columns. The columns of Minoan architecture have a distinctive profile (Figure 3.1). From a large cushioned capital at the top they taper toward a narrow base. This profile follows the logic of structure, as the weight of

Figure 3.1 Palace of Knossos, column, c. 1700–1400. Knossos, Greece.

Figure 3.2 Throne of King Minos, Palace of Knossos, Knossos (Greece), Late fifteenth century B.C.E.

the heavy entablature above is distributed to an increasingly narrow profile. (Frank Lloyd Wright appreciated the efficacy of the Minoan column, for it minimized the amount of ground space dedicated to structure.) Minoan columns were a feature of exterior façades, and also of the interiors whose liveliness derived from the painting schemes.

The Minoans left behind a fine legacy in fired and glazed pottery. They made items out of metal, such as knives, spears, and jewelry, and had an extensive system of producing textiles. Crete is covered with oak, cypress, fir, and cedar, but few wooden products remain. There was not much in the way of monumental sculpture.

The central ceremonial sequence of the palace contains a throne room, and from it, one of the rare examples of Minoan furniture (Figure 3.2). The throne itself is made of alabaster and likely imitated a common chair type made in wood or straw. This throne has no arms; the back is high, and carved with the naturalistic forms that are a feature of the wall behind it. The walls of the throne room were lined with benches of the same height as the throne, and also made of alabaster. Subsequent Greek furniture is made of wood, and it is probable that the Minoans had wooden furniture, of which this alabaster throne is the only trace. The word *throne* derives from the Greek *thronos*.

The important rooms of the palaces were richly decorated with a variety of wall paintings, including marine scenes and lively lines of men and women bearing offerings. One particularly grand fresco features a giant bull. At several points, the cornices of the palaces feature bull horns. Architectural historian Vincent Scully is one of those who argue that Knossos is important for its siting in relation to the landscape. Subsequent Greek temples take their cue from Knossos. Scully (1962) argues: "The mountain may have other characteristics of great sculptural force, such as rounded slopes, deep gullies, or a conical or pyramidal massing itself, but the double peaks or notched cleft seem essential to it. These features create a profile which is basically that of a pair of horns, but it may sometimes also suggest raised arms or wings, the female cleft, or even, at some sites, a pair of breasts." According to Scully's interpretation, Minoans saw in the landscape the profile of the sacred bull, and sited their cities accordingly.

Minoan history, and its age of grand building, came to an end around 1400 B.C.E., likely due to an earthquake or the exile or mass movement of people, setting the stage for the next episode in Greek history.

Mycenae

Mycenae is on mainland Greece and thus is the immediate forebear to classical Greece. Mycenae is the city for which the civilization itself is named. The history of Mycenae also features a beguiling cast of characters on whom countless myths would be based, including Agamemnon, Cassandra, and Clytemnestra.

The simple **megaron** is the foundation of Mycenaean architecture. It is a U-shaped structure, with a porch that features two columns **in antis**, flanked by two projecting side walls that follow a decorative system different from that of the columns. A hearth stood at the center of the singular chamber, open to the sky.

In contrast to the Minoans, the mainland cities responded to the landscape in a direct way. These early cities, and thus the first chapter in the history of Greek architecture, date to approximately 1400 B.C.E. They chose to locate their fortified cities on mountaintops, thus starting a tradition that saw meaning in the landscape. This was a way of locating themselves in relationship to the cosmos. Walls were built of **cyclopean** masonry, big blocks of irregularly shaped stones. These formidable walls were 20 feet thick and clearly defensive. Gated openings in the walls sharply limited access.

Palaces were elaborations of the vestigial megaron; they were larger, and some were formed from agglomerations of this basic architectural unit.

Tiryns sits on an outcropping of stone in the plain of Argos. The Argive plain is an agricultural area in the Peloponnese. It was occupied from the Bronze Age into the Mycenaean period, 1300–1400 B.C.E.

King Agamemnon dominates the list of important historical figures. He was married to Clytemnestra, and his children included Orestes, Electra, and Iphigeneia. He was the brother of Menelaus. Menelaus' wife was the beautiful Helen, and her preference for a man not her husband was the flashpoint that started the Trojan war. The tragic tribulations of Agamemnon's family, the House of Atreus, were featured in Homer's *Iliad* and *Odyssey*. His family members' individual contributions to history were the focus of plays written by Aeschylus, Euripides, and Sophocles.

Rather than the palaces, the most fantastic type of architecture exists outside of the citadel context. They were the beehive tombs. These deceptively simple structures hold subterranean **corbelled** domes; corbelling is a construction method in which each successive course or layer projects past the lower course. A corbelled arch is structurally a forerunner to the rounded arch. The tombs were approached from a **dromos**, an elongated entryway with high retaining walls, also known as **tholos** (plural **tholoi**). In fashioning these structures, a hillside was selected and then partially excavated. After the dromos, the dome was built, half buried in the ground; once the dome was completed, it was then completely buried with earth. Many exist, and one of the best preserved is the so-called Treasury of Atreus (it was a tomb, not a treasury). A straightforward rectangular burial chamber lies off the main rotunda.

The doorway is a classic post-and-lintel construction, flanked by two Mycenaean columns. In the space above the lintel, a relieving triangle was left, which reduced the weight on top of the lintel and helped distribute the weight to the sides. Sometimes this panel was sculpted, thus starting the tradition of decoration that crowns doorways. A similar relieving triangle embellishes the main gate to Mycenae, the famous Lion Gate. This is the first piece of monumental public sculpture in Greece. With its paired lions, it is reminiscent of Assyrian palaces. In the time period of the early Greeks, the Assyrians were prominent and formidable adversaries militarily, commercially, and artistically.

Mycenaean Greece has a direct relationship to classical Greece. It had a pantheon of gods, goddesses, and other mythical figures; these heroes and villains were the subjects of oral histories and represented in decorated pottery. Stories about the Trojan War were popular. The Greeks developed a graceful way of draping the body and an artistic strategy of developing forms in one material—say, wood—and transforming the shapes into stone. The end of the Bronze Age for the island of Crete and Mycenaean Greece marks the beginning of classical Greece.

CLASSICAL GREECE

Temple Development

The first Greek shrines followed the model of domestic architecture, the simple megaron. These modest structures hint at the riches that are to come. Mainland temples were also based on the megaron. What had been the hearth in a home became the statue of a deity in a temple.

The sources of Greek identity included the Greek language and the Greek Gods, including Zeus, Hera, Apollo, and Athena. Greece, the birthplace of democracy, saw the rise of the city-state, the **polis**. These disparate elements all contributed to the Panhellenic community that was Greece. It was an urban culture whose citizens were beholden to a combination of local allegiances and also to a regional and national Greek identity.

The development of the Greek temple was another way of forging a common identity, yet also an individual civic character that was based on the identification of a city with a god or goddess.

The Temple of Hera I, at Paestum, Italy, is an example of a Greek temple plan (Figure 3.3). The central hall, the **cella** or naos, is flanked by two porches, the pronaos (at the entrance) and the episthodomos (at the rear). The plan shows several of the early steps in the process of crafting a monumental architecture. As with other early Greek temples, there were a number of spatial arrangements that are awkward compositionally and whose problems would be solved by subsequent temple design. First among these problems was the central row of columns down the middle. In the desire to have a larger building, but unsure of how to span a larger distance, Greek architects and designers doubled the interior space with an intermediate row of columns. While this had the effect of increasing the size, it had the undesirable effect of creating a bifurcated interior with two equal long chambers. This layout was at odds with the building's function: to house a single statue.

William Dinsmoor wrote a standard text on Greek architecture, published in 1902. His *The*

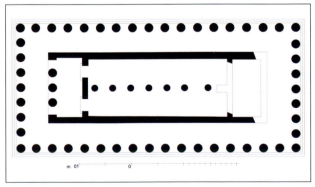

Figure 3.3 Temple of Hera I, 550 B.C.E. Paestum, Italy.

Architecture of Ancient Greece is still required reading for classicists. Writing about early temple design, he noted: "When a temple containing an inner row of columns had likewise a pronaos enclosed with *antae,* the inner row was usually recalled in the pronaos by a single post *in-antis.*" That is, the odd layouts of early Greek temples were reflected in their façades, which featured a column directly in the center.

The Temple of Apollo at Bassae represents a further development, in which two rows of columns create a central nave with two side aisles. From Pausanias, we know that Iktinos was the architect of the Temple of Apollo at Bassae. Pausanias referred to him as "contemporary of Perikles and architect of the Parthenon of Athens." Tzonis and Giannisi refer to Bassae as having "a strange dual conservative-revolutionary identity" (Tzonis and Giannisi, 2004). It had a new and unusual combination of orders—Doric outside, Ionic inside, and a single Corinthian column in the middle—which was perhaps the first column of its kind. Charles Robert Cockerell (1788–1863) visited Bassae in 1812 and did a drawing of the interior (Figure 3.4). It is an odd structure because the central nave leads to a single column and not a statue, and no statue or base has ever been found. The interior façade of the pronaos had three columns, which put a column in the center. The principal façade, accordingly, had nine columns. Eventually Greek architects reached a consensus that an even number of columns was ideal. Bassae also, exceptionally, faces north and has a side entrance that faces east.

The optical refinements of Greek architecture involve defying strict geometries in order to improve the visual perception of a building (Figure 3.5). The Parthenon was the building that most fully employed the potential of optical refinements. The horizontal lines of the Parthenon are slightly convex; the temple platform, the stylobate, bulges in the middle. The resulting curvature had optical and

Interior of the Temple at Phigaleia

Figure 3.4 Iktinos, Temple of Apollo, 450–425 B.C.E. Bassae, Greece. Interior.

functional effects. **Entasis** is the optical refinement of columns; it involves the outward swelling of the shaft. Additionally, the axes of column shafts were tilted slightly toward the center of the building.

Most famously, the location of triglyphs at the corners of the entablature was adjusted. Typically, triglyphs occurred along the centerline of a column, yet this would result in an awkward configuration at the building's corners; it seems logical that the entablature should end on a triglyph. At the Parthenon (and other temples), the corner column has the triglyph shifted off axis; the next triglyph is placed equidistant between the two columns, with the result that the spaces between the triglyphs, the metopes, vary. Yet this is imperceptible to the eye. The result of these manipulations is that while the actual building defies strict geometries, the perceived building is perfect.

Figure 3.5 Iktinos, Parthenon, 447–438 B.C.E. Athens, Greece.

We know very little about Greek domestic architecture. One restoration of a house's section shows a courtyard surrounded by zones of construction (Figure 3.6). Greek houses were important, and epics and myths refer to them, but because they were made of mud bricks, they have largely disappeared from the archaeological record. The section

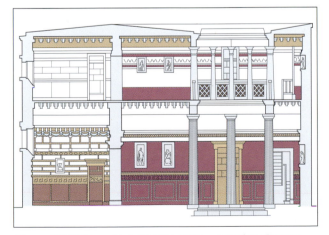

Figure 3.6 Maison de la Colline, 176 B.C.E. Delos, Greece. Conjectural building section.

of the so-called Maison de la Colline, a second-century B.C.E. house in Delos, documents one of the few examples of Greek domestic architecture. It is speculative, as little more than the foundation remains, but foundations in conjunction with models of houses give some as idea as to their three-dimensional projection. They were courtyard-centered houses, two-storied, with walls that were richly painted. A. W. Lawrence (1957) admits that the drawing is conjectural: "The restored section through a house at Delos, though unreliable in detail, must give a fair impression of late Hellenic decoration."

Poems extol the virtues of paintings, and there were many important painters, but we have almost no information on Greek wall painting, because the organic materials of the pigments have not lasted. With the exception of a few remnants, almost no ancient Greek furniture has come down, yet we know an extensive amount about Greek furniture. How?

Material Culture

When studying history, we, as twenty-first-century researchers, have no immediate access to the past. The past comes to us through oral, material, textual, and visual sources. Without sources, our knowledge of the past would be dim. For different time periods and places, the source materials vary greatly, and different source materials relay different types of information. A great deal about ancient Egypt is known because the society itself valued preserving items for eternity, and also because the climate is perfect for preservation. In sharp contrast, we have almost no information about Aztec or Khmer furniture; both were crafted largely out of wood and straw, and jungle environments are harsh on objects made of organic material.

Some cultures created things out of durable materials, such as marble.

Certain materials seem as if they would last, such as gold, yet although gold endures for a long time in the life of an individual, in historical terms it does not do well in terms of lasting for centuries.

History rarely bequeaths information on modest ways of living. To the extent that societies themselves set in motion the preservation process, as did the Egyptians, they rarely considered the objects of the lower and middling classes worthy of preservation. Which is why the subject of furniture in ancient Greece is such a delight. A wealth of information exists, not only about the objects but their use.

The Greeks had an extensive pottery-making industry. They found great utility in pottery in their daily lives, and they decorated their clay pots and vases with pictures. The material was inexpensive and durable. It was actually durable beyond their wildest dreams. Archaeologists love pottery because it is virtually indestructible. For almost all cultures, a great deal of valuable information is conveyed via the medium of pottery. Fired pottery can be thrown into a trash heap, and it will break, but the pieces can be pieced back together. The only way to destroy it is to grind it up.

Vase painting was a less exalted art form than wall painting. Whereas little to nothing is known about Greek wall painting, we have a comprehensive knowledge of vase paintings. Because many of the vases display furniture, we have a thorough knowledge of furniture. Though the information conveyed by this body of images is extensive, we need to realize that we are looking at representations of interiors and furniture and not the spaces and pieces themselves. It is certainly possible that pictorial conventions were at play that do not correspond to actual pieces of furniture.

For example, a drinking cup by the artist Onesimos shows the interior of a stable (Figure 3.7). The convention to indicate an interior is that an object, here a broom, hangs on the wall. Objects in vase paintings often look as though they are hanging in space. The other convention is that the ground plane, the floor, is visible at the bottom of the round "window" through which viewers are looking.

Some Greek vase paintings present versions of popular themes, such as the labors of Herakles or the Panathenaic Festival. A scholar interested in them has hundreds of similar images to examine. Yet some wonderful vase paintings are one-offs, singular images whose precise interpretation remains illusive. There is no definitive authoritative interpretation of the African groom but some likely assertions. The fact that an African individual is represented is significant, underscoring that the Greek and African worlds were in communication with each other. Many recent studies have explored the ancient concepts of race by looking at sources such as this. The Onesimos cup demonstrates that the world of images and objects contributes to constructions of racial and ethnic identity.

An achievement of Greek vase painting is the ability to capture a mood, a psychological moment that is complex and sometimes wry, on the unforgiv-

Figure 3.7 Onesimos, African Groom, 480 B.C.E.

ing medium of painted glaze on a spherical clay surface. Here, the horse appears ill at ease, not ready to bolt but a little testy. The African character, not terribly concerned, calms the horse with one confident hand on its back. One possible interpretation is that he holds a brush and that he is grooming the horse. He is possibly looking at the comb to see if any hairs are remaining; thus this image connects the human quality of diligence to this young man.

An example of the precise dating that is possible because of vase painting is the switch from black figure to red figure. Black figure refers to the method of painting black glaze on red clay. Details were then incised with a sharp instrument, revealing the red clay underneath. Red figure is the opposite of black figure in both technique and result. The artists drew in outline, then painted the background black, leaving the figures red, a color that more closely approximated the human skin tone (red-figure artists left the red clay to indicate the skin of Greeks and Africans alike). *The Dictionary of Art* dates black figure to approximately 625–480 B.C.E., and red figure to 500–320 B.C.E. (Turner 1996). White-ground has a light background, formed by applying a light slip of clay whitened with kaolinte.

A red-figure painting from 480 B.C.E. shows a male youth sitting on a stool (Figure 3.8). It is an image that speaks across the ages, as it appears to show a student engaged in an activity that would be familiar today. He has, no doubt, just opened his laptop and is poised to check his e-mail. Obviously this is not true, but this false familiarity is due to his engagement in an activity that relates human communication to the act of writing. He is practicing writing by using a stylus on an erasable wax table. The image conveys information about literacy, writing, and communication as they relate to a youth.

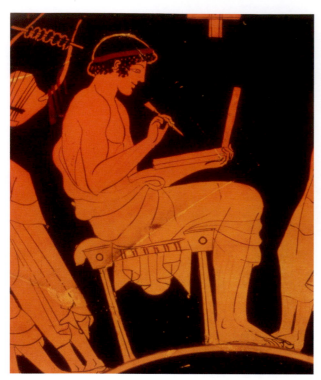

Figure 3.8 Douris. Kylix vase-painting detail, youth practicing writing. 480 B.C.E.

He sits on a square stool that has upright legs. The seat is a frame, connected to the legs with visible dowels, and whose actual support is made from caning or leather straps. The comfort of such a stool is that the straps flex and provide a more comfortable seat than does a hard surface. We can interpolate that this modest stool was appropriate seating for young men who were studying.

Sculptural reliefs constitute another source for information about furniture. A frieze from the Parthenon shows multiple figures sitting on stools. Stools could be exalted as well as pedestrian.

Over the years, many have been interested to test the knowledge of furniture derived from vase paintings by attempting to construct them. One example is a common type of stool that folds and is therefore transportable (Figure 3.9). Leather connects the horizontal rails and forms the seat that in turn could support a cushion. The legs take the form of a gazelle's legs, each side facing in a different direction. The direction of the animal feet em-

ploys a different strategy from that of the Egyptians. On a Greek piece of furniture, the front and back face in different directions; on an Egyptian piece of furniture, all the feet are poised as if to move in the same direction.

Klismos Chair

The signature piece of Greek furniture is the Klismos chair, presented on thousands of vase paintings. (The most prominent categories of vases are black figure and red figure, but there are also a significant number of white-ground paintings.) The Klismos chair is a technically accomplished piece of furniture. When discussing Greek art, people often discuss its grace, its perfection, and its relation to human proportions—qualities that also exist in the Klismos chair. It is one of those rare examples of a design that seems as though it could not be improved upon.

Greek architecture is anthropomorphic, with its proportions related to the human body. This is true of columns, the most obvious example being the caryatids of the Erechtheion, in which female bodies literally take the place of columns. The im-

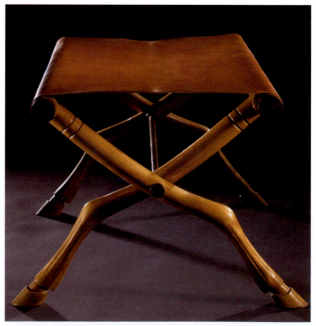

Figure 3.9 Stool reconstruction.

Figure 3.10 Red figure calyx krater.

portance of the proportions of the human body also relates to Greek furniture. In fact, many of the names of a chair (as with a vase) rely upon parts of the body: feet, legs, arms, back, seat.

A red-figure painting from a krater held in Berlin shows a beautiful moment in which a seated woman plays an aulos, a bi-valved flute whose sheath hangs on the wall (Figure 3.10). A woman in a short dress dances. With her extended arms, she forms the right edge of the vase-painting; the left edge is formed by an equally graceful figure, the Klismos chair shown in profile.

The Klismos chair has splayed legs, and its seat is usually represented with caning or leather straps, sometimes with a cushion placed on top of it.

The top rail of the chair back curves and conforms to the sitter's back, making it one of the earliest examples of the design of a piece of furniture related to the body's movement and function.

A reconstruction of the Klismos chair successfully re-creates how the chair was constructed out of wood (Figure 3.11). The chair has a central tapered splat that supports the curved back rail, aided by two side vertical supports. The most

problematic parts of the reconstruction were the splayed legs and lack of stabilizing stretchers. The chair, as crafted, is delicate and subject to fail at the legs. It is important to remember that we are

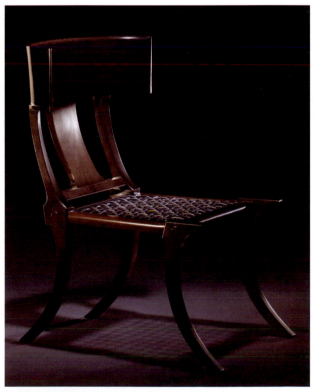

Figure 3.11 Klismos chair reconstruction.

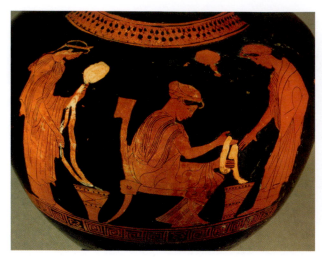

Figure 3.12 Red-figure vase painting.

although there is limited evidence to support this. Just as buildings are presented diagrammatically in vase paintings, it is possible that some of the actual details of the construction of the Klismos chair are not conveyed.

In a red-figure vase painting on a hydria also from Berlin, three women engage in activities related to working and weaving wool (Figure 3.12). The Klismos chair stands in profile. The dowel connections are visible and join seat frame to leg. The seat has no cushion.

A fifth-century Attic (from Athens) bell krater is one example which places a male figure on a Klismos chair (Figure 3.13). An older man (he has a beard) is seated and touchingly tips a krater of liquid for a thirsty child who stands at his feet. It is noteworthy that in these images (Figures 3.10, 3.12, and 3.13), the Klismos chair has a visible backrest that the seated figures to not take advantage of. They do not lean back and rest, but sit upright, actively engaged in playing an instrument, working wool, or quenching a child's thirst.

looking at images of the furniture, not the pieces themselves. One possibility is that the mode of representing the furniture departed from actual construction techniques; perhaps the chairs had stretchers and, for whatever reason, the vase painters eliminated them from their paintings. Some posit that the delicate profile of the Klismos suggests that it was forged in bronze and not wood,

Figure 3.13 Attic red-figure bell krater, c. 450–440 B.C.E.

Although both men and women use the Klismos chair, in vase paintings it appears more frequently in activities that women engage in, such as dancing, weaving, sewing, and placing cushions.

In these images, the Klismos chair is related to the arts of dancing and weaving. It is also witness to common daily activities, again weaving and caring for children. These images suggest that the Klismos chair, at least ideally, was used in the context of conducting work. Showing a Klismos chair in the context of dancing and weaving elevated those activities by relating them to an elegant piece of furniture. It is likely that common stools were most frequently used for daily activities.

Furnishing the Symposium

Multiple images show people setting up furniture for a social engagement that will occur after the mo-ment shown. One red-figure vase painting shows a satyr with a Klismos slung over his shoulder. **Satyrs** were human figures with goat legs, ears, horns, and tail, and who were usually involved in some sort of mischief. The Klismos chair dates to the late Archaic period, and its use was widespread in the classical period.

The Greeks had beds, made of wood, in a frame construction with attached legs. Like chairs, beds had either leather or cane strapping. A fifth-century red-figure vase painting shows a bed, couch, or settee, set up for the all-male, or mostly male, dining and drinking social engagement known as a **symposium** (Figure 3.14). In this painting, two men, one older, one younger, recline on a couch. They lean their arms on striped cushions. The younger man turns to speak with the older man. A three-legged table stands within arm's reach. On another painting of two reclining men, the older gentleman

Figure 3.14 Interior view of an Attic red figure cup. c. 420 B.C.E.

is having his head held by the younger man so that when he vomits it will fall into a krater (another vase) and not soil the bedclothes.

A tradition that departs greatly from modern custom is how Greeks dined in formal situations, which was sitting upright, in bed. Food and drink were placed on three-legged tables in front of the couches. The three-legged tables could be round or rectangular. The couches were arranged to form a U shape, with ranks of couches at right angles to each other. When women are shown in the context of a symposium, they are typically either servers, entertainers, or prostitutes.

A vase painting from an **amphora** shows a young man carrying a Klismos-type couch with a three-legged table attached to it (Figure 3.15). *Klismos couch* denotes a couch with the characteristic curved back of a Klismos chair. The low backrest looks flat, but testament to the accuracy of the vase painter, he has correctly depicted the curved rail in its side profile. It is a wooden couch with attached legs. There was a method to attach the table to the couch, although its exact mechanics are unclear. This youth is involved in setting up couches and tables for a social function. His nudity is a pictorial convention that elevates this daily activity to a higher artistic realm. Getting to the core of the matter, art historian Gloria Ferrari (2002) writes: "In the representation of manhood, the body takes center stage, naked because it is perfect."

A limestone statuette also exists that shows a three-legged table slung over a male figure's shoulder. One reason for the three-legged rectangular version of a table was precisely that it could be carried over a man's shoulder.

A few actual table legs, such as those shown in front of the couches, remain. Some are marble and some are metal (Figure 3.16). In a reconstruction, metal legs are attached to a separately manufactured top. Table tops were either of stone or

Figure 3.15 Pan Painter. Amphora red-figure vase-painting, 475–450 B.C.E.

wood. The legs are fluted like columns and have lion's paws. The lion's feet on Greek furniture were likely an "Oriental" (Mesopotamian) influence. Furniture also existed with turned legs, another Eastern influence. The Greeks broadly referred to the Middle East as the East, or Orient, and this tradition lives on in modern institutions such as the Oriental Institute in Chicago; its collections are Middle Eastern, not Asian.

A common piece of furniture in vase paintings, as in life, was the modest chest. A chest portrayed in a red-figure **hydria** produced in Athens was crafted from planks (Figure 3.17). The front is a frame with an infill panel that has modest decoration of rosettes and circles. The chest has a flat top and what appear to be attached legs. Chests are foremost useful storage devices, and they enter the narratives of vase paintings precisely because an object is held within them.

Figure 3.16 Metal and wood trident table reconstruction.

Another vase painting shows a lower chest with integral legs (as opposed to attached). A pattern decorates its side elevation (a pattern also found in textiles and architecture). A woman takes advantage of the flat surface and low height and sits on the chest.

Chests are one of the most important furniture

Figure 3.17 Hydria red-figure vase-painting, c. 490 B.C.E. Carpenter at work on the chest of a Danaë.

types. Because of their utility for holding things, they are found across the globe. A by-product of their design is that they provide a useful flat surface for sitting, dining, working, or sleeping. In the Greek realm, chests were gendered and metaphoric.

Art historian Gloria Ferrari writes about the representations of women and storage chests in vase paintings: "The footed chest is never far from the maiden. It sits on the ground, by her side, together with the wool basket." The use of the chest was not proscribed, but as an object that contains things, it was a space-enveloping piece of furniture. Smaller chests were related to women because they contained jewels, garments, and sewing equipment.

Just as women in vase paintings are shown cloaked and uncloaked, chests can be locked and they can be pried open. The supreme example of the chest as related to women, riches, and surprises is the story of Pandora's box.

ROME

Roman art and design, broadly defined, was inspired by Greece. The Romans were intimately familiar with Greek achievements in art, architecture, sculpture, and literature, and often compared their works based on their cultural predecessors. The invention of Roman design is that it brilliantly operated within the stylistic parameters initially set by Greece, yet took it in new directions.

The Etruscans were the ancient people who preceded the Romans. The art and architecture of the southern half of the Italian peninsula show that southern Italians had direct experience with Greek culture and with Greek colonies.

The Arch

Roman architecture was highly inventive, and much of the inventiveness was due to the discovery and use of the arch. Where Greek architecture was an architecture of the column and the post-and-lintel construction system, Roman architecture focused on the arch. Other civilizations have had the arch and not really explored its possibilities, including Greece. When an arch is projected three-dimensionally, it becomes a barrel vault. When it is rotated around a single point, it becomes a dome. With the arch, the barrel vault, and the dome, the Romans had a whole new architectural vocabulary at hand.

They also had a new material to accompany their explorations of form: concrete. Although Roman buildings often look as though built of stone, they were largely an architecture of bricks and concrete, faced with stone. Roman architects quickly saw the possibilities of the arch and concrete, and vaulting and use of the arch was widespread by the first century B.C.E.

Urban Character

The Roman Empire adopted the grid for city planning in its military outposts. Yet the capital city, Rome itself, was irregular, responding to topography, important sites, and routes of trade. One oddity is that, as far as city planning goes, Rome was not very Roman; the best examples of Roman city planning are found in Rome's colonies.

The public infrastructure of Greece had been fairly limited. In a Greek city, there was never any doubt that the most important building was the temple. In Rome, new building types provided the public with amenities in addition to religious services. The Roman building program included baths, theatees, amphitheaters, warehouses, and markets—all built on an unprecedented scale. Roman engineers also relied upon the arch to build aqueducts and bridges.

The Roman forum bears some similarities to the Greek **agora** and **stoa**, the Greek outdoor marketplace and public square, and the covered portico that delineated its perimeter. The Roman forum, an elongated rectangular space, was the civic and religious center. The Greek custom of public sculpture proceeds into the Roman period, most evident in the statues that lined the forum. There was a market, and a deceptively modest building type, the basilica, served as a combination stock exchange, general assembly room, and courtroom. And, of course, the most prominent structure was the center of religious ceremonies, the temple. Most Roman temples were similar to Greek temples to the extent that their primary function was the same—to house a cult statue.

Interiors

The Romans are broadly credited with a focus on interiors as carefully designed spaces. Greek temples, wonderful as they were, were figural objects meant to be viewed within the landscape. At close distance, it is clear that the Greek temple existed to house a statue. The development of temple interiors took a backseat to the development of the exteriors and the elaborate sculptural programs.

In Rome, even the forum was inward-looking, in comparison to civic developments that come after it. It was a conception of a public space as a single enclosed entity, almost a room itself. The Roman forum did not lie at the end of a grand open roadway. Citizens and visitors experienced them by walking through the urban fabric. One happened upon the forum, passing through an entryway, after which a grand articulated space opened up. The comparison is anachronistic, but as a process of experiencing an urban space, it is more like the experience of coming upon the atrium in an American shopping mall, which is a bit of a surprise and not made obvious by exterior markings.

The Pantheon

Rome achieved its greatest geographic expanse during the reign of the long-lived emperor Hadrian. It included North Africa and the Middle East up to the tenuous border with Persia; Hadrian's famous wall in England constituted the western edge of the empire; and it included all of France and Spain. Hadrian was a prodigious builder, and his masterpiece is undoubtedly the Pantheon. An oddly self-effacing building, its pediment reads "M. Agrippa made me," although actually it was funded by Hadrian.

The temple faces north, with a standard temple front that gives no hint of the shape of the building behind it. The rest of the exterior is unexceptional. The portico is made of monolithic, smoothly polished columns of Egyptian granite, with eight Corinthian capitals and a triangular pediment. There are two additional rows of four columns that make the porch a deep, ponderous entity. There are great bronze doors; the originals are still there.

The concrete dome is 4 feet thick at the top, swelling to 14 feet thick at the bottom. The dome contains one of the most magnificent spaces in the history of interiors (Figure 3.18). Surprisingly simple, it is a perfect half-dome, set upon a cylinder. It is 142 feet in height. It is one of the first examples of universal space, a giant column-free volume that does not house a myriad of functions; the primary purpose of its large volume is to impress. The hemisphere of the dome is divided into five tiers of coffers, lines that radiate outward from the center.

Figure 3.18 The Pantheon.

The drum is divided into two stories, also delineated with the **Corinthian** order. The floor does not respond to the round dome that hovers above it, but is a grid of squares with inset disks, made of granite, marble, and porphyry, the dark purple rock quarried in Egypt and transported to Rome at great expense. The grid is an additional feature that makes this building seem universal. A grid suggests that it is but a part of a larger pattern that extends far beyond this building. The interior, known as the rotunda, is richly ornamented, although the effect is still of simplicity.

A dome is subject to gravity. The round surface of the dome transfers the vertical forces and transforms them to lateral forces at the base; while the dome itself is subject to collapse, the greatest forces that need to be countered are at the base. The Pantheon counteracts the lateral forces of the dome with massive walls. This considerable mass is remarkably scarcely noticeable on the exterior, and imperceptible from the interior.

The building is superbly designed and required large amounts of labor and materials to build. With a daring design, it is an architectural feat. It is, after all, called the Pantheon, the temple of *all* the gods. It seems cosmic, as though it has a universal meaning. Yet it was a Roman monument, built by Romans. It is an architectural symbol of the heavens in which the Roman Empire and the cosmos were one.

The lighting of the Pantheon is superb. It needs no artificial light. Natural light, from the oculus, is adequate on sunny days and creates a moody and dim atmosphere on cloudy days. The atmosphere changes under inclement weather; rain pours through the oculus, the raindrops refract the light, and a shimmering column of water connects oculus to floor. The building relies upon a unity in visual and architectural terms, and it also served as a piece of propaganda of the empire. The center of the universe was in Rome.

Underscoring the extent of the geographic reach of the Roman Empire, Roman temples are also found in Baalbek, Lebanon; Pergamon, Turkey; Leptis Magna, Libya; and Thugga, Tunisia. It was the Emperor Hadrian who extended Rome into Africa. Part of his strategy to incorporate foreign lands into the empire was a grand building project that included establishing an architectural infrastructure in outposts. To court public support, a favored building type was the bathhouse, found in the Roman towns in Libya, Tunisia, Algeria, and Morocco. Hadrian reinforced the might of the Roman Empire by building monumental architecture in the colonies. This was also a populist move to win people over.

L. P. Hartley (1953) grandly wrote: "The past is a foreign country: they do things differently there." One of the pleasures of studying the past are those moments when one feels a human connection that traverses time. But there are instances when the past seems very strange. One such example comes to us from the Roman African town of Thugga. As with all Roman towns, one of the grandest buildings was the bathhouse, and the Bath of the Cyclops in Thugga sported a very elegant privy (Figure 3.19).

This marble latrine seated twelve and shows a high level of craft on the part of its creators. Marble is an unforgiving material to work with. They could have made this from wood, and there probably were wooden toilets, but for this location, it was made of a permanent material. The high level of technique also relates to the privy's connection to the city's plumbing. The privy was a social arena, and this is an example where modern practices depart from ancient ones. Clearly, the Romans operated with a different concept of privacy.

Baths were grand buildings, and some of the largest in the empire. To finance the building of a public bathhouse was a way for leaders to show their populist leanings. The sequence of bathing rooms followed a standard procedure of tepidar-

Figure 3.19 Bath of the Cyclops, toilets. Thugga (Tunisia).

ium, caldarium, and frigidarium. A bather was first to slowly warm up, to grow acclimated to the heat; one was then prepared for the hot bath, foggy with steam. A final dousing of cool, fresh water completed the invigorating bathing process in the frigidarium. Baths were separated for men and women, with the women's section usually being smaller. Grand baths also incorporated the Greek habit of an outdoor exercise area known as the **palestra**.

Domestic Architecture

Up until the Roman period, little is known about domestic architecture and certainly little about how families of modest means lived. This situation changes dramatically with Rome, where the materials that document Roman domesticity are extensive.

How? Regarding historical sources, the Egyptians used permanent materials, enjoyed a climate conducive to preservation, and themselves prepared items for an everlasting life. In Greece, ceramics are a useful resource, as they are indestructible. Our knowledge of Roman houses and their contents is largely due to one of history's greatest catastrophies, the eruption of Mount Vesuvius.

Pompeii lies fourteen miles southwest of the modern city of Naples, at the foot of the volcanic Mount Vesuvius. Pompeii and the seaport of Herculaneum were destroyed by a massive eruption that occurred on August 24, 79 C.E. A combination of lava and pumice blanketed the city to a depth of 9 feet. A rain of ashes followed, for a total depth of 23 feet. This deadly sludge fell so fast that humans and animals alike were trapped and buried alive.

Italian archaeologist Giuseppe Fiorelli developed a method of pouring plaster into the cavities formed in the volcanic ash where once there had been bodies that disintegrated.

The eruption preserved a large swath of the residential quarters, with the result that we know a lot about Roman domestic architecture and interiors. The tragedy also gives history a precise date; all buildings and artifacts from Pompeii and Herculaneum date prior to the auspicious date of 79 C.E.

The Roman House

The typical Roman house belonged to the larger category of Mediterranean courtyard-style houses (Figure 3.20). It followed a general approach to building that was suitable for the climates of the regions that surround the Mediterranean. A Roman house was similar to a Greek house in that both were centered on a courtyard. Openings connected rooms to the courtyard; openings to the street, doors or windows, were minimized.

The center of the house was the atrium, with an opening to the roof and a corresponding pool for collecting rainwater. This catch basin was sometimes elaborately decorated with mosaics. Besides being a judicious way to collect and store rainwater, the atrium let in sunlight yet kept out the direct force of winds.

There was an idealized Roman house plan that grew out of an Italian house, the domus. ("Italian" here means the vernacular way of constructing houses on the peninsula.) This general layout, of a rectangular structure with an opening in the center, recalls the ancient Greek megaron. Like the megaron, sometimes four corners delineated the corners of the opening.

A central room off the atrium held a small religious shrine. The principal room was the **tablinum**, the room where the head of the house received visitors and where the business of the household was conducted.

The house was inward-looking, and regimented in its layout. From front to rear, street entrance to garden, there was a general progression of openings that become successively larger. Correspondingly, the area devoted to structure becomes smaller, so that a house progresses from architecture to garden.

From the Greek, the Romans adopted the **peristyle**, the perimeter of columns that held up the roof of a covered colonnade. Running around three, if

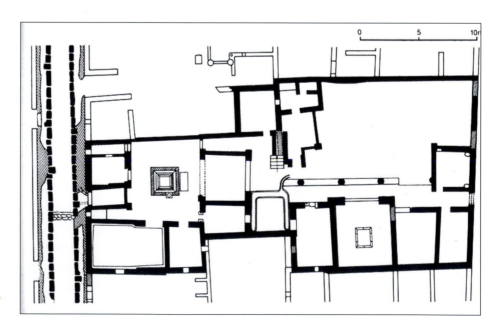

Figure 3.20 Plan of the House of M. Lucretius Fronto, Pompeii.

not four, sides of a rectangular space, the peristyle surrounded a space that usually centered on a fountain or other water feature.

The Greeks painted their house walls, but these schemes became very elaborate for wealthy Romans. For both wall paintings and mosaics, there were skilled artists who did the important work and apprentices who did the more prosaic infill work.

House exteriors did not receive the attention that interiors did; they were stuccoed and painted brick, with tiled hipped roofs. Over time, second stories became more common.

The desire and need for housing in Rome was great, and from ignominious beginnings, the Romans developed an apartment house, the **insula**. Roman houses housed extended families, servants, slaves, and tenants. Most single-family houses, therefore, acted as multiple-family units. Not many mod-

ifications were necessary to turn the Roman house into an apartment house, hotel, or brothel. The insula was also a response to the expanding Roman population.

Wealthy Romans developed another housing type, the villa, a sumptuous country house. In contrast to the inward focus of townhouses, villas had platforms, terraces, peristyles, and galleries that overlooked gardens and vistas.

Roman architecture was often symmetrically centered on an axis, and Roman architects increasingly relied upon the strategy of ending an axis on a curve, whereas the Greeks ended a prominent axis with a flat wall.

Hadrian's Villa in Tivoli is an extreme example of the other end of the scale of domestic architecture (Figure 3.21). It was a retreat for the emperor from Rome. The Empress Livy's rooms on the Palatine, the

Figure 3.21 Hadrian's Villa, near Tivoli, Italy. Model.

wife of the Emperor Augustus, were, in comparison, quite small.

Hadrian's Villa is an enigmatic design. Viewed in conjunction with the other major construction of Hadrian, the Pantheon, it is difficult to reconcile the two. One is his view of the cosmos, the world, and the place of the Roman Empire in administering it; the other is a private world that follows a different set of rules. Some of its pavilions are highly inventive, almost Baroque in the use of curves and countercurves.

Marguerite Yourcenar was a novelist, and her *Memoirs of Hadrian* was an imagined autobiography of the Emperor Hadrian. It is highly regarded for its research and tone, and is often cited as being as accurate as actual works of history. Her approach is appropriate to a time period that saw little utility in separating history from myth. About the emperor's villa, she has Hadrian write: "The villa was the tomb of my travels, the last encampment of the nomad, the equivalent, though in marble, of the tents and pavilions of the princes of Asia" (Yourcenar 1951). Yourcenar's scholarly musing is an explanation for the idiosyncratic nature of the design that follows no easily discernible plan. One theory is that the villa was a repository of his memories, a way for the emperor to revisit places he had visited in life, and the various pavilions are architectural versions of his most cherished memories. This interpretation stems from Hadrian's Roman biographer, Spartianus, who wrote: "His villa at Tibur was marvelously constructed, and he actually gave to parts of it the names of provinces and places of the greatest renown."

Art historian Indra Kagis McEwen writes: "Significantly enough, like the gradual accretions of memory itself, the Villa was not built all at once but was added to piece by piece over the period of years that spanned the period of its owner's reign. And although the pavilions in the linked sequence thus accrued over an Imperial lifetime are all discrete, with well-defined outlines, they ramble over the countryside in an overall assembly that has, like memory, no strict geometry and no clearly designated limit" (1994, p. 54).

Pompeii

Roman houses were richly decorated with wall paintings of a great variety. The painting was done directly on wet plaster. For a long time, Roman paintings were shoehorned into four designations. The usefulness of stylistic categories for Roman painting is disputed, but references to the four painting styles are frequent.

The First style: Painted stucco mimics other materials, such as marble and other stones (Figure 3.22). The French phrase "Trompe l'oeil," literally "trick of the eye," refers precisely to this approach to wall decoration. *The Dictionary of Art* dates the first style to 300–100 B.C.E. Because of the trove of wall paintings from Pompeii, they are virtually synonymous with late Republican–early Imperial Roman painting, or the period 100 B.C.E. to 100 C.E.

The Second style mimics architectural construction; thus there are columns, entablatures, and arches (Figure 3.23). The color palette is similar to that of the Minoans and Greeks. Red was the most popular color, in part because it was chemically stable and fairly easy to produce. The color is known as "Pompeian red." The general composition was to have a wainscot, about waist high or lower, with the area above divided into panels, framed with painted architectural moldings. Second-style painting differs from First-style painting in that the illusionist painting is enhanced with perspective and shading. It is roughly associated with the period 100 B.C.E. to 20 B.C.E.

The Third style shows an increasing amount of pictorial sophistication and the architecture represented is more fantastic; often it is unbuildable—that is, the frescoes show images of architecture that could never be. There are attenuated columns, gar-

Figure 3.22 Checkered mural, Triclinium, House of Aulus Trebius Valens, Pompeii, Italy, c. 70 C.E.

Figure 3.23 Second style room, Villa of the Mysteries, Pompeii (Italy), c. 60 B.C.E.

lands, birds, and vegetation. There are sometimes framed painted panels within the painted scenarios. Specific painters were responsible for these inset pieces. The Third style also includes landscapes. Green pigments were expensive and difficult to produce, hence the prevalence of reds, whites, and blacks. A wall painting such as *The Fruit Orchard* was obviously expensive (Figure 3.24). Republican Rome refers to a form of representative government in which there were patrician consuls. Augustus (63 B.C.E.–14 C.E.) was the adopted son of Julius Caesar. He attempted to transform Rome and make it architecturally worthy of the empire. He claimed that he found a city of brick and turned it into a city of marble. The Third style is related to reigns of Augustus and his successor, Tiberius, the son of his wife Livia. The third style is mannerist, was popular in the years 20–50 C.E., and often incorporates disembodied architectural features.

The styles are related to chronology, although

Figure 3.24 Third style mural from the cubiculum (bedroom), House of the Fruit Orchard, Pompeii, early first century C.E.

street and that were rented out. A food and wine shop has built-in amphorae (Figure 3.26). Pottery vessels were not just fine dinnerware, they were also industrial containers. Tabernae were essentially cafés or fast-food joints. Some public buildings, such as bathhouses, also had tabernae, or spaces for retail establishments, such as tailors. Part of the public infrastructure of Roman cities included raised sidewalks, paved streets, and stepping-stones for crossing streets.

Furniture

Roman furniture inherited Greek forms, and the general repertoire is the same: tables, beds, chairs, and stools. As a general rule, Roman furniture is more elaborate than Greek furniture.

The piece of furniture most associated with Rome is the couch. A couch, synonyms of which are bed and settee, is a horizontal surface for sitting or reclining, with arms at one or both ends. It was used at night for sleeping. It does not have a back. The Romans perfected the social art of dining while re-

there is also considerable overlap. The fourth style is associated with the reign of Claudius (c. 40–79 C.E.). Wall paintings were representational and often featured large scenes and panoramic vistas. They were full of figures, often in movement, and had luxurious foliage and other types of ornamentation. Fourth-style wall paintings often had painted paintings "hanging" as elements of their compositions. Many made overt references to theatre sets, one example being the Emperor Nero's Golden House, 65–68 C.E. (Figure 3.25).

In addition to the retail spaces centered on the forum and urban markets, there were auxiliary retail spaces in otherwise residential areas. These were often perimeter rooms of houses that fronted the

Figure 3.25 Fourth style room, Golden House of Nero (Domus Aurea Neronis), Rome (Italy), 66 C.E.

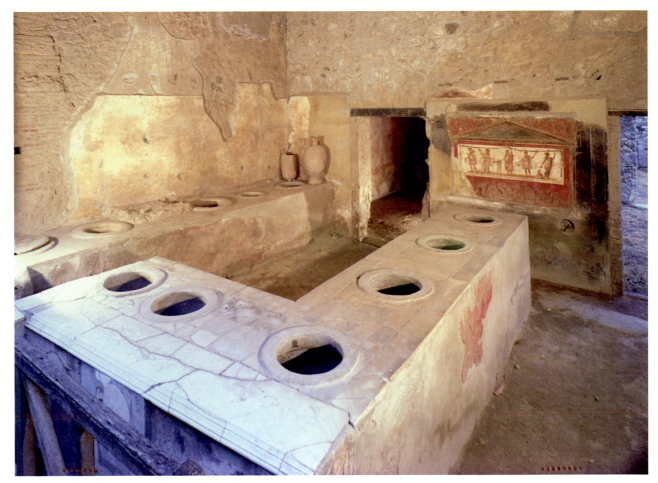

Figure 3.26 Food and wine shop, Pompeii.

clining. In fact, one Roman room takes its name, **triclinium,** from the standard dining configuration of three couches placed at right angles to one another. Sometimes the feet were made of ivory or metal, or wood covered with ivory. Cushions and blankets, placed on top of the couch, rendered it more comfortable.

A bronze couch survives from the Villa Boscoreale, and a wood and ivory couch from the site has been reconstructed in the Metropolitan Museum of Art in New York (Figure 3.27). It features a **fulcrum,** a headpiece for leaning on, which was a Roman invention. Beds were made from cypress wood; more luxurious beds were made from citrus wood and veneered, and sometimes inlaid with glass and tortoiseshell.

A variety of small tables served those who were reclining on couches. These include a small metal tripod table, similar to Greek tables (Figure 3.28).

Some tripods were folding armatures that when opened supported a top, of wood or marble, that held food or drink. There were also rectangular three-legged tables, with tops of marble or wood. Often the legs were manufactured separately from the tops, and of different materials.

Seating

The Romans inherited the Klismos chair, although it lost its central position and was only one of several seating options. The Roman **cathedra** chair is close to the Klismos chair in its form. The stalwart x-frame stool continued to prove its usefulness in formal and informal settings. A noble version of the simple stool, the **sella curulis,** featured more elaborate decoration. Marble thrones or stools were built-in and also used as free-standing pieces of furniture. The author of an early and comprehensive book on Roman furniture, Gisela Richter, wrote that

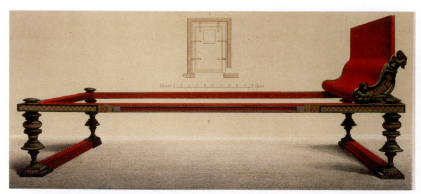

Figure 3.27 Bronze Couch, typical of late Republican and early Imperial periods, Boscoreale.

Figure 3.28 Trident table.

chairs "with turned legs supply a vivid picture of the constant variations that were introduced on a central theme, and indicate great fertility of invention" (Richter 1966, p. 98). One of these, a chair from a Pompeian wall painting of a woman playing an instrument, has curved back rails, painted decoration, and elaborately turned legs (Figure 3.29).

Barrel-formed chairs and thrones were made of wood, wicker, and marble. A barrel chair is simply a chair with a rounded back (in plan). There are no remains of these wicker chairs, but Early Christian and Byzantine thrones resemble them in their form. In his classic work on Roman gold and silver, D. E. Strong (1966) informs us that wealthier houses had some pieces of silver furniture. Bronze and wooden furniture was less costly.

The Romans enjoyed the use of marble tables and benches. Trestle tables, with a marble slab supported by two pedestals, were often used in gardens, and were remarkably similar to garden furniture today manufactured out of concrete.

CONCLUSION

When we look at ancient Greece, we often find ourselves marveling at their products, their majestic temples, their exquisite statues, and their well-crafted vases delineating scenes of myth and life, both played out in the world of things, that includes a vast reper-

Figure 3.29 Throne with turned legs, from a wall painting in a villa at Boscoreale.

toire of furniture. Roman history provides many distractions, from the violence of gladiatorial fights, the drudgery of military campaigns, the competence of engineering projects, and the epic destruction of Pompeii and Herculaneum. Rome took the art of monumental architecture in new directions, and Roman interiors developed an appreciation of luxury to a degree unknown in Europe. The Greeks and Romans competed against each other culturally and aesthetically. It is only in retrospect that subsequent generations could view their artistic productions together as the model for the millennia that followed.

Sources

Dinsmoor, William. *The Architecture of Ancient Greece*. London: B.T. Batsford, 1975 (1902).

Ferrari, Gloria. *Figures of Speech: Men and Maidens in Ancient Greece*. Chicago: University of Chicago Press, 2002.

Lawrence, A. W. *Greek Architecture*. Penguin: Baltimore, 1957.

McDonald, William and John Pinto. *Hadrian's Villa and Its Legacy*. New Haven: Yale University Press, 1995.

MacDonald McEwen, Indra Kagis. "Hadrian's rhetoric II: Thesaurus Eloquentiae, the villa at Tivoli." *Res* 25 (Spring 1994): 51–60.

Richter, Gisela. *The Furniture of the Greeks, Etruscans, and Romans*. London: Phaidon, 1966.

Robsjohn-Gibbings, T. H., and Carlton Pullin. *Furniture of Classical Greece*. New York: Knopf, 1963.

Rykwert, Joseph. *The Dancing Columns: On Order in Architecture*. Cambridge: MIT Press, 1996.

Schimmel, Norbert. *The Norbert Schimmel Collection*. Mainz: P. von Zabern, 1964.

Scully, Vincent. *The Earth, the Temple, and the Gods*. New Haven: Yale University Press, 1979 (1962).

Spartianus. *Historia Augusta*. trans. David Magie. Loeb Classical Library. London: Heinemann, 1932.

Strong, D. E. *Greek and Roman Gold and Silver Plate*. London: Methuen, 1966.

Turner, Jane. *The Dictionary of Art*. New York: Grove, 1996.

Tzonis, Alexander, and Phoebe Giannisi. *Classical Greek Architecture: The Construction of the Modern*. Paris: Flammarion, 2004.

Yourcenar, Marguerite. *Memoires of Hadrian*. New York: Farrar Strauss, 1963 (1951).

Vitruvius Pollo. *De Architectura*. trans. Ingrid Rowland and Thomas Noble Howe. New York: Cambridge University Press, 1999.

DISCUSSION AND REVIEW QUESTIONS

1. What are some examples of Greek design based on the human figure?
2. What are some examples of Greek design based on Egyptian or Mesopotamian art?
3. What are some examples of forms created out of one material that are then crafted out of a new material?
4. Describe the optical refinements of Greek temples?
5. What are the characteristics of a Roman house?
6. How does it respond to its climate? How is it sustainable (relies upon local materials, efficient in its use of energy and water)?
7. Compare a Plan of Hadrian's Villa to the Plan of Versailles. Using the plan as your evidence, what does each structure say about its owner? How is each one a different statement about the nation?
8. What are the similarities and differences between Greek and Roman architecture and design? Consider form, materials, and effect.
9. What is the Roman concept of monumental architecture? What is meant by Roman inventiveness?

CHAPTER 4

EARLY CHRISTIAN AND BYZANTINE

330–800

Early Christian

330–1453

Byzantine

Edward Gibbon famously employed the phrase "fall of the Roman Empire" in the title of his book *Rise and Fall of the Roman Empire*. Its grandiloquence is appropriate for the end of one of the world's great empires. Yet it promotes a picture of complete collapse, when life on the ground was, no doubt, less dramatic and more complicated. There were no immediate population shifts or definitive cataclysmic battles. People and stones did not go away.

Compared to the legacy of Greece and Rome, the works of the early Christians and the Byzantines are less easily grasped, because they lack the stylistic cohesiveness of the preceding periods. In fact, the word "Byzantine" is often used as a synonym for opaque. This is actually due to most people's lack of familiarity with the materials. The Early Christian and Byzantine periods, well studied in academic spheres, are less prevalent in popular media. The two most important historical factors to remember when looking at Early Christian and Byzantine art are the decline of Rome and the rise of Christ.

Regarding form and style, a great deal of continuity links the Roman period and the Early Christian and Byzantine periods that followed it. This is true in dress, painting, sculpture, and furniture. Regarding architecture, the new religion, Christianity, inherited most importantly two architectural forms from the Romans: the straightforward basilica and the luxuriant, centrally planned domed space. Various camps developed, each promoting theirs as the most appropriate to house the services that honor Christ. Architects and clergy have been fighting over the issue of the appropriate architectural form for Christianity ever since.

In seeking to establish an architectural identity for the new religion, some saw the best prototype to be the practical meeting hall of the basilica form. Others, dazzled by the brilliance of Roman baths and mausoleums, created complicated forms that rotated around a single point, a profusion of domes and half-domes, all brilliantly lit with a clerestory. Complications and idiosyncrasies abound. Those who worked with the more straightforward basilica often proceeded to make them as grand as possible. By adding a transept, the basilica became the Latin cross, the plan itself a representation of the cross on which Jesus was crucified.

EARLY CHRISTIAN

Early Christian is a term that designates the art and architecture of the first Christian communities. It does not refer to a specific national polity, nor does it correspond to a precise geography. When discussed in conjunction with the Byzantine Empire, which was a political and economic realm, Early Christian indicates Western Europe, or simply "the West," while Byzantine refers broadly to "the East." Early Christian churches are found in various parts of Europe, the Middle East, and North Africa.

The terms "Early Christian" and "Byzantine" are not synonymous, but related. Some artifacts are purely Early Christian, others are mostly Byzantine, and others, especially on the Italian peninsula, are both.

The earliest examples of architecture related to Christianity were not designed to house Christian services but were co-opted for that purpose. Dura Europos (in modern Syria) contains several sites that are considered the first structures associated with Christianity. Quite simply, those who espoused the renegade religion made do with holding services in typical Mediterranean courtyard houses. The situation changed dramatically in 313 C.E. when the Emperor Constantine issued the Edict of Milan, officially recognizing Christianity as a religion of the empire. With official sponsorship, the edict led to the first era of church building. And with the basilica, it had a form to take it into the future.

EARLY CHRISTIAN AND BYZANTINE CHURCHES

One way of understanding Early Christian and Byzantine churches is to consider, hypothetically, that Christianity was a client whose architect presented two philosophies of thought as to what the new architecture should be. One side promotes the basilica, sober and straightforward, well suited to the function at hand, a horizontal progression, the liturgical march to the apse. The alternative is the centrally planned church, with its symbolically resonant and heavenly dome. Should Christianity not have a house of equal grandeur to the pagan temples, and the building, centrally planned, perhaps with multiple domes, be imposing and bold yet still serve a congregation? For this question, the Pantheon, one of the most moving interior spaces of all time, was the building to beat.

While there is no direct evidence of architects and clergy discussing a particular commission and the most appropriate form for it, hypothetically it is as though there were those in the basilica camp promoting simplicity, and those in the centrally planned camp who felt that Christianity deserved the grandest structure imaginable. It is an argument—simplicity versus grandeur—that survives to the present day. There also exist fusions, basilicas that try to be grand and vertical, and centrally planned churches whose designers do everything to impose a bilateral axis, apse, sanctuary, and space for an audience onto a centrally planned design.

Constantine

Constantine was one of the four co-rulers who followed the Roman emperor Diocletian. He ruled the North from his capital at Trier, Germany. The new religion, Christianity, needed to develop its own building and design culture. The monuments and art of the third century mostly follow Roman aesthetics and constitute the swan song of the Roman Empire. The final Roman monuments are grand indeed, such as the Baths of Caracalla in Rome, 212 C.E.; the Basilica of Maxentius, 307 C.E.; and Diocletian's Palace at Split, 305 C.E. All these buildings are magnificent in scale and form, and are sumptuously outfitted with elaborate decoration.

Part of Constantine's early-fourth-century palace remains, the remarkable audience hall (Figure

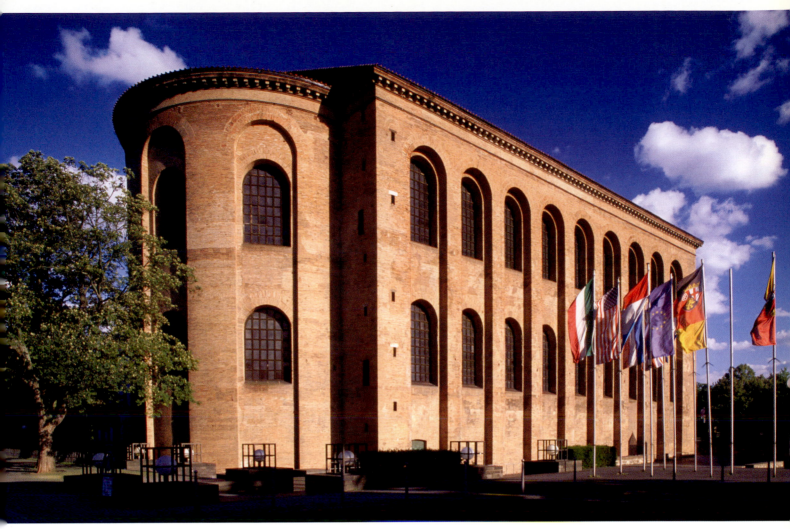

Figure 4.1 Basilica at Trier, Germany, 305–312, exterior.

4.1). While not built as a basilica in the religious sense, which it later became, it is one of the purest examples of the basilica form. Its interior rivals that of the Pantheon, though without awe-inspiring theatrical effects. Trier is a large structure, important in its size yet reticent in its decoration and confident in its tectonic simplicity. It is the epitome of restraint.

Its form could scarcely be simpler: a column-free rectangle with an apse at one end (Figure 4.2). Like the Pantheon, it is an ancient forerunner to modern buildings that seek to explore the idea of universal space, that a simple well-designed program can result in a building that ultimately serves multiple functions. The Basilica at Trier is a straightforward shell that encloses a large column-free space. Within a framework of simplicity, the plan does suggest certain uses. The rectangular area is the space for an audience (later, a congregation), the apse for a speaker, a statue, or an altar. The position of the apse at one end logically suggests that an entryway should be at the other end.

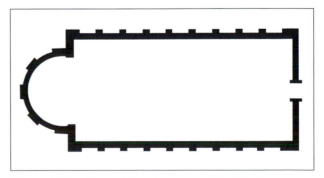

Figure 4.2 Basilica at Trier, Germany, 305–312, plan.

Structurally the building breaks no new ground, although its overall size is impressive. It is a simple load-bearing construction that initially had a timber roof. The exterior elevation is sober if odd; two rows of rounded windows suggest two floors, not the single space of the interior. (At one point, there were outer service galleries that ran around the circumference of the building.) These windows increase the amount of light and deliver it equally to the interior. This early building starts the quest for a vertical expression in basilica shapes. The vertical piers between the windows are expressed, while the spandrels underneath the windows are suppressed. Only the cornice suggests the classical roots of the basilica form. This prescient building looks forward to the nineteenth-century warehouse structures of Karl Friedrich Schinkel and Henry H. Richardson.

Early Christian Churches

The fourth and fifth centuries saw Early Christian churches built throughout Europe, the Middle East, and North Africa. The Church of the Holy Sepulchre in Jerusalem, 328–336 c.e., is a marvelously awkward structure that combines several forms, one of them a basilica, to house the congregation. Another famous Early Christian church is Old Saint Peter's, 333 c.e. (Old Saint Peter's was torn down for the present structure, built in the Renaissance.) A huge basilica was built on the site where his modest tomb was part of a cemetery. The basilica itself was 275 feet long and 190 feet wide. Yet another church that essentially retains its Early Christian form is Santa Maria Maggiore, Rome, 430 c.e.

Italy

Sant'Apollinare in Classe, Ravenna, 535–538 c.e., shows how Christian architects started with the basilica form and refined it to respond to the specifics of a Christian service (Figure 4.3). In plan, Sant' Apollinare is an elongated rectangle, entered at one end, with an apse at the other end. The apse creates a focal point, the perfect spot for an altar or a speaker, and eventually an image or sculpture of Christ. Here, bread and wine were transubstantiated into the body and blood of Christ. Relying upon the model of Old Saint Peter's, side aisles flank the central nave and allow visitors to proceed into the church without interrupting the service. What had been exterior walls at Trier became a screen of columns; a feature of Early Christian churches is that their builders felt quite free to avail themselves of the ready supply of Roman capitals and reuse them. In some churches, the entablature atop the columns was deep enough to walk on, a feature that would morph into an actual gallery in future churches.

The addition of side aisles renders the building grander, and a row of columns separates the aisles from the nave. The side aisles have their own roof, which allows for a row of windows (what had been the second story of windows at Trier) above the columns, known as a clerestory. This ingeniously allows outside light to enter directly into the nave, and further emphasizes the vertical emphasis of the structure and the consideration of light as a heavenly material. The side aisles are lit by their own set of windows. The straightforward timber roof echoed the pitch of classical temples.

In many Early Christian churches, as in Sant' Apollinare, a mosaic or fresco in the apse features a prominent story of the life of Christ. Thus, the most architecturally significant part of the structure underscores the most important figure of the religion. The apse provides a backdrop for the altar, the sanctuary, the holiest part of the structure, and the point from which the priest addresses the congregation.

Spain

While the Early Christian church is primarily associated with Italy, the churches of pre-Muslim Spain demonstrate that the forms traveled and the effects

Figure 4.3 Sant' Apollinare in Classe, Ravenna, Interior, view of nave, 535–538 C.E.

differed. The façade of the Basilica de San Julian de los Prados in Oviedo respects the Italian Early Christian attitude (Figure 4.4). The Oviedo façade is an honest expression of the building's section, projected forward and largely unadorned. It expresses the height of the nave and the side aisles with their sloping roofs. A central doorway indicates the presence of a central axis that leads to the apse.

The Early Christian church has a façade that expresses the building behind it, with a central nave, a triangular roof, a central door opening onto the axis that progresses directly through the nave, and the side aisles, subsidiary paths with a lowered elevation. The volume of the church, visible behind the façade, reveals the position of the transept.

The Spanish churches of the period depart from the basilica form with their robust development of the transept, crossing tower, and generally more complicated interior layouts. A famous Spanish example from this period is San Pedro de la Nave in El Campilo, Spain, 680–711 C.E. Some churches combine the basilica and the cruciform plan, or have apses at both ends of a basilica. San Fructuoso in Braga, Spain, seventh century, imaginatively combines a central plan with three horseshoe-shaped apsidal rooms (McClendon, 2005). Spanish Early Christian churches show a distance from classical prototypes. Exterior masses express interior spaces in the small but exquisitely proportioned churches of pre-Islamic Spain.

Figure 4.4 Basílica de San Julián de los Prados (Oviedo, Spain)

The term "Early Christian" is mostly used to describe buildings. There were also material artifacts, such as fashion, furniture, and household items from this period, although the fragmentary nature of the evidence tells us little. Early furniture and artifacts are typically classified as Byzantine.

The Byzantine Empire

There were three major Byzantine cities: Constantinople, Venice, and Ravenna. The Roman emperor Constantine (280?–337 C.E.) officially adopted Christianity and moved the capital to what had been Byzantium. The renamed Constantinople served as the capital and administrative center, and Venice was a bustling and vibrant center of trade. One of the most famous artistic links between Constantinople and Venice is that a statuary group of four horses that once ornamented Constantine's hippodrome was taken to Venice by Crusaders in 1204; it has since become a symbol of the city. The city of Ravenna served as the seat of the emperor's interests in the West, on the part of the Italian peninsula still remaining in the empire. Ravenna, home to many Early Christian monuments, also houses many Byzantine artworks.

In Ravenna, San Vitale was built during the reign of the Emperor Justinian. Justinian (483–565 C.E.) was a master builder. San Vitale was an attempt to prove that a centrally planned church, if large enough, could hold a sizable congregation and, more important, outperform the basilica form symbolically. In the military and political sphere, Justinian attempted to return to the borders of the empire as they had been under the Roman emperors Trajan and Hadrian. San Vitale in Ravenna, with its form and decoration, correspondingly attempts to restore the grandeur of Rome.

San Vitale is centrally planned, with a cupola supported on a tall drum. There is also an octagon. The sanctuary of San Vitale in Ravenna, the terminus of all processions, was dedicated in 547 C.E.

A famous mosaic in San Vitale shows Christ receiving a model of the church. One of the most intriguing and evocative figures in history was Justinian's wife, the Empress Theodora, an actress praised (and decried) for her beauty, strong personality, and intelligence. A mosaic from San Vitale in Ravenna dates to around 547 C.E. and shows the Empress Theodora accompanied by her attendants (Figure 4.5). This is one of a pair of celebrated mosaics that flank the altar; the other shows Justinian himself, resplendent in purple, yet with the piety of a saint. Emperor and head of the Church, he offers the host, and Theodora carries the wine chalice.

Figure 4.5 Empress Theodora and Her Attendants, c. 532–547. San Vitale, apse, Ravenna, mosaic.

Near the hem of Theodora's gown, the three magi are depicted bearing gifts.

The mosaics of Justinian and Theodora are marvelous examples of political rulers who deftly treaded the thin line between aggrandizing themselves and presenting themselves as pious and obedient followers. Justinian never visited Ravenna, but the existence of a mosaic dedicated to him indicates that Ravenna was nonetheless underscoring its allegiance to Constantinople and its contribution as an important component of the Byzantine Empire. Theodora and her attendants are a part of a procession, a ritual that enlivened the experience of being in a Byzantine church.

Byzantine artists distanced themselves, artistically, from Roman artistic practices. A feature of Roman and Greek religions is that worshipers prayed to a statue. At first, many Christians sought to avoid charges of idolatry, the worship of idols, by staying away from statuary and, above all, having a statue in the apse. This partially explains the lack of attention to statuary in-the-round in Byzantine art. Wall mosaics nicely played into the desire to have instructional motifs that would be intelligible to

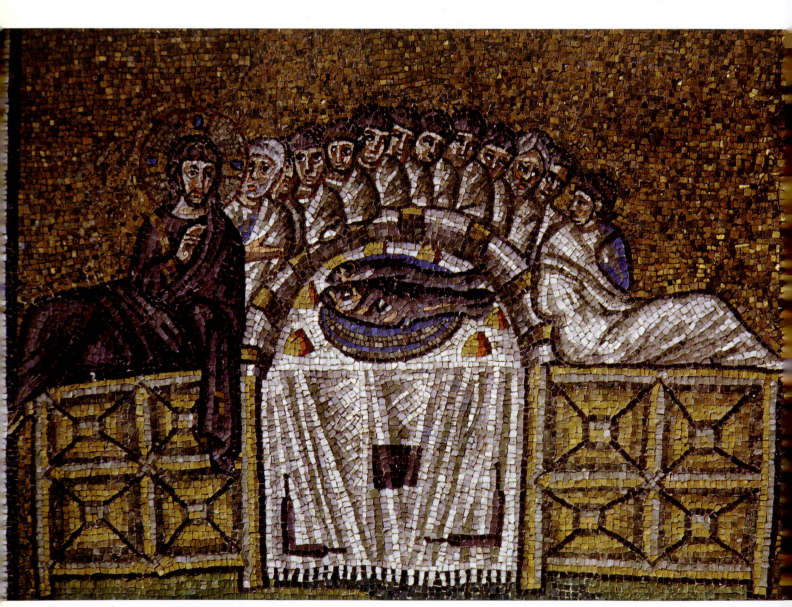

Figure 4.6 Sant' Apollinare in Classe—Ravenna, 520. Last supper mosaic.

their audience yet not repeat the sins of the Romans. Usually, the scenario was to have a representation of some important story from the life of Christ associated with the apse.

Sant'Apollinare in Classe was financed by a wealthy Ravennate, Julianos Argentarios. It contains a set of mosaics dedicated to the life of Christ, set against a golden background. The theme is Christ's miracles, including curing the blind. Such images circulated widely in the Byzantine period via the medium of illuminated manuscripts. A mosaic from Sant'Apollinare is a most unusual rendering of the familiar Christian Last Supper scene.

Christ and his disciples, all dressed in Roman-looking robes, are represented dining in the Roman symposium fashion, recumbent around a semicircular table that is draped with a tablecloth. Christ is the most dominant figure, gesturing as though orating at a Roman dinner party (Figure 4.6). The mosaic showing Jesus and his disciples at the Last Supper reinforces how historical events are seen through the lens of the culture doing the telling. By the time of the Renaissance, the fashion of eating while reclining in bed had dissipated from most parts of the world.

Byzantium

The Byzantine State, or Byzantium, constituted the longest political entity in Europe, lasting from 324 C.E. to 1453. Its primary distinction from its immediate predecessor, the Roman Empire, is that it was Christian. Byzantium was the name used by Greeks and Romans; Byzantines themselves referred to their state as the Roman Empire, as it was, effectively, a continuation of the Roman Empire. Culturally the heir to Greece and Rome, it followed the economic, legal, and administrative systems of Rome.

The word *Byzantine* itself, in modern parlance, is sometimes used to connote confusion, difficulty in understanding, remoteness and mystery. Actu-

ally, the Byzantine Empire was the model for many European medieval states, with its balancing of the roles of secular political leadership with religion.

Byzantine art is rich and evocative. It is Christian and humanist, and continues to speak to the present day. Highlights of Byzantine art are mosaics, ivories, illuminated manuscripts, and domed churches. Most liturgical manuscripts belonged to churches and monasteries, and were not in private hands. Their illustrations, known as illuminations, underscore the light they cast, metaphorically, on their subjects. Many of them look back to classical portraits but also provide invaluable information about Byzantine furniture and the outfitting of interiors. Both chronologically and stylistically, Byzantine art is a link that connects the Greco-Roman tradition, with its centrality of the human figure, to the Renaissance, which also focused largely on the human figure.

The Byzantine Empire is the political entity that inherited the remnants of the Roman Empire. Byzantine cultural productions are characterized by their Eastern influences, and the Empire did thrive economically because of trade with the East. The successor to the Roman Empire, under the direction of Constantine, abandoned Rome. Not only did Constantine recognize Christianity, but he moved the capital city of the Holy Roman Empire to the shores of the Bosphorus, to a city that he renamed. Byzantium was the Roman pagan city, Constantinople was the Byzantine Christian city, and Istanbul is the name of the Muslim city that now stands.

Constantine's city, Constantinople, dominates Byzantine art like no other. Constantine took what had been a politically insignificant city and made it the center of a rich empire. It became one of Europe's largest cities, with a population perhaps as high as 500,000. Constantine's ascendancy is paralleled by the descent of Rome, one of the most famous examples of which was the Sack of Rome, when it was plundered by Visigoths and Vandals.

The three periods of Byzantine art relate to the political structure of this new empire and its geographic reach. In the Early Byzantine phase, the state's borders followed the geographic outlines established by the Roman Empire. During this period, correspondingly, Byzantine art closely follows Roman traditions, although representing Christian themes and outlook.

The second phase, the Middle Byzantine period, increasingly exhibits Islamic influences. The Byzantine Empire lost its North African and Middle Eastern territories; various Italian states emerged that distanced themselves politically and culturally from Constantinople. The Byzantine Empire consolidated and retrenched to an area that is today Turkey, Greece, and the Balkans. This phase was medieval, more coherent stylistically, and resolute in its obligation to Christianity. The use of ivory and enamel was prevalent in the design of furniture and small precious objects.

In the Late Byzantine period, the last florescence, the empire had become a diminished polity, with Constantinople as its spiritual center and limited Greek territories.

Hagia Sophia

Constantine ruled from 306 to 327 C.E. His son, Constantius II, in an auspicious move, dedicated a Christian Cathedral, an early Hagia Sophia, as part of a complex that included a public urban space, church, and palace. The Emperor Justinian ascended the throne of the empire in 527 C.E. He and his architects turned their attention to the site first built on by Constantius. Richard Krautheimer, whose comprehensive work on Byzantine architecture (1996) is standard reading, wrote that "Byzantine architecture starts with Justinian." Justinian belongs to the ranks of the greatest patrons of architecture. What clearly rankled Justinian, and no doubt others, is that no Christian building rivaled the Pantheon.

Working with two architects, Anthemius of Tralles and Isidorus of Miletus, Justinian erected Hagia Sophia, the Church of the Holy Wisdom, in Constantinople between 532 and 537 C.E. Hagia Sophia was an updated manifestation of what the Romans knew how to do exceptionally well—make grand structures out of bricks and concrete.

The multidomed structure is the supreme symbol of Constantinople's ascendancy over Rome and constituted the Christian claim of the mantel of universal rule (Figure 4.7). In most respects, Hagia Sophia seeks to outdo the Pantheon. The beauty of the Pantheon lies in its simplicity and geometric purity: The Roman structure was a dome on a drum. Built on a massive scale, Hagia Sophia has a dome lifted onto four columns and connected to them with the ingenious device of **pendentives**. The plan of Hagia Sophia merges the longitudinal basilica with the centrally planned church by abutting the central dome with two half-domes. The assembly of domes rests largely on the four giant piers that sit within an outer shell. The space between the inner dome sequence and the outside wall is a perimeter of colonnaded arcades. It is therefore a double-shell construction. Some of the many innovations associated with Hagia Sophia are its unusual capitals, vaults, colonnaded arcades, carefully constructed interior pavements, and wall mosaics.

Hagia Sophia is the supreme architectural monument of the Byzantine empire. It is a hybrid of a congregational basilica and a multidomed and vaulted superstructure. Although there is a sanctuary located in an apse, a nave, and side aisles, this is not immediately apparent because of the overwhelming presence of the giant dome.

Forty round windows enliven the base of the dome and constitute a new type of clerestory. Once the dome is lifted up on columns, it is possible to have a bigger system of openings between spaces; to the east and west of the central dome, half-domes create an immense vaulted space.

Figure 4.7 Isidoros and Anthemios, Hagia Sophia, interior of Dome, 532–537 C.E.

The central dome of Hagia Sophia rises to a height of 55 feet above the floor, the largest vaulted space of the ancient and medieval world. It is the supreme example of a Byzantine church; many churches built after it used it as a model. And although it was designed and built as a church, it curiously becomes a model for Ottomon mosques as well (Mark and Ahmet 1992). Hagia Sophia is to the Byzantine Empire as the Pantheon was to Rome and the Parthenon to Greece.

The exterior is impressive in its size, with waves of domes that lead up to the central dome. Yet the real achievement of Anthemios and Isidorus was the interior. Yale art historian Robert Nelson writes: "During the nine hundred years of the Byzantine Empire that stretched ahead, no structure would surpass the size and grandeur of Hagia Sophia" (Nelson 2004). One interpretation of the complicated design is that the building explores a series of visual attributes from opposite viewpoints. It was the tallest building of its day, clearly expressing verticality, yet its central space also displays a strong hint of the horizontal. The first two bands of the interior elevations emphasize continuous horizontal lines. The two half-domes are balanced by two blind arches, flat elevations that appear as two-dimensional representations of a half-dome. In plan, the two half-domes appear as near equals to the central dome, yet because they rise to a lower elevation they are clearly lower in the building's architectural hierarchy.

A capital from Hagia Sophia detail shows shallow carving, a hint of the classical with **volutes**, and a spread of vegetal motifs (Figure 4.8). A Byzantine capital often looks like a pillow, its bulbous form reflecting the physical demands on a capital to distribute the weight of a stone entablature onto a single column. A profusion of shallow decoration, covering every morsel of a surface, is a feature of Byzantine art.

Part of the Byzantine attitude toward art is explained by the desire and necessity to distance itself from the idolatry that was associated with Roman paganism. Byzantine artists, although trained in artistic traditions that clearly derived from Rome, needed to establish a new direction for a Christian art. One way to do this was to focus on geometric patterns and floral designs. A mosaic floor shows the influence of Roman floor design and the use of tesserae (Figure 4.9). Byzantine artists incorporated

Figure 4.8 Isidoros and Anthemios, Hagia Sophia, capital detail, 532–537 C.E.

Figure 4.9 Mosaic

glass, semiprecious stones, and metals into their mosaics, which made them glisten. In Roman times, the mosaics brought life to the floors; Byzantine artists moved them to vertical surfaces that were sometimes curved and increased their color and sparkle.

Furniture

The furniture realm involves the reuse of Roman forms, sometimes unchanged, although with an increasing amount of invention and adaptation over time. Regarding the continuation of inherited forms, the X-frame stool survives with its useful form intact. Beds continue as well. The most ubiquitous piece of furniture was the chest, which, when outfitted with strong hinges and a lock, kept thieves at bay.

Throne of Maximian

The throne of Maximian is an ensemble that incorporates magnificent examples of ivory carving and is the high point of Byzantine furniture (Figure 4.10). Scottish Byzantinist David Talbot Rice (1903–1972) considered it an artistic link between Ravenna and the ivory-carving schools of Alexandria, Egypt. Made in 540 C.E., ten of the panels of the throne show scenes from the life of Joseph. The story of Joseph, not surprisingly, was popular in Egypt. Other details of the throne also suggest an Egyptian provenance.

The larger panels on the front of the throne show St. John the Baptist, looking particularly grand, and may have come from Constantinople. It is possible that either the artists for these panels came from Alexandria and Constantinople and

working their exacting craft on an expensive material. As a work of furniture, it was likely assembled by someone with experience creating chairs.

Maximian was archbishop from 545 to 553 C.E. When he sat in this chair, his feet touched the ground and his back was erect. The throne's back is not for leaning against—there is no place to rest the head. The sitter's hands and arms lie in dignified repose on the armrests, which is to say that the throne demanded a dignified public posture of its sitter. One could notice the Eastern flavor, literally in spices, metaphorically in art, such as the famed ivory panels of Alexandria, Antioch, and Palmyra.

Boxes, chests, and caskets made of ivory constitute the biggest cache of designed objects in Byzantine art and display the height of ivory carving.

Figure 4.10 Throne of Maximian, c. 540 C.E.

traveled about, or that the ivory panels were carved in those locations and transported as panels to Ravenna, where a talented craftsman assembled the parts and pieces into the masterful chair that stands before us today. Some of the lesser panels were done by other hands. The nonfigurative carved panels were stock items, produced en masse, and used as connectors.

The chair's form is reminiscent of a barrel chair, a form whose beginnings ultimately lie with the Roman cathedra chair. The throne of Maximian is carved on all sides, with a rounded back; this suggests that it was not placed against a wall but was instead a figural sculptural piece. The most prominent and elaborate panels face forward. The throne itself is similar in form and scale to other works. Its exceptional nature derives not from height, form, or scale, but from the expertise of the ivory carvers,

Figure 4.11 Illumination showing the scribe Ezra at work in a medieval armorium, from the Codex Amiatinus, late eighth century.

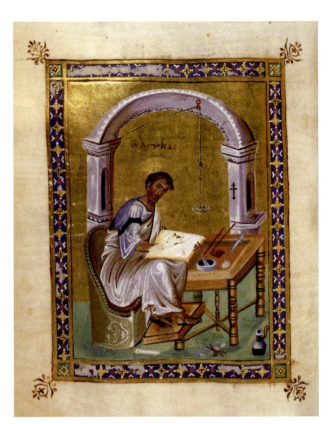

Figure 4.12 Miniature showing a chair and 5-legged table, mid-tenth century.

Although few examples survive, it is likely that there were also many simple wooden pieces.

An illumination that shows the scribe Ezra at work features a table, chair, footstool, and bookcase with doors (Figure 4.11). One of the primary functions of monasteries was copying texts, and the first libraries came from monasteries. This image shows the process of creating copies, and an armoire that holds completed works. The object that contained the illumination, a book, is represented in the illumination. The image can be considered a tribute to the importance of the book, collections of books, and the images they contained.

Another miniature, from the mid–tenth century, shows a man similarly at work, seated in a barrel chair (Figure 4.12). The chair and his robe convey the legacy of Rome. With his feet on a footstool, he works with a manuscript in hand; the five-legged worktable in front of him holds his supplies. A com-plicated metal lighting device extends an oil lamp directly over his work surface, directing its luminance to the pages of his book.

Medieval Furniture

While the throne of Maximian shows the highest level of what Byzantine furniture makers and ivory carvers were capable of, to understand how most people interacted with furniture, we turn to other sources. Two undated medieval stools, of uncertain provenance, demonstrate that most people's experience with furniture involved pieces that were strictly utilitarian. It is inspiring that even when someone sought to craft a piece of furniture as straightforwardly as possible, whose only purpose is to provide a sturdy seat, there is considerable variety in form, and a simple aesthetic result—even if the desire for a pleasing appearance was secondary.

One three-legged stool is anthropomorphic to the extent that its soft curves respond to the curves of a human figure whose posterior sat on it, and whose fingers clasped it in order to carry it from place to place (Figure 4.13). The integral handle indicates that this rough-and-ready stool was picked up, carried about, and set down so that its owner could get down to work. The method to render this stool rugged relies on neither hardware nor strengthened con-

Figure 4.13 Medieval stool

Figure 4.14 Medieval stool

nections; it relies on the inherent strength of the material from which it is made. A monoxylous work, it is made from a single piece of material. A leg is less likely to shear off when integral to the piece.

Another **monoxylous** stool cleverly takes advantages of tree branches to form its legs (Figure 4.14). The resulting form retains trace resemblance to the natural material from which it was created: a trunk with branches. The resulting piece resembles the three-legged stools that satyrs and other Greeks were fond of slinging over their shoulders, responding to yet another part of the human anatomy.

VIKINGS

In order to create monumental architecture and public sculpture, great wealth and stability are desirable. Societies that moved, herders, and hunter-gatherers such as the Berbers did not have the luxury or the necessity of permanent buildings, and thus turned their design energies to smaller-scale objects. Seagoing societies, pirates and Vikings, were skillful at many tasks, most notably the sophisticated knowledge of carpentry necessary to build a ship. This involved precise cutting, joints, and complicated geometries.

The Vikings were a migratory people, hunter-gatherers of the seas. In the 830s, the Vikings started raids that sometimes involved their wintering in the lands they attacked. Their knowledge of shipbuilding is evident in many aspects of their cultural productions. Even their streets were paved with wood.

Their ability working with wood is visible in a bed whose curved headboard and trapezoidal stretchers resemble the boats for which they were famous (Figure 4.15).

Figure 4.15 Viking bed.

CONCLUSION

In the thousand years after the end of the Roman Empire, Christianity became more important over time. While Early Christian basilicas lean toward the solemn, the multidomed church was pompous and emotive, with Hagia Sophia as the supreme example. Paintings and mosaics were important, yet sculpture almost not at all; relief carvings were shallow, focused on the surface. The heritage from Rome was both artistic and technical.

Furniture followed a similar path in its journey from ancient Rome to the Renaissance. Some forms existed virtually unchanged, such as the X-frame stool. Modest tables and chests continued to demonstrate utility. Some forms were adapted and made of new materials. Barrel chairs, which the Romans made in marble and straw, were covered with ivory. The habit of dining recumbent all but disappeared, as did the popularity of the public bathhouse.

The Early Christian and Byzantine periods inherited Roman forms and for centuries put them to contemporary use, in the process making them their own. The artists of these periods developed vibrant traditions of art, architecture, and the decorative arts. Not stylistically cohesive, the works from the time after Rome's implosion and before its rebirth in the Renaissance are known for multiple qualities. The works are secular and sacred, tender and brash, solemn and dazzling. It is no doubt that the combination of qualities resulted in a collection of works that are subjective enough to speak to individuals, yet universal enough to appeal to many.

Sources

Krautheimer, Richard. *Early Christian and Byzantine Architecture*. New Haven: Yale University Press, 1996.

Mark, Robert, and Ahmet Çakmet. *Hagia Sophia: From the Age of Justinian to the Present*. Cambridge: Cambridge University Press, 1992.

Matthews, Thomas. *The Art of Byzantium: Between Antiquity and the Renaissance*. London: Calmann and King, 1998.

McClendon, Charles. *Origins of Medieval Architecture*. New Haven: Yale University Press, 2005.

Nelson, Robert. *Hagia Sophia, 1850–1950: Holy Wisdom Modern Monument*. Chicago: University of Chicago Press, 2004.

Rice, David Talbot. *Art of the Byzantine Era*. New York: Praeger, 1966.

Graham-Campbell, James. *The Viking World*. London: Frances Lincoln, 1980.

Oxenstierna, Eric. *Die Wikinger*. Stuttgart: W. Kohlhammer, 1959.

Tryckare, Tre. *The Viking*. Gothenburg: Cagner and Co., 1966.

DISCUSSION AND REVIEW QUESTIONS

1. What were some of the important materials?
2. How is Early Christian and Byzantine art a continuation of Roman artforms?
3. How does the Throne of Maximian make its seated figure look visually prominent?
4. How would a viewer of the Throne of Maximian respond to it?
5. What do you imagine the throne's relationship to its architectural setting to be?
6. How important was comfort to those crafting the throne?
7. Compare Hagia Sophia to the Pantheon, considering both similarities and differences.
8. Discuss the basilica form versus the centrally planned form. What does each plan suggest about its use? How is each appropriate, or inappropriate, for certain types of religious services?

CHAPTER 5

ROMANESQUE AND ISLAMIC

800–1150	750–1492	1000–1200	1502–1736	1525–1750
Romanesque	Islamic Spain	Seljuq Empire	Safavid Dynasty	Mughal Era

There is no shortage of ways to understand the some one thousand years between the Fall of Rome, circa 330, and the Renaissance, the style inspired by ancient classicism. One could simply ignore seemingly singular achievements, consider them the results of minor trends, label the period "the Dark Ages," and proceed as quickly as possible to the Italian Renaissance. In belated deference to the craftsmen and artists who produced so many fine works during this period, whose economy of material teamed with a fearful spirituality, the term "the Dark Ages" has rightly fallen into disgrace. Another now-discredited approach was to emphasize the unintelligibility of the artifacts of this period and thereby dismiss them. Yet, when approached with patience, the study of the Medieval period, and the focus of this chapter, Romanesque and Islamic design, yields considerable riches.

For many people, Romanesque is not a pale version of the more florid Gothic that followed, it is the style they revere most. Henry Hobson Richardson, one of the most important American architects of the nineteenth century, worked almost exclusively in a Romanesque revival style. A seminal figure of his time, he saw the Romanesque style as the best

way to express the modern age. His work, and that of others, led to a building type as important in its era as the cathedral had been for France: the skyscraper.

Islamic design is an ongoing endeavor. Mosques continue to be built in traditional Islamic styles. Furniture and works of decorative art, from Africa to the Middle East to Asia, are still produced that can lay claim to being called Islamic.

This chapter considers Romanesque and Islamic design as parallel tracks, with separate beginnings and locations, that become intertwined by military operations, those of the European crusades into the Middle East and Islamic expansion into Spain and France. As with all military operations, there were horrible consequences for many people, yet the cultural results of this blending, in which Islam incorporated European forms, and in which southeastern Europe grew more Islamic, are often stunning. This is a testament to the powers of artistic creation. The greatest achievements of the Romanesque and Islamic periods are not found in freestanding pieces of furniture but in majestic buildings and the rich design legacies that they bequeathed to subsequent generations.

ROMANESQUE

Frankish control of Gaul (the Franks were a Germanic ethnic group) was a step toward establishing a stable order with a centralized authority, a political achievement not experienced by other European regions since the collapse of the Roman Empire. Two early pieces of furniture are inextricably linked to their famous occupants. Dagobert I and Charlemagne are rare figures of authority in a period known for its factions and a general shift toward feudalism. Few pieces of furniture survive from this period. These two exceptional chairs are best understood by considering a triad of strong ruler, uni-

fied government, and imposing chair. Transitional pieces between Medieval and Romanesque, they exhibit features of both.

Two Early Chairs

Dagobert I (605–639 C.E.) was a ruler with an unusual achievement during this period: he ruled over a united realm. He was a Frankish king who oversaw a period of prosperity, and he was a patron of the arts, specifically those involved in metalworking. The "throne" that makes its appearance here, really a chair, is made of metal (Figure 5.1).

The X-frame chair existed in Egypt, Nubia,

Figure 5.1 Throne of Dagobert (France), early seventh century; arms and back, 1125–1150.

Greece, and the Byzantine Empire. The most obvious precedent to Dagobert's chair is the Roman *sella curulis*. It is a modest type of chair, here rendered regal. In the second quarter of the twelfth century, the Abbot Suger, an advisor to King Louis VI, significantly altered what had been a folding bronze stool by adding on elaborate side and back panels. Dagobert's chair was both ecclesiastical and secular: It was an emperor's chair, and it resembled the X-frame chairs favored by popes.

Folding chairs had proven useful for military campaigns and also when noble households took up new quarters. This is a frontally oriented folding chair. When facing the chair, a user grasps the two arms, pulls them together, and it collapses in the middle. (This is in contrast to Chinese folding chairs, which fold laterally.)

Dagobert's chair exhibits several of the conflict-ing trends of the earliest years of the Romanesque period. Small in scale, its grandeur derives from the intricate details of its cast bronze and its compli-cated mechanical operations. It is unquestionably majestic, yet portable. Rather than being a typical example of its period, it is an example of the skill that can occur in unstable times. It presages both the imposing Gothic chair and the now ubiquitous director's chair, which it so straightforwardly re-sembles. The sturdy lion's paws provided a stable seat in a changing landscape. Its survival stems from its unusual material, and it operates as a stand-in for the innumerable wood chairs, similar, if inferior, that have not survived.

Charlemagne's throne is similarly famous be-cause of the person who sat in it (Figure 5.2). This piece of furniture confers authority on its user by its height, its material, and the social circumstances

Figure 5.2 Charlemagne's throne, Palatine Chapel, Aachen (Germany), 792–805.

of its use. Situated on a raised platform, it exhibits the increasing preoccupation with height, a primary means of conferring status and confirming authority. Charlemagne (742–814 C.E.) has a lofty place in history because of his success at creating a unified government. Planar in form, the shape of his throne stems from its grand material, marble sheets. Barely decorated, it also blurs the lines between ecclesiastical and secular furniture. It has several features in common with a number of Byzantine bishops' thrones.

The status that a throne confers upon its user derives from its context, and Charlemagne's throne has a grand context. Two of the finest constructions that resulted from the reign of Charlemagne are the palace and royal church at Aix-la-Chapelle (today Aachen), designed by Otto of Metz. Work on them began in 792 C.E. Only the chapel remains (Figure 5.3). The chapel that houses the throne owes its centrally planned form to ancient Roman monuments and is one of the key structures of the Carolingian period.

Figure 5.3 Detail, Odo von Metz, Palatine Chapel, Aix-la-Chapelle (Aachen, Germany), 792–805.

Figure 5.4 Fortifications, Aigues-Mortes, France, thirteenth century.

With its location in Germany, it is one of the last direct links to the ancient Roman presence in German lands. Yet the fact that French-speaking Charlemagne had his capital in Germany is also an early indication of the long periods in which French- and German-speaking people strove to form an alliance. The bicolored stonework is a dominant feature of the space and becomes one of the hallmarks of Romanesque architecture in Germany, France, Italy, and Spain.

A time period and a style are associated with Charlemagne: Carolingian. In his eponymous style, Carolingian, one sees the beginnings of the forms that became known as Romanesque. Charlemagne seemed to usher in an era of stability, grandeur, and consolidation, a cultural and political unity. But following his death, political, military, and economic pressure from the north and south returned.

Cities

Many medieval cities, well up to the early Gothic period, were heavily fortified, and Aigues-Mortes, in the southern French region of Languedoc-Roussilon, is a fine example (Figure 5.4). Aigues-Mortes was the port of embarkation for the two Crusades of Louis IX. Medieval cities became individual strongholds. Inside the walls, wattle-and-daub and timber construction were prevalent.

Although Aigues-Mortes followed a grid, a feature of many medieval towns was a narrow and winding street. One of the achievements of architectural historian Spiro Kostof's work is his examination of planned, and unplanned, medieval cities (Kostof 1995, pp. 349–351). The latter shared a characteristic with their Islamic cousins. Passageways in the Casbah had beguiling curves, surprising dead-end streets, and lacked an obvious logic. These quarters with their intimate scale provided charm and favored those familiar with their ins and outs. European Medieval town planning, similarly, confused strangers, another example of the defensive posture of so much construction of the Medieval period. The defensiveness and xenophobia had cultural and artistic ramifications as well.

Churches

The twelfth-century Cathedral of St. Foy at Conques, France, is known for the masterfully carved decorative program of the façade. Romanesque façades offer a simple menu of options for a public who led a hard life, and many of whom were illiter-

Figure 5.5 Detail of Tympanum, Saint Foy at Conques (France), 1124–1135.

ate. For those unable to read, the façade's reliefs, the carved capitals, and the sculpted **voussoirs** rendered the Bible's lessons visible. Acting as a sign, the message is prosaic and immediate: Going over the threshold and into the sanctuary of St. Foy was a step toward salvation. This is the spiritual direction represented by the central figure of Jesus; salvation lay in following him. The **tympanum**, whose subject is the weighing of souls, makes clear the available choices for parishioners and pilgrims alike. The consequence of not choosing the path of righteousness is also shown. The alternative is Hell, where a devil stands, club in hand, all too eager to feed souls into a dragon's mouth (Figure 5.5).

Romanesque church plans are a development from Early Christian church plans, but they were also inspired by rediscoveries of antiquities. The buildings largely follow the form of the basilica with an apse, only their designers explored new means to fashion architectural monumentality (Figure 5.6). The most significant addition was the **transept**. Adding the transept provided a central focus on the altar, and gave the building its overall shape. The building's interior became something to be walked around and experienced rather then perceived in an instant. And there was the considerable symbolic benefit that the plan of the church took on the shape of the crucifix.

A growing knowledge of architectural construction allowed for the addition of **side aisles**, part of a general enlargement process. The addition of side aisles made the plan laterally expansive. A masonry barrel vault roof often took the place of a wooden timber frame. On the longitudinal axis, the early Christian apse developed into a choir with an **ambulatory**. Side chapels were added. Viewed from the outside, the rounded mass of the rear elevation, made bulbous, plastic, and imposing, is known as the **chevet**. The prominent zone of the **narthex** corresponds in plan to the façade, the primary threshold through which one enters.

St. Sernin in Toulouse (France) is a paradigmatic example of the heights that Romanesque ecclesiastical architecture could reach, both literally and figuratively. The basilica shape was inherited; what was new was the nascent grandeur.

It is not incorrect to view the Romanesque cathedral as a predecessor to the Gothic cathedral, regarding both chronology and form. It is wrong, however, to view it merely as a forerunner, or Gothic poorly done. Romanesque churches were significant achievements in their own right, at once majestic and sobering. For many, Romanesque churches are among the finest examples of architectural form and interior space, due to the qualified simplicity of their design.

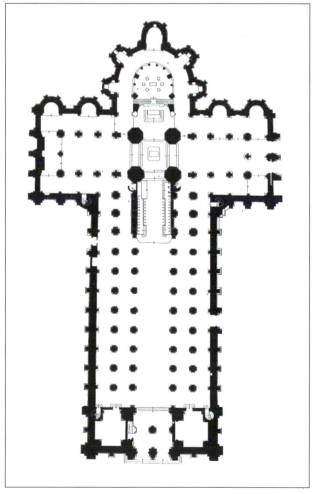

Figure 5.6 Saint Sernin, plan, Toulouse, France, 1080–1120.

Figure 5.7 Saint Sernin, elevation, Toulouse, France, 1080–1120.

Saint-Sernin's elevation is an honest projection of the building behind it, a more elaborate vertical surface than graced Early Christian church façades (Figure 5.7). There are indications of it being treated as a designed vertical surface, worthy of its own articulation, the foremost being the elaborate entryways and the giant oculus that is a forerunner to the Gothic stained-glass window.

Churches in the Romanesque period fall into three categories: urban pilgrimage sites, sprawling rural monasteries, and modest parish churches. St. Sernin is an example of an urban pilgrimage church. Famous monasteries such as Cluny were important economic, political, religious, and cultural centers. Every village, no matter how small, felt the religious impulse and did its part to construct a building worthy of God.

Regarding both scale and articulation of detail, a plan of a provincial church in Cézais, France, shows the other end of the spectrum (Figure 5.8). A minimal structure, it is not far removed from the humble basilica form of the Romans. Its primary gesture toward grandness is centered on the apse. Hundreds of Romanesque parish churches dot the French countryside and visiting them is one of life's pleasures. A tympanum from an equally modest church in Foussais-Payré, France, shows how the Crusades were important international events whose effects were felt worldwide and in the smallest village. The central scene shows Jesus having dinner at the house of Simon, one of the Pharisees. Above them looms an architectural representation of Jerusalem, looking suspiciously Romanesque.

A goal of the crusades, not realized, was to put

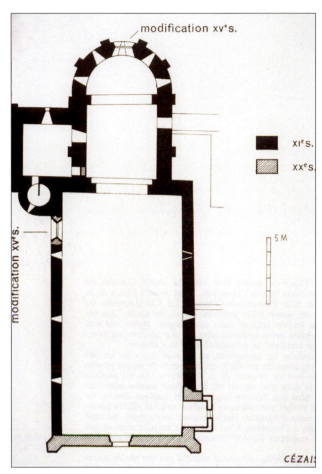

Figure 5.8 Saint-Hilaire Plan, Cézais, France, eleventh century

Christian monuments of the Holy Lands under European control.

Houses

A Romanesque house in Cluny, 1159, is one of the few extant houses of the period (Figure 5.9). It is a great material document of social history. The façade exhibits a high level of craftsmanship and can be analyzed. It indicates a separation of the commercial and residential functions. The smaller, private windows of the upper floor indicate the residential floor. The large opening on the ground floor clearly indicates the commercial space that lies behind it. The ground floor was the commercial sphere, with a large and welcoming opening, acces-

sible to the public. This made a spatial connection to street life.

The façade corresponds to an exceedingly simple, if logical, plan (Figure 5.10). This is a plan of another Romanesque house. The prominent room of the upper floor that fronts the street was a general-purpose room that served many functions. This confirms our knowledge about living spaces. There was an overall scarcity of resources, and rooms were not devoted to a single function.

Medieval cities were crowded, space was precious, and the linear footage along a street was at a premium. A feature of living in a Romanesque house, by today's standards, was a lack of privacy. There is little doubt that commercial areas served double duty and that nighttime found workers sleeping there. The large living space contained only one heating element, used for general warmth

Figure 5.9 Romanesque house, elevation, Cluny, France, 1159.

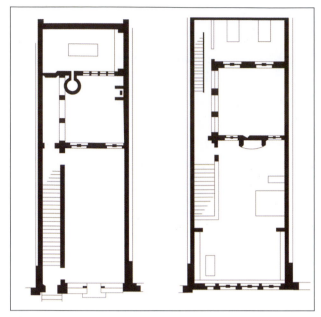

Figure 5.10 Romanesque house, plan, Cluny, France, 1159.

and cooking. The room itself was used for cooking, eating, entertaining, and, for countless numbers, sleeping at close quarters and all that entails. And now, after considering these activities, we turn to the furnishings that help make them possible.

Furniture

Chests

In her study on medieval furniture, Penelope Eames (1977) demonstrates the centrality of the chest: "In an age in which mobility and security for household possessions were primary considerations, the adaptability of the chest in its various forms made it the most indispensable single article of furniture. The chest was, at one and the same time, a piece of furniture and an article of luggage." A modest Romanesque chest confirms life's difficulty and is a practical response to real needs (Figure 5.11). Used for storage, transport, and other practical uses, most chests were made of sturdy and common woods, such as oak, walnut, poplar, and pine.

A chest is one of the most basic types of furniture. It is a space-containing object, meant to provide storage for objects. The practical people of the Middle Ages took note that a piece designed for storage also resulted in a work surface. Chests had secondary functions, their horizontal surface occasionally called into use for sitting, working, dining,

Figure 5.11 Romanesque chest.

or sleeping. A chest's probable use as a table indicates that households contained few pieces of furniture; the ones they did have performed double if not triple duty.

This piece is an example of plank construction, meaning simply that it was constructed from planks in a judicious manner; there is no attempt to hide the fact. The construction method remains visible in the final product. Plank construction indicates the availability of milled boards. The creator of this particular piece may have been a joiner, with most of his professional experience in architecture. It lacks the level of craftsmanship evident in Dagobert's chair.

This piece also bears traces of its history as a finished piece. It spent long periods of time in places where its owners were concerned about cleanliness. The floors that supported the chest were continually mopped, and mops, dripping with oily soap, slapped thousands of times against the chest's feet, resulting in their darkening over time. Cleanliness was a virtue, but treating this workhorse delicately was not. This chest had a long life, and like the people it served so well, and outlived, the form bears the scars of its tribulations.

Footed chests were desirable because they raised the contents off a cold and damp ground. Generally speaking, flat-lidded chests with feet were used for storage. For both private and commercial purposes, chests were the primary means of storage. Fairly large numbers survive, although not because they were deemed worthy of preservation. Because their *raison d'être* was storage, chests survived because their contents, long since dispersed, were considered valuable.

Chests with domed lids and flat bottoms were used for transport. They were indispensable when individuals prepared for travel and when noble households moved from one location to another. The curved top expelled rainwater, and protruding feet were a liability when transporting a piece of furniture, as they were likely to incur damage.

Eames argues convincingly that even a footed chest could have been used for transport if slipped into a **bahut**. This leather envelope protected the piece of furniture itself with a water-resistant wrapping. It also protected protruding feet from damage, thereby blurring the line between storage and transport chests. A considerable advantage to this procedure is that a household's contents could be transported without repacking.

In some Romanesque pieces, the straightforwardness of the undecorated chest gives way to a surprising profusion of applied ornament, and the ornament comes in the unexpected material of iron (Figure 5.12). Iron tracery is an applied means of adding decoration based on geometric designs, and figures of vegetation, animals, and exceptionally, human figures. This demonstrates a willingness to incorporate new materials that extended to decoration. In a time period known for restraint, when decoration motifs were created, they were often employed effusively and not sparingly. The plank construction remains visible, but barely.

The decoration gives the overall impression that it covers the entire object comprehensively. A series of horizontal lines binds the sides. On closer inspection, one sees that the pattern of lines responds to the chest, changing direction, running left, right, up, down, turning corners and recognizing the top and bottom, and the front and sides. This wrought-iron strapping runs perpendicular to the boards, providing additional strength, reinforcement, and stability. The lines and figures rise vertically in the front and run horizontally across the uprights. The wooden uprights become the legs.

A prominent lock is likely a later modification. Attached rings facilitated transport. Both decorative and functional, the ironwork had several functions, as hinges, locks, and a means to bind and

Figure 5.12 Chest, c. 1200–1250

strengthen the oak planks. In the Romanesque period, furniture had to resist the unwanted intruder. There is therefore continuity between a town's fortifications, the coat of mail that a knight wore, and the locks and metal bracing of a Romanesque chest.

The word **coffer**, in French *coffre*, indicates where money and valuables were stored. The phrase "the coffers of the Pope" (or King or President), still in use today, indicates the place where money is stored or, even more abstractly, the treasury. Money, like nearly everything else in this period, was stored in chests.

Another chest emphasizes furniture's debt to architecture, indicating that at least occasionally the same people created both (Figure 5.13). A **hutch** is a subset within the larger category of chests. It has uprights at its ends that also form the legs. Again, when decoration was employed, it came full force, spreading across every surface. When iron tracery was not needed or could not be afforded, another means to improve a chest's appearance was chip carving. Hutch designs favored motifs readily accomplished with the skilled use of a compass, chisel, and block. Examples are rondels and miniature Romanesque arches.

With certain pieces, a sure sign that a piece dates to the Romanesque period is the presence of the semicircular arch. The arches look exactly like the entryways of Romanesque churches, further emphasizing furniture's connection not just to architecture, but to ecclesiastic architecture. With this walnut hutch, an arcade of Romanesque arches constitutes the body of the piece, lifted well into the air, spanning a considerable distance, an achievement in the world of furniture that is the equivalent of the Roman bridges and aqueducts that were known features of the landscape of twelfth-century France. This particular piece is reminiscent of the Pont du Gard (Nîmes, France).

In French, the word used to denote Romanesque monuments, *roman,* is the same word that denotes ancient Roman monuments. Thus, the French term for the art, architecture, and furniture of this period emphasizes the continuity with ancient Rome, and the English term, Romanesque, emphasizes the differences. The builders of churches in Aquitaine were trying to emulate the grandeur of ancient Rome. Their knowledge of Rome was incomplete. Roman sites lay in ruins, with half-buried temples, and columns, capitals, and headless torsos strewn

Figure 5.13
Walnut Hutch.

about. Books on Rome, or, for that matter, any subject, were rare. Many people were illiterate and had no access to libraries. Romanesque works were inspired by Rome, but the results—buildings, sculpture, dress, and furniture—were not encyclopedic copies.

ISLAM

Islamic design, like Romanesque, is centered on religion. Without Islam there is no Islamic design, and without Mohammed, there is no Islam. The story begins with the Prophet, Mohammed, who lived from 570?–632 C.E. An explanation for the success and spread of Islam into Africa, Europe, and Asia was its ability to incorporate local architectural and decorative trends. Thus, Islam developed a series of regional variations that, when viewed collectively, are astonishing in their variety. In Mesopotamia, Persia, North Africa, Saharan Africa, Spain, and Anatolia, mosques were built that shared similar features: courtyard, **prayer hall**, **ablutions fountain**, and **qibla** wall with **mihrab**. The decorative motifs of interior and exterior façades, columns, floors, and ceilings varied greatly from region to region. As varied a style as has ever existed, Islam resists facile summarization.

Mosques

All mosques owe their form to the Prophet's farm in Medina and are in fact representations of it (Figure 5.14). The key elements can be seen in a recreation of Mohammed's farm, the first mosque. Important features of all mosques are the perimeter wall, the covered hall of columns that becomes the prayer hall, and the courtyard, which acts as both forecourt to the prayer hall and overflow space.

Middle East and North Africa

In Christian churches, a priest preaches to a congregation; hence the auditorium-like layout. In a mosque, the central activity is an individual praying, albeit multiplied hundreds of times. The apse that signals the direction to Mecca is correspondingly humanly scaled and significantly smaller than the central apse of Christian churches. A large single space, therefore, is not a priority. The Great Mosque of Damascus, Syria, initially converted from a Roman temple, displays the repetitious, cellular

Figure 5.14 Drawing, Prophet Mohammed's farm, Medina, Saudi Arabia, 707–709.

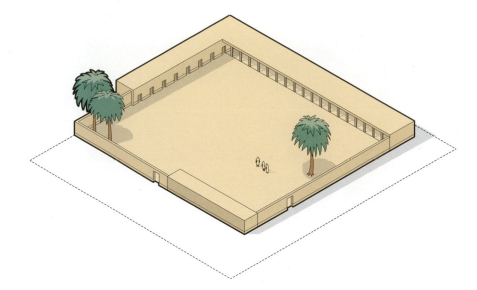

quality of mosques (Figure 5.15). Although Muslim imams also preach, the central activity around which a mosque is designed remains that of an individual, on a carpet, facing Mecca and praying to God.

As Islam spread, it merged with local traditions. A comprehensive look at the broad topic of Islamic architecture, interiors, and furnishings would require volumes. This chapter, therefore, more modestly seeks to present what is meant when people refer to Islamic design, and provides a summary

look at some of its forms, basic characteristics, and the more intriguing of its many meanings.

North Africa, like southern Europe, is blessed with an abundance of Roman ruins. Because of the drier climate, some of them are remarkably complete, and classical ruins grace Morocco, Tunisia, Libya, Egypt, Israel, Jordan, and Syria. Designers of Islamic mosques, like those of Romanesque churches, were oftentimes inspired to work within classical architectural languages. Sometimes they literally reused the ruins, incorporating Roman

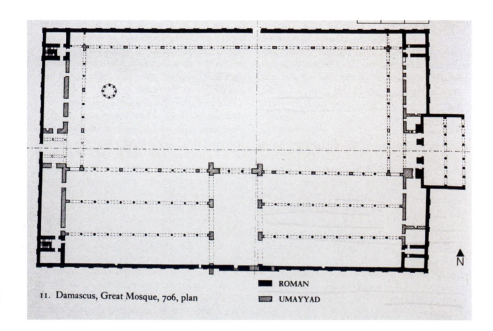

11. Damascus, Great Mosque, 706, plan

▮ ROMAN
▨ UMAYYAD

Figure 5.15 Plan, Great Mosque of Damascus, Syria, 705–711.

Figure 5.16 Interior, Prayer Hall, Great Mosque of Kairouan, Kairouan, Tunisia, 820–836.

columns and capitals (Figure 5.16). The fusion of classical architecture with Islam is obvious in the interior of the Prayer Hall of the Great Mosque of Kairouan. Kairouan is one of the key Islamic monuments. From its classical capitals spring a field of Islamic arches. The Islamic arch is pointed like a Gothic arch, but it is distinctive because its semi-spherical shape exceeds 180 degrees, as does a horse-shoe. Hence its other name, horseshoe arch.

Saharan and Sub-Saharan Africa

In Saharan and sub-Saharan Africa, Islam worked within indigenous African traditions. They used local materials and took advantage of local building traditions. In the Sahara, all things come from and return to the earth. Art in the region frequently venerates the humble mudfish. Soil dredged from the bottom of the Niger River dyes mud cloth black or ochre. Saharan mosques, appropriately, are made of mud, or more accurately, sun-dried mud bricks skim-coated with an outer layer of mud. The vertical divisions take the form of phallic fertility symbols whose existence as a recognizable form pre-dated Islam. This, along with the **toron,** or permanent pieces of scaffolding, are what create the buildings' distinctive exterior walls (Figure 5.17).

Figure 5.17 Great Mosque of Djenné, Djenné, Mali, fourteenth century. Restored, 1905.

The toron are also utilized during the annual resurfacing of the mosque, a communal activity. The archetypal Saharan mud mosque is the Great Mosque of Djenné.

Ottoman Empire

In Anatolia and regions of the Middle East under the Ottoman Empire, there occurs as audacious a case of cultural appropriation as the world has ever seen. Justinian's famed Christian temple, Hagia Sophia, was designed to outshine the pagan Pantheon. It was then converted to a mosque in the fifteenth century, and this church-turned-mosque became the prototype for hundreds of mosques that copy its domes, half-domes, clerestories, pendentives, and mosaics (Figure 5.18).

Persia

Persian mosques accomplished a form of architectural appropriation of a different sort. Isfahan (Iran) is a city filled with large-scale Islamic monuments and is today a UNESCO World Heritage site. The buildings at Isfahan harken back to Assyrian and Babylonian palaces and thereby render Islam as the logical inheritor of those ancient civilizations. This connection across millennia is achieved by a building material indigenous to the region: a brilliantly glazed blue brick (Figure 5.19). Isfahan had two important periods: It thrived under the Seljuq Turks (eleventh to twelfth centuries) and under the Persian Safavid dynasty (sixteenth to eighteenth centuries). The Persian mosques of the twelfth century incorporated the distinctive Assyrian form of crenellated walls.

Figure 5.18 Mosque of Sultan Ahmed I (Blue Mosque), Constantinople (Istanbul, Turkey) 1609–1617.

When comparing design motifs over time and geography, one of the more interesting occurrences is when decorative motifs travel and mutate. The process of transformation, however, varies from culture to culture. In Egypt, bundled reeds were used as columns. The form of bundled cylindrical elements tied together then became the schema of choice when columns were carved from stone. In Rome, painted plaster imitates stone. In Athens, Constantinople, and the Île-de-France, architectural motifs migrate from buildings to furniture. Often in the process, the motif looses its function, but the form remains. A skeuomorph is an object of utility that becomes a decorative form.

One of the most interesting aspects of the structures of Isfahan, and indeed of all Islam, are the vertical architectural surfaces that resemble carpets. Fields of patterns rework motifs that originated in textiles. And carpets, analogously, often portray architectural details. Thus, there are walls that look like carpets and carpets that look like walls. A frequent motif of individual prayer rugs is a single Islamic arch through which the person praying can peer, also indicating the direction to Mecca. Where walls resemble carpets, instead of staring at a flat vertical surface, a viewer stares at motifs that they associate with textiles. Innumerable decorative schemes fall under the rubric of Islamic design, but

Figure 5.19 Uzbekistan Khiva Tashkhavli Palace Harem.

the type of decoration prevalent at Isfahan is what most people mean when they refer to Islamic decoration. It is largely geometric, nonrepresentational, and often formed by tiles or mosaics.

The Mughal Empire

Despite ample Persian riches, it was the Mughals of the East who set the standard for Islamic luxury. In English, the word *mogul* still means people who combine business savvy and economic success with an unparalleled sense of luxury. Of note in this

corner of the Islamic world, today Pakistan and northwestern India, is that the most magnificent structures were not solely religious structures, but tombs and residential complexes that included ceremonial chambers, audience chambers, reception rooms, and reflecting pools.

A Muslim capital was established in the last years of the twelfth century, at Delhi, India. This was a significant milestone in Islam's eastward expansion. For more than 300 years, five dynasties successively ruled from Delhi, a period known as the Delhi Sultanate. The Delhi Sultanate is typically dated to 1200–1526 B.C.E. The first mosques in the Indian subcontinent were converted Indian temples, or new buildings constructed from reassembled Indian architectural fragments. A feature of these early mosques was the use of a decorative screen to separate the imam from the congregation. Building in Delhi, Agra, Fatehpur Sikri, Lucknow, and other locations, the early sultans established the foundation of Indo-Islamic architecture and design.

The following period is the era of the Mughal rulers, 1526–1707. Akbar (1556–1605) was a great patron of the arts, and his reign was the height of Mughal art. Art in this context means paintings, buildings, and illustrated texts. Akbar had the great Hindu epics, the *Ramayana* and the *Mahabharata*, lavishly illustrated. He built forts at Agra and Fatehpur Sikri that were fusions of indigenous forms and Islamic motifs.

Akbar's son, Jahangir (1605–1627), was also an important patron. Like his father, and his son after him, he built mosques, mausoleums, forts, palaces, hunting lodges, and pavilions. In comparison to other regional Islamic traditions, it is significant that the Mughal building programs included multiple secular building types.

While Akbar and his son, Jahangir, were active patrons, it was Jahangir's son, Shah Jahan (r. 1628–1658), who built the building that has a hallowed place in the world's collective imagination. Shah Jahan's wife was Mumtaz Mahal, and for her he built a monument of sandstone and white marble decorated with semiprecious stones. The Taj Mahal in Agra (India) is one of the most famous buildings in the world. In the widely reproduced photographic image of it, on postcards, calendars, and travel posters, it stands perfectly symmetrical, with its white marble domes reflected in a pool. The building today is synonymous with India, as the Eiffel Tower is with France. But it also stems from a compelling story. It is the touching monument that a grieving widower, Jahan, erected for his beloved wife.

Islamic Interiors and Furniture

Akbar and Shah Jahan were fabulously wealthy by any standard. A gouache owned by the Musée des Arts Asiatiques, Guimet in Paris shows two male figures on their knees (Figure 5.20). One has his knees together, the other sits cross-legged. Both sit on a raised platform. Sitting, kneeling, or lying on the ground in a warm climate is a perfectly adequate means of repose. Correspondingly, creative efforts focused on mats, carpets, and pillows. When chairs entered these realms, it was often the result of inter-

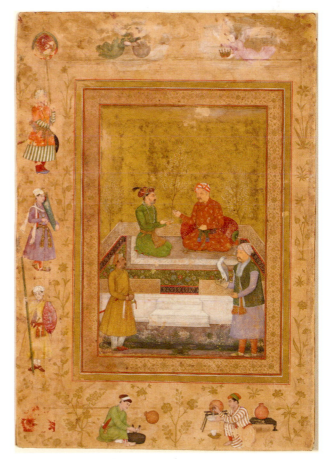

Figure 5.20 Shah Jahan, Gouache, India, 1620.

Figure 5.21 Khas Mahal, Daughter's pavilion, Agra, India, 1635.

national exchange, and a matter of status and cultural identification rather than necessity.

In the area that was the Mughal Empire, many residential and administrative functions were carried out in structures that can be best described as pleasure pavilions (Figure 5.21). What these pavilions have in common with a mosque's prayer hall is that multiple columns support the roof. The structure is a hypostyle hall, formally linked to Egyptian hypostyle halls (see Chapter 2). The word that originates from these pavilions is **diwan,** the root from which the modern English "divan" stems. Raised platforms frequently formed the perimeter of these columned pavilions, and they were smothered with cushions, pillows, and carpets. This comfortable setting frequently served as the audience chamber for government officials, the place where business was conducted. And just as the word *coffer* came to mean treasury, so too *diwan* came to mean an office and its related finance, or more specifically, a government's financial sector.

In photographs, Mughal pavilions today are portrayed as austere when they should be pictured in use. Assemblies of pillows, carpets, and tasseled cushions do not remain intact for centuries, so historical engravings are invaluable for re-creating this episode in the history of seating (Figure 5.22). Engravings from the nineteenth and twentieth centuries also hint as to seating practices and diwan layouts of previous periods.

Saharan nomads carried leather pillows with them, a means of making some of the more modest comforts of the diwan transportable. Whether carried by camel or horse, a leather pillow could make travel more comfortable. Also used for sitting on the ground around a fire, or when sleeping in a tent, leather was a favored water-resistant material of the medieval period.

As we have seen, there is a reason why, for this early period, Islamic furniture is practically an oxymoron. Many of the functions that were taken care of in the West by chairs and couches were accomplished with cushions, carpets, and other textiles. This is a cultural response to a warm climate where it is less necessary to distance oneself from the ground.

One piece of furniture, however, is essential to outfitting a mosque, and that is the **minbar** (Figure 5.23). A hybrid of a stair, a chair, and a pulpit, it is the stand from which the imam preaches. It is located immediately adjacent to the mihrab, the apse in the **qibla** wall. Usually made of wood and separate from the structure, some minbars are made of stone and built in. An elaborate minbar from the Great Mosque of Algiers even has wheels.

A great number of Islamic prayer stools are intended for use when reading the Koran. Some are collapsible and portable. The position of the back piece is designed to keep the reader alert while studying the Koran.

It is a mistake to oversimplify Islam, both as a religion and as a system of decoration. A trend is not dogma—thus it is with the Islamic stance on representation. No hard-and-fast rule prohibits visual representations, though this is interpreted differently in different places and time periods. It is true that geometric designs, whether formed of car-

KHORSHID'S DIWAN

Figure 5.22 Khorshid Effendi's Diwan, Suakin, Sudan, nineteenth century.

Figure 5.23 Mihrab and Minbar of the Friday Mosque of Nain, Iran. Tenth century.

pet fibers or glazed bricks, constitute the majority of Islamic decoration. Sometimes these patterns suggest flowers and other botanical motifs. Animals are portrayed less frequently. An exceptional aspect of Persian and Mughal design is that human figures are represented. Geometric designs and vegetal motifs are the most frequent subjects of Islamic decoration, with human figures being the least frequent.

In addition to this intriguing relationship between carpets and vertical architectural surfaces, there is a connection between residential architectural features and the human figure. In many areas of the Islamic world, in this case the historical trading center of Suakin (Sudan), houses were outfitted with a protruding bay window, or **roshan.** This hybrid space mediated between the public world of the street and the private world of the house. This created a space for women to observe city life yet be shielded from public visibility. In this sense, this architectural feature acted as does the veil; roshan

Figure 5.24a Algerian postcard. Women with veils.

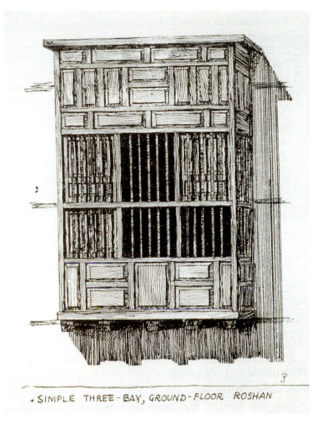

Figure 5.24b Roshan, Suakin, Sudan, nineteenth century.
The Coral Buildings of Suakin.

is to house as veil is to female body (Figures 5.24 a and b). Again, one should not confuse a widespread practice with dogma. Not all Islamic women are veiled; among the Tuareg of Mali, the men shield their faces from the public gaze.

Islamic Spain

Islamic designers of all sorts—architects, carpet weavers, and furniture craftsmen—were not shy about borrowing. In Islamic Spain the fullest fusion of Islamic and European models occurs, particularly when it comes to furniture. With Islamic Spain this chapter comes full circle; Romanesque becomes Islamic, and Islamic becomes Romanesque.

Jews, Christians, and Muslims thrived in Islamic Spain. Maria Rosa Menocal's *The Ornament of the World* is a well-written book that, in recovering a lost era, is at once general and specific. This section is indebted to her effort.

The story starts in Syria where the Umayyad dynasty, successors to Mohammed, ruled from Damascus. Damascus was an international place, with its Greek, Aramaean, Hebrew, and Arabic histories. The Umayyads were violently overthrown by a rival dynasty, the Abbasids. Most of the Umayyads were murdered and their residences plundered. The Abassids subsequently moved the center of their operations to Baghdad. An Umayyad survivor, the tenacious Abd al-Rahman, headed to the Iberian peninsula where he settled in Cordoba.

Medieval Spain was populated with Visigoths from the north and Berbers from the south—the Northern coast of Africa.

Al-Rahman and his followers created a brilliant European Islamic society that included a grand tradition of courtyard residences and rich furnishings. A descendant, Abd al-Rahman III, built Madinat al-Zahra, a hilltop structure that Menocal describes

Figure 5.25 Interior, Prayer Hall, Great Mosque of Córdoba, Spain, 785–966.

as the Versailles of Cordoba (Menocal, 2002, p. 36). A rival faction of Berbers destroyed it in 1009, but its tradition of orange groves, palm trees, fountains and pools was to live on in two even grander residential complexes.

Testament to the openness and multicultural quality of Islamic Spain comes from two cases in which the most important administrative position, vizier, analogous to prime minister, was held by a Jewish scholar. Hasdai Ibn Shaprut (915–975) and Samuel Ibn Nagrila (993–1056) served in the most important administrative position in Europe's Islamic caliphate.

The comingling of languages, religions, and artistic traditions of every sort—in food, clothes, songs, houses, and chests—took place not only on the Iberian peninsula, although certainly most vigorously there, but with increasing intensity far beyond the Pyrenees, into France. Several terms explicitly indicate the hybrid populations and the corresponding artistic productions. A "Mozarab" was a "wanna-be Arab," a Christian who took on Arabic manners and spoke Arabic. Similarly, "Mudejar" meant an Arab who lived in Christian areas of the city. "Moorish" refers generally to the late medieval hybrid artistic culture of Islamic Spain and North Africa.

The two most important buildings in Islamic Spain, one a mosque, one a sprawling residence, are associated with Cordoba and Granada, respectively. The Great Mosque of Cordoba was culturally complex from the start, with its recycled columns and capitals.

The prayer hall of the mosque incorporates both classical elements and **Moorish** arches (Figure 5.25). These arches employ the bicolored stone work, so prominent in Charlemagne's octagonal chapel in Aachen, that is a hallmark of Romanesque churches.

In the residential sphere, Ibn Ahmar built the Alhambra on the hills outside of Granada, 1250–1360. It consists of a series of pavilions and gardens, and the resulting ensemble is considered one of the two most important structures of Islamic Spain.

The centuries of the second millennium saw Islam, as the official religion, loosing ground in Spain, yet the cultural effects lived on. The Castilian monarchs who ruled from Seville continued to build in the style started with the Alhambra. Their primary residence was the Alcazar, Arabic for palace. Mostly built by Peter the Cruel, starting in 1364, this house included Quranic inscriptions in their lush wall decorations made of plaster, paint, and ceramic tile. Their mosque turned cathedral is the largest Gothic church in Europe, yet its plan remains that of an Islamic prayer hall. The Giralda received a new top, yet retained its clear identity as a one-time minaret. And adjacent to the church is a courtyard with fountains and an orange grove, entered through a stately horseshoe-shaped arch.

Moorish furniture clearly shows the fusion of Western forms and Islamic decoration. A typical piece of furniture in sixteenth-century Spain is the **vargueño.** Initially a chest on a stand, it served equally well as a desk. With both a writing surface and storage, it is a predecessor to the French *secrétaire* (Figure 5.26). The carving is detailed, the decoration profuse. Moorish chairs, in many respects,

Figure 5.26 Writing desk, Spain, sixteenth century.

resemble Italian and French chairs. Included in the group of Moorish seating is a folding chair, made of wood and leather, called **sillón frailero.** Highly decorated, they are also a sign of the itinerant quality of the people during this time period.

Writing about this medieval culture of tolerance, Menocal states: "In its moments of great achievement, medieval culture positively thrived on holding at least two, and often many more, contrary ideas at the same time. This was the chapter of Europe's culture when Jews, Christians, and Muslims lived side by side and, despite their intractable differences and enduring hostilities, nourished a complex culture of tolerance" (Menocal, p. 11).

CONCLUSION

In the period when Rome became ancient, two religions sought to establish themselves as world players with major architectural monuments. The designers of Christian churches collectively pursued a strategy of refining a particular schema. The creators of Muslim mosques took the opposite approach and operated within a bewildering number of regional vocabularies.

The Christian and Muslim worlds alike experienced a shift from a civic order to religious power, and from cities to feudal families. Feudalism was an economic and political system, and a hereditary one at that. From fortified urban structures, to residences, to locked chests, the emphasis was on protection. There were also some remarkable coincidences. Both Europe and the Islamic world used leather as an industrial material, prized for its durability and ability to repel water. Two words from the world of furniture, *coffer* and *diwan,* curiously enough, came to act as stand-ins for a highly desirable commodity: money.

In many respects, the period from the Fall of Rome to the rebirth known as the Renaissance was a period of introspection, in which the delicately delineated illuminated manuscript took the place of the heroic statue in a public square. In the world of the arts, Islam and the West developed in ways that are the exact opposite of how they are perceived today. The West, as represented by Romanesque churches, was unflinching and austere. Islam, in the many variants of its mosques and palaces, became known worldwide for its sensuousness, because of the richness of surfaces, from silk to mosaics, and the complexity of its decorative patterns.

Sources

Romanesque

Conant, Kenneth. *Carolingian and Romanesque Architecture: 800 to 1200.* Middlesex: Penguin, 1959.

Eames, Penelope. *Furniture in England, France, and the Netherlands from the Twelfth to the Fifteenth Century.* London: Furniture History Society, 1977.

Mercer, Eric. *Furniture 700–1700.* London: Weidenfeld & Nicolson, 1969.

Oursel, Raymond. *Living Architecture: Romanesque.* London: Oldbourne, 1967.

Seidel, Linda. *The Romanesque Facades of Aquitaine.* Chicago: University of Chicago Press, 1981.

Temple, Richard, ed. *Early Christian and Byzantine Art.* London: Element Books, 1990.

Islamic

Alloula, Malek. *The Colonial Harem.* Minneapolis: University of Minnesota Press, 1986.

Ettinghouse, Richard, et al. *Art and Architecture of Islam, 650–1250.* New Haven: Yale University Press, 1994.

Goitein, S. D. "Daily Life and the Individual" (1983), IV, from *A Mediterranean Society.* Berkeley: 1967–88, 105–138. University of California Press, 1967.

Greenlaw, Jean-Pierre. *The Coral Buildings of Suakin.* London: Wiley, 1995.

Kostof, Spiro. *A History of Architecture: Settings and Rituals.* Oxford: Oxford University Press, 1995.

Lewis, Bernard. *The Middle East: A Brief History of the Last 2000 Years.* New York: Scribner's, 1995.

Michell, George. *The Majesty of Mughal Decoration.* London: Thames and Hudson, 2007.

Sadan, Joseph. "Furniture, Islamic," *Dictionary of the Middle Ages.* New York, 1985, pp. 313–16.

Menocal, Maria Rosa. *The Ornament of the World: How Muslims, Jews, and Christians created a culture of Tolerance in Medieval Spain.* Boston: Little Brown, 2002.

DISCUSSION AND REVIEW QUESTIONS

1. In the nineteenth century, a significant number of architects professed their fondness for Romanesque churches. What is appealing about these buildings, if they are technologically less advanced than Gothic?

2. What are five vocabulary terms that refer to features of a church in plan?

3. What are some of the regional variations of Islamic architecture?

4. What are the standard features of a mosque? Corresponding vocabulary?

5. What are some of the variable features of a mosque that vary from place to place?

GOTHIC

800–1150	1140–1500	1150–1250	1230–1325
Romanesque and Norman	**Gothic**	**Early and High Gothic**	**Rayonnant**

By 1250, European design had changed dramatically and there existed what can reasonably be called the Gothic style. The building of French Gothic churches was part of a national surge of architectural expression. Gothic cathedrals of the Île de France are widely seen as one of the high points in the history of architecture. Initially associated with France, the effects of this new style quickly spread across Europe. Gothic architecture is important because it is an entire architectural system—plans, sections, façades, details—not derivative of the classical orders. Gothic furniture was closely allied with architecture in its forms, details, and in the vocabulary used to describe it. Over the course of the twelfth century, the interest in classical remains was spasmodic and in decline, although this was less pronounced in painting and sculpture.

Gothic is the last style of the medieval period, before the Renaissance. Gothic architecture and design becomes an entity in its own right, but it is also a bridge between Romanesque and Renaissance. One means of understanding Gothic is to examine it side by side with Romanesque; comparing arches, façades, and plans is a worthwhile endeavor. It is a grave mistake, however, to consider them as opposed. Gothic architecture grew out of Romanesque, and all the features for which Gothic architecture and design are known—flying buttresses, stained glass, ribbed vaults, and so on—existed in the Romanesque period.

It is a final florescence of the medieval period, but in some countries, most notably England, it marks the beginning of the Renaissance. Because of its technical achievements and spatial innovation, many people see in it the beginnings of architectural modernism.

For not the first time in art history, we employ a word that was initially meant derogatorily. The word *Gothic* was widely used in the sixteenth and seventeenth centuries to refer to art that was specifically not Italian and not Renaissance. In the eighteenth century, the term became neutrally descriptive.

As with much of the medieval period, rarely do we have information about artists, architects, woodworkers, and masons. We also have little information about people's reactions to art. This is in part the antimaterialist stance of a period where religion was everything and there was a disdain for manual labor.

CIVIC INFRASTRUCTURE

After the significant Roman urban-scaled endeavors, the return of European urbanism occurs in the Gothic period. Thus, the period known for one of the highlights of Western architecture is coincident with the reintroduction of urban design in the European arena. The achievements in the realm of urban design in the Gothic period have not received the attention lavished on Gothic cathedrals. Many histories of urban design consider all medieval towns to be an example of laissez-faire capitalism, with irregular streets and squares (Figure 6.1). There were several types of medieval town plans,

Figure 6.1 San Gimignano, medieval square, eleventh to thirteenth centuries. Tuscany, Italy.

but for our purposes here, one illustrates what most people think of when they think of medieval towns. San Gimignano, in the Italian region of Tuscany, has all the features of a medieval town. It grew up around trading routes that had existed for centuries. Town squares were not designed to follow strict geometries, but appear as a response to foot and vehicular traffic and often center on a public utility such as a well. Houses of irregular height and width line the square; the irregular fenestration reflects their interior layouts.

The Gothic period also sees a considerable number of new towns built, speculative real-estate ventures. These put to rest the notion that all medieval cities were irregular. Crisply rectilinear in plan, many of these towns had gates, defensive walls, and the central feature of medieval towns, the commercial street that runs its length from gate to gate. Competition for space along this street was fierce, so structures had narrow façades on the street; property lines extended backward from the street. The Gothic period is known for its religious monuments. The achievements in urban design, however, are also noteworthy. Over the course of the Gothic period, there was an increasing emphasis on civic government and its architectural infrastructure, such as libraries, town halls, hospitals, and universities. Few of these survive.

Beginning

Saint Denis is the patron saint of France because he was one of those responsible for converting Gauls to Christianity in the third century C.E. The conversion process did not run smoothly, and after being tortured on a hot grill, Denis was decapitated. According to Catholic tradition, he picked up his head and walked north until he reached the area where the church that was dedicated to him still stands. In addition to being the burial ground of St. Denis, the abbey church became the holding place for French kings, and it houses the remains of Louis XVI and Marie Antoinette. The abbey church of St. Denis is one of the most importance places for the nation of France, French Christianity, and the history of architecture.

The royal abbey, founded in the fifth century, was rebuilt in the Carolingian and Romanesque periods. The Abbot Suger was the head of the monastery of St. Denis from 1122 to 1151. The story of French Gothic typically begins with the Abbot and his abbey. Suger, famously, had the church remodeled, a move that set in place an architectural movement that redefined religious architecture and came to be known as Gothic. He is rightly considered the most important patron in the development of French Gothic.

Suger's efforts started in 1137. He left intact the central Carolingian and Romanesque hall, and added on to it at the front and rear (the hall itself was later replaced). To the front he added a new elevation, but it was his dazzling addition to the rear that was most impressive. He replaced the Carolingian apse, and his remodeling included an ambulatory and a new series of chapels (Figure 6.2). The design dispenses with the divisions between chapels, creating a continuous visual effect in which circulation, places for prayer, columns, walls, and ceiling are all part of a continuous whole.

The term *chevet* refers to an elaboration of what had been the apse in the Early Christian basilica. It is an agglomeration of chapels and ambulatory. In Romanesque churches it is sculptural and bulbous; Gothic churches follow the model of St. Denis, in which the chevet is an integral part of the overall church plan. The chevet at St. Denis includes three elements that constitute the foundation of what became Gothic architecture: Gothic arches, rib vaults, and flying buttresses.

Figure 6.2 Saint-Denis, view of ambulatory and choir, 1144.

Gothic Architecture

Romanesque architecture relies upon the Romanesque, or semispherical, arch. The barrel vault is an extrusion of the arch into three dimensions. A Romanesque church is essentially a barrel vault lifted onto walls. The height of a Romanesque arch is based on its width; in combining spatial elements with different dimensions, such as a nave and side aisles, it is difficult to roof the system because each rises to different heights. Gothic architecture relies upon a pointed arch whose width can be manipulated in order to maintain a consistent height.

When two barrel vaults intersect, the points of intersection are rib vaults. This is the Romanesque system of vaulting. Gothic architects realized that the vault is an entity that gathers and transfers forces, and it can be an element of design itself. Rather than two intersecting cylinders, the Gothic system is akin to an umbrella and its multiple spokes. The underside of a roof no longer follows a simple geometric form, but is an agglomeration of facets.

The pointed arch came into existence after 1150. Whether Gothic or Islamic, the pointed arch is an architectural and design element struck from two adjacent but separate circles. With less horizontal spread, it emphasizes the vertical.

The genius of Gothic architecture can be found in one of its constituent details: the Gothic rib. To the Gothic mind, ribs and groin vaults were plastic design elements. Innumerable vaults could spring from a column in many directions.

A masonry vault suspends heavy stones in the air, subject to the forces of gravity. As with all things in the earth's atmosphere, they are subject to the laws of physics. A barrel vault exerts tremendous lateral forces on the tops of walls, over time causing them to collapse outward. To counter this, walls can be made very thick or can be strengthened with piers. Knowledge of how to do this was learned in a trial-and-error process. Many Early Christian and Romanesque churches failed structurally and were rebuilt with stronger walls. Visiting Romanesque churches, one often observes walls that had started to precariously peel away from the church, only to be propped back into place by the external additions of piers or buttresses. Gothic architects took a necessity, the structural reinforcement of walls, and made it a virtue.

In Suger's remodeling of St. Denis, all the characteristically Gothic features were developed and put into place. An old material, glass, was used in new ways. Suger felt that expensive materials were appropriate for the buildings that housed the ritual of celebrating mass. The results were highly admired and copied, and began a movement of church building throughout France.

Notre Dame de Paris

Romanesque and Gothic churches are the result of several hundred years of building and rebuilding, and one of the charms of visiting them is teasing out the parts that derive from each epoch. Many Romanesque churches have minor Gothic additions. Similarly, many Gothic churches were built on top of Romanesque or Carolingian structures, and almost all have nineteenth- and twentieth-century repairs and restorations. The lively façade of St. Denis has a Romanesque band, a Gothic band, a crenellated cornice that recalls a feudal past, and significant modern restorations.

The Cathedral of Notre Dame de Paris (Our Lady of Paris) spectacularly sits on an island, Île de la Cité, in the center of Paris. It once had Gallo-Roman, **Merovingian,** and Carolingian forebears, yet because its founder, Bishop Maurice de Sully, had those pulled down, it mostly dates to the end of the early Gothic period.

The façade of Notre Dame dates to the period 1200–1250 and belongs to the mature phase of early Gothic façade development (Figure 6.3). No longer an amalgam of elements, the result of an additive process, the façade of Notre Dame has become a canvas or field to be designed and manipulated. It no longer slavishly represents the cross section of the building behind it, as had Early Christian churches. The façade is a thick and heavy wall with windows cut into its depth. Horizontal elements predominate. All these features are held in common with its Romanesque predecessors. The front elevation contrasts greatly with the side and rear elevations, which emphasize vertical elements and have expansive windows—two architecture moves that dematerialize the wall as the principal architectural element.

Figure 6.3 Notre Dame, façade, Paris. 1163–1250.

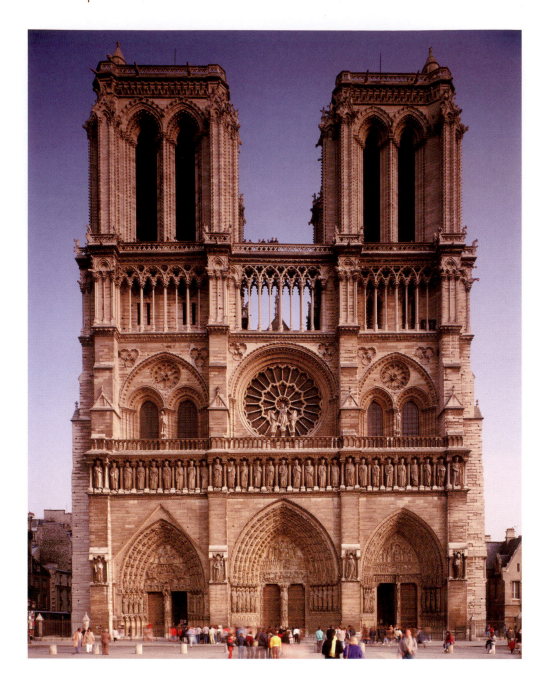

The design of the Gothic church front elevation can be considered an elaboration of the Romanesque scheme. Most, such as Notre Dame, have two towers, three portals, **arcading, voussoirs,** round windows, and **tympana.**

Notre Dame's tripartite composition relates to the presence of the nave and side aisles, yet in the façade, the three divisions are presented equally. The tripartite division of various parts of the Gothic architectural vocabulary, the **trefoil,** the nave with two side aisles, the three bays of the façade, all are consistent with a religious belief in the Christian Holy Trinity. From the baseline to the top of the cornice (below the towers), the front façade is a near-perfect square. The expression upward, so important in a Gothic church, in the elevation is relegated to several elements—the towers, the spires, and the use of the pointed Gothic arch. The towers are half the height of the square. Vertically the façade is divided into thirds; horizontally each succeeding band is of a narrower width, which subtly gives the impression of greater height.

Portal

Centuries before scholars began discussing buildings as signs (semiotics) and relating architecture to advertising, Gothic sculptors lavished their attention on the portals to churches (Figure 6.4). The sculptural programs of Gothic cathedrals focus less on torture, evil, and doomsday scenarios (characteristic of Romanesque churches), and there is both secular and religious iconography. Gothic cathedrals and their frontal elevations acted like billboards. Their façades, and specifically the sculptural programs of the façades, related to an audience that was mostly illiterate in words but not in visual imagery. The sculptural and decorative programs of Gothic

cathedrals announced to viewers, "Come, enter through these doors. Heavenly salvation awaits."

Interior Elevation

Gothic architects gave considerable attention to the development of interior elevations, and one of the results of the ponderous front elevation is that visitors walk through a heavy wall that is foreboding in both scale and iconography. Once inside, a visitor met an architectural system focused on height and light (Figure 6.5). Considerable attention was paid to the lateral façades of the nave (standing in the middle of the church, looking at the side elevations). As Gothic churches grew more complex, the areas flanking the nave developed into a complicated assembly that comprised a side aisle, a gallery above it, yet another gallery above that,

Figure 6.4 Notre Dame, central portal. thirteenth century, Paris.

Figure 6.5 Notre Dame, interior, nave, Paris. 1180–1220.

known as the **triforium,** and the clerestory above that. This was essentially an interior four-story elevation. The problem is that this configuration emphasized horizontal movement, physical and visual, and decreased the amount of space devoted to the clerestory. The clerestory is important because it is the one element of the interior elevation that lets in light directly from the exterior to the nave. The side aisles have fenestration, but by the time the light reaches across the side aisles and galleries to the nave, it is greatly diffused.

Part of what highlights the sanctuary is that light reaches the apse unobstructed. Hence, despite all the attention to glass and light, many Gothic cathedrals are quite dark, and the light, as it is, has a diaphanous quality.

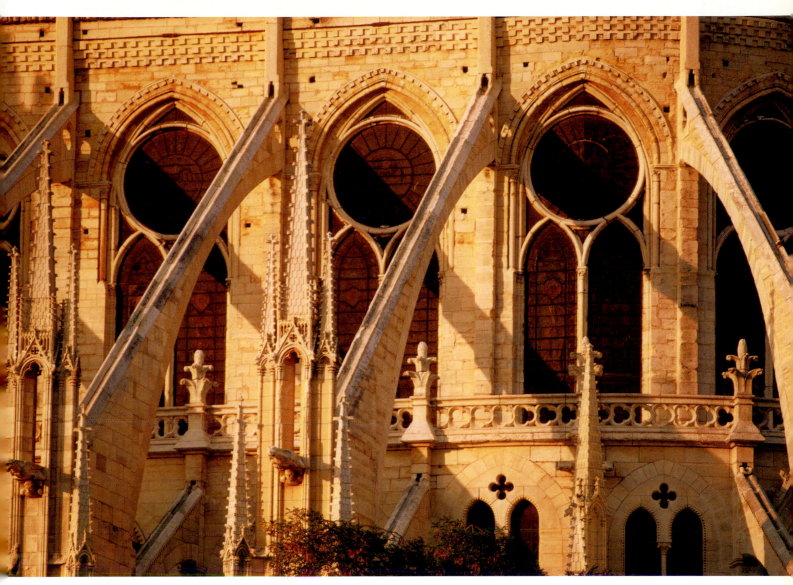

Figure 6.6 Notre Dame Cathedral, exterior of apse, northeast corner, with flying buttresses. Thirteenth century. Paris.

The solution to the "problem" of the side elevation at Notre Dame was to eliminate the triforium. This increased the depth of the clerestory and simplified, to great effect, the nave's interior elevations.

Flying Buttress

Beginnings are important in history books. Many people see in Gothic architecture the first glimmers of several key precepts of modern architecture. The two most important are related: the distinction made between columns and walls as structural features or as space-defining (non-load-bearing) elements; and the development of an all-glass or nearly all-glass curtain wall. What made this possible—

and one of the achievements of Gothic cathedrals— was the flying buttress (Figure 6.6).

The buttress had a humble beginning, as a correction used to prop up a leaning wall. Stone or brick walls that support interior barrel vaults tend to splay outward at the top over time. Eventually, they topple over and the building structurally fails. A buttress, essentially an applied pier, holds the wall in place and helps it maintain stability. This led to the discovery that the buttress could be designed in from the start. Eventually, it was discovered that the buttress could be lightened to the smallest possible profile and separated from the wall, the first step toward separating wall from structure.

The separation of structure from space-defining wall allowed architects to expand the area devoted to glass. Clerestories and stained-glass windows were not merely a means of letting in light. They delineated space in a new way and were central to the spiritual effect of a Gothic church.

Related to this is the development of a Gothic architectural detail, tracery. Tracery is not just a fussy decorative term. Two of the most common types of tracery, in architecture, interiors, and furniture, are **trefoil** and **quatrefoil.** Tracery involves a fundamentally different approach to defining space and using materials. The architects of Romanesque churches considered walls to be solid elements conceptually, and windows were punched into them. When adding windows to a wall, there is a limit to how many and how wide they can be. If the windows are too numerous, the wall will fail. A consequence of the flying buttress is its ability to increase the expanse of glass while still supporting the roof and propping up the wall. Yet glass cannot be produced in large pieces. The mullions between panes and sections of glass, instead of being remnants of a wall, are held together by the smallest of pieces possible, tracery—in stone or metal—whose only purpose was to hold the glass in place. Thus, the beginning of the modern skyscraper mullion, or glass-to-glass pressure connections, lies with Gothic tracery.

A characteristic of tracery in furniture is that the material—stone, metal, or wood—is relatively unimportant. The goal is the decorative form. Tracery sections are as delicate as possible in order to emphasize the pattern they create.

Bourges and High Gothic

Major French Gothic churches were built at Chartres, Amiens, Rheims, and Bourges. Saint-Etienne at Bourges, begun shortly before 1200, is a remarkable example of High Gothic architecture (Figure 6.7). Like Notre Dame, it belongs to the tradition associated with Paris in which the church, viewed in plan, is an integrated and unified composition. The development of the Christian church up to this point had been additive, starting with the basilica form, which is a rectangle with a semicircular apse at one end. Over time, the layout became increasingly complicated, with the addition of a transept, **narthex,** side aisles, and chapels. One of the achievements of Gothic design was to consolidate all these disparate elements as part of a unified plan.

Saint-Etienne at Bourges is 407 feet long and consists of a nave flanked by double side aisles. The piers lie mostly on the exterior and the side aisles run seamlessly into the ambulatory. The unity and harmony of the nave are achieved by vaults that extend over two bays. The nave elegantly becomes the choir. More so than with any other Gothic cathedral, the expression of the transept is suppressed.

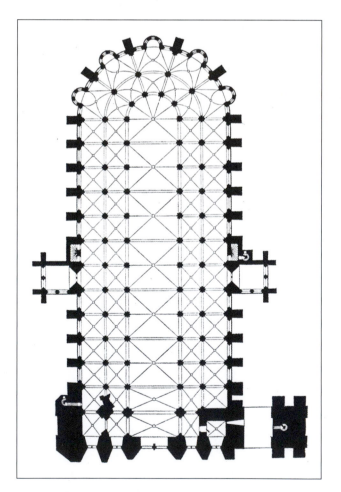

Figure 6.7 Bourges cathedral, plan, 1195–1250.

Figure 6.8 Pierre de Montreuil. Sainte-Chapelle, 1246–1248. Paris.

Sainte-Chapelle and Rayonnant

Louis IX reigned as king from 1226 to 1270. Known as one of the most pious and just kings, he was also an important patron of architecture. He was canonized in 1297. He expressed his religious devotion by participating in a craze of the late medieval period—the acquisition of holy relics. Saint-Louis paid great sums of money for Jesus' crown of thorns, a nail and a wooden piece of the cross, fragments from the spear that pierced Jesus' torso, the vinegar-soaked sponge, and pieces of Jesus' robe and shroud. Sainte-Chapelle was the private royal chapel built to house these famous relics. The cost of obtaining the relics far exceeded the construction costs.

Sainte-Chapelle is the best example of the **rayonnant** style (Figure 6.8). The distinguishing feature of rayonnant tracery is that lines radiate out from a single point. Unusual for a Gothic monument, the King's chapel is tiny. It has four small bays and a seven-sided apse. Because it was a private chapel, there was no need for side aisles. Essentially a single room, continuous walls of glass illuminate its interior. Three quarters of the height of the walls is luxuriously devoted to stained glass. With an extensive system of flying buttresses, the building's structural support is external and largely separated from the walls. The walls, therefore, are space-defining elements with little structural function. Sainte-Chapelle is one of the most important monuments of Gothic glass. It is an impressive space, tall in section and devoted to color and light. One of the most important achievements of Gothic architecture is the separation of a building's structure from space-defining walls and the development of nonstructural walls that are largely made of glass.

Wells Cathedral

Once the efforts of a group of architects and designers associated with a region achieves an across-the-board similarity, we have what historians refer to as a style. One feature of the development and dissemination of design styles is that they tend to appear in one region, then spread to another. It is conceivable that some architects and construction workers crossed the channel in both directions, and that the movement of workers was one of the mechanisms by which knowledge of the Gothic style was transmitted from France to England.

There is typically a time lag from region to region. For example, Gothic reigned in France in the period 1140–1230; elsewhere in Europe, it is associated with the period 1170–1250. Most countries developed regional variations.

While all European countries were affected by

the fashion to express devotion (and economic success) by erecting Gothic cathedrals to some extent, England made Gothic its own. One example is Wells Cathedral, whose construction began in 1174 (Figure 6.9). A general characteristic of English Gothic, evident at Lincoln Cathedral, is a delight in and profusion of surface ornamentation. Many vaults have extra ribs, taking what had been a structural element and making it decorative. English Gothic churches have more elaborate patterns of vaults than seen elsewhere. The decorative-versus-simplicity battle in England plays out between Lincoln (decorative) and Salisbury (simple).

The emphasis on verticality is less pronounced. Wells was an abbey church, surrounded by a lawn. The interior elevations recall Norman Romanesque; the walls are thick and solid. Horizontal lines are continuous, while verticals are broken, the opposite scenario of French cathedrals. The most unusual features are the strainer arches at the transept, dating to 1338.

By the mid-thirteenth century, Gothic cathedrals were being built throughout Europe. Germany joined the Gothic fray with the New Cathedral of Cologne in 1248. Spain embraced the Gothic style with major Gothic churches at Burgos (1222) and Toledo (1226).

A feature of Gothic outside of France (although also found in France) is an interest is column capitals formed with elaborate naturalistic foliages, such as those at Rheims. This became popular in England and Germany. This is significant because it underscores that Gothic architects developed an entire architectural vocabulary devoid of classic details. Deriving decorative motifs based on common plants was also a way of personalizing the international Gothic style and making it local. Foliate decorative patterns are also a feature of furniture and other designed objects.

Italian Gothic, like Italian Romanesque, fits oddly within the framework of European stylistic

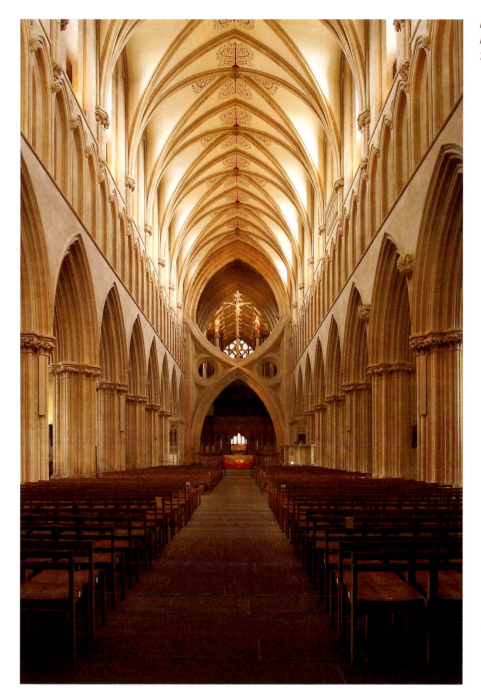

Figure 6.9 Wells Cathedral, interior, nave. Wells, England. 1174–1425.

developments. There was considerable Italian resistance to Gothic architecture. For Italians, the Roman artifacts they dealt with were real and not imagined. Thus, Italians never lost sight of what actual Roman ruins looked like. Similarly, the Byzantine impulse was strongly felt, so one particular branch of Italian Gothic, Venetian Gothic, combines Gothic forms with Byzantine decoration.

The aspect of Gothic architecture most conducive to the Italian mentality was the façade. Freed from literally expressing the building's form, the Italian Gothic façade was precisely that—a false front that shaped the space in front of the church. The façades of Italian Gothic churches acted on the urban scale, and (thinking of the Pantheon) Italian architects, not surprisingly, were always interested in expressing the dome and making it visible from the exterior.

INTERIORS AND FURNITURE

Interiors

When the most significant building interiors of an era are found in churches, it is clear that religious institutions had a great deal of power and money. Correspondingly, the greatest achievements and innovations are found in the building and outfitting of churches. Yet as we saw in our brief look at Gothic urban design, the period known for churches saw a gradual decline in the power of the church and the ascendancy of secular institutions, such as hospitals, libraries, universities, and town halls.

There are few domestic structures from the Gothic period, and very few examples of vernacular, or modest, Gothic houses. Paintings and illuminated manuscripts are an important source when examining the domestic world. Turning to the realm of interiors and furnishings, the most obvious observation is that Gothic furniture bears a remarkable continuity with Gothic architecture.

By the end of the Gothic period, designers had increasingly focused their attention on delineating the interiors of masonry buildings and increasing the amount of comfort. When working within masonry structures, there were two principal means of doing this: hanging tapestries and constructing paneling.

An early fifteenth-century French miniature shows Christin de Pisan offering her works, in the form of a book, to Isabel of Bavaria, and reveals details of a Gothic domestic interior and its furnishings (Figure 6.10). A barrel-vaulted roof caps a

Figure 6.10 Christin de Pisan offers her works to Isabel of Bavaria, early fifteenth century. French miniature.

room made of masonry walls. Tie beams and vertical king posts act as tension rods stabilizing the arches of the roof structure. Tapestries hang on the walls. The bed has a canopy, or tester, and is heavily draped for both warmth and privacy. This room, a bedroom, serves double duty as a sitting room during the day for a group of women.

Heavy bars at the window let in air and light but prevent outsiders from gaining access. This is a straightforward indication of another aspect of secular life: the ever-present danger of burglaries, and hence the defensive nature of houses. Gothic domestic interiors of palaces, castles, and houses are at the tail end of the great period of fortified castles. The invention of gunpowder and other elements of warfare rendered the house-as-fort prototype obsolete.

Isabel of Bavaria sits on an X-frame chair, the others on small stools. The room is sparsely furnished; even for the nobility, pieces of furniture were exceptional and prized.

Another valuable aspect of this image is that it shows a preference for richness in color, material, and decoration, mostly achieved with textiles. Gothic buildings seem somber today, because the color of the statuary has worn off and current taste does not allow for stone statuary to be painted. The visual abundance in a Gothic interior was provided

Figure 6.11 Wedding banquet with high table, cloth canopy, and display cabinet.

by the saturated colors of textiles that draped both house and body.

Our knowledge of secular attire comes almost exclusively from images such as this one. Isabel of Bavaria is richly adorned in a voluminous embroidered dress, cinched in at the waist. All the women wear the two-horned headdress, *truffeaux,* an extravagant style of headdress favored by many, and also a frequent target of scorn.

A scene of a wedding banquet presents a view of furniture involved with ritual and daily life during the Gothic period (Figure 6.11). Individual chairs were a rarity. The diners sit on benches behind draped trestle tables—no doubt hidden because of their inelegance and rudimentary construction. In some English great halls, a raised platform, or dais, distinguishes one end of the room where the noble family dines. Other European countries also had the custom of outfitting a dining room with a dais. Being seated along one side of the table allows for servers, who were plentiful, to serve from the other side. Other guests similarly sit on one side of the table.

The central figure wears a rich headdress decorated with two truffeaux, while her companions sport hennins, pointed cone headdresses. The servers wear tight-fitting, and revealing, hose and short jackets. A tall cabinet serves as a sideboard. The sideboard acted as a staging area for servers and also put the family's expensive serving pieces on display.

Carpentry

In a Gothic painting, a carpenter works with a plane (Figure 6.12). In front of his worktable stands the fruit of previous efforts, a partially constructed base cabinet. Again, bars protect the workshop from unwanted intruders. A woman unravels thread from a spindle. This image divides the labor force, with a man engaged with carpentry and a woman involved with weaving, underscoring the two primary means of articulating a Gothic interior, with carpentry and textiles.

Figure 6.12 Craftsman making linenfold panels, Gothic painting.

A surefire way to identify a piece of furniture or carpentry as Gothic is the linenfold motif, usually featured in wood constructions (Figure 6.13). This frequently occurring motif is a shape achievable with planing and carving. It is also a testament to the value of linen, and textiles in general. Gothic painting and sculpture paid considerable attention to the folds of drapery, and the linenfold motif in furniture is related to conventions of drapery folds in sculpture.

In Gothic churches, wooden choir stalls and other interior partitions were often freestanding and self-supporting. Their design, in form and detail, is consistent with architectural Gothic. The most prestigious and innovative architectural projects were churches; hence, the finest and most highly paid carpentry jobs were found in outfitting them. It is therefore not surprising that this led to furni-

Figure 6.13 A linenfold-paneled room, assembled mostly from Tudor-period interiors, c. 1475–1525.

ture production with strong visual ties to Gothic architecture. Many pieces of Gothic furniture are beholden to architecture, and in fact are designed like miniature buildings, such as choirs, buffets, and display cabinets. The Mathias choir stall from Hungary is a piece of furniture consistent with Gothic architecture. While the vertical divisions between the individual seats are structurally expressive, most of the attention is devoted to decorative work designed to make this piece look like the building it sat in (Figure 6.14). There are Gothic arches, crosses, finials, and quatrefoil tracery. The side panels are exceptionally delicate examples of wooden tracery.

Regarding function, the choir stall is taller than necessary. The sitter's head would rest about three-quarters of the way up the backrest. The remainder of the choir stall exists purely for visual effect.

Tracery, initially carved in stone, is here carved out of wood. Tracery did not exist solely to support glass. Elements of tracery are intended to be decorative. The form is important, in stone, wood, or metal. Details of Gothic tracery glory in curls, arches, and C and S curves. Expressing the nature of the material was unimportant.

Furniture

A Gothic chair looks as though a choir stall had been chopped off in slices, and one piece turned into a chair (Figure 6.15). Up to this historical point in time, the late fifteenth century, important chairs, such as thrones, highlighted the status of the sitter by using elegant materials and time-consuming and exacting workmanship. The Gothic chair, however, bestows status upon its sitter in a different

Figure 6.14 Mathias choir stalls, 1483. Hungary.

fashion: by exaggerating its scale. From Gothic architecture, furniture designers inherited an emphasis on height. The Gothic chair renders the person fortunate enough to be sitting in it high status and visual import by exaggerating their physical presence within a space. The combination of seated person (resplendently dressed) and chair presents an eye-catching ensemble that relates Gothic architectural principles to the human body.

The stylized linenfold motif identifies this as a work of the Gothic period, as do the finials. In this chair, a storage unit supports the seat. Pieces of furniture were scarce and precious in the Gothic period, and often had to take on several functions, here storage and seating. A cushion could be added to provide a modicum of comfort. The rest of the chair emphasizes visual effect over comfort. The chair exacted a precise vertical posture of its sitter, with arms at a dignified position of rest.

Gothic chairs were rare. Most people sat on benches, chests, or stools, and these common seating types were less elaborate. Rather than being consistent with Gothic, their straightforward forms are a testament to their utility. The X-frame stool is remarkably consistent from ancient Rome to the twentieth century. X-frame stools of various kinds existed on all continents. Gothic X-frame stools take the typical form and dress it with Gothic detailing (Figure 6.16).

Just as the stylistic influences of Gothic architecture can be seen across Europe, the work of French carpenters also made its mark on European furniture. A coronation chair from Westminster Abbey in London is an exceptional piece of furniture for an exceptional function: the ceremony to crown the monarch (Figure 6.17). It represents how craftsmen combined their knowledge of furniture making with architectural detailing. It has a commanding presence in a room, and is designed to receive the end of an architectural and visual axis. It is meant to be viewed frontally.

The vertical expression is achieved by lifting the seat itself atop two platforms. A triangular backdrop frames the head. The lion feet underscore the regal nature of the piece, and the polychrome decoration makes it a worthy focus of those gathered in the assembly room.

In the realm of decorative arts, the Gothic period exhibits a love of small, precious things made of exquisite materials. This is typically evident in the production of finely crafted reliquaries or chalices. When it was financially feasible, the same attention

Figure 6.15 Gothic bishop chair, c. 1500. France.

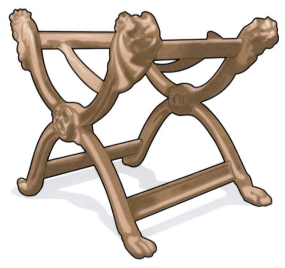

Figure 6.16 Folding X-stool, c. 1400.

Figure 6.17 Coronation chair, 1300. Westminster Abbey.

was turned to furniture, and a few exceptional pieces of metal furniture exist, made of bronze or silver. The throne of King Martin of Aragon shows architectural forms rendered in silver (Figure 6.18). Its creator employed the system of Gothic architectural detailing, which had an international appeal. Although certain accommodations were made for the material, the Gothic forms were applied with little regard for the unique qualities of metal. The decorative vocabulary remained unchanged. The emphasis is on effect and not an "honest" expression of materiality.

A seventeenth-century Gothic armchair from Hungary results from a different cultural context

Figure 6.19 Gothic arm chair, seventeenth century. Hungary.

(Figure 6.19). Stylistically, it looks both forward and backward. It shows a link to a Roman chair and also displays a similarity to a chair associated with the Renaissance, the sedia. Its nonrepresentational decoration suggests that by the seventeenth century, motifs associated with Islamic Spain had spread around Europe. Some artworks conform to the belief that Gothic, Renaissance, and Islamic are distinct categories, yet certain pieces display evidence of overlap.

CONCLUSION

The Gothic period is the tail end of the Middle Ages and the last period before the Renaissance. The inspired period of building cathedrals with

Figure 6.18 Silver throne of King Martin of Aragon, fourteenth century.

Gothic elements lasted for approximately three hundred years.

The church played a central role as a religious, political, economic, and cultural entity. Commissions for building and outfitting churches involved large outlays of cash and resulted in most of the high-end artwork. Yet the Gothic period saw the growing importance of royal patronage. Power was no longer the exclusive purview of monasteries. Gothic churches involved the input of nobles, merchants, and artisans.

During the Gothic period, the necessity for walled cities waned. Gothic domestic interiors are more elaborate and comfortable than Romanesque interiors. Yet the Gothic domestic realm is not the equivalent of the religious realm.

Gothic furniture comes from and is an extension of Gothic architecture. The distinctive features of Gothic architecture constitute the distinctive features of Gothic furniture: pointed arches, tracery, finials, trefoils, and quatrefoils. The techniques for stone carving also greatly increased over the course of the Gothic period.

The interior spaces of churches were carefully delineated to affect the mood and spirit of the religious visitor. If a visitor entered a Gothic cathedral on a bright day, the difference between the bright outside and the dim inside was noticeable. Before the pupils dilated, the visitor noticed the vertical orientation of the building and the details that composed it, and likely looked upward. Then, becoming accustomed to the light, the visitor noticed the existence of walls almost entirely of glass and brightly colored. There is a reason why Gothic cathedrals are known by the catchphrase "height and light."

Sources

Bony, Jean. *French Gothic Architecture of the 12th and 13th Centuries*. Berkeley: University of California Press, 1983.

Branner, Robert. *Gothic Architecture*. New York: G. Braziller, 1961.

Fitchen, John. *The Construction of the Gothic Cathedral*. Chicago: University of Chicago Press, 1981.

Frankl, Paul. *Gothic Architecture*. Harmondsworth: Penguin Books, 1962.

Mark, Robert. *Experiments in Gothic Structure*. Cambridge: MIT Press, 1982.

Martindale, Andrew. *Gothic Art: From the Twelfth to Fifteenth Centuries*. New York: Praeger, 1967.

Simson, Otto Georg von. *The Gothic Cathedral: The Origins of Gothic Architecture and the Medieval Concept of Order*. New York: Pantheon Books, 1956.

Wilson, Christopher. *The Gothic Cathedral*. London: Thames and Hudson, 1990.

Worringer, Wilhelm. *Form in Gothic*. New York: Schocken, 1927.

DISCUSSION AND REVIEW QUESTIONS

1. **What are the chief differences between Romanesque and Gothic?**
2. **What are the chief similarities between Romanesque and Gothic?**
3. **What are the elements of the Gothic design vocabulary that relate to the religious experience?**
4. **What are two technical achievements of the Gothic that predict modern developments?**
5. **How is Gothic furniture an extension of Gothic architecture?**
6. **How does a Gothic church seek to create a spiritual feeling in a viewer?**

THE AMERICAS

MEXICO	1500 B.C.E.–200 C.E.		200 C.E.–900 C.E.		900 C.E.–1521 C.E.	
	Preclassic		Classic		Postclassic	

PERU	1800–900 B.C.E.	900–200 B.C.E.	200 B.C.E.–600 C.E.	600–1000 C.E.	1000–1476 C.E.	1476–1534 C.E.
	Initial	Early Horizon	Early Intermediate	Middle Horizon	Late Intermediate	Late Horizon

This chapter represents a deficit and an attempt to address that deficit—namely, the role of indigenous American architecture and objects in a history of design. It is not a deficit in terms of high-quality objects for inclusion, but it is a deficit in the sense that these items have not traditionally taken a prominent role in design histories. There are many reasons for the relative lack of attention up until recent decades, and just as many sound reasons for righting the wrong.

But there are difficulties. For one, furniture as construed in the European way did not play a major role in pre-Columbian societies. Where there are hundreds of books on eighteenth-century English and French furniture, there is not a single book devoted to pre-Columbian furniture. The aesthetic impulse of many American groups presents itself in textiles, baskets, masks, headdresses, jewelry, sports equipment, and clay figurines—objects that standard design histories mostly ignore. Classified as crafts and not art or design, they were given a minor role.

Architectural survey books have added pre-Columbian monuments to their canon. The task of architectural historians was easier: the temples, pyra-mids, and cities of Mexico, Guatemala, and Peru fit anyone's idea of great architecture. In addition, problematic for the history of interiors and furnishings, Mesoamerican architects focused their efforts on building exteriors and sculpture. And there is the problem of preservation: Most objects made of impermanent materials have disappeared. Although pre-Columbian arts receive less coverage in traditional architecture, art, and design histories, it is not for lack of scholarly materials. Archaeologists, anthropologists, and historians have been skillfully working on these subjects for decades. The task that this chapter tackles is deciding how to include these materials in a history of design that focuses on furniture.

EARLY HISTORY

In prehistoric periods, to varying degrees, Europe, Asia, and Africa were connected. Shards of Chinese vases have been found in Africa; the Greeks and Romans knew and drew Africans, who figured into their myths and into their art; Europeans and Asians traveled and traded via the Silk Road, and later on ocean voyages. Yet there was little knowledge of or contact between Asia, Africa, and Europe and the Americas. The inhabitants of the pre-Columbian Americas had no knowledge of the Old World—Europe.

It is believed that physical contact between Asia and the New World (North and South America) occurred around 30,000 B.C.E., via the land bridge that connected Alaska and Asia. People of Asian ancestry crossed the Bering Strait and began the population of the Western Hemisphere. By 10,000 B.C.E., people lived along the length and breadth of North and South America, from the southern Andes to the Arctic Circle. They had stone points, fishing nets, sleeping mats, and pottery for both storage and cooking. Organized agriculture developed in some areas as early as 4000 B.C.E. (Kostof 1995, p. 233). By 1500 B.C.E., the range and depth of the production of objects constitute what can be termed the beginning of an American vision regarding artistic expression.

The varieties of domestic architecture were innumerable, with some houses sunken into the earth, some tucked underneath cliffs, some made of ice, stone, bricks, reeds, wood, or leather. Over time, a mosaic of cultures stretched across the Americas down to Antarctica—a patchwork quilt of languages and cultural practices. The first Americans were hunter-gatherers, and some groups stayed that way. But major urban civilizations developed, the largest the world had ever seen, and their metropolises included complicated, stratified societies and monumental architecture related to religious practices.

For historians of architecture and design, the cultures that developed permanent ritual complexes are compelling, as they also left significant historical remains. Some North American groups had earthworks, such as the Hopewell in the Ohio Valley, with their impressive Serpent Mound. The Hopewell mounds were burial sites containing human remains and grave objects, including smoking pipes, pottery, and copper jewelry. In southern Illinois,

near St. Louis, Cahokia was a large city centered on several giant mounds. The city had a population of about 20,000, and Monks Mound was the largest earthwork in North America.

While the possible subjects of this chapter are many, it will focus on the buildings and objects of two areas that had major urban centers: Mexico and Peru.

Columbus's voyage to the Americas in 1492 set in motion a series of events that would lead to the downfall of the societies he found; hence the term "pre-Columbian." Two of the expeditions in Columbus's wake, Hernando Cortés's conquest of the Aztecs in 1521 (Mexico) and Pizarro's conquest of the Incas (Peru) in 1536, completed the process set in motion by Columbus, and the results of that encounter are addressed at chapter's end.

When Columbus arrived, no national boundary lines separated the regions that are today the United States, Mexico, and Central America. "Mesoamerica" refers to the North American and Central American region. "Pre-Columbian" is a general term referring to any and all of the indigenous groups who predated the arrival of the Spanish-funded Italian explorer.

The challenge in writing this chapter concerns not only what pre-Columbian artifacts we should look at, but how we look at them. Art historian Esther Pasztory addresses the issue of Western viewers of pre-Columbian artifacts: "In order to reconstruct pre-Columbian aesthetics, one is forced to deal with the context as defined anthropologically. The most immediate issue is the function of art, which is said to be 'utilitarian' in traditional societies and 'free' in the modern West. While we can say that as an embodiment of value, status, taste, and intellect, art of all periods has a similar function, there is indeed a difference between implicit and explicit concepts of aesthetics. Pre-Columbian cultures whose arts survived in permanent media were complex, hierarchical societies defined as chiefdoms and states. Having limited systems of writing, artworks were the most important communicating media" (Pasztory 2005, p. 193). Looking carefully at designed objects is the first step in reconstructing a pre-Columbian aesthetic.

MEXICO

In the Preclassic period, the major site was San Lorenzo and the artworks of the Olmecs, including the colossal heads. The Classic period, covered in these pages, includes the major ethnic groups: Teotihuacán, the Toltecs, and the Maya. The Postclassic includes the Aztecs, those who were there at the time of the Spanish conquest.

Several major urban centers dominated life in ancient Mexico; their most impressive structures were pyramids. It is easy to see the connection between earth mounds and pyramids, with pyramids arriving later, architecturally constructed versions of the former, at once of the earth but reaching toward the sky.

Teotihuacán

100 B.C.E.-750 C.E.

In terms of scale and age, the most imposing ancient buildings in North America are found at Teotihuacán. They lie in the semi-arid Valley of Teotihuacán, north of present-day Mexico City. Teotihuacán was a major ritual center, a center of agriculture and trade with a bustling marketplace. As architectural historian Spiro Kostof (1995) eloquently wrote: "Nothing can prepare us for the size, conviction, and majesty of Teotihuacán" (p. 237). Their agricultural abilities must have been extensive enough to support the large population and allow for this complex culture to develop. At its height, Teotihuacán had a population of approximately 200,000, making it one of the largest cities in the world. The most spectacular buildings are two pyramids; they are surrounded by lower temples, platforms, and palaces

and residential areas that are equally significant for the history of design. The first age of inhabitation at Teotihuacán was in the period 100 B.C.E.–200 C.E., predating the Aztec capital, Tenochtitlan, by a thousand years.

Teotihuacán is built around a central axis. In one direction it trails off with no definitive formal conclusion; the other ends in the central ritual complex that includes the Pyramid of the Moon and the large Pyramid of the Sun. The Pyramid of the Sun is the largest pyramid in the Americas, and it is built directly on top of a four-chambered cave. Facing west, it is 705 feet square and 206 feet tall.

What the Pyramid of the Moon lacks in size, it makes up for with the precision of its construction. The Pyramid of the Moon marks the end of the central axis at Teotihuacán and faces south. Pyramids attract attention for their overall mass and their height. The surrounding buildings, smaller platforms, temples, and palaces emphasize the horizontal orientation and relate to the broad expanse of the valley, framed in the distance by low-lying mountains.

Pasztory wrote her dissertation on the murals at Teotihuacán and is the author of a highly regarded book on the ancient city; this chapter is indebted to her efforts (Pasztory 1976 and 1997). She considers the dominant aesthetic quality at Teotihuacán to be order and organization. The city was organized along an axis, with blocks laid out according to a grid. There was standardization of the city, its architecture, and its art. The buildings that made up the blocks followed suit.

In many ways, Teotihuacán was a forerunner to the Aztec empire; it was ancient and mythical to the Aztecs. Like the Aztecs, the people of Teotihuacán likely spoke Nahuatl. There was a cult of warriors, warfare, and human sacrifice. But it was not exactly the same as the Aztecs; there were differences. As a city, Teotihuacán was also organized differently than Mayan cities.

Unlike other Mesoamerican sites, the major monuments of Teotihuacán were built mostly at one time, and not in successive layers. The Pyramid of the Sun may have been built over a sacred natural site. Like the Aztec, Teotihuacán temples honored the gods. The Teotihuacán and the Aztecs may have had a god in common, Quetzalcoatl, the feathered serpent. The identification of the feathered serpent statues that exist in quantity at Teotihuacán with the Aztec god is under dispute. The Quetzal bird had long green tail feathers that the Mesoamericans incorporated into their dress. They also acted as a collar to the serpentine heads that are a prominent feature at Teotihuacán.

The Talud and the Tablero

Architecture varies greatly across Mesoamerica, yet there are aspects of its development that are variations on a single compositional scheme, outlined here. Using Pasztory's formulation, a frequent composition had two parts: the **talud** was a base, frequently sloped, that acted as the physical and visual support for a raised panel, the **tablero** (Figure 7.1). This panel features a prominent flat frame and a sunken inset field.

Apartments

The so-called palaces (a more accurate term might be apartments) reflect the horizontality of the land-

Figure 7.1 Palace of Quetzalpapalotl (Temple platforms), courtyard. Fourth to eighth centuries. Teotihuacán, Mexico.

Figure 7.2 Palace of Quetzalpapalotl (Priests' residence), courtyard, pier in elevation. Fourth to eighth centuries. Teotihuacán, Mexico.

scape; they focus on a courtyard, with rooms that open off the central space that was open to the sky (Figure 7.2).

The leaders of Teotihuacán, after the grand period of monument building, focused their efforts on the city's residential quarters; they turned to making apartments. Teotihuacán's residents lived in these courtyard houses that served as multifamily units. "Most of the population of Teotihuacán had lived in apartment compounds built on a grid plan" (Pasztory 1997, p. 33). Apartments had central patios with altars and a temple platform on one side of the court. The interior rooms of the apartment compounds were dark because they had no windows (Pasztory 1997, p. 47). The courtyard elevations are

a different riff on the Teotihuacán style moldings—the talud and tablero—and utilize the same profile as the temples. The variation is that the base is two steps, followed by flat, square piers. The piers support an elongated, framed panel (Figure 7.2). Across Teotihuacán's precincts, there are stone buildings and adobe buildings, but they share a similar composition and decoration.

Artists

To create, maintain, and continue the artistic traditions of religious and domestic life requires large numbers of masons, carvers, painters, and potters. The traditions of craft production were highly developed, and there were hundreds of workshops and thousands of artists. The markets of Teotihuacán sold the goods of artists and merchants, some of whom had traveled long distances. Artists, whose works were admired, were on the lower end of the social-economic scale, on the level of people who worked in agriculture.

The stone walls are similar to mural paintings. Many of the stones that constitute the buildings had originally been painted in vibrant colors, red being one of the most prominent (Figure 7.3). Yet a color scheme of red on red, with similar value and hue, emphasizes the compositional flatness. Pasztory broadly characterizes Teotihuacán art: "Lack of ostentation, simplicity, geometric form, and minimalism thus govern many Teotihuacán art forms from sculpture to pottery" (Pasztory 1997, p. 159).

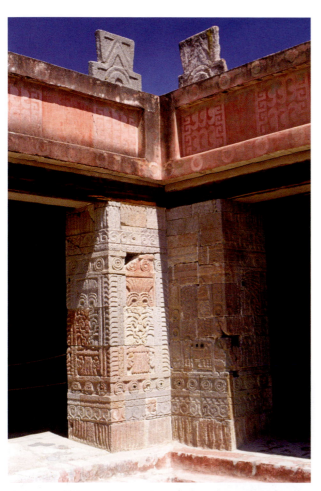

Figure 7.3 Palace of Quetzalpapalotl, corner detail of courtyard. Fourth to eighth centuries. Teotihuacán, Mexico.

Apartment complexes were surrounded by a high wall and accessed from a single entrance. The apartments, while pleasant, were not architecturally striking or innovative like the temples. They provided a high standard of living for a significant portion of the population. Some people were wealthy, others less so; Pasztory estimates that two thirds were poor. It was not an egalitarian society, but collective. Pasztory sees the apartments as "representations and embodiments of civic wealth and power" (Pasztory 1997, p. 52). At Teotihuacán, there were few representations of rulers. "The leaders of Teotihuacán were therefore consciously playing down their individuality and not advertising their dynastic legitimacy in arts" (Pasztory 1997, p. 56). While less spectacular than the pyramids, the courtyard houses are worthy of attention for their skilled use of materials, stone, paint, and an endless supply of sunlight.

ZAPOTECS

The Valley of Oaxaca lies in southern Mexico and was inhabited by the Zapotec people from approximately 1500 B.C.E. until the arrival of the Spanish.

Monte Albán

Monte Albán was the administrative center of the Zapotecs, centrally located in the Valley of Oaxaca. The grand plaza at Monte Albán sits on a level platform 985 by 656 feet. The plaza is ringed by three conjoined temples and other structures, including a ball court. The period 200–700 C.E. was the height of the Zapotecs at Monte Albán.

Ball Courts, Paraphernalia, and Trophies

Ball courts were a prominent feature of many Mesoamerican cities (Figures 7.4 and 7.5). Ball courts and the games played on them are noteworthy, both for their architecture and for the objects created for

Figure 7.4 Monte Albán, Ball Court, 200–950 c.e., Zapotec. Mexico.

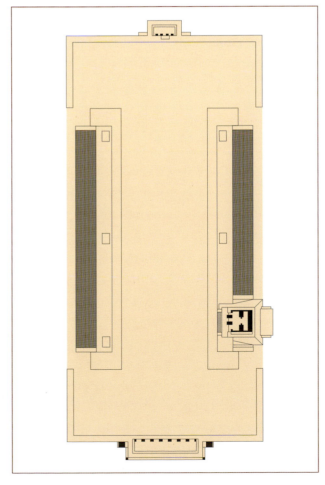

them, sports-related paraphernalia. A ball court from Monte Albán has two ranges of seats overlooking the central playing field. The sloped structures are reminiscent of pyramids, although they take the monumentality in a horizontal direction. These constructions, like pyramids, are compositions that involve shaping the landscape in addition to building on top of it. The playing field itself is characteristically I-shaped, a central field that opens up at each end.

In the Mesoamerican world, Mary Ellen Miller (2004) writes, ball games were played for some three thousand years. Later, this resulted in striking architectural works; most existing ball courts were built in the period 100 c.e.–1519. Outdoor ball courts were a prominent feature of the ceremonial cen-

Figure 7.5 Ball Court, Chichén-Itzá, tenth to thirteenth centuries. Maya-Toltec. Mexico

ters of Mesoamerican cities. An I-shaped ball court stood directly in front of the Aztec twin pyramid in Tenochtitlan.

Mesoamerican people saw the ball game as a rich metaphor that reflected their place in the world and its relation to celestial movements of the sun, moon, and Venus. The courts themselves were sacred areas, liminal places "where man and god met" (Miller, p. 23). They combined manipulated landscape with built architecture—the audience stands. Twentieth-century Mexican modernists were as impressed with the ball courts as with the flashier temples.

The category of ball game paraphernalia related to the games included hard rubber balls that fascinated the Spanish conquerors. The game itself is alternately described as relating to lacrosse, basketball, or jai alai; the goal was to get the ball through a vertical ring attached to the side of the court. Depending on the game, the ball was hit by hand or by a stick or paddle that was attached to the body. Murals and figurines of players inform us that players wore a U-shaped yoke around their waist.

Vertically oriented objects were attached to it, either the tall thin "palma" or the squatter "hacha." Their use is not exactly clear, which demonstrates the difficulty of interpreting objects without corroborating evidence. They may have been used to strike the ball. A variety of protective paddings, hand protectors, and knee pads were fashioned from soft, perishable materials.

Yet many yokes, palmas, and hachas were made of stone and carved. It is difficult to know if these are actual objects or commemorative versions of actual objects, trophies to commemorate a victory. In their creation of designed objects, the Mesoamericans of several areas had the habit of taking the form of simple, daily-use objects and making them into permanent form. In this transformation, the objects lost the ability to function in a mechanical or practical way, but gained the ability to function in a representative, commemorative, and emotive way. They were physical manifestations of prowess, vigor, and athletic ability.

Mitla

In the region surrounding Monté Alban, the Zapotec capital, there are numerous smaller villages and rural residences.

The courtyard interior of a palace from Mitla, a Zapotec site, is worthy of attention for the quality of its mosaics and carvings. Tourists in Mexico usually focus on the pyramids, yet the design of this interior space, open to the sky, reveals another kind of expertise. This is a carefully designed symmetrical space in which four low walls surround a courtyard; rooms open off this central space (Figure 7.6). The stone walls are faced with carefully dressed and carved stone, whose final delineation was turned over to the considerable talents of the stone carver. Everything emphasizes the horizontal: the low, broad openings, the broader lintels, and the rectangular panels that constitute the bulk of the façade.

These structures rely upon a façade profile that first appeared at Teotihuacán. Each panel has a broad, flat frame, and the frame emphasizes the field. There is a modestly sloped base. The talud supports two levels of framed panels that in turn support the uppermost, and most visually significant, tablero.

Considering the totality of the Zapotec courtyard, it functions as a testament to a stone carver's abilities and is illustrative of the social position of the artist. Within the tablero's border, the stone carvers and stone layers, it appears, were given free rein, each panel a testament to the artist's expertise. There is a sense of one-upmanship, with each panel being a version of a previous panel's motifs yet rendered more complicated. There are patterns, repetitions, and small-scale changes from side to side, panel to panel. This appears to be an example of artistic bravado, each artist trying to outdo the next.

Figure 7.6 Mitla, Zapotec.

Yet the individuality of artistic expression has its limits. Each panel is subsumed as part of an overall composition; the prominent corner moldings overhang and frame the entire elevation. There was a mediation between the collective effort and the ability of artists to express themselves individually. They were all working on one project. The upper panel floats in a display of virtuosity in which common stone is made extravagant by the number of man-hours spent skillfully shaping it.

MAYA

The Maya of the Classic Period are commonly dated to 300–900 C.E. The Maya occupied the areas that today lie in Southern Mexico, the Yucatán Peninsula, and Guatemala. They had impressive urban centers whose dominant buildings were religious temples on top of pyramids. The Mayan pyramids are not as massive or as tall as the Pyramid of the Sun in Teotihuacán, but they are impressive for their steep slope. Mayan pyramids were platforms for temples and also contained burial places. There is no indication that the Maya had extensive residential quarters of the city that consisted of apartment blocks made of durable materials, although the nobles and religious leaders lived in stone palaces.

Ancestors of the Maya continue to live in the region. Considerable visual evidence suggests that the temple structures on top of the pyramids bear a formal relationship to the classic Maya house. A temple, like a typical house, is a rectangular space of one to three rooms, approached laterally, with a central door in one of the long sides. There is a single range of rooms that may be interconnected.

Figure 7.7 El Castillo. Chichén-Itzá. Maya-Toltec. Eleventh to thirteenth centuries. Mexico.

Figure 7.8 Dwelling at Uxmal. Mérida, Yucatan Peninsula, Mexico.

Even the pitch of the stone temple roofs repeats the form of the thatched roofs of the Maya house (Figures 7.7 and 7.8).

Maya-Toltec

Chichén-Itzá is a Toltec site, far to the south of the Toltec heartland around Tula, north of Teotihuacán. The reason for the existence of a Toltec city surrounded by Mayan sites remains unresolved. Its artifacts are therefore usually interpreted as benefiting from both traditions.

Architecture

The central pyramid at Chichén-Itzá, now known as El Castillo, was a sacrificial temple related to the solar calendar (Figure 7.9).

The Temple of the Warriors is significant because it features a field of columns, which are no longer structural members, but stand-ins for human figures.

Designed Objects

A designed object represented on numerous sculptural reliefs and wall paintings is a footed raised platform. Nobles or gods are shown kneeling on

Figure 7.9 El Castillo, Chichén-Itzá, Mexico.

Figure 7.10 Stone altar. Chichén-Itzá, Mexico.

these low platforms, sometimes sitting on platforms on platforms. An altar is a version in stone of what must have been a common object (Figure 7.10).

Furniture

The jungles of the Yucatán Peninsula and Guatemala, in contrast to the more arid north, present terrible conditions for the preservation of artifacts, particularly anything made of biological materials, such as wood, leather, or textiles. These ritual centers were surrounded by bustling cities, their straw houses replete with items made of wood, reeds, grass, and leather, almost none of which survive. Today the pyramids sit in the middle of archaeological parks, a backdrop that gives little indication of what Mayan city life was like. Our knowledge of the life of the Maya is tilted in the direction of the elite, whose material culture is better preserved owing to their burial practices.

From the principal pyramid at Chichén-Itzá comes one of the few extant examples of ancient Maya-Toltec furniture: the Jaguar Throne (Figure 7.11). It is a mid-height seat, neither as low as African or Asian examples, nor as high as European chairs. There are no backrest or arms. Its chief function is to provide visual impact, with little obvious attention to comfort. This was a seat for ceremonial and not casual use.

All continents had furniture-making traditions that were zoomorphic: They incorporated animal parts as elements of their overall form. With an English Georgian armchair, the piece is foremost a chair, and one of its details is that the feet resemble lion paws. With the jaguar throne, the identification of the throne is foremost as a jaguar; its identification as a seat is secondary. Mayan religious practices included rituals that involved wearing masks and costumes. Pasztory (2005) writes generally about

Figure 7.11 Jaguar Throne. El Castillo. Chichén-Itzá. Maya-Toltec. Eleventh to thirteenth centuries. Mexico.

cultures with masking traditions: "An impersonation is not just the mask but the whole costume, dance, music, and songs" (p. 54). Herbert Cole (1985) similarly writes of the masked individual: "This *is* and *is not* a human being. So transformed, the being is saying: 'I am not myself.' Ambivalence and ambiguity exist in the presence of maskers." A masking tradition involves humans who dress as spirits, and this included using animal skins and body parts to adorn and transform their human bodies. A logical interpretation of the seat whose primary identification is as an animal is to consider the aesthetics of the masking performance. This was an exceptional piece of furniture; the role that the chair plays was not merely to support a human figure. Considering the masking tradition encourages an interpretation in which the assembly of figure and chair is read as an impressive visual totality; jaguar, seat, and human figure became one. The throne had the role of visually transforming the seated human figure.

In the case of the Jaguar Throne, while it is conceivably possible that there were wooden benches of a similar configuration, the decoration of a jaguar's head was likely limited to ceremonial pieces. Compared to other cultures' use of animal legs for feet, it is also notable that the Mayan seat is "walking" away from a viewer. With its head turned and its teeth bared, the asymmetry adds to the dynamic impression the piece makes on a viewer, particularly when it supported a human in elaborate dress and makeup.

The seat is similar to the common Chacmool sculptures found throughout the Toltec areas. A Chacmool sculpture features a human figure who is lying down on his back, face up, legs and arms bent, with a shallow bowl balanced on his stomach. This vessel was used either for offerings, as a brazier, or as the location of animal sacrifices. Chacmool figures were widespread at Chichén-Itzá.

AZTECS

The Aztecs were a cultural and political entity whose capital was Tenochtitlan (today Mexico City). For many, the Aztecs are synonymous with Mexico, although they were one of several ethnic groups.

They spoke Nahuatl, and one of the Aztec groups was the Mexica.

Tenochtitlan was the Aztec capital city, the home of Montezuma. The center of the city was on an island in the middle of a lake; causeways connected the island to the shores. The city was founded in 1325 and had grown considerably by 1487. At its center stood a great double pyramid, with a ball court in front of it (Figure 7.12). Hernán Cortés reported that the city had approximately 200,000 inhabitants.

The official religion of the state was polytheistic, and one of the significant deities was Huitzilopochtli. Huitzilopochtli was the sun god and god of war, and he brought the Mexica people to the island in the middle of the lake that became Tenochtitlan. Along the way, he fought successfully in several battles; his cult was associated with military success.

The Templo Mayor is the central temple in Tenochtitlan's center. It is an unusual double temple that Huitzilopochtli shared with Tlaloc, the god of rain and therefore the god of agriculture. Statues of Tlaloc, large and small, exist in great number. For a place with no shortage of art, sculpture, reliefs, and murals, it is surprising that Huitzilopochtli's form and appearance are mostly unknown. He was rarely portrayed, and most of the images of Huitzilopochtli were created post-conquest. One of the

Figure 7.12 Tenochtitlan with Templo Mayor. Mexico City, Mexico. Model.

few, and most significant, representations of him comes from the backrest of a seat, the so-called Throne of Montezuma.

The Throne of Montezuma

Elizabeth Boone's writing on the image of the Aztec god Huitzilopochtli addresses Aztec religion and art, and in so doing provides an invaluable account, summarized here, of one of the most important pieces of Aztec furniture.

The object is called Teocalli, or alternately the Throne of Montezuma (Figure 7.13). It is important as a rare example of Aztec furniture, and it bears one of the few representations of Huitzilopochtli. It is a "blocky symbol-laden monolith that probably functioned as a throne" (Boone 1989, p. 15). The throne has the distinctive profile of an Aztec stepped pyramid, with a steep incline and a rectangular block on top of a base. The backrest of the throne has one of the rare presentations of Huitzilo-

Figure 7.13 Teocalli, Throne of Montezuma, commemorative monument, stone, Post-classical period Aztec culture, 900–1521.

pochtli. Carved on the backrest is a composition centered on a sun disk with figures on each side. To the left is Huitzilopochtli in human form, identified by the hummingbird, and he is missing his left foot. He faces the figure who stands to the right, Montezuma. Understanding how god, ruler, image, and piece of furniture work together is crucial to interpreting this object.

Wrestling with the scenario of an important God who was visually absent, Boone examines the concepts of "teotl" and "teixiptla." The post-conquest Spanish translated "teotl" as god, saint, or devil. It was a "sacred and impersonal force or a concentration of power" (Boone 1989, p. 4). "Teixiptla" is referred to as an impersonator, substitute, image, incarnation, or actor—in other words, the physical representation. During performances and rituals, humans personified Huitzilopochtli. Thus there was a God, a sacred power, who was without form or physical attributes until a variety of representations (including dressed humans) were created. A god was not a person, but a force or a natural phenomenon. Similarly, Tlaloc was lightning, although represented in human form.

The rare representations of Huitzilopochtli are therefore images of actors impersonating the god. One shows him standing in front of a steeply raked and stepped pyramid. He wears a headdress of quetzal feathers that spring from a metallic band, and he has a hummingbird attached to the back of his head. His face has yellow and blue stripes, and his nose is turquoise. His body is painted blue, and he wears a blue cape and an outer apron of feathers. He carries a shield and spears; these are the identifying attributes of Huitzilopochtli, and the hummingbird is uniquely associated with him. He is sometimes represented missing his left foot, which is replaced with a serpent's head.

Boone writes that "the teotl can be defined—the 'god' as we think of him can be created—through the formulation of the teixiptla" (Boone 1989, p. 9).

Carvings of Huitzilopochtli are of human impersonators of Huitzilopochtli. Cecelia Klein, who teaches pre-Columbian and Latin American art history at UCLA, has proposed identities for the human figures represented on the throne. They are the ruler Ahuitzotl, dressed as Huitzilopochtli, and Montezuma, dressed as the Aztec god Tezcatlipoca. At the time of Montezuma's succession, Ahuitzotl was recently deceased. The throne's relief shows two rulers in the guise of gods.

The person who allegedly sat on this throne is Montezuma, who disastrously encountered Cortés. A more accurate transcription of his name, from Nahuatl into English, is Motecuhzoma Xocoyotzin, although his name is commonly spelled as Montezuma. And actually, the Montezuma who had the misfortune to rule when the Spanish arrived was Montezuma II.

Just how violent Aztec life was is a point of contention. There is no doubt that there was ritualized violence. Prisoners of war were sacrificed on the Templo Mayor, and many of the reliefs of Huitzilopochtli and other figures show them engaging in self-sacrifice through bloodletting. Blood was drawn by inserting bone awls into their ears. Additionally, prisoners of war were sacrificed, and Boone writes that "each war captive dispatched on the sacrificial stone before the shrine of Huitzilopochtli thus repeated symbolically the god's own victory over his adversaries" (Boone 1989, p. 2).

Pasztory (1983) reports that Ahuitzotl had 20,000 victims sacrificed (p. 53). Understanding how ritualized violence functioned within a society is a complicated endeavor for those outside of that society. A partial explanation comes from military strategy: When on battlefields, soldiers from the losing side either have to be killed on the field, freed, imprisoned, or enslaved. The Mesoamericans choose not to slaughter their enemies on the battlefields, but to capture them alive, dispatching them later to honor their gods.

A throne is associated with a ruler and frequently is the place where the ritual of succession occurs. In other cultures, a throne often takes a common form of seating and aggrandizes it—for example, Byzantine. That does not appear to be the case with the Aztec throne. The form owes its shape to the pyramid on which it likely stood. "Blood letting imagery associated with the Aztec Templo Mayor is part of the accession iconography of the Aztec rulers and visually fulfills their need to validate their descent and reign" (Boone 1989, p. 15). As a model of the building in which it functioned, this piece of furniture has an architectural design vocabulary.

As at other Mesoamerican sites, Tenochtitlan had large numbers of craftsmen—painters, stone carvers, metalworkers, furniture makers, and potters. A market-centered economy, correspondingly, had large numbers of merchants. Pasztory (1983) writes: "Wood was used for furniture, house posts, canoes, weapons, and tools, as well as for idols" (p. 76). What they created and traded has mostly disappeared from the archaeological record.

Tlaloc, the other god of the temple complex, was the god of agriculture. This helps explain why anthropologists have frequently found objects that look like seats, yet it is not clear if they were seats, sacrificial altars, or grinding stones. The context of the Templo Mayor underscores that the confusion between seat, altar, and grinding stone is not arbitrary. In these arenas, agriculture by way of grinding corn, military success by way of sacrifice, and religion by way of an altar, were all brought together by an object that looks like a seat and may have been one.

The talud-tablero composition gets a particular riff in a room from the main temple, the Templo Mayor. Lining the perimeter of a room is a stone bench (Figure 7.14). Here, the talud has become a built-in seat, with the tablero on the (missing) wall behind. Because often only the foundations remain, it is convenient for archaeologists, as the talud

Figure 7.14 Painted benches in the Temple of Eagle Warriors, Aztec, Templo Mayor. Mexico City, Mexico.

portion represents a complete sculptural panel. Archaeological work on rural residences in the area has confirmed that built-in benches were common.

Montezuma thought Cortés was the returning god Quetzalcoatl. It had been foreseen that the god Quetzalcoatl would return as a bearded man who opposed human sacrifice. When Cortés arrived, Montezuma and his followers initially thought he was their god, a case of mistaken identity that resulted in the end of the Aztec Empire. Cortés communicated with the ruler by way of his female companion, La Malinche, who translated for him. The story of Montezuma's mistaking Cortés could be a fabrication. Both sides had reason to support this version of the encounter. For the Spanish, the story is flattering and acts as justification for their destruction of the city and its temples. For the Aztecs, it presents the meeting as a predestined defeat, a fate that was out of their hands.

CENTRAL AMERICA

A feature of some Mesoamerican seats is that their exact use is not always clear, nor is it certain if they even were seats. The Isthmia region, including modern-day Costa Rica and Honduras, in the period 300–900 C.E. produced a large number of objects known as **metates**. These are stone-grinding platforms, made from porous volcanic rock, and some are found with their grinding stones, similar to rolling pins. Some bear traces of wear. Others do not. Initially, the favored form was a three-legged or tripod metate. Around 900 C.E., there was a preference for four-legged grinding platforms. Some are elaborate, with caryatids supporting the platform. Practically, these were used for grinding grain into flour. Yet the same form could serve as an altar, possibly for animal sacrifice. These are also forms that suggest they served as seats. It is therefore possible that these pieces of furniture served multiple ritual functions. Elaborate ones were decorated with birds and monkey figures.

PERU

Human inhabitants have been in the Andean region that is today Peru since 9000 BCE. From the initial period, the people of Cupisnique culture, 1500–200 B.C.E., created a beautiful type of designed object. Anthracite mirrors were highly polished black disks that adequately reflected whatever faced them.

In the 1920s, an archaeological discovery took place in the southern Peruvian desert, Paracas. Paracas means "sand that falls like rain." The Paracas were active toward the end of the Early Horizon period, in the years 300–200 B.C.E. Archaeologists discovered four hundred funerary bundles that contained layer upon layer of textiles. Mummies were also wrapped in fabrics and interred in baskets. Because they were protected by the dry climate, they survived 2,000 years in perfect condition. This cache constitutes a great artistic tradition, all the more valuable because it includes fragile objects that rarely survive. Some of the oldest existing textiles come from Peru.

The Paracas wove cotton textiles that they embroidered with wool. They also painted and dyed textiles. The motifs included geometric shapes and abstracted animal forms.

In the Early Intermediate period, the Nazca, living on the plains of Nazca, created artworks unlike anything found elsewhere in the world. The giant geoglyphs are symbols created using the earth itself as the artistic medium. They were created by removing a layer of the desert floor. The forms include precise straight lines and other geometric shapes, plants, animals, and insects, all at a colossal scale that can be best appreciated from the air. The Nazca built adobe architecture and also had developed traditions in textiles and ceramics.

From the Late Intermediate period, the Chimu are known for their delicate feather work. Feather panels and capes were made by painstakingly attaching feathers, one at a time, to a cotton backing (Figure 7.15). They were attached to form geometric patterns. As these delicate textiles were buried in tombs as in Paracas, they survive in a surprising number. In addition to using feathers to craft articles to adorn the human figure, panels were made that may have served as wall hangings or room dividers. They may have been used temporarily outdoors in celebrations.

Pre-Columbian scholar Nicholas Saunders (1999) terms feather work as belonging to an aesthetic of brilliance. He writes: "There is a wealth of evidence to suggest that indigenous Amerindians perceived their world as infused with a spiritual brilliance which manifested itself in natural phenomena—sun, moon, water, ice and rainbows; natural materials—minerals, feathers, pearls and shells, and artifacts made from such matter" (p. 245). The Chimu continued into the Late Horizon period and were one of the adversaries of the Inca.

At their height, the Inca ruled the area that is today Peru, Bolivia, Chile, Ecuador, and northern Argentina. They spoke Quechua, and their capital, Cuzco, is located in the highlands.

Many types of structures became shrines, including buildings, sites, a terrace, a fountain, and

Figure 7.15 Feather panel, Peru, c. 900–1476.

occasionally a seat (Niles 1999, p. 54). The departed were remembered after death at the places where they slept, farmed, rested, dreamed, drank, or lived" (p. 54). A chair could represent the person who, in life, sat on it.

The Inca empire is usually dated to 1438–1532. The Inca are known for the precision of their stone-masonry. Giant blocks of stone were cut, or dressed, to fit tightly against one another without mortar. Carolyn Dean examines the relationship between the outcroppings and the masonry walls that sit on top of them and are supported by them. For years, the architectural journal *Progressive Architecture* had a regular feature titled "divine details"; the point was not only to highlight an impressive detail, but that good details should also themselves carry a project's concept and have meaning. Relying upon Dean's work, the goal here is to consider Machu Picchu and other mountain sites from a different approach, looking at the details of their construc-

tion as works that reveal their creators' intentions and worldviews.

The Inca used outcrops of rock as the foundation of the structures they built (Figure 7.16). The resulting form was a combination of nature and architecture. Dean offers the following rationale: "According to a Quechua story told in the Andes today, the ancient Inka (Inca) of that area married Pachamama (Mother Earth) and produced human offspring. A trace of that union is still manifest in the ruins of Inca buildings in the form of rock outcrops—masses of bare rock protruding from the surface of the earth—that were integrated by Inka builders into masonry structures in the fifteenth and early sixteenth centuries throughout the Inka realm, an empire that eventually reached the greatest extent of any pre-Hispanic state in the Americas. By providing firm, petrous foundations for Inka structures, Mother Earth herself, called Pachamama by the Inka and other Quechua speakers, appears to

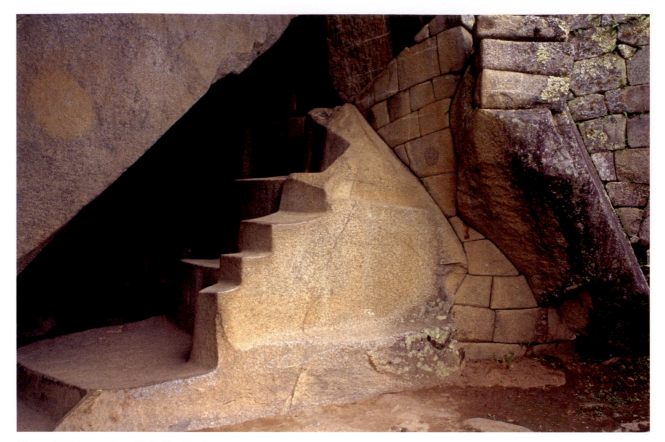

Figure 7.16 Inca ruins of Machu Picchu.

have readily consented to, if not actually joined in, the interface between nature and art; they exist simultaneously as parts of, and blur the boundary dividing, natural and built environments. As places of union between Inka and earth, integrated rock outcrops also served as powerful signs of belonging in a particular locale" (Dean 2007, p. 502).

Inca architecture and urban planning are usually rectilinear; when they break the pattern it is to respond to the earth's naturalistic form (Dean 2007, p. 508). Dean outlines the laborious process of roughing out the great stones with hammers and chisels, using progressively smaller and finer tools. It was a process that was time-consuming, although not technically difficult: A block was chiseled away, fitted into its eventual space, then removed, then, using the word Dean prefers, "nibbled" away, then replaced, until a perfect shape was achieved (Fig-

ures 7.17a and b). Some were quadrilateral, some polygonal.

The Inca ability with dressing stones is legendary. The blocks were individually cut to fit into the structures, using no mortar and with precise joints. Because the blocks are not of regular size, it is believed that this was done by trial and error, meaning that the blocks had to be continually lifted into place and then extracted, or that precise models of each block were first made.

The stool from the Field Museum of Natural History in Chicago is also known as the Inca throne (Figure 7.18). It is made of wood and painted, and features a carved, round seat. Two jaguars, headed in opposite directions, support the seat. It is a dynamic piece of furniture due to its assymetry and the animals' position. The jaguars have curled tails, bare their teeth, and are poised to bolt. It was an

Figure 7.17a Baths of the Incas, Tambo Machay.

Figure 7.17b Stone masonry wall of Inca ruins of Limatampu, Peru.

Figure 7.18 Jaguar throne.

important piece designed for the effect it would have on viewers, taking in an ensemble that included an elaborately clothed human figure.

The most famous of the Inca cities built on outcroppings is definitely Machu Picchu, mid-fifteenth to early sixteenth centuries. Machu Picchu is the Incan settlement situated in the Andes northwest of Cuzco. Because it was overlooked by the Spanish, it survived intact. The apex of its inhabitation was likely the sixteenth century. It was later abandoned and fell into disuse, its location known only by some locals. It was "rediscovered" by Hiram Bingham in 1911.

CONQUEST

In an age of specialization, Jerod Diamond, author of *Guns, Germs, and Steel: The Fates of Human Societies,* continues to tell big stories in terms of chronological and geographic scope. He writes: "The biggest population shift of modern times has been the colonization of the New World by Europeans,

and the resulting conquest, numerical reduction, or complete disappearance of most groups of Native Americans (American Indians)" (p. 67).

Mexico

The Relaciones Geographicas was the mapping project of Philip II of Spain. His administrators hired legions of Aztec artists to carry out the extensive project (Figure 7.19). The maps are representative of many things, including foremost the desire of Spain to use mapmaking as a tool of expressing and consolidating its power. But the maps are also representations of a *criollo*, or creole, identity. They are examples of a new art form, with both Aztec and Spanish precedents. The churches and crosses are obviously due to the imposition of European Christianity, but the artist used Aztec symbols to indicate road and river.

In Mexico, a generation after the conquest, the forced conversion was mostly complete; people had converted to Christianity and spoke Spanish.

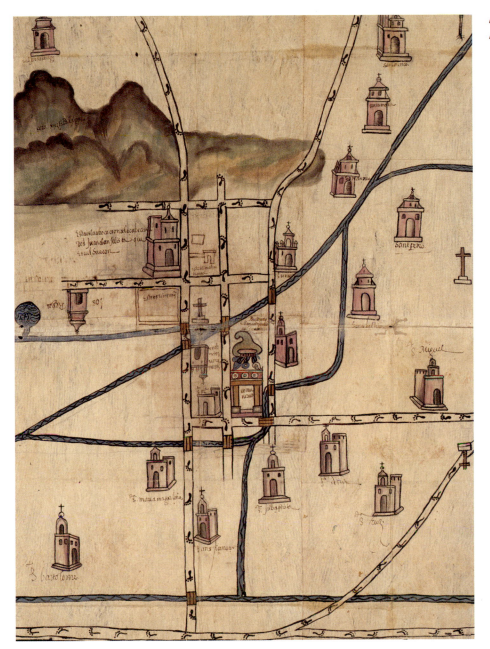

Figure 7.19 Culhuacan, Mexico, 1580.

Wheels, tiled roofs, horses, and other beasts of burden were commonplace (Kostof, p. 442). Mass destruction was followed by mass building. New cities were built on top of the old, churches on top of temples. Mexico City was built directly on top of the ruins of Tenochtitlan. Teotihuacán, Palenque, and Chichén Itzá were saved from destruction because they had already been abandoned.

A chest from 1650 is a modest object to represent the conquest, but its ubiquity is equally telling (Figure 7.20). In the century after the destruction of the Aztecs, Mexican furniture makers were largely working within the stylistic parameters of Spanish craftsmen, although with a recognition of locality. The chest is made of Mexican woods, mahogany, with orangewood and rosewood veneers. It has iron hardware. It was likely made in Pueblo de los Angeles, an important center for furniture manufacturing, and was probably meant for travel.

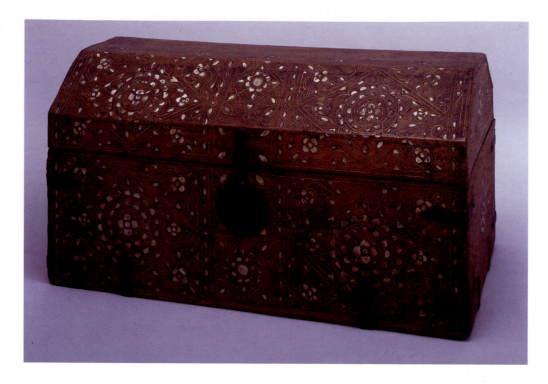

Figure 7.20 Mexican chest. 1650.

Peru

Francisco Pizarro landed in Peru in 1527. He returned in 1532 with a small force. The Spanish *conquistador* met the Inca emperor Atahuallpa in Cajamarca that year. Pizarro led a group of 168 soldiers. Atahuallpa being carried on a litter, sitting on a cushion on top of a stool, was in the middle of a giant tent city of 80,000 soldiers. Spanish witnesses report that among Atahuallpa's minions, many carried furniture covered in gold and silver. Within minutes, Pizarro's men killed Atahuallpa's attendants and imprisoned their emperor. How this could happen is one of history's great stories. The Peruvians were divided. Those people recently incorporated against their will into the Inca Empire were all too happy to see its leader captured. And Atahuallpa was politically weakened by a fratricidal war of succession with his brother Huascar. Technologically, the big point of Diamond's book is that the Spanish had steel swords, guns, and horses (Diamond 1997, p. 71).

At the height of their power, the Inca relied heavily on the symbolic use of objects seized in battle. Niles (1999) reports several methods of celebrating victory that involve objects, including turning the flayed skin of an enemy soldier into a drum, his teeth into a necklace, and drinking from a cup made of a victim's skull. Another means was physically trampling on the possessions of the vanquished: "In Inca military victories, the symbolic affirmation of victory and the granting of credit for the defeat were marked by the act of treading on captured enemies, booty, or the insignia (standards, banners, emblems) of foreign armies" (pp. 40–41). Booty is the category of objects seized in battle or siege. *Spolia* is the Roman term. The category of objects that became war monuments and trophies included exceptional pieces of furniture, such as a brass chair (p. 70). Niles writes: "It was the former custom of these Incas to bring back to Cuzco all the things they had seen that might cause admiration and wonder, so that the sight of these objects would enhance the fame of their deeds and would memorialize their accomplishments" (p. 70). An empty chair in this case was a sign of military victory, and denigrated the person who no longer had the right to sit in it.

This was a lesson that the Spanish did not need to be taught. There is a long history of **iconoclasm,** the destruction of art, particularly in the name of promoting a monotheistic religion, Christianity, over a "pagan" polytheistic religion. In 1533, the Spaniards sacked the Incan capital Cuzco. They rebuilt it, following the street lines and, in many cases, reusing the Incan foundations for their own buildings (Figure 7.21). The Incan practice of trampling on the possessions of the defeated enemy got an ironic translation into architecture.

The Spanish city was built on top of the Inca ruins, so that there are several areas where Spanish buildings appear to grow from the carefully cut large Inca stones. One purpose of *spolia* was to commemorate victory over an enemy. Another aspect was the belief that destruction ultimately results in regeneration.

CONCLUSION

The differences between the pre-Columbian societies and the modern world are striking. The prime example is ritualized sacrifice, an aesthetic performance in which the visual effect was paramount, as was the meaning of materials, foremost blood. In contrast, there was a Mesoamerican practice that is familiar to the modern age: ball games, complete with ball courts, souvenirs, trophies, and other sports-related paraphernalia. The Mesoamericans commemorated victory with stone mementos,

Figure 7.21 Cobbled street in Cuzco. Angled cut stones make up Inca wall.

whose forms, including knee pads and hand guards, were logical in a functional sense only when made from perishable, pliable materials. One cannot help but wonder what future civilizations will make of the quantity of bronze basketballs and footballs that fill today's trophy cases.

The massive and towering pyramids have lost none of their ability to impress. A means to connect earth and sky, in Mayan civilizations they also served as temple platforms. The temple structures atop the pyramids present a strategy of monumentalizing architecture: Work with a common form, such as the typical Mayan domestic structure, and translate it into permanent materials. Pyramids were exceptional features of the first American cities, because the other structures, such as the courtyard houses of Teotihuacán, emphasized the horizontal, with their overall form, their expansive elevations, their squat openings, and their prominent door heads.

In North and South America, a brilliant material was used for the finest objects; even though it is still commonplace, it is no longer used: feathers. It is amazing that so many works were produced using this exceedingly delicate material, and even more so that so many of them survive thanks to Peruvian burial practices.

Few seats from the pre-Columbian era exist, but those that do are dynamic, with twisting, turning, and snarling animals. Looking at a throne alone is but half the picture; it was meant to be experienced as part of a performance that featured a brilliantly made-up and costumed ruler.

Pre-Columbian artistic communities were large and numerous. Building and maintaining the houses, temples, and ball courts, with all the corresponding objects, required large numbers of masons, stone carvers, potters, woodworkers, weavers, painters, and furniture makers. The Spanish conquest of the Americas was a rupture in all traditions. But artists continued to produce art, and their blending of Span-

ish and indigenous motifs, coerced and voluntary, started a new era of American designed objects.

Sources

Boone, Elizabeth. "Incarnations of the Aztec Supernatural: The Image of Huitzilopochtli in Mexico and Europe." *Transactions of the American Philosophical Society* 79, no. 2 (1989): 1–107.

Cole, Herbert. *I Am Not Myself: The Art of African Masquerade*. Los Angeles: Museum of Cultural History, the University of California, 1985.

Dean, Carolyn. "The Inca Married the Earth: Integrated Outcrops and the Making of Place." *Art Bulletin* 89 (September 2007): 502–518.

Diamond, Jared. *Guns, Germs, and Steel: The Fates of Human Societies*. New York: Norton, 1997.

Klein, Cecelia. "Not Like Us and All the Same: Pre-Columbian Art History and the Construction of the Nonwest." *Res,* no. 42 (Autumn 2002): 131–138.

Kostof, Spiro. *A History of Architecture: Settings and Rituals*. Oxford: Oxford University Press, 1995.

Kubler, George. *The Art and Architecture of Ancient America*. Harmondsworth: Penguin, 1962.

Miller, Mary Ellen. *The Art of Mesoamerica: From Olmec to Aztec*. London: Thames and Hudson, 1986.

Miller, Mary Ellen. "The Ballgame." *Record of the Art Museum, Princeton University* 48, no. 2 (1989): 21–31.

Miller, Mary Ellen. *Courtly Art of the Ancient Maya*. San Francisco: Fine Arts Museum of San Francisco, 2004.

Niles, Susan. *The Shape of Inca History*. Iowa City: University of Iowa Press, 1999.

Pasztory, Esther. *Aztec Art*. New York: Abrams, 1983.

Pasztory, Esther. *Teotihuacan: An Experiment in Living*. Norman: University of Oklahoma Press, 1997.

Pasztory, Esther. *The Murals of Tepantitla, Teotihuacan*. New York: Garland, 1976.

Pasztory, Esther. *Thinking with Things*. Austin: University of Texas Press, 2005.

Protzen, Jean-Pierre, and Stella Nair. "Who Taught the Inca Stonemasons Their Skills?" *Journal of the Society of Architectural Historians* 56, no. 2 (June 1997): 146–167.

Saunders, Nicholas. "Biographies of Brilliance: Pearls, Transformations of Matter and Being, c. AD 1492." *World Archaeology* 31, no. 2 (October 1999): 243–257.

Young-Sanchez, Margaret. *Pre-Columbian Art in the Denver Art Museum Collection*. Denver: Denver Art Museum, 2003.

DISCUSSION AND REVIEW QUESTIONS

1. Think of examples, from any culture and time period, in which daily objects are commemorative and functionally useless when turned into a new material.
2. The topic of how violent the Aztec and Maya were is controversial. If today's world—and its cultural productions—were looked at by another civilization, would it be considered peaceful or violent?
3. Name some of the sites in Mexico.
4. What ethnic group was ruling the city that became Mexico City?
5. Name some of the ethnic groups in Peru that predated the arrival of the Spanish explorer Pizarro.
6. Name an unusual material that the Paracas made clothing and other textiles from.
7. What ethnic group was ruling the area that is now Peru when the Spanish arrived?

CHAPTER 8

FROM STUPA TO PAGODA AND FROM MAT TO CHAIR
CHINA, INDIA, AND CAMBODIA

	1600–1050 B.C.E.	1050–256 B.C.E.	221–206 B.C.E.	206 B.C.E.–220 C.E.	618–907 C.E.	1279–1368 C.E.	1368–1644 C.E.	1644–1912
CHINA								
	Shang dynasty	Zhou dynasty	Qin dynasty	Han dynasty	Tang dynasty	Yuan dynasty	Ming dynasty	Qing dynasty
					802–1431			
CAMBODIA								
					Angkor Period			

India and China play major roles in Asian history, both for their geographic heft and large populations. A difference between them is that in its early history, India was not a consolidated entity. India does, however, have the considerable distinction of having been the birthplace of Buddha. China is the world's longest continuous civilization, existing as a unified cultural and political entity for some 4,000 years without interruption. In the twenty-first century China has the world's largest population, but even in its earlier periods it had a significantly large population.

Cambodia is one of Southeast Asia's smaller countries, but from the ninth to twelfth centuries, it produced extremely fine examples of monumental architecture and sculpture. The Hindu and Buddhist sculptures bear comparison to other representational sculptures, such as those of ancient Greece and medieval Benin. They are informative about seating postures, just as reliefs from the temples bear the only traces of historic Cambodian furniture.

ARCHITECTURE AND SCULPTURE

China

China plays a significant role in the fossil record of the earliest human habitations, including the famous Peking Man. A long and productive neolithic period left a variety of archaeological remains, including geometric pottery.

In the fourth millennium B.C.E., a series of settlements lay in the area between the Yangzi River and the Yellow River. These naturally well-irrigated river valleys were conducive to agriculture. Initially there were no major urban centers, but small settlements dispersed over a large area. Pottery sherds and the remains of a kiln date to this period.

One of the earliest Chinese capitals, a proto-urban center, Zhengzhou, relied on the waters of the Yellow River. With Zhengzhou starts the tradition of each dynasty building its own capital city. A wall surrounded the rectilinear-shaped enclosure that contained platforms upon which buildings stood. Tombs have been found from this time period, known as Shang dynasty China.

Prior to the Zhou dynasty, there were numerous linguistic groups in China. Zhou rulers enforced the use of Chinese, thus creating a large, unified, linguistic geographical group. The Zhou had cast-iron production, and created two cities, Luoyang and Xian, that still exist today. The teacher and philosopher Confucius (551–479 B.C.E.) belongs to the Zhou period. The Zhou built a ritual ancestral temple complex at Fengchi, circa 1000, which is one of the earliest versions of a large-scaled building based on the typical Chinese courtyard house.

The English term "China" comes from the Qin dynasty (also referred to as the Ch'in dynasty). Chinese people today refer to the country as "China" or "Zhong guo." The latter first appeared in a Shang dynasty document, but it was a cultural and geographic term. It acquired a national meaning only in the twentieth century.

FROM STUPA TO PAGODA

Buddha is one of the names given to the teacher and enlightened one, also known as Gautama and Siddhartha. He lived in northern India and Nepal. The dates of his life are not certain, but one widely accepted scenario puts the years of his time on Earth as 480–400 B.C.E. The religion that resulted from his teachings, Buddhism, celebrates the enlightenment and eventual passage of Buddha and his followers into nirvana.

Tracing Buddhism's effect on art, architecture, and material culture is an endeavor that includes considering the natural landscape, the body, the represented body, building, and town planning; all are interrelated to a diagrammatic pattern known as the mandala, a common feature of many artworks and textile designs.

One of the vestigial means of finding meaning on Earth, proto-architecture, occurred when indigenous people picked out distinguishing landscape features and in them saw meaning. Ayer's Rock in

Australia, Sugarloaf Mountain in Brazil, and Chimney Rock in the United States are all examples of this. Sometimes the natural features are so extraordinary that it seems as though the landscapes themselves are a part of the selection process. Mountains and fantastic promontories stand out from their surroundings and clearly are important, a naturally occurring example of rarefied space.

India, Afghanistan, and Tibet

The next step for human involvement in creating meaning in landscape is to shape the landscape and natural materials. One of the earliest shifts from seeing meaning in landscape to shaping landscape involves the burial places of Buddha's relics. He died at Kushinagar, his body was cremated, his remains buried, and the mound of earth that covered his remains became venerated. Over time, the mound of earth was faced with either bricks or stone, thereby rendered permanent and more monumental, and evolved into a **stupa**. The Stupa

Figure 8.1 Stupa at Sarnath, Darnek. Northern India, Third century C.E.

Figure 8.2 *Stupa 3 and entrance gate. Buddhist sanctuary at Sanchi, India. Second-first century* B.C.E.

at Sarnath, Darnek, in India, is a simple yet powerful creation that reveals the honest expression of facing a mound of earth with permanent material (Figure 8.1).

Another early stupa, the Stupa at Sanchi, is a more elaborate architectural composition that intertwines site, setting, and ritual (Figure 8.2). Buddhism was largely a religion of meditation, involving recitation in front of a stupa, sculpture, or images, and later a pagoda, that housed Buddhist relics. The ritual of visiting a stupa was to circumnavigate the mound clockwise. This was a processional homage and also a somatic activity that cleared the mind of extraneous thoughts. At Sanchi, gateways to the precinct stand at the four cardinal points. The gate at the front blocks direct access and prompts visitors to begin their meditative walk.

The practice of visiting a stupa relates to a diagram that tells how followers of Buddhism understand themselves, their place on Earth, and Earth's place in the cosmos. Over the course of centuries, stupas were built through the area that is now India and Nepal and gradually spread eastward. While early stupas were solid, they were followed with structures that featured hollow domes. Stupas became more elaborate and architectural practice increasingly emphasized the vertical. Sometimes the dome is emphasized with a pole at its apex, furthering the vertical thrust of the structure. One way of involving stupas with impermanent ritual was to attach a banner to the **chattri,** drawing more attention to the stupa's highest point. Hanging a banner on a stupa was a further means of personalizing the experience of visiting the stupa. The banners that flew on stupas are some of the oldest surviving Asian textiles, today protected in museums.

Figure 8.3 Interior view of cave. Ajanta, India.

An example of incorporating naturally occurring forms and rendering them more elaborate occurs at the caves of Ajanta (Figure 8.3). There, the stupa sits within an interior space, yet the process of circumnavigating around the stupa remains. A limit to the stupa as the sole element of Buddhist architecture is that there was no worship space separate from the stupa. The caves of Ajanta provided a vocabulary and form for a larger space to house multiple devotees, and formed the basis of subsequent Buddhist temples with rectangular halls.

Some caves were utilized as they were; some are a combination of found configuration and elaborately carved-out architectural compositions. In the kingdom of Bamiyan, today Afghanistan, in the seventh century, two colossal statues, the tallest 165 feet, were sculpted out of rock in giant niches. Over time, statues of Buddha were placed in front of the stupa, sometimes on top of the stupa, sometimes carved into the face of the stupa. Sometimes, the Buddha statue sits alone, taking the place of the stupa. This is full circle, where once the bodily remains of Buddha were represented by a mound of earth, there is now a statue that more literally evokes his physiognomy.

A mandala is a design that features a circle circumscribed within a square, as did the rounded mound of the stupa. The circle is the heavenly realm and the connection of Earth to cosmos. The square represents the domain of humanity. This diagram is related to the layout of a variety of designed forms, including carpets, temples, and cities (Figure 8.4).

China

As Buddhism spread eastward into China in the beginning of the Han dynasty, the religious practice and the buildings that supported it became **sinicized**—that is, rendered Chinese. Courtyard houses were donated and converted to temples, thereby merging established Chinese architectural forms with a new subculture. In the development of the stupa, it was the Chinese emphasis on the vertical expression that created a new type of Buddhist building, the pagoda.

As the building of stupas spread into Thailand, Cambodia, and Indonesia, they became more elaborate and more vertical. The vertical expression be-

came the focus of Chinese design attention. The Chinese were familiar with the vertical construction of towers, made of either timber or brick, so, consequently, the pagoda is a hybrid structure of the stupa and Chinese tower building technology.

One of the earliest Chinese monasteries to feature a pagoda is the Songyue Monastery on Mount Song, Henan (Figure 8.5). Its pagoda, which unusually has twelve sides, dates to 523. The pagoda form became popular, and hundreds of them were built in China, Korea, and Japan. Like the stupa, the pagoda housed Buddhist relics. The pagoda at Songyue is the earliest extant pagoda in China. It is a prime example of the process by which cultural influences from outside China merged with Chinese indigenous construction techniques and shapes. Having developed the technology, and custom, of creating watchtowers, the Chinese were able to apply their

Figure 8.4 Mandala scroll. Tibet, Asia, sixteenth century.

Figure 8.5 Pagoda of Songyue Monastery, Mount Song, Henan, China, 523 C.E.

knowledge to create a vertically oriented religious structure, the pagoda. Fu Xinian writes that by the late fifth and sixth centuries, Buddhist architecture had become Chinese architecture.

Qin Shi Huangdi is the Chinese emperor who unified China. The discovery of his tomb in the twentieth century is one of the greatest finds of Chinese archaeology (Figure 8.6). The cavernous complex has rammed-earth foundations and walls. It is populated by an army of 6,000 life-size terra-cotta warriors, accompanied by dogs and horses. The actual tomb of the emperor has not been opened.

The Great Wall

As a visual icon in the modern world, the Great Wall is virtually synonymous with China (Figure 8.7). An architectural wonder and an engineering marvel, it is also an accomplished example of landscape utilization and manipulation.

Qin Shi Huangdi, founder of the Qin dynasty, declared himself emperor, consolidated power, and built some 3,000 miles of the wall in the third century B.C.E. The wall's entire length is estimated at between 3,000 and 4,000 miles. In photographs, the wall looks like a giant singular entity, unraveling over the northern Chinese mountainous landscape, but it is actually a defensive network and made of constituent parts. Initially made of rammed earth and rubble, its ramparts were strengthened over the years with stone and brick. It mostly follows the ridgelines of mountains and hills.

There are two principal elements to the wall: the defensive walls themselves, topped with a roadway, and the watchtowers. The towers and walls were built in separate phases and were remodeled and strengthened in separate phases, a building

Figure 8.6 Tomb of Qin Shi Huangdi, Lishan, Shanxi, 206 B.C.E.

Figure 8.7 Great Wall, originally constructed third century B.C.E. Reconstructed in the Ming dynasty, fourteenth to seventeenth centuries, C.E.

process that resulted in some odd intersections. The crenellated towers occur approximately every hundred yards and feature arrow slits, underscoring the wall's defensive purpose. In addition to arrows, the Chinese shot cannons from atop the wall.

The wall's purpose was to keep Mongol and Turkic raiders at bay, and it is often considered a military failure. That view is tempered by the position that the Wall was one part of a foreign trade policy that included both offensive and accommodationist strategies. Monumental in scale, it was not designed to be the monument it became, but to

simply and powerfully thwart the efforts of nighttime raiders. It is therefore considered by many as a symbol of Chinese xenophobia, the most obvious expression of a desire to keep foreigners out. Traditionally, the Great Wall did not play the role of national symbol until the twentieth century, when, in the context of the Japanese invasion, it became a symbol of Chinese nationalism.

Large stretches of the wall were also built during the subsequent Han dynasty, although most of what is seen today was built in the Ming period, the last dynasty to devote major resources to maintaining it. Other achievements during the Ming period include ceramics and furniture. Because of its immense scale, it is today considered a singular type of Chinese monument.

A new capital city built for the Han dynasty was Ch'ang-an (Figure 8.8). Noting that religious structures, such as temples and pagodas, were not major elements in the urban environment, Spiro Kostof (1995) writes: "Unlike their Indian neighbors, the Chinese had little sympathy for the mystical or the infinite. Theirs was basically a secular, intellectual order; unmoved by any need to search for some ultimate truth, they plotted their own precise, clearcut place on earth." Chinese urban layouts share overall spatial principles with the layout of a stupa

precinct—the reliance on the four cardinal directions, the placement of important structures in the center, and a rectilinear layout, surrounded by a wall. Major pathways lead directly from gates to the all-important center.

Cambodia

Cambodia is one of Asia's smaller countries, yet from the ninth to twelfth centuries, the small inland region produced magnificent works of urbanism, architecture, and sculpture. It is difficult to pinpoint the circumstances necessary to produce great art, though this likely includes political stability, central authority, and financial resources. These circum-

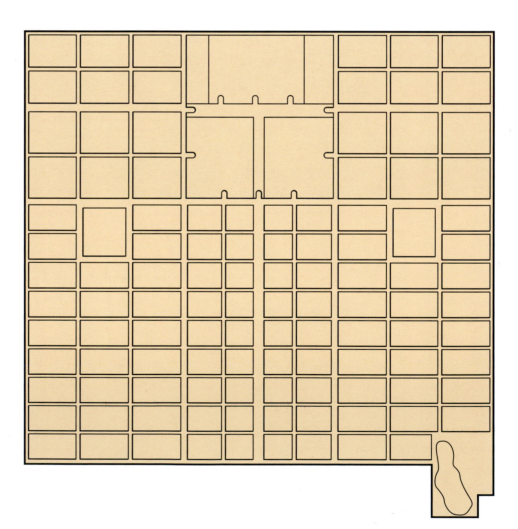

Figure 8.8 Chang'an, city plan, Tang dynasty, 618–907 C.E., China.

Figure 8.9 Angkor Wat, 1100–1150.

stances were present in the Mekong River valley, but nothing was affirmatively predictive of the wonders that would arise.

Helen Jessup articulates the circumstances aligning themselves in the Mekong River valley that allowed a political and economic entity to become a cultural one as well: "What is of interest in the study of art and architecture is the extent to which the consolidation and centralization of power resulted in the desire among the leaders to create symbols of material and spiritual power in permanent form" (Jessup 2004).

The region drew its wealth from agriculture, including wet rice cultivation made possible by fertile lands fed by two rivers, the Mekong and the Tonlé Sap. The connection to river-faring international trade had cultural implications as well.

The great period of temple building, the Angkor period, is generally considered to start with the reign of Jayavarman II in 802 c.e. The Angkor period is roughly contemporary with the Carolingian and Romanesque periods in Europe.

In terms of urban design, the cities built in the Khmer Empire are rectilinear and huge. The Khmer Empire was a dominant polity in the twelfth century in Southeast Asia. Khmer refers to the language and people, and Cambodia is the name of the modern country. Khmer cities were larger than contemporary European medieval cities; all of ancient Rome would fit nicely within the borders of the largest Angkorian city, Angkor Thom.

Angkor Wat is the masterwork of the region, perfect in its architectonic expression and in the quality of many of its details (Figure 8.9). It was built by Suryavarman II (1113–1145), one of the great builders in Cambodian history. It exceeded in scale and complexity the temples that preceded it, many of which were also impressive.

The central temple complexes relate to the stupa and also to Mount Mehru, the mythological home of Hindu gods. The center is surrounded by a moat, which likely was part of a vast irrigation system, but symbolically referred to the primordial sea, the cosmic ocean from which life began. The moat at Angkor Thom is 300 feet wide.

The moat of Angkor Wat is 623 feet. The temple faces west, with additional entrances at the north, east, and south sides. What remains today is the religious complex that lay at the heart of an immense city. As a layout, the Khmer religious centers have several points in common with the Indian stupa complexes; foremost they are rectilinear, with a ver-

tically dominant structure at the center and based on the cardinal directions. (Chinese cities follow this basic scheme as well, although a palace, a secular structure and not a religious structure, takes center stage.)

The main structure consists of five vertical towers, configured in a **quincunx** layout. They are in ascending height, with the highest in the center. Galleries line the perimeter (Figure 8.10). The windows are filled with vertical elements carved from stone. The forms clearly derive from wooden originals (Figure 8.11). Similarly, the roofs, also made of stone, resemble clay tiles.

In the Cambodian historic cities, most of the secular buildings that surrounded the central complex were made of perishable materials, and there-

Figure 8.10 Angkor Wat. 1100–1150 C.E. Temple courtyard.

Figure 8.11 Bakong, 881 C.E. Cambodia.

fore they have not survived. The stone galleries hint at the form of the wooden residential architecture. As for the climate being conducive to preserving artifacts, few places are as detrimental; Cambodia is hot, humid, and wet. This is the perfect condition to ensure that all vegetal materials, wood and textiles, will perish. And, in fact, the Cambodian jungle even does an amazing job at eating into stone temples as well.

After Suryavarman, Jayavarman VII was Cambodia's most important patron. He reigned from 1181 to 1218, and he ruled over the largest swath of territory. His capital is Angkor Thom, which literally means "Great City." It is larger than Angkor Wat, and the principal temple is known as the Bayon.

A statue of Jayavarman VII makes obvious that the Khmer were as skilled in freestanding sculpture as they were in architecture (Figure 8.12). For the history of furniture, it is significant, for it demonstrates that accomplished societies can develop in which pieces of furniture play a small role and where there are many traditions of sitting. The sculptor's skill is exhibited in the naturalistic treatment of the torso, and the king is imbued with two qualities: He is powerful and humane. His power derives from his broad shoulders and strong chest. Being represented in a posture that clearly invites comparisons to Buddha is hardly a gesture of modesty, yet it does demonstrate the king's authority as a religious figure.

The statue's highest achievement is its presentation of Jayavarman VII as a humble and spiritual figure, the embodiment of serenity. The statue is appealing because of the benign expression on his face. The downcast eyes suggest that the king had

Figure 8.12 Jayavarman VII in meditation.

achieved something of the wisdom and compassion of Buddha.

The sculptural program of his temple, the Bayon, at Angkor Thom, is unlike that found elsewhere in Cambodia; invaluably, many of the reliefs represent scenes from daily life. Some represent carefully delineated **howdahs,** the saddle and platform structure in which nobles sat when riding an elephant. One sculptural relief shows several people using a variety of chairs and tables, a rare representation of historic Khmer furniture (Figure 8.13). Another piece of furniture shown in several reliefs is a **palanquin.** A palanquin is a chair attached to horizontal poles and used for carrying someone about. A Cambodian nineteenth-century palanquin bears some relationship to pieces represented at Angkor Thom (Figure 8.14). The more recent palanquin is essentially a platform with a backrest. The rings underneath the platform are for the poles that are borne by carriers.

Figure 8.13 Angkor Thom. Relief. Late twelfth–early thirteenth centuries.

Figure 8.14 A nineteenth-century palanquin. Cambodia.

Chinese Courtyard House

The history of building in Cambodia consists of a series of monumental works of religious architecture. Equally important in China is the development of a secular building type, the Chinese courtyard house. Chronologically, the earliest examples of Chinese houses still standing postdate the temples of Angkor. Looking at historic Chinese architecture, several distinct types emerge. There is the accidental monument, the Great Wall, which stands out because of its uniqueness. In contrast, hundreds of iterations of the pagoda form lend distinctive profiles to the Chinese landscape and play an important role in the practice of Buddhism in China and in the region. Regarding architecture, it is not always a series of individual monuments that are significant, but also the development and widespread use of the

Chinese courtyard house, as a type, for buildings both modest and grand. The development of this dwelling type includes a modular system, which is what renders the courtyard house almost modern. The Chinese courtyard house is the essential unit of most Chinese architecture, with its emphasis on symmetry, axiality, and rectilinearity. Incidentally, these are qualities that it shares with city planning.

A few examples of Yuan dynasty houses remain, and additional information comes from paintings. From the Ming dynasty, numerous examples exist. Most of the early pieces of furniture, discussed below, come from the Ming dynasty. Thirty-one courtyard houses stand in the village of Ding, and one was built in 1593 (Figure 8.15). It has a central courtyard with ceramic seats and an entry at the southeast corner. This building, in the northern Shanxi Province, has a main building that stands separately from the buildings that house the side rooms. Winters are cold in Shanxi, so the courtyard is long on the north-south axis, to receive maximum sunlight. This relatively modest house has a single courtyard.

In the system of the Chinese courtyard house, the unit of a courtyard and its central hall could be multiplied depending on the need and wealth of the owner and the size of the extended family. A drawing of a Qing dynasty courtyard house in Beijing delineates two courtyards (Figure 8.16). The entrance, as with the Ding house, is at the southeast corner, and the building is oriented on its north-south axis.

The first strip of buildings, nearest the street, has a room for receiving guests, and vendors might proceed no farther into the house. A screen or wall blocks visual access into the house and causes a visi-

tor to enter the house on an oblique angle. The Chinese courtyard house looks inward, to the courtyard, with few openings to the surrounding streets.

The courtyard house is the dominant type of residential building in China, and monumental Chinese architecture, palaces and temples, are based on it, including the Forbidden City and the Yonghe Palace in Beijing.

Across the first courtyard lies the main residential building with its central room. The interior of the house was separated from the raucous street life. In more elaborate courtyard houses, there was an increasing level of privacy, with the most private spaces set farthest back from the front. The increasing level of privacy is reflected in the furnishings.

The central room, the Ming **Jian,** is located in the center of the main hall. The entire main hall is often raised on a platform, including the central

Figure 8.15 Wang family courtyard. Seventeenth century classic-style residences, Shanxi province.

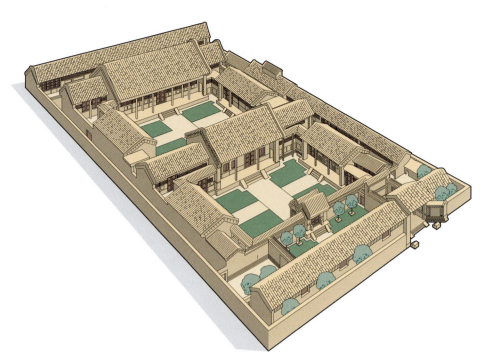

Figure 8.16 Courtyard house Beijing. Qing dynasty.

room. This was a house, but also a social arena with elaborate rules of decorum that involved pieces of furniture—who sat where and with whom. There was a strict system of hierarchy. The final courtyard was for women, and the buildings behind it for servants. Many guests would never proceed to the women's courtyard.

Ideally, the Chinese courtyard house and temples and palaces based on it are oriented north-south. Initially earth and timber-frame constructions, the houses became more elaborate over time and came to include bronze fittings and ceramic roof tiles.

Yunnan Province is the southwesternmost province in China and is known for its impressively rugged landscape. It was once part of the Silk Road, which is one reason why it developed an ethnically diverse population. In southern provinces such as Yunnan, the courtyard arrangement was adjusted to respond to climatic differences. Courtyard houses in the north were composed of freestanding pavilions set within the walls of the compound. Houses in the warmer and wetter south had smaller courtyards and their pavilions and halls were often contiguous. In this regard, they were similar to

Mediterranean courtyard houses. The entire property was built up, with the courtyards as openings within the overall structure.

Despite considerable demographic and economic changes in Qing China, the popularity of the courtyard house grew, and it proved to be a resilient and pliant form that incorporated changes and responded to new conditions. A decline in timber resulted in the once wooden structures being built of a combination of timber, bricks, stone, stucco, and tile.

China was slowly becoming more urban and exposure to Western commodities increased. The courtyard house as a prototype was remarkably strong. Even ethnic groups such as the Zhuang, who lived in houses on stilts, and the Li, who had boat-shaped houses, adopted features of the courtyard house, such as ceramic tiles and distinctive roof profiles.

Urban areas saw the development of two- and three-story houses, and also houses with shops in the front. Until the second half of the twentieth century, the courtyard house was the dominant form for rural and urban residential architecture.

A reconstruction of a Ming room at the Metropolitan Museum of Art gives an idea of the planning principles that dictated the form of the central pavilions of a courtyard house. The pieces of furniture are Ming and the room was built by Chinese craftsmen. This rectangular room would lie perpendicular to the central north-south axis that dominated the house's layout.

CHINESE CLASSICAL FURNITURE

Many achievements date to the Ming dynasty, rebuilding the Great Wall among them, but for the history of designed objects, the Ming dynasty also has a special place. Long esteemed for the high quality of its bronzes and porcelain, it plays an equally important role for the development of high-quality furniture.

In fact, most of what is now considered Chinese furniture, also known as Chinese classical furniture, traces its origins to the late Ming dynasty. Pieces from the subsequent Qing dynasty also fit into this category, and they continue forms whose profiles were set in the Ming period. The Ming dynasty was the great age of Chinese furniture.

Some pieces of Ming furniture were similar to furniture that existed before the Ming period, although there is little knowledge of these pieces and few extant works. Classical Chinese furniture had its origins in the Song dynasty (960–1279), but it reached its highest expression in the subsequent Ming and Qing dynasties.

There were several categories of furniture: hardwood furniture, lacquered furniture, softwood furniture, and pieces made of other materials, such as porcelain, stone, and bamboo. Here we are mostly concerned with hardwood furniture, as this constitutes what most consider to be classical Chinese furniture.

Ming chairs came about as part of a general shift from a mat mode of sitting to a chair mode. In the former, people sat on the ground, on mats or rugs. In the latter, their bodies were elevated, and they sat on chairs with their legs pendant. This was exceptional in East Asia, where, as in other regions of the world, people sat low to the ground, on mats or on low platforms. The Cambodian statue of Jayavarman II demonstrates the spread of Buddhism, and that it is entirely possible to sit comfortably, in a dignified manner, and have status without using a chair. In fact, there are entire cultures that develop sophisticated systems of furnishing in which the chair plays no role. Cambodia, like most of Asia with the exception of China, did not adopt tall chairs until the twentieth century.

The Triumph of the Chair

Initially, the Chinese, like other Asians, sat on the ground, on mats on the ground, or on low platforms. People also slept on mats. Corresponding to the mat mode of living, tables were low to the ground. During the time period of the mat mode, furniture types were limited.

Three major developments took place in Song dynasty China (960–1126). One, a framework with an infill panel became the major structural system for furniture. Two, furniture became an important aspect of interior layouts. Three, and most significant, the chair mode, or sitting on a tall chair, with legs pendant, gradually became the norm. The adoption of the chair mode of sitting had implications for all other pieces of furniture and architecture as well. The details of exactly how this came about are somewhat murky. Xiao Hu states that people started to sit on high chairs in the period 200–500 C.E. Art historian Craig Clunas posits that a key date for the change from mat sitting to chair sitting occurred around 1000 C.E., a development he refers to as the triumph of the chair.

The specific circumstances of the development of the high yoke-back chair are unclear, but several sources suggest a connection of Chinese exposure to "foreign" influence. This also begins the introduction of "minority" cultures into China. This is a straightforward explanation: The early Chinese had contact with foreign chair-using people, they admired the pieces, and they copied them.

Why would tall chairs come about? Three reasons: function, comfort, and status. In a recent and admirably researched publication, Sarah Handler writes that even in the period of the mat mode of living, there were functional reasons why some people sat on high chairs; for example, women weavers needed to free their feet to operate trestles (Handler 2001). The comfort that chairs can provide derives from the desire to lift the human body off the ground and separate it from cold and damp. And there is status: In situations that involve a group of people, one or more individuals are to be singled out and afforded a higher rank. A tall chair aids in this process: It forces the sitter to sit upright and assume a noble posture, and it renders him or her more visible. Whether housing a teacher, a deity, a noble, or a guest, a tall chair bestows status on its sitter.

Hardwood Furniture

A note about chronology: Furniture in this chapter is generally classified as classical Ming furniture. The first piece considered was initially owned by Gustav Ecke, one of the Europeans who brought attention to Chinese hardwood furniture in the mid-twentieth century (Figure 8.17). It is an excellent example of a tall yoke-back chair, although its exact date is unknown. In some cases precise dates confirm that a piece comes from the Ming period. In other cases, as here, the piece is stylistically Ming although it chronologically belongs to a later period.

Figure 8.17 Yoke-back chair. Huali wood.

The yoke-back chair receives its name because of its distinctive curved top rail, with upturned ends that extend beyond the vertical supports. Textile chair runners were placed on top of the chair, folded over the top, and tied to the upturned top rail extensions. Made of silk or cotton, chair runners were a way to update chairs and have them respond to seasonal changes.

The modern term "side chair" denotes a chair without arms. Side chairs were more common than armchairs, discussed on the following page, and they likely predated armchairs. This chair has many of the features of a classic Ming chair. It is made of huali wood, a tropical hardwood.

The seat is a fixed-frame, meaning that it does not fold. The advantage of a frame seat is that the infill panel can be changed. The existence of a series of holes in many pieces suggests that the wooden frames once supported cane seats. For the seat frame, four pieces of wood are mitred at the corners—that is, cut and connected at forty-five-degree angles, with mortise (hole) and tenon (protrusion) connections. In early Ming furniture, the tenons were visible. Over time, as the methods for constructing the pieces became more sophisticated, means were developed to conceal the tenons.

A curved **splat** dominates the backrest. The splat is the broad flat piece of wood that forms the centerpiece of the back and supports the top rail. It leans slightly backward, following the subtle profile of an S-curve. This provides a modicum of comfort, as it allows the chair to "give" when a person sits in it. The chair also provides room for the broader expanse of the sitter's chest and shoulders, while its lower register approaches the body more closely, corresponding to the slender area of the sitter's waist. This classic Chinese yoke-back chair is a forerunner of twentieth-century chairs in which designers respond to the human physiology.

Stretchers connect the four chair legs and stabilize the chair, a configuration known as a box-stretcher. The front stretcher has a surface to rest the feet on, recognizing that a sitter would likely use a stretcher close to the ground as a place to rest the feet. An integrated footrest means that the seated figure is entirely lifted off the ground.

A classical writer of the Ming period, Gao Ling, writing in 1591, referred to a broad armchair as a meditation chair (Handler 2001, p. 57). He stipulated that a meditation chair should be half as wide as the yoke-back chair (Figure 8.18). The name "meditation chair" prompts visions of repose and serenity, a stance reinforced by the restraint exhibited in the chair's form, materials, and lack of decoration. This chair name connects secular chairs to

Figure 8.18 Yoke-back chair.

the spiritual realm. The vertical arm supports are frugally continuous with the front legs; similarly, the verticals of the seat back are continuations of the rear legs. The cross sections of all elements are rectangular. With its reliance on simple if not severe geometries, this chair has a modern aesthetic.

Huali wood is a tropical hardwood from Guangdong and Guangxi. Its color ranges from golden to reddish and orange tones. It has a close, dense, and heavy grain, the density being what makes it hard. Harder woods are difficult to work with, but the trade-off is that they are durable and resistant to pests. Many Chinese hardwood pieces were covered with a clear finish. Ming pieces did not rely on glue or metal nails.

In the distant past, huali wood grew in southern China. The deforestation of China has been going on for centuries, so possibly even during Ming times the prized wood was imported. Most of the tropical hardwoods came from India and Indochina. Huali wood is usually translated as rosewood, although it is a slightly different species. Other tropical hardwoods are sandalwood and satinwood. Huang-huali wood is huali wood with a distinctive yellow cast.

The fact that chairs exist in pairs makes reference to the resolutely symmetrical nature of the Chinese courtyard house. Furniture was moved, and many historical paintings show house furniture set up in a garden or on a terrace. But when placed in their proper locations, Chinese chairs were lined up against a wall, parallel to the wall, and symmetrically placed. When the parallel configuration did not work, pieces of furniture were placed at crisp right angles to one another. In public areas, they were ideally arranged symmetrically. The placement of the furniture was an extension of the rigid architectural layout of the Chinese courtyard house.

A pair of armchairs are made of huali wood and date to the late Ming dynasty, 1550–1600 (Figure 8.19). The pieces have round profiles. The foot rails display a considerable amount of wear. Ming furniture also exists whose individual elements are made with rectangular profiles.

In modern Chinese, an important chair type is *guan mao shi yi,* or "official hat-shaped chairs," because the top horizontal rail of the chair back resembles the distinctive profile of winged hats of Ming officials. As with other yoke-back chairs, the top rail extends beyond the vertical supports with its characteristic bend and lively profile, and is used for the attachment of chair runners. The verticals of the chair back are continuous with the rear legs; they pass through the seat, a construction process that renders the chair sturdy.

A tall chair confers status upon its sitter. A chair with arms, in the company of chairs without arms,

Figure 8.19 Armchairs. Huali wood.

Figure 8.20 Table.

The English terminology for "an" and "zhuo" can be waistless, or inset, and waisted, or at the corner (Shixiang 1990, p. 19). The splayed legs and stretchers are circular in their cross section. The apron (the piece hanging below the tabletop itself) curves downward and has a slot, into which the leg fits snugly, stabilizing the whole piece. Craftsmen also made stools similar to this table, the difference being that the legs are shorter. These relatively simple pieces of furniture belong to the category George Kates calls "the general repertory of household furniture" (Kates 1948, p. xi).

The various iterations of the yoke-back chair represent one major category of Chinese chairs. Another is the round-back armchair (Figure 8.21). Also known as horseshoe-back chairs, the signifying element is a continuous back and arm rail. Round-back chairs also exist in pairs, indicating that they were placed formally in houses. The four vertical posts that support the arms are contiguous with the

has higher status. Inviting a guest to sit down was, and is, a sign of politeness. People of a higher status typically sit in higher, grander chairs.

The move from the mat-mode to the chair-mode level of sitting had many cultural and architectural repercussions. Beds, discussed below, also rose in height. The use of high chairs and beds affected other pieces of furniture. This resulted in taller rooms and correspondingly higher tables.

Small tables had many uses, and generally, pieces of Chinese furniture were not limited to single uses. What in modern times is referred to as an occasional table (Figure 8.20) is the adjunct to the tall yoke-back chair. This type of table, even though known as a wine table, could be used to display items, such as a single vase, and used for dining. Historian Wang Shixiang divides tables into two categories: tables with set-in legs (such as this one) and tables with legs at the corners. The former, with inset legs, is an "an" type of table. The latter has legs at the corner, which Wang Shixiang classifies as "zhuo."

Figure 8.21 Round-back chair.

legs. Multiple joined pieces, however, come together to form the curved arm-and-back piece. The bottom front rail shows signs of wear.

Lacquer, Ceramic, and Bamboo Furniture

There is a whole other category of furniture separate from hardwood pieces—pieces that were usually lacquered in either monochrome or polychrome.

Chinese furniture aficionado Sarah Handler (2001) writes: "The traditional folding armchair leads a double life: it folds away into transportable luggage and sets up with all the stability and grandeur needed to comfort an emperor. It is a protean object, momentarily beautiful and practical, but constructed for imminent metamorphosis. Through its long life it is an elegant vagabond." It is likely that the fixed-frame, curved-back armchair actually derived from an older folding chair, which in turn derived from a simple folding chair that dates back to the second century c.e. Folding chairs and stools were important and existed in both hardwood and lacquer versions (Figure 8.22). Emperors, generals, and other nobles used folding chairs when traveling. As Chinese emperors were known to go on extended inspection tours, their entourage included folding chairs. These chairs were also used outside the house and set up in the garden.

Many were made of huali wood. The horseshoe-shaped, curved-back rail is the piece that it has in common with other round-back chairs (nonfolding). This curved back-and-arm rail is supported by a curved splat and curved armrest supports. The splat is divided into three panels and has a subtle S-curve (some folding curved-back chairs utilize a C-curved splat). Above the seat, this lively chair is all curves; below the seat, it is all straight lines. The front legs start at the base and extend to the rear, yet at the seat they curve dramatically and powerfully upward and forward.

Figure 8.22 Folding chair. Red lacquer on wood. China. Sixteenth century.

A Chinese folding chair folds differently than does the folding chair of the Egyptian/Greek/Roman tradition. For a person standing in front of the chair, the latter folds perpendicular to the human body. With the Asian chair, the fold runs parallel to the width of the body, following the line from shoulder to shoulder. Because there are so many moving parts, pieces of metal hardware reinforce the connections.

This practical chair for travel and informal use also found formal uses inside. Lacquered red and gold, it is a prestige item. Similar chairs are shown in paintings in residential use—as a writing chair, for dining, and to offer to guests. As with other chairs, they could be covered with textiles or animal hides. Folding stools existed for quotidian purposes.

An interesting side note is that Philip II of Spain possessed a folding Chinese chair.

Lacquer pieces were also known as palace pieces—the exceptional pieces that were available only to the wealthy. These grand pieces were elaborately decorated. One is lacquered red with gold and black accents—that is, polychrome (Figure 8.23). Called a throne, this is a platform with side and back panels. The apron that hangs below the sitting platform is continuous with the curved legs. A more elaborate type of chair leg than the horse hoof is the curving elephant trunk.

Such pieces are known as thrones, although the owner may have not been royal in the modern sense. A throne is a platform for sitting, in lotus or semi-lotus, or with one or both legs hanging down. Different time periods have been interested in different aspects of Chinese furniture. European aesthetes, from the initial stages of contact in the thirteenth century through the nineteenth century, were most interested in polychrome lacquer pieces, with highly elaborate forms, lively profiles, and profuse decoration. The prevailing attitude was that the more exotic, the better. Over time, Chinese furniture makers noticed that certain types were more appealing to foreign customers; they therefore started making pieces explicitly for the export market. It is not surprising that those who lived in Europe during periods that celebrated elaborate compositions and complex forms, such as the Rococo and Victorian, preferred elaborate Chinese pieces. These consumers' conceptions of Chinese furniture were tainted by their own tastes. Chinese furniture makers responded to their market and made highly decorated pieces, whose new owners mistakenly concluded that such pieces were typical. Chinese furniture makers had always produced the simpler pieces, but they did not appeal to foreign buyers until the twentieth century. Then it was the austere hardwood pieces that found a willing audience in the West.

Another category of Chinese furniture consists

Figure 8.23 Imperial throne. Qing dynasty, 1736–1795.

of a material not used in Europe for furniture—ceramics. These durable seats were most often used in gardens and could also serve as a seat or table. Sometimes such pieces had receptacles for hot coals to warm them. There was also an extensive production of bamboo furniture, which was considerably less expensive and which is not considered here.

Platforms

Boxlike platforms existed, and also platforms with legs. Just as small bronze boxes in the kitchen functioned as hot plates, to keep dishes warm, so a large boxlike platform for sitting had the possibility of being warmed underneath with toasty braziers. When a platform has had sides and back extensions added, it becomes a couch; the line between platform, couch, and bed is not always distinct.

Couches

Both couches and beds are in fact raised platforms (Figure 8.24). As a general rule of thumb, couches

Figure 8.24 Couch. Ming dynasty.

were associated with males and canopied beds with women. This relates to their placement within the courtyard house. The gendering of bed and couch refers to their social use during the day. At night, both sexes used both platform types. Couches, like beds, were seen from the front, approached on axis, and symmetrically placed within the room.

This particular couch is waisted with a visual separation between the frame and legs (Figure 8.24). Frequently, railings were added at a later date, and sometimes they remained removable. Often the back rail is ever so slightly higher. The Ming period preferred platforms with four legs instead of boxlike platforms, which had been popular in the Tang dynasty. The legs are thick, and continuous with the **spandrel,** rendering this couch particularly sturdy. The spandrel is the horizontal element below the seat that spans the space between the legs.

Beds

These versatile and adaptable pieces of furniture accommodated many activities. All Chinese beds were used for sleeping at night and sitting during the day. They were intended for multiple people. Whereas chairs were for formal engagements, couches were for intimates. Those sitting on the couch sat either in a lotus or semilotus position, or with one or both legs pendant.

A variety of accoutrements expanded the comfort and range of activities that took place on these platforms. Cushions and blankets, mats, bolsters, and armrests were added and taken away. If large enough, tables and trays with dishes of food could be placed on top of the platform, or alternately, food and drinks could be placed on small auxiliary tables within arm's reach. Couches of this type appear in several wood-block illustrations dated to the end of the Ming dynasty.

Texts and illustrations inform us that beds existed at least as early as the Han dynasty. When a platform was long enough for sleeping as well as sitting, it became a bed. Deep platforms were also double beds. The bed stood on axis in the center of a room. Some beds were very large, virtually rooms

Figure 8.25 Six-post canopy bed. Early seventeenth century.

within rooms. A canopied bed was the most important piece of furniture in a household. Some had full railings on three sides and partial railings on the front (Figure 8.25). As with couches, frequently the rear panel was higher. Open patterned panels constitute the railings. The decorative motifs of the infill panels also existed in architectural work. A continuous open wanzi motif enlivens the railings, a pattern that symbolized immortality and infinity, and indirectly, fertility.

Canopied beds had either four or six posts. Beds with six posts, such as the one in Figure 8.25, required that the curtains hung inside the framework. The textiles were sometimes elaborate, making the brightly colored ensemble a visual and figural element in the house. Hangings were made of cotton or silk, and people in warmer climates made use of the canopy to hang mosquito netting. As with couches, beds served as a social space during the day, the sleeping quarters at night, and the place for romantic encounters.

Located in the rear of the house, the canopied bed was the realm of women. Beds dominated a woman's room and were sometimes a significant part of a woman's dowry. Incense could perfume the bed linens. At night the curtains were pulled and the bed was completely enclosed. During the day, they were drawn to the side.

Tables

The classic **zhuo table** is a table with legs at the corners (Figure 8.26). These tables served many

Figure 8.26 Kang table. Ming dynasty.

purposes, from display to writing to serving food. A couch table could be placed in front of a couch or a bed.

This type is also known as a **kang table**. Historically, a kang was a built-in platform of a northern Chinese house, a hollow brick form with a fire underneath. This heated surface was ideal for sleeping on wintry nights. Originally, kang tables were small tables placed on top of the kang platform. But the term came to be used for low rectangular tables placed in front of couches or beds. A kang table is a forerunner of the Western coffee table, but in order to understand its versatility, one need only think of the myriad uses the coffee table lends itself to.

This table is waisted and has horse-hoof feet. Tables, like chairs, require stretchers to stabilize them. Stretchers at the ground or even higher up can interfere with a person's legs or feet. The solution of waisted tables is that the stretcher becomes an integral part of the tabletop, separated with the waist by a reveal strip. The purpose of the waist is to smoothly integrate the structural reinforcement of a stretcher or spandrel into the overall design.

If well made, the horse-hoof shape is crafted from a single piece of wood, rather than having a slice added on. The roster of creatures who lend their profiles to furniture designs in China includes elephants, horses, and the praying mantis. The praying mantis "leg" is modeled on the insect's bent "arms" and bends back in a distinctive double-curve.

The wine or occasional table (as seen in Figure 8.20), although well thought out in its detailing, belongs to the category of modest pieces of furniture. All the separate pieces are visible as separate pieces, and there is no attempt to integrate them into part of an overall design. It is a table with inset legs and no waist, and therefore visible stretchers.

The sixteenth-century table in Figure 8.27 is an elegant piece, far removed in style from the rudimentary need for a horizontal surface. It was used as a writing table, for calligraphy and painting on long scrolls (thus fulfilling the function of a desk), for dining, and for display.

Square tables were used for dining and playing games. The names for square tables relate to their overall size and the number of people they sat. There are thus four-immortals tables, six-immortals tables,

Figure 8.27 High table.
Sixteenth century.

and eight-immortals tables. The eight-immortals table sat two people on each side. Square tables exist with both inset legs and legs at the corners.

Chests

One of the characteristics of storage devices is that often they were made in two parts, with the possibility of the top and the bottom being used separately (Figure 8.28). They were used to store a variety of items, including clothes that were stored carefully folded. Clothes were not hung.

CONCLUSION

In early Asian history, India and China play important roles. A form initially associated with India and Buddha, the stupa, took hold across Southeast Asia.

When combined by the Chinese with the structural technology to build watchtowers, the pagoda arose, which similarly became an important architectural prototype and spread to Korea and Japan.

In the domestic realm, the Chinese courtyard house had a prominent role. Equally influential were the objects created for the interiors of these houses, and the development of Ming-style furniture is one of the highlights in the history of furniture. Because of its quality in design and construction, Ming dynasty furniture is most often compared to English and French eighteenth-century furniture.

In more recent history, when other Asian countries started expanding their repertoire of furniture forms, they developed furniture pieces that exhibit an awareness of the forms developed in Ming China. This topic is explored in Chapters 13 and 18.

In China we are concerned with the contents of

Figure 8.28 Clothes cupboard. Qing dynasty.

the domestic world, and indeed the houses themselves. In Cambodia, our attention is drawn to items connected to religion, such as the monumental temple complexes and statuary of the Angkor period.

Sources

Clunas, Craig. *Chinese Furniture*. London: Victoria and Albert Museum, 1988.

Ecke, Gustav. *Chinese Domestic Furniture*. Rutland, VT: Charles E. Tuttle, 1944.

Handler, Sarah. *Austere Luminosity of Chinese Classical Furniture*. Berkeley: University of California Press, 2001.

Jessup, Helen. *Art and Architecture of Cambodia*. London: Thames and Hudson, 2004.

Kates, George. *Chinese Household Furniture*. New York: Dover, 1948.

Kates, George. *The Years That Were Fat*. Cambridge: MIT Press, 1952.

Murthy, K. Krishna. *Ancient Indian Furniture*. Delhi: Sundeep Prakashan, 1982.

Shixiang, Wang. *Connoisseurship of Chinese Furniture*. Hong Kong: 1990.

Steinhardt, Nancy, et al. *Chinese Architecture*. New Haven: Yale University Press, 2002.

DISCUSSION AND REVIEW QUESTIONS

1. Compare the Chinese house to the Roman courtyard house. What are the similarities and differences?
2. What were the regional differences of the Chinese courtyard house?
3. Look at a piece of furniture such as a chair. How does a piece of furniture suggest the kind of architecture in which it stood?
4. What were some of the ramifications of the adoption of sitting in tall chairs, with legs pendant?
5. What are some Asian-designed objects that involve sitting and yet, in the West, are not considered pieces of furniture?

CHAPTER 9

RENAISSANCE

1400–1500	1500–1520	1520–1600	1400–1500	1500–1600	1600–1700
Early Renaissance	High Renaissance	Late Renaissance	Quattrocento	Cinquecento	Seicento

The chronological and artistic period known as the Renaissance had many influences, but foremost it was, as its name implies, a historic revival. Renaissance literally means rebirth, and refers to the period, roughly 1400–1600, when artists, architects, and artisans looked to ancient Greece and Rome. As both an artistic and intellectual movement, validation was sought in ancient art and architecture. The look to the antique encompassed most artistic realms, including painting and sculpture. For architecture, the most important building types were churches and private palaces.

God and religion, and fear of them, had been a unifying force of Gothic society. In the Renaissance, the unitary focus on God was joined by an interest in humanity, meaning increased attention on the individual and human secular institutions. Most art histories present the Renaissance in sharp contrast to the medieval period, or Gothic; these distinctions are less obvious in England. Some historians bristle at the presentation of the Renaissance as a departure from medieval traditions, or a rebirth of antiquity, and focus on the continuity that existed in many areas of life. This is especially true of the Italian peninsula, where the knowledge of Roman ruins was a constant feature of medieval life.

The first works we now recognize as belonging to the Renaissance were in northern Italy, and the movement quickly spread to other regions and become a continentwide phenomenon. To some scholars, the shift from a God-centered concept of the world to a man- and individual-centered concept of the world constitutes the first step toward the modern age.

Innumerable scientific achievements impacted on the arts. In sculpture and painting, there was an increased attention to the "reality" of the human form; in painting, art increasingly mimicked the processes of the human eye. This also exhibited itself in architecture with the creation and widespread adoption of the **one-point perspective**. The one-point perspective is the drawing method of three-dimensional representation in which items are shortened as they proceed into the distance, often aided by a grid that disappeared into a vanishing point.

One of the many paradoxes that arise when studying the Renaissance is that its leaders constructed the foundation of modern civil and civic society by relying on the idea of the perfectibility of man, yet they looked to the past. Unlike those involved in other revivals, Renaissance artists did not seek to re-create the past and were exceedingly inventive in their use of classic forms. The ancient world served as an inspiration, a point of departure, but not a template.

For those who were not wealthy or politically connected, or who lived modestly in rural areas, the revolutionary changes wrought by Renaissance artists were less important. Interiors, particularly of churches, were more or less viewed from the lens of antiquity. Yet for furniture, there is no Renaissance cabinetmaker who was lauded as were Michelangelo and Raphael.

The Renaissance was an artistic rebirth, and it also related to momentous political and medical events. By the end of the fifteenth century, most of Europe had recovered from the bubonic plague that had decimated the continent in the mid-fourteenth century. France had recovered from the Hundred Years War and the Byzantine Empire had collapsed, giving way to the Ottoman Empire.

Europe beyond the Alps followed with rapt attention the goings-on in Italy. Whereas Italy had firsthand knowledge of the ancients, most of Europe knew it secondhand. Flemish, French, and German Renaissance architecture and design is the result of blending local vernacular traditions with imported Italian Renaissance forms.

Figure 9.1 Albrecht Dürer's house. Nuremburg, Germany. 1495.

ARCHITECTURE

Germany

Dürer

Albrecht Dürer (1471–1528), the foremost German Renaissance painter, also contributed to the development of engraving. In 1495, Dürer established himself in Nuremberg. His house presents a different side of the Renaissance. It demonstrates that in certain areas of life and art, such as domestic architecture, interiors, and furnishings, there was a great deal of continuity from medieval traditions into the period known as the Renaissance.

Figure 9.1 shows a building that bridges the gap between medieval and Renaissance. Still standing, at first glance it looks medieval. It fronts directly onto the street and fills out its lot lines. The upper floors overhang the lower floors, and its most notable features are the exuberant timber-framing of the façades and the steeply pitched roof, the products of centuries of evolution. Yet it is a large and imposing house that stands out from its less illustrious neighbors. The interior features simple rooms, although all the walls have been plastered, their structure hidden (Figure 9.2). Its furnishings include classic Renaissance pieces, such as a trestle table, X-frame chairs, and a storage cabinet.

Albrecht Dürer is an exception to the assertion

Figure 9.2 Dürer's house, interior.

that there is no such thing as a great Northern Renaissance painter. Furniture pieces are important in configuring the interiors of this comfortable house. The interiors are not rigorously studied in their design but respond to the specific demands for a place to sleep, write, sit, and paint.

Italy

Palazzo Davanzati

An examination of the Renaissance typically begins with Florence, home to Brunelleschi, Donatello, and Masaccio. In the fifteenth century, the city's administration had evolved to a point where there was an increased attention to buildings that served as a public infrastructure. This was a move away from absolute rule and gestures in the direction of democracy. The city and the buildings that composed it reflected the gradual shift toward participatory government. The town hall of Florence, the Palazzo Vecchio; its public companion, the Loggia della Signoria; and the Baptistry were three of the public structures that rendered the city grander than its rivals, Pisa and Siena. Another artistic high point considered a beginning of the Renaissance was Ghiberti's commission for the bronze doors of the Baptistry.

The sources for the Renaissance palazzo included traditional Tuscan farmhouses, the watchtowers for which San Gimignano was famous, as well as ancient prototypes. By the mid-fourteenth century, the townhouse, the Palazzo, was becoming something grander, more elegant, and civilized.

Revolutionary Palaces

An analogous structure in Italy to Dürer's house is the Palazzo Davanzati, a transitional house between the Middle Ages and the Renaissance. The Palazzo Davanzati, from the late fourteenth century, sports the first Renaissance interior. Its tall exterior also hints of the façade developments to come. Its façade is regularized and topped off with an open gallery on the roof. A **string course** delineates each floor. The ground floor is rusticated and houses shops. A deep cornice, vaguely classical-looking, crowns the top. The residential floors are above the ground floor; the most important is the first residential floor, the **piano nobile**. Subsequent floors decrease in height. This building mitigated the needs of one noble family and the general citizenry; it provided prestige and comfort for the family and lent an elegant façade to the street. Its interiors are at once rich and austere (Figure 9.3).

In Italy, the important social units were families, such as the Pazzi, the Medici, the Gonzaga, the Pitti. The Palazzo Medici was another significant step in the development of the Renaissance palazzo. It is grand, symmetrical, and relied on classical forms and proportions for its considerable street presence.

Italy was not yet unified, so most of the cities acted as city-states, with the Vatican, in Rome, as a particularly significant player. Florence was a city of bankers and merchants, with considerable ties to the agricultural life of the countryside.

Filippo Brunelleschi (1377–1446) is the most important figure of the early Renaissance. The Renaissance, as viewed from his architectural efforts, relied on the classical system in which all details are related to other details, and the entire building, by way of proportion. Brunelleschi is credited with having invented the one-point perspective. At San Lorenzo and the Foundling Hospital, he put arches on top of columns, something the Romans rarely did.

From 1420 to 1436, Brunelleschi was working on the Florence Cathedral. How to roof the cross of nave and transept? Renaissance architects wanted to do this with a dome. For the city's most important structure, he devised a double-shelled dome, with Gothic vaulting and tension rings at the base that counteract the lateral forces. With this building, and the others that followed, Florentine archi-

Figure 9.3 Palazzo Davanzati. Florence.

tects were making a significant departure from international Gothic developments.

Leon Battista Alberti (1404–1472) was an architect and architectural theorist. He had a well-rounded education in the classics. His primary architectural treatise, the *Ten Books of Architecture* (1452), was a way of making the classic text of the Roman Virtruvius current. In the realm of urban design, he was one of those who advocated that public spaces, like the buildings that fronted them, should be conceptualized and designed.

Urban Design

Michelangelo

The Capitoline Hill is one of the seven hills of Rome. It provides a spectacular view of the Roman forum and also of medieval and Renaissance Rome; the dome of St. Peter's can be glimpsed in the distance. Michelangelo famously redesigned it. Michelangelo never had a blank slate on which to work; all his projects grew out of existing projects started by others. And none was so daunting as the redesign of the Campidoglio, as it is known in

Figure 9.4 The Piazza del Campidoglio and the Cordonata, Rome, by Canaletto.

Italian. His design process is a classic Renaissance design story in which there is a dramatic contrast between medieval urban and architectural traditions and those of the Renaissance. Through the genius of one architect, a new approach to urban space was about to arise.

The project consisted of the Guild Hall, essentially a town hall with a palace for the senators at an awkward eighty-degree angle to it. Michelangelo's solution was to provide a new face for the Guild Hall and move its tower to the center (Figure 9.4). He grafted a new façade onto the Palace of the Sen-

ators and mirrored it with a matching palace. The really ingenious move was to also place the new structure at eighty degrees, making a virtue out of an oddity. For the center of the trapezoidal piazza, he devised a slightly raised oval, from which radiate curvilinear lines. Renaissance architects were well aware that a circular form had the benefit of accepting axes from varying angles. The oval regularizes the buildings. An imposing giant order of pilasters dominates the palace façades.

Renaissance Church design is a continuation of the Early Christian Church basilica form, as it survived through the Middle Ages, with some gestures toward the international Gothic style, and an increased desire to bring the Renaissance qualities of perfection of form, and idealization, into the ecclesiastical realm.

The Latin-cross plan had taken root and proved difficult to dislodge, as much as Renaissance architects were to try. To the architectural mind, the perfectability of form mirrored a spiritual awakening, although this proved a difficult sell to their clients, the church. A rare example of a centrally planned church is Santa Maria della Consolazione in Todi. Many Renaissance architects tried their hand at crafting a centrally planned church—Michelangelo, Bramante, Leonardo da Vinci—so it is therefore difficult to know for certain who the designer of Todi was. The best example of a perfectly symmetrical geometry was likely designed under Bramante's influence. It is similar to designs for centrally planned buildings by Leonardo da Vinci.

Some artworks are perfect examples of a particular artistic concept; they themselves appear as a manifestation of an artistic ideal. So it is with Santa Maria della Consolazione. Many Renaissance architects, at one point in their careers, expressed a desire to see a project through that relied upon simple geometries, an artistic move in keeping with the overall desire to create a perfect solution. And a part of this was the necessity of achieving symmetry— often in contexts which made that difficult. The centrally planned church was difficult because it lacked an obvious entrance—and an obvious destination, the altar. Additionally, it did not indicate the location of a congregation.

The plan of Todi is relentless in its pursuit of symmetry (Figure 9.5). The entry is barely indicated by one apse that is made of line segments; the others are curved. Inside, all four interior elevations appear the same. Nothing mars the perfect interior, and the stairways are discreetly tucked into the poché of the

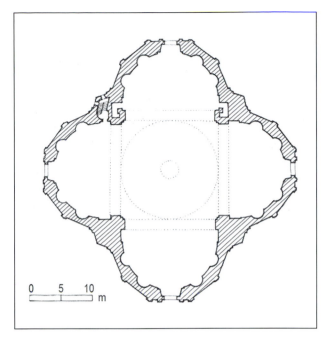

Figure 9.5 Santa Maria della Consolazione. Todi. 1494-1518.

walls. The plan gives no hint of the location of the altar, the priest, the congregation, and the principal entry.

Todi is not only bilaterally symmetrical (two halves of a composition are mirror images of each other), it is radially symmetrical around a central point. The expression of the front façade and its correlate, the apse, is suppressed to the point of being inconsequential. All four elevations of Todi are almost exactly the same.

Todi's forms are simple: a square, a dome, and four half domes. Yet the articulation of its façade ripples over four nearly identical elevations, bringing the pieces together into a unitary composition (Figure 9.6). Its classical detailing is simple in design, inspired in its use. The building sits like a sculpture, upright in the landscape, with no encumbrances. The church is a masterstroke of simplicity. This building stands today more as a statement about architecture than a response to the functional needs of a church. It is a remarkable event in the history of architecture when all the ostensible programmatic

Figure 9.6 Santa Maria della Consolazione, 1494–1518, Todi.

functions of a building are secondary to a relentless pursuit of the perfect form.

DaVinci and Bramante

Santa Maria della Consolazione is the closest incarnation of the Renaissance architectural spirit. Collectively, the works of Raphael, Bramante, and Leonardo da Vinci present varied approaches— abstract, ideal, and pragmatic. The year 1500 was a benchmark of the High Renaissance. Leonardo da Vinci (1452–1519) was an architect, painter, and inventor. The painter of the *Mona Lisa*, 1503–1506, he painted several fresco cycles throughout his life. The High Renaissance architect Donato Bramante (1444–1514) was one of those named as architect of St. Peter's.

Some works are included in the Renaissance because they are transitions (Dürer's House) or important breakthroughs (the Campidoglio); studying them, one imagines the designer grappling with the problem at hand and arriving at a brilliant solution. This is true of every project that Michelangelo turned to, including his work on the Campidoglio and the buildings that he designed for it.

Architectural developments, in addition to being inspired by classical form, are characterized by a striving toward perfection, with perfection being defined as pure geometries and centrally planned buildings.

INTERIORS

Walls, Floors, and Ceilings

The standard composition of a Renaissance residential wall divided it into horizontal bands and fields. Starting at the intersection of wall and floor, a woodwork base made the initial transition from horizontal to vertical. Above the base was a dado-line (waist high or higher). This band encircled the room and visually supported the main field, which extended up to the juncture of wall and ceiling. A cornice mediated the wall-to-ceiling transition and frequently featured a decorated frieze. The frieze was sometimes three-dimensional, more frequently painted. Most walls were plaster, simply painted or featuring frescoes. Frescoes were representational or architectural.

The most expensive options for treating a wall included marble or wood paneling, but these were rare in houses. Walls that were not elaborately painted had wall-hangings whose supporting hooks were at the bottom of the frieze. Walls hangings were made of leather or fabric, relatively simply or embroidered and gilded. Elaborate tapestries with narrative scenes were the purview of only the wealthiest homes. The ubiquity of textile wall-hangings is indicated by the presence of walls that were painted or tiled to resemble hanging fabric, such as the Palazzo Davanzati.

Floors were most commonly made of wood. Fancier rooms had brick or tiled floors; marble floors in houses were rare, because of the weight. Some houses had Turkish carpets, although they were not common.

There were many famous commissions for replacing a simple timber ceiling with a grand one. Looking at these projects reveals the Renaissance approach toward the horizontal plane of the ceiling. The ceiling, like an elevation, became a field to be designed, yet it followed its own parameters. It was foremost considered a piece of architecture. In one type of construction, the joists running in one direction were visually dominant. These parallel timbers spanned the length of the room and literally supported the floor above. An alternate ceiling strategy emphasized the cross-beams as well, which turned the ceiling into a plane of rectangular panels. If the cross-beams' depth was emphasized, the ceiling became a waffle-grid of recesses, or coffers (not to be confused with storage chests of the same name). Some beams were carved with classical details; they were more frequently painted. There were also vaulted ceilings, an architectural element that some grand houses and villas shared with churches.

The first step of the architect working on a prominent ceiling commission was to construct a conceptual grid or framework that established the ceiling as an architectural entity, lent order to a blank upside-down horizontal plane, and divided it into smaller areas to be designed. Some spaces within the framework were then turned over to painters, with the paintings being subordinate to the architectural system. Some plaster ceilings make a nonliteral gesture toward representing beams and joists. The real ones were covered up, then idealized and painted. They were classical in their detailing, although ancient ceilings did not look like the Renaissance ceilings that ostensibly paid them homage.

Figure 9.7 Michelangelo. Sistine Chapel.

Michelangelo

Michelangelo famously took the plain plaster ceiling of the Sistine Chapel and painted it himself to look like architecture, a singular endeavor of heroic proportions (Figure 9.7). Part of his scheme was to wittingly make visual statements about the status of the arts of architecture and painting. Some figures step outside of their "assigned" panels.

The Renaissance approach to ceiling design was unlike that of the ancient's, unlike that of the Middle Ages, and unlike that of the Baroque period that followed it.

Inigo Jones

Inigo Jones is the central figure credited with introducing Italian Renaissance architecture to England. Banqueting House in London was one of the buildings that did this, and it still stands in contrast to its neighbors. The rectilinear elements of the ceiling establish a grid (Figure 9.8). They appear as structural beams, reminiscent of timber ceilings, yet decorated and gilded to the hilt. They also can be read as an oblique reference to Roman coffered ceilings. Rubens did the celebrated paintings that are an integral part of the composition.

Figure 9.8 Inigo Jones. Banqueting House, with paintings by Rubens, 1573–1652. Whitehall, London.

Gradually, over the period of some 200 years known as the Renaissance, the approach to ceilings changes. The geometries become less rigid. In Carraci's ceiling for the Palazzo Farnese, the panels resemble picture frames and the scenes within them are given more visual importance. In many cases, the narrative scenes trump the architecture.

The Study

In her book on the Italian Renaissance, art historian Dora Thornton addresses a single room type: the study. A study could be a small low-ceilinged area in a house's mezzanine, a monk's cellular room, or part of a bed-chamber delineated with a wood partition made by a carpenter for that purpose.

Carpenters also constructed free-standing booths that served as private studies within the context of a larger space, such as a church.

Studies were often outfitted with built-in desks and benches that were continuous with a raised platform. For those involved in trade, a study accessible to a house's visitors served as a place for meeting with vendors and discussing and signing contracts. For others, it was a place of solitude, for reflecting, reading, and writing.

As free-standing furnishings became more common, a desk or a simple trestle table served as the work surface. A movable bench, stool, or X-frame chair provided seating. A lectern was a shallow storage unit with a sloping top that acted as the writing surface. It sat on top of the desk or table, and its storage space held pens, ink, paper, and other writing supplies. Travelers found lecterns particularly useful.

The objects that completed a study could include a small collection of contemporary artworks, antiquities, and exotic souvenirs. Pen knives, seals, spectacles, and magnifying glasses were common accessories. Some surprising objects found in a study included a mirror and a reading cushion to rest one's forearms against.

An important function of a study was to store and display books. Shelves were built in, recessed, or surface mounted. A free-standing piece of furniture, a cabinet with shelves and doors, was a secure way to store valuable books. Thornton writes that "The evolution of the cabinet as a piece of furniture was the single most important development in the history of the study in Renaissance Italy, for it demonstrated the importance of collecting as a form of interior decoration" (Thornton 1997, p. 74). Cabinets and chests that held books, either in private homes, churches, or town halls, were the forerunners to libraries.

Considering a single room type such as the study underscores the role that rooms and interior furnishings played in the development of ways of thinking about and interacting with the world. Dora Thornton writes: "Reading, studying and thinking were considered by Renaissance writers to be free and pleasurable pursuits which gave shape and elegance to one's leisure, so that a study represented the ideal of making the pleasures of thinking and working continuous with the rest of one's existence" (Thornton 1997, p. 2). The celebrated Renaissance focus on the individual was encouraged by a place whose objects were configured to encourage careful, informed thought.

Raphael

In the periods that followed the Renaissance, the interior became a completely designed space, with an integration of all the constituent elements. In the Renaissance, the full integration of interior design elements does occur in churches, less so in houses. In many respects, the Renaissance domestic interior remained, as it had been in the Middle Ages, a collection of disparate elements. By modern standards, a Renaissance interior was sparingly furnished.

The painter and architect Raphael (1483–1520) was influenced by da Vinci and Michelangelo. For Pope Julius II, he did a series of rooms in his Vatican apartments. These projects involved painting wall and ceiling frescoes. They are known as the **Stanze**, which means, simply, rooms. The most famous was the Stanza della Segnatura, which includes Raphael's painting *The School of Athens*.

Raphael's *stanze* in the Vatican was an inspired set of interiors that follows Renaissance principles. But the furnishings of the suite of rooms were not a part of the design, and in fact were at odds with it.

Palazzo interiors were the product of almost continual rebuilding and remodeling. Furniture and tapestries, therefore, played an important role in shaping the use and disposition of rooms. Renaissance rooms usually had beamed ceilings and also had prominent fireplaces. The ensemble of fireplace, mantel, and overmantel was a favored site of elaborate decoration. Where Renaissance interiors depart from medieval practices is that there is an increasing tendency to mask the actual structure—ceiling, beams and joists, floorboards, walls of studs and lath—and present a unified plane to those in the room. These unified planes became blank canvases awaiting artistry.

FURNITURE

Two strands of Renaissance furniture stand out: One strand comprises pieces of furniture that are clearly derivative of Renaissance architecture; the other constitutes the continuation of medieval forms. The former is chiefly large cabinets and beds; the latter includes tables, chairs, and stools. Information on medieval Italian furniture is sparse, although we know that there were tables, chairs, stools, and chests. The invention in 1322 of the saw mill eased the production of furniture based on planks. Harold Eberlein, the author of an early twentieth-century work on Italian Renaissance interiors and furniture, emphasized a central duality to his subject matter: it was complex or simple. He wrote: "The Italian Renaissance interior was either richly ornate with all the wealth of polychrome treatment that could be applied to walls and ceiling . . . or else it was severely simple, and even austere with points of concentrated enrichment only where they would give the greatest emphasis" (Eberlein 1916, p. vii). High contrast characterized a Renaissance interior, regarding color and surface articulation. Individual pieces were sometimes elaborate, but the overall effect of simplicity was achieved with a judicious use of elaborate objects within a straight-forwardly articulated space.

Large-Scale Architectural Furniture

One category of designed objects includes large ponderous items that attract a viewer's attention. Eberlein explained, "Few rooms could stand many of the more ornate pieces of Renaissance cabinet work, whether polychrome or carved, and it was not intended they should. To have had more than a few would have been like trying to make an entire dinner on plum pudding" (Eberlein 1916, p. ix).

A feature of one class of Renaissance furniture pieces, including wardrobes and large chests, is that they are resolutely architectural, with a clear architectonic profile, and their detailing relies on the classical architectural vocabulary. Knowledge of Italian Renaissance architecture circulated around Europe via the printed book; hence, the invention of the mechanical printing press in Germany in 1439 impacted furniture design, as well. Furniture designers had access to a precise grammar of ornament, with classical capitals, fluting, putti, caryatids, and so on.

Cupboards and Wardrobes

Many big Renaissance pieces of furniture resemble buildings. They have a base, multiple stories and columns, and an overhanging cornice. Meticulously designed, their elevations promote multiple readings. Sometimes they combine furniture detailing with architectural detailing. On one particularly impressive piece shows doors open to reveal an elaborate scene crafted out of veneers (Figure 9.9). The marquetry scene exploits the impression of depth with a false perspective.

The two two-storied pavilions can visually predominate, or the giant order of columns, a motif borrowed from Michelangelo's buildings on the Campidoglio, can be read as the visually dominant elements. The overall cabinet can look like it comprises two two-story pavilions set on a base; an

Figure 9.9 Grand cabinet. Seventeenth century.

alternate reading is of a three-story piece. The rows of lozenges, ovals, and rectangles can also be read to stand in for framing columns.

The local engagement with the imported Italian style is found in the infill panels: non-architectural motifs, a surfeit of marquetry and parquetry.

Edward Lucie-Smith (1979) writes that such pieces of furniture "are in every detail like miniature renaissance palaces—far more correctly classical than the buildings which were being erected simultaneously by German architects" (1979, p. 55). Printed pattern-books served as guides to making furniture. The list of architects whose careers were largely due to their publications includes Peter Flötner in Germany, Jacques Androuet du

Cerceau I and Hugues Sambin in France, and Hans Vredeman de Vries and Theodore de Bry in the Netherlands.

The new style required a higher level of expertise in woodworking and resulted in a growing distinction worldwide among joiners, carpenters, and turners.

Joiners did rough carpentry work; carpenters were involved in house building, such as paneling and built-in pieces; and turners worked on smaller projects, such as pieces of furniture. One piece of evidence of this comes from the American continent, when on August 30, 1568, the City of Mexico issued separate ordinances for carpenters, sculptors, joiners, and makers of stringed instruments. By the end of the sixteenth century, it was possible to discuss national trends in furniture design and growing distinctions among the wood-working trades.

Beds

For those fortunate enough not to sleep on the floor, an essential item was a mattress, a textile bag stuffed with straw or feathers. A frame lifted the mattress off the floor, and there were multiple examples of the resulting space (between frame and floor) being used by a lower mattress and frame on wheels—a trundle bed.

More elaborate beds had tall headboards with an overhanging cornice. The visual dominance of a bed in a bedroom was furthered by the custom of surrounding it with auxiliary pieces of furniture, a chest at the foot of the bed, and benches at the sides. The benches had hinged lids which opened to reveal storage. These benches also provided seating, indicating that beds and bedrooms had a social function during the day. The custom of surrounding a bed with a chest and benches led to the construction of closed platforms that supported the mattress. Wider on three sides than the mattress, there was a space between the mattress and platform's edge for guests to sit. Storage spaces lay underneath the guest's seat cushions. Bed curtains were not attached to beds (Thornton 1991, p. 111–120).

The Renaissance bed differed significantly from the Roman bed. It was no longer used for dining and was monumental in size, form, and decoration.

Chests and Cassoni

In the fifteenth century, the chest remained one of the most important and numerous pieces of furniture. Over the course of the sixteenth century, its central role in a household's inventory of furnishings lessened. A storage device, it was also a means to transport items. The rounded top indicates the possibility that this piece was envisioned to stand outside; rounded tops evaded rainwater.

In less exalted households, a chest was frequently one of the few pieces of furniture and was called to serve many uses. A synonym is *coffer*. What distinguishes a coffer, sometimes, is that it was used to store money and valuable items; hence the phrase "the coffers of the pope," in which a piece of furniture is used as a stand-in for the papal treasury, or Chaucer's line from *The Canterbury Tales,* "Yet hadde he but litel gold in cofre," in which a nearly empty coffer is a sign of poverty.

Within the domestic realm, the Italian **cassone** demonstrates how a piece of furniture did not just serve functional purposes but was also a player in a familial, social, and ritual network (Figure 9.10). Many modern furniture traditions date back to this piece of furniture.

The Italian verb *accasàre* means to marry off, and a cassone, a large *cassa* (box or chest) is a piece of furniture that was part of the process. A cassone traditionally held items that were to serve a prospective bride in her marriage. As the bride decamped from her familial home to that of her husband's, the cassoni were carried through the streets, a public affirmation of the transference of property and wealth from one family to another, and a symbol that hereafter the young lady's home was with her new family. This chest therefore had both a private and a public function. Once ensconced in its new home, the cassone often took its place at the foot of the marriage bed. It had a functional use and also served as a visual tie to the woman's birth family.

Art historian Cristelle Baskins wrote an entire book on cassoni. If the private study was mostly a male realm, Baskins states that "the cassone became a microcosm of the household, but also synecdochically, a figure for the wife herself" (Baskins 1998, p. 2). The cassone, like the house, contained locked-up things that were watched over and cared for by

Figure 9.10 French Renaissance cassone.

women. These elegant chests might contain items of the bride's wardrobe, fine linens, purses, bags, scissors, gloves, and prayer books. The circulation and collection of these consumer goods was related to the wealth that stemmed from Renaissance trade. Symbolically, a cassone was related to its owner's reproductive contribution to her family and the social alliance and financial arrangement between two families. Cassoni were usually made in pairs; commissioning them was an expensive endeavor reserved for wealthy families. Cassoni were most popular in the fifteenth century, and their manufacture and use declined in the sixteenth century, as did the importance of chests generally.

Elaborate cassoni featured painted or carved panels. These allegorical stories relate to courtship and marriage. Sometimes these allegories appear odd for modern viewers, such as the Rape of Daphne, but in their context, they underscored faithfulness within the bonds of marriage. These lavishly decorated chests were made in Italy in the fourteenth to

sixteenth centuries; Florence was an important center of production for both the cases and the painted panels. Commissioning and owning cassoni was initially an Italian practice, but over time some individuals continent-wide admired and purchased the carefully crafted storage units.

Cassapanche and Credenzas

A **cassapanca** recognizes that chests were often used as seating (Figure 9.11). It is a piece that is designed for two purposes: storage and seating. Slightly higher than a chest, it is essentially a storage chest to which a back and arms have been added.

A **credenza** is a storage unit with a higher elevation than a chest (Figure 9.12). A credenza is a storage item, but its primary purpose is for the display of items. Some credenzas had stepped shelves to make even more precious objects visible. Credenzas were also initially associated with Florence. The display of expensive objects publicly affirmed a family's status.

Figure 9.11 Cassapanca (combined chest and seat).

Renaissance palazzi did not have closets. Grand houses had storerooms on the upper floors, but on lower floors, items were stored in cabinets or wardrobes (Figure 9.13). In many places of the world today, apartments do not have built-in closets and items of clothing continue to be stored in cabinets.

As one of the finer pieces of Renaissance furniture, it is appropriate to ask if this piece is indicative of a general Renaissance design approach toward objects. It is. The approach seen here is to accept a tried-and-true form and make it more valuable by covering its forms and surfaces with decoration. This presents the Renaissance solution to taking a common object and rendering it grand. This method takes a form known to be successful in workshops and farms, and decorates it to the hilt to render it acceptable for use in fine houses.

A chest, a cassapanca, a credenza, and a cabinet—each is of increasing height, and all are storage items. Drawers are used, yet entire chests of drawers were not common. While in no literal way does this constitute a forerunner of the twentieth-century office panel system, it does constitute a series of pieces of furniture, of increasing height, that were used to furnish a room, with a practical function and making a visual impact. The list of items that could be called upon to resolve the furnishing of a room had increased significantly from the medieval period.

Figure 9.12 Florentine credenza, seventeenth century.

Figure 9.13 Wardrobe, c. 1580.

Surface-Forming Furniture

Tables

A **trestle** table is a table whose horizontal surface is supported by a system of uprights, at the ends, and stabilizing cross-pieces. (Other types of tables are legged tables, plinth tables, and pedestal tables.) On an Italian **refectory table**, the uprights are end panels (Figure 9.14). The trestle table had a clear ancient Roman precedent, and trestle tables were widespread throughout the Italian peninsula. They were frequently found in convents, but were not limited to religious contexts. This table makes scant reference to Renaissance architecture. Its form presents an honest response to the need of supporting a horizontal work or dining surface. Two horizontal rails stabilize the panels. Such tables are translations into wood of Roman marble tables and benches that were used in gardens.

Renaissance furniture relied less on metal strapping and metal nails, as did medieval pieces, and more on wood pins and dovetail joints. Tables, if they had legs, generally had rails.

Figure 9.14 Refectory table, Italy.

Seating

Unlike the other arts and the rare cabinet, furniture for sitting rarely took its inspiration from antique models. Those pieces that existed in ancient Rome were prevalent in the Renaissance not because they were rediscovered but because they never went away. There were three categories of seating: stools, benches, and chairs.

Stools

Sgabello literally means stool, although the term also denotes specifically Renaissance upper-class stools and small-scale chairs. For those at the lower end of the economic spectrum, the stool was the most common type of seating device. The most comprehensive book to date on Italian Renaissance interiors and furnishings is by Peter Thornton, the father of Dora Thornton. Much of the information about seating, other pieces, and Renaissance interiors presented here comes from his work.

The construction of a stool was simple; some were carved from solid pieces of wood, some from planks simply cut and assembled. The word stool is a misnomer as this category contains several elegant and elaborate pieces that provided seating in refined locations.

What all Italian Renaissance stools have in common is an ancestor in a common utilitarian seat, what Peter Thornton calls an "old-fashioned milking stool" (Thornton 1991, p. 168). Simple stools consisted of a seat, round, octagonal, square, or rectangular, supported by three or four legs.

Figure 9.15 shows an example of a stool whose relief decoration and painting render it appropriate for the public rooms of a palazzo.

Examples of straightforward stools, with attached backs, are visible in Figure 9.16.

Another type of stool was the box stool, made from five boards (four sides and the seat) with the feet integral to the sides. The flat surfaces of a box-stool were rife for decoration. Some box stools were painted, carved, or inlaid with intarsia. Some stools featured a backboard, which blurs the line between chair and stool. Some stools were wide enough to

Figure 9.16 Sgabello chair, c. 1560. Italy.

Figure 9.15 Stool. Sgabello, Italy.

seat two in close proximity, which blurs the line between stool and bench.

It is odd to name a chair sgabello, using a word that means stool, but the etymology reveals the history of design; a back was once upon a time added to a stool (Figure 9.16). The notches in the front and rear planks hint at legs.

Sgabelli were useful at social functions, in a public realm. They demanded no small amount of dexterity of the people who used them. An awkward move and seated person and chair together would topple over. They were not intended for relaxing, but for a place of rest within the context of a public function. The small scale and delicacy of sgabelli contrast with the imposing cabinets and wardrobes.

Although cushions were used and limited upholstery on seats and arm rests, no fully upholstered piece of furniture made an appearance in the Renaissance.

Furniture buyers did not purchase elegant chairs in large numbers; a collection of matching sgabelli in the Louvre is exceptional. Rooms that needed to accommodate many people did so with a variety of chair types, often combining armed chairs with sgabelli and benches.

When furnishing a room, a strict hierarchy of seating types reigned that mirrored the hierarchy of secular and religious life. The most elegant (and therefore of the highest status) type of chairs was the armed sedia, followed by the X-frame chair, followed by a sgabello with a back, followed by a backless sgabello, and finally modest stools and benches. Stools were useful in homes of the wealthy and homes of the poor.

Benches

Benches, fixed (built-in), and free-standing, provided multiple seating. There were benches with and without backs. Most benches had hinged seats, providing access to storage below the seats. Thornton writes that most seating was provided by stools and benches until 1500, after which a variety of chair types became common (Thornton 1991, p. 174).

The X-Frame Chair

In the context of the Italian Renaissance, the X-frame chair seems to be yet another example of an ancient object rediscovered and embraced by fifteenth-century artisans. While it is true that there were ancient X-frame chairs, this is a case of an item whose continual utility is evidenced by the fact that it existed in ancient Rome, through the medieval period, through to the Renaissance.

A chair provides a horizontal surface for a human figure to sit upon at a decent height above the ground (at lower heights, it is then a stool). This makes the human figure appear important and separates it from the cold and damp of the ground. If the seated figure were a static (or "dead") load, the task of distributing the weight to the ground would be simple. Yet because the seated human figure fidgets, moving constantly from side to side, the chair as a designed object is subjected to lateral tensile forces as well as vertical compressive forces. Hence, a chair is complicated structurally and requires lateral bracing.

The continual appearance of the X-frame chair throughout history is testament to its ability to respond to the complicated forces of the seated figure. This is not an example of a simple solution; the construction of an X-frame is difficult and exacting and requires a skilled carpenter. It is an example of a form that endures over time because knowledge of how to build it becomes widespread.

An X-frame chair was comfortable and transportable. Comfort here is a relative term, meaning comfort as opposed to sitting on a rock or log.

In fifteenth- and sixteenth-century Italian cities, even wealthy families owned few pieces of furniture, although many owned several homes. Prominent families typically owned a town house and a villa in the countryside (for example, the Palazzo Farnese in Rome and the Villa Farnese). Furniture was frequently moved from house to house; hence the foldable and transportable X-frame chair was a useful addition to a household. Pieces of furniture were also periodically moved within a house—for example, from public rooms to storerooms on upper stories. Another development over the two hundred years of the Renaissance is that families were less likely to move along with all their furnishings.

The Savonarola Chair

The Dominican monk Girolamo Savonarola was a religious figure who fought the powerful Florentine Medici family. The Medici family fell in 1494 and was replaced as the rulers of Florence. Savonarola's reign was to be short-lived; he was executed in 1498.

He abhorred the excesses of the wealthy and powerful, and sought to lead the church down a simpler path. The church and its followers, he felt, should lead lives marked by self-discipline and self-denial. Restraint was one of the qualities that the arts sponsored by the state, the church, and the wealthy should reflect. The chair named after him, Savonarola, does precisely that (Figure 9.17). It is not an example of simplicity as a matter of economic necessity, but as a contemplated goal in itself. The austere lines of the chair reflect the religious attitude of asceticism. This chair raises what is a perennially recurring question among the religious: Should art forms associated with a religion espouse

Figure 9.18 Savonarola chair.

Figure 9.17 Folding Savonarola chair. c. 1500.

virtues of simplicity, piety, discipline, and denial, or should they glorify God with grand impressive gestures?

A different Savonarola chair takes a more complicated approach. Some decoration covers the simple forms of the chair and the backrest (Figure 9.18).

Previously, we enumerated several functions of a chair: to raise the seated human figure off the ground, provide a modicum of comfort, avoid contact with damp and cold, and in some cases to be transportable. Added to this list is another function, a symbolic one: A chair should look like a chair. A challenge chair designers face is that their designs should be intelligible to those looking at them.

Figure 9.19 Dante chair.

The Sedia

The standard Renaissance armchair is referred to with the Italian word that simply translates as "chair": the sedia (Figure 9.20). Sedia means chair, but it also indicates a Renaissance armchair. This type of chair is similar to some late Roman chairs that we know of from wall paintings.

It is also important in that it starts what will be a long line of chairs. In fact most European seating from the time of the Renaissance onward is based on the sedia.

The sedia is a combination of plank and turned construction. The legs of the chair are decorated by being turned and carved during fabrication. The front legs stabilize the chair and continue through the seat to become the arm supports; similarly, the

Dante Chair

The starting point of the Dante chair is the X-frame chair, which had existed on the Italian peninsula for some 1,500 years. This is not a new design, but a revised version of a tested form. Many Dante chairs take the form of a folding X-frame and elaborate on it, although they themselves do not always fold (Figure 9.19). Thus, the original derived out of the need to be transportable, but the form in itself became desirable and recognizable, outside of its ability to fold.

As with the heavily decorated sgabello, with the Dante chair, we observe the furniture designers working with a recognizable form and applying decoration to it. X-frame chairs of the Dante variety are synonymous with the Renaissance throughout Europe.

Additionally, there were modest chairs that folded fore-and-aft—the X was visible on their side profiles.

Figure 9.20 Renaissance chair, Sedia, Italy.

rear legs continue through the seat to form the backrest. Horizontal stretchers stabilize the chair against lateral forces. The front stretcher is raised. A seated human figure would likely want to raise his or her legs and possibly rest them on the front stretcher; this is made impossible on the sedia by the front rail's elevated position.

It is not fully upholstered, and thumbtacks hold down the leather that is attached over padding. They also form a part of the decoration. This chair's verticals and horizontals are all true. They are nearly vertical and horizontal, and connect at crisp right angles. There is some evidence that chairs of this type were imported from Spain and France (Thornton 1991, p. 186).

CONCLUSION

The knowledge of Renaissance forms circulated around Europe. Books were published and some pieces of furniture were exported. More important, craftsmen knowledgeable of Italian Renaissance techniques traveled and took their knowledge with them. Italian Renaissance decorative styles came to France first during the reigns of Charles VIII and Francis I. This was an outcome based upon French political and military incursions into Italy. Italian craftsmen also traveled to France. A neighborhood developed in Paris that became known for furniture: the Faubourg Saint-Antoine.

England experienced continental Renaissance design at a remove from Italy; many of the furniture makers in England who produced Renaissance pieces were themselves Flemish. England is almost always more eclectic than the continent, but the reign of Henry VIII saw an interest in a particularly pure form of Renaissance art.

Over the period of the 200 years known as the Renaissance, there was a progression from simple and functional to decorated.

Renaissance furniture was more comfortable, and numerous, than medieval furniture. While not fully integrated into the design of interiors, some exceptional Renaissance pieces display the full virtuosity of carvers, sculptors, and gilders. Renaissance craftsmen established the essential roster of European furniture that would be further developed in the Baroque and Rococo periods.

Sources

Baskins, Cristelle. *Cassone Painting, Humanism, and Gender in Early Modern Italy*. Cambridge: Cambridge University Press, 1998.

Baskins, Cristelle, ed. *The Medieval Marriage Scene: Prudence, Passion, Policy*. Tempe: Arizona Center for Medieval and Renaissance Studies, 2005.

Boroli, Marcella. *Il mobile del rinascimento*. Novara: Istituto Geographico De Agostini, 1985.

Eberlein, Harold Donaldson. *Interiors, Fireplaces, and Furniture of the Italian Renaissance*. New York: Paul Wenzel and Maurice Krakow, 1916.

Ghelardini, Armando. *Il mobile italiano dal medioevo all'ottocento*. Milan: Bramante Editrice, 1970.

Mende, Matthias. *The Dürer House in Nuremberg*. Nuremberg: Verlag Hans Carl Nürnberg, 1991.

Thornton, Dora. *The Scholar in His Study: Ownership and Experience in Renaissance Italy*. New Haven: Yale University Press, 1997.

Thornton, Peter. *The Italian Renaissance Interior*. New York: Abrams, 1991.

Waddy, Patricia. *Seventeenth-Century Roman Palaces: Use and Art of the Plan*. Cambridge: MIT Press, 1990.

DISCUSSION AND REVIEW QUESTIONS

1. Look at a Renaissance plan or façade. With the drawing as your evidence, explain how Renaissance designers designed. What was important to them? How does this differ from other design approaches, such as how people design today?

2. What was the attraction to centrally planned buildings? Why were they problematic for churches?

3. What are examples of forms, in furniture, art, or architecture, that were not reinventions but medieval holdovers?

4. How was the Renaissance a dramatic break from the medieval period?

5. Who are some of the major Renaissance architects and artists?

CHAPTER 10

BAROQUE

1600–1720	1600–1700	1600–1700	1603–1649
Baroque	**Seventeenth century**	**Seicento**	**Jacobean**

The Baroque period is known for its convergence of patronage and prodigious artistic talent. Two centers of increased wealth and the prestige they sought were significant: the Italian noble class and the French monarchy.

Art historians use the terms "seventeenth century" and "Baroque" synonymously. Baroque, in common parlance, means elaborate. Often historians of art and design discuss the economic, religious, and political factors that lie behind the art—that is, they examine how the context was important and related to the artworks produced. This is also true with Baroque art. But, significantly, there is also the phenomenon of those active in the arts reacting to the stylistic traditions they inherited. What we have is a style that can be interpreted as reacting to another style. It is difficult to understand the genesis of Baroque forms without first understanding the Renaissance. As happens when studying styles in progression, many of the elements that become the hallmark of Baroque design are also present in late-Renaissance design; thus a predecessor to the Baroque are the late-Renaissance mannerist tendencies as seen in the work of Giulio Romano and Michelangelo.

As for the political and religious context, continual discord between Catholics and Protestants, throughout Europe, marred the seventeenth century. In France, the Edict of Nantes of 1598 sought to decisively put the religious wrangling to rest, yet failed to do so. Regarding economic power and trade, the seventeenth century saw a shift in which the chief rivals for leadership in international trade were the Netherlands and Portugal. By the end of the century, the contest was between the Netherlands and England.

International contacts between Europe and the rest of the world had existed since the fifteenth century, but in the seventeenth century the effects were deeply felt and widespread. For furniture and the decorative arts, this resulted in new materials, such as tortoiseshell, ivory, brass, silver, and semiprecious stones. Increased trade in wood involved both native European timbers and also exotic hardwoods, foremost ebony.

The seventeenth century was an important time for interiors and furnishings, more important than the Renaissance had been. There was a move from heavy oak cupboards to lacquered cabinets. The desire for comfort increased, resulting in more heavily upholstered pieces of furniture.

ITALY

Architecture

In Italy, the two major Baroque artistic figures were Francesco Borromini (1599–1667) and Gianlorenzo Bernini (1598–1680); they frequently competed against each other for the same projects. With projects that were geographically close, each tried to out-do the other.

Borromini

A church Borromini designed, San Carlo alle Quattro Fontane, dates to 1634. Designed and built for the Spanish Trinitarians, it is a seminal work of Baroque architecture, and is worthy of study in its façade, in plan, and in its interior. It is also compelling as a work of urban design. It stands at the intersection of two streets, and each of the four buildings at the corners sports a fountain—hence the church's

Figure 10.1 Francesco Borromini. San Carlo alle Quattro Fontane. Rome, Italy.

unusual name (Figure 10.1). The fountain is visible in the plan and to the extreme left of the façade.

The façade contains many of the elements that predominated in Italian Renaissance façades. In its detailing, the façade relies on classical elements— columns, pilasters, niches, bases, and Corinthian capitals. Yet the façade of San Carlo bends and breaks in ways no Roman temple ever did. The other aspect that represents a departure from Renaissance elevations is the depth of the façade. The cornices are deep and hang over the rest of the façade, both at mid-height and at the top, casting the building in deep shadow. Rather than meekly lining the street, the curvy façade has a lively relationship to it. Compared to a Renaissance church elevation, it stands out from its context. The façade no longer expresses a central nave and side aisles. Instead it reads as a Baroque take on the idea of a church façade. Baroque architects frequently used the broken pediment. At San Carlo, it curves and projects into the public space of the street. With its deep niches and scrolled gable, the façade expresses movement as does the interior.

Borromini was trained as a stone carver. Unlike his rival Bernini, he was an architect, not a painter and sculptor. The plan of San Carlo is startling: The geometric purity of the Renaissance is gone (Figure 10.2). Compared to Todi, geometric complexity and plasticity have replaced simplicity and solidity. There is nothing rectilinear in the plan; even the curves are complex. It relies on ovals and elliptical shapes. Half domes hang over the altar and the side apses. The dome has windows at its lower edge and a lantern lets in light. San Carlo is a very small church with an astonishing amount of visual activity.

It bears comparison to the Renaissance church in Todi because it is not a version of the basilica/ Latin cross plan, but a Baroque version of a centrally planned church. The entrance is on one of the narrow sides. It vaguely resembles a Greek cross, with concave corners and concave apses at the entry, altar, and sides. Yet there is no individuation of parts; everything seems to flow together.

Another tour de force of Borromini's planning abilities was Sant' Ivo, also in Rome. It was built in

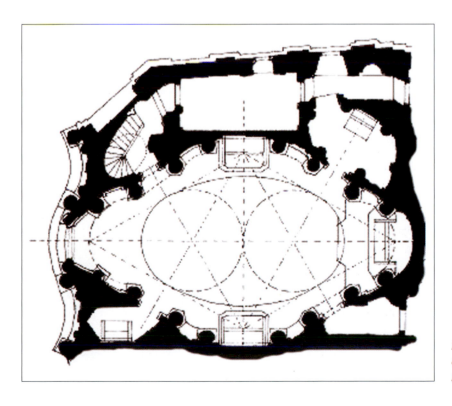

Figure 10.2 Francesco Borromini. Plan of San Carlo alle Quattro Fontane, Rome, Italy.

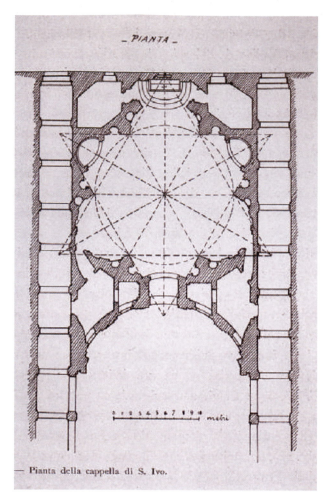

Figure 10.3 Francesco Borromini. Sant' Ivo della Sapienza, Rome, Italy.

1642–1662 as part of a complex by Giacomo della Porta for the University of Rome. It underscores that Borromini was interested in ovals, circles, and stars, but not the standard basilica form. Sant' Ivo takes the form of a six-sided star, formed from the intersection of two equilateral triangles (Figure 10.3). Each point of the resulting six-sided star receives an apse. The interior elevation comprises alternating convex and concave curves, and straight pieces, which results in an undulating interior façade.

Bernini

Gianlorenzo Bernini (1598–1680) is the major figure of Italian Baroque sculpture and architec-

ture. Although Borromini at one point worked for Bernini, they became fierce rivals. Bernini was a sculptor before he turned to architecture. Bernini's sculpture of Apollo and Daphne catches the mythological figures not in studied reflection, but caught up in the most emotional moment of the narrative from Ovid's *Metamorphoses* (Figure 10.4). Apollo is in hot pursuit of Daphne. The story is dramatic and involves one figure running, another fleeing. It is a trenchant moment filled with action and emotion. It portrays unbridled violence. She resists his attempts by turning into a tree. In addition, the sculpture of Apollo and Daphne is asymmetrical with no obvious front elevation. It encourages its viewers to walk around it. Bernini began as a sculptor, and many see in his architectural designs the mind of a sculptor at work.

Figure 10.4 Gianlorenzo Bernini. Apollo and Daphne.

Figure 10.5 Gianlorenzo Bernini. Piazza San Pietro, 1667. Rome, Italy.

Michelangelo's *David* also takes as its subject a narrative that involves two adversaries; yet Michelangelo's *David* barely hints at the most dramatic part of the story: David's slaying of Goliath. Emotion, in the Bernini sculpture, is explicit. Looking at Baroque artworks helps explain that when people discuss interiors and furnishings, they rely upon the same vocabulary, judging the works to be emotional, jubilant, or seductive.

In Bernini's time, the public space in front of St. Peter's Basilica in Rome was a sorry lot. The Vatican Palace, to the north, was an asymmetrical mess on its exterior. To the south and east stood a smattering of irregular, undistinguished buildings, and

the basilica itself was in the process of being remodeled. In order to complete the transformation of the Vatican, the square in front of the basilica had to be addressed. The public space needed to hold thousands for special events, such as Easter when the Pope directly addresses the crowd from the central balcony. The new piazza needed to be huge, yet not overpower the cathedral.

Bernini's design for the Piazza San Pietro in 1667, the urban space in front of St. Peter's, derives its perimeter lines from complex geometries and overlapping forms, yet it meshes with the Renaissance church with its careful classical detailing (Figure 10.5).

Bernini's composition has three parts. As an ensemble, it acted as a giant vestibule to the church, an outdoor room to prepare visitors for the act of visiting the church that housed the relics and tomb of St. Peter. Most visitors, including pilgrims, approached St. Peter's from the bridge over the Tiber River. The first element was a simple urban space, a forecourt (unbuilt in Bernini's time and not realized until Mussolini's urban intervention in the twentieth century).

Then visitors reached the centerpiece of the design, the huge oval space wider than the church itself. The colonnades that form the perimeter of the oval piazza have columns that are slightly smaller than those of the giant order of Carlo Maderno's façade. There are four rows of unfluted, massive Tuscan columns made of travertine. The piazza is self-contained in a way.

These outstretched arms express not the distress of Christ on the cross but the encompassing embrace of a motherly church. Completed with an Egyptian obelisk placed by Fontana, the piazza gave ordinary people an extraordinary experience.

A feature of many Baroque artworks, paintings, buildings, and sculpture is that the works are not meant to be viewed from a single vantage point. Although there appears to be the single focal point of the obelisk, it is not the center of a circle but the focus of a complex shape derived from several overlapping circles. The giant colonnade is resolutely classical in its details, Baroque in its forms.

Finally, immediately in front of the church, low wings enclose a trapezoidal space. Eventual movement toward the church, up a broad flight of stairs, reinforces the Baroque love of movement, and the dome disappears from view. Before entering the church, visitors have navigated their way through the piazza, moving both laterally and vertically.

Architectural historian Spiro Kostof (1995) writes: "Bernini absorbs us into a palpable world of devotion, ravishes our senses, persuades us through visual testimony instead of rational argument or abstracted passion. Architecture, painting, sculpture—all the arts and every device of theatrical illusion work together to sweep us into a realm of unashamed emotionalism" (p. 509).

It is a more aggressive piece of urban design than any achieved during the Renaissance. With narrow parts and expansive parts, it compresses visitors at some points (the vestibule, the space in front of the church) and releases them at others.

Michelangelo and Bramante had been given the task of fashioning for Christianity a basilica in western Europe that could rival the Pantheon. Bernini created the public space in front, worthy of it. Bernini is to the Baroque what Michelangelo was to the Renaissance.

Residential Interiors

Architectural historian Patricia Waddy writes that visitors to residential interiors experienced continual movement, an experience that contrasted to the act of viewing a more somber exterior. The architectural part of an interior ensemble acted as a stable framework—for people, furnishings, and therefore a variety of uses. Waddy writes: "The organization of the whole palace involves relationships of various sorts among the parts. There may be some underlying organizing armature, or each connection may be seen as an isolated incident. Axes of organization may or may not be the same as axes of vision or movement. Symmetry may be present with respect to a wall (a picture-like field) or with respect to a spatial axis. The three-dimensional organization of a palace may involve vertically continuous walls or other supports, or it may involve transformations from level to level. Interior order and exterior order may or may not coincide." Examples of palaces that exhibit these features include the Palazzo Barberini and the Palazzo Borghese.

CENTRAL AND NORTHERN EUROPE

Baroque churches became a dominant feature in many towns, large and small, in Germany, Austria, and Switzerland.

Churches

In Germany, Dominikus Zimmermann designed a pilgrimage church, known as Die Wies, in Steingaden (Figure 10.6). The ceiling is painted to go away, as though the building opens to the sky. This introduces a new element into the art of interior

Figure 10.6 Dominikus Zimmermann, Die Wies, Steingaden, Germany.

decoration; Renaissance artists, under the right cir-cumstances, also appreciated a good trick—false perspectives and the like. A standard part of the Baroque architectural vocabulary is to paint ele-ments to deliberately give a false impression. Thus, a painted ceiling pretends to be a window, or the sky itself. The ceiling at Die Wies is a rich composi-tion of color, detail, and form.

Figure 10.7 Johann Bernhard Fischer von Erlach. Karlskirche, 1723. Vienna, Austria. Interior, looking at dome.

Figure 10.8 Johann Bernhard Fischer von Erlach. Schönbrunn Palace. Vienna, Austria.

German churches relate to Italian Baroque churches because they also rely on complex geometries, rich decorative schemes, and illusionistic painting to achieve effects, most prominently in the ceiling. As a designed interior, there is an overall continuity; some wall elements flow seamlessly onto the ceiling. All details are part of a dynamically designed whole.

The spread of Baroque design into central and northern Europe confirms that Gothic had lost its hold, and the supremacy of classical detailing reigned. In Vienna, Johann Bernhard Fischer von Erlach (1656–1723) was the designer of the Karlskirche (Figure 10.7), a major Baroque monument. It encourages its visitors to look up at the dome, where a variety of figures and objects, freed from the weight of gravity, float around haphazardly. It is a painting with an illusionistic view upward into the skies and heaven. The plan is an oval. The over-

hanging cornice forms a distinctive break from the wall's surface. A ring of windows encircles the dome, followed by an entablature that frames the ceiling and that combines oval windows, at the top of which is a lantern, also a source of sunlight.

The decoration of the walls is with restrained, gilded Corinthian pilasters, which, in addition to the streaming sunlight, draw attention to the visual complexity of the dome.

The association of Baroque design with curves is correct. Yet there are also resolutely rectilinear examples of Baroque architecture particularly outside of Italy, one of them being Fischer von Erlach's Schönbrunn Palace in Vienna (Figure 10.8). In such structures, one finds the essence of Baroque design, the emotion, the restlessness, the movement, and the depth expressed in rectilinear projects. The palace itself is no flat block, but a figural object that both recedes and progresses into space.

Gardens

Garden design was important in the Baroque period. Landscape designers further developed an approach to landscape that started in the Renaissance and that used nature as a raw material. Baroque garden design also explored many of the design principles that Bernini developed for his urban design for the Vatican. The gardens of Schönbrun extend off into the distance. They are an important presence, and an integral part of the palace design. They appear to cut through a natural-looking forest, setting up a relationship between designed nature and natural nature. Just as many Baroque objects are considered to proceed forward into space, Baroque gardens aggressively march off into the distance, if not to infinity itself.

Neumann and Tiepolo

Johann Balthasar Neumann (1687–1753) was a German military engineer who became an accomplished architect with the encouragement of his chief patron, the Prince-Bishop of Würzburg. One of Neumann's largest works is the home of the Bishop, Das Residenz, built in 1735. It is a huge structure with a sober exterior, which gives little indication of the Baroque and Rococo delights that lie within it. This building and its interiors prove the fact that there is not always a precise dividing line between Baroque and Rococo art. In some circles, Rococo is considered as a final, if delicate, version of Baroque. There are many examples of Baroque buildings that were refashioned with Rococo interiors.

One of the finest Baroque ceilings is the collaboration of the German architect Neumann and Italian painter and frescoist Giovanni Battista Tiepolo (1696–1770). They worked together on the stairwell, the Treppenhaus, of Das Residenz (Figure 10.9). Stairways were a natural focus of Baroque designers, because their function involved both horizontal and vertical movement. This is the giant ceremonial staircase where guests, after having left their carriages, would mount the stairs to reach the suites of rooms on the upper, principal floor.

The central figure of the painted ceiling of the Treppenhaus is Apollo. In one vignette of the composition, Tiepolo painted those who contributed to the project: the architect Neumann, the stucco decorator Antonio Bossi, Tiepolo himself, his son Giandomenico Tiepolo, and his painting assistant, Franz Ignaz Roth. Tiepolo also grandly included his client, the resident of Das Residenz, Prince-Bishop Karl Philipp von Greiffenklau. Known as the Apotheosis von Greiffenklau, it shows the Prince-Bishop accompanied by the allegorical figure of Fame, who leads him to Apollo (Pedrocco 2002, pp. 137–140).

Guests first climbed a single flight of stairs, then arrived at a landing, from which two more flights rose to meet the second floor. This means that the viewers of the painting were themselves in continual motion, viewing the painting from changing vantage points.

Tiepolo was the most renowned painter of eighteenth-century Italy. Born in Venice, he was internationally successful, known for his contemporary, less rigid approach to classicism. He was in Würzburg from 1750 to 1753, working with his sons and assistants.

In the Garden Hall, on the first floor and overlooking the palace's garden, an oval ring of columns stands within the room's perimeter (Figure 10.10). A gap between the columns and wall adds depth to the space. From them springs the rippled ceiling whose decorative stucco work spills out of the architectural framework. A giant border of white-on-white plaster frames a flattened dome. The richly designed stucco work acts as a transition from the vertical to horizontal, a feat that is then taken over

Figure 10.9 Johann Balthasar Neumann, Giovanni Battista Tiepolo. Das Residenz. Stairwell. Würzburg, Germany.

with painting. The painted ceiling features a landscape and sky and numerous figures. The ceiling is painted not to be there, with clouds and spectacular rays of light coming from many directions. Nature in this garden hall is beguiling and menacing.

The sun god is the subject of another room, the Kaisersaal, in the complex. There, Apollo is seen conducting Beatrice of Burgundy to the Genius of the German Nation (1751).

Neumann also collaborated on the Kaisersaal

Figure 10.10 Johann Balthasar Neumann, Giovanni Battista Tiepolo. Das Residenz, Garden Hall. Würzburg, Germany.

with Tiepolo (Figure 10.11). It represents a lighter approach, predictive of the Rococo fascination with less significant moments in time. Pink, blue, and gold dominate the color palette, signaling a trend that moves away from the saturated colors of early Baroque design. The detail features a central oval frame, formed of both curved and straight elements, but certain figures from the painting defy the framing device and step out of and over the frame. Heavy elements miraculously float in midair, brusquely defying gravity. Certain elements recede back into space, while others spill forward toward the viewer. Neumann's and Tiepolo's interiors had undulating lines; they were dynamic and spatially complex, sometimes disturbingly so.

FRANCE

In France, the major Baroque buildings were not churches but residences. Versailles is a residence of the state, a work of architecture with a charge to express the French national character. French architects worked with Baroque fervor, not as an expression of religious sentiment but to express national power.

Figure 10.11 Giovanni Battista Tiepolo. Residenz, Ceiling of Kaisersaal. Würzburg, Germany.

Louis XIV

One historical figure is particularly related to French Baroque, and that is Louis XIV, both for how he lived and the art he patronized. Louis XIV consolidated the development of a French national style as part of a political program. Art and design were called into service of an absolute ruler. French artist Rigaud painted Louis XIV in 1702 (Figure 10.12). This is a portrait of political might: high-heeled shoes, flowing wig, heavy draperies, and gold are all signs of a powerful monarch at the height of his powers. There is nothing effeminate about this man. The background is not parallel to the picture plane, and Louis addresses his viewers at an oblique direction. This is the portrait of one of Europe's most powerful monarchs, using every-thing at his control—dress, coiffeur—to make a strong impression. The drapery is heavy and, like the heavy curtains behind the king, it peels back at several points to reveal ornate possessions. The colors include strong reds, blacks, and oranges.

The Louvre

Before Versailles became the center of the design world, considerable attention was paid to completing the eastern portion of the Louvre. In this project, the competing architectural approaches of Italy and France came head to head. Bernini's Louvre featured the geometry he was known for, a central oval and flanking curved wings, and a colossal order sitting on a tiered base. This project, and two subsequent projects Bernini designed, were rejected.

Louis XIV and his advisors decided on a restrained classical building, suggesting that the French conception of Baroque architectural design departed from the Italian. The project that stands in Paris today is the result of Le Vau, Le Brun, and Claude Perrault. Its Baroque features are the depth of its façade and its rhythmic use of paired columns.

French designers were aware of Italian achievements, yet they also furthered a local nationalistic agenda. Louis XIV had a director of building, Jean-Baptiste Colbert, who brought Gianlorenzo Bernini to Paris. French designers were important in establishing the reputation of France for crafting highly developed gardens, buildings, interiors, and furnishings.

Figure 10.12 Rigaud. Portrait of Louis XIV. 1702.

Vaux

An early work, a seminal piece of French Baroque architecture, was by the architect Louis Le Vau (1612–1670). Vaux-le-Vicomte, a country house or chateaux, was designed for Louis XIV's finance minister, Nicolas Fouquet (Figure 10.13). A bulbous central mass protrudes from the building, aggressively asserting itself forward into space. It corresponds to the most important interior room, an oval salon. The chateau at Vaux is a forerunner to Versailles, where all the design elements were first experimented with.

As at Schönbrunn, the architecture is an integral part of the garden design. André Le Nôtre (1613–1700) designed Vaux's gardens, which established the guidelines for the French approach to palace garden design. The interiors survive intact and are a good example of interior design of the time of Louis XIV, prior to major construction at Versailles. The same trio of designers who worked at Vaux, Le Vau, Charles Lebrun, and Le Nôtre, also worked at Versailles. Le Vau's purposely inconsistent use of the architectural orders in Vaux-le-Vicomte was something that the young Louis XIV admired.

When Louis XIV visited Vaux, he was impressed with its design but wary of its cost. Ensuing investigations led to the imprisonment of Fouquet, and the three designers set to work remodeling the royal residence at Versailles.

Versailles

Louis XIV considered himself the world's most powerful leader, and he sought an architectural backdrop that not only reflected that power but added to it. The siting of the seat of government away from Paris put all under his roof and under his control. Part of his power was the awe that those

Figure 10.13 Louis Le Vau. Vaux-le-Vicomte. Maincy, France.

who visited Versailles felt at the richness of the architecture, the opulent interiors, the expensive furniture, and the clothing of the nobles inside the palace.

At the core was the old chateau Louis XIII had built in 1624, a brick and stone structure. In the 1660s, Louis XIV had had it enlarged by Le Vau, Le Nôtre, and others. In 1677, Louis XIV decided to move the court and the nation's administration to the former hunting lodge that lies some 20 kilometers southwest of Paris. Thirty-six thousand workers labored to create a place that would eventually house 100,000 people.

Versailles' growing opulence reflected the economic and political consolidation of the country.

Versailles became the seat of the French government in 1682. It became the model that other European monarchies sought to emulate, and also nobles in the French provinces. Versailles was the center of the design world.

The new palace needed to be furnished, so Louis XIV was also instrumental in promoting several manufacturing enterprises. He started a furniture manufactory, the Gobelins, to create furniture and tapestries for the royal palaces. Over the seventeenth century, the quantity of furniture found in a palace greatly increased.

Gardens

As at Vaux, André Le Nôtre was responsible for the garden design. Le Nôtre's signature move was to create a work of environmental greatness that included earthworks, pools and fountains, topiary, clipped hedges, and geometric flower beds (Figure 10.14). The axial relations of the garden and the building were one, an integrated whole that relied heavily on symmetry. The gardens impressed European nobles and every royal family did what they could to imitate them. Le Nôtre regularly used an open-ended perspective, which symbolized Louis XIV's ambitions for France. The iconography of the garden sculpture brazenly connected Louis XIV to Apollo the Sun God.

Baroque gardens represent a particular treatment of nature, where nature is an architectural material that can be used, cut up, or reconfigured to provide dramatic effects. Part of this effect were pools, canals, and extensive waterworks. The extent to which nature is tamed, and forced into submission by art, reflected French mastery over the elements and scientific achievements. The French attitude to nature, as espoused by landscape design-

Figure 10.14 Gardens of Versailles.

Figure 10.15 Louis Le Vau. Garden façade. Versailles. France.

ers such as Le Nôtre, was antithetical to the English tradition. French Baroque gardens continued trends that originated in the Italian Renaissance, yet on an unimagined scale. It is fair to describe the French Baroque garden as an Italian Renaissance garden on steroids.

In the wake of Versailles, the designers of palaces around the world sought to emulate it, including the Nymphenburg in Munich, the Zwinger in Dresden, and Peter the Great's palaces in St. Petersburg. L'Enfant's urban plan for Washington, D.C., is formally related to Le Nôtre's garden designs.

Versailles was the most significant, and certainly the largest, if not the most artistically innovative project of Baroque France. Louis Le Vau worked with the existing chateau that had already been enlarged. Le Vau refashioned its garden façade with a new structure that from the perspective of a visitor in the garden completely enveloped the original building and its entry court. Three blocks form the basis of Le Vau's design. The center block was set back with a terrace. The rhythm of "solid-recession-solid" invites nature into the building, and subtly projects building into nature. A stately row of Ionic pilasters integrates the three blocks of Le Vau's design. They sit on a rusticated base.

The Palace

Le Vau's work at Versailles had an Italianate flat roof with a balustrade instead of a steeped French roof (Figure 10.15). Le Vau's façades did not rely upon curves for their effect, but there was a real depth to them. The porticoes protruded and the window wells receded. The profusion of ornament around the windows was deeply carved and figural, the opposite of the flat early-Renaissance surfaces. The statuary on the rooftop continue the lines of pilasters. Le Vau's first major project for Versailles consisted of simple cubical forms that were beautifully detailed. Its delicate composition did not last long.

After Le Vau's death, his position as principal architect at Versailles was taken by Jules Hardouin Mansart (1619–1690).

Mansart's refashioning resulted in a dazzling interior space that marks the beginning of a Rococo sensibility, yet some consider that his additions robbed the complex of the refinement it had reached under Le Vau's watch, particularly concerning the building's massing and its formal relationship to the garden.

Mansart tripled the length of the garden façade. He filled in the recessed central block and made it flush with the flanking blocks in order to build the centerpiece of his remodeling, the Galerie des Glaces. New wings to the north and south of Le Vau's building created a huge structure whose overall façade extended some 600 yards.

Interiors

The consideration of Mansart's work at Versailles is more favorable from the perspective of its interiors and furnishings. Le Vau, Mansart, and Le Brun, a painter and architect who supervised many of the decorations, were responsible for a remarkable set of rooms that functioned as a central part of the French state apparatus. Their work included new apartments for the king and queen, a grand staircase, a suite of seven public rooms named after the planets, and the centerpiece, the Gallerie des Glaces.

The apartments for the king and queen used stucco, gilding, and paint to create illusionistic scenes on the walls and ceilings. Marble covered the floors, and velvet was used as wallcovering and upholstery. Le Brun and Le Vau collaborated on the Stairway of the Ambassadors, a deft composition that also created illusionistic architecture by combining marble panels and paint. This vertical circulation space made an impressive first impression on foreign dignitaries to the French court.

The next step of the spatial and sensual experience of visiting Versailles included a suite of seven public rooms that similarly combined painted architecture, marble floors, and opulent furnishings.

The staircase and the salons were preparation for the culmination of a visit to Versailles: a long gallery overlooking the gardens, known as the Galerie des Glaces, or Hall of Mirrors. Mansart filled in Le Vau's terrace in order to construct this gallery and two adjacent salons. Designwise it was conventional, yet it was built with an unprecedented scale and level of opulence.

It is a long gallery crowned with a barrel vault. Arched windows overlook the manicured gardens and are literally reflected by a wall of similarly arched mirrors framed with the same architectural details. Candelabra, both free-standing and ceiling-hung, illuminated gilded capitals, illusionistic ceiling paintings, and a complete suite of silver furniture. The room is a negotiation between the use of a classical vocabulary and the desire for Baroque dramatic effects. The space was further enlivened by its occupants, exquisitely dressed, powdered, bejeweled, perfumed, and coifed men and women.

Mirrors were costly. Poor families could not afford them, and wealthier families publicly announced their status with a single hallway mirror. To construct an entire room that used mirrors freely, as an unlimited architectural material, and then to fill that room with silver furniture, was an expression of wealth meant to impress and intimidate.

Later, Mansart designed the royal chapel, with Robert de Cotte doing the stucco work (Figure 10.16). A painted vaulted ceiling combines large amounts of white space with gilding and natural light.

Under Louis XIV and the artists he employed, the arts were central to his political strategy. They were a means to centralize authority and create unity. They expressed both the king's and the state's power to both domestic and European audiences. Louis XIV's involvement with art, architecture, and design is likely the most extensive control that a state has ever wielded over the arts. Legions of artists, gardeners, and craftsmen were all marshaled into serving the glory of France.

British art historian Anthony Blunt felt that at Versailles, sometimes the parts are more impressive than the whole. He singled out the interiors and furnishings by Le Vau, Le Brun, and Mansart for praise.

Figure 10.16 Robert de Cotte. Royal Chapel. Versailles. France.

"But if the principles are not original, the application of them is so brilliant as to produce quite new results. The scale, the richness of the materials, the delicacy of the detail, the ingenious relation of the three rooms to each other, all make of this suite something far more impressive than any earlier work in this style" (Blunt, p. 229). French Baroque design did not follow in form the complex geometries of Bernini and Borromini.

In 1665, Bernini returned to Italy. The only project he completed in France was a bust of Louis XIV.

Louis XIV and his artists gave the Baroque style a secular twist, an aspect where it departed from the Italian Baroque tradition. Most of the great French commissions were related to building and furnishing royal palaces. The result was that Versailles dominated France and France dominated Europe.

Furniture

The development of French Baroque furniture had started when Henry IV (1553–1610), the first Bourbon king, set up furniture workshops in the Louvre. In furniture design, there was a shift from functional to decorative pieces. While seat furniture followed the models of the previous period, there was a growing multiplicity of furniture types that would be expanded even further in subsequent periods. Furniture of the late sixteenth century increasingly complemented the interiors.

Under the administration of Louis XIV and Colbert, the Parisian furniture industry was organized into a system with three components: royal workshops, the guilds, and the neighborhood—the Faubourg Saint-Antoine. Colbert founded the Gobelins factory in 1667 under the direction of Charles Le Brun. Its charge was to provide furnishings, paintings, and tapestries for royal households. As a royal workshop, its furniture makers were allowed to have apprentices and employ foreigners. The Savonnerie was the French carpet factory that became a royal workshop, also under Le Brun's leadership. The royal workshops of the Louvre produced various types of artworks and furnishings destined for royal palaces.

The guilds, predecessors to professional organizations and unions, were not allowed to hire foreigners. Auslander describes their operation as somewhere between free-trade and regulated manufacturing (Auslander 1996, p. 95).

The Faubourg Saint-Antoine is where most Parisian furniture makers set up shop who were not affiliated with the royal workshops or members of the guild. They were not part of the apprentice system. The results of their efforts ranged from pedestrian to good.

A topic that concerns historians of design is the matter of style. Why do things look the way they do, and why do those parameters change over time? Looking at Baroque furniture raises the issue of the evolution of styles. Considering first Renaissance furniture, then Baroque, then later Regency, Rococo, and Neoclassical, each style appears to engender the next in an evolutionary way, and the reference to nature is explicit. Sherrill Whiton, one of the early historians of interior design and furniture, was emphasizing precisely this point with a diagram that compares Baroque, Regency, and Rococo chair legs (Figure 10.17). The diagram treats the evolution of furniture scientifically, with each succeeding leg becoming increasingly curved and light.

One of the finest books written on furniture takes as its subject the development of French furniture prior to the twentieth century. Its skilled author, art historian, and one-time furniture maker Leora Auslander, is as adept at presenting a myriad of hard facts as she is with delivering nuanced interpretations. This chapter and the next rely heavily upon her efforts.

Women had a limited but significant role in the furniture industry. They did not typically work in the wood trades but did find employment as sanders, varnishers, and gilders. The art of upholstery, because it centered on textiles, was open to women.

Figure 10.17 Typical French Baroque, Regency, and Rococo chair legs.

Figure 10.18 Baroque armchair, c. 1680. France. From The National Trust Collection, UK.

The tasks that women were allowed to practice were not particularly creative but required a meticulous attention to detail (Auslander, 131). Auslander mentions several instances in which a woman inherited a workshop from her husband. Sometimes she ran the shop after her husband's death. It was not uncommon for these masters' widows to marry journeymen furniture makers.

The Baroque armchair is consistent with the aesthetics of other areas of Baroque art, such as sculpture and architecture (Figure 10.18). The Baroque armchair owes its overall form to the Renaissance sedia. The nature of the visual relationship between the two is that almost every element of the chair in the Baroque version has become more complicated in form, position, and decoration. The back, still straight across the top, is no longer up-right but leans backward. The arms curve in both their vertical and horizontal expressions. The legs, contiguous with the arms, are straight yet richly carved and decorated. The stretchers are no longer straight rails, but form an X- or I-shape, with pieces that have been turned, curved, and decorated. The amount of upholstery has increased. In comparison to the Renaissance sedia, the chair is dynamic. It has the presence of a work of Baroque sculpture; it leans back and protrudes forward into a room. Though solidly square and massive, it appears as if it could move.

A Regency armchair, in comparison to the standard Baroque one, is decidedly lighter (Figure 10.19). Regency is the transitional style between Baroque and Rococo. The curves of the Regency chair are pronounced, and the elements are more delicate,

Figure 10.19 Regency armchair. Louis XV. France.

with smaller profiles. The back itself is now curved and slightly tilts back. The legs have a pronounced curve to them. The X-shaped cross-stretcher is delicate and lightweight. Regency, also discussed in the next chapter, refers to the time when Louis XV was too young to reign, so the country was led by the regent.

A Baroque side chair has no arms, a curved back, severely raked rear legs, and straight although turned front legs, with the characteristic cross-stretcher (Figure 10.20). Generally speaking, sofas and chairs are lower to the ground. The back takes the form of a **bouchon**.

The Louis XIV **canopé**, a variety of sofa, has curved arms, and decorative carving frames the top and sides (Figure 10.21). The furniture associated with the Sun King, Louis XIV, inaugurates a system in France in which important pieces of furniture are labeled according to the reigning monarch. The most important styles of eighteenth-century France are, therefore, Louis XIV, Louis XV, and Louis XVI. A canopé is a descendant of the Roman couch or bed, to the extent that its user could recline while in the company of others. It is equally likely that the French sofa was a laterally expanded version of an armchair; they were decorated with all the design elements of chairs.

A gilded footstool was a handy piece of furniture. They typically had legs that were elaborately carved, while the stretchers twist and turn. Such pieces served as footstools, and also as seats, without armrests to encumber a voluminous gown.

The Baroque **console** c. 1680 shown in Figure 10.22 is a furniture piece that would be placed in an entry hall, likely with a mirror above it, and wall-mounted candle sticks. Mirrors were a sign of wealth, and were often paired with a console table. Two separate pieces, and additional accessories, became an ensemble. Consoles were marble- or wood-topped side tables. The mirror, like the ceiling, opened up and visually (not literally) broke through the architectural framework. This was an example of designers integrating pieces of furniture and interiors in a way not done previously. Pieces of furniture were no longer placed in isolation around a room.

The specialization of those involved in carpentry that started in the Renaissance continued. The main distinction remained between those who worked on the carpentry of buildings, and those who did furniture (Auslander, 77–85). Sawyers prepared lumber in the mill. Turners specialized in lathe work, producing legs, columns, and banisters. Sculptors specialized in carved panels, legs, and arms. *Menuisiers en bâtiment* did built-in cabinetry,

Figure 10.20 Baroque side chair.

Figure 10.21 Canopé, Louis XIV. France.

Figure 10.22 Baroque console, c. 1680. France.

staircases, doors, and moldings. They also created the chassis on which furniture makers crafted furniture. Carpenters who specialized in furniture created weight-bearing structures, including chairs, stools, and sofas.

Before the late seventeenth-century, most of the wood carpenters used to make furniture was European. Starting in the early eighteenth century, woods from Africa, the East and West Indies, and the Americas, were increasingly popular.

At the pinnacle of the hierarchical system of furniture makers was the **ébénist.** This talented furniture maker did the finest work, and focused on pieces with large surfaces (desks and tables) and larger space-containing items (wardrobes). The name of the profession indicates that they were initially associated with veneers, such as ebony, but they became masters of all sorts of marquetry. They did not make chairs; they were designers, and much of their work involved coordinating the labor of others. These allied professionals included metal workers. Bronze hardware and mounts became increasingly visible parts of furniture designs. Bronzes had to be cast, chiseled, filed, and polished. After

being attached by the ébenist, the mounts were gilded by a gilder. Marble similarly had to be cut, polished, and mounted. In addition to upholstering chairs and sofas, upholsterers provided draperies, bed cloths, and wall fabrics.

Veneered Furniture

Queen Marie de Médicis introduced the taste for ebony furniture. In France, the material lent its name to carpenters who specialized in veneered furniture. The most prominent of the ébénistes was André-Charles Boulle (1642–1732). His workshop created a wide variety of pieces but was known for its elaborate armoires (Figure 10.23). Boulle was the most celebrated of Louis XIV's furniture makers. He also worked for other members of the French royal family, other nobles, and Philip V of Spain. Boulle, his workshop, and his followers and imitators took polychrome wood marquetry to new levels. In addition to his celebrated furniture pieces, he did marquetry and parquetry floors, wainscoting, and paneling. Boulle and his numerous assistants became as knowledgeable about metal as wood. His ormolu mounts, larger than most, were integrated

Figure 10.23 André-Charles Boulle. Wardrobe. Boulle work. France.

elements of his designs. Ebony, pewter, brass, tortoiseshell, copper, mother-of-pearl, and colored foils were some of his favored materials. The subjects of his marquetry stemmed from classical mythology, but he also created popular scenes with secular references, such as *singerie.*

In crafting his furniture designs, he worked with inherited forms, but with his opulent decoration, he took those recognizable forms to a higher level. His work is credited with popularizing three furniture types: the console, the bureau plat, and the bas d'armoire. Over the decades of his workshop's

prominence, his pieces became lighter, more sculptural, and therefore more dynamic. His incorporation of the cabriole leg took his designs from the Baroque period into Regency. Spanning two centuries, Boulle's workshop was active for 80 years, first with Boulle, later with his sons, the most prominent of whom was Charles-Joseph Boulle (1688–1754). Boulle's influence is mostly seen in three stylistic periods—Baroque, Regency, and Rococo—yet some Neoclassical pieces were clearly inspired by his methods. He is known for a body of work that is internally consistent.

The term "Boulle work" came to indicate works in the style of Boulle and those done by his many imitators.

Boulle relied heavily on the use of **ormolu**, gilded bronze ornaments that were attached to furniture pieces. The process of gilding bronze involved heating mercury, which produced poisonous fumes detrimental to the health of those working with it. The production of furniture for the wealthy involved the death of those making it; it was therefore emblematic of a style that catered to the needs of the rich at the expense of the life of those who produced them.

Foreign influences on European furniture design increased over the course of the seventeenth century. From India came the habit of caning furniture. Travelers to China and Japan noticed with interest superior skill in lacquering. Lacquering in Europe was frequently referred to as **japanning.** John Stalker and George Parker wrote and published a book in 1688 titled *A Treatise of Japanning and Varnishing.* The topic of exoticism and Chinoiserie is covered in Chapter 11.

Pondering the existence of simple pieces of furniture within grand houses, Edward Lucie-Smith (1979) writes: "These small pieces represent an element of informality that had infiltrated what was still a very formal structure of living. Often they must have disrupted the grandiose decorative schemes of which the larger pieces of furniture in the same rooms formed an important part. One has a rather touching vision of people camping out amid their socially necessary but comfortable splendours, making themselves at home as best they could" (p. 87).

Furniture histories usually focus on more accomplished pieces, but common sense tells us that the greatest number of pieces were ordinary, utilitarian furniture. Much of this is virtually dateless and without obvious national characteristics. "Certain pieces of furniture, because of their essential practicality and usefulness, began during this period to achieve definitive forms which they were to retain for many years. Skilled but unsophisticated country craftsmen, usually joiners rather than cabinet-makers, repeated the same designs again and again, without changing them much, because they had been found to be the best for a particular purpose. A good deal of furniture thus escaped from the influence of fashion and, however unconsciously, responded only to the principle of fitness for use" (Lucie-Smith 1979, p. 91).

Because the industry was dependent on royal patronage and reputation, there was little advertising, although selling was important. **Marchands merciérs** were sellers, not producers, of furniture. They sold ready-made pieces, not at fixed prices, and sold on credit (Auslander 1996, p. 100). They increasingly functioned as taste masters, and in this capacity they served as early decorators. In addition to furniture, they sold clocks, mirrors, artworks, and porcelain. One of the most famous was Edmé-François Gersaint. The painter Antoine Watteau created a sign for him that became one of the most important works of eighteenth-century French painting.

The number of pieces of small furniture—such as tables, stands, stools—that were deployed in a room increased. The Baroque style gradually lost some of its essential characteristics in the aftermath of Louis XIV. The subsequent Regency and Louis XVI styles, in the first half of the eighteenth century, took design in a different direction. During this period, there was a decline in royal patronage and an increase in private residential work. This shift worked in favor of the marchands merciérs and the unallied furniture makers of the Faubourg Saint-Antoine.

CONCLUSION

Baroque art, architecture, and design are related to the Renaissance, which, appropriately enough, also began in Italy. Yet Austria, Germany, France, and England themselves became major centers of Baroque design. Like Renaissance design, Baroque design was inspired by antiquity, but this was true of details more than overall forms. Baroque architects favored centrally planned churches and classical façades, but in new configurations.

Baroque forms arose from mathematically complicated geometries that involved overlapping shapes and multiple focal points. Forms, like color palettes and compositional strategies, were neither pure nor distinct. In discussing Baroque artworks, most historians emphasize movement and emotion. The success at indicating movement is all the more significant in that buildings, paintings, sculptures, interiors, and furnishings rarely literally move. Yet one cannot describe Baroque art without verbs. The works bend, break, melt, flow, retreat, advance, ravish—and above all, they twist, turn, and curve.

Bernini was the major Baroque figure in Italy. The major figure in France was not himself a designer but the patron who marshaled their efforts, Louis XIV. He was responsible for rich decorative schemes and a national building program as ambitious as the world has ever seen. The works associated with Louis XIV, including interiors and furnishings, fostered the connection between design and national pride, wealth, and power.

Common Baroque features included illusionistic painting, ceilings painted to open to the sky, and a focus on stairways, domes, and deep façades. Mirrors and veneered furniture were popular for their dazzling effects. From gardens to candlesticks, Baroque designs were complex, plastic, and asymmetric. While clearly designed, the underlying order of a Baroque artwork is not easily discernible. The Baroque designed object was visually active, a remarkable feat because the activity was done by the viewer yet prompted by an incredibly complex object.

Sources

Auslander, Leora. *Taste and Power: Furnishing Modern France.* Berkeley: University of California Press, 1996.

Ballon, Hilary. *Louis Le Vau, Mazarin's College, Colbert's Revenge.* Princeton: Princeton University Press, 1999.

Ballon, Hilary. *The Paris of Henri IV: Architecture and Urbanism.* Cambridge: MIT Press, 1991.

Blunt, Anthony. *Art and Architecture in France, 1500–1700.* New Haven: Yale University Press, 1999.

Gerbino, Anthony. "The Library of François Blondel, 1618–1686." *Architectural History* 45 (2002): 289–324.

Lucie-Smith, Edward. *Furniture: A Concise History.* London: Thames and Hudson, 1979.

Pedrocco, Filippo. *Tiepolo: The Complete Paintings.* New York: Rizzoli, 2002.

Waddy, Patricia. *Seventeenth-Century Roman Palaces: Use and Art of the Plan.* Cambridge: MIT Press, 1990.

DISCUSSION AND REVIEW QUESTIONS

1. Put a Renaissance artwork next to a Baroque artwork—two portraits, two sculptures, two ceilings, or two armchairs. What are the significant differences between them?

2. What are the primary characteristics of a Baroque artwork?

3. People generally describe Baroque art as emotional. How do static objects create emotion? Give some examples.

4. A significant feature of Baroque art is its dynamism; pieces seem to be moving. How do static objects simulate motion?

5. A development of the late twentieth century is the idea that gender is constructed and not innate—that is, different societies developed their own concepts about gender. How did seventeenth-century France define masculinity?

6. What was the Baroque attitude toward nature, as evidenced by the gardens of Versailles?

7. List some of the materials used in the construction of Boulle works.

8. Do you think it is inevitable that an artistic period of simplicity is followed by one of complexity?

9. How do Regency pieces of furniture differ from Baroque pieces?

10. What role did mirrors play in interiors?

CHAPTER 11

ROCOCO

1643–1700	1700–1730	1730–1760	1760–1789
Baroque	Regency	Rococo	Neoclassical

The Enlightenment is a magnificent chapter in history in which the forces of many disciplines come together. The emphasis of the name of this intellectual movement, in three languages—Enlightenment, Sîecle des lumières, Aufklarung—was on light. This seems right, as those active in science, philosophy, politics, and the arts focused on changing the status quo. The Enlightenment was the force that shined light on its subjects and saw them in a new way. After the Renaissance, many feel that it was the defining moment in the creation of a modern emancipated public, based on reason and thought, and opposed to monarchy and theocracy. With the assistance of Enlightenment thinkers, Europe recrafted democracy, promoted equality, promised individual liberty, and endeavored to build a secular state and moral code. The reliance on reason was central.

Enlightenment polemicists were idealists, and reality often failed to live up to promises. Just a few points: It was unquestionably Eurocentric, and some see it as an apology for colonialism. Equality was an ideal that excluded many, including women and nonwhites.

There was no direct artistic equivalent of the Enlightenment, and yet the artworks of the period were inevitably caught up in the desire to craft a new world, intellectually, materially, and artistically. Artistic production of the eighteenth century was characterized by rapid stylistic change. Four distinguishable styles presented in succession: Baroque, Regency, Rococo, and Neoclassical. This represents a modern trend, the speeding up of stylistic change, which will be the case from this point forward.

Rococo is the primary stylistic legacy of the mid-eighteenth century. It is inextricably associated with France, yet the artistic force was strongly felt in Austria, England, Germany, Italy, and elsewhere. It occurred during the reign of Louis XV and the early years of Louis XVI's reign. Compositionally, Rococo artists favored asymmetrical designs. The style was most prevalent in the decorative arts, painting, sculpture, interiors, and fashion. Its formal qualities were often undetectable in architectural exteriors. Considered an elite art, its subject matter and visual impression was not ponderous but light.

This book has presented some marvelous pieces of furniture. Yet it has been constantly necessary to qualify that, for example, while the Renaissance saw great achievements in art and architecture, strides in interiors and furnishings were of a lesser degree. With the eighteenth century the importance of designed objects ascends. For the first time in this book, there is a period, the Rococo, whose greatest achievements were in interiors and furnishings. According to many connoisseurs, eighteenth-century English and French furniture are among the finest objects ever crafted.

The word *rocaille,* in use in France in the eighteenth century, literally referred to "rock work." Its use to describe a range of artistic productions is a twentieth-century invention. Rococo is another example of a word now used to refer to a body of work, including a number of important furniture pieces, that was not used in that sense in its own time. When French citizens in the eighteenth century said *"rocaille,"* they often meant it as an insult.

FROM BAROQUE TO ROCOCO: REGENCY

When Louis XIV died in 1715, it could be said that the Baroque died with him. Louis XV was a young boy and would not begin his reign until 1723. The period in which the country was ruled by a regent is known as Regency or Régence (not to be confused with English regency). It was a transitional style between Baroque and Rococo. It is often difficult to distinguish the differences between Rococo and French Regency pieces if seen out of context, although when they are placed side by side, the differences are evident. Generally speaking, Rococo curves are more pronounced, and the profiles are lighter than they were in Regency pieces. Once he arrived on the throne, Louis XV reigned from 1723 to 1774.

Cressent

Charles Cressent (1685–1768) was one of the most successful and prolific furniture designers. He is one of the relatively few cabinetmakers whose name is known. He started working during the reign of Louix XIV and became a leading cabinetmaker in the Regency period. Cressent specialized in fine marquetry work. **Marquetry** work involves creating scenes using pieces of veneer. Geometric marquetry is called **parquetry**. A French commode

Figure 11.1 Charles Cressent, Commode. c. 1745.

Figure 11.2 Rococo commode. France.

by Cressent is now in the Louvre in Paris (Figure 11.1).

Boulle and Boulle Work

André-Charles Boulle (1642–1732) was the favorite cabinetmaker for Louis XIV. His work moves into the Regency and Rococo periods. He made **armoires**, large-door cabinets that served the function of a closet, commode, and desk. Because he did not do seating, Boulle work pieces typically were lined up against a wall. An ébéniste, he worked with veneers and incorporated ivory, shell, brass, pewter, and silver. The tops were marble. The surfaces were painted, stained, sanded, lacquered, varnished, and gilded. Boulle work was continued by his four sons and imitated by others. Although initially the term "Boulle work" indicated pieces by Boulle or his workshop, it came to denote objects that resembled his. Extraordinarily expensive, in twenty-first-century

monetary terms, they would cost in the hundreds of thousands of dollars. A Boulle work chest of drawers, or commode, was made for Louis XIV in 1708 (Figure 11.2).

Ormolu mounts were decorative devices that protected the edges of veneered furniture (Figure 11.3). Veneered furniture is most likely to chip at its fragile edges, so both Cressent and Boulle relied heavily on the use of ormolu mounts. As the process of gilding bronze endangered the workers engaged in the process, it is thus a detail of furniture in which workers produced objects for the very rich and paid with their lives. It is worthwhile to remember that Regency and Rococo design were associated with the rich, and that this is the century that was marching headlong toward the French Revolution. As early as 1750, there were protests against the extravagance of the Rococo, and calls for artistic reform existed side by side with calls for political reform.

Figure 11.3 Ormolu mount. France.

ROCOCO

Rococo is often used as a shortcut to describe the works of the *ancien régime*. The phrase refers to prerevolutionary France and its political system of absolute monarchy. Design criticism of the period initiated a trend that haunts the consideration of interiors and furnishings to the present day: that works that are decorative are decadent, frivolous, vapid, and less important than other types of art—certainly not the argument of this book.

Historical Background

Art historian Matthew Craske prioritizes the economic and social causes of stylistic change over the course of the eighteenth century. Unprecedented economic growth and the effects of urbanization contributed to the prevalence of Rococo art. He writes: "A perplexing cocktail of positive and negative attitudes to urban growth arose concurrently not only in society at large but also in the minds of individuals" (Craske 1997, p. 12). The discussion of styles as discrete entities relates to the birth of a consumer culture. There were new means to advertise, market, and merchandise works. Also significant was the eventual rise of the public art museum; the first public rooms of the Louvre Museum opened in 1793. Materials were available that had previously been rare or nonexistent, including tulip wood, zebra wood, and ebony.

Emphasizing Effect Over Process

Art historian Marian Hobson articulated a way of considering the French arts, seeing in them a unity that extends from costume to theater to painting. Her point is that Rococo artists, in many fields, had a similar approach to illusion, with the result being an emphasis on effect (Hobson 1982). Her concept is best grasped by first considering a painting. For example, an artist is in a room, brush and palette in hand. In front stands a canvas on an easel, on which he or she will paint. Posing in front is the subject, the live person. In summary, this idealized setup presents artist, artwork, and live person.

One way of broadly considering Western art, admittedly a simplification, is that artists sought to mimic optical process; when Italian Renaissance artist Raphael painted a portrait, he endeavored to make the artwork—the image he created on a canvas—resemble as closely as possible the live body (one example being his portrait of Baldassare Castiglione, painted in 1514–1515). A portraitist in eighteenth-century France, according to Hobson's thinking, took a different tack. For example, the artist François Boucher (1703–1770) created his famous portrait of Madame de Pompadour in 1756. Boucher and Jean-Honoré Fragonard (1732–1806) were two of the most technically accomplished, and successful, Rococo artists. The emphasis of Boucher's work was no longer merely resemblance but the masterful tricks the artist could achieve on the canvas in order to render it as dazzling as possible (Figure 11.4). Effect on the canvas trumped verisimilitude. In the portrait of Madame de Pompadour, the artist emphasized the shimmering fabric, and the sprays of flowers and ribbons. The attention to the artwork, over fidelity to the subject, had obvious implications for theater and opera, where performance was everything. The focus on operatic effect was demonstrated by the popularity of castrated opera singers, **castrati,** in Italy and France. Male sopranos took the leading roles, playing heroic figures. No one thought that Julius Caesar, a popular operatic role, was a soprano, but French audiences preferred having a male soprano, in a powdered wig and resplendently dressed, portray him. The emphasis was on the brilliance of the performance, the sustained high notes, and not the actor's resemblance, in appearance or voice, to the historical figure.

Costume, makeup, and the art of wig-making followed suit. The towering wigs, the powder, the perfume—the goal was not to trick anybody into thinking that these attributes were real. In an introductory essay to an issue about the cultural meanings of hair, the art historian Angela Rosenthal (2004) writes: "In Europe, eighteenth-century individuals well-understood the potential of hair—be it powdered, dyed, curled, feathered, piled up to dizzying heights, or set into memorial jewelry—to communicate central cultural concerns" (p. 8). Wigs were an artistic realm where wig-masters displayed their expertise; it was also a realm where conceptions of race, ethnicity, nationality, and gender were explored.

Figure 11.4 François Boucher. Portrait of Madame de Pompadour.

Architecture and the French Hôtel

Architecture, interiors, and furnishings are not representational arts. A set of interiors does not represent something else, whereas Boucher's portrait of Madame de Pompadour does represent something other than itself, the "real" de Pompadour. The interior arts were consistent with the other arts to the degree that they also exploited the art of illusion and emphasized surface and effect.

Town mansions in Paris are known as *hôtels*; they were not an invention of the seventeenth century, although associated with it. Unlike Italian Renaissance *palazzi,* in which a large architectural block fills out the lot line, the hôtel has a strip of construction on the street, followed by a courtyard, which is in turn followed by the main body of the house. Architectural historian Michael Dennis sees in this building type the beginning of a suburban mentality (Dennis 1986). The first band is a screen that separates the house itself from street life. If space is permitting, there is an even more private and green garden in the back. The house is an object within a garden and separated from the urban fabric. The courtyard was the cour d'honneur.

Considering the relationship of building to garden and the sumptuousness of a building's interiors, Spiro Kostof (1995) recognized the importance of this time period: "There is general agreement that something critical happened in the course of the eighteenth century to jar Western architecture loose from its moorings and set it adrift toward an unpredictable future" (p. 547).

Boffrand

Gabriel-Germaine Boffrand (1667–1754) was a pupil of Jules Hardouin Mansart, Louis XIV's chief architect. Boffrand's Hôtel Amelot, 1717, is a rare plan that looks Rococo (Figure 11.5). That is because the oval courtyard dominates. The oval shape

affects the other parts of the building, causing them to bend and adapt their walls to the curvilinear geometry. Yet the layout of the house remains that of a standard hôtel: The street façade is followed by a zone of service buildings. The body of the house straddles the space between two outdoor spaces: the courtyard and the garden.

In 1735, Boffrand designed an oval room that was inserted into the existing Hôtel de Soubise in Paris (Figure 11.6). Boffrand's remodeling of the Hôtel de Soubise is considered one of the best Rococo interiors. The walls and ceiling were outfitted with white panels and a pale blue flattish domed ceiling. Gilded cupids frolic in the room John Pile (2004) calls "an astonishing display of Rococo virtuosity" (p. 177). Boffrand created an intimate space with imaginary pictorial realms.

Prior to this project, Boffrand was an unknown architect. Arguably the first work of Rococo design, his widely admired rooms were considered modern

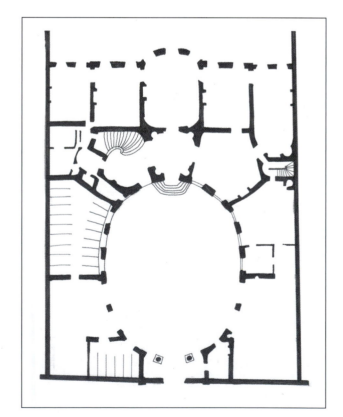

Figure 11.5 Boffrand Plan.

Figure 11.6 Germain Boffrand. L'hotel de Soubise, Paris.

in their time, as there was no classical detailing. They spawned legions of imitations.

Boffrand's room is oval in plan; its elevations are formed by a series of large rounded arches that alternate with smaller panels, also capped with a rounded arch. A system is adhered to: The larger rounded arches contain doors, mirrors, or windows. In classical architectural design, which Boffrand's room approximates in its composition, columns or piers supported the roof, with expanses of wall between them. The circular Temple of Vesta in Rome is the classical building closest in shape to the room at Soubise.

The smaller panels are vestiges of columns or piers, meaning that they would be structural elements, while the larger arches would be the intercolumnar spaces, or walls. Mirrors are positioned directly opposite the windows.

The mirror in the center of the photograph reflects a smaller oval panel. The large mirror over the fireplace reflects a window, itself centered within an arched panel. The large oval panels are at various levels of transparency. They allow for literal entrance and egress, through doors, yet the doors are opaque. Some rounded arches sport windows that allow for visual or imagined egress, yet glass panes restrain a moving body. Some of the arches frame mirrors, which allow for virtual egress: Reflected bodies look as though they are entering and leaving, yet it is an illusion. In Rococo interior layouts, mirrors were often positioned to diagonally reflect mirrors in other rooms, resulting in an infinite blur of expanded space.

The Soubise interior wall elevations suppress the differences between pier and wall. Everything becomes an undulating surface, articulated with the same system of gilded panels and stucco decoration. Doors and piers alike (architectural elements with different functions) receive the same decoration.

If the smaller panels are manipulated piers or columns, the triangular forms above them are either pendentives, the structural elements that distribute a ceiling's weight to the walls, or oversized capitals. Yet in Boffrand's composition, the "structural" elements are painted canvases, the least structural material possible.

Even the use of paint was consistent with the emphasis on effect and illusion, and the disinterest in representing real objects and materials. Wood in a Rococo interior was not a natural material whose inherent qualities were highlighted; it was a surface awaiting decoration. The application of white paint to woodwork and plaster alike rendered the materials unimportant.

Cuvilliés

Soubise deemphasizes structure by making piers and alternating panels of nearly equal visual weight. An equally accomplished room in Munich, Germany, takes the approach one step further. French Rococo interior design had a strong influence throughout Europe, particularly in Germany and Austria. The existence of French Rococo design in the Bavarian capital suggests two competing attitudes. One was the rise of a cosmopolitan culture. The Bavarian nobility wanted to operate on an international scale, and a clear signal of this was to embrace the latest trend in interior design. At the same time that Rococo decorating represented an urban, international culture, outside of France it was also considered an example of French affectedness, kowtowing to luxury, and a danger to German artistic traditions. Depending on the interpretation, it could be evidence of French cultural imperialism, the style connected to Europe's dominant commercial, cultural, and military power.

François Cuvilliés (1695–1768) was a French architect of Flemish origin, active in Bavaria. His first royal post in Munich was as "court dwarf." A little person, his artistic aptitude was quickly recognized, and he was sent to work for four years under the supervision of French architect and designer Jacques-François Blondel (1704–1774). He returned to Germany, where he produced several modest but influential projects. Credited with having introduced the French hôtel to Munich, he had the good fortune to be working within the parameters of French Rococo at the height of its popularity.

His works were at once restrained and ornate. The Amalienburg is a small garden palace on the grounds of the larger Nymphenburg Palace in Munich, built in the years 1734–1739. It has a subdued exterior, and the corners of the room are rounded.

Like Soubise, the principal room is circular and has windows that open to the garden (Figure 11.7). Stucco work, mirrors, a chandelier, and pieces of Rococo furniture, stools and consoles, constitute an ensemble design that is light and airy.

In this application of the latest French style,

nothing remotely resembles classical architecture, scarcely hinting at columns or pilasters. The decoration is applied, with no indication of the buildings' structure. This interior was non-architectural.

In designing the elevations, Cuvilliés expanded each rounded arch to be as wide as possible. The "structure" is reduced to the narrow vertical elements between them. Tellingly, the vertical lines do not fulfill a structural role. Instead of distributing weight to the floor, they turn into a decorative element: the mirror's frame. The Rococo wall, in the designs of Boffrand and Cuvilliés, two of the biggest names in Rococo design, has become a surface to be lavishly articulated; it no longer represents

structure. All surface, it is the opposite of the post-and-lintel structure at Stonehenge. Several of the infill panels are filled with a grid.

A detail from Amalienburg highlights the predominance of asymmetry (Figure 11.8). Trees, vines, swags, and urns are nestled into a bevy of S and C curves. Even the silver grid is canted to respond to swags. A favorite device of Rococo designers was the use of a grid. As Barbara Stafford (2007) writes, "The inlay, mesh, net, lattice, and grid: all pose the problem of fit" (p. 136). Although custom-made for the project, the use of the grid suggests that it was a material, like wallpaper, that could be used at will, and employed to solve the problem of an undecorated

Figure 11.7 François Cuvilliés, Amalienburg. Munich, 1734–1739.

Figure 11.8 Amalienburg Castle. Detail. Nymphenburg, Germany.

schemes demonstrated both the architect's and the client's mastery of the universe of goods and their control of the dominant cultural paradigm. The coherent decorative statement evinced a cultural competence in marked contrast to the fumbling uncertainty of those outside the orbit of polite society" (Scott 1995, p. 109).

The brothers Hoppenhaupt crafted similarly integrated designs for rooms for Frederick the Great in Potsdam, outside of Berlin. The desire of German nobles to participate in the latest style was evidence of French supremacy in the decorative arts.

Rococo was an art movement mostly associated with interiors, furnishings, the decorative arts, and graphics. It scarcely made an impact on urban design. This does not mean that no building was done on the urban or architectural scale, simply that those projects do not exhibit characteristics that can be defined as Rococo. Many Rococo interior designs were fitted into buildings whose exteriors were Baroque or something else. Versailles, Schönbrunn in Vienna, and the Residenz in Würzburg are all Baroque palaces with extensive Rococo interiors.

space. Allegorical figures are the only allusion to classicism. Some items lean into the distance; others break the frame and advance forward.

Cuvilliés also did the *Reichen Zimmer* (Ornate Rooms) at the Residenz in Munich, another example of integrated decoration. In German Rococo works, the designer acted autonomously, and actually had more control than with French commissions, resulting in a complete integration of architecture, furniture, and interior decoration. In his remodeling projects, he gave his German clients what they desired: the new-look *goût nouveau*.

Katie Scott is the author of a book on Rococo interiors. She describes the goal of a Rococo decorator, as articulated by Blondel, the mentor of Cuvilliés: "Interior decoration should, above all else, create a unified impression, analogous in this to the exterior treatment of the hotel. Coordinated decorative

Louis XV Furniture

The furniture production that started under Louis XIV continued under Louis XV. The number of Louis XV distinct furniture types was enormous, a departure from the Renaissance. When outfitting a room, patrons and their assistants—designers and merchants—could choose from a large selection of pieces. With a whole range of specific furniture types came a heightened sense of comfort, luxury, and decorum.

Fauteuil

The chair in Figure 11.9 is an extremely elegant piece of furniture, an object in the history of design that perfectly meets its own design criteria. The aggressiveness of the Baroque chair is gone. In contrast to Baroque and Regency chairs, the cross-stretchers have been eliminated. A Louis XV chair, also known as **Louis Quinze**, stands lightly on its legs. Yet it seems at rest because of the perfection of its proportions, lines, and silhouette. It is all curves. The back is lifted off the seat, the arms are curved, the legs are curved, and the back is curved. The curves are not segments of perfect circles but the result of a complicated geometry.

The color scheme of the chair's upholstery employs a single color against a white background. The pattern of the textile looks symmetrical or at least balanced, yet closer inspection reveals that it is not. In the progression from the Renaissance sedia to this chair, furniture design became consistently lighter and more curvilinear. The **cabriole** leg, the vertical support with a gentle S curve, was fully developed.

Figure 11.9 French Rococo Louis XV chair.

This armchair is known as a **fauteuil,** an armchair with upholstered seat, lifted back, and open padded arms. *Fauteuil* literally means armchair in French, but it is commonly used to refer to Louis XV and Louis XVI chairs. Delicate cresting in the center completes the top rail. A seated person's arms rest on **manchettes,** small upholstered pads. The legs have carved knees that are formed of scrollwork, as are the feet. The back takes the shape of a **cartouche**.

Bergère

A more informal chair was the **bergère** (Figure 11.10). The bergère is a larger, commodious armchair, with enclosed back and arms. *Bergère* literally means farmer's wife, and the naming of the chair relies upon an idealized idea that a farmer's wife, after milking the cows, might rest for a moment in such a chair. Of course, this is nonsense. Chairs of this type were out of the price range of most farmers. A bergère had a separately upholstered seat cushion and a full backrest, and the upholstery of the arms is continuous with the back. A profusion of curves in the legs, seat, and back hid the effect of its substantial weight-supporting structure.

A pet project of the queen is related to the bergère. Marie Antoinette's architect, Richard Mique, built for her a rustic house on the grounds of Versailles. The Hameau, or hamlet, was built in 1783. Modeled after a farmhouse, it was a retreat for the queen and her attendants, where they could escape from Versailles' spotlight, dress in simple clothes, and enjoy the pleasure of milking cows.

Furniture in midcentury was less likely to be moved about from house to house, a fact evident in the delicate leg profiles. Pieces were made in large numbers, so there are many examples of rooms being furnished with matching furniture, or furniture **en suite**. Art historian Mimi Hellman wrote an article in 2007 that addresses the importance of matching pieces of furniture: "Many of the basic

Figure 11.10 French Rococo
Louis XV bergères, c. 1775.

elements of a well-appointed social space—couches and chairs, commodes and tables, tea sets and vases, decorative paintings—were designed as groups of objects that were either identical or closely coordinated in medium, color, style, or figurative motif. A sustained interest in matching first emerged in upholstery design during the seventeenth century, and by the early eighteenth century it was a widely practiced formal strategy" (p. 130). The appeal of matched sets was evident when families reupholstered mismatched pieces—using a single textile. Some families combined Louis XV and Louis XVI pieces, blending them together with a monochromatic color scheme.

Performing Objects

Furniture was not just a reflection of wealth but also a social player. The elite lived according to an elaborate system of etiquette that accommodated moments of formality and informality, and with pieces of furniture acting as social brokers. The social structure was rigid, but the more rigid the structure, the more intense the appeal of improvisation.

The **confidant** demonstrates how a piece of furniture was a player in social life (Figure 11.11). A large seating unit, it was usually positioned against a wall or in a niche. The confidant encourages sitters to sit close to one another yet be separated. Although they faced in different directions, the possibility existed of whispering to each other. The separating devices maintained decorum, but the sanctioned closeness allowed for a hushed intimacy. This was perfectly in fitting with themes addressed by artists, including Antoine Watteau (1684–1721), whose paintings highlight seemingly innocuous moments of conversation or casual activities like playing cards and blowing bubbles.

In another article by Hellman, she cleverly considers French furniture not as static objects but as agents. The art of leisure, as it related to furniture, looked easy, but, Hellman argues, was actually difficult and learned. Furniture was at the heart of eighteenth-century French elite culture. They were important artistically and socially, and played a pivotal role in the development of a French national identity that presented itself to the world in terms of its artistic achievements.

The aesthetics of eighteenth-century French interiors are widely studied. All components of an interior—wall and ceiling treatments, draperies, and furnishings and fittings—were carefully considered. Hellman describes the delineation of interiors and furnishings as a two-part system, one part fixed, the other movable. The fixed part included the architectural envelope, the walls made of paneling or **boiserie**, fireplaces, and some pieces of furniture. For all practical purposes, heavy pieces were not moved, including **consoles** with marble tops. These pieces constituted the architectural backdrop, the stage set for the "actors," which includes furniture and people interacting with them. The second system involved the lightweight objects, dressing tables, music stands, coffee and chocolate services, and individual seat furniture—all objects that moved about (Hellman 1999, pp. 419–20).

Hellman argues that pieces of furniture acted on the people who used them, rather than the other way around. She writes: "Tables, chairs, and other decorative objects were social actors that both facilitated and, in a sense, monitored the leisure acts of privileged society. Through strategically designed aspects of form and function, furniture appeared to accommodate and flatter its users as they pursued such activities as reading, writing, conversing, eating, dressing, and game playing. Through the same design qualities, however, furniture also structured and delimited the behavior and appearance of individuals according to culturally specific codes of social conduct" (Hellman 1999, p. 416).

That these obsessively designed interiors were comfortable, Hellman calls "a central mythology" of eighteenth-century French culture (Hellman 1999, p. 420). The French considered the achievement in interiors and furnishings to be uniquely French. While the artistic achievement is undis-

Figure 11.11 French Rococo confidant.

Figure 11.12 Armchair, Louis XV.

puted, the comfort, *commodité,* is another matter.

Genevieve Souchal's book from 1961 is an example of the mythology of the comfort and grace of eighteenth-century furniture that Hellman feels is misguided. On the opening page, Souchal (1961) writes: "Never, even during the Renaissance, had the art of living developed so high a degree of fastidiousness, and certainly comfort and elegance had never previously been so effectively allied as they were then" (p. 7).

A **voyeuse,** or conversation chair, is an armchair whose upper back is padded as an armrest (Figure 11.12). The chair could be used for private in-house performances. One person was seated, while another stood behind, leaning on the backrest, ostensibly listening to the performers. This scenario was useful for those watching a card game.

François Boucher's painting of 1747 is titled *Are They Thinking About the Grape? (Pensent-ils au*

raisin?). It depicts an amorous pair; she feeds him a grape, and the barely hidden subtext is that they are thinking of something else. A voyeuse is the furniture equivalent to Boucher's painting. If a man were standing behind a seated woman and he leaned forward—allegedly interested in the performance—he was perfectly positioned to stare down the décolletage of her dress.

There is no doubt that the aesthetic and artistic transformation of France, begun by Louis XIV and consolidated by Louis XV and Louis XVI, was admired and emulated by all the European courts. The French cemented their place as the world authorities on artistic matters. But Hellman stresses that the apparent ease and comfort of eighteenth-century French furniture was just that, an appearance. Pieces of furniture could ease, or hinder, the desire to appear knowledgeable and graceful.

Beds and Daybeds

Beds were important objects of the French state's political apparatus. Versailles was outfitted with state beds for the king and queen. The daily witnessing of the **levée,** watching the monarchs rise from their beds and start the day, was a reaffirmation that the country, which was synonymous with the royal family, was doing well.

The German-born American anthropologist Franz Boas (1858–1942) introduced into the popular realm the connection between culture and language, specifically looking at vocabulary elaboration. He noted that the Eskimos (Inuit) had innumerable words for snow. There is a question as to the accuracy of Boas's observation (the discrepancy rests on the Inuit use of prefixes and suffixes), yet the concept of vocabulary elaboration became mythologized. Boas's undisputed point was that snow was important to the Inuit. The Inuit were linguistically responding to their natural environment; the eighteenth-century French were building

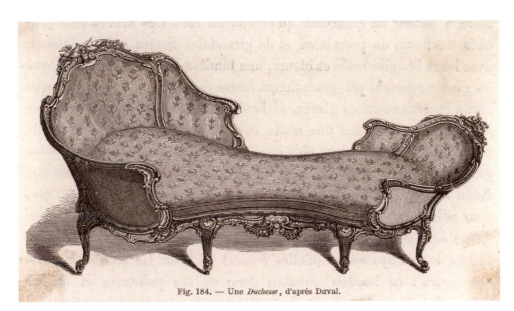

Fig. 184. — Une *Duchesse*, d'après Duval.

Figure 11.13 French
Rococo meridienne.

their own, literally, with their interiors and furnishings, and linguistically, with hundreds of words that refer to distinct furniture types.

In the private realm, a series of pieces allowed a person to recline while in the company of others. A **meridienne** provided a place for a person to relax, artfully arranged perpendicular to the viewing angle of visitors (Figure 11.13). This encouraged a sitter to be at ease in a social setting, yet it did not encourage total relaxation. **Chaise longue, settée, canapé, duchesse,** and **duchesse brisée** are some of the terms that refer to specific types of sofas and couches. A meridienne was an example of seat furniture that no longer lined walls but occupied a prominent place in the center of a room.

Flat Surface and Space-Containing Furniture

A **bureau plat** is today known as a table desk, meaning that it has no apron, front panel, or side drawers that rest on the floor (Figure 11.14). A graceful piece of furniture, it looks like a table. (This type was less popular with the English, who preferred library desks, heavy-looking desks with fronts that extended down to the floor.)

Another important category of Rococo furniture was mechanical furniture (discussed later). A high level of craftsmanship was exhibited in exceedingly complex pieces, such as a rolltop desk. A rolltop desk, **bureau à cylinder,** was a writing desk that responded to the increasing need for storage.

There were numerous varieties of **commodes,** a piece that provided storage and a surface for the display of objects. A commode was the standard chest of drawers. Taller chests were uncommon

Figure 11.14 Rococo desk, bureau plat (table desk). France.

Figure 11.15 Console.

(Figure 11.1). A commode typically had two, three, or four drawers; some had doors.

A **console** leaning against a wall is the epitome of a Rococo furniture ensemble (Figure 11.15). The ensemble consisted of a mirror, hung in the center of an architectural panel, a console placed beneath it, and candles at its sides. A console looks as though it is unstable, defying one of the definitions of what a piece of furniture should be: a freestanding piece of furniture. A console is half a table, although reflected in a mirror it appears to be a whole table. This is strange, as then the "correct" table was an illusion, the "real" table incomplete. Consoles, or side tables, were for display and contained no storage. There are curves everywhere, gilded wood, ormolu mounts, and a stone top.

A **gueridon** was a small, ornate pedestal table that often served as a stand for a candelabra. Candles were the primary source of light; hence candlesticks, candelabras, and wall brackets were numerous. Paired with a mirror, the ensemble of a reflecting mirror and a shiny candelabra in crystal or metal was an ideal source of flickering light.

Rococo pieces required the work of many trades.

Charpentiers, carpenters, did rough carpentry. They were responsible for creating a chair's **chassis,** or framework of a chair. **Menuisiers** were artisans of more refined work; they made chairs, carved pieces, mirror frames, and console tables. These groups collaborated with those who specialized in marble, and finishers who did sanding, painting, varnishing, and lacquering. A gilder provided hardware, locks, drawer pulls, and mounts. They collaborated with another group, upholsterers.

As in the Baroque period, **ébénistes** were the highest level of furniture makers, and they crafted veneered pieces. Their professional name stems from one of the veneers they worked with, ebony. Ébénistes also excelled at the complicated mechanical pieces that were the pride of a Rococo household.

The father-and-son firm of Abraham Roentgen (1711–1793) and David Roentgen (1743–1807) operated out of a town close to Cologne, Germany. Their accomplished workshop sold pieces throughout Germany and France. David Roentgen sold several pieces to Marie-Antoinette. Specific pieces were made for card-playing, writing, reading, working, sewing, and eating. English furniture makers also became adept at copying French pieces and brought the Rococo style across the English Channel.

Some mechanical pieces were complicated, delicate, and technically complex. *Sprezzatura* is a musical term, yet it also refers to any art form in which the final result makes the difficult process look easy. A dressing and writing table made by the Roentgen workshop is as much a technical accomplishment as an aesthetic one (Figure 11.16). When open, it resembles a NASA command center as much as a piece of furniture (Figure 11.17). Thinking of Hellman's work, this desk demanded that a user was knowledgeable about its operations, and also graceful to use it correctly and not appear clumsy.

Figure 11.16 Roentgen. Dressing table, closed.

Figure 11.17 Roentgen. Dressing table, open.

Chinoiserie

Chinoiserie refers to Western imitations or evocations of Chinese art, a western style inspired by China. These works were popular in the seventeenth, eighteenth, and nineteenth centuries. The pieces were often standard European shapes, such as consoles and commodes, decorated with Chinese motifs. A manual to assist those interested in Chinoiserie came when William Chambers published his *Designs for Chinese Buildings, Furniture, Dress, etc.* in 1757.

The **cabinet** shown in Figure 11.18 is not a piece of Chinese furniture but one of the many examples of European decoration inspired by a fanciful idea of China. Exoticism and interest in foreign lands were prominent in art, opera, and the decorative arts. Chinese wallpapers, real and imitation, were popular.

Chinoiserie was the most prevalent of the foreign interests, but there were others. Those active in the decorative arts showed considerable interest in Turkey, India, and Persia. The minor trend of monkey motifs used in the decorative and graphic arts is

Figure 11.18 Lady being Perfumed by Monkeys, from La Grande Singerie, c. 1735 (painted panel), artist Christophe Huet (1700–1759).

Figure 11.19 Japanned console.

known as **Singerie.** Art historian and artist Elizabeth Liebman provocatively suggests that monkey pictures were anything but innocent: "The animals in these images do not wear the collar of the organ grinder's gentle companion; rather, they are masculine brutes, shackled at the pelvis in order to restrain the impulses of a body bereft of reason" (Liebman 2003, p. 137).

If a piece of furniture was **japanned,** that meant that it was lacquered. Japanned pieces were popular in England, France, Germany, and the United States. A wooden two-drawer console owned by the Victoria and Albert Museum is a French piece finished to look Eastern (Figure 11.19). It has a marble top, veneered and lacquered sides, and ormolu mounts. Its pictorial composition, spread out over the five panels of its sides and front, vaguely resembles a Japanese screen. In addition, there was the fashion of purchasing Chinese and Japanese screens and taking them apart and using them for new pieces of furniture and in interior ensembles.

Maria-Theresa (1717–1780) was the mother of Marie-Antoinette and fifteen other children. She coped with her grief over the death of her husband by having his studio remodeled. The room of her palace in Vienna, Schönbrunn, was outfitted with lacquered Chinese panels that alternated with European-style paintings. Finished in 1772, it was called the "Vieux-Laque Zimmer" and became a popular place to show palace visitors. Michael Yonan (2004) discusses the specific meanings that the use of Chinoiserie could entail. About the room in Maria-Theresa's royal residence, he writes that "the specific possibilities inherent to China brought it a greater prominence in her court imagery. Vienna's position as leader not of a monarchical state but of a multicultural, polyglot empire had a useful parallel in the mythical China, one that allowed for nuances of meaning" (p. 662). While Chinoiserie was often used in superficial ways ignorant of Chinese and Asian history, occasionally the political reasons that underlay its use were knowledgeable and complex.

Decorative Arts and Graphics

An offshoot of Chinoiserie was the popularity of resetting Chinese vases in French-made ormolu mounts (Smentek 2007). The favored vases were monochromatic porcelain jars. The preference for monochromes and single-color schemes was an extension of the interest in matched sets (Figure 11.20). The mounts include swirling bulrushes, finials, and multiple swirls. Europeans had imported Chinese vases for centuries, most famously the blue and white variety. The monochromes popular in France in the eighteenth century were made in China in the late 1600s or early 1700s. Few made it to Europe, and their scarcity increased their value for the French. Many were produced for the domestic Chinese market. Creating monochromes was exacting work: The hard part was getting the color even, something less important in patterned work.

Figure 11.20 Chinese vases in French mounts.

The process of resetting the vases involved a lot of work. One reason for the mounts is that they may have hidden chips or cracks. The process of cutting the vases was exacting, arduous, and occasionally hazardous. The mounts were commissioned by **marchands merciers,** the sales force admired for their discerning taste. An artisan made a model in

Figure 11.21 Silver sauceboat, probably by Nicholas Sprimont. London, England, 1745.

wax, wood, or terra-cotta, from which the bronze caster made the various parts of the mounts. A **ciseleur** (chaser) did the filing and finishing of the raw bronze cast, and a **doreur** (gilder) gilded the bronze. The result of all the effort is that the Chinese vases looked French.

Rococo artists loved sea shells. Real sea shells were encrusted into the walls of garden grottoes, resulting in the rough-textured work called "rocaille." Some objects were created by fitting real shells with metal mounts. Artists were fond of drawing shells. Shells were made of a hard luminescent material. The resulting objects looked natural and effortless because they were natural. Shells, pearls, and mother-of-pearl were popular Rococo materials. Shells had a connection to classicism as the ancients were similarly enamored of shells.

Shells were also an inspiration for some pieces. A shell made of silver is a curious thing. A sauceboat in the form of a shell goes a long way to look natural (Figure 11.21). In Sprimont's piece, what is natural in nature was painstakingly manufactured. If logic is thrown out the window, the sauceboat looks like something that could wash up on shore. It is an improvement on nature because it is more perfect than nature; it is nature conceived by a Rococo artist and lacking nature's flaws. Creating a shell-shaped silver sauceboat was technologically difficult. This piece was part of an increasingly elaborate table service, in which pieces were created for exceedingly specific purposes.

Rococo forms were popular in graphics because they represented the latest fashion and because they often included forms that could exist nowhere except on paper. Artist and designer Juste-Aurèle Meissonier (1695–1750) published hundreds of engravings showing wall panels, candlesticks, and furniture designs, often of fantastic and unbuildable shapes. Flowing curves predominate, the layouts were asymmetric, yet they appear designed. Many forms derived from shells and foliage. The graphic

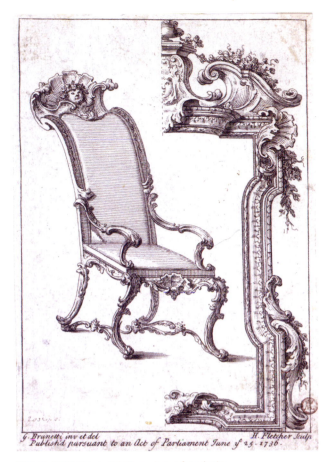

G. Brunetti inv et del
Publish'd pursuant to an Act of Parliament June y.e 25. 1730.
H. Fletcher Sculp

Figure 11.22 Brunetti. Drawing of a chair.

world of Meissonier was delicate, light, and florid.

Rococo graphic works exist in large numbers. They were frequently collected in pattern books, works that assembled examples of several designers, with the intention that they could be copied. The medium of two-dimensional representation was ideal, because it allowed the artistic imagination free rein, unfettered by practicality. It is difficult to imagine that Gaetano Brunetti's drawing of a chair, from a book published in London, could exist anywhere but on paper (Figure 11.22). Yet the carefully delineated frame could easily inspire a graphic artist.

Similarly, a London trade card is a graphic exploration of Rococo aesthetics and was likely inspired by a design in a pattern book (Figure 11.23). A trade card was a business advertisement; it included a field of text surrounded by a fantastic frame. The framing device is all curves and coun-

Figure 11.23 Trade card.

tercurves, with swags, vines, and tendrils, a semblance of nature that the natural world could never produce. The appeal of a Rococo graphic is that it was visually dynamic. The represented form fused nature and architecture, yet as a composition it was both attractive and unsettling. The eye has no place to rest, and there is no focal point—just an interminable series of curves and countercurves.

CONCLUSION

The taste for Rococo pieces survived into the early years of the reign of Louis XVI (1774–1779), although the pieces started to morph into forms associated with Neoclassicism. One of the anomalies of France in the eighteenth century involves the association of styles with political movements. Although Neoclassicism is generally associated with the Enlightenment, the French Revolution, and political reforms critical of the monarchy, its supporters included Louis XVI, Marie Antoinette, Madame

de Pompadour, and Madame du Barry, the last two the king's official mistresses. Neoclassical artists positioned themselves in opposition to Rococo, claiming that their creations were moral and not frivolous (see Chapter 14).

Rococo, a style aimed toward the very rich, also affected the tastes of the middle classes. Those in the middle and lower classes strongly felt the desire to emulate the nobility. Those on the lower rungs of the social ladder experienced Rococo design primarily through simplified decorative arts objects, such as French provincial chairs.

Material objects always exist within a cultural context. Hellman stresses that "objects were agents that highlighted and enhanced the attributes of others in a social system" (Hellman 1999, p. 434). Her work stresses that comfortable-looking items were not necessarily easy to use. An equally important observation is that items that gave an appearance of effortlessness were often exceedingly difficult to craft.

The designs created during the reigns of Louis XIV, XV, and XVI are prime examples of art being produced in service to the state. Art did not merely reflect state power, it was a tool of its implementation. The relation of art to state unravels in the following chapters, with an increasing number of individuals who grab the artistic reins for their own purposes and explorations.

Rococo design was a continuation of artistic explorations that started in Baroque Italy. The move away from classicism, the exploration of increasingly complicated geometries, and the preference for lighter profiles all reached their height in the Rococo period. The period that followed Rococo, Neoclassicism, was a repudiation of the art and objects that are the subject of this chapter. Yet Neoclassical furniture makers continued the attention to pleasing proportions and the high level of quality in construction. Neoclassical designers sought to craft a style that was the opposite of Rococo. With their attention to delicate, well-made forms, they joined their predecessors in continuing the tradition of fine furniture. The period 1716–1793, leading up to the French Revolution, was the golden age of French furniture.

Sources

Coffin, Sarah, et al. *Rococo: The Continuing Curve: 1730–2008*. New York: Assouline, 2008.

Dennis, Michael. *Court and Garden: From the French Hôtel to the City of Modern Architecture*. Cambridge: MIT Press, 1986.

Gallet, Michel, et al. *Germain Boffrand, 1667–1754*. Paris: Herscher, 1986.

Goodman, Dena, and Kathryn Norberg, eds. *Furnishing the Eighteenth Century*. New York: Routledge, 2007.

Hellman, Mimi. "Furniture, Sociability, and the Work of Leisure in Eighteenth Century France." *Eighteenth-Century Studies* 32.4 (1999): 415–445.

Hellman. "The Joy of Sets." From Goodman and Norberg's *Furnishing the Eighteenth Century*. New York: Routledge, 2007, pp. 129–153.

Hobson, Marian. *The Object of Art: the Theory of Illusion in Eighteenth-Century France*. New York: Cambridge University Press, 1982.

Koda, Harold, and Andrew Bolton. *Dangerous Liaisons: Fashion and Furniture in the Eighteenth Century*. New Haven: Yale University Press, 2006.

Kraske, Matthew. *Art in Europe, 1700–1830*. Oxford: Oxford University Press, 1997.

Levey, Michael. *Rococo to Revolution*. New York: Praeger, 1966.

Liebman, Elizabeth. "Unspeakable Passions: The Civil and Savage Lessons of Early Modern Animal Representations," from Richard Meyer, *Representing the Passions*. Los Angeles: Getty Publications, 2003.

Rosenblum, Robert. *Transformations in Late Eighteenth Century Art*. Princeton: Princeton University Press, 1967.

Rosenthal, Angela. "Raising Hair." *Eighteenth-Century Studies* vol. 38, no. 1 (Fall 2004): 1–16.

Scott, Katie. *The Rococo Interior*. New Haven: Yale University Press, 1995.

Smentek, Kristel. *Rococo Exotic: French Mounted Porcelains and the Allure of the East*. New York: Frick Collection, 2007.

Souchal, Genevieve. *French Eighteenth-Century Furniture*. New York: Putnam's, 1961.

Stafford, Barbara Maria. *Echo Objects: The Cognitive Work of Images*. Chicago: University of Chicago Press, 2007.

Stafford, Barbara Maria, and Frances Terpak. *Devices of Wonder: From the World in a Box to Images on a Screen*. Santa Monica: Getty Trust Publications, 2001.

Yonan, Michael. "Veneers of Authority: Chinese Lacquers in Maria Theresa's Vienna." *Eighteenth-Century Studies* vol. 37, no. 4 (Summer 2004): 652–672.

DISCUSSION AND REVIEW QUESTIONS

1. Name some specific types of furniture and their intended uses.
2. How did French furniture demand that its users be graceful?
3. How are Louis XV pieces different from Louis XIV?
4. How are Louis XVI pieces different from Louis XV?
5. What makes Louis XV pieces seem graceful?
6. What are the characteristics of Rococo architecture?
7. How do Rococo works, furniture, and architecture relate to Baroque pieces?
8. What was modern about Rococo design?
9. What similarities exist between Rococo furniture design and painting?

CHAPTER 12

ENGLAND

1500–1558	1558–1603	1603–1625	1625–1649	1640–1660	1660–1689
Tudor	Elizabethan	Jacobean	Caroloean	Cromwellian	Restoration

1689–1702	1702–1714	1714–1750	1750–1770	1770–1810
William and Mary	Queen Anne	Early Georgian	Middle Georgian	Late Georgian

A parade of fascinating and enigmatic monarchs, including Mary Queen of Scots, Henry VIII, Elizabeth I, and James I, dominate English history. The history of decorative styles and furniture is, appropriately enough, named after the rulers. Elizabethan is named for Elizabeth I, Jacobean named for James I, and so forth. The system is widely used.

Confusing the nomenclature issue is that the English were well aware of continental developments, and figures such as Inigo Jones and Christopher Wren ensured that some of the finest examples of Renaissance and Baroque architecture are found on the banks of the Thames. Design students thus find two systems at work, sometimes used concurrently. In some quarters, one hears about English Renaissance and English Baroque, one also, more commonly, hears references to styles based on the rulers, such as Elizabethan and Georgian.

No hard-and-fast rule predominates, but generally, the continental terms of medieval, Renaissance, and Neoclassical are used in conjunction with architecture, and the ruler-based names relate to furniture and the decorative arts. The English design nomenclature is also important for English colo-

nies—for example, Australia, Canada, Kenya, New Zealand, South Africa, and the United States. These countries rely on the English system, although they make it their own, with modifications.

An exceptional quality of English art and design, throughout the ages, is that there is not a singular home-grown English invention. English artists and designers worked marvelously with continental styles, such as classicism, Gothic, and Renaissance, adapting them to local needs and infusing them with local design motifs. A central feature of English design is its ability to adapt styles created elsewhere. The lack of categorical purity in no way indicates a lack of quality in art, architecture, interiors, and furniture. There was less internal design consistency than there was in France or Italy, yet seventeenth- and eighteenth-century English furniture is an unqualified high point in the history of designed objects.

TUDOR

Little early medieval furniture exists, so the exploration of English furniture starts with the reigns of the Tudor monarchs. The list of significant Tudor monarchs includes Henry VII, Henry VIII, Edward VI, and Queen Mary.

For architecture, the word Tudor is associated with timber frame construction (Figure 12.1). This type of half-timber construction, or **wattle-and-daub**, is found throughout much of Europe; in Germany called **fachwerk**, it is often found in typical medieval buildings, especially vernacular town buildings. But there is no neat correlation or distinction between Tudor and medieval. Tudor is chronologically the period in which Italian Renaissance forms started to appear. In Italy, the arrival of the Renaissance and its reinvented classicism was the death knell of medieval and Gothic forms. Across the Channel, the distinctions were less obvious.

Architectural historian Maurice Howard offers a counterpoint to the typical architectural history of the sixteenth and seventeenth centuries. Many works understandably focus on important churches and the official building and furnishing programs of Henry VIII. Another major center of English design history is the country house. Discussion of these stately manors often focuses on the degree to which designs were true to, or deviated from, continental fashions of classicism. Design innovations, however, were not only the result of new commissions. Howard suggests that: "far more importantly, there was a lot of making new from old materials: the flooring of halls open to the roof to create at least one more private space; the deployment of visible signs of lux-

Figure 12.1 Tudor-style timber-frame houses in Laycock, Wiltshire, England.

ury and comfort such as the fireplace (its stack often prominent for display purposes on the main façade of the house) and glazed windows; all these things customized old structures into modern dwellings" (Howard 2007, p. 2). The building legacy of England as it emerged from the medieval period includes innumerable informal structures that modestly line roads and face small town squares. These buildings were constantly being repaired and repainted. The elements of timber-frame buildings came from England's medieval past, and the honest architectural vocabulary proved flexible in responding to new functional demands.

The Great Hall and Its Furnishings

Mark Girouard's book from 1978, *Life in the English Country House*, is required reading for anyone interested in English domestic architecture. In his work, which combines architectural history and social history, a medieval household is defined as several hundred people, with a noble and his family at the center. The most important architectural features of a medieval manor house or castle were a giant dining hall, called the Great Hall, its kitchen, and a chapel. The house was essentially a small village whose inhabitants ate communally; hence the need for a large dining space (Girouard 1978, p. 27). Female servants were responsible for cooking, cleaning, and setting up for meals.

At the end of the medieval period, the Elizabethan household inherited a means of dining in which a nobleman and his family ate in a large rectangular room, still referred to as the Great Hall. One end of the room had a raised platform, called the **dais**, on which the family ate. The other end of the room had a screen, a porous wall, sometimes of columns or arches. Initially, screens were made of wood and were removable. This created a passageway, behind the screen, that allowed servants and others to cross the room without disrupting the festivities.

The nobles ate on the dais, sitting behind a fabric-covered table, the table most likely being boards on trestles. Diners sat on one side of the narrow table and were served by attendants working on the other. Typically, only the sovereign or lord sat in a chair, with the others seated on stools and benches. The typical Tudor chair, the **settle chair**, was box shaped, similar in some respects to the Italian Renaissance sedia, as it had a straight back and arms.

Tables were removed after the meal. The continual setting up and dismantling of the dining furniture was a tradition that was to live on in **gate-leg tables**. This table with a folding top was a space saver. Unfolded, a leg shaped like a gate swung out and supported the top.

A palace inventory from 1547, near the end of Henry VIII's reign, indicates that a great deal of the royal furniture was imported. Henry VIII in particular employed a vast retinue of artists, architects, and craftsmen who were Flemish, French, German, and Italian—one of the mechanisms by which continental styles traveled to the British Isles. Ralph Fastnedge (1955) writes that Flemish designers operating in England furthered "a florid Flemish interpretation of the Renaissance."

Over time, the architectural entity of a country house became less feudal and castle-like, and lost the features that made it resemble a village. By the Elizabethan era, the English country house became a single-family house, albeit with servants and the members of an extended family, the type of household associated with wealthy families today.

ELIZABETHAN

The Elizabethan period (1558–1603) was an age of great wealth that resulted in an increase in furniture and fine furniture production. It was also a time in which England flexed her diplomatic and military muscles. A decisive moment was the defeat of the Spanish armada by the English in 1588. The

Elizabethan period was characterized by significant cultural achievements, including the buildings of Inigo Jones and the plays of William Shakespeare.

Furniture

As new Renaissance construction techniques became prevalent in England, sophisticated Elizabethan pieces increasingly relied on wood-on-wood connections, or mortise-and-tenon. The use of iron nails was associated with medieval, Romanesque, and Gothic furniture.

In furniture, as in architecture, the English were initially resistant to wholeheartedly embracing Renaissance models. The English Renaissance held on to Gothic forms for a longer time than did the rest of Europe, until 1550. Renaissance ideas flowed northward from Italy and France into Holland and Flanders, and finally to the British Isles. The result is that Flemish influences remained strong in England, and similarly, English influences appeared in Flanders.

Elizabethan furniture in many cases takes existing medieval forms and overlays them with a profusion of decoration and ornamental work.

Tables

By 1550, there were framed tables, meaning that the top was created with a frame with cut boards filling in the frame, as opposed to parallel board or plank construction. Some tables were of considerable size.

A signature piece of the Elizabethan period is the Elizabethan table, with its characteristic bulbous leg (Figure 12.2). The round cup-and-cover form

Figure 12.2 Elizabethan table.

was also known as a melon motif. Bulbous legs were a feature of beds, sideboards, and tables. This legged table had rails close to the ground. Elizabethan legs are often capped with classical Ionic capitals on top of the cup-and-cover, a hint of the tentative assimilation of classical and medieval forms.

The English had draw-top desks and sloped desks (the French preferred flat desks). Tables served occasional duty as desks. The height of the popularity of the bulbous leg lasted approximately seventy-five years.

Chairs and Chests

Elizabethan X-frame chairs existed, as well as Gothic chairs and thrones. Another Elizabethan chair is the **Wainscot** chair (Figure 12.3). It bears similarities to its contemporary, the Italian Renaissance sedia. It is boxy, with turned legs and richly carved panels.

Its close-to-the-ground stretchers render it a sturdy piece of furniture, able to withstand the rigors of travel. When Elizabeth I traveled about the British Isles, she took a number of furnishings with her, including chests and wall hangings. Mark Girouard (1978) wrote: "A great household on the move was a familiar sight on medieval highways. It was also an impressive one. The number of people involved was unlikely to be less than one hundred, and could rise to well over five hundred in the case of a royal or semi-royal household. These numbers moved in three contingents of increasing size, probably spaced out several hours, or even days apart" (p. 14). The English vocabulary makes a distinction between a chest, which has a flat top, meaning that it might be stacked, and a coffer, which has a round top to throw off the rain and to keep other items from being piled on top of it. Chests remained

Figure 12.3 Elizabethan Wainscot chair.

important pieces of furniture; they were called into use for storage, as seating, as tables, and as beds. Chests were made from boards that remained visible. More elaborate chests were carved with tracery.

Beds

One of the most important furniture types of sixteenth-century England was the bed, and the grandest of Elizabethan beds is the Great Bed of Ware, 1590 (Figure 12.4). It has many of the signature characteristics of Elizabethan design—foremost its all-encompassing surface decoration.

Castles, churches, and dark-stained, heavy furniture give a false impression that Elizabethan life was somber. An installation in the Victorian and Albert Museum in London of the Great Bed of Ware presented it draped in full color. The medieval love of pageantry and bright color continued into the Elizabethan period in costumes and household textiles.

Beds were large, luxurious, and extravagant in a time period often known for scarcity. Houses were otherwise sparsely furnished. Beds were used as couches, for entertaining guests and friends during the day. Beds had a weight and consequence not seen on other pieces of furniture. Bed linens and draperies were expensive, and often finer than many pieces of furniture.

The Great Bed of Ware, like other Elizabethan beds, is architectural, with columns, arches, and a **tester** that looks like a cornice. A tester is the architectural canopy that caps off the bed. The bed's decoration is attributed to the Dutch architect and painter Hans Vredeman de Vries (1527–1606). Vredeman

Figure 12.4 Hans Vredeman de Vries. Great Bed of Ware.

de Vries was known more for his publications, pattern books filled with elaborate engravings, than his buildings. Pattern books were the medium by which continental design ideas and forms circulated. They were published with the intent that their designs would be copied. Some architects, like Vredeman de Vries, specialized in pattern books. The Great Bed of Ware, like Vredeman de Vries's other works, imagined and realized, has Dutch, Flemish, and Italian influences. In her book on dreams in the English Renaissance, Elizabethan historian Carole Levin informs us that "the expression of politicians getting into bed together was a common one then as now" (Levin 2008, p. 5). The heavy bed drapery provided warmth in the winter and also privacy, rendering the bed virtually a room within a room.

Architecture

Inigo Jones is commonly credited with having introduced Renaissance architecture to England. A feature of his work is that it relies heavily on Jones's admiration for the Italian Renaissance architect Andrea Palladio, and it constitutes a distancing from English architectural traditions.

The common understanding is that Jones and the Jacobean period he is associated with constitute the English Renaissance. An extension of this line of thinking is therefore that the preceding period, Elizabethan, is analogous to medieval. That characterization is problematic. An examination of Elizabethan architecture demonstrates that some English architects prior to Jones were innovative and aware of continental trends, although a feature of their work is that it relies heavily on updating homegrown traditions rather than importing new foreign ones.

The leading architect of the Elizabethan period was Robert Smythson (1534?–1614), and the first Elizabethan great house is Longleat, begun in 1568. Smythson's training as a mason is evident in his buildings, known for their blocky massing.

Another feature of his architectural interiors was ornamental **strapwork**, a decorative design formed of overlapping bands. His masterpiece is unquestionably Wollaton Hall, 1580–1588, a fusion of medieval and Renaissance forms, with a surprising amount of windows, a rigorously designed symmetrical façade, and innovations in interior planning that left the medieval castle far behind.

The plan of Wollaton reveals the multiple features that Smythson skillfully incorporated into the design. The Renaissance features include the fact that the house is essentially symmetrical on all four sides, a gesture to the Villa Rotunda that Alice Friedman (1989) called "mirror-image symmetry" (p. 93). The Great Hall at Wollaton was still a necessity in Smythson's time, yet it was not a feature of the Italian houses he admired, nor was it obvious how it could be incorporated into a Renaissance plan. It was a large, asymmetrical, rectangular entity, with dissimilar ends, approached off-axis and oriented perpendicularly to the axis of approach.

Smythson rotated the Great Hall ninety degrees from the central axis, although to arrive at it actually required visitors to make three ninety-degree turns (Friedman 1989, p. 93). Friedman wrote: "Wollaton Hall and its occupants frequently appear to be split between two different worlds. In appearance, the house itself draws on both Gothic and classical traditions, uniting a trabeated surface of pilastered orders with a centralized tower distinguished by its castlelike bartizan turrets. The plan brings together traditional English sequences of rooms and Palladian axial symmetry, but these two very different planning strategies are never integrated—the mazelike spaces of the hall, screens passage, and service rooms on the ground floor are a world apart from the open and airy formal rooms above. Moreover, in the running of their household, the Elizabethan Willoughbys often seem torn between the old ways and the new" (p. 9).

Smythson's other major country house was Hardwick Hall (1591–1597). Gothic detailing overlays simple forms and a central rectangular block. Its clever plan also incorporates an asymmetrical hall. Smythson's residential designs at the end of his life took a different turn. They were decidedly more traditional, leaving Wollaton and Hardwick Hall as his most innovative projects.

JACOBEAN

The Jacobean period corresponds to the reign of James I. Roughly analogous to continental Baroque, it is also characterized by the continuation of Elizabethan forms. In fact, some stylistically Elizabethan pieces continued to be manufactured during the Jacobean period with their forms unchanged. In general, compared to Elizabethan, Jacobean is more elaborate in its decoration and its profiles are visually lighter, although exceptions abound.

James I (1566–1625) is the monarch for whom the King James version of the Bible is named. He was the son of Queen Mary.

Interiors

Plaster ceilings and paneling are features of Jacobean interiors. What they have in common is that both are an articulated surface set in front of or below the physical structure. Timbered ceilings existed in the Jacobean period, but plaster ceilings became more common. A plaster ceiling is essentially a dropped ceiling, hung beneath the beamed ceiling that it hides. The physical structure of the ceiling is not visible. The ceiling of the Victoria and Albert Museum's Jacobean room features strapwork.

Paneling came into use in the early sixteenth century and became prominent in the Jacobean period; the Tudor habit of timber with plaster infill was largely left behind in the construction of rich people's houses. The increased reliance on paneling for vertical surfaces echoes the use of plaster on ceilings (Figure 12.5). Paneling is a carefully crafted surface that hides the structural wall behind it. There were many names for those who worked in wood, among them arkwright, smith, cooper, and joiner. Work on paneling was one of a joiner's areas of expertise.

Figure 12.5 Hans Vredeman de Vries. Jacobean room, 1606. Oak paneling, carved pilasters and overmantle, limestone fireplace. Molded plaster ceiling, with Elizabethan furniture, Table and chairs.

At the end of the Jacobean period, there are instances of paneling being painted white. James Ayres has researched the varieties of painting schemes used in historic British interiors. They include painting walls to look like tapestries and painting panels to imitate marble. Blackwork, which was inspired by the popularity of blackwork embroidery in textiles, featured elaborate patterns in black on a white background. In the eighteenth century, some patrons preferred murals, large-scale pictorial compositions, often landscapes, that covered entire wall surfaces (Ayres 2003, pp. 125–164).

Furniture

A Jacobean sideboard is dated to the reign of James I. It is similar to an Elizabethan sideboard, although its overall massing is lighter and its individual parts, such as the cup-and-cover vertical supports, are significantly smaller (Figure 12.6).

Jacobean furniture, still massive, was lighter than Elizabethan pieces. In many cases, it is impossible for the casual viewer to distinguish Elizabethan from Jacobean pieces. This is also because Elizabethan pieces continued to exist and were moved into Jacobean structures, and also because some furniture makers continued to make Elizabethan-style pieces. The use of cushions increased, and there were fully upholstered and partially upholstered pieces.

Chairs

Unassuming common tripod stools were holdovers from the medieval period. Around 1500, these simple seats were rendered elaborate with the

Figure 12.6 Jacobean sideboard. Early seventeenth century.

addition of turned elements (Figure 12.7). Fast-nedge (1955) described those covered with a profusion of decoration as "curious and rather monstrous" (p. 24). They were indicative of a desire to rely upon turned pieces rather than chip carving as the source of decoration. The technology of the lathe drove the design, evident in the piece's name: turned chair.

Upholstery was infrequent in the Elizabethan period. Some X-framed chairs were elaborately upholstered (Figure 12.8). The long-standing form of the X-frame chair was retained, yet the upholstered version was not collapsible. Simpler, folding versions of the X-frame chair continued to demonstrate their utility (Thornton 1978, pp. 184–185). Chairs became increasingly elaborate, with tassels and fringes and arched cresting.

In the Jacobean period, the Farthingale chair was popular. A side chair with an upholstered seat, without arms and with a low back, it was useful for

Figure 12.8 Jacobean X-shaped chair and footstool.

women wearing voluminous dresses. It was also called a "back chair." Some had front legs that protruded above the seat framing to hold the cushion in place. Historian of the decorative arts Peter Thornton (1978) wrote: "Although the farthingale chair was much used for relaxing in comfortable circumstances, it was the standard chair of its time and was also used for dining" (p. 187).

Wainscot chairs continued to be produced, with slight differences between the Elizabethan and Jacobean versions. The Wainscot chair's top was surmounted by a crest. In the Jacobean period, the cresting was atop the side rails; in the Elizabethan period, it lay between the side rails. The armrests sloped downward.

Walnut and beech became increasingly popular. A feature of many Jacobean pieces was twisting on the stretchers, also called **ball turning**. (Twisted stretchers, legs and columns were a feature of Italian Baroque design.) Clients frequently purchased sets of two armchairs with six or more side chairs.

Figure 12.7 Jacobean thrown or turned chair.

A Jacobean sleeping chair has adjustable wings (Figure 12.9). Other details of its design are consistent with continental Renaissance and Baroque chairs.

Because people kept their furniture and traditional-looking pieces (i.e., Elizabethan) continued to be made, many Elizabethan and Jacobean pieces look similar to the untrained eye. While the Jacobean period saw many innovations, some conservative pieces display an allegiance to previous forms.

Architecture

The most prominent architect of the Jacobean period was Inigo Jones, the figure credited with having introduced Italian High Renaissance into England; his work is often compared to that of the architect he admired and emulated, Andrea Palladio. Like the Italian Renaissance architect, Jones was a student of antiquity, and he brought several publications on Palladio back with him to England after his travels in Italy.

Jones's designs were consistent and rigorous forms of High Renaissance. He designed Queen's House at Greenwich (1616–1635) and Banqueting House (1619–1622). His work on Queen's House at Greenwich was an exercise in simplicity. Like Palladio, Jones was interested in the perfection of geometric shapes.

The rambling Whitehall Palace had originally been owned by a cardinal who was forced to relinquish it to Henry VIII. Its finest structure was also the only part to survive a fire in 1698, the exquisite Banqueting House. Contemporary drawings of Banqueting House, part of a larger complex intended to rival Versailles, show the sharp contrast between the medieval vernacular and the Renaissance England that Jones promoted. It is a single room with a double-story height—and with a single purpose, as its name suggests. Today the building is surrounded by a lot of grand buildings that vie for the viewer's attention, but in its day, its grand classical exterior, with Ionic and Corinthian orders, stood in sharp contrast to the context of timber-framed irregular buildings.

Jacobean architecture can also be seen as consistent with French architectural developments. In their embrace of luxury, the styles of the late seventeenth and eighteenth centuries reflect the influence of Louis XIV.

Figure 12.9 Sleeping chair.

Cromwellian and Restoration

Because the furniture classification system used in England is based on rulers, the Jacobean period is followed by Carolean (1625–1649), Cromwellian (1649–1660), and Restoration (1660–1689). Cromwellian refers to the figure of Oliver Cromwell

(1649–1660), and his movement is known as the Puritan rebellion. Cromwell was the English statesman who led parliamentary forces in the English civil wars and played a central role in overthrowing Charles I. In his movement, the Puritans opposed the monarchy and sought to purify the church of England of idolatrous (i.e., Roman Catholic) ways. The separation from Rome came in 1534, and a century later, the Puritans sought to further the division.

Cromwellian is not a distinct style, and it intermittently expresses the austerity promoted by its leading political figure. A Cromwellian side chair is a variation of the Jacobean Farthingale chair (Figure 12.10).

The Puritan movement didn't long survive the loss of Cromwell, and a restoration of the monarchy came next, with the rulers Charles II and James II. The stylistic period related to their reigns is known as Restoration. Charles and James were contemporaries of the French king Louis XIV. They restored the English monarchy to power and, like most European royals, they wanted to emulate the French king, his palace, and its furnishings. English Restoration is known for its lavishness and its engagement with continental Baroque movements. Restoration generally refers to Baroque-looking forms and a return to the opulence associated with the monarchy that was frowned on by Cromwell. The persecution of the Puritans in this period was one of the factors that drove some people to emigrate to the North American colonies (Chapter 13).

In Restoration England, the Mortlake Tapestry Industry was important, filling a role similar to that in France of the Gobelins Tapestry. Furniture forms were inherited from previous eras rather than invented. Circa 1660, after the Restoration, oval and round tables became a feature of private rooms used exclusively for dining. Nobles tended to eat in their private chambers, and the great age of communal dining in the Great Hall was over. Gate-

Figure 12.10 Cromwellian maple and oak side chair. 1650-1680.

legged tables and tables devoted to games were popular.

The recognition of continental developments reared its head in the growing use of glass and mirrors, most of which came from Venice. The fashion for glass-lined rooms was due to the fame of the Galeries des Glaces at Versailles. Paneled walls took the place of walls covered with tapestry hangings. Part of the need for ostentatious display was met by importing Chinese vases and Oriental rugs.

The Restoration court had an "Indian" taste for lacquered pieces and Oriental porcelains. Some furniture in China was made for European markets. Some pieces made in England were sent to China for lacquering, as the European lacquerers had yet to figure out how to successfully emulate Chinese techniques. Many furniture designers expressed their admiration for Chinese and Japanese lacquers and sought to uncover the secrets of their techniques.

The important architects of the day were John Vanbrugh and Nicholas Hawksmoore. Their classically detailed buildings are not always stylistically consistent with the furnishings they contained.

The brief reign of Queen Caroline was not a stylistically unique period. For most people, the reigns that were accompanied by significant artistic developments are Jacobean, followed by William and Mary and Queen Anne.

The Great Fire of London in 1666 was a catastrophic event. It prompted a large amount of building and created a demand for a fresh infusion of furniture. The fire seemed to be the perfect opportunity to institute a Baroque urban design, and Christopher Wren (1632–1723) created one, but it was not meant to be. Most of Wren's suggestions for the redesign of London were unrealized.

After the fire, fifty-one churches were built in the years leading up to 1700. Wren was in charge of the reconstruction of the city's religious infrastructure. Most of his churches were externally modest, with surprises to be found in their interiors. Wren produced a specifically English version of French and Italian design, sometimes described as Baroque, yet more restrained and disciplined than more elaborate Italian examples. One of the joys of visiting Wren's many London churches is to see the hand of one architect present in many buildings.

Wren traveled to Paris, where he met Bernini. He never traveled to Italy, but he was aware and knowledgeable of Italian Baroque through publications.

William and Mary

William and Mary was a style of furniture influenced by French and Dutch taste. A high-backed upholstered settee was part of the lavish furnishings of a house's public rooms (Figure 12.11). Such pieces

Figure 12.11 William and Mary settee, 1690–1700.

were formally placed around a room's perimeter. This settee was probably meant for Henry VIII's palace, Hampton Court. It has curves everywhere: in its back profile, in the outward curve of the wings, in the scrolled arms, and in the characteristic feature of William and Mary furniture, the perfectly curved cross-stretcher. A formal piece meant to impress, its shapes are simplified in comparison to the most elaborate Baroque pieces.

The cross-stretchers also existed on tall chests, dressing tables, desks, tables, and chairs (Figures 12.12 and 12.13). Most have straight turned legs (like Baroque pieces), but late William and Mary pieces have cabriole legs. Some pieces have ball feet, and others have the ball-and-claw foot. Dining room chairs had an open splat and a cresting rail, although the splat was moving toward the solid

Figure 12.13 William and Mary table.

splat characteristic of the subsequent Queen Anne period (discussed later).

A dresser was essentially a chest of drawers set on top of a table, and some were manufactured in two parts that were later connected; hence its straightforward name: chest-on-chest or chest-on-stand. A chest-on-chest has relatively little carving, with the decoration relegated to the art of the turner. Other than a cornice, there is little overt classical detailing. These pieces were copied in English colonies, where the chest-on-chest was known as a highboy.

Some William and Mary pieces were influenced by Boulle work, with a predilection toward gilding and lacquering. A subset of William and Mary furniture was silver furniture, either gilded or, more rarely, solid silver. In England, France, Italy, and Spain, there were examples of solid silver furniture. Extraordinarily valuable, few survive.

For upholstered furniture, the printed calico **chintz** was popular. William and Mary pieces related to Baroque design with their curves, yet they were simpler in profile, form, and decoration, and therefore predictive of the style to come, Queen Anne.

Figure 12.12 William and Mary chest-on-stand.

Queen Anne

The common use of the stylistic name "Queen Anne" is evidence of the occasionally arbitrary nature of artistic nomenclature. The historical Queen Anne herself was not an important monarch, nor was she particularly interested in or important for the arts, let alone furniture. (Nor does Queen Anne furniture relate to the nineteenth-century domestic architecture in the United States known as Queen Anne.)

Yet for many, a Queen Anne chair is unrivaled, on a par with the Ming armchair and the Louis XV fauteuil. What binds all three together, interestingly enough, is the cabriole leg. It follows a crisp curving line, practical, modest, and elegant. Queen Anne pieces were contemporary with the vigorous Baroque architecture of John Vanbrugh, with which they had little in common.

Queen Anne pieces are known for their restraint and beautiful proportions. Fastnedge (1955) described them as "extremely graceful articles of furniture; they exhibit the rich taste of the period, with its sense of elaborate display." By the time of Queen Anne, the ponderousness of Elizabethan and Jacobean furniture was a distant memory. A Queen Anne tea table has no stretchers (Figure 12.14). Furniture was no longer made ruddy for travel. The pieces were almost modern in their simplicity of form and lack of decoration. The profiles were as thin as they could be.

There is no one-to-one correspondence between the continental style of Baroque and English Queen Anne, but there is a stylistic relationship. Knowing that Queen Anne appeared at the same time as the late Baroque period, one detects a similar vision of lightness, grace, and elegance. France was moving away from Baroque forms to Regency and Rococo; England had Queen Anne.

A Queen Anne chair has the cabriole leg with an undecorated knee and slipper feet. The knees of a chair is the point where leg meets seat frame. The backrest has a solid central splat, in the shape of a vase. The back rail curves. The design's success is demonstrated by the fact that they are still manufactured (Figure 12.15).

In a different economic and artistic context of the Queen Anne period, the Windsor chair arose (Figure 12.16). Designed for modest circumstances, it was enormously successful. The Windsor chair has no stylistic relationship to other Queen Anne furnishings. The Windsor was a well-designed rural chair that proved to be a stalwart of modest houses. Endlessly copied, it did particularly well in the English colonies; there are many varieties of the Windsor chair. The original type was bow-backed, in which a bent hoop acts as the top rail; the comb-back variety has a straight top rail.

The other features of the Windsor chair are its saddle seat, turned legs, and stretchers. It was made as an armchair, a side chair, and as a settee. It is another example of a piece of furniture whose features stem from the widespread use of a lathe. Ayres (2003) informs us that another name for the Windsor chair is "stick-back seat" (p. 171). He writes:

Figure 12.14 Queen Anne tea table.

Figure 12.15 Queen Anne side chair.

Figure 12.16 Windsor chair.

"Although chairs of this type are now inseparably associated with the town of Windsor, stick-back chairs were in fact made in many parts of England as well as Scotland, Ireland, and Wales" (p. 172).

Making an individual Windsor chair was not an easy task. Because these chairs relied upon standardized forms made from common materials, they were popular throughout the British Isles. Soon after their introduction, they started appearing in English colonies worldwide.

GEORGIAN

Georgian is related to Neoclassicism. A feature of English design is that whereas France and Germany experienced the significant design interlude of the Rococo, which was not at all classical, classicism in England never went away. Georgian design was sometimes exceedingly plain, with nothing but the proportions and massing related to the classical tradition.

Supplies of mahogany from Hispaniola (Haiti) to England increased, with the result that mahogany is a common Georgian wood. It is a hard, close-grained tropical wood with a dark reddish color. Georgian pieces frequently had shell ornamentation on the knee, apron, or top. Chairs become lower,

Figure 12.17 Georgian chest-on-chest.

ing allegiances to England in the reigns of the three kings George. The German-born George I was not an enthusiastic supporter of London's arts scene, as his political and cultural ties were oriented toward Germany. George II, the last English king born in Germany, was better suited—temperamentally and linguistically—to attending to the English side of his international duties. His heir, George III, managed to be both nativist and internationalist, supporting English arts and keeping his eye on continental developments.

Hanson seeks to recuperate the reputation of the people, in many professions, who collected as a serious hobby in Georgian England. He proposes "a new framework for understanding the arts in the early modern period, a more malleable and far less tidy framework that stresses the virtuoso's fascination with objects in all their learned array" (Hanson 2008).

People collected coins, cameos, prints, antiquities, fossils, shells, and dried insects. The growing number of objects people collected required more tables, desks, and bookcases for their sorting, storage, and display. Georgian furniture manufacturers

more square, and robust. The top rails were straight or bow-shaped. A Georgian dresser has a classical broken pediment (Figure 12.17). Many leg types are found in Georgian pieces, curved and straight. An American Georgian knee-hole desk demonstrates the popularity of Georgian furniture and architecture in English colonies (Figure 12.18). Alternating concave and convex shell carvings top the three vertical divisions. Additional Georgian pieces are discussed in Chapter 13.

In a book that argues for a reassessment of the **virtuoso,** or enlightened collector and knowledge seeker, art historian Craig Hanson traces the vary-

Figure 12.18 Rare Chippendale Block and Shell Carved Mahogany Chest of Drawers. From Newport, Rhode Island, 1755–1785.

were happy to meet the demand. The scholarly pursuit of collecting ushered in a period in which physical objects were seen by some as conveying information, constituting knowledge, and proving their owner's erudite sensibility. The historian of art and science Barbara Stafford writes that "crammed shelves and drawers, with their capricious jumps in logic and disconcerting omissions, resembled the apparent disorganization of talk" (Stafford 1994, p. 238). Pieces of furniture were admired for their strong elegant profiles in an era that experienced an increase in both the quantity and quality of objects, found and designed.

Chippendale, Hepplewhite, and Sheraton

In the late eighteenth century, three furniture designers revolutionized the furniture industry with their designs, their publications, and their business practices. Before Chippendale, Hepplewhite, and Sheraton, most furniture makers worked by type and not by measured drawings.

Chippendale

Thomas Chippendale (1718–1779) was the son of a carpenter, and he became the head of an extensive business that made English furniture. His company also imported French furniture. In 1754, he published the *Gentleman and Cabinet Maker's Director*. Prior to Chippendale, although designers produced similar-looking pieces, most work was custom. His book standardized the product line, with the result that clients knew exactly what they were getting. His book was a first in that it documented almost every type of English household furniture.

    He was a designer, an author, and a manufacturer. His production was vast: He produced or drew almost the entirety of English furniture. Among his many pieces, three principal strands stand out: Gothic (Figure 12.19), a restrained version of Rococo (which

Figure 12.19 Thomas Chippendale. Gothic armchair.

Figure 12.20 Thomas Chippendale. Ribbon-back side chair.

Figure 12.21 Thomas Chippendale. Chinese-style side chair.

was not particularly faithful to French Rococo) (Figure 12.20), and his version of Chinoiserie (which was not particularly faithful to Chinese design) (Figure 12.21). In contrast to previous periods and designers, Chippendale's work is characterized by its variety and breadth. He is also known for refashioning the furniture business. He responded to the market's desire for well-made, sturdy, and practical furniture. His reasonably priced pieces allowed middle-class clients to enjoy decorative pieces.

Despite the breadth of his firm's output, when most people think of a Chippendale chair, they are referring to the armchair with the ribband, belonging to his so-called Rococo furniture.

When the firm was headed by his son, Neoclassical pieces became a more prominent part of the product line. Chippendale's supremacy in the furniture business was as much due to his business acumen as his talent as a designer. Chippendale did not stamp his furniture, so pieces referred to as Chippendale can indicate designs by Chippendale, the work of his company, or the work of his legions of imitators. Chippendale's encyclopedic book facilitated the process of imitating its author's designs and ensured that Chippendale imitations would be found across the globe.

Hepplewhite

Although George Hepplewhite (d. 1786) was not as prolific as Chippendale, nor his "line" as broad, he also created a wide variety of designs. He published them in his *The Cabinet Maker and Upholsterer's Guide* (1788). Hepplewhite is mostly known for delicate chairs whose backs take a shield or oval form (Figure 12.22). For his settee designs, he relied on the same characteristic shield form. His settees are literally based on multiplying the single unit of a chair. This was an innovation as it created the possibility of having multiple pieces of furniture with a similar look.

Sheraton

Thomas Sheraton (1751–1806) created pieces that were rectilinear, of a smaller scale and with delicate refined profiles. His chairs are known for their straight legs and backs (Figure 12.23). His uphol-stered pieces were simple, with light padding (Figure 12.24). Although he also published a catalog of his work, *Cabinet Maker and Upholsterer's Drawing Book* (1791), Sheraton was more of a designer and less of a businessman.

The works of Hepplewhite and Sheraton were firmly attached to the international Neoclassical aesthetic.

Prior to Chippendale, Hepplewhite, and Sheraton, most commissions were **bespoke**—clients ordered furniture in individually negotiated trans-actions whose details concerned style and price. With their publications, the three late-eighteenth-century designers and authors revolutionized the furniture business with a standardized product line and ready-made objects. This opened up the possibility of furniture being produced in quantity, in advance, and warehoused, waiting for eventual sale. The nineteenth-century furniture business was in-debted to the publications, practices, and products of Chippendale, Hepplewhite, and Sheraton.

Figure 12.22 George Hepplewhite. Side chair.

Figure 12.23 Sheraton chairs.

Figure 12.24 Sheraton sofa.

CONCLUSION

Ayres's recent work makes a valuable contribution to the study of interiors because he examines more modest structures. He writes: "Above all, the carpets, curtains and wallpaper which today provide vehicles for color and pattern in the home were largely absent from the pre-industrial vernacular interior. Most people did without such comforts and embellishments or made do with painted carpets (floor clothes or painted boards) and stenciled walls (in place of patterned wallpaper)" (Ayres 2003, p. 209).

Yet English design is mostly known for its grand country houses and their furnishings. When looking at English design, one must keep one eye on the continent and one eye on the British Isles. Architecture is generally known as Renaissance, Baroque, and so forth; furniture and the decorative arts as Elizabethan, Jacobean, and so forth. The dual nomenclature is appropriate because, more so than

for any of the great European powers, there is less internal design consistency within English design movements. The variations are endless, exceptions to the rule many. Yet this is no indication of a lack of mastery, for English design brilliance abounds.

This chapter covers a long chronological stretch, from Tudor to Georgian, the medieval period to the beginning of the modern age, and from castle to country house. The eclipse of the medieval era was heralded in ways modest and grand: Nails were eschewed in favor of elegant timber-on-timber connections, and a variety of new construction methods for floors, walls, and ceilings were developed that hid the structurally honest, if crude, timber-frame construction. The age of Shakespeare was the age of Elizabeth I, a monarch whose dresses confirm her understanding of the importance of a dazzling appearance. For designed objects, the drift toward opulence frequently resulted in new takes on medieval forms. Triangular stools, and the X-frame chair were overlain with great quantities of decoration. The somber interiors of churches and houses were contrasted by bright textiles associated with pageants and fairs.

The Elizabethan architect Robert Smythson displayed an astute ability to develop a uniquely English style of large country houses that grew out of English traditions. Yet his designs exhibit an awareness of continental (French and Italian) traditions. Smythson, for his ability to synthesize, represents one type of English architectural achievement. Inigo Jones represents another; Jones's buildings show the architect's ability to develop original designs absolutely in keeping with Italian Renaissance traditions.

In the Jacobean period, to which Jones belonged, furniture stalwarts such as the X-frame chair and the Farthingale chair continued to be useful. Yet there was a distancing from the primacy of structure, be it medieval or Gothic. Parquet floors lay on top of floor joists, plaster ceilings hung from rafters, paneled walls hid framing systems, and the extensive use of upholstery enveloped a chair's chassis. Christopher Wren continued the English architectural attitude toward continental developments initiated by Jones—to master the vocabulary, employ it skillfully, but not slavishly copy it. The result is that Wren's works are classical and scarcely look Baroque.

Whatever reticence English architects felt toward Baroque design was not seen in the works of furniture designers. With silver furniture, mirrored walls, and curvilinear William and Mary pieces, England experienced the Baroque period to the fullest extent—from the inside of buildings.

Queen Anne furniture is a highlight of the history of furniture owing to its technical and aesthetic perfection. It neither hides nor glorifies its structure, but exhibits an absolute understanding of it. A Queen Anne tea table has the lightness of French Rococo without the decoration. An important odd-

ity, for a place rife with exceptions, is the Windsor chair, known for its simplicity yet not all that easy to craft.

An important subtheme of this chapter is the transmission of design information. The efforts of Hans Vredeman de Vries prove the importance of the printed image; he was more influential for his published drawings, and the designs they inspired, than his own works. The key role of the printed design book came full circle in the late eighteenth century when a trio of designer-authors intuitively understood that their reputations would be based as much on those who copied their works as on their own creations. It is poetic justice that Chippendale, Hepplewhite, and Sheraton gave the world the means to copy their designs, for copying, adopting, adapting, and changing is something that English architects and designers had been doing masterfully for centuries.

Sources

Ayres, James. *Domestic Interiors: The British Tradition 1500–1850*. New Haven: Yale University Press, 2003.

Boynton, L. "The Hardwick Hall Inventory of 1601." *Furniture History*, vii (1971), pp. 1–40.

Dutton, Ralph. *The English Interior: 1500–1900*. London: Batsford Ltd., 1948.

Fastnedge, Ralph. *English Furniture Styles: From 1500–1830*. Harmondsworth: Penguin, 1955.

Friedman, Alice. *House and Household in Elizabethan England: Wollaton Hall and the Willoughby Family*. Chicago: University of Chicago Press, 1989.

Girouard, Mark. *Life in the English Country House: A Social and Architectural History*. New Haven: Yale University Press, 1978.

Hanson, Craig Ashley. *The English Virtuoso: Art, Medicine, and Antiquarianism in the Age of Empiricism*. Chicago: University of Chicago Press, 2008.

Howard, Maurice. *The Building of Elizabethan and Jacobean England*. New Haven: Yale University Press, 2007.

Levin, Carole. *Dreaming the English Renaissance*. New York: Palgrove Macmillan, 2008.

Levin, Carole. *The Reign of Elizabeth I*. New York: Palgrove Macmillan, 2002.

Lloyd, Nathaniel. *A History of the English House: From Primitive Times to the Victorian Period*. London: The Architectural Press, 1975.

Mercer, Eric. *Furniture 700–1700*. New York: Meredith Press, 1969.

Pointon, Marcia. *Hanging the Head: Portraiture and Social Formation in Eighteenth-Century England*. New Haven: Yale University Press, 1993.

Stafford, Barbara. *Artful Science: Enlightenment Entertainment and the Eclipse of Visual Education*. Cambridge: MIT Press, 1994.

Thornton, Peter. *Seventeenth-Century Interior Decoration in England, France, and Holland*. New Haven: Yale University Press, 1978.

DISCUSSION AND REVIEW QUESTIONS

1. What are the general characteristics of Tudor design?

2. What are the general characteristics of Elizabethan design? How do these forms represent power? What is the concept of elite design being employed in Elizabethan pieces?

3. How do Jacobean pieces differ from Elizabethan pieces?

4. What are the general characteristics of Georgian design?

5. What are the general characteristics of William and Mary design?

6. What are the general characteristics of Queen Anne design? How does Queen Anne design differ from Elizabethan?

7. What is an example of a rural chair, from the Queen Anne period, that has no identifiable Queen Anne characteristics?

8. Who are the three furniture designers and manufacturers of the late eighteenth century who revolutionized the furniture industry?

CHAPTER 13

IN THE COLONIES

1608–1720
UNITED STATES
Early American

1720–1790

Georgian

1790–1820

Federal

Colonial is a curious word. On the one hand, it refers to a style of furniture, interiors, and architecture that evokes feelings of nostalgia and tradition in the United States. On the other hand, it refers to a political and economic system that many people consider to be repressive. Ultimately, these two meanings are related, with the former arising from the latter. Art historian Mimi Hellman bemoans the fact that historians who look at major cultural preoccupations, such as colonialism, imperialism, and nationalism, tend to ignore the world of objects (Hellman 1999, p. 2). This chapter responds to her call and explores the relationship between colonialism and colonial furnishings.

This approach represents a change from how "colonial" is traditionally covered in design histories. What follows forges a global perspective by looking at a variety of colonial experiences from around the world. The purpose is to relate today's international environment to historical developments.

An American dictionary definition from 1993 gives an old-fashioned view of the North American/English colonial phenomenon:

Colonial: 1. of, concerning, or pertaining to a colony or colonies. 2. of, concerning, or pertaining to colonialism; colonialistic. 3. pertaining to the 13 British colonies that became the United States of America, or to their period. 4. Ecol. forming a colony. 5. Architecture, Furniture. a. noting or pertaining to the styles of architecture, ornament, and furnishings of the British colonies in America in the seventeenth and eighteenth centuries, mainly adapted to local materials and demands from prevailing English styles. b. noting or pertaining to various imitations of the work of American colonial artisans." (*Random House,* 1993)

In contrast, two academics, University of Chicago anthropologists John and Jean Comaroff, provide a multifaceted definition of colonialism. A two-volume work lays out their lifework and presents, if not a definition of colonialism, a theoretical approach to its multiple iterations. In theorizing colonialism, they list several attributes of the worldwide colonial encounter. Colonialism was, first and foremost, a political and economic system that involved actual agents—that is, the people who conducted colonialism's business, including soldiers, missionaries, traders, bureaucrats, artists, and scientists. Colonialism, the Comaroffs (and countless others) argue, had as many effects on the Metropole (London, Paris, Amsterdam, Lisbon) as on the periphery (India, West Africa, East Indies, Macao). Colonialism, as a governmental initiative and as an idea, stood on a foundation of binary oppositions: near and far, center and periphery, black and white, ruler and ruled, modern and tradition, art and craft, Christian and pagan, and so on. Yet the categories that colonialism thrived on were ruptured, compromised, blurred, and reinvented, because they were based all along on discontinuities and contradictions.

This chapter starts by juxtaposing these two different conceptual positions of colonialism—one that has been, in the traditional American context, the common one in relationship to furnishings and the decorative arts, and one that is based on the writings of anthropologists. These dueling definitions suggest new directions in conceptualizing colonialism, appropriate to the twenty-first century, and that start seeing material objects as players in complex societal and political relationships. This new approach is historically significant and also pertains to the present day, in which globalism and multiculturalism are important topics.

Colonialism was a political and economic system that had profound cultural implications. It was a governmental system in which one country controlled another and thereby expanded its sphere of influence. It was often brutal. Looking at colonial artifacts is a testament to the ability of those involved in the arts to create beautiful things often out of terrible circumstances. This includes architecture, decorative arts, interiors, and furnishings.

Different colonial experiences around the world played out differently. As for cultural productions, what is consistent is that colonialism was the process by which cultures intermingled. Terms such as *syncretism* and *hybridity* refer to the culture-making processes in which two or more cultures and their stylistic and craft traditions came together. This

process was often highly inventive and veered off into unexpected directions, sometimes producing objects not found in either of the original contexts.

Stylistic change occurs when traditions travel from mother country to colony; this is sometimes admired, sometimes abhorred. Some see the resulting hybrid culture as an artistic achievement that mirrors the biological process of the mixing of races and ethnic groups. One of the features of many colonial developments is the colonial time lag—which posits that most colonial achievements occurred in the colonies at a later date than in Europe.

ENGLISH COLONIAL

In the United States, *colonial* usually refers to English colonial, although significant portions of the Americas were colonized by the Dutch, French, and Spanish. (Around the world, there were Dutch, English, French, Portuguese, and Spanish colonies. Danes, Germans, and Russians played smaller colonial roles.) The word *colonial* in the United States now has a neutral tone, largely because of the close political relationship between the United States and the United Kingdom; the press regularly refers to it as a "special relationship." It is worth remembering that initially England was an avowed enemy of the United States, and France her greatest ally. Buildings and objects were created in recognizable styles, and part of what it meant to be American, English, French, democratic or royalist, was played out in the realm of aesthetics.

For the early periods in the United States, the following terms can be used: Jacobean, Cromwellian, William and Mary, Queen Anne, and Georgian. Colonial refers to the early days of the American colonial encounter, while Shaker, Pennsylvania "Dutch," and the works of Iowa's Amana colonies are stylistically, although not chronologically, related. *Federal* is the term that refers to the American version of Neoclassicism.

United States

Although there were Europeans in the Americas from the time of the late fifteenth century, their lives were harsh. The terms Renaissance, Baroque, and Rococo are not used to refer to American colonial pieces. The works the early settlers produced were a response to limited resources rather than to stylistic influences, and had little in common with ornate European artworks, although they were produced at same time.

With few exceptions, the earliest extant American pieces are from the seventeenth century. Known as **colonial** or **early American,** they are simple, hardy pieces that are ingenious responses to difficult living situations. Pieces of furniture were few and valuable. A table-chair is a chair that folds into a table and that boasts a small storage area under the seat (Figure 13.1). It exhibits an accomplished level of workmanship, made from milled lumber, with no parts stemming from a lathe. As with many early American colonial pieces, it is mostly devoid of stylistic flourishes. It responded to immediate needs. Table-chairs were particularly useful in taverns and inns. When a single piece of furniture has multiple functions, as seating, as storage, and as a horizontal surface, it is an indication that furniture was rare. Incidentally, this single piece of furniture responded to the three essential functions of furniture: space-enveloping (storage), supporting a human figure (seating), and providing a horizontal surface (for work or display).

A large number of early pieces were made of pine, but also cherry, oak, and hickory. A feature of Hadley chests is that some were made from wide boards (Figure 13.2). The austerity of colonial life, from the houses to the ways of living, appealed to the Puritans. The Puritans originated with the Protestant English religious reform movement that opposed both Roman Catholicism and the Church of England. The persecution of the Puritans in England was one of the factors that contributed to the

Figure 13.1 American colonial folding table.

Figure 13.2 Hadley chest. Connecticut.

establishment of North American colonies, and various strains of New England Puritanism developed.

A Hadley chest, so named for the Hadley region of Massachusetts, is typically a chest on top of two drawers, with a flip top. Shallow relief carving, mostly floral decorations and biblical references, cover a surface that was further embellished with paint. The Hadley chest is a mediation between the desire to have simply crafted objects and the desire to embellish these objects and make them beautiful.

Some pieces are found in English colonies that are called Jacobean or Cromwellian. American Jacobean sideboards are simplified versions of English sideboards.

In large part due to the arrival of skilled chair and cabinet makers from England, Pennsylvania and New England had burgeoning furniture-manufacturing centers; by 1720, imports of English furniture had declined significantly.

In 1730, almost all American mirrors were imported; by 1740, many of them were locally produced. Virginia and Maryland were responsible for a large amount of the imports.

In response to the growing capacity of Americans to produce their own furniture, in the late seventeenth and early eighteenth centuries, England sought to protect its export trade in manufactured items, including furniture. Laws were passed to force colonists to purchase English goods, thereby supporting the English furniture industry at the expense of the nascent American one. American imports of English furniture, chairs, cabinets, and upholstered pieces mostly went to wealthy homes. American producers and consumers resisted these laws.

The English ports of the American east coast stretched from New England to South Carolina. The colonies were increasingly selling to one another, and also abroad.

Furniture historian Edward Cooke (1996) writes: "Furniture making, like other Connecticut crafts of

Figure 13.3 William and Mary sideboard, Connecticut. c. 1710–1727.

the late colonial and early national period, was not simply an economic task, a means to supplement an income or increase self-sufficiency. Rather it was an essential part of the region's mixed agricultural economy from the earliest settlements. Making chests, chairs, and tables was one facet of the agricultural cycle and fit in neatly with the responsibilities of animal and grain husbandry" (p. 199).

William and Mary

Throughout the 1730s, many British-American towns were large and prosperous and had a variety of specialized craftsmen, some from England. Unlike those active in England, American cabinetmakers were not members of guilds; they were independent businessmen. The development of regional traits was largely due to their freedom to explore personal expression within the boundaries of a retail economy based on stylistic type and object.

By the early eighteenth century, the situation had changed from the early colonial period and furniture makers were working clearly within European stylistic conventions. The finer American William and Mary pieces are nearly indistinguishable from their European forebears. Many pieces have all the standard William and Mary features: the unique curved stretcher, the bun feet, and the scalloped apron (Figure 13.3). A William and Mary high chest of drawers relies on a combination of form and applied decoration—paint—to achieve its grandeur.

Queen Anne

Experts can distinguish English from American pieces although their task is made easier because actual English pieces of furniture were rare in the American colonies. Because information was available in accurate, printed form, many pieces, such as tea tables and chairs, are high in quality and similar to English pieces. American Queen Anne pieces have characteristic features, such as slipper feet, cabriole legs, and other attributes that contribute to a graceful economy of line. Initially, some furniture makers who were trained in England immigrated. Those who felt that their employment options in Europe were stymied were attracted by the promise of a better life. Once in North America, they continued to produce the types of pieces they were familiar with.

Windsor chairs, the workhorses of English agriculture, proved to function well in modest American settings. Many forms of these chairs developed in the American colonial context (Figure 13.4). A Windsor settee shows the chair form expanded laterally to become a settee. This is a piece at home in a rough-and-tumble environment. Windsor chairs also appeared in other English colonies, including South Africa, Australia, and New Zealand.

By 1810–1820, the United States was fully recovered from the Revolutionary War, whose crowning moment was the Declaration of Independence of 1776. The first decades of the nineteenth century saw the new country and its artisans ready to participate in the world's economy. Some Windsor

Figure 13.4 Windsor settee. American.

pieces belie the humble circumstances of their intended context and are elaborate renditions of a modest furniture type. A Windsor settee has turned legs, spindle backs, and carved plank seats. Made with simple joinery techniques and repetition of parts, it is an early nonindustrial version of mass production. Windsor pieces were often painted.

Georgian

The cultural productions of the reigns of the English monarchs, George I, George II, and George III, are referred to as "Georgian." A simplified form of classicism, Georgian design is characterized by symmetry, restrained decoration, and heavy-looking forms.

Architecture

The English colonies use the same nomenclature for furniture and architectural styles; hence there is English Georgian and American Georgian. Although the term "Georgian" refers to the English kings, it is felicitous that the first American president was also named George. Around 1776 in the United States, when George Washington became president, was also the era of American Georgian architecture and furniture. Georgian is a classical style.

Figure 13.5 The William Trent House, 1719. Trenton, New Jersey.

In American Georgian buildings, the classical legacy of Georgian design is subtly apparent. A Georgian house in Trenton, New Jersey, has a classical cornice and is proportioned perfectly according to classical principles (Figure 13.5). Being made of local brick or wood places it in the local American context. Although no columns support its roof, with its proportions and fenestration, it is as though six columns were once there and have disappeared, leaving behind a robust structure with the dignity and presence of a Greek temple.

Furniture

Many Georgian furniture pieces are staunch, resolute, and earnest. An American Georgian highboy has little obvious classical detailing (Figure 13.6). The legs firmly support the base and the cornice protrudes, giving the piece an architectural profile. The broad plinth supports a base unit of five drawers. The top piece also has five drawers. This is known as a chest-on-chest. The diagonally cut corners are fluted like columns. The proportions and the detailing classify it as Georgian.

The delicately scrolled brass **escutcheons,** in a bat-wing shape, are neatly aligned and constitute the bulk of the ornamentation. Scalloping, or carving in the form of a seashell, was popular in Georgian pieces because it had a classical prototype. Scalloping was also an impressive design that could be created easily with a radius and a gouging tool. The former could be as simple as a pencil and string or, later, a protractor.

Dressing tables, also known as **lowboys,** often accompanied high chests. The taller chests held linens and apparel, while the dressing table held personal items such as combs, ribbons, jewelry, and cosmetics.

Georgian upholstered pieces share the same weighty presence and substantial profile as highboys. They make their presence known in a room. A **camelback** sofa, also known as a **humpback** sofa, has a pronounced curve to its back, vaguely remi-

Figure 13.6 Georgian chest of drawers, highboy.

niscent of Baroque pediments, and stands firmly on curved legs (Fig. 13.7). The armrests curve like classical scrolls. Yet the reference to classicism is indirect. The Georgian sofa is restrained in its decoration. Its sharply defined profile gives it a clear, recognizable shape.

Georgian armchairs or wing chairs became staples of the American furniture scene. By the late eighteenth century, skilled cabinetmakers were active in Boston, Philadelphia, and Charleston. They produced chairs with the same curved back and scrolled arms as sofas, and which were usually fully upholstered. They were comfortable pieces for people of means, or for people who wanted to imitate, at least for an hour or two, the lifestyle of people of means. Wing chairs were often paired in front of a

Figure 13.7 Georgian sofa, Chippendale-style. c. 1770. Philadelphia.

fireplace, responding to the symmetrical architecture with their placement. Georgian furniture, as a group, employs a range of details, but certainly a good indication that a piece is Georgian is the characteristic ball-and-claw foot. Sometimes the knees of armchairs also feature the Georgian scallop.

The wings themselves, purportedly to protect the sitter from drafts, in practice were used to lean against when napping. Sometimes they rolled horizontally; sometimes they were curved and shaped in the vertical dimension as well. Some Georgian chairs and chests have slipper feet, and exceptionally, Georgian chairs have rear cabriole legs (Kotz 1997, p. 212). Some Georgian wing chairs had back-swept rear legs, a Baroque touch. Sometimes thumb tacks held down the upholstery and by highlighting the edges further delineated the form.

A Bombé chest demonstrates the high level of quality that American furniture makers achieved in the late eighteenth century and early nineteenth (Figure 13.8). It also demonstrates that Georgian is a broad category containing many pieces. The Bombé profile curves in two directions and is difficult to achieve. This is one of the most Baroque-looking American pieces. With no classical detailing,

it has curved legs and the characteristic Bombé swell in its profile. The chest stands solidly on the ground, a very different approach to a piece of furniture and its relationship to the ground plane than the Queen Anne tea table. Georgian pieces share the quality of solidity with their architectural backdrop. Swelled or Bombé chests were popular in Boston and Newport in the mid-eighteenth century, despite their cost.

Figure 13.8 Bombé chest. American.

Other Colonial Furniture

In contexts that required hardier pieces, **ladder-back** and **banister-back** chairs were popular. They were sturdy, useful, and easy to produce (Figures 13.9 and 13.10). With cane seating, they were relatively inexpensive. A ladder-back chair is named for the horizontal rails of the backrest that resemble a ladder. Initially, it is probable that carpenters who produced ladders also utilized their skills making chairs. Alternately, it is possible that some chairs were made using leftover lumber. Banister-back chairs have a similar manufacturing history. Their backs are formed with vertical supports that resemble a stair railing and its vertical supports, the balusters. Sometimes the baluster form was made by

Figure 13.10 Bannister-back, chair.

turning on a lathe; sometimes it was cut out in profile from planks.

Shakers

Artworks are often connected to religion, with Chinese pagodas, Mayan temples, and Gothic cathedrals as obvious examples. The work of the Shakers in the United States adds a different wrinkle to the connection between design and spirituality. In the late eighteenth century, the predominant contextual note for furniture is that the United States was gradually moving from an era of privation to an era of wealth. Economic prosperity often was represented by the increased use of European styles. For the Shakers, design was a religious and moral statement about restraint and austerity. Journalist and author Adam Gopnik (2006) referred to the works of the Shakers as "so magically austere that they

Figure 13.9 Ladder-back, Cape Coast chair. South Africa.

continue to astonish our eyes and our sense of form" (pp. 162–68). Many of their pieces are breathtakingly beautiful and simple. (It is logical that twentieth-century modernists, who appreciated minimalism, admired Shaker pieces.) Shakers shared property, and their communities were an early exploration of socialism. Shaker design reached its height around 1830.

The group's founder, Ann Lee, was from the North of England. In 1774, she and her husband immigrated to New York (Larkin 1995, p. 3). Lee and her followers saw a connection between chasteness, charity, organization, cleanliness, and some form of communal living. Her order had disciples who were eventually spread throughout New England in the late eighteenth century and the early nineteenth century. There were not many of them, approximately 5,000, but the enduring popularity of their artistic productions exceeds what is expected from a small community.

Shaker design is not the same as colonial design, although in many respects they are similar. Early colonial designers often created objects in an arena of scarcity; it was all they could do. Their simple creations were the result of a lack of material resources and the time they could devote to crafting furniture. Shakers made a virtue of simplicity. Neither technologically nor stylistically innovative, they made ordinary pieces extraordinarily well. In some Shaker pieces, there is a connection to Neoclassicism, to the extent that lines were simple, forms crisp, and edges hard. What came to be known as the Shaker style, in housing, dress, and furniture, was not different from that of other American creations, yet Shaker creations trod the fine line between the normal and the extraordinary. Author John Shea (1971) writes that "the Shakers' individuality and disdain of 'worldly superfluity' produced new techniques which made their furniture lighter, stronger, and more practical than that constructed by other craftsmen" (p. 65). They were antiworldly

and anticommercial, while also quite commercial; many of the items were specifically created for sale, initially for lower- to middle-class markets.

Shaker products are stylistically related to Pennsylvania Dutch, Quakers across the country, and Amish in Amana, Iowa (who eventually progressed from making pieces of furniture to refrigerators and microwaves).

Shaker design is surprisingly asymmetrical (Figure 13.11), a feature that departs significantly from contemporary Neoclassical design. The ancient Greeks and their Renaissance imitators saw beauty in the proportions of the human body; they sought to imbue their objects with that beauty by relying upon human proportions. The Shaker creed rejected the idea that formed objects should reflect the human body; instead they relied on repetition and the grid. Many pieces are arrhythmically broken up. Objects responded directly to the intended functions; Shaker products looked like useful objects that followed a functional and nonhuman law of design.

Figure 13.11 Shaker sewing desk with drawers. United States.

South Africa

South Africa is unique for a number of reasons and its artworks are examples of hybridity of a different sort. For one, the Dutch and the English in this area were competing interests. This is not unusual; different European parties fought for many colonies over the centuries. This can be a source of cultural richness, in addition to causing strife. What was unusual in South Africa is that the Dutch and the English interests remained as relative equals for much of the area's history. This is reflected in the nation's official languages, English and Afrikaans, a Dutch-based dialect. The indigenous context on the southern tip of the African continent was equally varied.

Significant European settlement started in Capetown with the Dutch merchant Jan van Riebeeck, who arrived in 1652. van Riebeeck came with a party of eighty-two men and eight women. He either brought a lathe with him or one arrived shortly after his arrival, as many types of spindle (turned) chairs were in production as early as 1700.

South Africa has a rich heritage in the decorative arts, and one of them is furniture. The forms are clearly European, but the break from Europe happened early. A feature of some colonial arenas is that forms continue to live on in the colonies after they have expired or become less fashionable in the home country. African carpenters became familiar with European furniture types and the methods necessary to produce them. The integration and spread of European forms in South Africa was quite complete, so that many indigenous practices virtually ceased to exist, from building to clothing. The extermination of local traditions and their replacement with hybrids or European ones was a tumultuous process.

The topic of European-style furniture in South Africa is well studied and documented. In contrast, there are no books devoted to English furniture in Kenya, Nigeria, and Gold Coast (Ghana). While the situation in South Africa was in many respects unique, certain developments are probably indicative of continent-wide practices. These include the differences between city- and country-made furniture, the presence of actual European pieces on the coast and their absence in the countryside, and the effects of nineteenth-century transportation developments in changing the first two. We can, by inference, consider them as indicative of furniture trends in other African regions as well.

Cape Country

South Africa, like much of Africa, saw little utility in and therefore ignored Baroque and Rococo design developments, including furniture. There are two principal categories of South African European furniture: Cape Coast furniture and Cape Country furniture. Author Mary Alexander Cook is one of the people who appreciate the latter for its combination of good design and simple decoration. Country furniture in South Africa can be called "Country," "Platteland," or simply "traditional furniture." About the relationship between country furniture and city furniture, with its more obvious ties to European styles, she writes: "It can be regarded simply as a parallel manifestation of the same trends, limited in its expression by the nature of local materials and by the less skilled techniques, simpler tools, and lower standards of training of the country workman" (Cook 1980).

Petrus Borcherds was born in 1786, and his memoir describes the dire living conditions of many South Africans of European descent: "The occupants, when in the Karoo, reside in small houses, or rather huts, consisting generally of but one room with a fire place and a small entrance hall, adjoining their sheep-folds (kraals), which are so situated that those inside the dwelling can easily protect all points by their muskets against rapacious animals or robbers" (Borcherds 1861).

Many South African country houses were simply

furnished with only a few chairs and small tables, such as tea tables. Often people slept on the floor, or on benches or mattresses. There was not always a bed or a dining room table.

The flagship of country furniture is the Tulbagh chair. It is unique to South Africa, as was its stylistic follower, the Tulbagh transitional chair. The lineage of these pieces starts with the English Queen Anne chair, although they are like it in another respect as well: The naming of the Tulbagh chair is similar to the naming of Queen Anne furniture; the name has stuck in the popular consciousness, with no logical explanation for it. There are two possible origins for the name of the Tulbagh chair: Tulbagh is a geographic designation, and there was a Governor Ryk Tulbagh. There is no evidence that Governor Tulbagh had anything to do with the chair's design, nor is it geographically limited to Tulbagh. The Tulbagh chair came about in the late seventeenth century, and its back resembles the vase-shaped central splat of the Queen Anne chair. Initially, the Tulbagh chair had a cane back. This was not a feature of the European Queen Anne chair, and therefore is one of the African chair's defining characteristics. Tulbagh chairs were not exact copies of European Queen Anne chairs—there is no cabriole leg. The Tulbagh chair has a box stretcher, and the chairs range from ornate to simple. The Tulbagh transitional chair is made of wood, sometimes from a mixture of woods (Figure 13.12). The stalwart of the countryside, more elaborate versions stood on turned legs.

Its boxy frame resembles the Jacobean Farthingale chair; chairs similar to the Farthingdale chair were also created in the Netherlands, and it is likely that the importation of this form to South Africa came from Dutch craftsmen.

The transitional Tulbagh chair drops the ornateness of the Tulbagh chair but maintains the sturdy box stretchers. The legs, stretchers, and back were not turned. The squat legs are tapered and ex-tend past the seat frame to form cushion knobs. Only the top rail is shaped; not a crest rail, it rests between the verticals.

In the eighteenth and nineteenth centuries, sets of chairs were rare; even if a household had ten to twelve chairs, they were mostly different. Tulbagh and transitional Tulbagh chairs were initially made of local woods, yellowwood, and stinkwood.

A specific type of transitional Tulbagh chair developed in the late eighteenth century. As they were made from the wood of lemon or orange citrus trees, they were called Lemoenhout chairs. Small and low, they have the same square proportions of the transitional chairs. They do not have a true box stretcher, as the side stretchers were elevated. The seat side rails were also higher; this was because they were connected by a mortise-and-tenon, and the connections were stronger if they were not on the same level. Lemoenhout chairs were sanded literally

Figure 13.12 Lemoenhout chair, rough with web seat.

by scrubbing them with sand; some were bleached and many were painted. Wired seats could be configured to incorporate patterns, such as spokes of a wheel. The pattern of the wiring was an area where the indigenous craftsmen innovated.

Despite an increase in furniture imports, seldom did imported furniture make it beyond Capetown into the countryside. Real Queen Anne chairs were seen only in the towns. Functionally, aesthetically, and economically, there was little place for flamboyance. Initially, people in the countryside could not afford European furniture, so they relied upon indigenous furniture. Country furniture makers were usually active in other professions and could not devote all their time to crafting furniture. In addition to the higher cost of imported works, transport was difficult. Simply put, the coast and the African interior were two different cultural and economic worlds. The so-called Cape Country furniture, therefore, developed a distinct character and followed its own path of development. Country pieces used different woods and were created using simpler tools.

Over decades of change, the dynamics of furniture trade and production in South Africa varied. For one, the increase in imports of English furniture to Capetown came at the expense of locally made furniture. A general increase in trade included an increase in the quantity of timber shipped to Africa. Mahogany took a big share of the imported timber, with an important role for rosewood from Brazil, and ebony, satinwood, and zebra wood from the Netherlands East Indies. Although not immediately apparent, there is a relationship between the slave trade and the production of furniture. Slaving ships left Africa bound for Brazil, the United States, and the West Indies, all three of whom had copious supplies of timber. The ships had to return to Africa with their cargo holds filled, and timber was one of the New World products that sold well in Africa. So human cargo left in one direction, with the raw material of timber return-

ing in the other direction. The result is that much African colonial furniture and architecture is made of North and South American timber. The growth in African timber imports coincided with a gradual depletion of African timber supplies.

Cape Coast

The initial creators of European-style furniture were Europeans, in the cities and in the countryside, and they hired Europeans, Africans, and Asians as their assistants. Many of the Asian assistants were Malaysian, called Malay or inaccurately Chinese. The presence of Malaysian furniture makers, operating in an environment in which the major interactions were between the Dutch, English, and indigenous African ethnic groups, represents the ethnic complexity of the colonial environment and the rich genealogy of the pieces they made.

Neoclassicism

Simplified versions of Neoclassical pieces, however, were contemporary with the Tulbagh and Tulbagh transitional chairs. Neoclassicism in South Africa is another strand in the complicated ethnic web of South African furniture. South Africans were familiar with Dutch, English, and French variants of Neoclassicism. From 1795 onward, many of the British who arrived brought Neoclassical furniture with them. Eventually, Neoclassicism made its mark on country furniture, especially in cupboards. A Cape County cupboard is Georgian in its detailing. Its form is rectilinear, resulting in a well-designed unyielding form, with a pediment and classically detailed feet and cornice (Figure 13.13).

Triangular pedimented cupboards were a feature of wealthier homes. Riversdale is a region in the Western Cape where craftsmen excelled at making them. The tapered legs shown in this cupboard are known as Riversdale block feet. They are identified as having three flutes, echoing classical triglyphs. The cornice overhangs. A defining feature of

Figure 13.13 Triangular split-pediment cupboard. Late nineteenth century.

German Neoclassical (and Biedermeier) pieces was a distinct contrast between cherry or mahogany (orange or reddish in color) and ebony or ebonized (black or near black) wood as accents. Riversdale pieces achieve the contrast by juxtaposing infill panels of yellowwood with dark stinkwood framing. Yellowwood trees are huge, growing to 150 feet in height. The dark-hued stinkwood is so named because it emits an unpleasant odor upon being felled that dissipates over time. Sometimes these cupboards were made with imported teak, although Africa also grows teak. Similarly, most ebony was imported, although it also grows in South Africa. The Riversdale cupboard has a visible closing strip. Cupboards and wardrobes were standard features of European households in South Africa, as chests

of drawers or dressers were not common until the late nineteenth century. Metal escutcheons were rarely used in early colonial Africa.

A limited number of Indo-Portuguese chairs from Ceylon, Goa, and Bombay made their way to Capetown but not into the countryside. Wealthier urban families had Chinese and Japanese furniture, lacquered pieces, part of the fashion for chinoiserie. Few survive. They arrived thanks to the routing of the ships of the Dutch East India Company.

The industrial revolution of the nineteenth century impacted the production of Cape Country furniture in a negative way. The arrival of railroads made it easier to import furniture made in South African cities, and also European furniture. At the same time as the railroads arrived, the number of roads from the coast to the interior increased, also facilitating transport of furniture to the interior. Locally made country furniture was therefore in decline.

Australia

The first fleet arrived at Sydney Cove in January 1788. John Earnshaw, a self-described amateur, wrote a book titled *Early Sydney Cabinetmakers,* which he published in 1971. It, and other books like it, does a good job of documenting the rich world of nineteenth-century furniture making in Australia. These books, however, are primarily interested in form and style and are written to promote the collecting of furniture. They do not consider their subject from a social perspective, as a body of cultural artifacts to be interpreted. For example, there is little information on the ethnic makeup of either creators or users of the furniture, and no consideration of the impact that European art forms had on indigenous arts. Indigenous Australians (of non-European background) are not even mentioned in passing. Nonetheless, Earnshaw's book provides the background for future scholars, and most of the information presented here benefited from his efforts.

Australia's history of European furniture differs from those of other English colonies, India, South Africa, and North America, because the starting date of the European presence is at the tail end of the eighteenth century. A feature of its colonial history is that it seems speeded up. Australian history bypasses any developments such as Elizabethan, Jacobean, Baroque, and Rococo.

In Earnshaw's telling, the 1790s were lean and hungry years, yet by 1800, furniture reflected a sense of stability. In the early years of the Australian settlement, before and after 1800, households were modest and furnishings consisted of chests, stools, tables, and beds. Convicts owned less. One of the unique characteristics of Britain's colonization of Australia is that it relied heavily on relocating prisoners, or convicts, to relieve pressure from Britain's prison population. The European population in 1800 was less than 5,000.

The first lathes on the island-continent were manual, spring-bow, or treadle-driven (operated by moving paddles with the feet). By 1810, New South Wales had a European population of 10,000, and Earnshaw surmises that the professional lines drawn between the activities of cabinetmakers, carpenters, and joiners were not distinct. Few English pieces arrived with the immigrants, so the production of European furniture was mostly by local furniture makers. Knowledge was passed down to the next generation through the apprentice system. Most workshops had only a few apprentices. Apprentices started working in their early teenage years, twelve hours a day, six days a week, with a contracted indenture of approximately seven years.

What gave early Australian colonial furniture its unique character was its material: Australian cedar wood. Red cedar wood grew plentifully on the eastern coast of Australia, providing materials for the local furniture industry. It was felled in sufficient quantity that by 1795 there were Australian cedar exports to India. The terms *cedar* and *mahogany* were frequently used interchangeably. Loggers almost completely depleted Australian cedar forests less than a hundred years after the arrival of the Europeans.

A cedar sideboard is stylistically indicative of early colonial cedar work (Figure 13.14). Simply made pieces met most people's needs.

Figure 13.14 Red cedar sideboard. Australia.

Australian Neoclassicism

Noris Ioannou describes a pine settee from the Barossa valley as vernacular Biedermeier. Once the economic success of Australia seemed inevitable, other ethnic groups, from Europe and Asia, immigrated to the island and brought their artistic traditions with them. In Figure 13.15, the settee's classicism is barely discernible, and is limited to the klismos form of the backrest and the scrolled arms and feet. The cut-out tulip motif provides the vernacular element, a German invention with no classical precedent.

As early as the first decade of the nineteenth century, some pieces were made in simplified versions of the global style of Neoclassicism. A fully scrolled Neoclassical armchair from 1840, in cedar wood, is evidence that some furniture operations by midcentury produced high-quality work and maintained global standards (Figure 13.16). It has the klismos back, scrolled arms, straight front legs, and raked rear legs. By 1840, powered woodworking machines in Australia changed the way furniture was made. Initially, there was an uneasy coexistence of Europeans and indigenous Australians. By 1840, there were first- and second-generation Australians of European descent and handmade furniture became a thing of the past.

In 1850, the European population stood at 260,000, and consequently both local production and furniture imports increased to meet demand. The midcentury saw the beginning of organized labor, and the furniture industry, like the country at large, sought to distance itself from its convict past by excluding convicts from the furniture trade. Two industries were largely responsible for the economic boom of the 1850s—gold mining and wool ranching. This economic activity brought about the existence of furniture middlemen and warehouses devoted to stockpiling furniture. Most furniture had been utilitarian before 1850, but Australians, from a distance, followed reports about the Exhibition in London of 1851. Victorian pieces were imported and their arrival marked the decline in the appreciation, and therefore production, of both colonial and Neoclassical works.

Figure 13.15 Pine settee, with German motifs. Southern Australian.

Figure 13.16 Early Colonial scrolled armchair, neo-classical. Cedar. Australia.

Figure 13.17 Prie-dieu chair, red cedar.

A cedar hall side chair has all the ambiguities of the Victorian age; based on a Jacobean chair, it is covered with carving made by machines (Figure 13.17). Adding to the diversity of the Australian furniture scene, in the 1870s, Chinese furniture makers started to arrive. In 1890, Australia had 72 furniture workshops, 19 of which were Chinese, and these 19 workshops employed 386 Chinese workers. Nineteenth-century Australia had a diverse workforce to produce the myriad Victorian styles that popular taste demanded.

INDIA

Vasco de Gama's voyage of 1497–1498 delivered him to Calcutta in 1498, and he returned to Portugal to great acclaim in 1499. In the late fifteenth century, European trade with West Africa flourished, and Columbus sailed to the Americas. Indigenous Americans are called Indians because India was ostensibly Columbus's goal. The Italian explorer Marco Polo (1254–1324) was the first European to travel widely in Asia and to record his impressions. Polo's book, whose English title was *The Travels of Marco Polo,* brought discovery and foreign travel to a wide audience.

The Portuguese crown was attracted by the trade that expeditions to India promised to deliver. A fifteenth-century cliché provided a rhetorical answer to a query as to why the Portuguese were embarking on these costly and life-threatening endeavors: "We seek Christians and Spices." That is, the voyages were in the name of God and had an economic motive. Indian spices, small in volume, high in value, were ideal commercial items. The reasons for European expansion are not easily explained. In addition to economic, religious, and political motives, expeditions provided outlets for restless young men. Expeditions were attractive to the proverbial younger sons who did not benefit from the European inheritance system that favored firstborn males. Oceangoing voyages to East Asia acted as a release valve from social and economic pressures at home. Individuals caught up in the Portuguese colonial drive made little distinction between religion, economics, politics, and personal ambition.

A technological innovation made possible the extension of Europe's global reach. The caravel, developed in the 1440s, utilized the triangular sails that allowed sailors to tack against the wind. Before the Europeans' arrival, Arab traders had been trading up and down the East African seaboard, also known as the Swahili coast.

In the nineteenth century, India was primarily an English colony, and the vision of India as the jewel in the crown of the British Empire has stuck in the public consciousness. Yet in the earlier period, there were competing Dutch and Portuguese interests. The early Portuguese colonial experience was more cooperative and interactive than dominating. The goal was not territorial expansion but access to trade.

The influence and impact of the Portuguese on the whole of India, regarding authoritarian power and cultural productions, was relatively minor, with a few exceptions. The Portuguese and Dutch presence on the Indian coast resulted in some fantastic pieces of furniture—some of which stayed in India, some of which were shipped to England—that started appearing the world over.

India had a population in 1600 of some 150,000,000, with 110,000,000 of those being in the Mughal Empire. The Mughal Empire was inland and not dependent upon coastal trade (Pearson 1987, p. 23). It was a different cultural and economic world from the coast.

The principal Portuguese trading center was the city of Goa. There was little European cultural impact outside of Goa. A characteristic of international trading centers like Goa was a social mobility not found either in inland Indian areas or the European home countries.

Coastal India traded in cotton, indigo, pepper, cinnamon, intoxicants, wool, silks, and gold bullion. From China came silks and porcelain. Coastal Indian trade included ebony, slaves, ivory, beads, horses, pearls, carpets, dyes, opium, copper, rice, and rubies.

Hindu artists in India learned to do European-style portraiture, one step in the process of creating a multinational artistic world. Adding to the cultural mix, there were other Europeans—Italians, Germans, French, English, Flemings—and Africans. Few Portuguese women traveled to the Indian colonies; consequently, a significant mixed-race population arose.

Portuguese in India had been urban poor or peasants, and were not rooted in Portuguese high culture. In sixteenth-century Portugal, chairs were unusual and were typically reserved for the head of the family. Portuguese sat on the floor, spoons were rare, and forks unknown.

Western-style seats did not traditionally exist in India, as people sat on the ground, on mats, cushions, or on drum seats made from a variety of materials. The Dutch, British, French, and Portuguese inhabitants of the early trading centers were the first to commission elevated seats from local carpenters, who were happy to oblige. These European forms were made out of "foreign" materials (non-European) and with "exotic" decoration. The resulting objects were interestingly exotic to both Indians and Europeans.

Figure 13.18 Hand carved chair. India, 1660–1680.

Figure 13.19 Five-legged armchair. India. c. 1785.

The standard chair was likely based on a Dutch original box chair—the same chair that inspired the Tulbagh chair (Figure 13.18). Initially, Dutch craftsmen oversaw Indian artisans and slaves who, in short order, took over their business. Because of their affiliation with the Dutch East India Company, these chairs were exported around the world, a few to Africa, many to the Netherlands, and some to England. The Dutch East India Company was founded in 1602, and remained an important economic and cultural force until its dissolution in 1799. Its charter was to protect and promote Dutch trade to India and to the islands of the Indian Ocean, including Indonesia. Initially a commercial venture, its activities had major political, military, and cultural implications.

The Indian chairs that arrived in England caused mass confusion some hundred years after their arrival. Because of their dark appearance and profuse decoration they were misidentified as English, from the Tudor, Elizabethan, or Jacobean periods.

Ivory work was made in Vizagapatam, Murshidabad, and Travancore, on the East Coast of India (Figure 13.19). These cities had traditionally been centers of Hindu ivory work, and they became known for producing ivory-veneered furniture. Some five-legged chairs were made to rotate and serve as barber chairs. Another explanation for the unusual form is that they were translations of round straw drum chairs. These five-legged chairs are exceptional examples of the inventiveness of Indian furniture. Indonesian furniture makers later copied them.

Figure 13.20 Cedar Cabinet. Goa, India. Late seventeenth century.

Another branch of Indian furniture was influenced by the Muslim preference for geometric decoration (Figure 13.20). In this category seating was rare; most pieces were highly decorated storage items.

Though it was not initially a center of locally made furniture, by the late eighteenth century, Bombay was producing furniture in quantities large enough to export to other parts of India and abroad. Bombay blackwood furniture was made from blackwood from the Malabar coast. The furniture of Bombay carvers is related to architectural work, especially the sort typical in Ahmedabad. Every visible surface was carved, a confluence of Indian tradition and Victorian taste. Flamboyant carving was central to the concept of quality. Bombay blackwood furniture was exhibited at the Great Exhibi-

tion of 1851. It gradually fell out of favor, because it was difficult to clean and aesthetically did not conform to the modernizing trends that characterize the tail end of the nineteenth century.

The Coromandel Coast of India was another source of carved ebony furniture. It is the southeastern tip of India, on the Bay of Bengal. Ebony pieces were first made in India, and in Ceylon, Batavia, and the Dutch East Indies in the second half of the eighteenth century. Typical products were chairs, tables, beds, and chests. The common feature of this production is that they are covered with dense low-relief carving of foliage. They often have twisted stretchers and legs. Their backs are further embellished, sometimes with finials. The decoration has an affinity with carving traditions of southern India, drawn from Hindu mythology.

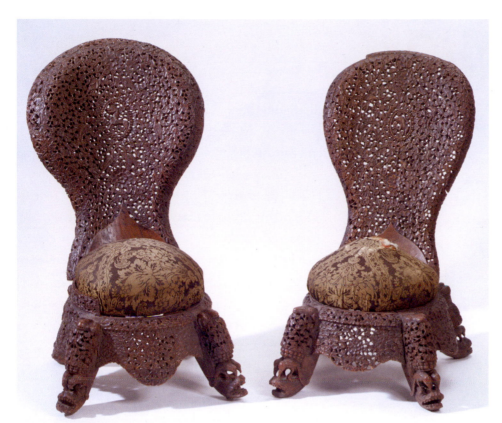

Figure 13.21 Pierced blackwood chairs. Bombay, India. c. 1870.

Two prie-dieu chairs from 1870 are Victorian both chronologically and stylistically (Figure 13.21). They are made from carved and pierced Bombay blackwood. Their concave, balloon-shaped backs fit into a slot of the seat, secured with a giant tenon. Foliate designs that incorporate birds cover every visible surface. Carved and pierced aprons extend below the seats. The legs have beast heads at top and bottom. Sprung cushions add a touch of comfort and are attached to the seats.

SPANISH COLONIAL

European-style furniture was introduced to South and Central America in the sixteenth century, following the Spanish conquest. Initially, the items were imported; then they were made by local furniture makers. The pieces included X-frame chairs, chairs similar to the Renaissance sedia, trestle tables, beds, and chests (Figure 13.22).

Latin America

The year 1500 marks an important time around the world. The Renaissance was flowering in Italy, the Ming dynasty was in full swing in China, and the Mughals were consolidating their power in the inland Indian region. The late fifteenth century also brought Europe into contact with South America, Asia, and Africa.

Hernán Cortés took the Aztec capital of Tenochtitlán, and the Spanish Hapsburg royal regime ruled New Spain for nearly 200 years, 1521–1700. In 1535, the Spanish king Charles V installed a viceroy to represent the Spanish crown in New Spain (today Mexico). In Latin America, the Spanish sought to build and furnish in the styles they were familiar with, which resulted in a significant amount of Baroque architecture, interiors, and furniture. Sometimes by intention, sometimes by necessity, the results were hybrids that incorporated indigenous techniques.

Figure 13.22 Spanish colonial furniture. Mexico.

colonial theorizing on the inherent ambivalence of colonial objects that were part of a fractured counterdiscourse.

Plateresque or, in Spanish, Plateresco refers to the highly ornamented Spanish design of the sixteenth century. It is found in architecture, interiors, and furnishings. Related to Baroque art, Plateresque works frequently take Renaissance forms and embellish them with decoration, often Islamic motifs. This highly decorative style became prevalent in the Americas. *Mudejar* refers to Islamic-influenced design in Spain, and it is used infrequently in reference to American works. A Plateresque chair from Mexico has the form of a Renaissance chair, and it is opulent in its finishes, detailing, and applied decoration (Figure 13.23).

Charles II (r. 1665–1700) was the last Hapsburg

The official aesthetic of Baroque New Spain centered on religious imagery, the building of churches, and the painting and sculpture they held. But the secular realm was equally important, with portraits of kings and viceroys, and secular objects including furniture. Art historian Michael Schreffler examines representation's role in the production of a visual and spatial order, with all its forms and symbols. In 1492, Antonion de Nebrija wrote that language always accompanies empire; Schreffler argues that there was also an official aesthetic that included paintings, interiors, and furnishings.

Some interpret the objects as proof of a growing Creole patriotism. Yet objects of royal propaganda were contested in the New World (North America) in ways that they were not in the Old World (Europe). The position they held regarding nationalism was tenuous. This dovetails with post-

Figure 13.23 Armchair. Mexico.

king. While his life's work has been seen as a monarchy in decline, it can also be seen as a final expression of Spanish power in the Americas. **Churrigueresque** refers to late Spanish Baroque design, in Spain and throughout Latin America of the seventeenth and eighteenth centuries. Named for three brothers from Barcelona, Spain, it is a continuation of the stylistic trend started in Plateresque, only it is even more elaborate. The use of pattern in Churrigueresque allowed for furniture makers in the Americas to occasionally incorporate indigenous motifs.

FRENCH COLONIAL

France was a major colonial power whose ascendancy on the world stage coincided with the lessening of Dutch and Portuguese power. In addition to a large swath of North America, which resulted in the famous Louisiana Purchase of 1803, France had outposts on several Caribbean islands, including Guadeloupe, Martinique, and Saint-Domingue (today Haiti). France had substantial colonial holdings in Africa and Asia. In Africa, most of West Africa and parts of central Africa and the island of Madagascar were under French colonial control. In Asia, France had considerable presence on the eastern coast of India and, in Southeast Asia, controlled Vietnam, Cambodia, and Laos.

West Africa

The standards of design established by the French monarchy, from Louis XIV to Napoleon, Baroque through Neoclassical, had an enormous impact on monarchies around the world. Court taste also influenced design within France. People in the French provinces looked to the latest styles from Versailles and sought to emulate them—hence the term *provincial*. The word refers to pieces made simpler and

for people of more modest means. Some nobles in the French countryside were able to afford fairly accurate versions of royal designs; for those of more modest means, simplified pieces were appealing. This included middle-class merchants, craftsmen, well-off farmers, and other successful professionals. This is the trickle-down effect of design, in which the elite establish the standards of taste that the middle classes seek to emulate. While "provincial" implies a rural version, some people, then and now, preferred the simplified versions of Regency and Rococo designs. Many Rococo designs are too elaborate in their appearance and difficult aesthetically to incorporate into a household.

French provincial furniture is more likely solid than veneered. Many chairs had rush seats and unattached cushions. French provincial pieces also made their way to the French colonies. In these new locations, they represented the home country, and they were elegant and sturdy.

Senegal, the westernmost part of the continent, was the center of France's West African interests. A mid-nineteenth-century watercolor was published in a book written by David Boilat, a mixed-race African priest. One of the book's ethnic portraits, it shows the interior of a home that belongs to the *habitants,* the name given to the mixed-race, or Creole, class that grew up in several West African coastal trading centers (Figure 13.24). The print of the watercolor clearly shows a European-style home, with a fireplace, stone floor (or wood floor stenciled to look like stone), windows, European artwork framed and hung on the wall, and heavy draperies. The women of the habitant class were known as *signares*, a word of Portuguese derivation. In artworks, a signare is distinguished by her pointed headdresses; the headdress indicates that she did not carry items on her head. This signare sits on a type of ladder-back chair common in French provincial contexts. The print presents her as an

Figure 13.24 David Boilat, *Esquisses Senegalaises, Signare, 1853.*

African woman, comfortably seated, and she is at home.

GERMAN COLONIAL

The German colonial initiative started late and never reached the scale of other European powers. Part of this was due to the late date of German unification, 1871. Germany had several colonies in sub-Saharan Africa, including Cameroon, Togo, Namibia, and Tanzania. Despite Germany's modest colonial holdings, an important colonial event occurred in Germany: the "Scramble for Africa." This phrase refers to the Berlin Conference of 1884–1885, in which European powers divided up Africa into spheres of European control.

Germany also had some Asian colonies, in New Guinea, Samoa, the Solomon Islands, and the Marshall Islands. Germany was stripped of all its colonies at the end of World War I, in 1918.

Namibia

There are scenarios and features common to colonial situations, yet there are also distinctions in how the colonial relationship played out from place to place. The political effects range from relatively benign (English Hong Kong) to nefarious (Belgian Congo). Yet the cultural productions are always interesting.

A late-nineteenth-century house in Namibia, formerly South West Africa, shows one attitude of those embedded in colonialism, which is to try to re-create the home country as much as possible, building structures that remind their inhabitants of home (Figure 13.25). In the cities of Luderitz and Swakopmund, a feeling of nostalgia reigns, and there is little understanding of the local context in culture or climate. Germans built houses in a style that climatically made sense in the Bavarian Alps, but that made little sense in the deserts of South West Africa.

CONCLUSION

Across colonial contexts, the earliest designs, buildings, and furniture were an initial response to harsh conditions and limited resources; they constituted a fight for survival. The prosperity that later developed was reflected in the ability of furniture makers to interact with European styles. Yet some religious groups, the Shakers and the Puritans, retained the simplicity of the early objects and made aesthetic austerity a virtue.

Artistic traditions traveled by three principal means: furniture pieces that arrived with the colonists; trained furniture makers who emigrated, usu-

Figure 13.25 Goerke Haus. Namibia. 1909.

ally for economic reasons; and publications, such as those of Chippendale, Hepplewhite, and Sheraton, discussed in Chapter 12. The transmission of design information had implications other than design dissemination. The general characteristics of colonial design include the colonial time lag: Artistic movements that originated in Europe took time to spread around the world; thus, Neoclassicism occurs at an earlier date in England than it does in Australia. An extension of the temporal delay is that some traditional forms lived on in colonies when their usefulness in the home country had expired, such as the resilient Tulbagh chair. African craftsmen kept alive a form associated with the sixteenth and seventeenth centuries in the Netherlands and England.

Colonial pieces were rarely exact copies of European originals. The transformation came about because of new materials: cedar in Australia, stinkwood in South Africa, and ebony in India. Colonial production was characterized by a freedom from rules—European artistic guilds had little control over colonial areas, where the demarcation between professions was less distinct. This resulted in another colonial characteristic: the freedom among furniture manufacturers to innovate.

The logistics of oceangoing and local transport had the result that those in international trading centers, such as Charleston, Capetown, Sydney, and Goa, had exposure to actual European items, while those in the countryside did not—and they therefore relied on local furniture makers. This resulted in differences between city and country furniture.

The nature of the interaction between colonizer and colonized varied from continent to continent. Africa and English North America saw little utility in Baroque and Rococo forms; Latin America, by force, did. The early presence of the Dutch and Portuguese in India and Africa was marked by cooperation (prompted by necessity as much as goodwill), resulting in some highly inventive pieces that combined European forms with Hindu decorative motifs. Sometimes colonialism resulted in cultural obliteration, as in Australia and the United States, where English styles were faithfully reproduced, with indigenous traditions having little impact on them.

Ethnic complexity is a feature of colonial furniture, and the plethora of words for mixed-race people—habitants, Creole, coloured, mestiço—is evidence of the fascination with racial and cultural mixing. Because Islamic motifs were prevalent in Spanish Baroque forms, when those forms traveled to the Americas, the geometric patterns went as well, although the explicit relationship to Islam was lost.

In many countries, European art forms were a means by which colonial elites, of all races and ethnicities, expressed their status. Neoclassicism (Chapter 14) is likely the first international style. Curiously, even though it was itself a revival, for areas with no previous classical tradition, it was a means of expressing refinement, grandeur, and progress. Several inventions of the nineteenth century—railroads, industrial manufacturing processes, and steamships—were blunt tools whose effects reached all corners of the globe.

Sources

Baarsen, Reinier. *Courts and Colonies: The William and Mary Style in Holland, England, and America*. New York: Cooper-Hewitt Museum, 1988.

Baraitser, Michael, and Anton Obholzer. *Cape Country Furniture*: Cape Town: Struik Publishers, 1978.

Baraitser, Michael, and Anton Obholzer. *Cape Antique Furniture*. Cape Town: Struik Publishers, 2004.

Borcherds, Petrus. *An Autobiographical Memoir*. Cape Town: Africana Connoisseurs Press, 1963 [1861].

Buttsworth, John. *Australian Colonial Furniture*. Drummoyne, New South Wales: Colonial Living Press, 1987.

Comaroff, Jean, and John Comaroff. *Of Revelation and Revolution: Christianity, Colonialism, and Consciousness in South Africa*. Chicago: University of Chicago Press, 1991.

Cook, Mary Alexander. *The Cape Kitchen: A Description of Its Position, Lay-Out, Fittings, and Utensils*. Stellenbosch: Stellenbosch Museum, 1975.

Cook, Mary Alexander. *The Old Buildings of the Cape: A Survey and Description of Old Buildings in the Western Province*. Cape Town: Balkema, 1980.

Cooke, Edward. *Making Furniture in Preindustrial America*. Baltimore: Johns Hopkins University Press, 1996.

Craig, Clifford, Kevin Fahy, and E. Graeme Robertson. *Early Colonial Furniture in New South Wales and Van Diemen's Land*. Melbourne: Georgian House, 1972.

Fahy, Kevin, Christina Simpson, and Andrew Simpson. *Nineteenth Century Australian Furniture*. Sydney: David Ell Press, 1985.

Fairbanks, Jonathan, and Elizabeth Bates. *American Furniture: 1620 to the Present*. New York: Richard Marek, 1981.

Fehr, William. *Treasures at the Castle of Good Hope*. Cape Town: Castle Art Collection, 1963.

Gopnik, Adam. "Shining Tree of Life," *The New Yorker* 82, no. 1 (2006): pp. 162–168.

Ioannou, Noris. *The Barossa Folk: Germanic Furniture and Craft Traditions in Australia*. Roseville East: Craftsman House, 1995.

Jaffer, Amin. *Furniture From British India and Ceylon.* Salem: Peabody Essex Museum, 2001.

Kirk, John. *American Furniture: Understanding Styles, Construction, and Quality.* New York: Abrams, 2000.

Kotz, Suzanne, ed. *Dallas Museum of Art: A Guide to the Collection.* Seattle: Marquand, 1997.

Larkin, David. *The Essential Book of Shaker: Discovering the Design, Function, and Form.* New York: Rizzoli, 1995.

Pearson, M. N. *The Portuguese in India.* Cambridge: Cambridge University Press, 1987.

Peters, Walter. *Baukunst in Südwestafrika: 1884–1914.* Windhoek: John Meinert, 1981.

Random House Unabridged Dictionary, 2nd edition, 1993.

Schreffler, Michael. *The Art of Allegiance: Visual Culture and Imperial Power in Baroque New Spain.* University Park: Pennsylvania State University Press, 2007.

Shea, John. *The American Shakers and Their Furniture.* New York: Van Nostrand Reinhold, 1971.

Shipway, Verna Cook, and Warren Shipway. *Mexican Interiors.* New York: Architectural Book Publishing, 1962.

van Onselen, L. E. *Cape Antique Furniture.* Cape Town: Howard Timmins, 1959.

Veenendall, Jan. *Furniture from Indonesia, Sri Lanka, and India During the Dutch Period.* Delft: Volkenkundig Museum Nusantara, 1985.

DISCUSSION AND REVIEW QUESTIONS

1. What are the mechanisms by which styles travel around the world?
2. What are some of the causes for stylistic changes in the colonial era?
3. What are some of the general characteristics of artistic production in the colonial era?
4. What are some of the unique circumstances of specific colonial areas?
5. When is the last time you heard the word "colonial" used and what was the context?
6. Go to a local museum. How are the artifacts presented? What is emphasized in the presentation?
7. Think of one example of each of the following: an English colony, a French colony, a German colony, a Portuguese colony, and a Spanish colony. Talk about the regional differences in furniture and interior design.
8. Parts of the United States were, at one time, culturally if not politically English, Dutch, French, German, Russian, and Spanish. Name some of these areas.

CHAPTER 14

NEOCLASSICAL

1760–1789	1789	1789–1804	1804–1820	1830–1870	1780–1830
FRANCE					
Louis XVI	Goût Grec	French Revolution	Directoire	Empire	Restoration

1780–1830	1776		1810–1837		1815–1848		1772–1792	1810–1844
UNITED STATES			**ENGLAND**		**GERMANY**		**SWEDEN**	
Federal	American Revolution		Regency		Biedermeier		Gustavian	Karl Johan

Neoclassicism is a broad term for the artistic tradition whose artists reacted against Rococo art by embracing simplicity and geometric purity. It was related to political reform and sought its inspiration in antiquity. *Neoclassical* describes several movements of the late eighteenth and nineteenth centuries. As with the Renaissance, it was a period whose artists looked to the ancient world for their grounding and sometimes did so with archaeological precision.

Any artistic movement grows out of the preceding period to some extent, even a revolutionary style based on rejecting the status quo. So it is with Rococo and Neoclassical. Neoclassical was the opposite, a rejection of everything Rococo. But it also grew out of that period, so, not surprisingly, the earliest Neoclassical works seem Rococo in their expression, regarding the amount of decoration. Nonetheless, these were the pieces that started the process of artistic change.

For any period, it is worthwhile to consider cultural artifacts in political terms, but for no other period is this as true as for the Neoclassical. It was a historical revival firmly connected to contemporary politics. Neoclassicism is associated with the Age of Reason, the Enlightenment, and the French and American Revolutions.

FRANCE

The most important contextual note in France about Neoclassicism is that a new way of creating art was related to a new way of governing the country. In the French political theater, the art-politics relationship is odd, and rife with complications, discrepancies, and ambiguities. The art-equals-politics style that was considered as the antithesis of the monarchy was born in the period of Louis XVI and Marie Antoinette. The style that came to signal the excesses of the monarchy and the aristocracy was first heavily supported by the monarchy. In the nineteenth century, after the Republican experiment of the Directory, the new emperor, Napoleon, took up Neoclassicism with gusto. After him, so too did the restored Bourbon monarchy.

Louis XVI

The craze for all things Rococo had ebbed by the mid–eighteenth century and was decidedly out of fashion by 1760. In its place came a new style that looked to antiquity, particularly ancient Greece. Known as *goût grec,* or Greek taste, the first Neoclassical iteration occurred in the final decades of the French monarchy, or *ancien régime.*

The features of the new design approach included simpler materials, a lack of applied surface ornamentation, and a preference for symmetry and pure forms. Functionally, the Louis XVI Neoclassical armchair, or fauteuil, played the same role in seating arrangements as had its predecessor, the Louis XV armchair. Yet aesthetically, the Neoclassical Louis XVI is a departure from previous developments in French furniture (Figure 14.1). Most curves are gone. The legs are straight, and the back is square and only slightly off vertical. The detailing of scrolls and fluting is classical. What this piece shares with its Rococo predecessor is the lightness of its profile.

Figure 14.2 George Jacobs, Louis XVI armchair, 1770. France.

Figure 14.1 Gilt Louis XVI chair with tapestry upholstery, France.

Many furniture designers worked within the Neoclassical idiom, one of the more accomplished being Georges Jacob (1770–1841), who created several pieces for Louis XVI. His armchair is weighty, broad, and sits close to the ground (Figure 14.2). Jacob, a politically astute man, managed to continue his career after the revolution. Other artists associated with the king and queen had to flee the country.

Later works reflected the changes in taste within the Neoclassical idiom. The pieces became more austere, the lines straighter, the patterns simpler. A Louis XVI side chair (no arms) has a rounded seat. Its legs, seat, and backrest are elaborately carved, yet the piece manages to convey simplicity (Figure 14.3). The exposed wood is monochromatically painted to look like gold. Monochromatic textiles were popular.

Figure 14.3 Louis XVI side chair. France.

Directoire and Empire

The postrevolutionary style was known as **Directoire**. This was the Republican, representative government that had been the goal of the revolutionaries. Directoire pieces continued the trends started in the reign of Louis XVI.

When Napoleon came to power in 1799, he co-opted the Neoclassical style. He became emperor in 1804, and the style of his reign, and its imitators, is now known as **Empire**. The distinctions between Directoire and Empire were incremental. In both, the detailing was classical. The profiles were light. Rococo curves, complexity, and ambiguity were a thing of the past.

David, Juliette Récamier, and Napoleon

Charles Percier was commisioned, through one of his students, Louis Berthault, to refashion the interiors of the home of the banker M. Récamier. His young wife, Madame Récamier, was painted by the painter Jacques-Louis David (1748–1825). David's painting is important because of its integration of fashion and furnishings, and for the visual qualities of the painting itself. In the painting, Juliette Récamier reclines on a settee, which came to be known as a "Récamier" (Figure 14.4). Luc de Nanteuil writes that the settee was made by the famed Neoclassical furniture designer Georges Jacob (Nanteuil 1985, p. 132). Her feet are bare, which offended some people who thought it inappropriate for a formal and public portrait. She wears an empire gown, a close approximation of ancient dress, her hair curled like a Roman lady's. The fashion term *empire waist* originated in the Napoleonic empire with dresses such as the one worn by Juliette Récamier. David's composition employs simplicity in several respects.

Just as many Neoclassical artists were intrigued by the possibilities of simple geometries, David reduced his pictorial composition to the simplest possible elements: the horizontal and the vertical. The subtle dynamism of the painting, however, derives from Récamier's reclining figure. The curves of her body, her formal yet relaxed posture, and the draping of her gown contrast with the rigid X-Y axis established by settee and lamp.

David was the most celebrated artist of his day, a fierce critic of the Rococo style and a tireless proponent of Neoclassicism and political reform. Juliette Récamier, as painted by David, is somber, serious, and intelligent. The moment captured is not psychologically complex, a singularity that Nanteuil notices in other aspects of the painting as well: "The décor is even more neutral than in David's other portraits. The vertical blends into the hori-

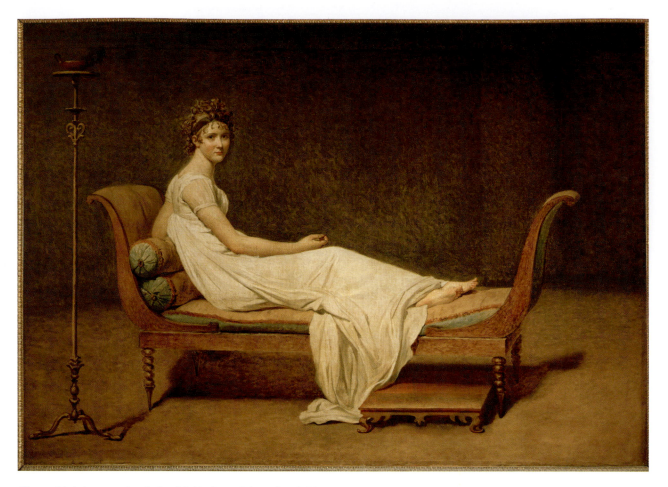

Figure 14.4 Jacques-Louis David. Madame Récamier, 1780.

zontal and the tones are in harmony, rather than in contrast. David tried to represent his model in that spirit of simplicity which attracted him to Greek art, and which inspired the fashions of the time. Juliette's long floating gown barely outlines her body and its folds fall softly to the foot of the stool" (Nanteuil 1985, p. 132). Many Neoclassical painters were successful—Vien, Mengs, Kauffmann—but Jacques-Louis David was able to fuse the taste of the day with a moral clarity and a fervent belief in artistic and political reform.

David turned his talents to representing the hero of the moment, Napoleon. The Italian Neoclassical sculptor Canova did a larger-than-life sculpture of the leader that portrayed him as a Roman god. Napoleon was embarrassed by the overt heroicism of the nearly nude statue and stashed it away. David,

in contrast, deftly worked with the Emperor's physiognomy and visage, yet never losing sight of his subject's heroic quality.

From Throne to Desk

David's portrait of Napoleon was his last painting of the Emperor (Nanteuil 1985, p. 146). In portraiture of the time, it was fashionable for people to pose as classical heroes and heroines. In David's painting, modern history replaces antiquity as the supplier of heroes (Figure 14.5). David's portrait of Napoleon has clarity and dramatic intensity. Like his Bourbon predecessors, Napoleon was a patron of the arts, personally responsible for commissioning a great deal of Neoclassical architecture, interiors, furnishings, paintings, sculpture, and fashion. Philippe Bordes (2005) writes: "Napoleon thor-

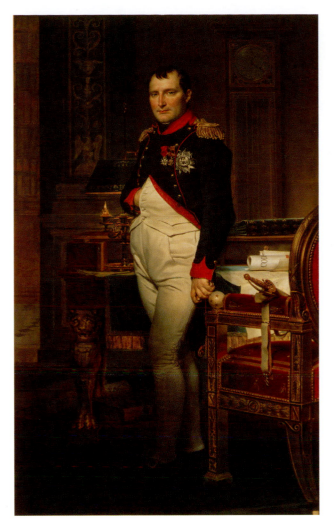

Figure 14.5 Jacques-Louis David. Portrait of Napoleon in his study, 1812.

oughly believed that impressive pomp and splendor could be used to political advantage and that encouragement of the luxury trades had a favorable impact on the national economy" (p. 65). Although the style of choice differed, Napoleon took a cue from Louis XIV with his belief that the arts were a political tool, for himself and for France.

In David's painting, the leader of the nation was working tirelessly for his citizens. It is an eerily calm view of a general. He is shown in his study at the Tuileries palace, which is completely outfitted with Neoclassical furniture: a chair, desk, and clock. David was knowledgeable about Neoclassical furniture (Nanteuil 1985, p. 146). The color palette, of furniture, costume, and painting, relies upon a restrained use of primary colors. The empire chair is red and gold, and the Emperor's uniform combines white, red, blue, and gold. Napoleon had previously hired David to design uniforms for him.

Numerous paintings and engravings show the emperor on his throne, some by David, but David's painting of the Emperor in his study is significant because a desk has usurped the throne as the piece of furniture associated with the nation's ruler. Napoleon played the imperial card too, showing himself resplendently dressed and surrounded with all the trappings of empire. But David's canvas portrays him as the tireless worker. Hugh Honour (1977) writes: "The candles have burnt low, the clock shows that it is 4:13 in the morning and the Emperor stands by the writing table where he has been working on the legal code, with a volume of Plutarch at his feet" (p. 179). Typical for David and other Neoclassical painters, the background is parallel to the picture plane and the wall is also classically detailed.

Architecture and Interiors

Charles Percier (1764–1838) and Pierre-François-Léonard Fontaine (1762–1853) met as students and became leading figures of interior design and architecture, with the support of the Emperor and his Empress. Publications of their work, including Percier's *Recueil des Arts décoratifs* (1801), made them well known in England and Germany.

One of the gems of their work was a redesign of the interiors of a chateau for Napoleon's wife, the Empress Josephine, the Chateau de Malmaison, 1801–1812. Percier and Fontaine draped the walls and ceilings of the dining room at Malmaison to look like a tent (Figure 14.6). The conceit, not totally convincing, is that this is a tent of a Roman commander, perhaps Marcus Aurelius, on a military campaign in foreign lands. Percier and Fontaine are

Figure 14.6 Charles Percier and Pierre-François Fontaine. Chateau de Malmaison. France.

considered the first interior designers in the modern sense in that they designed everything within sight. They were architects, yet they were less concerned with structure and more concerned with decorative effect. They designed the furniture, walls, ceilings, fireplace, lighting, and all accessories. Mario Praz was an Italian historian of the decorative arts whose writings are at once old-fashioned, perceptive, and forward-looking. About the first interior designers, he writes: "The line drawings of interior decorations by Percier and Fontaine combine the inspiration of classical antiquity with a Renaissance clarity" (Praz 1964, p. 185). Art historians of Neoclassicism frequently reduce it in their discussion to a simple straight line.

Claude-Nicolas Ledoux (1736–1806) was a major French Neoclassical architect, his chief com-mission being thirty-seven tollhouses. He was another of the politically astute architects who had royal commissions yet was able to stay in France after the revolution.

Furniture

A French empire trident table is one of the works whose creator sought to accurately re-create a classical piece (Figure 14.7). More of a reproduction than a reinvention, it resembles actual Greek and Roman three-legged tables. The Louis XVI penchant for gilding all wood surfaces gradually gave way to a preference for ebonized wood and natural wood. Some Neoclassical artists of this period increased their efforts to be faithful to ancient models. The excavations at Herculaneum and Pompeii

Figure 14.7 Empire three-legged table. France.

began in 1748, and this provided a fresh impetus for the craze for classical stylings. The ensuing publications provided accurate information about actual Roman artworks.

The last of the Napoleonic Wars included Napoleon's disastrous decision to invade Russia in 1812, the year of David's portrait. This marked the beginning of his decline, and he was forced to abdicate in 1814. Napoleon tried to return to power, but in the Battle of Waterloo in 1815, he lost to an English-Prussian coalition. His fate was sealed and he spent the rest of his years in exile. The Empire Style outlived the Emperor.

UNITED STATES

During the period that Neoclassicism was raging in Europe, Americans were no longer fighting the elements for survival but were fully able to engage with international design currents. Just as Neoclas-

sicism in France was related to democracy, so it was in the United States. Historian of the decorative arts Gerald Ward (2006) wrote: "Classicism permeated almost every aspect of life and thought in America. Its impact was felt in government, education, architecture, and dress, as well as furnishings, as citizens sought to emulate and recapture the virtues of the ancient Greeks and the Republic of Rome" (p. 89).

With their nearly coincident revolutions, the United States and France were on parallel tracks politically and artistically. Famous American political figures such as Thomas Jefferson and Benjamin Franklin spent extended periods of time in France. Both countries overthrew their monarchs at approximately the same time—France deposed Louis XVI, the United States George III. There were parallel revolutions, in 1776 in the United States, and in 1789 in France. France and the United States, by the end of the eighteenth century and the beginning of the nineteenth, were great allies, and it was England that most Americans viewed with distrust and suspicion. France and the United States had a similar ideology in their desire to establish a representative government, and both found in Neoclassicism the design that represented their political aspirations.

Benjamin Franklin (1706–1790) spent eight years in France, from 1776 to 1785. He was followed by Thomas Jefferson (1743–1826), a draftsman of the Declaration of Independence and the third American president. Jefferson was an important politician, and is also known for his role in fostering the American version of Neoclassicism. (Neoclassical buildings that resemble his works are sometimes referred to as **Jeffersonian**.) From 1784 to 1789, Jefferson served as ambassador to France, underscoring the strength of the Franco-American alliance. Few significant political achievements stem from Jefferson's time in Paris, but while there, he immersed himself in French art and architecture. He left shortly before the violence of the revolution began.

Jefferson designed a state capitol for Virginia, in Richmond, and the campus of the University of Virginia (1817–1826). His own house, Monticello (1796–1809), is formally related to two famous European classically inspired residences: the Italian Renaissance Villa Rotunda and its English eighteenth-century cousin, Chiswick. But Monticello was also an inventive work of design. It looks like a one-story building, but it actually has a second story of bedrooms and a lower service floor. An alcove bed borrows a configuration from Malmaison (Figure 14.8). It opened onto Jefferson's bedroom and his office.

Figure 14.8 Thomas Jefferson. Monticello, bedroom.

Once the Declaration of Independence was signed in 1776, the United States was no longer officially a colony. American architects soon started taking the steps to establish the foundling profession. Benjamin Latrobe and Charles Bulfinch are considered the fathers of American architecture. Latrobe (1764–1820) was born in Britain but carried out his career in the United States. He knew Thomas Jefferson, who hired him to finish the United States Capitol. Latrobe's most accomplished work was for the Basilica of the Assumption of the Blessed Virgin Mary, in Baltimore in 1805. The dome of the basilica carefully replicates the dome of the Pantheon. Latrobe also designed a plausible copy of the klismos chair (Figure 14.9) Bulfinch (1763–1844) was the architect of the Massachusetts State Capitol (1795–1797). He had visited England, where he saw firsthand the work of the Adams brothers.

The visible similarities between European and American Neoclassicism suggest that designers were reaching across the ocean and building upon a shared tradition. American Georgian houses followed the parameters of English Georgian houses. They were symmetrical, with classical detailing in the cornices and the pediments, pilasters, and windows. Southern plantations also followed the model of English country houses, although they were less elaborate.

Federal

Federal was the American strand of Neoclassicism. There were considerable numbers of pieces influenced by the Neoclassical work of English furniture designers Sheraton, Hepplewhite, and Chippendale (Figure 14.9). Black horsehair was a favored upholstery textile for Neoclassical chairs. Publications played an important role in the international spread of Neoclassicism and in providing accurate information about its forms and details. Robert Adams published engravings of his projects, and he, along with Thomas Hope and George Smith, published

Figure 14.9 Benjamin Henry Latrobe, side chair, c. 1790–1820. United States.

builder's guides. Knowledge of actual antiquity came from many sources, including Jean-Françoise de Neufforge's *Receuil élémentaire d'architecture*. James Stuart and Nicholas Revett traveled to Athens in 1751, and their publication of 1762, *The Antiquities of Athens*, provided much-needed information about Greek monuments. *The Society of London Cabinet-Makers' Book of Prices* (1788), provided technical information for producers, rather than consumers, of furniture (Clouston 1975, p. 131). English and French publications made their way to the United States and were largely responsible for the creation of American Empire. Jefferson himself collected many of these books in his library at Monticello.

A common American Empire armchair has curved armrests and straight legs. The elements are ancient, but the form is nineteenth-century American (Figure 14.10).

Figure 14.10 Empire armchair. United States.

Classical lyres, a musical instrument resembling a harp, and crowns of laurel leaves were favorite Neoclassical motifs. Napoleon co-opted the laurel wreath as his personal insignia, a connection between his reign and France and the Roman Empire. The use of symbols was a significant feature of Neoclassical furniture, with Eagles being a favored American motif. An American pedestal table from 1815 has the finishes typical of American Neoclassical furniture: a clear finish on the wood, with prominent black and gold accents (Figure 14.11).

Daybeds were a favorite item of Neoclassical designers, and they exist in great variety. This was, in part, due to David's iconic image of Juliette Récamier. A Lanniere bed has sphinxes, acanthus leaves, and a restrained use of gilding (Figure 14.12).

Daybeds were used for napping or for reclining while in the company of others.

Samuel McIntire (1757–1811) was an American furniture maker whose father was a carpenter. Early in his career, he carved ship figureheads. He mostly made furniture according to the designs of others. He started out working in the colonial Georgian tradition and gradually developed a leaner style consistent with American Federal.

Duncan Phyfe (1768–1854) was the Scottish-born American cabinetmaker who is considered one of the finest American furniture makers. In 1792, he moved to New York. He was a successful businessman, with many employees. He was a major proponent of Neoclassicism in the United States, and he counted John Jacob Astor among his clients. His signature piece was a sofa or daybed (Figure 14.13), of which he designed innumerable variations. Neoclassical pieces were configured differently as a part of furniture arrangements. Praz notes: "Furniture was no longer fused with wall decoration but regained an independence that soon led to virtual isolation" (Praz 1964, p. 160). Pieces were used as movable objects in a room, and this

Figure 14.11 American pedestal table.

Figure 14.12 Charles Honore Lanniere. Daybed. United States.

Figure 14.13 Récamier sofa. United States.

Figure 14.14 Hitchcock chair, 1825–1850. United States.

the Greek klismos chair. A member of the British royal family and himself a furniture maker, David Linley, states, "In America the Greek style was readily adopted as a means of embodying the democratic principles of the new republic" (Linley 1993, p. 54). Yet in England, Neoclassicism was related to an opulent resurgence of the monarchy.

ENGLAND

Regency relates to the political structure in which a regent stands in for an underage heir to the throne. Theoretically, it can pertain to any regency. There were two significant furniture styles known as Regency: French Regency, which ushered in the Rococo, and English Regency, which was related to Neoclassicism.

English Regency is the English version of Neoclassicism. Considerable stylistic similarities link French Directoire, American Federal, and English Regency, largely due to the international market for books on antiquities, architecture, and design.

would be characteristic of the use of furniture throughout the nineteenth century.

Lambert Hitchcock (1795–1852) was another successful furniture maker whose efforts made Neoclassicism part of the American design mainstream. Neoclassicism, in contrast to Rococo, was not intended to be another elite style. In that regard, Hitchcock, working out of Connecticut, is mostly known for having created a chair made out of wood with a common rush seat. His chairs were painted black and then stenciled. Known as Hitchcock chairs, they were popular with people of modest means (Figure 14.14). Hitchcock chairs are a ubiquitous part of the American furniture vocabulary, all the while maintaining a striking resemblance to

Architecture and Interiors

English regency design is known as a restrained form of classicism, with occasional instances of uncharacteristic exoticism. Two projects by John Nash (1752–1835) exemplify this bifurcated aspect of Regency design. One is Regent's Park and the other is the Royal Pavilion at Brighton. Nash's Regent's Park is a grand urban gesture linked to capitalism; it was a Neoclassical façade with unexceptional row houses behind it.

Lord Burlington (1694–1753) owned a substantial property in the outskirts of London. Burlington designed his own house, Chiswick, in 1725. It is a building clearly modeled on Palladio's Villa Rotunda, with Neoclassical interiors and furniture. David Linley (1993) acknowledged Lord Burlington's role in setting the foundation for Neoclassi-

Figure 14.15 Robert Adam. Syon House. Isleworth, England.

cism: "Palladianism, pioneered by Lord Burlington and his circle, ushered in a new era of design blending English practicality with the purest classical ideals" (p. 43).

The central octagon acts as the figural and functional center of the project (Jefferson's Monticello also employs an octagon). Yet the house is no longer situated in a formal parklike setting, such as Versailles, but within an informal picturesque English garden. Romanticism was the cross-disciplinary movement that involved artists, poets, authors, and landscape designers. As it highlighted the capri-ciousness of nature and accidental forms, it was, in certain respects, a rejection of Neoclassicism. Yet in the English context, such as Chiswick's garden, a classically detailed house stood within a picturesque landscape, a setting that brought together two contrary movements. Another interpretation of Chiswick is that it was a gesture to express English democratic freedoms. The Neopalladian house was a counteroffensive to the Rococo, and the English garden was an alternative to the French formal garden. Certain commonalities aside, while they occasionally overlapped, Romanticism and Neo-

Figure 14.16 Robert Smirke. British Museum. London.

classicism are typically presented as distinct artistic entities.

The Adam brothers were Scotsmen who worked out of London. Robert Adam (1728–1792) was the chief designer, while James Adam (1730–1794) was the business partner. One focused on design, the other on commerce and practical matters.

The overall body of work of the Adams brothers contains Rococo projects and Neoclassical projects. The Rococo projects stem from earlier in their career. Of their Neoclassical work, one of their most accomplished was Syon House (Figure 14.15). Significantly, when designing the home for the Duke of Northumberland, Robert Adam referred to Neoclassicism as the French style.

Their other Neoclassical masterwork is Osterley Park, from the same time period, 1762–1769. Their designs often inventively combined several

classical traditions. Much of their work was Neoclassical, yet they were not directly copying the ancients but relating to it through the works of Renaissance architect Palladio. They also could be inventive with their use of the classical vocabulary, such as combining Ionic pilasters with a Doric entablature, or Ionic details with coffered ceilings. After experiments with dynamic shapes and deeply cut Baroque and Rococo carving, the Adam brothers later in their career created surfaces that were once again flat.

Robert Smirke (1780–1867) designed the British Museum in 1824 (Figure 14.16). Smirke's Museum looks correctly classical, yet its Greek temple front sprouts substantial side wings. The entry capped with a pediment leads directly to a very un-Greek dome. It is a large building, a Napoleonic-style project of public infrastructure on an urban scale.

Figure 14.17 Jacob Desmalter. Throne of Emperor Napoleon I Bonaparte. Empire armchair, Egyptian influence, 1803–1813.

Furniture and Graphics

A sideline of Neoclassical artists was a renewed interest in Egyptian artifacts, and again there was a Napoleonic connection. Napoleon's expedition to Egypt in 1798 had cultural ramifications. The resulting publications, the twenty-one-volume *Description d'Egypte,* made available detailed information about Egyptian antiquities. The desire was not necessarily to re-create Egyptian forms but to include Egyptian motifs in a Neoclassical design, such as the use of Egyptian sphinx heads on a chair's front legs (Figure 14.17). Desmalter's chair has lion's-paw feet, scrolls, and classical fluting. There were many strands of Neoclassicism, including Greek, Roman, and Egyptian. Some artists took the desire to imitate the ancients to extremes. Hancarville did an etching in which he sought to faithfully re-create on paper the drawing technique of a red-figure Greek vase painter (Figure 14.18).

Figure 14.18 Pierre-François Hancarville. Hercules and a companion in combat with centaurs. 1766–1767.

Figure 14.19 Karl Friedrich Schinkel. Altes Museum. 1824–1830. Berlin.

GERMANY

German history presents a complicated scenario, as early-nineteenth-century Germany was not a unified country. German Neoclassicism is commonly considered in light of Karl Friedrich Schinkel in Prussia and Leo von Klenze in Bavaria; both were talented architects and painters. Yet even Schinkel, the Neoclassical architect *par excellence*, made a significant number of Gothic Revival designs. With his fanciful and accomplished designs for theater and opera, he experimented with Egyptian and Aztec forms.

Karl Friedrich Schinkel (1781–1841) designed the Altes Museum, a cubic mass that is a highly inventive project. A blocky form, it is not a re-creation of an actual classical building, for it is an abstraction of classicism. It uses a Greek temple's side elevation as a front elevation (Figure 14.19). Schinkel's patron was Friedrich Wilhelm III, for whom he designed singular public buildings—not urban complexes, nonetheless they were deftly suited to their urban environment.

One reason for singling out the Greeks for praise, as Schinkel did, is that they used columns structurally, whereas the Romans used them decoratively.

A corollary to Schinkel's interest in ancient Greece was the art critic Joachim Winckelmann, who passionately defended the supremacy of Greek art. Schinkel's inventive use of classicism with the Altes Museum, like Smirke's British Museum, demonstrates that those operating within Neoclassical stylistics were not copying the past but working creatively with its vocabulary. And in architecture, Neoclassical was often related to public buildings such as museums and libraries.

A chair by Schinkel is light-years away from Rococo extravagance (Figure 14.20). With its economical use of materials and straight legs, it is a visual essay in restraint.

shoot, some very simple pieces show no classical detailing at all.

Unlike other manifestations of Neoclassicism, Biedermeier was not particularly political. Biedermeier occurred when Romanticism was in full swing, such as the poetry of Byron. Biedermeier intersected with Romanticism in the field of landscape painting. Many Biedermeier paintings featured interior views. Indoors were comfortable, serene, and leisurely, and the outdoors were inviting and accessible.

Biedermeier furniture was most often made in red and blond woods, such as mahogany, and cherry, but also ash and walnut, and a characteristic was an orange or reddish color. Many pieces are particularly sparse or simple, sometimes austere. Chairs are

Figure 14.20 Two chairs in the living room of Charlottenhof designed by Schinkel.

Biedermeier

Biedermeier refers to a middle-class art whose geographic scope included Austria, the Czech lands, Germany, Denmark, and Poland. Its chronological benchmarks are the Congress of Vienna in 1815, which resolved the Napoleonic wars, to the various European revolutions of 1848. The term "Biedermeier" was not used until the late nineteenth century, and, as with many stylistic terms, was initially a term of derision. "Bieder" means conventional, and "Maier" or "Meyer" is one of the commonest of German surnames, such as the names Jones or Smith in English.

Initially, German Biedermeier furniture was the rural version of Neoclassical furniture. It was simple and restrained. Details were ebonized (stained to simulate ebony), such as columns and trim pieces. Gilding was limited. While it was a Neoclassical off-

Figure 14.21 Biedermeier secretaire. Germany. Nineteenth century.

Figure 14.22 Biedermeier sofa. Germany.

streamlined, elegantly functional. This is a style of furniture associated with the bourgeoisie and the provinces. Biedermeier is to Neoclassical as French provincial is to Rococo.

While initially created for a rural middle class, the pieces found fans, and customers, in the upper classes as well. On the occasion of an exhibition devoted to Biedermeier furniture, Hans Ottomeyer wrote: "Biedermeier is here interpreted not as a lowly product of bourgeois taste but rather as a highly cultivated and refined quest for simplicity and purity of form that has its roots in the late eighteenth century" (Ottomeyer 2006, p. 39).

A Biedermeier secretaire is mostly naturally finished wood, with columns, pilasters, and restrained use of metal (Figure 14.21). A Biedermeier sofa is an essay in simplicity (Figure 14.22). It is scarcely recognizable as classical, except for the curved ends and the outlines of the feet. Its design is abstract, relying on geometry, a clear finish, and a lack of ornamentation.

SWEDEN

Swedish art historian Johan Cederlund relates that Neoclassicism was late in arriving at the Scandinavian country, and that the preference for Rococo designs was enduring (Cederlund 2006, p. 170). There was also considerable overlap between the two periods, with many Swedish projects that exhibit both Rococo and Neoclassical characteristics.

When Neoclassicism did arrive, it was largely due to the interests of King Gustav III. Gustav III's favorite architect was Jean Eric Rehn, and Rehn traveled to Italy. While there, he saw firsthand classical, Renaissance, and Neoclassical works. "Rehn's travels initiated a new period in Swedish art history. His exposure to the ancient world and to its echoes in contemporary work definitely shaped not only his own personal artistic development but also that of Sweden" (Cederlund 2006, p. 172).

Swedish Neoclassicism is so inextricably intertwined with Gustav III that the style is also referred to as Gustavian. The architect Erik Palmstedt designed the Court Theater at Gripsholm in 1781, a project that skillfully adapts a rotunda that looks like the Roman Pantheon to be a theater, complete with a generous backstage. The Swedish king's passion for Neoclassicism is evidence that France dominated the world in design matters. Gustav III imitated XVI's bedroom stylistically and also initiated the practice of the levée, the publicly viewed awakening of the monarch. Cederlund writes that "more than a few of his foreign guests found this outdated practice strange" (Cederlund 2006, p. 177).

The French-Swedish connection continued into the nineteenth century. The childless King Karl XIII adopted French field marshal Jean Baptiste Berndadotte, who ruled Sweden as Karl Johan. Empire design in Sweden is known as Karl Johan (Cederlund 2006, p. 228). The Swedish interest in Neoclassicism was far-reaching, and included architecture, and the decorative arts, including furnishings.

NEOCLASSICISM AND ROMANTICISM

There is little scholarly consensus on the relationship between Neoclassicism and Romanticism. One school of thought considers them as opposed artistic movements and neatly chronologically distinct, with Romanticism following Neoclassicism. Another school of thought considers them as contemporary and alike, in sentiment if not in form. In the imagined battle of classicists over Romantics, the former are beholden to a state-sponsored institutionalized art. Their academic art is elite, emotionally cold, and flat. The latter are a group of individualists, and their works are colorful, emotional, and visually bold.

Hugh Honour belongs to the older school of thought, yet his work is more nuanced than is commonly thought, as he notes the connections that

bind Romanticism to Neoclassicism. He argues that Neoclassicism has more in common with Romanticism than Neoclassicism does to Rococo. He writes that the stylistic change from Neoclassicism to Romanticism (which he sees as successive, and not contemporary, movements) was not "the result of a reaction comparable with that which led to the rejection of the Rococo fifty years earlier. The Neoclassical movement contained within itself the seeds of most of the Romantic forms that were to destroy it" (Honour 1977, p. 186).

The Rococo-Neoclassicism divide was often reduced to an opposition between a curve and a straight line. Another strand of scholars presents Neoclassicism-Romantic schism in terms of the contrast between line and color. Art historian Andrew Carrington Shelton, writing about the painter Ingres, sees the supposed divide in a different way. He writes: "What was at stake in the great debates over line versus color and classicism versus Romanticism in the 1830s and 1840s was not so much a theoretical position as the personal power and prestige of those who came to embody each cause" (Shelton 2001, p. 719).

The Biedermeier furniture exhibit held at the Milwaukee Art Museum in 2006 emphasized the connections between Romanticism and classicism, or at least the German vernacular version of it, Biedermeier (Ottomeyer 2006). It included many examples of works by known classicists, such as Schinkel, who produced decidedly Romantic works, with Gothic ruins set within foreboding Romantic landscapes.

CONCLUSION

Even though Romanticism and Neoclassicism are often presented as contrary movements, some projects combined aspects of each, a complexity that was a harbinger of the multiple modes of stylistic expression that was to dominate the second half of the nineteenth century.

Neoclassicism, in its various forms, can be seen as the end of a series of stylistic traditions that date back to antiquity. Its effects were found across the design spectrum, from designed objects, to dresses, paintings, and buildings. Neoclassicism provided a resolute answer to the question What should the world be? Its proponents displayed a sincerity and aesthetic surety that the world would not quickly find again. Neoclassical architects and designers were responding to a political call to arms that was local (Paris, Washington, or Berlin), yet their projects also stressed that classicism was a universal design language, based on simple massing and symmetry, and opposed to changing tastes and fashion.

Neoclassicism is the last of a series of big artistic movements in which each seems a reaction against the previous generation. Stylistically there is a linear progression from Renaissance, to Baroque, to Regency, to Rococo, to Neoclassicism. This trajectory, however, was at an end. Instead of seeing Neoclassicism as the end of a progression, Gerald Ward sees it as the harbinger of what was to come: "Neoclassicism was the first of many successive yet overlapping revival styles that would come to typify the eclecticism of the nineteenth century. While many of the later revivals were similarly linked to moralistic leanings or social movements, none captured the imagination and profoundly influenced the shape and look of the entire country to the extent of Neoclassicism" (Ward 2006, p. 92). From that perspective, Neoclassicism was to be usurped into a nineteenth-century mélange of historical revivals.

Sources

Bordes, Philippe. *Jacques-Louis David: Empire to Exile*. New Haven: Yale University Press, 2005.

Brookner, Anita. *Jacques-Louis David*. New York: Harper and Row, 1980.

Brookner. *Romanticism and Its Discontents*. New York: Farrar, Straus and Giroux, 2000.

Cederlund, Johan. *Classical Swedish Architecture and Interiors, 1650–1840*. New York: Norton, 2006.

Clouston, K. Warren. *The Chippendale Period in English Furniture*. Ilkley: EP Publishing, 1975.

Fastnedge, Ralph. *Sheraton Furniture*. London: Faber and Faber, 1962.

Honour, Hugh. *Neo-classicism*. London: Penguin, 1977.

Levey, Michael. *Rococo to Revolution: Major Trends in Eighteenth-Century Painting*. London: Thames and Hudson, 1966.

Linley, David. *Classical Furniture*. New York: Abrams, 1993.

Nanteuil, Luc de. *Jacques-Louis David*. New York: Abrams, 1985.

Ottomeyer, Hans, Klaus Albrecht Schroder, and Laurie Winters. *Biedermeier: The Invention of Simplicity*, exhibition catalog. Milwaukee: Milwaukee Art Museum, 2006.

Pile, John. *A History of Interior Design*. New York: Wiley, 2000.

Praz, Mario. *An Illustrated History of Furnishing*. New York: George Braziller, 1964.

Shelton, Andrew Carrington. "Art, Politics, and the Politics of Art: Ingres's Saint Symphorien at the 1834 Salon." *Art Bulletin* vol. 83, no. 4 (December 2001): 711–739.

Ward, Gerald. "Neoclassicism and the New Nation: The Late Eighteenth and Early Nineteenth Centuries," in *American Decorative Arts and Sculpture*. Boston: Museum of Fine Arts, 2006.

DISCUSSION AND REVIEW QUESTIONS

1. What are some Neoclassical buildings in your area?

2. List some of the many alternate names for styles or movements related to Neoclassicism.

3. In its approach to antiquity, how does Neoclassicism compare with the Renaissance?

4. What were some of the national strains of Neoclassicism and some of each country's unique characteristics?

5. How did early Neoclassical works in France retain some Rococo elements?

6. When designing, what was important to Neoclassical designers? What was unimportant? Chiswick was an exception; there weren't many Neoclassical houses built. Any idea why?

7. Discuss elements of Neoclassicism from across the arts—painting, fashion, furniture design, and architecture. What were the common interests?

8. What is the name for middle-class Neoclassical furniture from Germany and surrounding countries?

CHAPTER 15

VICTORIAN AND HISTORICAL REVIVALS

1837–1901	1820–1929	1750–1939	1842–1914	1850–1905	1825–1900
Victorian	Egyptian Revival	Gothic Revival	Greek Revival	Renaissance Revival	Romanesque Revival

In the Victorian period, the universal standards of taste were collapsing in the phenomenon known as the battle of styles. The nineteenth century ushered in the modernist movement, yet it did so in a complex and contradictory way. The era that gave us modernism was also known for a myriad of historical revivals. Often the styles were precisely that—styles divorced from the cultural contexts that originally produced them. The nineteenth century began with Neoclassicism, the last universally accepted style, and then proceeded into an à-la-carte menu of styles in the middle of the century. Deep-seated antipathies pitted the proponents of Neoclassicism against the champions of Gothic Revival. The plurality of design choices gave little indication that modernism was to arrive at the end of the century.

"Victorian" literally refers to anything in the decorative arts and architecture produced during the reign of Queen Victoria (1837–1901). The profusion of styles was particularly strong, and strongly fought, in England. While the prominent English Victorian style was Gothic Revival, no one style was universally accepted.

Throughout history, technology has significantly impacted the arts and furniture making, from the development of the arch, to paper, to planed lumber. Yet the nineteenth century was besot with technological innovations, any one of which had the potential to significantly alter the way people lived and did business; collectively, these inventions wrenched the world from what we now view as history into the modern era.

Many of the innovations involved communications and media. The nineteenth century started out with sailing ships, relying on the same means of propulsion that had been used for millennia, not essentially different from the feluccas that had been sailing the Nile since time immemorial. The century ended with steam-powered ships, no longer dependent on weather conditions and made from steel, not wood. The dramatic change in the design environment was also due to the explosive population growth and urbanization that accompanied industrialization.

Iron had also been around for centuries, but sophisticated manufacturing techniques greatly increased its use; it became an important architectural material and made an appearance in furniture. Steel was similarly used in greater quantities. Running water, flush toilets, central heating, first gas then electric lighting, whale oil then kerosene, milled lumber—all affected the world of design. Glass was made in factories in large sheets, just one of the many factors that made a new building type possible—the skyscraper.

With the considerable wisdom of hindsight when looking at nineteenth-century architecture and design, one finds the seeds of modernism all over the place, from Schinkel's Bauakademie in Berlin, 1831, to Henry Hobson Richardson's Glesner House in Chicago, 1885. At first it seems curious that an era greatly impacted by technological achievement was, in the realm of design, defined by historicity and a multitude of competing styles. All artistic movements owe something to the period that preceded them, even if by contrast. There were early indications of the revolution to come. When the nineteenth century is carefully examined, the specter of modernism raises its head in the most unlikely places.

One explanation for the persistence of historical styles in the nineteenth century involves the education and training of designers. Nineteenth-century architects and designers were trained in their respective disciplines and traditions, and like most artists and craftspeople, they knew of no way to respond to world conditions and change except, initially, from within those traditions. Thus we have the phenomena of Romanesque skyscrapers and Turkish baths in steamships.

A rationale for the historic look of designed objects is that the new technologies implicitly promised to improve the lives of the lower and middle classes. Evidence of this prophecy's fulfillment is the existence of decorated objects that previously were handcrafted, expensive, and available only to the wealthiest. Some new machine-made objects were affordable. Inventions were supposed to provide luxury, or at least the appearance of it, for people for whom expensive-looking baubles were previously out of reach.

QUEEN VICTORIA

The nineteenth century and Queen Victoria (1819–1901) are essentially synonymous. The monarch, whose given name connotes etiquette and decorum, lived her years almost perfectly within the 1800s. She was born when the world was in the throes of Neoclassicism, and she came of age and to the throne when that period was nearing its end. She lived to see only one year of the twentieth century. As "Victorian era" refers to anything made during her long reign, one frequently finds objects referred to as Victorian that do not stylistically look Victorian. Generally speaking, regarding style, "Victorian" refers to articles that are elaborate in their decoration, utilize a dark and sometimes somber color palette, and freely make use of historical precedents, often in combination. Regarding the configuration of interiors, Victorian design is characterized by an increase in the overall number of objects, and their complexity, that figured in the decorative schemes of lower-, middle-, and upper-class homes. These material attributes are frequently superimposed with an idea of sexual and moral propriety that largely stemmed from the Queen herself (notwithstanding the notoriety surrounding her likely affair with her personal servant, John Brown). Despite its considerable popularity, to many (a big group, including all the modernists) "Victorian" connoted the depths of bad taste, allegedly playing into the desire of unsophisticated people for efflorescent decoration, and a frenzy of decorative excess.

HISTORIC REVIVALS

The nineteenth century started out with Neoclassicism, which was also an artistic movement inspired by the past, but the height of the era of competing historic styles started in earnest in 1830.

Gothic Revival

Gothic Revival was the most important of the mid-century historic revivals. This is largely due to its prominent place in England and France and the English colonies, including Australia, South Africa, and the United States. For proponents of Gothic Revival, it was not one of an array of choices but the way that architecture, interiors, and designed objects should be done.

In England, Gothic Revival was a means of announcing Englishness. Michael McCarthy dates the beginning of the Gothic Revival in England to the late eighteenth century and the figure Horace Walpole (McCarthy 1987). Walpole created a series of Gothic-inspired **follies**, pavilions with little purpose other than to act as eye-catching accents in picturesque English gardens. For his own home, Strawberry Hill in Twickenham, Walpole created an important set of Gothic Revival interiors. They garnered a lot of attention in his day and also served as inspiration for nineteenth-century Gothic Revivalists.

High Victorian Gothic began with two publications by John Ruskin, *The Seven Lamps of Architecture* (1849) and *The Stones of Venice* (1851). Ruskin promoted medieval European architecture, especially that of northern Italy. His writings connect design to moralistic theories and consider buildings as shells awaiting agglomerations of ornament. In *The Seven Lamps,* Ruskin outlined his belief that ornament is the vital component that distinguishes architecture from mere building. Ornament was central to Ruskin's thought.

Gothic Revival had the advantage that it was related to Christianity from its beginnings, unlike Pagan classicism and Egyptian design. Mid-nineteenth-century England built large numbers of churches, which created the need for large numbers of architects, designers, and craftsmen familiar with medieval detailing. Ruskin fostered the idea that good design was moral and related to piety and rectitude, all of which, to his mind, was best expressed in Gothic forms.

Augustus Welby Northmore Pugin (1812–1852) was, like Ruskin, a writer, but as an accomplished furniture designer and sometime architect, he was able to see his ideas translated into forms. He attacked classicism as being inappropriate, meaning too foreign (meaning too Italian), for England. Pugin is the figure at the center of nineteenth-century English Gothic Revival. For Pugin and his followers, Gothic Revival became the symbol of Protestant Christianity, England, and its empire. He came to prominence when he successfully did the furnishings for George IV's apartments in Windsor castle. He designed built-ins and freestanding pieces of furniture. Astonishingly, he started his work for the king when he was fifteen years old.

Pugin's signature project was his work on the Houses of Parliament. He collaborated with the architect Charles Barry (1795–1860) on the prominent project, focusing on the interiors. His designs for furniture, ceramics, textiles, stained glass, and wallpaper reveal that he was an accomplished artist, devoted to various phases of medieval architecture and design. The Houses of Parliament, while in the Gothic Revival style, was a building with an incredibly complex program that included extended administrative functions and audience rooms, and also acted as architectural symbol of the nation. The complex building contains the House of Commons and the Chamber of the Lords.

It is sometimes difficult to reconcile Pugin's rhetoric with his artistic production. For example, he often calls for simplicity and his complex designs seem at odds with that. An octagonal table by Pugin has Gothic arches that spring from a square base (Figure 15.1). No replica of a medieval piece, its complicated forms and elaborate carving

Figure 15.1 A.W.N. Pugin. Table, Houses of Parliament. c. 1844–1852.

came from Pugin's imagination. Such pieces appear exceedingly elaborate to modern eyes, but one must understand the context in which they were created.

In 1836, Pugin published *Contrasts,* in which he compares the medieval period to the nineteenth century; invariably, the nineteenth century pales in comparison. In 1841, he published *The True Principles of Pointed or Christian Architecture*. This publication was a culmination of his design thought; it was no less than an impassioned design manifesto. While Pugin, his projects, and his publications were influential, they often had the result of influencing people to copy his decorations without understanding the theoretical underpinnings. Pugin was one of many philosophically opposed to revivalism, and he was particularly harsh in his criticism of Egyptian revival. Gothic held such a hallowed place in the English psyche that it was, according to Ruskin's and Pugin's logic, above the stylistic fray.

Pugin's sometime business partner, Barry, was first instrumental in introducing a restrained form of Italianate architecture to nineteenth-century London, sometimes referred to as Renaissance Re-

vival. Open-minded regarding styles, he was in part responsible for introducing eclecticism and making it semirespectable. An accomplished artist, he also worked within the Greek revival realm. Barry and Pugin worked together on several occasions. Barry focused on the architecture, letting Pugin turn his talents to the interiors and furnishings. The most famous of the Barry/Pugin collaborations was the New Palace of Westminster, now the Houses of Parliament (Figure 15.2).

A fireplace from the Houses of Parliament combines stone, wood, iron, brass, and tile (Figure 15.3). **Polychromy** was the natural result of using many materials. In compositions that featured multiple materials, each retained its inherent color.

Germany

The promotion of Gothic in England reverberated across Europe and around the world. Neuschwanstein, Ludwig II of Bavaria's fairy-tale-looking castle, is just one of many projects constructed in a late Gothic Revival. Work on the castle started in 1869. And while Karl Friedrich Schinkel and Leo von

Figure 15.2 Charles Barry and A.W.N. Pugin. The Houses of Parliament, London. England.

Klenze are mostly known as Neoclassical architects, they also did Gothic buildings and paintings.

France

In France, also midcentury, Eugène Viollet-le-Duc (1814–1879) played a similar role as Ruskin and Pugin, writing the publications that supported the adoption of Gothic architecture and that remained the central texts for the movement. Viollet-le-Duc published the *Dictionnaire raisonné de l'architecture française* in 1854, and *Entretiens sur l'architecture*. An important distinction between the French and

English approaches to Gothic stems from their initial defenders: Whereas Ruskin saw architecture as ornament, Viollet-le-Duc saw it as structure.

Eugène Viollet-le-Duc was a French architect and preservationist. His knowledge of Gothic was learned on the job while working on the restoration of several cathedrals in the 1840s and 1850s; he oversaw the restoration work on Ste. Madeleine, in Vezelay, and St. Denis, Sainte-Chapelle, and Notre Dame in Paris. He vehemently excoriated eclecticism and sought to establish the basis of a modern Gothic architecture, although his own works occasionally combined Gothic shapes with details that

are distinctly Byzantine or Early Christian. Interested in prefabrication, he enthusiastically promoted the use of iron, although he himself used it sparingly. His publications, widely read and influential, were central to relating Gothic Revival in France to French nationalism. The French version of Gothic Revival did not spread to France's colonies to the extent that English Gothic Revival did.

South Africa

In English colonies, the use of Gothic Revival was a way to connect with the homeland and affirm English heritage. For Anglophone South Africans, it simultaneously differentiated them as a group distinct from the Dutch-influenced Afrikaans population. It also provided an architectural vocabulary that served as a racial divider. Eighteenth- and nineteenth-century European travel accounts regularly, and erroneously, commented on the superiority of European architecture over the indigenous varieties. A Gothic Revival house in Durban relies heavily on forms associated with churches in its salon, down to the inclusion of a stained-glass window.

United States

Across the pond in the United States, employing Gothic Revival also served as a means to affirm the new country's English traditions (the sore feelings left by the American Revolution having been largely forgotten). American Gothic Revival was also related to several key tendencies of **Romanticism**. Romanticism started out as a literary movement that emphasized emotion and intuition, while relying less on the appeal to reason. It was most important in poetry and fiction, with Lord Byron's poetry as the prime example. But there were a number of painters whose subject matter and method of representing landscapes resonated with Romantic poetry and placed them firmly in the American fold. The relationship of Romantic landscape painting and Gothic Revival architecture had a strong European precedent in the paintings of Caspar David Friedrich and Karl Friedrich Schinkel.

Landscape paintings relate obviously to gardening, and particularly to the informal English garden that was usurping the primacy of the French formal garden. Reinforcing the connection between informal gardens and Gothic Revival, many English country gardens included either real Gothic ruins or constructed Gothic follies.

The Hudson River School was a loosely organized group of mid-nineteenth-century American landscape painters. Their paintings provided a visual affirmation of Edmund Burke's (1729–1797) *A Philosophical Enquiry into the Origin of our Ideas of the Sublime and the Beautiful,* published in 1756. Many of the paintings are views of the Hudson River

Valley, although also of other American landscapes featuring rugged mountains, steep cliffs, and the occasional waterfall. In these paintings, the skies often appear as if on the verge of a thunderstorm. The height of the Hudson River School activity came in the 1850s and 1860s, and Thomas Cole (1801–1848) was the key figure. Their pastoral paintings sometimes looked sentimental and nostalgic, and by the 1870s they were considered old-fashioned. Yet a closer look reveals that their naturalistic landscapes included factories with billowing smokestacks and railroads cutting across otherwise pristine landscapes (Wallach 2002). They were not as out of touch with the times as their contemporaries suspected and, in fact, within the discrete conventions of landscape paintings, made explicit the tension between nature and industrialization.

Romantic landscape painting connects to American Gothic architecture and furniture design in two ways: in the manner in which architects represented their buildings, sited in natural settings reminiscent of landscape paintings, and in the buildings' designs themselves.

A leading figure in American Gothic Revival was Richard Upjohn (1802–1878). A feature of Gothic Revival is a picturesque asymmetry, which can be evident in plan, elevation, or in the rendering technique.

Upjohn started out as an English cabinetmaker in 1819, later emigrating to the United States, where he began his career as an architect. He combined his knowledge of English Gothic with the New England vernacular, thereby creating a strand of American Gothic. Upjohn designed several churches throughout his career, including Trinity Church in Boston. His publication *Rural Architecture* made his standardized church designs available across the country. Gothic Revival was certainly deemed appropriate for churches, but it also made its mark in the realm of domestic architecture. Residential projects became the center of his large and successful practice. Upjohn promoted the perception of the architect as a professional and honorable person. He played a major role in founding the American Institute of Architects in 1857, and served as its first president. Looking at the totality of Upjohn's career, house, church, and office all figure equally, related to honor, rectitude, and the visual vocabulary of Gothic Revival.

Alexander Jackson Davis (1803–1892) dabbled in Egyptian Revival, Italianate, and Tudor Revival, but he is mostly known for turning his design talents to creating modest yet picturesque Gothic houses in the United States. Davis rendered some of his buildings within Romantic-looking landscapes. This connected American architecture to European artistic developments, yet with a distinct American slant. Prior to Davis, most architectural views were hard-edged, more a result of drafting and engraving than rendering and painting. Davis's houses were irregular in plan and elevation, and featured a judicious use of towers, turrets, pinnacles, finials, and gables. His only book, *Rural Residences,* was published in 1838.

Andrew Jackson Downing (1815–1852) also worked with the Gothic Revival architectural vocabulary in his efforts at fashioning well-designed, modest American houses. He and Davis collaborated on pattern books, the success of which contributed to the spread of Victorian Gothic throughout the United States (Figure 15.4).

Figure 15.4 Gothic Revival house, Holly Springs, Mississippi, 1857.

Figure 15.5 Frank Furness. Pennsylvania Academy of the Fine Arts, Philadelphia, 1871–1876.

A response to a positive economic climate, growing urban populations, and a desire to create a public infrastructure that improved the mind as well as the body resulted in a great wave of museum building across much of the globe. Many of these buildings were in Gothic Revival, such as Thomas Deane and Benjamin Woodward's Oxford Museum, Oxford, England, 1855. Frank Furness's Pennsylvania Academy of Fine Arts, in Philadelphia, is a particularly inventive take on Gothic architecture (Figure 15.5). Furness incorporated glass, stone, and metals,

and responded to the program of an art museum, a building type for which European churches provided no obvious solution.

Crawford Riddell was an American furniture maker, active in the years 1837–1849 in Philadelphia. He created a huge 13-foot-tall Gothic Revival bed, commissioned by Henry Clay, the favorite to win the presidential election that year (Kotz 1997, p. 224). Clay lost, and the giant bed found another client. Gothic Revival frequently had religious and moral associations, and in Riddell's design, Gothic

Figure 15.6 Gothic revival side chair. United States.

became presidential. A Gothic Revival side chair is unlike the boxy chairs of the Gothic era (Figure 15.6). With turned legs, it cleverly utilizes a Gothic pointed arch as its back, which in turn is composed of three Gothic arches. Eclecticism sneaks in the piece by way of the textile used for the upholstery. It features a laurel wreath, which was a classical motif that Napoleon Bonaparte adopted as his personal insignia. This Gothic Revival chair is upholstered with a Neoclassical textile.

Egyptian Revival

Egyptian Revival was one of the more prominent of the exotic revivals. It was less highly theorized than Gothic Revival and proved to be a remarkably persistent if minor trend. The fashion, also known lightheartedly as Egyptomania, received a boost with Napoleon's campaign to Egypt of 1798. Egyptian Revival was never a serious movement like Neoclassicism or Greek Revival. Twentieth-century historian James Curl gives the subject a weightiness that many Victorians never did: "Probably no culture (even those of Central America) has produced such mighty works of architecture that are so stark, so basic, so grand, so instantly memorable, as did ancient Egypt. The pyramid, the obelisk, the pylon, and the symmetrical temple are pure shapes that are best seen within a luminously clear landscape, set amid Horatian verdure, where the colours are strong, and the light is not dissipated in mist or in haze" (Curl 1982).

British designer Christopher Dresser (1834–1904) was a prolific artist. Multitalented, he designed ceramics, glass, metalwork, furniture, carpets, fabrics, and wallpapers. He was internationally successful, as his designs sold in Europe, America, and Japan. Dresser's primary design affiliation is with English Arts and Crafts. Accordingly, many of his designs refer to English medieval art, but he also belongs to the significant subgroup of those in the reform movement who expressed a serious interest in Japanese art.

Unlike some who contributed to the English cult of **Japonisme**, Dresser traveled to Japan. He freely mixed historical sources, and he was known to draw upon Islamic, Greek, and Egyptian motifs. He was a writer and theorist, although less well known than William Morris. His writings promote honesty, regularity, and angularity. A theorist in tune with the times, Dresser sought to improve

Figure 15.7 Thebes stool, by William Birch and B. North & Sons Ltd. Mahogany and leather. London, England, 1840.

popular taste by refining it, not overturning its underlying premises.

One effect of the plurality of styles available to architects and designers is that many experimented. While Pugin is irrevocably linked to Gothic, and Richardson to Romanesque, some designers made a career out of switching stylistic alliances. And many well-regarded designers, at least occasionally, drifted into foreign design milieus.

Thus, avowed Neoclassicists Schinkel and von Klenze experimented with Gothic, Egyptian, and Byzantine forms. Tiffany, usually associated with art nouveau, also has Egyptian Revival pieces to his name. Little opprobrium was associated with crossing stylistic borders, as when Christopher Dresser, usually considered as belonging to English Arts and Crafts, created an Egyptian stool (Figure 15.7).

Byzantine Revival and Turkish Revival

John Nash (1752–1835) was a prolific English architect and urban designer, and his works are associated with the glamour of the Regency era. Working with the landscape designer Humphry Repton, he designed a series of country houses whose exteriors were consistent with the desire for picturesque landscapes. Nash made use of several different styles throughout his career. He did work in Tudor, Gothic, Renaissance, and Greek Revival, and his country houses include castle-like forms and detailing.

Regency is a term that relates to the political structure in which a regent stands in for an under-age heir to the throne. Theoretically, it can pertain to any regency. There are two significant furniture styles known as regency: French Regency (1715–1723) and English Regency (1811–1830). French

Figure 15.8 John Nash. Royal Pavilion at Brighton. Exterior, salon.

Regency is a transitional style related to rococo. English Regency is a branch of Neoclassicism, although, as John Pile points out, "the most curious aspect of Regency design is its seemingly inconsistent vacillation between the restraint of classicism and the exuberance of fancy" (Pile 2004, p. 229). Nash's work represents both ends of the Regency design spectrum.

Park Crescent, Nash's project of 1812, proved him to be an accomplished urban designer. It was a circular band of classically detailed attached houses. It is a confident work of architecture, urban design, landscape design, and was also a successful real es-

tate venture. When he was in his sixties, Nash's career took off in a new direction when he started working for the crown and stopped taking on private clients. His show piece was his transformation of the Royal Pavilion at Brighton (Figure 15.8). It had a cast-iron structural system, and some of the metal columns sprouted palm fronds at the ceiling. The Brighton Pavilion is a tour de force of exotic decoration in its exteriors, interiors, and lavish furnishings.

Critics of historic revivals decried the superficial emphasis on style and inclusion of exotic elements. The superficiality was sometimes true, but the designers were often interested in exploiting specific qualities of the culture in reference. Turkish Revival often overlapped with Byzantine or Islamic, and was sometimes referred to as **Saracenic**.

Turkish revival exteriors, interiors, and furnishings existed within a popular culture milieu in which Turkey (and more generally the Middle East and the Islamic world) was considered a highly sensual environment, full of mystery and intrigue, comforts and pleasures, and a freedom from (Western) cultural restraints.

Part of the nineteenth-century fascination was fueled by the continuation of eighteenth-century interests, such as a Mozart opera, and the writings of Mary Wortley Montagu (1689–1762). Many composers were interested in **Janissary**, or Turkish, music and incorporated snippets into European opera. There were several prominent productions of Mozart's "The Abduction from the Seraglio."

Montagu was the wife of the British ambassador to Constantinople. She published a popular memoir based on fifty-two letters, written from the Turkish capital, that described a world in which she, as a woman, was able to enter the harem and circulate freely. The veil, in Montagu's telling, allowed her to hide her smallpox scars, freely associate with Turkish women and eunuchs, and also, if momentarily, hide her ethnicity as a non-Arab.

Another British ambassador, the explorer Richard Burton (1821–1890), and his wife, Isabel Burton (1831–1896), spent extensive periods of time abroad, and their writings satiated the desire for scintillating tales from the Middle East. Burton was a respected translator of *The Arabian Nights* and many ethnographic studies, in which he unflinchingly described the sexual practices of North Africans and Arabs. He and his wife traveled widely, and he had an astonishing talent for languages, reportedly learning twenty-five of them (Kennedy 2005). They traveled to North Africa, the Middle East, India, and Pakistan. For Burton, as for Montagu, the veil was an opportunity to hide his identity most famously when he, in disguise, was one of the few Europeans to make the pilgrimage to Mecca, an account of which he published, his *Pilgrimage to El-Medinah and Mecca,* in 1855. Not many Britons could afford to travel to Turkey, but they could vicariously enjoy its pleasures by going to the opera, reading memoirs, and lounging on extravagantly upholstered pieces of Turkish furniture (Figure 15.9). Isabel Burton also wrote her memoirs and translated several texts.

To twenty-first-century Westerners, the nineteenth-century representation of the Middle East is nearly the exact opposite of how the Middle East is evoked in today's popular media. Victorian Britons developed their concepts of the Middle East from sources that highlighted the sensual side of life. What is consistent in the popular references to Turkey and the Middle East is that the harem, veils, and generally Arabic dress were emphasized for their ability to allow Westerners to move freely in the Middle East, unrecognized as foreigners.

The popularity of so-called Turkish daybeds and occasional chairs played off of the general associations of Turkey with luxury and comfort. They were almost completely upholstered and tufted, and outfitted with yards of fringe and tassels. Freestanding pieces of furniture were not standard features of Turkish interiors, so the European "Turkish" pieces are hybrids between the desire for pieces of furniture and a fanciful and idealized image of people lolling about in a harem or bath house.

Stage Design

The varieties of nineteenth-century historic revivals were endless. There were Venetian Gothic, Pisan Romanesque, and Pompeian Revivals. Egyptian

Revival and Turkish Revival were two of the more prominent of the minor trends. Others were Assyrian Revival, Ottoman Revival, and Aztec Revival; they are typically grouped together under the catch-all phrase "exoticism." Neoclassical architect Karl Friedrich Schinkel was an accomplished stage designer. He did a series of well-received Egyptian Revival stage sets for an 1816 production of Mozart's *The Magic Flute* (Figure 15.10). He also designed four sets for an opera that is rarely produced today, Gaspare Spontini's *Fernand Cortez,* in 1818. The style of Schinkel's designs can only be referred to as Aztec Revival. The title of the set from the first act, "Temple of the Peruvians," does not make much historical or geographic sense, as Cortés was in Mexico. One feature of exoticism was the tendency to combine elements, especially when the artist was not familiar with the cultures being portrayed. At the front of the stage, Schinkel places a statue that resembles the Hindu deity Shiva.

Figure 15.10 Karl Friedrich Schinkel. Garden with Sphinx, stage design for Mozart's The Magic Flute, 1815.

THE INDUSTRIAL REVOLUTION

A brief look at the population changes of three cities, from South America, Africa, and Asia, makes clear that the convergence of population growth, urbanization, and industrialization was a worldwide phenomenon that affected all aspects of life, including design.

In 1810, Buenos Aires declared itself independent from Spain. A modest growth in population followed the split, and the number of inhabitants of the city reached 60,000 in 1826 and 90,000 in 1854 (Pendergast 2002). The city established itself as the social and economic center of Argentina over the next few decades. In 1862, Buenos Aires became Argentina's capital, and the transformation of the city thereafter was phenomenal. Argentina became integral in the world economy, exporting wheat, wool, beef, and other agricultural products that fueled its economic boom. Because of the increase in trade, Buenos Aires grew rapidly as hundreds of thousands of immigrants migrated to the city from Europe from the 1880s to the 1930s. By 1930, 3 million people lived in the city, almost a third of Argentina's total population.

In 1860, Cairo was home to 295,000 people. Less than forty years later, its population had almost doubled; the ancient city had an estimated 590,000 inhabitants in 1897 (Mitchell 1998, p. 38). The period between the two world wars saw a steady if not spectacular increase in the large cities of northern Africa. By the time of the 1927 census, Cairo became the first African city with a population that exceeded one million (Hance 1970, pp. 212–217).

Shanghai had a population of 149,000 in 1860. A scant forty years later, its population quadrupled to 651,000 (Mitchell 1998, p. 42). The British were influential in Shanghai, but they were even more influential in another Chinese city, Hong Kong. In the 1860s, Hong Kong's population grew significantly as a result of migration from mainland China and its economy continued to flourish (Domschke 1986, pp. 621–22). As with many world cities, the period of population growth coincided with an emergent infrastructure, including telegraph systems and street lighting (Pendergast 2002, pp. 95–112).

Different regions of the globe industrialized at different rates and at different times, but the specter of technologically driven change was worldwide. Victorian design, in its many manifestations, was an attempt to mediate, hide, or glorify those changes.

The Industrial Revolution is most often presented in an urban context, with visions of London and endless smokestacks, rows of textile workers in steel-framed buildings, and giant stockyards in Chicago, Omaha, and St. Louis. Yet it had an equally profound effect on small towns and villages. African coastal cities had been cosmopolitan for centuries, yet it took the arrival of railroads to connect cities of the interior with global economic and cultural trends. Smaller cities were about a day's train ride away from a major metropolitan center. The industrialization of some countries occurred at a later date.

The relationship between industrial processes and design is evident in several projects. Joseph Paxton (1803–1865) created the iron-and-glass Crystal Palace, London, in 1851. It was important for its

Figure 15.11 John Paxton, Crystal Palace, London, 1851.

materials—nothing could be more modern than iron and glass—and for its contents, the displays of decorative art objects from around the world (Figure 15.11). In Paris, Henri Labrouste (1801–1875) created the Library of St. Geneviève and also the Bibliothèque Nationale, both of which relied on an innovative metal structural system. Those who felt that the reliance on historical revivals was leading architecture down the wrong path often saw better results, to their minds, when they turned to engineering projects and industrial buildings. The Eiffel Tower is the prime example of the triumph of engineering. Some thirty years after the Crystal Palace in London, a Crystal Palace was built in Petropolis, Brazil. Built in France in 1879, it was then erected in Brazil in 1884, part of a horticulture exhibit. Like its English predecessor, it had the desired effect of dazzling visitors with its form, materials, and contents.

A single designed object has all the contradictions, for better and for worse, of Victorian art and industry. It was also used by the woman for whom the century is named. Queen Victoria's railroad car features a surprising mixture of industrial technology and hyperdecorated materials. Her private railway carriage was padded and tufted, with heavy draperies and no shortage of fringe and tassels (Figure 15.12). The tufted white silk ceiling was designed with acoustics in mind. Her carriage is scarcely recognizable as a railway car, which evidently was the idea.

Figure 15.12 Queen Victoria's railway carriage, 1869. England.

Ships

A historian of Victorian decorative arts, John Gloag, posits that the Victorian age outlived Queen Victoria, lasting until World War I (Gloag 1973). There is no better example of the contradictory impulses of the Victorian approach to design than the outfitting of ocean liners. Technologically, the ships of the first decades of the twentieth century were highly advanced; they were the largest and the fastest. Their engineering was complicated, as they featured running water, electricity, elevators, and swimming pools. Yet their interiors, based on hotel designs of the period, were a riot of historical styles.

The shipping industry was an economic powerhouse at the center of the world economy. Prime economic statistics involve the movement of goods and people, and shipping was the venue for both. Shipping was also connected to immigration. For both strategic and symbolic reasons, passenger ships had military ties, as in wartime they transported troops. Although not planned for these purposes, the ships became tools in international relations. Because of their extreme visibility, many details about their form received the input of national leaders, such as Edward VII, Edward VIII, and Kaiser Wilhelm II (Wealleans 2006). Important symbols of national pride, the press followed their every move, and hundreds of thousands of people lined beaches and quays to get a glimpse of them when they steamed by. They were popular subjects for newspaper and magazine articles in their day, and curiously, these projects live on via the delicate medium of photography.

Mèwes and Davis, the London architecture and interiors firm headed by Charles Mèwes and Arthur Davis, was one of the most successful firms of its day. They had two prominent shipping companies as clients: the German Hamburg-America Line and the English Cunard Line. Ship interiors were true interiors projects, as they were not intended to be permanent. The most optimistic projections by their owners and designers were that they might serve for forty years; they were expected to turn a profit in less than ten years.

Mèwes and Davis both studied in France and their designs are based on eighteenth-century French architecture. Yet it is not true that the shipbuilders and designers made no contribution to innovative design. They were at the center of the reconciliation between design and technology. Fierce promoters of traditional styles, they created workplaces with incredibly complex programs, spaces carefully crafted to respond to specific business functions, and they embraced new technologies and materials. In fact, the message that their ship designs communicated to potential passengers was comfort, and this meant electric lighting, elevators, and indoor plumbing. Their designs also incorporated modern materials such as metal, glass, linoleum, and plastic laminate.

Traditional architecture, interiors, and furnishings played a robust part in the world economy. The aspect of ship design that has received considerable attention is how their designs and layouts reflect class and gender models of the time, and in fact, ship interiors make this quite obvious. While it is now ubiquitous that French furnishings of the Louis XV and Louis XVI periods connote luxury, particularly in the hospitality industry, this was not predestined. This came about because of the popularity of the late-nineteenth-century hotel and ship interiors.

The designers of the ship interiors worked independently, yet they inadvertently created a system that utilized almost the entirety of historically inspired designs at their disposal. The most important public rooms, the first-class lounges and dining rooms, were in Louis XV and Louis XVI styles sometimes combined. Often the men's smoking room, particularly on English ships, was Tudor,

Elizabethan, or Jacobean. The English ship *Titanic* featured a Turkish bath (Figure 15.13) and the German liner *Imperator* had a Pompeian swimming pool (Figure 15.14).

Figure 15.13 Harland and Wolff, Titanic's Turkish baths, 1909.

FURNITURE

The general features of Victorian furniture include its elaborate surface decoration and a myriad of stylistic references, sometimes combining details from several epochs in a single piece. New materials and manufacturing techniques also figured in the designs.

Rococo Revival

John Henry Belter (1804–1863) was a furniture designer and manufacturer. Born in Germany, he immigrated to New York City, where he spent his entire professional career. From 1845 on, he worked almost exclusively in a mode that was referred to as Rococo Revival. Now his works are considered the essence of Victorian design. The pieces at which he excelled do not really constitute a faithful revival of

Figure 15.14 Charles Mèwes. Imperator's swimming pool. Hamburg.

Figure 15.15 John Henry Belter. Laminated rosewood sofa, 1856.

the Rococo (Figure 15.15). This style originated in England in the 1820s and spread to Germany and France in the 1830s. Belter had a knack for responding to popular taste. His designs were visually compelling, well built, relatively lightweight, and surprisingly sturdy. He worked in a combination of solid and laminated wood. His three-stage manufacturing process included a combination of contoured shaping, punched decoration, and carving. He created dynamic pieces that curved in several planes. He embellished already-curved shapes with arabesques, scrolls, foliage, flowers, fruit, and vegetables. Mostly using machines, he was able to create pieces that looked hand-carved. The rear elevations of his pieces were equally well attended to. The pieces were sculptural in that they were meant to be walked around. Furnished with wheels in the Victorian fashion, they could be moved about within a parlor and pulled up for a conversation grouping. They were not visually related to a specific and fixed architectural location. During Belter's time, Americans started the habit of purchasing furniture *en suite,* a set of sofa and armchairs for parlors, a bed with matching chest and dressing table for bedrooms. Belter's parlor and boudoir suites, with their expressive ornamentation, appealed to a well-to-do clientele. Some of the pieces made by his many imitators were more affordable.

Victorian Horned Furniture

The Victorian approach to design was eclectic, and people appreciated novelty items known as conversation pieces. This resulted in some odd pieces of

Figure 15.16 San Antonio horn table, 1880–1890.

furniture, such as the minor but nonetheless significant trend in Texas of horned furniture. The pieces show an appreciation of unusual materials and forms (Figure 15.16).

Cast-Iron Furniture

Industrial manufacturing techniques made **cast-iron** furniture possible (Figure 15.17). For a while cast iron was immensely popular, seen as a wondrous modern material. Some buildings were built entirely out of cast iron, although eventually a series of fires proved its weakness as an architectural material and its popularity declined.

Cast-iron garden furniture also had a sustained period of popularity. The iron itself could be formed into endless shapes and patterns, such as Gothic

Figure 15.17 Cast-iron veranda furniture, c. 1880.

arches. Cast iron was frequently molded to imitate bamboo; the back panels of the iron bench resemble caning. These pieces make no distinction between the living and the mechanical.

Victorian Decorating

A feature of Victorian interiors is the juxtaposition of bizarre things that have no logical relationship, and it is precisely that quality that makes them memorable. These include curios, the oddly shaped figurine, and other miscellaneous bric-a-brac. A popular open shelving unit for mementos was called a **whatnot**. The jarring juxtapositions prompt reflection and new trains of thought. Objects in a Victorian interior also acted as repositories of memories.

Victorian design was related to personal memory, collective knowledge, and the importance of new materials and media. The overall quantity of stuff that people owned and that houses contained increased greatly. The Victorian decorating approach was well-poised to handle large quantities of objects (this in contrast to modernism, which was an aesthetic at odds with dealing with large personal inventories).

The hallway and stairwell of a house by Church, Vaux and Withers amazingly holds together as a work of design, given the disparate elements it combines (Figure 15.18). They include: Assyrian stencils, a Buddha statue, Gothic arches, Moorish claustra work, African spears, Chinese vases, and Turkish carpets. The Victorian salon was the focus of design attention, and it managed to be simultaneously formal and comfortable (Figure 15.19).

Regarding the affordability of decorative arts objects and their distribution across class lines, the collaboration of new industrial manufacturing processes and designers largely succeeded. This was the

Figure 15.18 Church, Vaux and Withers hallway. New York, 1872.

Figure 15.19 Victorian domestic interior. Nineteenth century.

beginning of a consumer culture, and Victorian parlors accommodated the increasing number of objects. Several economists, most notably Thorsten Veblen, anointed the second half of the nineteenth century as the age of conspicuous consumption. Up until the nineteenth century, design had been the purview of the elite. The Industrial Revolution promised to increase the standard of living of the lower and middle classes. While the Industrial Revolution created as many problems as solutions, objects became affordable to people who in previous centuries would have led lives deprived of shiny bibelots. Complaints about the degraded quality of Victorian design notwithstanding, it was the beginning of the democratization of design. And the effects of Victorian design are still being felt. To many,

John Belter pieces were the pinnacle of beauty, luxury, and refinement. To purchase a Belter furniture suite was not merely a response to the functional need for seating, it was an announcement that socially one had arrived.

Reactions Against Victorian Design

Robert Kerr (1823–1904), a Victorian architect, gained greater renown as a critic. In 1860, he read a paper, "The Battle of the Styles," whose title became the catchphrase for Victorian architecture and design. Regarding design, there was little consensus, and fierce criticism of Victorian approaches began in the Victoria era.

The debate surrounding the appropriateness of Victorian design abated little in 100 years, for in the

1960s, American architectural historian John Summerson felt the need to address the issue and put it to rest once and for all (he didn't). Four lectures he gave in March of 1968 at Columbia University prominently tackled the question of the validity of Victorian design. These famous lectures became the basis of a book (Summerson 1970). Summerson provocatively asked if "early and mid-Victorian architecture was, in its own time and in the eyes of its own best-informed critics, horribly unsuccessful" (Summerson 1970). Summerson's *Victorian Architecture* does not make for a suspenseful read; early on, he answers his rhetorical question about the value of Victorian aesthetics: "Where the Victorians are concerned it would be very much safer to begin, at least, on the assumption that it was wrong." Summerson was writing in the late 1960s, when modernism was still going strong, a movement antithetical to Victorian design principles. Summerson was not alone; critics of Victorian design were and are many. Perhaps the reason Summerson felt the need to address Victorian architecture is that it remains popular among non-academics, those for whom modernism is a tough sell. Some of the words used to describe Victorian design are *unintelligible, garish, deplorable, monstrous, ambiguous,* and *vulgar*. The revulsion that many critics feel about Victorian design exceeds in intensity that of critics of previous epochs when discussing the styles that preceded their own.

Other twentieth-century writers felt the same. Summerson dismissed all Victorian architecture up to 1870 as a failure. Humphrey House in 1948 pinpointed Victorian design's underlying premise that, he felt, doomed it to failure. Victorian architects and designers, he regretted, were trying to combine, in form and detail, elements that were simply incompatible. All Victorian architects, according to House—and he lamented the fact—had to position their work in relationship to style. They either had to announce their belief in the superiority of one style (e.g., Pugin), or affirm the validity of mixing styles, known as eclecticism (e.g., Nash).

Professional Organizations and Design Schools

Until a Cornell architectural historian wrote her book, the story of the rise of professional organizations in the nineteenth century was mostly untold (Woods 1999). Eighteenth-century guilds were forerunners to two important developments of the nineteenth century: the establishment of professional organizations and design education programs.

The organization that became the American Institute of Architects was started in 1857, and its initial members included Andrew Jackson Davis, Richard Morris Hunt, Richard Upjohn, and Calvert Vaux. An important responsibility of a professional organization was to establish the standards for the profession.

Of equal importance was the opening of architecture and design schools. Tuskegee Institute was founded in 1881, with Booker T. Washington as its first teacher (Figure 15.20). The Rhode Island School of Design opened in 1877. The development of professional organizations and schools and academies was important for architecture and interior design, and this two-pronged development occurred worldwide.

Romanesque Revival and Modernism

The importance of the work of Henry Hobson Richardson is underscored by the fact that a style bears his name, Richardsonian Romanesque. He made a significant contribution to modernism, but some twentieth-century historians of modernism felt that his work was in need of redemption. They offered lengthy explanations, clarifying that Richardson's work should not be lumped casually together with other historical revivals. Richardson's masonry

Figure 15.20 Tuskegee Institute, architecture studio.

buildings look to French Romanesque architecture, with occasional Byzantine flourishes. He used Romanesque forms, most notably semispherical Romanesque arches, but he unified them in compositions that were commensurate with their modern functions. He was more interested in functional planning and shaping volumes than in historical details.

The J. J. Glesner House was built in 1885–1887 (Figure 15.21). Startling severe elevations line two streets; it sits on a corner lot. There are few openings. The garden side is invisible to the street and much different in character. The house's interior spaces intrude into the garden, with several protuberances that also have large windows. The asymmetrical plan and the arched entryway—the most obviously Romanesque feature—were among the elements that Louis Sullivan and Frank Lloyd Wright admired.

Paul Clifford Larson stresses that Richardson's buildings are not easy to pigeonhole: "Some of Richardson's admirers pursued his archeological

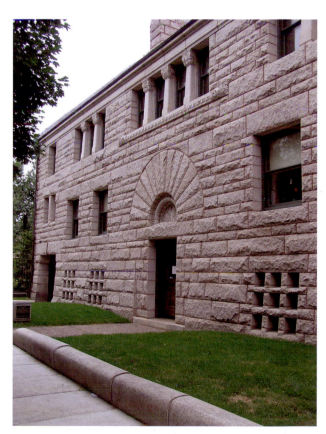

Figure 15.21 H.H. Richardson, Glessner House, Chicago, 1885-1887.

interests and others his search for distinctively American form; some championed his picturesque compositional schemes and others his penchant for simplification; some enlarged on the exuberance of his detailing and others on his respect for primal volumes" (Larson 1988).

The underlying rationale for the adoption of Romanesque forms by the early skyscraper designers is not immediately apparent. In architecture circles, Richardson's Marshall Field Warehouse, 1885–1887, in Chicago, was widely admired and became an architectural pilgrimage site. It had an abbreviated cornice and rows and columns of segmental arches. The windows were arranged logically to express the structure's steel frame. The façade, of rough-cut American stone, was no longer hiding or dressing up

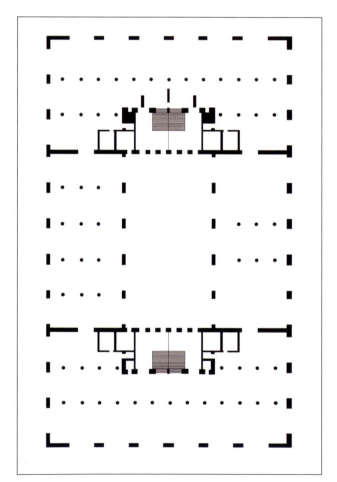

Figure 15.22 H.H. Richardson. Marshall Field's Warehouse, Chicago.

the structure, but was integral to it. Working within a historical idiom, Richardson found a solution that avoided the fripperies of Victorian design. Cass Gilbert, Burnham and Root, and Louis Sullivan were influenced by Richardson and specifically the Marshall Field's Warehouse. This building has a central position in the history of American architecture and interiors. It has open floors supported by a regular grid of columns (Figure 15.22). Sullivan considered it a monument to trade, noting that a new kind of commerce required a new kind of structure.

It is curious that Louis Sullivan is known for the saying "form follows function." When compared to other great building types of the late nineteenth century, opera houses, newspaper offices, and train stations, skyscrapers were essentially functionless. They provided wide-open leased spaces that, once leased, were outfitted in tune with the renters' needs. Skyscrapers were important because they changed the world's cityscapes, and they also made possible the twentieth-century field of corporate interior design, which, in turn, exponentially increased the demand for office furniture. Tenants leased empty floor plates that had to be designed and built. Because tenants changed over time, especially in the United States, a building's interiors had to be periodically reconfigured.

CONCLUSION

Robert Kerr, not a well-known figure today, was not only prescient with his perceptions about nineteenth-century design, he was wise about what was to come. He placed the blur of nineteenth-century styles into three categories: the eclectic, the followers of Pugin and other Gothic revivalists, and the early modernists. This is an astute and productive way of making sense of an era that defies organization. On the one hand, designers of the Victorian era were buried in the past, yet on the other, they were marching triumphantly toward the future.

Sources

Brooks, Chris. *The Gothic Revival*. London: Phaidon, 1999.

Curl, James. *The Egyptian Revival*. London: George Allen and Unwin, 1982.

Curl, James. *Victorian Architecture: Its Practical Aspects*. Newton Abbot: David and Charles, 1973.

Domschke, Eliane, and Doreen Goyer. *The Handbook of National Population Censuses*. Westport: Greenwood Press, 1986.

Edwards, Clive. *Victorian Furniture: Technology and Design*. New York: St. Martin's, 1993.

Fergusson, James, and Robert Kerr. *History of the Modern Styles of Architecture*. New York: Dodd, Mead, and Company, 1891.

Gloag, John. *Victorian Comfort: A Social History of Design from 1830–1900*. Newton Abbot: David and Charles, 1973.

Hance, William. *Population, Migration, and Urbanization in Africa*. New York: Columbia University Press, 1970.

Jenner, Michael. *Victorian Britain*. London: Weidenfeld and Nicholson, 1999.

Kennedy, Dane. *The Highly Civilized World: Richard Burton and the Victorian World*. Cambridge: Harvard University Press, 2005.

Kotz, Suzanne. *Dallas Museum of Art: A Guide to the Collection*. Seattle: Marquand Books, 1997.

Larson, Paul Clifford, ed. *The Spirit of H.H. Richardson*. Ames: Iowa State University Press, 1988.

McCarthy, Michael. *The Origins of the Gothic Revival*. New Haven: Yale University Press, 1987.

Mitchell, Brian. *International Historical Statistics Africa, Asia and Oceania, 1750–1993*. New York: Stockton Press, 1998.

O'Gorman, James. *The Architecture of Frank Furness*. Philadelphia: Philadelphia Museum of Art, 1973.

Peck, Amelia, ed. *Alexander Jackson Davis: American Architect 1803–1892*. New York: Rizzoli, 1992.

Pendergast, Sara, and Tom Pendergast. *Worldmark Encyclopedia of National Economies*. Farmington Hills: Gale Group, 2002.

Summerson, John. *Victorian Architecture: Four Studies in Evaluation*. New York: Columbia University Press, 1970.

Veblen, Thorstein. *The Theory of the Leisure Class*. New York: Modern Library, 1934.

Wallach, Alan. "Thomas Cole's Rivers in the Catskills as Antipastoral." *Art Bulletin* 84 (June 2002): 334–350.

Wealleans, Anne. *Designing Liners: A History of Interior Design Afloat*. Abingdon: Routledge, 2006.

Woods, Mary. *From Craft to Profession: The Practice of Architecture in Nineteenth-Century America*. Berkeley: University of California Press, 1999.

DISCUSSION AND REVIEW QUESTIONS

1. What are some examples of design developments directly related to technological improvements? What were some of the nineteenth-century inventions?

2. What are some examples of design developments that seem to ignore technological developments?

3. What is an example of a historic revival where a specific quality or historical reference is being explored?

4. What is an example of a historic revival that seems superficial, more related to an appreciation of the form rather than a deep understanding of history?

5. How can nationalism be related to design?

6. The Victorians sometimes used a name for a particular historical revival, yet today we normally use a different term. What is an example?

7. What were some of the major historical revivals?

8. What were some of the minor historical revivals?

9. Describe the major trends in Victorian decorating. What specifically did critics dislike about Victorian design?

CHAPTER 16

REFORM MOVEMENTS
ARTS AND CRAFTS

1860–1910

British Arts and Crafts

1910–1930

American Arts and Crafts

Arts and Crafts was an influential English movement of the second half of the nineteenth century that had worldwide implications and a lasting effect on design. Artists, architects, furniture designers, and patrons were closely related to the school of painting known as the pre-Raphaelites. Arts and Crafts designers sought to counter two prevailing trends, one economic and technological, the other cultural and moral, that dominated the nineteenth century. The first was the Industrial Revolution and its effects; the second was Victorian design. Arts and Crafts designers sought to renew design by looking at an idealized preindustrial world.

Although Victorian pieces were popular with the general public, among artists and designers there was a backlash against (what they perceived to be) ostentation, display, and mindless historicism. This artistic revolt took several forms, which are the subject of this and following chapters. In England, the anti-Victorian reaction was generally referred to as the reform movement, as a broad category, with Arts and Crafts as a specific subgroup of the larger trend.

ARTS AND CRAFTS

Criticism of Victorian design and all it stood for came about almost immediately. One of the strongest reactions to it was Arts and Crafts. Even the long-standing work of the American Shakers was an aesthetic rebuff to all things Victorian. Art Nouveau and the Secessionists, covered later, were also reactions against Victorian design.

It is occasionally difficult to reconcile all the tenets of the Arts and Crafts designers regarding the use of historical forms. On the one hand, they decried historicism; on the other, they extolled the virtues of the medieval era. Understanding the historical context of nineteenth-century Britain aids this effort. The writers William Morris, John Ruskin, and Pugin objected to trends in which historic forms were grafted onto new structures with little thought given to their history and meaning. They disliked anything that fell under the broad rubric of Victorian design and the "recent" continental periods Baroque and Rococo. The English reformists and their followers cherished the medieval side of the Italian Renaissance, yet they chastised the highly developed side; hence the name of the painting movement, the pre-Raphaelites (before Raphael).

The leaders and followers of the Arts and Crafts movement felt that two of the biggest scourges of the day, the Industrial Revolution and Victorian design, could be remedied by a return to what they considered good design. They sought to counteract the ugly side of industrialization—the degradation of modern (nineteenth-century) life. In addition to looking favorably at the medieval period, they admired humble objects and those with the knowledge of how to craft them.

These reformists were critical of industrial techniques and their ability to cheaply produce vapid ornament. Their aesthetically minded activities can also be seen in the context of the muckrakers, the journalists who were investigating dubious business practices by factories and their owners. Other sympathetically aligned movements were Romanticism (in painting and literature), the garden city movement, the Chicago School, and Prairie Style.

A major focus of their efforts was the unity of the arts, in contrast to the hierarchy that dominated previous periods. This represented a major shift in how those involved with high art—painting, sculpture, architecture—viewed the "lower" arts—furniture and other designed objects. They sought to elevate the status of craftsmanship to the level it once enjoyed (as they perceived it) in the medieval period. This would lead to a reintegration of art, artifacts, and life, only on a higher plane.

For inspiration, they turned to German tribes, Icelandic sagas, Celtic tales, and the story of King Arthur. Although Arts and Crafts enthusiasts objected to the indiscriminate use of historical forms, they objected to history less emphatically than those affiliated with Art Nouveau and the Vienna Secession. There was frequent overlap between Arts and Crafts and Gothic Revival, particularly as both found common ground in the writings of theorist John Ruskin. The 1850s, 1860s, and 1870s were the prime years of the Gothic Revival.

Both movements admired simplicity and directness, although defined in a nineteenth-century way. The exhortation of directness extended to moral virtues, social organization, and methods of fabrication—in other words, an integrated approach to life. Yet there were differences between Arts and Crafts and Gothic Revival. The latter was an explicit return to medieval forms; Arts and Crafts was contemporary design loosely based on the principles and production methods of the medieval period.

An achievement of the Arts and Crafts movement was that it managed to be intellectual and populist at the same time. There was an urban, sophisticated side to it, but also a down-to-earth, rural side to it. Its followers included accomplished artists and amateurs.

The pre-Raphaelites were the group of English artists interested in medieval subject matter. Usually the term refers to those whose principal activity was painting, in contrast to those involved with decorative objects. Dante Gabriel Rossetti is the most famous of the group. The pre-Raphaelites felt an affinity for the decorative arts, and they collaborated with furniture makers. One product of these joint ventures, Morris and Company's hand-painted chests and bureaus, sold extremely well.

John Ruskin

John Ruskin (1819–1900) was an artist and collector, but he is mostly known as the author of *The Seven Lamps of Architecture* (1849) and *The Stones of Venice* (1851–1853). These two publications constituted the theoretical backbone of Arts and Crafts. Ruskin's Christian faith was a foundation of all his writings. He was important as a philosopher and as an aesthetic advisor. He strongly objected to industrially produced objects. He did not proclaim that all ornament was bad; he objected to meaningless ornament, and his writings provided a way to instill ornament with meaning. Arts and Crafts also showed the way for those involved with design to imbue their projects with meaning. One of the principal design strategies involved ornament, specifically ornament that made local references, incorporating motifs based on local flora. The inspiration could lie in the English countryside, the Midwestern prairie, the Hudson River Valley, California, or New Zealand.

Arts and Crafts architects, a distinguished group including Philip Webb, and C. F. A. Voysey, discussed in this chapter, approached design in a way that resulted in buildings with irregular and strong geometric profiles. Their buildings were characterized by irregular fenestration and a seemingly ad hoc agglomeration of gables, windows, and chimneys. Houses were designed from the inside out. This was the opposite of the Renaissance and Palladian approach to design, in which the architect developed a pleasing overall form—in plan and elevation—and assigned functions to rooms. The suite of rooms behind a Renaissance façade was ingeniously worked out within the constraints presented by the system of fenestration. The Arts and Crafts approach was simultaneously modern, a forerunner to functionalism, and vernacular, the straightforward method of designing agricultural buildings based on need. At the level of a building's details, Arts and Crafts supporters called for a return to handcrafted pieces.

William Morris

Unquestionably, the central figure in English Arts and Crafts was William Morris (1834–1896). He was important as a designer, as a spokesman for the movement, and as a successful businessman; many of his designs are still in production. Morris was a designer, writer, reformer, and poet. At the start of his career, he worked for Gothic Revival architect George Edmund Street (1824–1881); one of Morris's coworkers was Philip Webb. In 1861, Morris founded a firm with Webb. In 1875, it became Morris and Company, which specialized in a broad array of designed products, including stained glass, furniture, wallpapers, and textiles.

The members of the coterie of reformists took different paths. Morris's friend Edward Burne-Jones became a painter. Although Morris studied architecture and started his career in that profession, he devoted his energies to poetry and two-dimensional designs. Ruskin's writings influenced Morris and Webb alike.

People with a desire for Victorian decoration liked Morris's designs, and they also appealed to designers (Figure 16.1). Designers, aesthetes, and the public alike responded to Morris and Company's products.

William Morris made designs for fabrics, wallpapers, and graphics based on nature. Seeking to recuperate the degraded state of design, the company started producing wallpapers in 1862. Their greatest long-lasting success was as a source of well-

Figure 16.1 William Morris. "Cray," upholstery textile, 1884.

conceived flat patterns for textiles and wallpapers. Van der Post explains the lasting appeal of the firm's designs: "The development of Morris' patterns, from early medieval-inspired wallpapers to subtle repeating designs of English garden flowers drawn ten years later for wallpapers and printed textiles, shows his increasing preoccupation with nature and a growing confidence in his own intuitive powers as a pattern designer and botanical draughtsman" (van der Post 2003, p. 6). Morris's accomplished designs remained popular throughout the career of the firm's founder.

Morris himself was talented at designing and exhibited a knack for marshaling the talents of others. The Morris Chair is a sturdy wooden armchair, probably designed by others in the employ of Morris and Company (Figure 16.2). It is a logical piece of furniture, based on traditional inexpensive chairs and made comfortable with unattached cushions. A reworking of a common chair type, it was itself endless copied. It was found to be useful as porch

Figure 16.3 Philip Webb. Chair. 1870-1890. Cushion covers by William Morris.

furniture, for summer resorts, and for those who wanted to incorporate unpretentious pieces of furniture into the living rooms of their homes.

Morris's company also produced an adjustable armchair (Figure 16.3). Webb designed this popular piece for the company based on an original bought in the countryside. The back moves and is secured on a metal ratchet. The ebonized finish relates to Anglo-Japanese pieces. The bobbin turning on the legs, spindles, and stretchers is a traditional form that dates to the Jacobean period. The wheels are a Victorian touch. The cushions are made of stamped woolen plush velvet. This piece shows how Morris and Company designers synthesized influences from several sources into a cohesive "new" whole. It was sold by catalog, and was eventually copied by several American furniture companies. It is from a suite of furniture for a family in Bath, England, and it was designed for the guest bedroom.

Morris had an intellectual side that he pursued in addition to designing. He studied at Oxford, and he and his wife were great readers. In addition to his other areas of success, Morris was a successful poet. The enterprising Morris could apply his energies to reading, writing, managing, and designing.

Figure 16.2 William Morris. Morris chair, 1866.

Figure 16.4 Philip Webb. Red House, 1859–1960. Kent, England.

His firm benefited from the popularity of Gothic Revival, especially in church architecture. Huge numbers of Gothic Revival churches were built in England in the nineteenth century, and they required stained-glass windows. Stained glass became one of Morris and Company's specialties. Morris's stained-glass designs were similar to his textile designs; they looked appropriate but were actually contemporary versions of traditional motifs. Morris was also concerned with preserving historic buildings (Donovan 2008).

Morris promoted in words and deeds the close relationship between art and craft. His writings articulated the advantages to this approach, and his firm put the idea into action. He regularly collaborated with painters and craftsmen. The reason that graphics, typeface, printing, and books play an important role in Arts and Crafts stems from the unity of the high arts and craftwork. The underlying ra-

tionale was that if artists (mostly painters) were encouraged to apply their talents to ordinary objects, everything improved.

With their use of complicated patterns in textiles, wallpapers, and title pages, Arts and Crafts designs today seem both traditional and visually complex, but a keen eye discerns how they significantly departed from the Victorian love of clutter. Morris demonstrated his commitment to graphics and publishing with his last project, Kelmscott Press, established in 1888.

Philip Webb

Philip Webb (1831–1915) was an English architect and designer and one of the reformists concerned about the effects of manufacturing. He met William Morris in Street's office and they both became involved with the pre-Raphaelites.

Webb started his own practice in 1859, and his first commission was Morris's house, Red House in Kent. As Webb often did, he developed most of the detailing himself. Red House is so named because of its redbrick walls and tiles (Figure 16.4). It has little ornamentation and is designed from the inside out, meaning that the exterior elements are the result of internal function, a process much admired by modernists. Windows correspondingly relate to rooms behind them and are not subordinate to a symmetrical façade.

The living room of Red House looks like a barn, with a loft (not for hay), exposed rafters, and ladder (Figure 16.5). Yet careful scrutiny reveals that it is scrupulously designed and displays several surprising hints of modernism. The artworks and shelves coalesce into a horizontal band above the chair rail. The paintings are not framed and hung on a wall, but form a continuous horizontal zone. They extend to the corners and nestle directly against the built-in storage unit. The walls are white, and the built-in bookshelves are structural. Furniture was upholstered with Morris fabric.

The principles that govern the house's designs are also evident in details, such as the cabinet doors. They are functionally simple, with a straightforward emphasis on visible hardware and clean white paint. This house, and others like it, reflect vernacular architecture and structures from agricultural environments.

Figure 16.5 The Settle designed by Morris and added to by Philip Webb in the Drawing Room of the Red House.

Figure 16.6 Philip Webb. Sideboard, 1862. For Morris, Marshall, Faulkner, and Co.

Webb did many tasteful country houses. He was more of an architect and furniture designer than a designer of textile patterns. A signature move of his, in his houses, was the use of paneling painted white.

Webb was a natural fit for Morris's business, as he was anti–Industrial Revolution and anticommercialism. Influenced by Ruskin's writings, Webb idealized the medieval period. Like the other reformists, he opposed the Victorian parade of styles—Egyptian Revival, Turkish Revival, Venetian Gothic Revival, and so forth. He rejected historicism and purist forms of Greek and Gothic Revival. He favored tradition, not history. By looking to the medieval past, relating to the landscape, and seeking inspiration in vernacular architecture, one could, according to Webb's way of thinking, rediscover the essence of English character. The revival of art was related to social change, and Webb became a socialist. Unlike Morris, he was not a writer.

A sideboard by Webb is made of ebonized wood that has been painted and gilded (Figure 16.6). It has stamped leather and brass and copper hardware. The joints remain visible and the hardware is prominent. A signature detail is the use of metal strap hinges on cabinet doors; they are obvious, functional, and medieval. Sheila Kirk delineates the fine line of Webb's design, which is not a strict revival yet is related to history: "Webb's early pieces have no overtly Gothic ornament yet they do call to mind the Middle Ages" (Kirk 2005, p. 50).

Webb's sideboard relies on a grid for its well-proportioned composition. All the elements come in threes and twos. An almost perfect square is divided into two, a base and a top. Each half is in turn

divided into three sections, each of those sections divided into three, with those modular units left as single pieces, or divided into two or three. It is simple in its overall visual effect, yet painstakingly hand-painted. Now in the collection of the Victoria and Albert Museum, it was initially sold by catalog.

Webb designed a side table, one of which was owned by the artist Edward Burne-Jones (Figure 16.7). Castle-like crenellations enliven its apron, and its legs take the form of columns. The subtle medieval references give it a sturdy appearance, but it is a carefully designed and crafted piece.

Kirk also articulates how Webb, when designing furniture or architecture, demanded a high level of precision that was more modern than medieval: "Webb never aimed for a primitive, rustic effect. He insisted on good workmanship, and on a smooth but not highly polished finish" (Kirk 2005, p. 51). When modernists arrive on the scene, they frequently praised the finishes achieved by Arts and Crafts designers such as Philip Webb.

Morris and Company

One of the most popular pieces of Morris and Company was the Sussex chair, named after a country

Figure 16.8 Philip Webb. Sussex chair, 1860. For Morris and Company.

Figure 16.9 William Morris. Kelmscott Manor. London. Originally built, 1570. Interior design by Morris, 1871.

chair from Sussex (Figure 16.8). Like the adjustable chair, a Morris associate found a chair in the country and thought it suitable for the Morris line. One chair was purchased, and Morris designers set about redesigning it. Simply detailed turned elements constitute the frame, and it features a simple rush seat. William and Jane Morris used Sussex chairs in Red House and Kelmscott House, and Edward Burne-Jones likewise owned Sussex chairs. It was a modest chair, also used at English colleges. In homes, it found use as a dining room chair or as a side chair in living rooms.

Jane Morris

Jane Morris, née Burden (1839–1914), was a muse for the pre-Raphaelites. As students, Rossetti, Burne-Jones, and Morris had all been struck by her beauty.

Prolific interior design author Elizabeth Wilhide (1991) wrote: "Her particular type of beauty was so strongly associated with the Pre-Raphaelite vision that it was difficult to tell which came first" (p. 15). Morris painted Jane, using her to model as Guinevere. She fell in love with, was engaged to, and married William Morris. Jane Morris was not formally well educated, but she was intelligent and a voracious reader. She naturally came by the timeless beauty many of the pre-Raphaelite painters sought in a model.

Initially, the Morrises lived full-time at Red House, but in 1865 they moved back to London to be closer to their booming business. Kelmscott Manor was a sixteenth-century house redecorated by William Morris in 1871 (Figure 16.9). Morris's decorating scheme left the medieval structure intact, yet he simplified the visual effect of the old house with his selection of furnishings and finishes. He decorated the place with simple pieces of furniture—upholstered in Morris textiles and painted the walls. Interior draperies hang at a consistent height and bring order to a group of otherwise disperate elements that includes Sussex chairs, a Wainscot chair, and a hearth with a Gothic arch.

Jane Morris posed for Rossetti (1828–1882) several times, and at some point their relationship became intimate. What was once an illicit affair became public knowledge (Wilhide 1991, pp. 15–26). William

Figure 16.11 Dante Gabriel Rossetti. Rossetti chair, 1870–1890.

and Jane Morris remained married, and just how incensed he was over his wife's affair remains a mystery. Amazingly, he later commissioned Rossetti to paint his wife's portrait, the very same scenario that prompted their initial indiscretion (Figure 16.10).

Rossetti, of Italian background, never visited Italy. When the pre-Raphaelites had formed as a group in 1848, Rossetti was friends with William Morris and Edward Burne-Jones. Rossetti later was employed by Morris, primarily working on the stained-glass windows for churches. The popularity of Gothic Revival resulted in many commissions for stained glass, in houses and churches.

The Rossetti chair was named for the artist, and he is listed as its designer (Figure 16.11). It is possible that other Morris designers assisted in its creation.

Figure 16.10 Dante Gabriel Rossetti. "The Day Dream," 1880.

In the case of Arts and Crafts, while their rhetoric praised a return to a simple life and the necessity of designing well for humble households, their own lives were unconventional, with the triangular relationship of William Morris, Jane Morris, and Rossetti as the prime example.

May Morris

Morris and Company offered a three-paneled screen with embroidered canvas panels (Figure 16.12). It relies upon a simple frame-and-panel system. The screens were sold as kits or already completed by catalog. John Henry Dearle was Morris's assistant, and he later became artistic director. May Morris (1862–1938), William and Jane Morris's youngest daughter, directed the embroidery shop from 1885 to 1896. The inclusion of the humble pastime of embroidery as part of the Arts and Crafts aesthetic sphere added to its popularity, particularly among women.

Other Arts and Crafts Designers

Edwin Godwin (1833–1886) was an English architect, designer, and writer (Soros 1999, p. 15)—a major figure in the Arts and Crafts movement. The breadth of his stylistic interests resulted in a lack of consistency in his overall body of work, which, depending on one's viewpoint, was a point for or against him. Susan Soros, the editor of an exhibition catalog on his work (1999), writes: "Domestic interior decoration played a significant role in Godwin's career. He was responsible for many highly original interior designs, ranging from an elaborate Gothic Revival scheme of decoration for an Irish castle to a

Figure 16.12 John Henry Dearle. Screen, 1885–1910. For Morris and Co.

severe minimally furnished, Japanese-inspired interior for an artist's house-studio in London" (p. 185).

Although he expressed his allegiance to Ruskin, his attraction to Japanese art made him an unusual voice in the English reform movements. His pieces were a fusion of Arts and Crafts and Japanese motifs and themes. Gridlike and modular, his Anglo-Japanese furniture was more imaginative than ethnographic.

Charles Eastlake (1836–1906) was a British architect, historian, and theorist. He didn't build furniture himself, but had furniture made to his specifications that were sold under his name. Through his publications, he was as successful in the United States as in his native country.

As was expected of a knowledgeable person in design, he was influenced by Pugin and Ruskin. Eastlake himself wrote a book that covered Pugin's area of expertise, *History of the Gothic Revival* (1877). He had previously written a book that ensured his ongoing relevance, *Hints on Household Taste* (1868).

Eastlake's furniture was severe-looking. In many respects, his pieces resemble Victorian pieces, which is how they are often described, only with less decoration. He achieved the severe look by utilizing flat decorative planes. One of his concerns was the ease of cleaning; hence his predilection for flat patterns. Eastlake's use of the word "taste" in his title is telling: He did not overturn trends and stylistic preferences, but assisted people in decorating their homes simply and tastefully. Eastlake's designs were received as the opposite of John Henry Belter's, yet there is a resemblance. Some Eastlake pieces look like Belter's work, stripped of ornament.

The Second Generation of Arts and Crafts

Morris, Webb, Rossetti, and Godwin represent the first generation of English Arts and Crafts. A second generation of English Arts and Crafts includes several talented architects and furniture designers whose careers take them into the twentieth century.

Voysey

Charles Francis Annesley Voysey (1875–1910) was an English architect who designed and built a small number of beautifully designed country houses in the period 1890–1910. His work was traditional, vernacular, and subtly revolutionary. Familiar with Pugin's publications, Voysey later produced work that mostly eliminated any lingering Gothic traces.

He had an architectural practice, and his career was an example of the cross-disciplinary nature of those involved in Arts and Crafts. Hitchmough (1995) writes that "Voysey's versatility as a designer went beyond that of any of his contemporaries, in both range and duration" (p. 141). Voysey was successful as a designer of furniture and wallpapers. When the opportunity arose, he designed houses, interiors, details, furniture, carpets, draperies, and wall coverings.

Like his colleagues in Arts and Crafts, Voysey (1894) lamented the state of design: "The intemperate indulgence in display and elaboration, in gilding and veneer, and the feverish thirst for artificial excitement, are all part and parcel of our proverbial restlessness. Too much luxury is death to the artistic soul" (pp. 415–418).

The residence he designed for himself, called The Orchard, finished in 1899, is remarkably simple in its façade (Figure 16.13). It fits into the local vernacular of farm buildings, yet there is a clarity in its composition that is the result of careful design work, not lack of attention. Similarly, little clutter detracts from the simplicity of the Voysey interior (Figure 16.14). The stairway is framed by a built-in screen formed by vertical slats, a detail also found in the works of Wright, Sullivan, and Mackintosh. The room has white walls and a continuous

Figure 16.13 Charles F.A. Voysey. The Orchard, 1899. Chorley Wood, England.

Figure 16.14 Charles F.A. Voysey. The Orchard, 1899. Chorley Wood, England.

dado line, the line that delineates the horizontal zones of the wall. The paintings were placed with care. The furniture was simple, and the bricks were inexpensive.

There are subtle historical references in Voysey's work. Some Gothic details are apparent in the detailing, such as the long strap hinges that many Arts and Crafts designers used. Yet Voysey considered himself on the periphery of Arts and Crafts. He did not vociferously oppose the machine as did most Arts and Crafts designers.

The clarity of his plans, the relative lack of decoration, the simplicity of his elevations, and the liberal use of white paint are collectively the features that made him one of the most forward-looking of those associated with Arts and Crafts. Hitchmough writes: "Voysey's architectural language was deliberately restrained. Where his designs were innovative they were also founded on reason rather than on a contrived attempt to be different" (p. 171). A source of his simplicity was his fondness for indigenous materials. His considerable success with elaborate wallpapers was not anticipated by the sparse exteriors of his buildings (Figure 16.15).

Lutyens

Edwin Lutyens (1894–1944) had a career that lasted so long that he outlived Arts and Crafts. He started out doing country houses, skillfully set within gardens. He was a traditionalist, more interested in

Figure 16.15 C.F.A. Voysey Design for a wallpaper showing water snakes for Essex and Company

vernacular country forms than were his contemporaries. For the gardens of his projects, he designed garden furniture that is still manufactured.

The end of his career took him in a different direction. Always a critic of modernism, when he received the commission for the English Viceroy's House in New Delhi, India, he combined European Baroque planning with Mughal decoration. Because of his output in the 1930s and 1940s, he is also covered in Chapter 22.

C. R. Ashbee (1863–1942) was a mainstream Arts and Crafts designer, architect, and theorist. He was a well-known figure in the Arts and Crafts circle in London. He made many types of furniture, known for their simplicity, literal and figural weight, and reliance on the simple panel-and-frame system. He also designed houses, many of which reveal his admiration for Voysey's projects. After Morris died, Ashbee started his own printing press in 1896.

M. H. Baillie Scott (1865–1945) was a British architect, and a designer of interiors and furniture. He was a major figure in British Arts and Crafts. He belonged to the second generation of designers, and the role he saw for himself is suggested by the house he designed for his family. He named it Red House, after Philip Webb's house for William Morris. In the plan of Baillie Scott's Red House, he made the clever link between a medieval feature, the great hall, and the modern open space. Baillie Scott wrote articles espousing his design philosophy. As a consequence of these articles, he was well known in Germany. As with the work of Mackmurdo, some see his projects to be aligned with Art Nouveau.

Arthur Heygate Mackmurdo (1851–1942) had one foot in Arts and Crafts, one foot in Art Nouveau. Mostly a furniture designer, he was a strong proponent of the effectiveness of a total environment—meaning that one designer did the architectural envelope and all the objects within it. His Arts and Crafts work was more delicate than Ashbee's, and his work reveals an increasing interest in natural forms. He explored natural motifs in his silhouettes, carving, tracery, and textiles. He is mentioned in Chapter 19.

Mackintosh

Charles Rennie Mackintosh is mostly discussed in another chapter, but it is worth mentioning him here, as he is often found in works on Arts and Crafts (Figure 16.16). Some of his pieces have a distinct reference to Arts and Crafts projects. He

Figure 16.16 Charles Rennie Mackintosh. Armchair, 1917.

was sympathetic to the reformists, and they admired his work.

GERMANY

In Germany, Arts and Crafts was initially related to nationalism and German unification in 1871. While nothing of the pervasiveness of English Arts and Crafts emerged, the work of English architects in designing logical and comfortable houses was greatly admired, foremost by Hermann Muthesius (1861–1927). His book *Das Englische Haus* (1904–1905) is a testament to the virtues of the English house. The book discusses favorably many of the Arts and Crafts designers mentioned in this chapter. The desire to present alternatives to Victorian design was strongly felt in Germany.

One of the most significant figures was Bruno Paul (1874–1968), a German architect and furniture designer. He studied at the Kunstgewerbeschule in Dresden. His early career was involved with promoting finely crafted pieces of furniture and decorative arts. His name is associated with Jugendstil, although as he avoided the exaggerated Art Nouveau effects, his work is also associated with Arts and Crafts. German Arts and Crafts was more integrated with other movements, as its adherents less stridently separated themselves from industrial manufacturing processes. Paul's work later developed into a neo-Biedermeier phase, and eventually he was considered a modernist who created several competent ship interiors. Austrian Arts and Crafts, similarly, blurred the lines with those involved with other movements, and the nascent Arts and Crafts movement was quietly superseded by Jugendstil (Chapter 19) adherents and the Secessionists (Chapter 20). Other German design activities took on the onus of design reform, an effort that ultimately paved the way for modernism.

Elsewhere around the world, there were varying degrees of dissatisfaction with Victorian design, and everyone had to cope with the bevy of new inventions and industrialization, urbanization, and population growth. It was mostly in the British Isles and former English colonies, such as the United States, Australia, Canada, and New Zealand, that these impulses consolidated into forms that can rightly be referred to as Arts and Crafts.

UNITED STATES

The Arts and Crafts movement in the United States had a more direct relationship to the people of rural areas. In England, William Morris and Philip Webb had to look to the medieval period for the kind of craftsmanship they wanted to emulate. In the English colonies, such as Australia, New Zealand, and the United States, the time when hardy people fought for survival was recent, scarcely 100 years in the past. In many cases, the American craft traditions were ongoing.

Greene and Greene

Charles Sumner Greene (1868–1957) and Henry Mather Greene (1870–1954) started a firm they called Greene and Greene. It was the preeminent firm of the American Arts and Crafts movement, and their most prominent project the Gamble House, 1908–1909. The Gamble House was made of wood, low to the ground, bungalow-inspired, with long overhangs. As was often the case with Greene and Greene houses, it was modified as it was being built.

American Arts and Crafts related to a literary movement that similarly extolled the virtues of simple living, self-reliance, and the importance of the individual. The works of Henry David Thoreau, Ralph Waldo Emerson, and Walt Whitman also see the heart of American individualism as residing in the countryside. Another connection to Arts and Crafts was the work of reformists such as Jane Addams, whose Hull House was a home for the poor. To the extent that she also sought to counter

Figure 16.17 Connie Dalrymple. Hand-carved sideboard. Wellington, New Zealand, 1900-1910

the negative effects of the Industrial Revolution, her work was related to what the Arts and Crafts designers did in the realm of design. Another distinction between the British and American strains of Arts and Crafts is that American design, in general, was less influenced by Art Nouveau for the simple reason that Art Nouveau, with the notable exception of the works of Tiffany, was less important.

NEW ZEALAND

Ann Calhoun writes that the Arts and Crafts movement in New Zealand "was always linked to its British parent but also had a legitimate personality of its own" (Calhoun 2000). In addition to expressing a cultural and political allegiance to Great Britain, three features individuate New Zealand Arts and Crafts. Women had a significant role in the British Arts and Crafts movement, but they played an even

more prominent role in New Zealand, where the majority of students attending design schools were women. The New Zealand designs made reference to local flora and fauna, and significantly, some pieces incorporated Maori design motifs.

Many design schools were established in New Zealand in the 1870s, 1880s, and 1890s. An aspect of Arts and Crafts that broadened its appeal was its recognition and encouragement of amateur artists. William Morris's daughter May Morris designed embroidery, wallpaper, and jewelry and led the embroidery workshop. Her prominence in the field in England was one of the factors that encouraged women to attend design schools in New Zealand.

One piece from New Zealand looks decidedly Victorian, combining the details of two movements, Arts and Crafts and Art Nouveau, that were, in theory, ideologically opposed (Figure 16.17). Another work incorporates Maori design motifs, an activity not at the center of English Arts and Crafts, although certainly sympathetic to its respect for premodern cultures.

CONCLUSION

Despite occasional points of convergence, the Gothic Revival movement and Arts and Crafts were distinct entities. Arts and Crafts was not a historic revival, and in fact, its supporters opposed historicism. A useful way of conceptualizing Arts and Crafts is to consider that tradition and modernity were two sides of one coin.

The unity of the arts was not just theorized, it was realized, with graphics and book publishing playing major roles. In Arts and Crafts graphics, the graphic simplicity responded to a moral and religious appreciation of restraint. This concern for the common good, often with a religious basis, resulted in many progressive elements of Arts and Crafts, such as a concern with countering the effects of industrialization. The Arts and Crafts movements around the world skillfully blended politics, poetry, socialism, and the design of finely crafted objects.

The comparison is anachronistic, but Arts and Crafts played a role in the nineteenth century similar to that played by sustainability and green design in the twenty-first. Both movements were prompted by a concern about the environment and the ill-planned effects of technology and industry. Seeking a solution, designers looked to nature.

By 1910, Arts and Crafts in Europe had started going out of fashion, with its last remnants expiring in the 1930s.

Sources

Calhoun, Ann. *The Arts and Crafts Movement in New Zealand, 1870–1940, Women Make Their Mark*. Auckland: Auckland University Press, 2000.

Donovan, Andrea. *William Morris and the Society for the Protection of Ancient Buildings*. New York: Routledge, 2008.

Durant, Stuart. *CFA Voysey*. New York: St. Martin's Press, 1992.

Eisenman, Stephen. *Design in the Age of Darwin: from William Morris to Frank Lloyd Wright*. Evanston: Mary and Leigh Block Museum, 2008.

Fiell, Charlotte. *William Morris 1834–1896*. Cologne: Taschen, 1999.

Gebhard, David. *Charles F. A. Voysey Architect*. Los Angeles: Hennessey and Ingalls, 1975.

Haigh, Diane. *Baillie Scott: the Artistic House*. London: Academy Editions, 1995.

Hitchmough, Wendy. *CFA Voysey*. London: Phaidon, 1995.

Kirk, Sheila. *Philip Webb: Pioneer of Arts and Crafts Architecture*. Hoboken: Wiley, 2005.

Soros, Susan. *The Secular Furniture of E. W. Godwin*. New Haven: Yale University Press, 1999.

Soros, Susan, ed. *E. W. Godwin: Aesthetic Movement Architect and Designer*. New Haven: Yale University Press, 1999.

Todd, Pamela. *The Arts and Crafts Companion*. New York: Bulfinch, 2004.

Van der Post, Lucia. *William Morris and Morris and Co*. New York: Abrams, 2003.

Voysey, Charles F. A. *Journal of the Royal Institute of British Architects*, vol. 1 (1894): 415–416.

Wilhide, Elizabeth. *William Morris: Décor and Design*. New York: Abrams, 1991.

DISCUSSION AND REVIEW QUESTIONS

1. How did the reformists feel about history?
2. What was the relationship between Arts and Crafts and Gothic Revival?
3. What were some of the distinguishing characteristics of Arts and Crafts in Britain, New Zealand, and the United States?
4. What were some aligned interests in other professional areas?
5. Who were some of the figures whose works crossed over into Art Nouveau?
6. What was modern about Arts and Crafts?
7. What was elitist about Arts and Crafts? Populist?
8. What was the role of women in Arts and Crafts?
9. How would you relate Arts and Crafts in terms of today's environmental problems and the involvement of the design community?

CHAPTER 17

AFRICA

747-664 B.C.E.	Eighth to thirteenth centuries	1881
Twenty-fifth dynasty and Nubian control of Egypt	Empire of Ghana	Scramble for Africa; Berlin conference

1960's	1994	
Independence for most African countries	Democratic elections in South Africa and the end of Apartheid	

This chapter focuses on African traditional furniture pieces. This is not this book's first African chapter. There have been several. Egypt is in Africa. And, of course, Nubia is also covered in Chapter 2. Neolithic Africa is well represented in the historical record. Many of the other chapters have African connections. The second-largest continent, almost all styles and time periods are represented in Africa. There is African French Provincial, Art Nouveau, Art Deco, modernism, and postmodernism.

There is no clean dividing line between African traditional and other artistic genres. "Traditional" forms also responded to the vagaries of capitalist production and supply and demand. They were created in the countryside and in urban centers. Even if stylistically conservative—not always the case—their creators responded to and embraced technological innovations. These are not timeless pieces removed from chronology, but the category "traditional" does adequately refer to works that cannot easily and reasonably be identified by other stylistic terms, such as "art deco" or "modern."

The artists involved with creating modest pieces were curiously freed from many constrictions. Because their work received less scrutiny, they largely operated outside of aristocratic and religious control. While they did not enjoy the use of expensive materials and had to produce their products quickly, those involved with crafting simple objects experienced the emancipation of artists who participate in the marketplace. More important for the artisans was functioning within a capitalist framework, and an economy that was embroiled in colonialism for much of its early history.

The nineteenth century plays a big role in this chapter. The nineteenth century saw tremendous changes of a mind-boggling degree in many parts of the world, all the more so for Africa. It was also the period in which the horror of the slave trade was to thankfully wind down, although the specter of colonialism was on the horizon. As historians of culture, we are in the awkward position of decrying the injustice of colonialism, yet marveling at the brilliance and creativity of many caught up in it—the presence of English, Dutch, Portuguese, and German colonials prompted the creation of many wonderful objects.

A note on chronology. Most African furniture pieces, with some exceptions, can only be dated back to the mid-nineteenth century. We should reflect on why this is so. For one, Africans and Europeans started collecting African furniture pieces in earnest in the twentieth century. Because many of these pieces were modest, they were not, until recently, deemed worthy of being collected, cataloged, and preserved. Also, many pieces were removed from their initial cultural contexts, and little documentation exists to confirm the dates of their creation and purchase. In the absence of corroborating data, most pieces that are obviously old can only be dated with certainty back to the mid-nineteenth century. Descriptions of objects in European travel accounts suggest that the forms of many utilitarian objects go back centuries. For most of the pieces in this chapter, the type of precise dating found in other chapters is not possible. What is known is that the rate of stylistic change in the twentieth century speeded up as new technologies and new materials were available.

Jared Diamond points out that Africa is the most diverse continent on earth ethnically and linguistically (in contrast to China, for which the Chinese language acts as a source of common identity). One quarter of the world's languages are spoken in Africa, the continent that stretches almost from Antarctica to Mediterranean temperate zones and includes deserts, jungles, and snow-covered mountains (Diamond 1997, p. 377). Africa has fifty-four countries, each one having from two to a hundred or more ethnic groups, often with widely dissimilar languages. Most of Africa was colonized by the Dutch, English, French, German, Italian, and Portuguese, and several places were colonized by multiple European countries. Senegal, for example, was initially explored by the Portuguese and the Dutch. In the colonial era, they were followed by the English and finally the French; Senegal became independent in the 1960s. Germany lost

its African colonies in World War I. Cameroon, to give one example, was turned over to the British and the French. Overlying the category of domestic and foreign ethnicity is religion, where the main players are Christian, Islamic, and indigenous.

This chapter is not a comprehensive look at African furniture pieces but a representative sampling of some fine pieces, some typical pieces, and some pieces that display the unique qualities of African designed objects, those that render them different from Western and Asian pieces.

THE CLASSIC AFRICAN HOUSE

African architecture can be round, ovoid, square, or rectangular; made of stones, brick, mud, wood, or straw; and it can incorporate a myriad of different patterns by which ethnic groups distinguish themselves. The kind of architecture that Africa is most known for is a modest structure made of reeds or rush.

A Round House

The classic African round house, to many, is not only the essence of African architecture, it has iconic status; it means Africa (Figure 17.1). There are countless regional variations, but several ethnic groups from across the continent have something formally similar to this standard straw structure. The Wolof and Lebu ethnic groups of Senegal, West Africa, are related and both have a tradition of round houses. It is difficult although not impossible to trace this important building type in its various permutations throughout history. The difficulty arises because it is made of impermanent materials and these structures were never intended to last decades, let alone hundreds of years. But visual evidence for this type of structure, as suggested by the d'Hastrel engraving, gives some idea of what a Lebu/

Figure 17.1 Adolphe d'Hastrel. The village of Dakar, 1851.

Wolof dwelling looked like in the mid-nineteenth century.

In ancient Africa, Egyptian and Roman artists who created mosaics represented their permanent architecture as different from the autochthonous varieties. The artists were apparently fascinated by the latter's organic materials and soft curvilinear geometries. There is similarity between how workers constructed dwellings in the past and in the present, although it is unlikely that the processes are exactly the same. Yet, some knowledge of ancient practices can be inferred by contemporary building methods that produce similar-looking buildings.

Roy Sieber, an American curator and scholar, wrote: "For Africans, as for us, the house is the center of the world. However, to the African the sense of space at that center is not necessarily interior space, for most African houses are not lived in in the sense we usually use that phrase. An African 'home' is not the semi-sealed, closed container for a nuclear family that the West has come to consider it. Rather it often sprawls, housing an extended family and domestic animals: hunting dogs; goats and chickens as scavengers and food; goats, cattle or horses as wealth. There are no pets. Spread over a sizable area, often fenced in and at times with a gateway, the home/compound is at the same time a unit in the larger village" (Sieber 1980, p. 15). d'Hastrel's early view of the village that became the capital of Senegal, Dakar, correspondingly shows a collection of individual dwellings that are connected with a palisade of reed fences.

Another d'Hastrel drawing is a rare historical view of the inside of a Wolof straw dwelling (Figure 17.2). The walls and domed roof are made of straw, enlivened with a simple pattern. A single opening acts as the means of egress and lets in light. There are no windows. Some structures of this type have a threshold over which one must step in order to enter, although this one does not.

Figure 17.2 Interior at a chief's house, Dakar. Nineteenth century.

This engraving shows the interior of an African dwelling, yet the single piece of furniture is a European **bedstead,** with a reed mat laid over it. Mats such as these are also laid upon the ground, for sitting outside. This is the home of a chief, who may be demonstrating his social prominence with a European piece of furniture. On the far right, the artist himself sits on a stool, close to the ground, no doubt a modest piece of furniture. A few objects hang on the wall.

A Square House

A 1942 photograph of a Wolof house was created approximately 100 years later than the d'Hastrel view (Figure 17.3). The fishing village of N'dar Toute lies across the Senegal River from the city of Saint-Louis, Senegal's second-largest city. The town plan is gridded, which in part explains why these Wolof houses are rectilinear. The differences between the two structures are subtle but significant. The footprint of an individual house in the fishing village is square, not round; the walls, still of straw, are part of a framed construction method, and the door is made of milled lumber. When making Wolof houses, the straw roof is constructed as a separate element that is later placed on top of the walls. Square houses are also traditionally African, and there is no clean break between historic architectural styles and modern ones. Traditional African dwellings are often written about as if they have undergone no stylistic changes from time immemorial, but Africans were quick to adopt new materials when they became available, such as milled lumber and, later, corrugated metal, concrete block, and glass block.

Figure 17.3 House of a Wolof fisherman, Saint-Louis. Photograph, 1942.

DESIGNED OBJECTS BEFORE INDUSTRIALIZATION

A nineteenth-century engraving shows a weaver weaving (Figure 17.4). The artist's composition captures a beguiling combination of a mode of sitting, a human figure, a modification to the landscape, and two pieces of equipment, a loom and sun shade. Responding to the functional needs of a weaver, this is a complex if forthright designed object. These looms produce long narrow strips of cloth that can the be sewn together to make blankets and other cloths. Many African ethnic groups

Figure 17.4 African weaver. Nineteenth-century engraving.

weave this way; the most famous variety is the **Kente cloth** of Ghana, which, like the round house, has become virtually synonymous with Africa.

A hole has been dug in the ground, over which stands the loom. The male weaver sits with his legs in the hole, operating the poles that raise the warp strings. A separate structure, a woven mat on stilts, shields him from the sun. Mats, made of grass, straw, or reeds, are a common feature in Africa, and they exist continentwide. Sieber dates their appearance prior to sustained European contact, to at least the ninth century c.e. (Sieber 1980, p. 5). Mats can be used for sleeping at night and sitting during the day. They act as covers and rugs, as wall hangings and space dividers. Because of their usefulness, many Africans travel with one rolled up. They are a common article that nomads such as the Tuaregs use, after pitching a tent, to furnish the interior. Across Africa, it is common to entertain guests outside by unrolling a mat on the ground. The deceptively simple designed object of a weaver's apparatus uses a mat as a sunshade, as part of an ensemble that incorporates both man-made and found objects.

INDUSTRIALIZATION IN AFRICA

Nineteenth-century Africa got a crash course in industrialization, as did much of the world. Many regions experienced a shift toward market agriculture. Imported cast iron quickly found its place on a continent that had been forging iron, in smaller quantities, for centuries. Railroads transformed the African landscape, literally and symbolically, as they did everywhere. People in inland towns and villages, which had been days if not weeks away from urban areas and coastal trading centers, suddenly found that travel to a major city was only a day away, and relatively inexpensive. Colonialism had many effects on African populations, one of them being access to European transportation and communication technologies, such as railroads, airplanes, the telegraph, and photography.

The Railroad

Towns along railroad lines thrived from the traffic in people, goods, and therefore new forms and ideas

Figure 17.5 Railway station. Rufisque, Senegal. Late nineteenth century.

(Figure 17.5). The railway station in Rufisque, Senegal, is a building made of a combination of local and imported building products. Rufisque was an important trading center for eighteenth-century North Atlantic seagoing trade, and the railroad continued that tradition.

Railways, iron manufacturing, steamships, airplanes, electricity, and telegraphs often arrived due to governmental support, yet one art form needed no prompting to ensure its success. Shortly after its invention in France in 1839, Daguerre's photographic process appeared in Africa, and Africans quickly took to it as both producers and consumers.

Photography

Africans initially embraced the pictorial revolution for private portraiture. In the coastal trading city of Saint-Louis du Sénégal, Amadi Coumba responded to the event of having his photographic portrait taken by dressing in his best clothes and jewelry (Figure 17.6). In his case, it meant pairing a **bou-bou,** the flowing African gown, with a French jacket, and a ring and a bracelet. His head was freshly shaved and his beard combed.

Coumba enters the historic record simply because he had his portrait taken, and the photograph entered the collections of the Institute Fondamental d'Afrique Noire, the research institute affiliated with the University of Dakar. A postmodern interpretation of the photograph is that it mediates Coumba's identity, in which he seeks to reconcile his African heritage (the bou-bou) with the French cultural influences (the jacket) that connected him to international trade. Coumba probably viewed the event of having his portrait taken in a personal way. The interaction with a photographer left him with a two-dimensional likeness that he could, in turn, give to a loved one. No direct evidence documents Coumba's reaction to having his portrait taken. The

Figure 17.6 Portrait of Amadi Coumba. Saint-Louis. Early twentieth century.

suppositions offered here are to stress that when photography entered Africa, it became a new player in a society that had complicated familial and social relationships. Even in previous centuries, Africa was connected to the world's economy with trade in consumer items and the circulation of images.

Corrugated Metal

A photograph from Liberia, West Africa, shows a house under construction (Figure 17.7). Ethnically and historically, Liberia is an unusual country, as it was mostly populated with repatriated African-American slaves. Its modern history began in 1821 with the first arrival of African-Americans. The

Figure 17.7 House under construction, Liberia, 1907.

United States did not officially have any African colonies, but Liberia comes close. The capital city, Monrovia, was named for the American president James Monroe. In 1847, Liberia declared itself a sovereign state.

In the photograph, construction workers are building a house using the balloon-framing system, over which they attach corrugated metal sheeting. The African-Americans who moved to Liberia took with them their familiarity with and knowledge of Southern American houses and agricultural buildings. Author Bernard Herman writes: "The most powerful architectural concept behind the mansion houses of Liberia is authority" (Belcher/Herman 1988, p. 129). When given the opportunity to build houses in Africa, they built the type that responded to their notions of utility, comfort, and status.

FURNITURE

African furniture exists in great variety and relates to hundreds of ethnic groups. African furniture could also be classified by type or by country. The intent here is not a comprehensive survey of African furniture and designed objects, but a representative sample.

Stools and Chairs

African seating is a broad category, with the most ubiquitous piece being the stool. There are numerous types, from simple to grand, but one characteristic, across the board, is that they are low to the ground compared to Western objects designed for sitting.

Ethiopia

From Ethiopia, in the horn of Africa, comes a seat made of two planks (Figure 17.8). The top one fits into a slot in the bottom one, forming the backrest. The chair is therefore demountable and transportable. A person sits in this chair leaning against the backrest with legs extended. The bottom piece, if well constructed, has the feet integral to the bottom plank, a feat achieved only with a great deal of reduction carving. If the feet are attached, they are likely to shear off.

Figure 17.8 Stool with back. Twentieth century, Ethiopia.

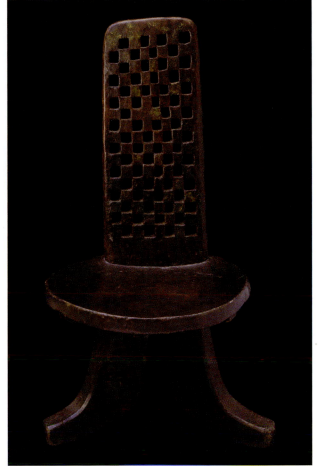

Figure 17.9 Wood chair. Ethiopia.

Laure Meyer (1995), writing about simple African objects, probes the relationship between function and form. She writes that an aesthetic sensibility "shows itself first in the elegance or fitness of the forms, which, in and of themselves, provide simple visual pleasure without recourse to ornamentation. This elegance, however, is never an end in itself, but emphasizes the functionality of the object by subordinating and adapting itself to it. Simple, pure forms are designed with an unerring sense of line" (Meyer 1995, p. 9). Meyer's comment is an ode to the aesthetic of some African pieces, but there are other approaches and methods for understanding these pieces.

The largest group of African seats are stools, and the most prominent type of stools are round.

In these stools, the seat retains its round shape from the tree log from which it is created. Another wooden chair is also from Ethiopia (Figure 17.9). The legs curve and the round seat is low to the ground. The round seat contrasts with the rectilinear form and pattern of the back. This one is a "chair" because it has a back, yet it is essentially a stool to which a backrest has been added.

Ghana

An example of the richness of forms found within one ethnic group, this chapter includes three distinct types of seats created by the Ashanti, one of the Ghanaian ethnic groups. The Ashanti are one of the largest of Ghana's fifty ethnic groups, and they

Figure 17.10 Ashanti stool. Ghana.

are a subdivision of the larger Akan group. The modern country of Ghana is the southernmost remnant of one of Africa's historical polities, the Empire of Ghana, which was dominant in the region in the eighth to thirteenth centuries.

A simple Ashanti wood stool is transportable in another way (Figure 17.10). One end gently tapers into a handle so that it can be slung over one's shoulder. In some situations, a man who goes visiting friends, to work, or to a village meeting, takes his chair with him. A person could sit perpendicular to the stool, with knees sharply bent, although a small child could use the handle as a backrest. Other Ghanaian pieces are discussed later in the chapter.

Côte d'Ivoire, Nigeria, and Congo

A Senufo stool from Côte d'Ivoire is made from a single section of a tree log (Figure 17.11). The laborious process of reduction carving ensures the piece's stability. This piece belongs to the category of works

that Philip Ravenhill (1991) wrote about when he proposed a distinction between utilitarian pieces and those with a clear aesthetic intent. He wrote about a work that "combines a response to a need for functional usefulness with a response to an additional need—the need to surpass mere function by inventing form and seeking further refinement" (Ravenhill 1991, p. 4). The Senufo are a subset of an ethnic group known as Voltaic. Senufo come from the Savannah regions in the north of the country of Côte d'Ivoire. This Senufo stool is unornamented, yet its carefully crafted form exceeds the most straightforward means of crafting a modest, low-to-the-ground seat. The stool gently curves in two directions, like a saddle.

Nigeria is the most populous country in Africa, and the Nupe are one of Nigeria's smaller ethnic groups. They are associated with the Nupe River. A Nupe stool also derives its overall form from a log's cross section (Figure 17.12). The legs, more than needed for the purpose of support, have become the

Figure 17.11 Senufo stool. Ivory Coast.

Figure 17.13 Tetela stool. Congo.

Figure 17.12 Nupe stool. Nigeria.

chief decorative item of the stool. The top, in low-relief carving, displays a common Islamic motif. The decoration is geometric and not representational. Stools similar to this one are not limited to Nigeria, but are made in several central African countries. The process of chip carving gives Nupe furniture feet a distinctive faceted surface. The Nupe also created beds, painstakingly crafting a platform from a large piece of wood; the contiguous feet similarly taper inward toward the ground.

A Tetela stool from Congo takes the process of reduction carving as far as it can go, when working with a log segment (Figure 17.13). The amount removed in this stool approaches the point when structural failure will occur. The result is a lightweight, elegant piece. The Shona of Zimbabwe create stools similar to this one.

Across Africa, countless varieties of carved stools are created from a single piece of wood. The round base and seat are consistent, yet the forms and patterns that enliven the space between the seat and the ground is left to the creativity of the artist.

These cylindrical stools range from spool-shaped ones that are relatively simple, to elaborate ones in which caryatids support the seat. Carefully ornamented stools are a part of the regalia of nobles and chiefs. Elaborate stools are associated with leadership. A further sign of a person's status occurs when someone travels with a stool bearer, a person designated to carry the stool and set it up. This practice is also recognition that not all houses will have a sufficient number of seats for guests.

Furniture and Seated Figures in Sculpture

A Senufo-Baule sculpture from Ivory Coast takes as its subject a mother and child seated on a round stool (Figure 17.14). She has a crested hairstyle and bare breasts. Sculptures of a mother and child are common in Senufo art, and found in the Ivory Coast, Mali, and Burkina Faso. The meanings vary, but in the most general way, this sculptural grouping relates maternity to fertility and abundance. The stool has two rear legs. What is interesting is that the mother's legs take the place of the stool's front legs. Many African artworks, including furniture, are anthropomorphic, with human figures or body parts taking the functional role of furniture pieces. Nowhere is this so obvious as when human legs literally stand in for furniture legs. Human figure and piece of furniture work together in this tandem piece. Yet the substitution of the human legs for the stool legs makes this sculpture visually precarious. The mother is solidly placed, yet also appears as if about to rise.

Backrests and Thrones

The Kuba are another one of some 300 ethnic groups in Congo, and the descendants of the former African kingdom of Kuba. A Kuba backrest is meant for reclining, close to the ground, with legs extended

Figure 17.14 Mother with child. Senufo-Baule sculpture. Ivory Coast.

(Figure 17.15). Upholstery tacks cover the entirety of its large, sweeping curve. This decorative surface treatment also makes the backrest tactile. A backrest is a furniture type virtually unknown in the West. In Africa, it is typically made from a piece of wood, braced to sit at a 45-degree angle with the ground. The most famous of Kuba artworks are not pieces of furniture, but their textiles with geometric patterns. The Ngombe, also from Congo, make chairs with legs that utilize the same gentle curve of the backrest and are similarly covered with tacks, sometimes in contrasting colors.

Figure 17.15 Kuba backrest. Wood with brass tacks. Congo.

Any chair, even when void of an occupant, is related to the human figure, more so than tables and chests, which have a purpose removed from humanity, to support or store things. The formula chair = person is of special importance in the case of Ghanaian thrones. Among the Ashanti, a stool can be related to the soul of an individual, an important leader, or even to all the Ashanti people.

Ghanaian Thrones

There are two principal methods for understanding African household objects. One involves appreciating them for their aesthetic qualities. The other seeks to understand them in their own terms, by delving into the ethnological details of their cultural context. Books about African furniture are few, but in 1971, a Ghanaian Catholic bishop, Peter Sarpong, devoted an entire book to one type of seating, *The Sacred Stool of the Akan*. In most societies, death does not end a person's participation in the world of the living. Yet unique to the Akan of Ghana is that

ancestor worship centers around a piece of furniture, a stool.

Most Ghanaian houses have a stool, and more stools than chairs. A Ghanaian stool is formed by two horizontal planes, a base and a top, with a decorated support between them (Figure 17.16). The base is stepped in two or three layers. The top, or seat, exceeds the base in length and is curved. This crescent shape symbolizes a mother's embrace. The depth of the stool is one quarter its worth. The curved seat makes it comfortable to carry the stool on the back; it is never meant to be carried on the head. It is alternately translated as "stool" or "throne," and as with most translations, neither is perfect. The word "stool" relates to its form: It is low to the ground and there is no back or armrest. "Throne" is more appropriate to its function, as the literal and symbolic seat of a chief in a public setting that is an artistic achievement of a craftsman. A great deal of time is spent crafting a Ghanaian stool, which is a work of art, a religious object, and a functioning piece of furniture.

Innumerable forms and decorations bridge the space between the top and the base (Sarpong 1971, p. 7). Upon reaching agreement with a client, the craftsman shows his expertise by how he designs and carves the middle portion. The symbolism of this decorative field is vast and prone to differing opinions and multiple interpretations.

The stool's undercarriage functionally needs to support the seat, which it sometimes does with a single trunk, sometimes with three. A common configuration of the middle part is a sphere with a hole in it, sometimes placed in front of a stout support. There are anthropomorphic seats and zoomorphic seats. Of the latter, elephants, leopards, and porcupines are considered most appropriate for this dignified and prized piece.

Men craft these stools, and they should be exemplary citizens, having peaceful relations with wife and parents (Sarpong 1971, p. 13). The relationship between client and craftsman was important, as it

repeated the relationship between the founder of the Ashanti kingdom and his priest. In no other group's foundation myth does a piece of furniture play such an important role. The foundation myth of the Ashanti kingdom is also the foundation myth of the Golden Stool, the first and most important of all Ghanaian stools.

The chief in the foundation myth is Osei-Tutu. He assumes leadership in Kumasi, and his military successes involve his consolidating power, vanquishing enemies, and exerting authority over a region that bears a geographic and cultural relationship with contemporary Ghana. Through the intervention of his priest, Anokye, at a summit of leaders, a stool falls from the sky accompanied by darkness and thunder. This wooden stool is covered with gold. It lands on Osei-Tutu's knee. This stool is the center of the national consciousness and the institution of the Golden Stool. A common stool in its form, with its gilding and exceptional provenance, it became the symbol of the unified nation.

The tradition of these stools became widespread over time, with many variations. Every Akan can have a stool. There are white stools, silver stools, golden stools, and blackened stools. White stools are left unfinished save for being washed and white-washed. Silver stools are white stools plated with silver. Golden stools are white stools covered with gold leaf. There are men's stools, women's stools, and children's stools. A groom frequently gives his bride a stool, as does a host his or her guest. There are stools for poor men, priests, attendants, and stool carriers.

Outside of functional use, the most important use a stool has is the role it plays after death, after going through the process of being blackened. The stool selected for blackening is typically a stool that was frequently and repeatedly used by the deceased, such as the stool in the bathroom used for daily bathing or the stool sat upon while eating.

The blackening of the stool is a ritual of both practical conservation and symbolic consecration. There are several explanations for the choice of the black finish. As the color white is related to happier times, black as the symbolic color of death is appropriate. Black is also frightening, and therefore commands respect. A functional explanation is that as part of the veneration, libations are poured on the stool, including eggs and blood. They would stain a white stool, but they add to the patina of a soot-blackened stool.

The centrality of this stool to the Ashanti reveals itself in many ways. The stool, related to the foundation myth, is a symbol of the nation. It is the symbol of a chief. Chiefs, appropriately enough, can be *enstooled* or *destooled*. But the stool will ultimately serve as the resting place for its owner's soul. While published information on African furniture is scarce, the exception is the Ghanaian throne.

Sarpong admits that Ghanaians are not so strict about a stool's uses today. The scenario outlined here about the use of the throne was true in historic periods and remains true. Yet the rules and practices of use are, no doubt, more flexible and less stringently applied today. The Ghanaian stool is second only to the kente cloth as an artwork associated with Ghana. A great number of the stools produced today are made explicitly for the tourist market.

Yet for a book that looks at designed objects, the majority of which are pieces of furniture, it is appropriate to expend much textual space on a common furniture type that becomes a symbol of the nation and also the final resting place of the soul in the afterlife.

On a traditional Ghanaian throne, the occupant sits perpendicular to its mass. The grandeur comes from the extent of the carving and its overall form. There is little concern for support or comfort in the way of cushions or upholstery, although a mat, a hide, or a textile is frequently placed on top of the throne. This throne is meant for sitting upright, in a public arena, and not for lounging in private. While the base and seat resemble planks, these thrones are traditionally carved from a single piece of wood. These stools are related to political and spiritual functions.

Ghanaian thrones can be appreciated for their artistry, but Michele Coquet (1998) provided an interpretation that is possible only with an in-depth knowledge of their political and spiritual purposes. She wrote: "The personal seat is conceived as the site where one of the spiritual principles of its user dwells. This principle is called sunsum by the Ashanti. Each time he sits on it, the owner transmits a little of this principle to the object. In this respect, the Akan chief's stool is doubly vested with *sunsum*: that of the owner and that of the founder of the lineage the chief represents. In that sense, the stool must also be regarded both as the receptacle of the spiritual principle of *sunsum,* which all the chiefs of the same lineage transmit from one to the other, and as the receptacle of power itself" (Coquet 1998, p. 132). When a throne was not being used by the chief, it was typically laid on its side. The throne operates as a stand-in for royalty, in an individual way but also in a collective way.

A chief's stool was the repository of his soul. After his death, his stool was preserved in a shrine. An enshrined stool commemorated the deceased, provided refuge for his soul, and functioned as ancestor figures did in other cultures.

Another type of Ashanti chair from Ghana is based on a European chair (Figure 17.17). Its occupant sits high off the ground, with a backrest and curved arms. Thumbtacks cover its surface, a sign of wealth that also affects the visual and tactile experience of the chair. Sieber (1980) surmises that the Portuguese first introduced the European armchair to the Gold Coast (Ghana) in 1481 (p. 159). This is a typical example of the chronological information that is available, and not available, about historic African furniture (Coquet 1998, p. 98). While it is likely that some European furniture accompanied the early explorers in the fifteenth and sixteenth centuries, this information is based on textual references. Existing pieces can only be dated with certainty to the mid-nineteenth century.

This chair is sometimes referred to as an **elbow chair** in recognition that, unlike a stool, the chair provides a place for users to rest their arms. The elbow chair easily found a place in a culture in which seats related to status. Its form indicates that

Figure 17.17 Ashanti elbow chair. Ghana.

it was initially based on a folding European chair. In Ghana, these chairs were known as *akonkromfi* or praying mantis chairs because of the crossed configuration of the legs. It is not an exact copy of a European chair, but a reinterpretation made by an African craftsman.

Beds, Baskets, Gourds, and Buckets

There are several categories of items that in Africa take on functions that in other places are accomplished by furniture. Baskets are used for storing clothes, and historically gourds, or calabashes, were also used as storage items; these were largely replaced in the twentieth century with plastic buckets. Particularly in the Islamic parts of Africa, many Africans sit and sleep on foam cushions placed directly on the ground.

Beds

Traditional African beds existed in great variety; they are all essentially raised platforms whose chief purpose is to raise the sleeping figure off the ground (Figure 17.18). In warm climates, the air circulation underneath the bed is desirable; in cool climates, a bed separates the body from the damp. Bedposts or

Figure 17.18 Chief's bed. Bamboo, wood, and wicker. Cameroon.

testers, and prominent head- and footboards, were typically not features of indigenous African beds. Most African furniture pieces were freestanding and movable, with an exception for built-in sleeping platforms in cultures that construct with bricks. Mats, mattresses, and blankets rendered these earthen platforms more comfortable. There were also a variety of wooden beds. Some are carved from a single piece of wood, including the legs, while others employ a wooden frame. A companion object to the bed is the headrest, found in several African ethnic groups. Headrests were also used in ancient Egypt for the same purpose: to maintain elaborate hairstyles.

Sieber also reports that among the Senufo, beds are occasionally used as biers or catafalques, for the display of the remains of a loved one during a formal mourning period (Sieber 1980, p. 105). This is an important symbolic and ritual use that takes on a different meaning from its daily use as a piece of furniture. Historic African beds are rarely made today, and the traditional means of creating mattresses has been replaced with foam.

Baskets

For many African groups, baskets fulfill a role elsewhere taken by pieces of furniture. Baskets are durable, lightweight, and inexpensive. Large baskets are used to store clothes, and smaller baskets are used to contain cooking utensils and foodstuffs. Prior to the introduction of mass-produced items, hand-made baskets were extremely useful. Across Africa, different ethnic groups have different traditions regarding the gender association of certain arts. Among the Tutsi, women are associated with the art of basket making. Baskets figure among the objects exchanged as a part of marriage rituals. Large and small Tutsi baskets from Rwanda and Burundi are created with a spiral technique (Figure 17.19). Coiled baskets are made from a spiral of

Figure 17.19 Tutsi baskets in Umulenzi Design. Late twenti-eth century. Rwanda/Burundi.

fibers or bundled grasses. Subsequent coils are sewn to the previous ones. This spiral method lends itself to the iconic profile of the tapering tops. It also provides a framework for incorporating geometric patterns. Spiral weaving or coiling exists in other parts of the continent, particularly in central and southern Africa.

Crossed or checkered weaving predominates in West Africa. The baskets can be decorated with black zigzag forms, and red is occasionally used as well.

European Furniture

This chapter is mostly concerned with indigenous African furniture traditions. The topic of European forms in Africa, which are many, is covered in Chapter 13, "In the Colonies." Two examples from Cape County, South Africa, give an idea of the vari-ety of European examples in Africa. One chair employs a framing system seen in both Dutch and English vernacular furniture.

This formal relationship between a South Afri-can chair and English and Dutch furniture is logical, as England and the Netherlands are the European countries whose presence has dominated South Africa since the seventeenth century. The seat is made from a frame, and stretchers connect the legs at nearly ground level (Figure 17.20). The system of stretchers securely ties the legs together, making this a sturdy piece of furniture. The seat is caned. Other than the local materials, there is little indige-nous influence in this chair.

Another Cape County piece is particularly ele-gant, and intended for those who led a comfortable life. These two examples of European furniture in South Africa demonstrate that lifestyles among the Europeans varied greatly, with the distinctions due to class and wealth, which were directly reflected in furniture. It also reflects the difference between the lifestyles of Afro-Europeans in South African cities and those who lived in the countryside. It is an ac-curate rendition of a Neoclassical chair, in which giant scrolls constitute the arms (Figure 17.21). With no stretchers, this is a less sturdy piece of fur-niture. The existence of an extremely elegant Neo-classical chair in South Africa indicates that many Europeans were no longer merely surviving but en-joying a comfortable if not luxurious life. This piece suggests an Afro-European desire to participate in the early-nineteenth-century international craze for Neoclassical pieces.

The effects of the European presence in South African were extensive, more so than elsewhere on the continent. African indigenous traditions were greatly impacted; for example, the classic round house no longer exists in South Africa, although it exists elsewhere on the continent.

Figure 17.20 Early box-frame chair. Cape County, South Africa.

A Basotho house, from the Apartheid era (1948–1994), shows how domestic architecture can operate in a variety of cultural and political contexts simultaneously (Figure 17.22). The subject of Basotho houses and their contents is covered in Gary van Wyk's book (van Wyk 1998). As for its form, this is a simple rectangular house made of concrete blocks that are found throughout South Africa. In the apartheid era, the regime outlawed the flag of the African National Congress (ANC). The owners of one house, the Masilelas, like many others, painted the house using the colors of the ANC flag—green, red, and black—yet combined them with other colors and motifs. The effect departed enough from the features of the flag so that the owner could not get in trouble for painting the house to look like the flag, yet it was clearly recognizable to those in the

know. The exterior decoration of this house personally individuated this house, and it was also a political statement, a sign of Basotho nationalism and anti-apartheid resistance.

The painting scheme relies on decorative schemes with a long history. The patterns relate to the view of agricultural fields seen from hilltops. These patterns traditionally existed on textiles and baskets before they became fodder for house decoration. One of the characteristics of African architecture is that many architectural motifs are also found in textiles, baskets, and ceramics.

CONCLUSION

The Masilelas' house and its contents are important to relate the political role that designed objects can

Figure 17.21 Sabre-leg stinkwood armchair. Grahamstown, Cape County, South Africa.

Figure 17.22 Home on Walregat Farm. South Africa.

play. As a point of comparison, Louis XIV marshaled all the arts—architecture, interiors, furnishings, painting, and costume—to serve his political goal: to embolden France and present himself as its embodiment. Cultural productions in Baroque France were at his command, to represent, constitute, and implement his power. The comparison between Louis XIV and the Masilelas is purposely ludicrous—a comparison between one of the world's most powerful people and two of its least: a king and two people living in the apartheid regime. But that's the point.

Most of history suggests that it takes state support and great wealth to produce art (Egypt, Rome, Cambodia). Many of the pieces in this chapter suggest that while that is often true, it is not always true. Designed objects can be tools of repression, but they can also be agents of resistance. Making, purchasing, and collecting objects can also be a means of empowerment.

Sources

Baraitser, Michael, and Anton Obholzer. *Cape County Furniture*. Capetown: C. Struik Publishers, 1978.

Belcher, Max, and Bernard Herman. *A Land and Life Remembered: Americo-Liberian Folk Architecture*. Athens: University of Georgia Press, 1988.

Blier, Suzanne. *Butabu: Adobe Architecture of West Africa*. New York: Princeton Architectural Press, 2004.

Coquet, Michèle. *African Royal Court Art*. Chicago: University of Chicago Press, 1998.

Diamond, Jared. *Guns, Germs, and Steel*. New York: Norton, 1997.

Garlake, Peter. *Early Art and Architecture of Africa*. Oxford: Oxford University Press, 2002.

Ginzberg, Marc. *African Forms*. New York: Abbeville, 2000.

Mazrui, Ali. *The Africans: A Triple Heritage*. Boston: Little Brown, 1986.

Meyer, Laure. *Art and Craft in Africa: Everyday Life Ritual Court Art*. Paris: Terrail, 1995.

Nelson, Steven. *From Cameroon to Paris: Mousgoum Architecture in and out of Africa*. Chicago: University of Chicago Press, 2007.

Phillips, Tom. *Africa: The Art of a Continent*. New York: Guggenheim Museum, 1996.

Ravenhill, Philip. *The Art of the Personal Object*. Seattle: Washington University Press, 1991.

Sarpong, Peter. *Sacred Stools of the Akan*. Accra: Ghana Publishing, 1971.

Sieber, Roy. *African Furniture and Household Objects*. Bloomington: Indiana University Press, 1980.

van Wyk, Gary N. *African Painted Houses: Basotho Dwellings of Southern Africa*. New York: Abrams, 1998.

DISCUSSION AND STUDY QUESTIONS

1. How are African furniture pieces different from Western and Asian pieces?

2. Has looking at African pieces prompted you to consider pieces from your own ethnic group in a different manner? Think of examples where the formula seat = person applies.

3. What do you know about Africa?

4. When you hear about Africa in the news, how do you characterize it?

5. What are your ways of defining if something is authentic?

6. As a general group, in what ways do pieces of African furniture differ from Western or Asian pieces? Are there any general characteristics that many pieces share?

7. What designs from other chapters can also be considered African?

8. How did the artists and designers involved in African artistic production respond to technological change?

CHAPTER 18

JAPAN AND JAPANISME

1603–1867	1853	1868–1912
Edo	Matthew Perry's negotiations with Japan	Meiji period

Approaching the topic of Japan and its art, Mimi Hall Yiengpruksawan (2001) cautions against conjuring a romantic notion of a Japanese spirit and to see it expressed in artworks and objects (pp. 105–122). Such interpretations, she fears, too often include generalizations and vague ruminations about Zen Buddhism. In a similar vein, John Dower (1998) warns against considering Japan as having a "unique, unchanging cultural essence" (pp. 2–3). His admonition could pertain to any non-Western culture viewed by the West, yet particularly with Japan, there is a widespread and persistent temptation to attribute to its designed forms some intangible quality that renders it fundamentally different from Western art.

Yiengpruksawan and Dower make an important point: There is not a unitary essence to Japanese design. Looking at the totality of Japanese arts across centuries, the variables are many. Although this chapter on Japan starts with the Imperial Villa at Katsura—and it is a great example of Japanese historic architecture—that iconic structure does not define the nature of Japanese architecture and design, as it is often purported to do.

Japonisme usually refers to the cult of Japan and Japanese art in the second half of the nineteenth century. This chapter considers the wider context of Japanese items that traversed the globe in many centuries, and their role as inspiration and model for Western art forms and objects.

ARCHITECTURE

The building types of historic Japanese architecture include **Shinto** shrines and Buddhist temples, castles, palaces, and other governmental buildings, vernacular domestic architecture, and the homes of nobles. An idea of the variety of Japanese architecture, in terms of size, material, and decorative effect, is presented by three different structures. The Castle of Edo is a huge structure built on massive stone foundations, with stone walls and wide moats. North of Edo is the Toshogu Shrine, known for its sumptuous decoration. And the Great Buddha Hall of Todaiji, in Nara, is one of the central buildings of Japanese Buddhism and was the largest timber-frame building in the world.

Figure 18.1 Katsura Imperial Villa, 1620. South side exterior elevation. Kyoto, Japan.

The Imperial Villa at Katsura

A monumental structure, such as the Imperial Palace at Kyoto, 804 c.e., focuses on a great hall that is part of a grand symmetrical complex. A contrasting design approach is represented by a structure that lies on the edge of Kyoto, in Katsura. The Detached Villa, begun in 1620, with its informal tea houses, presents another side of historic Japanese architecture, one that is asymmetrical, informal, and introspective. It has a rustic and reflective quality to its design that larger structures lack. Constructed over a period of approximately fifty years, it was largely completed by 1663.

Sited on the Katsura River, the villa is a country pleasure house with tea pavilions, all connected by a meandering path made of stepping-stones (Figure 18.1). Views are carefully controlled, as is the general construction of the plantings and site work that constitute its gardens. The studied manipulation of sight lines, and nature itself, is not immediately apparent. One interpretation of its gardens and their various features is that they relate to passages from the *Tale of Genjii*, the classic eleventh-century work of Japanese literature. Melissa McCormick discusses the "culture of Genji" in her 2003 article. She writes: "The Tale of Genji for the first time in history, came to embody a kind of timeless aristocratic social body in the capital." In its overall plan and in its details, Katsura is an unassuming study in serenity. The buildings relied upon construction techniques that have stood the test of time. In many respects, some of its pavilions are elaborations of a vestigial hut. Posts sit directly on stone foundations, and the wood is mostly unpolished and unfinished, some with tree bark.

Its design is attributed to Kobori Enshu (1579–1647), a tea master and garden designer, although this is under dispute. The building part of the principal complex is made of three sections, or *shoins*. The original structure is now known as the Old Shoin.

Old Shoin

Modernist architects and designers cherish Katsura, sometimes to the detriment of understanding its historical context and its formal complexity. The Japanese architect Arata Isozaki, writing in 1983, notes: "The many layers of design realized in the Katsura palace have made it an almost constant object of study, especially for the members of the modernist movement in Japan. In their attempts to read the design of the Katsura palace along functionalist lines, they base their analysis on its growth in terms of specific responses to material needs. In so doing, they have developed a unified position which transforms the real Katsura, lifting it out of its actual existence into the realm of myth" (Isozaki 1983, p. 2). Bruno Taut, Walter Gropius, Kenzo Tange, and countless others visited Katsura and wrote about it in rapturous terms.

The modernists saw in Katsura support for their own design concepts. The publications by Taut, Gropius, and later Tange, although spanning a time period of thirty years, are at similar pains to make the building look cubist. The books feature high-contrast black-and-white photographs that frequently cut off the pitched roofs, a traditional element at odds with a modernist vision of Katsura. In the Old Shoin, their preferred part of the complex, they saw the **shoji** paper screens as harbingers of one of the most important modernist attributes: transparency.

Kenzo Tange is one of the most successful Japanese architects of the post–World War II period. He opines: "The Katsura Palace reveals a simple, straightforward spirit of freedom, never blatantly insistent, but nonetheless tenacious and compelling. There is a marvelous balance between stillness and movement, between the aristocratic and the common, between perfection of form and sheer invention" (Tange 1960, p. 32). Although he wrote in the 1960s, the qualities he emphasizes—simplicity, perfection of form, and the spirit of freedom—are the very qualities that the Bauhaus apologists, such as Gropius and van der Rohe, emphasized when discussing the German work of the 1920s and 1930s.

At Katsura, simplicity relates to form and materials. Most of the materials are left plain and undressed, and this includes bamboo, rough-cut stones, and loose gravel.

It could be said that each artistic movement has its own Katsura, that designers of any epoch will find what they are looking for: Modernists will see the geometric simplicity, transparency, and honest use of materials; postmodernists will see the historic references, the complexity, and the delightful incongruity of certain details. Looking at the same architectural complex, Isozaki (some twenty years after Tange) sees ambivalence. In describing the structure, he writes that "there is no single governing style or design principle to be found in the Katsura. Both the buildings and the garden contain a mixture of styles and construction techniques. This is the source of the ambiguity of the Katsura" (Isozaki 1983, p. 12). Isozaki is also a product of his time. He is often classified as a postmodernist, a movement known for eclecticism, among other attributes. Appropriately enough for his generation, he does not see Katsura as a harbinger of modernism but a multilayered, multifaceted work of architecture.

New Goten

The New Goten Pavilion, the third shoin of Katsura's main structure, features a tea- and food-preparation area that is on a dais (Figure 18.2). The dais is raised and proportioned to have three mats, trimmed with edging. Where the dais steps up, the gridded ceiling steps down. Built-in cabinets and shelves are a part of this complex portion of the structure. The type of staggered or displaced shelves at Katsura is known simply as the Katsura shelf; similar shelves are found elsewhere in the complex. Yokobori Yoichi writes that "the term **tansu** is primarily applicable to cabinetry created during the post-fire Edo period (1657–1868), which became a

time of frenetic rebuilding and innovation" (Yoichi in Moss, 2007). Yoichi is referring to the great fire in Edo (later Tokyo) that nearly leveled the city in 1657; a positive outcome of the conflagration was that it prompted a new wave of building.

An opaque, comb-shaped window illuminates the space. Below the window, a built-in desk corresponds in its dimensions to two mats. Panels underneath the window can be removed to increase ventilation. There are both sliding doors and hinged doors in the complex.

Shōkintei Pavilion

The Shōkintei Pavilion is separate from the Shoin complex and lies across the pond, ideally reached by rowing in a small boat. The pavilion comprises several rooms, and each section, in turn, is composed of a variety of modular elements, the floors based on

Figure 18.2 Katsura Imperial Villa, 1620. Dais in first room. Kyoto, Japan.

Figure 18.3 Katsura Imperial Villa, 1620. Interior. Kyoto, Japan.

the dimensions of the **tatami** mat, a straw mat of approximately 3 by 6 feet (Figure 18.3). Tatami matting introduced a system of modularity into Japanese architecture. Standard dimensions and modular units are features of furniture, mats, and building components. This systemization of design into modular units occurred earlier in Japan than elsewhere. Kazuko Koizumi is a pioneer in the field of the study of traditional Japanese furniture. On the subject of walls in historic Japanese architecture, he wrote: "partitions had nothing of the solidity of Western or Chinese walls" (1986, p. 11). At Katsura, many of the walls are formed by sliding screens, shoji panels of wood and paper. Some panels are fixed, others are movable. Sliding screens separate the rooms, and several partitions of the Shōkintei Pavilion are decorated with a white-and-indigo checkerboard. One room has displaced shelves,

with cabinets above. Windows let in carefully filtered light low to the ground plane.

FOREIGNERS

The first known European in Japan was Francis Xavier (1506–1552), who arrived in 1549. A Spanish monk, he traveled to Japan after a stop in Goa, India, with the goal of finding converts in both places.

The Japanese in Mexico

Rokuemon Hasekura (1571–1622) was the first Japanese ambassador to New Spain (Mexico). No long-lasting political initiatives are attributed to his tenure, but his presence in North America did start a new trend in furniture design. He initiated a fashion

Figure 18.4 Biombo screen with scenes from Horace. Mexico. 1740–1760.

among the elite, Spanish, Mexicans, and foreigners of importing folding Japanese screens. This had the predictable effect that innovative local furniture workshops started producing their own "Japanese" screens. A screen was called a **biombo**; in Japanese, *byo* means protection and *bu* means wind. A screen in the collection of the Dallas Museum of Art, made by a Mexican furniture maker, incorporates scenes made by a Flemish artist based on the Roman writer Horace (Figure 18.4). Made between 1740 and 1760, it was owned by the viceroy, the Spanish king's representative.

Art historian Michael Schreffler discusses three different biombos, baroque Mexican folding screens inspired by Japanese imports (Schreffler 2007). One screen displays a view of the vice-regal palace on the Main Plaza of Mexico City. The palace is shown on a screen, its façade folding like the screen on which it is represented. Another Mexican biombo is a panoramic view of the city. Collectively, the images underscore the Spanish presence in New Spain. They are a sign of imperial power and announce the new country's allegiance to the Spanish Hapsburgs. Furniture traveled from one place to another and acquired new meanings in the process, a part of the global transmission of forms, images, and the ideas associated with them. They impacted what Mexican carpenters made, as folding screens became a part of their vocabulary of products.

The Dutch in Japan

The situation changed after Francis Xavier and Rokuemon Hasekura. The Tokugawa Shogunate, also known as the Edo period (1603–1867), is known for its central authority, stability, and sustained economic growth. Culturally, it is known for its fear of foreigners and considerable efforts to restrict their movement in Japan. Simply put, Japan shut itself off from the outside world. The Tokugawa Shogunate expelled the Christian missionaries that they did not execute, and traders' movements were circumscribed. The Shogunate tightly controlled commerce, trading only with the Chinese and the Dutch, whom they further controlled by limiting their access to the southern port of Nagasaki. Trade with Koreans was also carefully controlled.

The Dutch were the only Europeans allowed to trade with Japan, and they were confined to a foreigner's compound. A print from 1800 shows the living conditions of seventeenth-century Dutch traders in Japan. A view of the upper floor of their quarters in Nagasaki is one of a series, from a scroll painted by a Japanese artist and meant for a shogunal official (Figure 18.5). The subject matter is the Dutch amusing themselves in a variety of ways; this was meant to amuse Japanese viewers by highlighting the activities of foreigners and their strange ways. The artist employed a compositional strategy, seen in several Japanese media, in which there is a rigid framework, here provided by the house, the bays of its openings, and the tatami mats, visible in the interior. Arrayed across the framework, a variety of human figures mill about in an informal way.

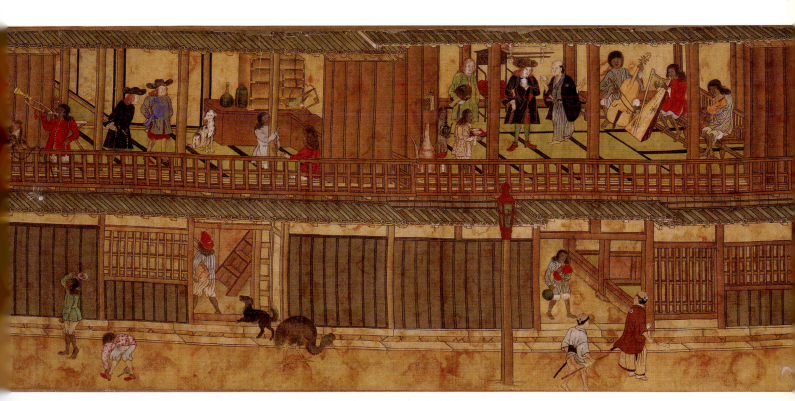

Figure 18.5 Unknown. Dutch in Nagasaki, with Javanese servants, 1800. Wood-block print, nineteenth century.

Javanese servants are playing a violin, a cello, and a harp; two little people serve tea; and the Dutch stand with their calves visible, wearing shoes even though they are inside. The courtly Japanese man who converses with one of them does not. Behind and between the two Dutch men is another foreign interloper, a tall imposing Chinese hat chair. No one deigns to sit in it. This print is a representation of otherness from a nineteenth-century Japanese perspective.

URBAN AND URBANE LIVING— FURNISHINGS IN PRINTS

Edo (modern-day Tokyo) was founded in the seventeenth century. Osaka was a center of commerce and Kyoto was the imperial capital. By 1750, Edo had a population of more than a million. To escape from the pressures of living in a crowded city, people engaged in pleasurable activities that included walks in the countryside and promenades along the river. Houses of prostitution and kabuki theaters also served as sources of entertainment. Many prints took as their subject matter professional dancers, actors, and geishas. The figures wear flowing kimonos and have ovoid faces—they are all curves.

A related genre are the **ukiyo-e** paintings that similarly took as their subject matter secular pleasures. Many were paintings on silk or paper fixed to screens. Oil paintings with these subjects were rare; prints of these subjects were common.

An 1825 print also relies on the compositional strategy of the framework provided by a house, which is set against a casual grouping of human figures involved in various activities (Figure 18.6). A popular print meant for sale, it is also informative about domestic architecture and its furnishings, or lack thereof. The timber house is delineated with a series of vertical lines that represent columns and balustrades. The human figures include three

Figure 18.6 Utagawa Toyokuni. Ladies in Waiting with Boy Prostitutes in Female Attire, 1825. Color wood-block print.

Figure 18.7 Shelves. Cabinet. Wood with gold and black lacquer. Japan.

ladies-in-waiting, who are visiting a brothel for boy prostitutes, also in ladies' attire, who are entertaining them. One woman picks her teeth, one of the boys plays an instrument, two servants kneel, and a woman carries a sake pot. Several of the figures kneel on cushions; there is not a lick of formal furniture in sight, showing that it was possible to be engaged in a variety of casual activities, in a nicely furnished dwelling, without any furniture.

FURNITURE

As in all of Asia, the imprint of China was felt in monumental architecture and furnishings. Although Chinese furniture was imported into Japan during the Chinese Sui and Tang periods, prior to the twentieth century, the use of chairs never really took hold. Before chairs, the most important furniture types were platforms, mats, beds, and storage chests with no legs. There were some low chairs.

Traditionally, Japanese lived at the floor level and chairs were not a part of most Japanese households. Additionally, many of the living and social functions that require pieces of furniture in other cultures were taken care of by built-in cabinetry in Japan. And finally, the Japanese household was relatively austere in its overall size, the quantity of objects it contained, and their complexity. Certain pieces, which in the Japanese context are considered furniture, would not be considered furniture in the West, such as trays, pots, and kettles. Often, the line between architecture and furniture is blurred. There were also lanterns, floor mats, and curtains.

To the extent that Japanese furniture existed, it was part of an overall system in which there was a continuity from building to interiors to furnishings. A feature of Japanese carpentry is finely crafted joints.

Among the earliest Japanese pieces were bookshelves, either built-in or freestanding (Figure 18.7).

The standard layout of a shelving unit was to have a staggered midlevel shelf, either in the food-preparation area as at Katsura, or on a freestanding piece designed for display. The staggered shelf emphasized the piece's asymmetry. Shelving units sat close to the ground.

Many Japanese furniture pieces are asymmetrical, in contrast to Chinese design. A desirable feature of asymmetry is that it provides a sense of dynamism, especially when contrasted with the fixity of a symmetrical design. Koizumi (1986) writes: "A sensitivity to just such subtleties lies at the heart of the Japanese genius for design" (Koizumi 1986, p. 12). The staggered midlevel shelf became a signifying feature of Japanese furniture, both by Japanese artisans and by those who emulated them. The staggered shelf became a regular feature of European Arts and Crafts and Art Nouveau furniture.

Figure 18.9 Clothes chest.

Figure 18.8 Table, 1670–1690. Wood, lacquer, mother-of-pearl.

When homes did have furniture, such as tables, they were low to the ground and often used without chairs. One nineteenth-century print shows a courtesan working at a table. She's painting and has her supplies spread out in front of her on a low table at which she kneels. While most tables were used for practical purposes—eating or painting, for example—a limited number were used exclusively for display. A five-legged table meant to hold a vase is similar to Chinese pieces (Figure 18.8). Because most pieces of furniture were experienced by a person seated at floor level and not far away, the fronts of the pieces were prominent; often there was little attention to the sides and back. Other features are linearity and blocklike forms, similar to the residential architecture. Koizumi writes that there was "little stirring after complicated effects" (Koizumi 1986, p. 12).

Boxes and Chests

One of the largest categories of early Japanese furniture was space-containing items, such as chests. In the seventeenth century, the repositioning of wealth from a samurai-based economy to a merchant-based economy also added to the growing usefulness and demand for a variety of chests. Oceangoing trade required chests for general storage, and also the storage of personal items such as clothes.

This category is directly related in its details and construction to built-in cabinetry. In fact, the word for chests, *tansu,* also refers to Japanese wooden cabinetry. The range of chest types is extensive, with both functional and regional variations (Figure 18.9). Chests and boxes were often stacked one on top of the other. Some pieces had metal fittings and hardware.

Figure 18.10 Stairway chest.

Chests were made to hold kitchen utensils, spices, sewing equipment, tea services, and money (Koizumi 1986, pp. 75–80). Captains, barbers, and eyeglass salesmen all had personalized commercial chests, often with small drawers. A box for storing writing instruments in effect functioned like a briefcase. A cash box was effectively a cash register.

A prime example of the close relationship between carpentry and furniture making is the existence of the Japanese stairway chest (Figure 18.10). With a combination of drawers, sliding doors, and hinged doors, these pieces economically served multiple functions.

Screens

Lacquer screens were a means of defining space and providing temporary privacy without resorting to weighty permanent partitions. Europeans were fond of collecting these items, whose surface treatments they admired, and transporting them back to their home countries (Figure 18.11). At first glance, it appears that a screen's six vertically oriented panels bear no relationship to the scene painted on them (Koizumi 1986, pp. 91–94). Close inspection reveals that each panel was carefully considered.

There are several cases of Europeans who bought lacquered screens and had them reconstituted into pieces of European furniture. Japanese lacquer techniques impressed European buyers. Europeans also bought the highly complex, carefully crafted chests, and sometimes the chests too were incorporated into the design of new ensemble pieces. A Japanese lacquer chest with a Dutch stand underscores the extent of the Dutch-Japanese cultural interactions (Figure 18.12). It also makes clear the difference between a mat-level mode of living in Japan and the chair-level mode

Figure 18.11 Unknown. Screen, 1670–1700. Wood, black, gold, silver, and red lacquer.

in the Netherlands. Europeans affected furniture production with their tastes. Because they sought exotic oddities, they bought the most elaborate pieces and eschewed simple pieces—which Japanese furniture makers made in great quantity. Furniture makers responded to market forces and increasingly crafted highly decorated pieces specifically to be sold to Europeans.

Chairs

When chairs started to make inroads into Japanese households, they were often modeled on Chinese chairs, such as a Japanese chair that is a fairly faithful reproduction of a Chinese folding chair (Figure 18.13). Koizumi writes that bentwood folding chairs were first introduced into Japan by the Chinese, and later by Western traders operating out of Macao (Koizumi 1986, p. 170). The full integration of the chair into the Japanese way of living did not come until the twentieth century.

Figure 18.12 Japanese lacquer chest, 1630. Dutch stand, 1700.

Figure 18.13 Bentwood chair.

THE OPENING OF OLD JAPAN

The ban on foreigners continued up to the mid-nineteenth century. The year the Utagawa woodblock was printed, 1825, was also the year that an edict was issued that stipulated that foreigners who landed in Japan illegally were to be arrested or killed and their ships destroyed. The purpose was not only to keep out foreigners but to keep the Japanese from having knowledge of the outside. Japanese ships were designed to be unstable on long oceangoing trips and hence preclude international contact. Despite attempts to limit foreign contact with Japan, and Japanese contact with foreigners,

some adventuresome Japanese gained firsthand knowledge of the West, specifically the United States, by traveling with the *Kuroshio* current. *Kuroshio,* in Japanese, literally means "black tide"; it is analogous to the North Atlantic gulf stream and flows northeastward from Japan to North America. Some Japanese sailors drifted to the East (the United States). Japanese sailors who traveled to foreign countries were barred from reentry to Japan. Yet sailors are typically a rebellious lot, and some discovered ways to sneak back by way of Russian and Chinese ships.

Manjiro

The evocative story of a shipwrecked Japanese sailor has no direct relationship to design, although it is a story of cultural transmission that captivated both sides of the Pacific. Manjiro (1827–1898) was from Shikoku, and when he was fourteen, he was on a twenty-four-foot boat that got caught in a strong current and a storm; the boat capsized and he was stranded on Bird Island, Torishima, where he endured six months of deprivation. An American captain, William Whitfield, rescued him and took him to Hawaii. After they sailed around South America, Manjiro arrived in Massachusetts. In the United States, he was known alternately as John Mung or John Manjiro. On board a whaling vessel, he worked as a cook and navigator. He displayed a facility with learning English and navigation. Author Christopher Benfey (2003) writes about Manjiro and other examples of Japanese-American cultural migration in his highly readable book *The Great Wave*.

In 1851, Manjiro returned to Japan, and Benfey reports that he carried with him a camera and a sewing machine, bought in the United States, to give to his mother. This simple act of gift giving illustrates the technological divide between Japan and the United States. Back in Japan, Manjiro started his career working as a naval instructor and interpreter. He acted as a conduit for Japanese eager to hear about the United States, and for Americans curious to observe him firsthand. From 1854 onward, he worked as an interpreter and negotiator. He was part of the team who negotiated with Matthew Perry. In 1860, the Treaty of Amity between the United States and Japan was largely concerned with trade (Benfey 2003, p. 39).

Commodore Perry

The seminal date of Japan's contact with the West occurred when the American Commodore Matthew Perry sailed to Japan in 1853. His voyage and the ensuing treaty marks the end of Japan's isolation, its opening to the world, and the beginning of the modern era. Benfey (2003) writes: "The irony

was that just as Bostonians were falling in love with Old Japan, Japan was reinventing herself as a modern state, evolving in the space of 25 years from a feudal backwater to an international power. This is the period known as the Meiji Era (1868–1912), which corresponds almost year for year to America's Gilded Age. The parallel rise of the two young nations, the United States and the 'New' Japan, initiated some of the major power struggles—both military and economic—of the twentieth century" (pp. xii–xiv).

Commodore Perry's arrival in 1853 signaled that Japan had decided to join the world community and embrace the technological advancements of the nineteenth century. There was no turning back. Japan entered the Industrial Age and adopted a constitutional government.

The year 1868 is when the Emperor Meiji was restored to the throne. The opening that began with Commodore Perry's delegation was complete, and from that time forward, there was a ratcheting up of the efforts to modernize Japan. The restoration of imperial rule signified the emergence of a modern state. Yiengpruksawan writes: "Since the political and cultural base of Japan in the middle of the nineteenth century derived from a worldview—a cognitive order—that was not European at a time when Europe and the United States in effect controlled the world, it is not surprising that the policy among modernizers initially was to borrow from Europe what Japan was seen to lack" (Yiengpruksawan 2001, p. 11). One way to achieve this was modernization through emulation. The buying practices of foreigners influenced Japanese design.

International Exhibitions and Museums

The nineteenth century is known as the great age of international exhibitions and museums, intertwined endeavors related to the official promotion of the decorative arts. The seminal moment was the 1851 Great Exhibition in the Crystal Palace, London. The central structure of the exhibition was Joseph Paxton's glass-and-steel building. The temporary building resulted in the permanent South Kensington Museum. Among all the exhibits, national displays of the decorative arts were particularly popular. The South Kensington Museum was renamed the Victoria and Albert Museum in 1899, and many of the images in this book come from its collections.

Countries around the world saw that participating in international exhibitions was a way to promote their products and arts, and to instill a sense of national pride for both visiting and home audiences. The exhibitions often resulted in museums; the development of exhibitions and permanent museums often went hand in hand.

Japan began to export wares in 1859, and part of the reason for Japan's interest in international exhibitions was to maintain a competitive advantage against her trading partners—and sometime enemies—China and Russia. Japanese products were shown in the following international venues: Exhibition of Industrial Art, Dublin, 1853; International Exhibition, London, 1862; the Vienna World Exhibition of 1873; the Centennial Exhibition, Philadelphia, 1876; the World's Columbian Exposition, Chicago, 1893; the Paris World Exposition of 1900; and the Louisiana Purchase Exhibition, St. Louis, 1904.

The Japanese government also sponsored exhibitions in Japan with the home audience in mind: the First Industrial Exhibition, Tokyo, 1877; the Second National Industrial Exhibition, Tokyo, 1881; the Third National Industrial Exhibition, Tokyo, 1890; the Fourth National Industrial Exhibition, Kyoto, 1895; and the Fifth National Industrial Exhibition, Osaka, 1903.

The list of prominent museums built in the nineteenth century include: the Oxford University Museum, Oxford; the Natural History Museum, London; the Metropolitan Museum of Art, New York, 1874–1880; the Museum of Fine Arts, Boston, 1909; and the Smithsonian, Washington, D.C., 1855.

Japanese participation in several prominent exhibitions, or world's fairs, was part of a program to promote Japanese decorative arts, ceramics, furniture, smaller lacquer ware, and also prints, especially woodblocks. Not surprisingly, American and European audiences who saw these objects considered them as representative of Japanese art.

Japonisme

French critic Philippe Burty (1830–1890) coined the phrase "Japonisme" in 1872.

Japonisme refers to European art influenced by Japan. It was part of a general interest in "exotic" cultures, and in that respect it is related to Chinoiserie. The cult of Japan and Japanese art was most prominent in Britain, although it became a cultural force worldwide.

Tackling Japanisme as the subject of her book, Ayako Ono (2003) writes: "Japonisme is considered

Figure 18.14 Charles F. A. Voysey. Wallpaper for Essex, 1887-1930.

Figure 18.15 Unknown. Japanese futon cover, 1880–1910.

a phenomenon whose influence spread widely throughout western pictorial art, sculpture, craft, fashion, design, architecture, photographs, theatre and music in the second half of the nineteenth century. It is quite hard to make a clear definition of Japonisme because of the breadth of the phenomenon, but it could be generally agreed upon that is an attempt to understand and adapt the essential qualities of Japanese art" (p. 1). Benfey enlarges the list to include more popular subjects, such as judo, geishas, and samurai.

Many American and European designers and artists collected artworks and were influenced by them. Louis Comfort Tiffany collected Japanese ceramics. Aubrey Beardsley (1872–1898) created pen-and-ink drawings that display a thorough knowledge of Japanese woodcuts. Neither C.F.A. Voysey's writings nor those of others about him emphasize Japan's influence on his work, although the visual evidence for this is considerable. Many of his

colleagues associated with the the Arts and Crafts or Art Nouveau movements were known collectors of Japanese art (Figures 18.14 and 18. 15).

Anglo-Japanese Furniture

Sometime between 1890 and 1900, the Bombay Art Furniture Establishment, so noted on an attached brass plaque, made a magazine rack in the Anglo-Japanese style (Figure 18.16). It is fashioned of rosewood and ebony with an inset lacquer panel that features birds and foliage. Spandrels act as brackets, supporting the superstructure, and are formed of three cubes. The Anglo-Japanese style is an offshoot of the English Arts and Crafts movement. English reformers, including William Morris, felt that the general state of design needed to be rehabilitated, although there was little consensus on how this goal was to be achieved. A significant although modest number of Arts and Crafts designers had an expressed interest in Japanese design and created works known as Anglo-Japanese. English Arts and Crafts artists appreciated Japanese design because of its accomplished construction methods, reliance on simple geometries, and restrained decoration. Japanese artists also incorporated motifs based on local flora into their designs, a design practice in step with the Arts and Crafts belief that art should relate to its locale context, be it England, New Zealand, or the United States.

Anglo-Japanese pieces were not accurate representations of actual Japanese furniture pieces. They resemble more closely Chippendale's versions of Chinese pieces. The creation of Anglo-Japanese pieces in India was in response to the British in India who, knowledgeable about changing patterns of taste, were less enamored of Victorian design, and especially Bombay blackwood design. To trace the trajectory of stylistic influences: Indian Anglo-Japanese design is Japanese-inspired design, in India, by way of the British Arts and Crafts move-

Figure 18.16 Magazine rack, The Bombay Art Furniture Company.

ment (Jaffer 2001, p. 359). About the variety of Asian furniture styles, Peter Moss (2007) writes: "Furniture has led almost as peripatetic an existence as any other aspect of social dispersion. It has traveled far and wide, influenced whole cultures, cross-pollinated others and evolved unique geographic styles as a result of its exposure to outside influence" (Moss 2007, p. 6).

Artists and Designers

Among those who can be considered in the Japonisme fold are the Americans Mary Cassatt (1845–1926) and James McNeil Whistler (1834–1903); and the French Edgar Degas (1834–1917), Edouard Manet (1832–1883), Claude Monet (1840–1926), Henri de Toulouse-Lautrec (1864–1901), and Vincent van Gogh (1853–1890). In England, the major figures included Christopher Dresser (1834–1904) and Edward Godwin (1833–1886). Dresser, who actually traveled to Japan, wrote several books, including *Japan, Its Architecture, Art and Art-Manufactures* (1882).

Conder (discussed below) was a good friend of Godwin, who collected Japanese prints. It seems odd that so many figures associated with English Arts and Crafts made references to Japanese motifs in their work. One of the creeds of the Arts and Crafts movement was against the vapid use of historical forms (with the prime example being Nash's Royal Pavilion at Brighton). Arts and Crafts aficionados were interested in restoring medieval woodworking techniques, so they were appreciative of Japanese woodworking techniques and judicious use of decoration.

The Japanese exhibit at the World's Columbian Exposition of 1893 in Chicago was a popular destination. The foreign interest in Japanese art affected the kind of art that was produced, and what was exhibited, both in Japan and abroad. The types of artworks that foreign connoisseurs were interested in also shaped the general knowledge about Japanese arts. Foreigners collected and preferred prints. This fixation gave Japanese prints a prominence abroad that they did not enjoy at home. American designer Louis Comfort Tiffany, like many others, additionally preferred historical Japanese works to contemporary ones—a preference that irked many contemporary (nineteenth-century) Japanese artists. One result of this is that Japanese paintings, especially contemporary paintings, did not sell well abroad although they were popular in exhibitions in Japan. For over a century, Japanese artists and craftsmen have grappled with a foreign preference for historic or traditional Japanese art forms and a dismissal of contemporary works.

Josiah Conder and Modern Japanese Architecture

Alice Tseng wrote an accomplished article on Josiah Conder and the Museum at Ueno, and most of the information presented here is drawn from her article. Ueno was Japan's first public park. An international exhibition took place in the park, and it ultimately resulted in a museum. Exhibitions whose subject was Japan, abroad and at home, showed lacquers, bronzes, porcelain, Western-style oil paintings, and traditional Japanese prints and ink paintings. Japan had a tradition of timber architecture. Once the building program of the Japanese government included major projects, like railway stations and world-class museums, it was unclear how to design large-scale Japanese buildings in brick, concrete, stone, metal, and glass, the materials of the new (nineteenth-century) age. To help in this endeavor, the Japanese government hired the young English architect Josiah Conder, who arrived in Japan in 1877. Conder's entire career was connected to Japan, and he is widely referred to as the father of modern Japanese architecture.

Conder's building was designed for the Second National Industrial Exhibition in Tokyo in 1881. It reopened in 1882 as a museum. He collaborated with students who had studied with him, and it was built by Japanese workmen. Tseng (2004) writes: "The building was in many ways the embodiment of the complex power relations between a non-Western nation that struggled to maintain its independence and a host of Western nations encroaching on this right. A product of the alliance between a foreign expert and his Japanese host, the museum in Ueno engaged the idea of nation-building and its architectural expression from both sides" (Tseng 2004, p. 472).

Many aspects of the design are absolutely foreign to the Japanese architecture tradition. Conder was influenced, in part, by the British architecture of the Raj, and some of these Saracenic motifs made their way into his designs. Saracenic motifs originated with Islamic design, yet in the period of historic revivals they were generically associated with Asia. Conder's own museum was destroyed by an earthquake in 1923. Many of Conder's students became architects and constitute the second generation of Japanese modern students.

While the Japanese architects Tōkuma Katayama (1854–1917) and Kingo Tatsuno challenged the primacy of Western architects active in late-nineteenth-century Japan, they continued to design in an international Beaux-Arts style, sometimes with gestures to Japanese design in the decoration. Katayama was a student of Conder's at the College of Technology (Tseng 2004, pp. 490–491). A prolific architect, his career was cemented with prominent commissions for three national museums: the Hyōkeikan Museum in Tokyo, 1901–1908 (Figure 18.17); the Kyoto National Museum in Kyoto, 1892–1895; and the Nara National Museum, in 1892–1894.

Several critics noted that Western-trained Japanese architects had no magical formula for making reference to the history of Japanese architecture when doing large modern buildings. Chuta Ito (1868–1954) was an architect, architectural critic, and architectural historian. He was critical of the West-leaning work of Katayama and Tatsuno, although some of his projects were seen by others as reflecting international Art Nouveau trends.

Prairie Style

Frank Lloyd Wright belongs in the ranks of those enamored of Japanese art. He collected Japanese prints and is responsible for the most famous work of architecture by an American in Japan, the Imperial Hotel, 1913–1923. The imprint of Japanese design is evident in many of those whose works are known as Prairie Style. This is especially evident in their exterior renderings of buildings. Many of the perspective renderings of Wright's houses were ac-

Figure 18.17 Tōkuma Katayama. Hyōkeikan Museum, Tokyo, Japan. 1901–1908.

tually done by Marion Mahoney Griffin (1871–1961). Marion Mahoney was the first licensed female architect in Illinois. Her distinctive style of rendering derived from her familiarity with Japanese woodblock prints. In 1895, she started working for Wright. In her lush renderings, Mahoney surrounded Wright's buildings with flowing vegetation, using a compositional technique that resembled the use of nature in the Japanese prints (Kruty 2007). Her technique asserted that Wright's designs, although in the Midwestern prairie, were inextricably connected to nature. Many of the drawings published in the *Wasmuth Portfolio,* the 1910 German publication that helped establish Wright's international reputation, were done by Mahoney.

She married Walter Burley Griffin (1876–1937) and her career was to remain connected to Asia, although not specifically Japan. The effectiveness of her renderings was proven again when her husband won the prestigious international competition to design a new Australian city, Canberra. It is widely thought that the jury's decision was largely based on the appeal of her renderings. The Griffins moved to Australia and later to Lucknow, India, where they did several projects.

CONCLUSION

Akira Kurosawa, the foremost Japanese filmmaker, released a film in 1951, *Rashômon,* a crime drama set in twelfth-century Japan. In the film, a samurai is killed and his wife raped. Four witnesses then proceed to give their account of the crime, and each version is different and contradicts the others. This masterful film, a high point of Japanese cinema, also made a wider contribution to twentieth-century intellectual thought. It contributed to a philosophical debate about the nature of truth and the meaning of history. The film suggests that historical reality is not something that can be accessed, but only approached obliquely through tellings and retellings. The film questions objectivity and focuses on the constructed nature of narrative, including historical narratives.

Kurosawa's film relates to this historical project and, in fact, any history, because it suggests that twenty-first-century inhabitants can experience history only through certain venues. It is a fruitful endeavor to understand the past by looking at designed objects, but they are only a part of the story. Different viewers of Katsura see different things in it. Most of the antique Japanese pieces available today are from the more recent past, even when they repeat and reiterate forms that had existed for centuries.

While modernity is too often posited as a Western construct exported from the West, this chapter demonstrates that Japan constructed its own modernity. Furthermore, part of what is globally considered as modernity was achieved because of Japanese contributions. For centuries, Japanese designers have been grappling with a classic problem of the modern age: how to deal with national identity in a time of change and in an increasingly global world.

Sources

Benfey, Christopher. *The Great Wave: Gilded Age Misfits, Japanese Eccentrics, and the Opening of Old Japan*. New York: Random House, 2003.

Clarke, Rosy. *Japanese Antique Furniture*. New York: Weatherhill, 1983.

Hashimoto, Fumio. *Architecture in the Shoin Style: Japanese Feudal Residences*. Tokyo: Kodansha, 1981.

Dower, John. "Sizing Up (and Breaking Down) Japan," in Helen Hardacre, ed., *The Postwar Developments of Japanese Studies in the United States*. Leiden: Brill, 1998.

Isozaki, Arata. *Katsura Villa: Space and Form*. New York: Rizzoli, 1983.

Jaffer, Amin. *Furniture from British India and Ceylon*. Salem: Peabody Essex Museum, 2001.

Koizumi, Kazuko. *Traditional Japanese Furniture*. Tokyo: Kodansha, 1986.

Kruty, Paul. *Marion Mahony and Millikin Place*. St. Louis: Walter Burley Griffin Society of America, 2007.

Lerski, Hanna. "Josiah Conder's Bank of Japan, Tokyo." *Journal of the Society of Architectural Historians* 38 (October, 1979): 271–274.

McCormick, Melissa. "Genji Goes West: The 1510 Genji Album and the Visualization of Court and Capital." *Art Bulletin* 85 (March 2003): 54–85.

Moss, Peter. *Asian Furniture: A Directory and Sourcebook*. London: Thames and Hudson, 2007.

Mueller, Laura. *Competition and Collaboration: Japanese Prints of the Utagawa School*. Boston: Brill, 2007.

Mueller, Laura. *Strong Women Beautiful Men: Japanese Portrait Prints from the Toledo Museum of Art*. Toledo: Toledo Museum of Art, 2005.

Ono, Ayako. *Japonisme in Britain*. London: Routledge, 2003.

Schreffler, Michael. *The Art of Allegiance: Visual Culture and Power in Baroque New Spain*. University Park: Pennsylvania State University Press, 2007.

Tange, Kenzo. *Katsura: Tradition and Creation in Japanese Architecture*. New Haven: Yale University Press, 1971.

Tensley, Sarah, and Chiharu Watabe. *20th Century Design History*. Tokyo: Petit Grand Publishing, 2005.

Tseng, Alice. "Styling Japan: The Case of Josiah Conder and the Museum at Ueno, Tokyo." *The Journal of the Society of Architectural Historians* 63, no. 4 (December 2004): 472–497.

Waithall, Anne. *Weak Body of a Useless Woman: Matsuo Taseko*. Chicago: University of Chicago Press, 1998.

Yiengpruksawan, Mimi Hall. "Japanese Art History 2001: The State and Stakes of Research." *Art Bulletin* 83 (March 2001): 105–122.

DISCUSSION AND STUDY QUESTIONS

1. As a group, how do Japanese designs differ from Chinese designs?
2. As a group, how do Japanese designs differ from European designs?
3. What are some of the varieties within the realm of Japanese design?
4. Considering furniture and houses, what are the general characteristics that many ascribe to Japanese designs?
5. What are the two architectural features of traditional Japanese designs that modernists were fond of?
6. What household objects take the role of furniture in Japan, yet would not be considered furniture in other countries?
7. What are the significant Japanese vocabulary words that relate to domestic architecture that are used in the West?

CHAPTER 19

ART NOUVEAU

1890–1910

Art Nouveau (Europe)

1900–1920

Art Nouveau (Latin America)

Art nouveau literally means "new art." A decorative style that flourished in the late nineteenth century, its prominent artworks were in architecture, interiors, graphics, and the decorative arts, including furniture. The single most important principle motivating Art Nouveau artists was the belief that artistic forms should take their inspiration from nature; flowers, vines, birds, and insects all served as source materials. Compositionally, this meant that Art Nouveau works followed a sinuous asymmetrical line. The promotion of Art Nouveau was part of a general reaction against nineteenth-century historicism (Aubry 1996, p. 13). To reinforce the dramatic break with the past, Art Nouveau artists rejected classical design and, in fact, most all historical precedent. The corollary to rejecting the past was that Art Nouveau artists embraced new materials. Using them, they successfully fashioned a new decorative system. Art Nouveau pieces were highly ornamented, yet the elaborate forms quietly nurtured the seeds of modernism.

In the beginning, the philosophical underpinnings of the new art came from three principal figures: William Morris, John Ruskin, and Eugène Viollet-le-Duc. From Morris came the commitment to the unity of the arts. That unity was to be achieved by abolishing the distinction between major and minor arts. Art Nouveau is one of the few periods whose greatest achievements are found in interiors and designed objects. The European architects associated with Art Nouveau were all accomplished furniture designers.

The lack of specific recognizable historic references made it an ideal candidate to become the first international style. Forms whose origins lie in Art Nouveau grace all continents. *Jugendstil* is the German variant, and the word *Modernisme,* in Catalan Spain, refers to Art Nouveau artworks (Permanyer 1999, p. 9).

Samuel Bing opened a gallery in Paris called "L'Art Nouveau" in 1895 (Borsi 1996, p. 36). This auspicious moment is considered the formal beginning of the movement, yet hints of Art Nouveau, in a variety of art forms and especially graphics, came as early as 1884. Henri Toulouse-Lautrec's posters played an important role in the dissemination of Art Nouveau into the French graphic sphere. Following the lead of the Arts and Crafts movement, Art Nouveau artists rejected Victorian design, its throngs of souvenirs, its eclecticism, and its promiscuous combination of historical styles. Those active in many fields—furniture design, jewelry, and advertising—revealed the influence of the new style whose rallying point was nature and its luminescent botanicals. Nature became a cleansing device, sweeping buildings, interiors, paintings, and books of superficial historical references.

ENGLISH BEGINNINGS

Many of the artistic themes held dear by Art Nouveau artists came from the Arts and Crafts polemical writings of Morris and Ruskin. A rallying cry for both Arts and Crafts and Art Nouveau was the need to counteract nineteenth-century historicism. Compositionally, the design strategy of artists in both movements was two-pronged, in which a rigorous structure was offset with fields of ornamental decoration inspired by local flora and fauna. Both movements frequently required a high level of craftsmanship and promoted a unified approach to design, allowing for no distinctions between major and minor arts. In theory, a pendant necklace was as worthy of attention as a painting.

The painter and poet William Blake (1757–1827) inspired artists in both movements. His illustrated book of poetry *Songs of Innocence* combines image and text in a closed graphic whose border recognizes the page's edge. A border creates a field within it, a blank space through which the artist can let meander an asymmetrical composition. Rococo designs did not consistently unite form and text the way Blake did, so his work served as a valuable link between Rococo and Art Nouveau.

The pre-Raphaelite painters, including Dante Gabriel Rossetti, were on good terms with the Arts and Crafts designers and frequently collaborated with them. The languid human figures that popu-

late their paintings anticipate the highly stylized human forms of Art Nouveau. The actual physical frames of the pre-Raphaelites continue the look and details of the paintings within them, underscoring the unity between the art of painting and the craftsmanship of building a wooden frame. Similarly, Art Nouveau two-dimensional works were often put in Art Nouveau frames.

The color palette of the American painter James McNeill Whistler's (1834–1903) Peacock Room of 1876–1877 includes purples, greens, and dark woods. These colors, and the featured animal, the peacock, were favorites of Art Nouveau artists. Charles Voysey (1857–1941) took Arts and Crafts in a modern direction by reducing his buildings to recognizable geometric shapes. His rooms flowed together, and his plans were rationally and simply organized. Yet he juxtaposed the rigor of his architecture with exuberant fields of two-dimensional decoration. His numerous wallpapers and textile designs reveal his training under the watchful eye of Arthur Heygate Mackmurdo (1851–1942). Voysey frequently included lilies, tulips, and egrets in his compositions, revealing his familiarity with Japanese prints. In fact, it was likely due to the ongoing success of English Arts and Crafts members such as Voysey that Art Nouveau, despite its English beginnings, never really took hold in Britain.

There were two principal English Art Nouveau artists: Arthur Heygate Mackmurdo and Aubrey Beardsley. Mackmurdo designed most of his furniture with right angles and relied on standard chair profiles. His famous chair of 1881 is unexceptional except for the appearance of Art Nouveau tracery in the back panel. This chair appears some ten years before the date normally given for the start of Art Nouveau. Two years later, in 1883, Mackmurdo used the same flaming flowers to embellish the title page he created for the book *Wren's City Churches*. The motifs also figure on the binding, combined with the softly curved typeface that became synonymous with Art Nouveau (Borsi 1996, pp. 22–23).

Aubrey Beardsley (1872–1898) is known for his pen-and-ink drawings. Beardsley, along with Whistler and Oscar Wilde, formed a trio of fashionable dandies, elite men who were wittily risqué and connected Art Nouveau to a world of drama, literature, and art. Beardsley's drawings, like Blake's, recognize the page's limit, but they also deny it with billowing asymmetric forms that are rendered dramatic by relying on large areas filled with pure black ink. He continued a tradition started with Morris's black-and-white woodcuts, and from it made something new.

Sharp lines delineate Beardsley's stylized figures. These expressive silhouettes were also well suited for mechanical reproduction. A master of linear Art Nouveau, Beardsley created popular illustrations for Wilde's play *Salomé* that brought the graphic side of Art Nouveau to a large audience.

Art Nouveau differs from the earlier aesthetic movements in two important respects. Arts and Crafts looked to medieval history, while Art Nouveau artists, theoretically, eschewed all traditional forms. Arts and Crafts was a knee-jerk reaction against the Industrial Revolution and the manufacturing processes that Art Nouveau artists embraced.

BELGIUM

Victor Horta (1861–1947), from Belgium, was an architect, designer, and teacher. Most of his buildings are in Brussels, the place where Art Nouveau left the pages of books and started turning into buildings. Particularly during the period 1893–1903, he worked in what came to be known as the Art Nouveau style. His designs revolutionized the design world in Belgium and their impact was felt all around the world. He is widely recognized as the single most important person in the development of Art Nouveau. His interiors are remarkable for their stylistic unity.

The Hôtel van Etvelde is stylistically his most modern project (Figure 19.1). In the stairway hall, structure, railings, walls, ceilings, and hardware all contribute to an integrated design. The goal of a unified interior is achieved.

The purview of Horta's design focus included wall paneling, ceilings, window details, light fixtures, furniture, and hardware (Aubry 1996, p. 56). His designs are the opposite of eclecticism. No assemblage of disparate items, everything in sight adheres to the same clean aesthetic. In plan, his designs are early explorations of the open plan. Horta's interest in the publications of Viollet-le-Duc reveals itself in his use of both cast and wrought iron. His metal forms are sinuous. Many of his projects treat iron as a ductile material, combining it with glass (Borsi 1996, p. 36).

Although he was born in Ghent, most all of Horta's design explorations were played out among several town-house designs in Brussels. His major projects include the private residences the Hôtel Tassel, 1892–1893, and the Hôtel Solvay, 1895–1900 ("Hôtel" in these cases indicates a private home). Horta was interested in the possibilities presented by metal, and he combined metal with wood and glass in his organically inspired compositions. For the balustrade of the Hôtel Solvay, wood and metal swirl together, only to be bolted to the marble stair tread (Figure 19.2). A ceiling fixture by Horta for the same project displays an aspect of Art Nouveau designs that the more florid compositions overshadow: its reliance on a strictly controlled system as a backdrop to the flourishes (Borsi 1996, pp. 61–64). The ceiling is divided into rectangular panels of equal measure and regularly placed. At the juncture between two of them, a light fixture hangs, its lengthy support a bundle of parallel metal tubes of equal diameter (Figure 19.3). At the bottom, the

Figure 19.1 Victor Horta. Hôtel van Etvelde, 1895–1897.

Figure 19.2 Victor Horta. Hôtel Solvay, balustrade detail, 1898–1901.

Figure 19.3 Victor Horta. Hôtel Solvay, ceiling detail and lamp, 1898–1901.

tubes bend and curl like a bouquet of lilies—only, instead of flowers, the stems sprout glass shades and electric lamps.

Horta's house designs served an elite clientele. The Maison du Peuple (1896–1899), in contrast, was the headquarters of the Belgian Socialist Party. Also known as The House of the People, it was an early sign of modern architects' interest in the masses and the ability of design to affect the social good (Borsi 1996, pp. 67–74). The Maison du Peuple also shows how Art Nouveau, with its prescient use of glass and metal, was an early sign of modernism that spread across late nineteenth-century developments. Horta essentially developed a **curtain-wall** structure of metal and glass. The central portion of the curved façade sports a broad expanse of glass held together by a nonstructural metal framing system (Aubry 1996, p. 15). This transparent exterior

wall also indicates a separation of structure from wall, and it was accompanied by the use of interior metal columns, visible in the auditorium's interior (Puttemans 1974, p. 64–65). Even though the skyscraper had its debut in Chicago, Horta's unusual building shows that European designers were working with the same elements—metal, glass, and the separation of structure from wall.

Henry Van de Velde (1863–1957) trained as a painter, and his early paintings are vaguely reminiscent of the French impressionists. Influenced by the written works of William Morris, he explored the relationship between aesthetics and moral qualities by looking at nature and common materials.

The design philosophy he articulated relied on a crucial distinction between **ornamentation** and **ornament**. Ornamentation was attached, a flat composition on flat planes. Ornament was inherent, a logical outcome of a form or material and revealing of its inner structure. A desk by Van de Velde is a sculptural presence in a room; the curves are extensions of the volumes that house various functions—closed and open storage, writing and transaction surfaces (Figure 19.4). The curves also respond anthropomorphically to the seated human figure; the storage and writing areas are within arm's reach of the user. This desk and chair set is a notable work of Art Nouveau design and an advancement in the history of office furniture. It recognizes the need for storage areas. Function aside, the desk is ornament, according to Van de Velde's thinking, because its decorative qualities derive from its forms and materials.

Ornamentation, according to Van de Velde's mind, was applied and flat, an application of the two-dimensional graphic traditions of Blake and Beardsley to the world of materials. Van de Velde did many designs for wall tiles, evidence of his interest in industrial manufacturing processes and producing well-designed, moderately priced materials. The glaze on ceramic wall tiles is not inherent to the ceramic material but is clearly applied.

Van de Velde's work for a tobacco shop in Berlin resulted in a total designed environment (Figure 19.5). A side chair employs the same easy segmented curves, yet stands on its own as a well-designed piece (Figure 19.6).

One of the major figures in developing Belgian Art Nouveau, Van de Velde had a significant second act in his career. He played a role in developing modernism as an educator and administrator. He went to Weimar, Germany, where he reorganized the Kunstgewerbeschule (Arts and Crafts School), thus setting the foundations for its reorganization, and radical refashioning, into the Bauhaus. When most designers considered Art Nouveau artists passé, Walter Gropius continued to admire him (Sembach 1989, pp. 28–30).

Figure 19.4 Henry Van de Velde. Oak and leather desk and chair, 1897.

Figure 19.5 Henry Van de Velde. "Tabaccheria dell'Havana." Tobacco shop, 1899. Berlin.

Figure 19.6 Henry Van de Velde. Chair, 1895–1900.

In Belgium, the new forms constituted a nationalist design anthem that was decidedly anti-French. This aspect of Art Nouveau was lost when the style migrated to other countries. Initiated by Horta and a small cadre of Belgian designers, Art Nouveau forms multiplied and spread across the globe.

FRANCE

Art historian Domenico Quaranta, in an anthology on twentieth-century art (2006), points out that France had consolidated its position as the arts center of Europe, with Paris its focal point. Paris captivated artists from around the globe with its museums and the support it lent artists with an ambitious exhibition schedule (pp. 112–113). In the opening years of the twentieth century, while the legacy of Impressionists remained strong in the capital, a tendency of many French artists was to seek locations where they could work in France's provinces. France was a major center of European Art Nouveau, primarily in two cities: Paris and Nancy.

Nancy

The city of Nancy was the artistic and intellectual center of the province of Lorraine, the state that has passed several times back and forth between French and German control in its long history. It had been a consolation prize for the deposed Polish king Stanislas Leszczynski in the mid–eighteenth century, who made it a center of Rococo art and design. This fostered a climate that appreciated the arts, and in the late twentieth century Nancy became one of two French centers for Art Nouveau. Formally established in 1901, the School of Nancy was an association of artists, artisans, and manufacturers.

Emile Gallé (1846–1904), one of the founders, became Nancy's foremost glassmaker, potter, and furniture designer. For his glass work, he worked with acid-resistant materials, metal foils, colored oxides, and a studied use of air bubbles. In all his designs, Gallé made use of the academic training he undertook in botany and mineralogy in Weimar, Germany. Visiting London's museums and private galleries, he saw firsthand collections of Chinese, Japanese, and Islamic ceramics.

He was fond of incorporating water lilies into his designs, and several pieces gave the impression that a dragon fly had just alighted. He first exhibited at the Exposition Universelle of 1878. In 1884, he exhibited at the Union Centrale des Arts Décoratifs in Paris. He brought his interest in unusual materials and organic forms to his furniture designs, in which he employed complex marquetry using exotic woods and mother-of-pearl inlays. An ovoid firescreen displays the complex geometry, the feeling of balance that is achieved despite a lack of symmetry, and the ever-present vines, cattails, and

Figure 19.7 Emile Gallé. Firescreen.

tendrils (Figure 19.7). The complexity of the overall shape was apparent when creating working drawings for Art Nouveau shapes. To mathematically describe an ovoid profile, and give instructions of how to construct it with compasses, was a complicated mathematical exercise. Thus, the effortless appearance of an Art Nouveau piece belies the difficulty of constructing it.

Gallé's firescreen creates a sense of movement, even though it is a static piece. Things are growing, and the passage of time is represented, long term, with one vine growing around another. Time is also frozen; a picture in marquetry depicts a branch bending in the wind—a transient act of nature is captured for eternity. Françoise Aubry (1996) refers to this temporal quality: "The essence of Art

Nouveau is ultimately encapsulated in the image of a frozen, enchanted, winter garden" (p. 21).

As the head of a successful company that by 1894 had more than 300 employees, Gallé was the artist behind his company's Art Nouveau products and the businessman who oversaw their production and distribution. Gallé's exhibit at the Exposition Universelle of 1900 was a triumphant retrospective of his career. French author Philippe Jullian wrote an entire book (1974) devoted to the Exposition, which he describes as an ephemeral city that "may be considered an important stage in the history of art, for it was the capital of Art Nouveau, a movement of which it marked both the apotheosis and the decline" (p. 17).

Also from Nancy was Louis Majorelle (1859–1926), a French cabinetmaker who was the son of a cabinetmaker. His father specialized in making reproductions of eighteenth-century pieces. Late-eighteenth-century French furniture was a highlight of French decorative arts, and the Majorelle family brought that expertise in craftsmanship to the early twentieth century.

Majorelle studied painting at the École des Beaux Arts, returning to Nancy to work in the family business. Under Gallé's influence, he started producing pieces in the Art Nouveau style, with the period 1898–1908 being his most productive years. His armchair is made from carved walnut stained dark (Figure 19.8). Also exhibited at the Exposition Universelle of 1900 in Paris, it is an iconic piece of French Art Nouveau. Majorelle incorporated naturalistic forms, yet his compositions are more abstract than Gallé's. His works were sumptuous, made of expensive materials, and featured the meticulous craftsmanship he learned from his father. A master craftsman in wood, his designs took the French expertise in marquetry and carving into the Art Nouveau fold.

After 1908 he started mass-producing furniture

Figure 19.8 Louis Majorelle. Armchair, 1900.

and the quality of his pieces declined. The year 1914 finds Majorelle in Paris working as a decorator. He abandoned Art Nouveau and started producing more restrained work. The relationship between Art Nouveau and the 1920s style Art Deco is under dispute (Aubry 1996, p. 209). Some consider Art Deco as an artistic reaction against Art Nouveau. The totality of Majorelle's career suggests overlap between the two. His later work is more rectilinear and includes many vaguely Art Deco–looking pieces. The last decades of Majorelle's career are symptomatic of the plight of most artists connected to Art Nouveau. They were once themselves leaders of the artistic vanguard and fiercely critical of the design status quo and popular taste. By the ends of their careers, they were in turn the object of scorn in a design world that had moved in other artistic directions.

Paris

Hector Guimard (1867–1942) was a French architect, furniture designer, and writer. He attended the École Nationale des Arts Décoratifs, and also later the École des Beaux-Arts, where he did not finish his studies. He was influenced by Viollet-le-Duc, particularly his studies of exposed cast-iron columns. Guimard traveled to Brussels, where he met Victor Horta. During the period 1899–1914, his works developed into full-blown Art Nouveau. In 1896, he entered a competition to design the Paris Métro stations; he did not win, but the head of the Métro, a fan of Art Nouveau, gave Guimard the commission anyway, a propitious decision. This extensive project included hundreds of small projects throughout Paris. Some of the designs were just steps and railings, some were decorated shields, and some featured glass roofs shaped like butterfly wings (Figure 19.9). Art Nouveau features of his designs include stalks that blossom into lamps (Figure 19.10). Although based on vegetal forms, his lamps were metal, modern, and made for a sophisticated transportation system. They were also modular and mass-produced. For the Métro, he designed standardized cast-iron fittings. Guimard's work for the Paris Métro is a wonderful expression of Art Nouveau in France that would have a lasting impact on the face Paris presents to the world. One of the features of Art Nouveau was the synthesis of furnishings and

Figure 19.9 Hector Guimard. Paris Métro entrances, Paris, 1900.

Figure 19.10 Hector Guimard. Paris Métro entrances, lamp detail. Paris, 1900.

décor. Guimard was an accomplished designer of residential furniture and street furniture.

Professionally active in the beginning of the twentieth century, Guimard was no fan of modernism. Guimard, like many others, was interested in Viollet-le-Duc, minus the interest in history.

Art Nouveau works look so decorative that it is not immediately obvious that they were technologically advanced. Art Nouveau artists married industrial processes with the desire to look to nature to create beauty. Guimard's designs look handcrafted, if not organically grown but they were produced in factories.

Style, Artists, and Art Nouveau

When looking at a body of work that comes to be known as a style—and there is no better example of a style than Art Nouveau—an issue is the historical status of the individuals who contributed to crafting that style. Many serious art historians dismiss outright the notion of style. Their point, and it is a good one, is that style is a convention of historians looking at the past. Artists of a specific time period rarely feel they are fulfilling the requirements of a style. For, obviously, a style cannot predate the artists whose works gave rise to that style. Some artists are so thoroughly associated with Art Nouveau that they seem to be its essence, to embody it, as though the style could not have existed without them. The notion of style is useful when looking at the careers of Victor Horta, Emile Gallé, and Hector Guimard.

SPAIN

Artists work and produce artworks that respond to their clients' needs, realize their own goals, and resonate with trends and concerns of their day. Certain artists—Horta, Gallé, Guimard—were astonishingly in step with the precepts that came to be known as Art Nouveau.

Another category concerns individuals who make important artistic contributions, yet their talent is so deep, complex, and contradictory that their relationship to a single style is tenuous. A discussion of Art Nouveau is incomplete without mention of Antoni Gaudí and Louis Sullivan. Yet to present their creative processes and works as derivative of a movement established by others is to grossly underestimate their talent.

Antoni Gaudí

Antoni Gaudí (1852–1926) was a Spanish Catalan architect. He was knowledgeable of medieval history and craftsmanship. His early works indicate that he was interested in ornamental motifs, systems of ornament, and experimentation—like so many others, he read Ruskin and Viollet-le-Duc. He was up front about his inspiration from historic forms, including medieval and Gothic, although in transforming them he sought to create a Catalan regional style.

Gaudí imaginatively experimented with ornament, construction, and pre-fabrication. He used glazed tiles (*azulejos*). In designs for a factory and stables, he developed a roofing system that relied on parabolic arches. He worked in wrought iron and investigated steel frames.

Figure 19.11 Antoni Gaudí. Casa Batlló. Façade detail. Barcelona, 1904–1910.

A criticism of Gaudí's brilliant compositions is that he could not be imitated easily. There was something deeply personal and subjective about his compositions that is sometimes downright bizarre. William Curtis calls Gaudí "one of the most curious and original architects of the past two hundred years" (Curtis 1996, p. 60).

Gaudí's work has moments of fantasy and represents an early connection to the artistic movement of Surrealism; his built forms appear to melt, bend, and sway, as objects do in dreams. Gaudí designed a wavelike façade for an apartment house, the Casa Batlló (Figure 19.11). Glass, masonry, ceramic tile, wood, and metal all appear to effortlessly flow to-

gether, yet achieving this required a high level of skill and attention from the construction workers (Permanyer 1999, pp. 60–61). Fellow Catalan Salvador Dalí felt a connection to Gaudí's work, admiring the occasional use of nightmarish elements.

The development of Gaudí's interior spaces became increasingly fluid. The plan of the Casa Batlló demonstrates that for Gaudí, the possibilities offered by flowing forms inspired his design work in elevation and in plan (Figure 19.12). Shimomura (1992) writes: "For Gaudí, interior design was first and foremost the construction of space. The transitions between rooms and staircases weave together freely in both fast and slow motion, and his expres-

to modern. Although he represented an old-fashioned approach to decoration, he pushed the boundaries of what was structurally possible. His talent exceeds any attempt to define it.

UNITED STATES

Art Nouveau did not exist in the United States as a full-blown movement, the way it did in Belgium and France. But the works of Louis Sullivan, and even more so Louis Comfort Tiffany, reflect its worldwide influence. Louis Henri Sullivan (1856–1924) was an architect and writer. Before opening up his own office, Sullivan worked for Frank Furness in Philadelphia and William Le Baron Jenney in Chicago.

The most important phase of his architecture was when he created a series of early skyscrapers in the 1890s. He was an incredibly gifted designer, architect, and drawer, and his partnership with Dankmar Adler allowed him to focus on his architecture. The organization of their office presents a typical scenario for architectural partnerships: One partner focuses on design (Sullivan) and one on business (Adler). Sullivan recounted the story of his youth and design inspiration in a book, *The Autobiography of an Idea*. He went to Paris and studied at the École des Beaux Arts; his work is more of a reaction against Beaux Arts planning than an iteration of it. But he was something of a snob, proud of the French spelling of his first and middle names. His architecture expresses Sullivan's ambitious goals: to create an architecture appropriate to the new age, to create an American, if not Midwestern, strain of architecture and, in the process, to derive an entirely new system of ornamental decoration. Sullivan's accomplished ornament was based on American, not European, flora and was decidedly unclassical.

Sullivan was one of the founding fathers of modernism, with his vociferous disavowal of historically imitative buildings, his desire to express the struc-

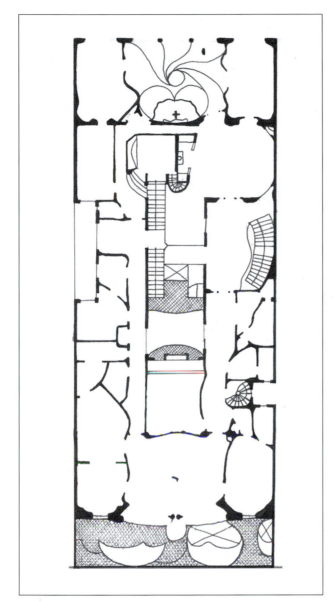

Figure 19.12 Antoni Gaudí. Casa Batlló. 1904-1907, Barcelona.

sive use of light makes those transitions visual. In short, the main theme of Casa Batlló is the functional continuity of space" (p. 52).

His early projects include two commissions by the Güell family, the Palau Güell, 1886–1891, and the Parque Güell, 1900–1914. These were followed by two apartment houses, the Casa Batlló, 1904–1906, and the Casa Milá, Barcelona, 1906–1910.

Gaudí did furniture designs for interiors, and also street furniture. His work ranges from eclectic

Figure 19.13 Louis Henri Sullivan. Carson Pirie Scott Store, Chicago, Illinois.

tural frame and emphasize verticality, and his creation of an American architectural idiom. Yet any review of his work that denies his system of ornament is omitting a major part of his design. His expressive buildings were highly decorative.

His major buildings include the Auditorium, 1889, an opera house and hotel ingeniously contained within a steel-framed office building. Of his high-rises, two of the most significant structures are the Wainwright Building in St. Louis, 1890–1891, and the Guaranty Building in Buffalo, 1894–1896. Because of their height, they are technological achievements, but their façades are also expressive explorations of verticality. His last major project

was the Carson Pirie Scott Store, 1898–1904. It is one of his most poetic projects, in which a cellular superstructure grows out of an elaborately decorated two-story base (Figures 19.13 and 19.14).

Louis Comfort Tiffany came from a family of jewelers, merchants, and designers. Tiffany traveled to Nancy, where he visited Gallé's factory. His father's firm opened a Paris branch that sold jewelry, lamps, and small art objects. Tiffany traveled in Europe and North Africa. During his travels, he focused on Romanesque art and Islamic and Japanese ceramics, using them as points of departure for his experiments with stained glass. He created many lamps (Figure 19.15). The ten-light lily fits squarely

Figure 19.14 Louis Henri Sullivan. Carson Pirie Scott building, Chicago, Illinois.

Figure 19.15 Louis Comfort Tiffany. Ten-light lily, 1900s.

Figure 19.16 Louis Comfort Tiffany. Chair, 1905.

in the Art Nouveau fold with its use of a favored flower. It was made of metal and glass.

Initially creating interior designs that were heavily influenced by the Aesthetic Movements, over time Tiffany's work turned in the direction of Art Nouveau. He is the most Art Nouveau of any American artist. Tiffany had a prominent exhibit at the World's Columbian Exposition of 1893. He contributed a glass curtain to the Palacio de Bellas Artes in Mexico City in 1915. As with many Art Nouveau artists, he found himself at odds with cubism and modernism. Although mostly known for his works in glass, lamps, vases, and windows, Tiffany also worked as an interior decorator, designing rooms in which all the elements adhered to a central scheme, and this included furniture (Figure 19.16).

GLOBAL

Belgium and France are the countries most frequently associated with Art Nouveau, but also Germany, England, the Czech Republic, and, in a limited way, the United States. In Belgium, the new style expressed a political and nationalist agenda. In Spain, it was given a Catalan regional twist. When it became an international artistic phenomenon, it was often evoked straightforwardly as the most up-to-date style of the times. This is ironic, because its effects were felt later in other regions of the world.

When most Europeans were no longer building in the Art Nouveau style, Art Nouveau buildings were still being erected in South America, Africa, and Asia. It could be considered the first international style, as it flourished in Turkey, Argentina, Brazil, and Japan. Brazilian Eliseu Visconti (1867–1944) was an accomplished Art Nouveau designer. He studied in Paris and completed numerous Art Nouveau projects in Rio de Janeiro. In the best tradition of the new style, he sought to eliminate the distance between architecture and elements of the decorative arts.

Figure 19.17 Antonin Balsanek. Municipal House. Prague, Czechoslavakia, 1913.

Czech Republic

Prague was Eastern Europe's major center of Art Nouveau, although the Czech version of the international style followed a different path. For Art Nouveau artists in Belgium and France, historic styles were anathema. In Prague, the earliest leanings toward an Art Nouveau outlook came from architects who worked within identifiable period styles. Art Nouveau contributed to the creation of modern Czech art. It was followed by a more progressive architectural style that bore the same name as the movement in painting, Cubism. In the works of Antonin Balsanek (1865–1921), the divisions between historic styles, Secession, and Art Nouveau were not pronounced (Figure 19.17).

Usually described as Art Nouveau, Balsanek's Municipal House reveals his familiarity with a number of contemporary and historical design idioms. The color palette of deep blues, purples, and sepias was decidedly Art Nouveau. Several of the painted human figures are dressed in patterned robes and offset with gold, a strategy perfected by Secessionist painter Gustav Klimt. One of the rounded arches frames a classically detailed aedicule that features a mirror and an air grille. Art Nouveau, Secession, and classicism are distinct artistic traditions with differing design philosophies. Yet a Balsanek interior design deftly blends them together.

Turkey

The last quarter of the nineteenth century saw an enormous amount of new construction in Istanbul. The historic eclecticism of the nineteenth century followed its own path along the banks of the Bosporus, in which Ottoman Revival buildings competed with other historically based styles. The building pace continued unabated, and the opening of the Istanbul Academy of Fine Arts in 1901 gave the design world an additional boost. In the first decades of the twentieth century, Istanbul became its own center of Art Nouveau. Turkish Art Nouveau was enriched by the international mix of the architects, which included Turks, Greeks, Italians, and others; this fascinating subject is the focus of a book by architectural historian Diana Barillari, upon which this section is based. Italian architect Raimondo D'Aronco (1857–1932) spent twenty years of his long career designing in Istanbul. Turkey inherited not the Belgian and French variety of Art Nouveau but the Italian permutation of it known as "Stile Liberty." Many of the forms of Stile Liberty in Italy and Turkey are recognizable as Art Nouveau, yet many of the meanings that were so important in Belgium and France, notably the antipathy toward historicism, lost their currency when moved to Europe's eastern border. A style created to replace historicism, in Turkey and Italy, happily blended with it.

The hundreds of Art Nouveau buildings in Istanbul range from superficial facsimiles to inspired meditations. Much of the construction was due to speculative development of rental buildings in which Art Nouveau was a cheap cosmetic finish to distinguish one landlord's buildings from those of competitors. Art Nouveau decoration fulfilled the capitalist intention of attracting customers or, in the case of apartment buildings, tenants.

The Art Nouveau features of buildings in Istanbul are generally limited to the façades, with little change in plan, or in the buildings behind the façades. This lends the façades a sculptural quality created from the abutment of projecting volumes and recessed volumes. Bay windows and prominently jutting cornices were popular features that furthered the plastic quality of the façades. Yet the building materials were conventional, and the fenestration was achieved using standard rectangular casement windows. The metal structure was hidden, not expressed, nor was metal combined with glass to produce broad areas of transparency; the use of metal was limited to balcony railings. Curved façades were rare.

The Gümüşsu Palas is one such example. It bears strong stylistic traces of Italian neo-Baroque façades, with its cornice, classical proportioning, and exaggerated (and fake) rustication, part of the interminable list of nineteenth-century historical revivals. Art Nouveau sculptures have been grafted onto a Baroque-style façade, a process Barillari (1996) calls "sculptural and decorative overkill." Art Nouveau buildings in Istanbul, some inspired, some pedestrian, underscore that Art Nouveau truly became a style, a recognizable grouping of features that could be imitated. In some cases, the new results were divorced from the style's original ideological underpinnings. Even if superficial, Art Nouveau designs were successful in creating a fresh new look, popular with the public, landlords, and tenants alike.

Japan

Chuta Ito (1868–1954) first studied architecture, then studied architectural history, eventually becoming one of Japan's first and foremost architectural historians. A tireless promoter of Asian and Japanese architecture, he opposed the neo-Baroque designs proposed for many prominent sites, including the design for the new parliament building, the Diet. These buildings were not only the work of expatriate architects but also that of Japanese followers of Josiah Condor (refer to Chapter 18).

Knowing that Ito supported creating a new urban Japanese architecture, we must consider his own designs from a different perspective. European Art Nouveau artists counted among their inspirations Japanese art. Many of the Art Nouveau artists, as well as the English Arts and Crafts artists they admired, collected Japanese prints and glassware. So Art Nouveau was in part a modern style based on Japanese decorative traditions. The common description of the Aritomo House as Art Nouveau is recognition of the "foreigners" of the style that was known by a French word. But Art Nouveau in Japan was simultaneously a homegrown approach that transformed Japanese visual themes appropriate for the modern period.

Peru

The major Latin American cities that were greatly affected by Art Nouveau were Rio de Janeiro, Mexico City, Havana, and Buenos Aires. The presence of an Art Nouveau structure in Lima, Peru, is evidence of the style's quick spread around the world, even to those places not typically associated with it. Peru is home to South America's oldest traditions of large-scale urbanism and architecture, its major sites including the Nazca Plains, Machu Picchu, and Cuzco. The capital, Lima, on the western seaboard, was founded in 1535. Peru achieved her independence from Spain in 1822, so by 1890 the Spanish colonial legacy was neither an immediate concern nor long forgotten. In the late nineteenth and early twentieth centuries, many Peruvian artists received travel grants to Europe, which lent them firsthand knowledge of European artistic movements, from Impressionism to Art Nouveau. Familiarity with European capital cities also aided in the project of constructing historically inspired buildings.

In the 1910s, Art Nouveau in Peru existed mostly in furniture and the decorative arts (Garcia Bryce, 1973). There were only a handful of Art Nouveau buildings, and often the occurrence of Art Nouveau was limited to doors, windows, balconies, and gates. A major Art Nouveau structure was built in 1915 by two brothers who worked as builders, the Hermanos Maspero. Their Casa Barragán was a popular hotel.

Figure 19.18 Fotografia Courret, Lima, Peru.

The new technology of photography was enormously popular and quickly spread all around the world, needing little governmental support. In many places, the art and business of photography linked up with Art Nouveau. The paper mats that framed photographs were often decorated with borders of tendrils and swirls. Photographic studios were outfitted with Art Nouveau interiors or, as in Lima, were situated in a building whose exterior was confidently decorated in the latest style, Art Nouveau (Figure 19.18). Fotografia Courret is a direct example of the kind of Art Nouveau structure built in Paris, usually private houses, such as the one owned by Toulouse-Lautrec's favored subject, Yvette Guilbert.

It was customary to paint advertisements directly onto buildings, but Art Nouveau precepts facilitated the process of combining building and text. Art Nouveau graphic layouts promoted the integration of text, border, and figural elements. The Fotografia Courret is a prime example of Art Nouveau in its massing, details, materials, and typography. It does not mix much with traditional architectural detailing (as in Turkey). The column capitals appear as traditional capitals from a distance, yet close inspection reveals them as twisting swirls of foliage. Local carpenters made the interior display cases.

The metal balcony railings and wooden door panels also have a clear Art Nouveau heritage. The deeply cut swirls of the plaster decoration owe some debt to the neo-Baroque style, yet studiously avoid classical elements. Not all buildings reveal the history of their locales. Fotografía Courret announces that one client, operating out of the capital city of a country with a long and rich architectural tradition, linked his fortunes to the new technology of photography and felt that the best architectural expression for his business was Art Nouveau.

CONCLUSION

In a design history, the presence of a major stylistic revolution prompts a basic question: Is the revolution due to new technologies, materials, or aesthetic expression? As an aesthetic statement, Art Nouveau shared with other avant-garde movements a distaste for a superficial use of the past. Henry-Russell Hitchcock wrote: "Art Nouveau was actually the first stage of modern architecture in Europe, if modern architecture be understood as implying primarily the total rejection of historicism." Art Nouveau artists switched allegiances from history to nature.

Art Nouveau, as a style, was well-poised to become the first international style. Art Nouveau was not aloof, was not elite, and was immensely popular. Its motifs avoided any direct historical connection, and its two-dimensional variety guaranteed its quick dispersal as a new graphic device. It resonated with a wide audience and had both commercial appeal and domestic success.

The most creative years for Art Nouveau in Europe was the period 1893–1905. It appeared later in other places around the globe, but by the 1920s its creative energies were spent.

To the extent that artists focused on nature, Art Nouveau bears similarity to Arts and Crafts, Prairie School, the detailing of Chicago School skyscrapers, and Japanese woodcuts. Unlike Arts and Crafts followers, Art Nouveau supporters embraced new technologies, new materials such as glass and metal, and industrial production. Many Art Nouveau objects were electrified. Yet, quick as a wink, the movement heralded as fresh and new was itself criticized as superficial and elitist, qualities all too often associated with decoration. Alastair Duncan, who has written books on both Art Deco and Art Nouveau, described the sense of relief many felt when interest in Art Nouveau dissipated, noting that many considered it "a grave and mercifully brief transgression against good taste" (Duncan 1984). The reign of Art Nouveau was not long, some twenty-five years split before and after the turn of the twentieth century.

Sources

Aubry, Françoise, and Jos Vandenbreeden. *Horta: Art Nouveau to Modernism*. Ghent: Ludion, 1996.

Barillari, Diana. *Istanbul 1900: Art-Nouveau Architecture and Interiors*. New York: Rizzoli, 1996.

Borsi, Franco, and Paolo Portoghesi. *Victor Horta*. Braine-l'Allend: J. M. Collet, 1996.

Curtis, William. *Modern Architecture Since 1900*. New York: Wiley, 1996.

Duncan, Alastair. *Art Nouveau Furniture*. New York: Clarkson N. Potter, 1984.

García Bryce, José. *Art Nouveau en Lima: Galería del Banco Continental*. Lima: La Galería, 1973.

Hitchcock, Henry-Russell. *Architecture: Nineteenth and Twentieth Centuries*. Baltimore: Penguin, 1963.

Jullian, Philippe. *The Triumph of Art Nouveau: Paris Exhibition 1900*. London: Phaidon, 1974.

Loyer, François. *Paul Hankar: La Naissance de l'Art Nouveau*. Brussels: Archives d'Architecture Moderne, 1986.

Permanyer, Lluís. *Barcelona Art Nouveau*. New York: Rizzoli, 1999.

Puttemans, Pierre. *Architecture Moderne en Belgique*. Brussels: Marc Vokaer, 1974.

Quaranta, Domenico. "Art Nouveau and the Parisian Crucible of the Avant-gardes/Paris 1900–1910," from *Art of the Twentieth Century: 1900–1919*. Milan: Skira, 2006.

Sembach, Klaus-Jürgen. *Henry Van De Velde*. New York: Rizzoli, 1989.

Shimomura, Junichi. *Art Nouveau Architecture: Residential Masterpieces 1892–1911*. San Francisco: Cadence Books, 1992.

Ulmer, Renate. *Art Nouveau: Symbolismus und Jugendstil in Frankreich*. Darmstadt: Arnoldsche, 1999.

DISCUSSION AND REVIEW QUESTIONS

1. What are the general characteristics of Art Nouveau?
2. How were Art Nouveau works modern?
3. Art Nouveau is often described as a decorative style. Why?
4. What are some of the regional variations of Art Nouveau?
5. What were some of the favored flora and fauna used by Art Nouveau artists?
6. How is Art Nouveau a repudiation of Victorian design?
7. Who was the American designer whose work is closely related to Art Nouveau?
8. Who were the Belgian Art Nouveau designers? Who were the major French Art Nouveau designers?
9. How did Art Nouveau artists respond to technology?

PROTOMODERNISM

1897–1935	1917–1932	1914–1935	1868–1928	1867–1959
Vienna Secession	De Stijl	Russian Constructivism	Charles Rennie Mackintosh	Frank Lloyd Wright

Modernism had many roots, causes, and influences. What binds the various projects in this chapter together is that they aesthetically straddle the nineteenth and twentieth centuries. These transitional projects contain the seeds of modernism. That is, some of these works are predictive of the modernism to come, but it is a mistake to view their forms as introductory exercises, for the ongoing popularity of Hoffmann, Klimt, and Wright suggests that these designers, artists, and architects achieved something significant in their works, a new sensibility and timelessness. Equally important is their shared belief that decorative motifs are carriers of meaning and not necessarily antithetical to artistic expression. In the correct hands, decoration did not mask meaning but enhanced it. Equally important for their popularity is that it was not necessary to be an enlightened member of the **avant-garde** to appreciate their works. "Avant-garde" refers to any group of artists who are experimental or unorthodox. In the case of the early modernists, it means those who experimented with forms and ideas—and their clients—before they were widely accepted.

These are the artists, architects, and painters whose projects gave rise to modernism. Yet to label these merely transitional works would be a mistake, as this group includes some real masterpieces, all discussed below, the Palais Stoclet, the Postparkasse, and the Glasgow School of Art.

We start by first looking at the works of the Vienna Secession movement, which are the most formally predictive of the modernism to come. For such a diverse cast of characters, it is surprising that when citing their influences, the artists of the Secession mention time and time again the writings of Arts and Crafts theorists Morris and Ruskin.

VIENNA SECESSION

The design revolution known as the Vienna Secession came about in a period in which there were significant achievements in many fields, including art history, psychology, and philosophy. In many respects, the works of Sigmund Freud, Alois Riegl, and Ludwig Wittgenstein provide the intellectual context in which the aesthetically oriented Secessionists thrived.

453

"Secession" is the noun of the verb "to secede, to leave." It has an aggressive and negative connotation. In art, it refers to a group of artists who withdrew from an academic institution or artistic movement. Members of the artistic community were fed up with Victorian historicism, an eclectic synthesis of styles. Secession groups sprouted up all over Europe, the most important ones in Berlin, Munich, and Vienna. In Vienna, the Secession movement comprised nineteen artists who favored an experimental approach in the arts. The Vienna group included Klimt, Hoffmann, Olbrich, and Kolomon Moser. They favored developing new forms that related to modern life with no ties to traditional design or historic styles.

Riegl (1858–1905) is an important art historian, responsible for establishing the modern parameters of the discipline. Even though he lived only five years in the twentieth century, his thought places him more in the camp of the twentieth century than in the nineteenth. Riegl believed that an artist's individual works are part of a historical development. When stylistic changes occur within that development, they are not, according to Riegl, a response to outside pressures. Rather, Riegl's writings stress that what is important when looking at art is the internal urgency, dynamics, and formal ordering of a movement or period. In architecture, this means that building should be self-contained entities. The term associated with Riegl's line of thought is Kunstwollen, usually translated as will-to-form, or artistic volition.

Philosopher Ludwig Wittgenstein (1889–1951) was a young man in Vienna when the Secessionists were at their height. His only book, the *Tractatus,* was published in 1922. His thought, a repudiation of traditional philosophy, is one of the beginnings of the twentieth-century push to understand cultural phenomena in terms of language and linguistics. There is no one-to-one correlation between his philosophy and Secessionist design, but he was an integral part of the arts world.

Of those active in the arts world, the writings of two, Otto Wagner and Adolf Loos, were most significant in defining the ethos of their era. With his theory of architecture, Wagner was the intellectual father of the Secessionist group. He represented a consensus—most of the Secessionists were looking for a modern (and Austrian) national style that was also appropriate for the masses. Loos espoused a provocative theory of culture and design, discussed below, that was extreme in its pronouncements.

For those active in the arts, there were two poles, one the decorative Secessionist pole, represented by three institutions, and the other the austere dogmatism of Loos. Three institutions provided the infrastructure that supported the Secessionists: the Kunstgewerbeschule (School of Arts and Crafts), the Vienna Secession, and the Wiener Werkstätte. The prominence of the School of Arts and Crafts underscores the Secessionist support for Gesamtkunstwerk, or unity of the arts. A core belief of this approach to the arts is that household objects were worthy of design attention. The Vienna Secession literally was an exhibition building, and the public face of their artistic philosophy. The Wiener Werkstätte was a commercial organization allied with the Secessionists. These three entities were the institutions that supported the Secessionists in their desire to prompt a regeneration of the arts. Those associated with these three groups were more decorative, in varying degrees, in their outlook and in their professional activities.

The Secession Building: An Exhibition Hall

The Secessionists were idealistic, sometimes to the extreme. The artistic positions that the Secessionists tried to maintain were sometimes tenuous. Their reasons for protesting against historicism are clear, but understanding their antipathy toward Art Nouveau is tricky. Historicism, for them, meant the

Figure 20.1 Josef Maria Olbrich. Secession Building, Vienna, Austria, 1897–1898.

grand nineteenth-century buildings of the Ring-strasse, Vienna's major urban design that relied heavily on historical revival architecture. The project was Austria's answer to Haussmann's refashioning of Paris, which similarly provided modern civic infrastructure (roads, sewers, and lights) in traditional garb.

With encouragement from Klimt, Olbrich received the commission to design the Secession Building, a work that established Olbrich as a major force in Austrian design and a progressive architect (Figure 20.1). The Secession Building was an exhibition building; one of the complaints of the artists had been a lack of exposure through exhibitions.

The city of Vienna donated the site. The building, solemn but festive, relies upon simple forms and is a prime example of a protomodern building. The Secession Building acted as a built design manifesto. The phrase "Ver Sacrum" ("The Rite of Spring"), emblazoned on its façade, was a clear call for a new approach. "Ver Sacrum" was also the name of the monthly design journal of the Secessionists that was published from 1898 to 1903. On the building, gilded leaves cover an open dome; the use of vegetal motifs is something that the Secessionists had in common with Arts and Crafts, Art Nouveau, and Prairie Style.

The Secession Building was formed from pure geometries; it had glistening white walls, and several flat planes that were then turned over to artists for decoration. The signature building of the movement, it was home to art exhibits for years. Celebratory and exuberant, its cornices hint of classicism.

The Wiener Werkstätte, the Viennese workshops, was a commercial confederation that existed from 1903 to 1932. The Werkstätte was a business proposition, seeking to find commissions for those associated with the Secession movement. A cooperative group of painters, sculptors, architects, and designers sought to counter the aesthetic devaluation that they saw everywhere. Part of the Secessionist creed was that everyday objects were worthy of consideration by artists as aesthetic objects. They felt that art could touch, revive, and improve all aspects of life. This line of thinking combines the worlds of high art and daily life, and is clearly based on the writings of William Morris. The cooperative believed in simplicity, and good design for the masses. The workshops functioned as a guild with the practical virtue of putting artists in touch with potential clients.

Joseph Maria Olbrich (1867–1908) had a career that lasted only a decade, but while professionally active he was an ardent contributor to the antihistoricist movement. An accomplished artist as well as an architect, he worked for Otto Wagner. At first, Olbrich's works display the influence of the Jugendstil designs that were becoming popular. He was on friendly terms with Josef Hoffmann, Gustav Klimt, and Kolomon Moser, his cofounder of the anti-academic Secession. One of Olbrich's most prominent commissions involved designing a number of houses at the Mathildenhöhe artists' colony in Darmstadt, Germany.

Unity of the Arts

Sometimes there are epochs in which art and architecture appear as if in tandem—Neoclassicism comes to mind. The paintings by the neoclassical artist David are perfectly in concert with the buildings of the neoclassical architect Leo von Klenze. With the Secessionists, there is a connection between visual artists and designers, yet it is less obvious. Members of both disciplines were concerned with the same issues. Yet the paintings of Gustav Klimt, the most well-known painter associated with the movement, are visual expressions that are emotional, psychological, and sexual.

Gustav Klimt (1862–1918) came from a humble background and became an accomplished academic painter. He was first a leading figure in Austrian Jugendstil. He was the first president of the Vienna Secession movement, founded in 1897. He studied in Vienna and did interior decorations for several buildings. His foreign influences include the English artist Aubrey Beardsley. The imprint of many historically styles is evident in his work, specifically Mycenaean, Byzantine, and Egyptian, and recent artistic movements, including Impressionism, realism, and abstraction.

Klimt felt that architectural decorations, such as mosaics and friezes, constituted a highly valued art form and his paintings were often part of a decorating ensemble. He designed a frieze with mosaics for the dining room of the Palais Stoclet in Brussels. With his *in situ* projects, he demonstrated the publicly stated Secessionist belief that there should be a symbiosis between art and design (as a point of contrast, while Renaissance artists painted panels destined to decorate cassoni, they did not consider cabinet-makers their equals).

He supported himself mostly as a portraitist. His paintings of Adele Bloch-Bauer came from a period in which he used gold encrustation. As Beardsley used black ink to dramatic effect, Klimt used gold. His paintings reveal his experience as a designer of jewelry and textiles. Spare lines form his figures, often contrasted by richly patterned robes, and Klimt himself was fond of wearing caftans. Klimt's over-the-top decoration presents another aspect of Secessionist style, one explanation of which is Freudian psychology—and Freud was from Vienna.

Klimt's paintings have more to do with the subconscious than questions of how to make twentieth-century buildings. The tectonic explorations of Olbrich and Hoffmann do little to prepare one for the visual profusion of decorative themes that dominate Klimt's paintings. *The Kiss* (1907–1908), includes enamel, gold inlay, and colored glass (Figure 20.2). For a painting that reveals relatively little flesh, it is surprisingly erotic. Were his paintings sexist? By all accounts, Klimt was a womanizer. He never married. His frank portrayal of nudes was shocking to many, and his works are often explicitly sexual.

Artists are often controversial figures with both supporters and detractors. While some saw Klimt as the hope of a new age, others saw in his paintings scandalous images of sexuality. To many he was an early modernist; to others he was an example of fin-de-siècle decadence. Rumors about his private life were abundant, and included uncountable girlfriends, illegitimate children, and syphilis. This affirmed some people's suspicions that his paintings, despite their technical virtuosity and gorgeous sur-

Figure 20.2 Gustav Klimt. The Kiss.

faces, were a harbinger of the breakdown of the moral order in the waning days of the Hapsburg Empire.

The Secessionist group started to splinter, and Klimt and a group of painters left because of their desire to support the linkages between art and commerce. Although the Secession Building survived, the 1930s and the rise of the Nazis in Austria put an end to the movement as a progressive force for positive change. Klimt is one of the major twentieth-century modern painters. Although he was a rebellious figure, his paintings met with strong public approval.

Figure 20.3 Otto Wagner. Austrian Post Office Savings Bank, banking hall, 1904–1906.

Otto Wagner

Otto Wagner (1841–1918) was an architect, urban planner, designer, teacher, and writer. A key figure in the development of twentieth-century modernism, his career lasted for over half a century. He studied at the Bauakademie in Berlin, where he admired Schinkel's buildings. He explored the integration of decoration with underlying forms and considered these in relationship to programmatic function. He worked with Olbrich on an ambitious unified urban transportation system, completed in 1901. This involved local train stations, entrances and exits, and for the Donaukanal, bridges and viaducts. One of Wagner and Obrich's most impres-

sive designs is the entrance to Karlsplatz Station. The projects of urban infrastructure were made of iron, stone, and brickwork.

Wagner disseminated his thoughts about modern architecture as a teacher and a writer. He taught at the Akademie der Bildenden Künste in Vienna. In 1895, he published a book titled *Moderne Architektur* in which he makes clear his disdain for the division of architecture into styles. A subsequent publication, *Baukunst unserer Zeit* (1914), reinforced his commitment to reforming design.

The Postsparkasse, or Post Office Savings Bank, Vienna, 1904, is made of glass and aluminum and is one of the monuments of the early modern move-

Figure 20.4 Otto Wagner. Armchair, 1902-1904.

ment (Figure 20.3). John Pile calls its banking hall the first truly modern interior. The Post Office Savings Bank resembles a church with a double-height central nave, complete with clerestory, and side aisles. Unlike Paxton's Crystal Palace (mentioned in Chapter 15), which combined technology with Victorian detailing, Wagner's banking hall was a frank and straightforward solution to a program.

Some of the public institution monumentality derives from its symmetry. Wagner took a form the public was familiar with, train sheds, and applied it to another equally important public institution. The use of glass in the Savings Bank is a literal comment about financial transparency. The floor is also made of translucent glass bricks. A restrained version of Secessionist decoration enlivens the floor.

Wagner was not formally a member of the Secession. He thought design should display an understanding of purpose and good choices in materials. Materials should be available, workable, durable, and economical. This would result in good, simple detailing. For Wagner, the form that arises from following these principles would be pleasing and understandable.

There is an industrial and engineering side to his work, not always evident in the designs of the Secessionists. Even when he worked with wood—for example, his chairs—his work has an industrial aesthetic. Bolt heads, in his architecture and in his furniture, are visible (Figure 20.4).

Josef Hoffmann

Josef Hoffmann (1870–1956), another Austrian architect and designer, enjoyed a career that spanned fifty years. His long life allowed him to realize a potential that escaped Olbrich. Hoffmann is one of the most important furniture and interior designers of the twentieth century.

He started studying in Brno, worked in Würzburg, and then studied again in Vienna, under Wagner. He was a fan of English Arts and Crafts, and admired the work of Charles Rennie Mackintosh. While in Wagner's office, Hoffmann joined the newly founded Vienna Secession. He became a professor at the Kunstgewerbeschule. A multitalented designer, his creations include furniture, jewelry, dresses, book bindings, posters, textiles, and wallpapers. The year 1900 saw a dramatic shift in Hoffmann's work: He moved away from the curvilinear forms that make some early Secessionist pieces nearly indistinguishable from Art Nouveau, and his work becomes restrained and sober. Among his many successes in this period were the Puckersdorf Sanatorium of 1903–1906 and the Fledermaus Cabaret of 1908. The Fledermaus table and chairs set became a staple of café design worldwide.

The Palais Stoclet in Brussels, Belgium (1905–1911), with its sumptuous interiors, is a highlight

Figure 20.5 Josef Hoffmann. Palais Stoclet, dining room, with mosaics by Gustav Klimt, 1905–1911.

in Hoffmann's career. Adolphe Stoclet was a Belgian financier who had seen Hoffmann's work in Vienna. A wealthy and sophisticated art collector, Stoclet commissioned Hoffmann to build him a house. It has a stunning sequence of public rooms, including a dining room with mosaics by Klimt (Figure 20.5). (Hoffmann did the interiors for Klimt's atelier.) For the Palais Stoclet, Hoffmann specified the furniture, carpets, fittings, lamps, tableware, and linens. Many of the furnishings were made by Hoffmann and his colleagues at the Wiener Werkstätte. The building proves that those working within the Vienna Secessionist style were capable of producing an exclusive and cosmopolitan house. The Palais Stoclet was formal, informal, sophisticated, and modern. One of the most signifi-

Figure 20.6 Josef Hoffmann. Palais Stoclet, music room. Sketch, 1905–1911.

cant residential interiors of the twentieth century, it appealed to an international audience of those in the know.

Hoffmann's early work relied on the clarity of classical composition. The Palais Stoclet is a forward-looking design whose music room particularly anticipates Art Deco (Figure 20.6). Planes, in Hoffmann's designs, are not just the result of volumes and forms, but flat entities that delimit a two-dimensional space that can and should be emphasized. The exterior relies on gilt bronze moldings to frame and emphasize the square masses. The most important rooms protrude and thereby express themselves in the façades and the overall volume. Hoffmann's design process, from the inside out, lent the house its notable asymmetrical massing.

He made the cube and the square the trademark of his design. Hoffmann liked drawing on graph paper. He explored rectilinear ordering systems, and he was interested in the possibilities presented by permutations of simple forms, particularly squares. The square was a favored motif for him, and he used it to great effect in fabrics, carpets, and furniture. One of Hoffmans's significant institutional projects was the Puckersdorf Sanatorium. An armchair from the project was called "Sitzmachine," or "Sitting Machine" (Figure 20.7). It was later mass produced.

The Fledermaus chair (Fledermaus is German for bat) was used in the Fledermaus Cabaret (Figure 20.8). Fledermaus chairs and tables were also mass produced.

Hoffmann's works often show an understated interest in classical composition. He was in tune with artistic advances, aware of De Stijl and Le Corbusier, whose designs he promoted. He was most interested in design and visual treatment, and less interested in structural innovations. For Hoffmann, the process of artistic creativity was important (in contrast to Loos, discussed next).

He was influenced by the writings of John Ruskin, William Morris, and Otto Wagner. Al-

Figure 20.7 Josef Hoffmann. Armchairs, "Sitzmachine," 1908.

Figure 20.8 Josef Hoffmann. Fledermaus Chair, c. 1907.

though World War II put an end to his career, many of Hoffmann's textiles and furniture pieces are still in production.

Adolf Loos

If Olbrich, Hoffmann, Klimt, and Wagner constitute one strand of early Viennese modernism, an opposing force is represented by the formidable figure of Adolf Loos. Loos (1870–1933) was an Austrian architect and theorist. As a theorist, his writings had a lasting impact few designers achieve. A fierce critic of the Secessionist movement, he instead promoted the functionalist approach. He was argumentative, and one of the most important figures of the early modern movement. Functionalism is a design method in which the overriding concern is the building, or object, in use. It is generally associated with European modernists of the 1920s and 1930s.

Loos came to his pragmatic design philosophy from the family profession. His father worked as a

Figure 20.9 Adolf Loos. American Bar, Kärnter Passage, Vienna, Austria, 1908.

mason, and Loos was certified to work as a brick-layer. He studied in Brünn (now Brno), Reichen-berg, and Vienna. In 1893, he traveled to Chicago where he visited the Columbian Exposition. Dur-ing his three years in the United States, he visited New York, Philadelphia, and St. Louis.

For the American Bar in Vienna's Kärntner passageway, done in 1908, Loos favored rich mate-rials (Figure 20.9), reddish-brown coralwood, trans-lucent yellow onyx panels, and leather (Bock 2007, p. 45). The bar has a coffered ceiling of veined mar-ble. It also uses electric lights and mirrors to expand the space, but the mirrors start above the level of eye sight, so patrons cannot see their personal reflec-tions. He usually paneled his rooms up to the dado level. This small, cozy bar had a clublike elegance.

Loos designed few pieces of furniture. He was usually happy to specify simple pieces designed by others; he was fond of Thonet's bentwood chairs. Part of a general project to redecorate a Viennese apartment, he designed a bedroom armoire for Gustav Turnowsky, c. 1900 (Figure 20.10). Loos admired the frame-and-panel system because, he noted, centuries of use had perfected the form

Figure 20.10 Adolf Loos. Armoire for Gustav Turnowsky's apartment, Vienna, c. 1900.

taking the idea of Gesamtkunstwerk too far, to Loos's mind. In contrast to the Secessionists, Loos opposed the idea of style. He limited his own design activity. He promoted the idea that designs should look anonymous and that design should be reserved. For the bedroom Loos designed for his wife, all the closets were concealed and he specified white fur for the flooring material.

During Loos's stay in Paris, he designed a house for the American entertainer Josephine Baker. Loos's house for Baker provides a restrained backdrop for a spectacular person (Figure 20.11). He believed that house exteriors should be discreet, and the functions of interior spaces should dictate a building's exterior form. Modernists believed that the internal and the exterior manifestation became out of whack in the nineteenth century. The alternating black and white marble bands obliquely refer to African decorative motifs.

The entry sequence of Loos' Baker House is important. The rectangle in the upper portion of the exploded axonometric is a swimming pool with underwater windows. Surrounded by a walkway, Baker could swim while her guests gazed at her body, shimmering in the water like an exotic fish.

It is no surprise that Loos was critical of Art Nouveau. That he was a severe critic of the Vienna Secessionists requires explanation. This seems odd as, especially in his early works such as the American Bar, his projects bear a strong resemblance to Secessionist works. He loathed the projects of Klimt, Hoffmann, and Olbrich. He sought beauty in form, not ornament. His buildings and interiors display a sense of rectangular control. The sense of control resulted from a design process that subordinated creativity to function.

Despite his impassioned rhetoric, he did sometimes use a restricted, stripped-down classicism. In full command of a simplified aesthetic, his buildings anticipated Bauhaus designs by nearly a decade.

(Gravagnuolo 1982, p. 99). Loos's chest has straight lines and angles, and honestly displays its structure. Loos opposed decoration, and also the idea of a personal intuitive style, anything approaching kitsch, or that which could not be rationalized. He strongly expressed his opinions in a lecture that was later widely published. In "Ornament and Crime" he equates the superfluous use of decoration with a lower state of human development. In her *Dictionary of Art* (1996) entry on Loos, Yehuda Safran states that Loos first presented his materials in a talk in 1910, which he then published in 1913 (p. 652).

Adolf Loos fought for truth in design and sought that which was genuine. He was against the prestigious buildings on the Ringstrasse. Loos was an adversary of Hoffmann and Van de Velde, the latter because Loos disapproved of the fact that he designed women's clothes to match his interiors—

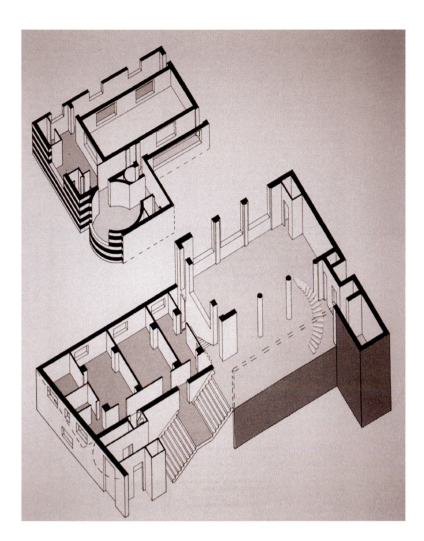

Figure 20.11 Adolf Loos. Josephine Baker House.

DE STIJL

The argument over the role of ornament was sidestepped by proponents of De Stijl and Russian Constructivism. The approach of the designers of these two movements had no real place for ornament. "De Stijl" literally means "the Style" in Dutch. It was a movement of avant-garde Dutch artists, designers, architects, urban designers, graphic artists, industrial designers, musicians, and writers. It was also the name of a periodical founded by Theo van Doesburg in 1917. Across disciplinary divides, De Stijl artists explored their fascination with elementary components—circles, triangles, and squares, primary colors, and flat surfaces. They sought to reduce compositions to horizontal and vertical lines. In many respects, this movement was related to,

and aware of, Expressionism, Cubism, Futurism, and Dada. The major artist of the period was Piet Mondrian; the major architect and designer was Gerrit Rietveld (1888–1964).

RUSSIAN CONSTRUCTIVISM

Postrevolutionary Russia was a work in progress in all respects, so while the new social, political, and economic system was loosely related to architectural modernism, there was no easy correlation. The 1920s is an interlude—after the Revolution but before the rise of Joseph Stalin's totalitarian regime. What would the architecture be that represented a dramatic break with the past? During this hopeful period, several highly experimental forms of modernism briefly thrived. Significant achievements occurred in graphics, posters, flyers, and pamphlets. Built buildings were few.

Vladimir Tatlin (1885–1953) started out as a painter and attended the Moscow School of Painting, Sculpture, and Architecture. Initially he painted icons, displaying his skill with Russian traditional painting techniques. He worked for a while as a stage designer. He grew increasingly aware of the avant-garde developments of Western European art. Influenced by the October Revolution of 1917, he joined the cadre of architects who sought to express the spirit of the revolution in architecture. Tatlin's Monument to the Third International, 1919–1920, was a spiral tower with technologically derived forms. The movement associated with Tatlin, Constructivism (or Russian Constructivism), involved artists who pursued a program of rational design based on functional processes, the tectonics of reinforced concrete, the possibilities of metal, and the utopian ideals appropriate to a socialist society.

Konstantin Melnikov (1890–1974) was a Russian modernist architect, mostly active in the 1920s. He built six workers' clubs in the period 1927–1929 in the Moscow area. His own house in Krivoarbatskiy Lane was built in 1927–1929. He sought a new way of designing buildings that was to emerge from Russian traditions and Russian mysticism, rather than relying on importing Western European technologies and styles. Initially, his work was in step with the dramatic break from tsarist society to the Soviet socialist society. After a short period of time, mass taste and official doctrine meant that the officially sanctioned Soviet architecture became a bombastic version of classicism. From 1938, Melnikov was not allowed to practice because his design aesthetic was sharply at odds with the new Soviet realist style.

Le Corbusier built a building in Moscow, 1928–1936. The problems he had seeing his building built were a harbinger of the difficulties that modernism was to have in the Soviet Union.

MACKINTOSH

Charles Rennie Mackintosh (1868–1928) resists easy categorization, and in fact, Mackintosh's works are frequently found in books on Arts and Crafts,

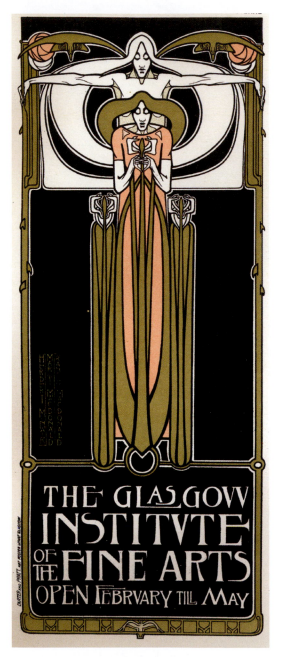

Figure 20.12 Charles Rennie Mackintosh. Watercolor for the Glasgow Institute, 1896-1898.

Figure 20.13 Charles Rennie Mackintosh. Willow Tea Rooms, Room de Luxe. Glasgow, Scotland, 1904.

Art Nouveau, or even Prairie Style. (Junichi Shimomura includes Mackintosh in a book on Art Nouveau residential architecture; Shinomura 1992.) Mackintosh's graphic work shows the connections between his work and both Arts and Crafts and Art Nouveau two-dimensional works. A watercolor for the Glasgow Institute features a central robed female figure (Figure 20.12). The style of this graphic work bears comparison to Beardsley, Klimt, and Rossetti, and blurs the line between commercial and fine art (Kaplan 1996, p. 301).

His early design work includes a series of tearooms. A later project, the Willow Tea Rooms (Figure 20.13), was in a fashionable area of Glasgow. Roger Billcliffe calls the Room de Luxe, or Ladies Room "one of the most precious interiors that Mackintosh ever designed" (Billcliffe 1984, p. 108).

In 1897, he won a competition to design a new building for the School of Art in Glasgow (Figure 20.14). Unquestionably Mackintosh's masterwork,

it is known for its façade, its details, its interiors, and its furnishings. But it is also a building superbly suited to its site, largely due to its design in section.

A pedestrian walking along Renfrew Street first notices the contrast between the massive stone framework and the broad expanses of industrial-looking glass. The system of broad windows indicates an independent invention from Horta's metal-and-glass exploration for the Maison du Peuple in Brussels. Mackintosh's façade is yet another European example of developments related to the Chicago School's exploration of frame and glass. This building is one step toward the creation of all-glass structures. The massing and the glass relate this to warehouses and factories, yet they are nowhere else designed with such care.

The windows of the School of Art are contrasted by a stern masonry framework. The massive masonry itself is contrasted by iron elements, tensile decorative pieces that stretch into slender threads.

Figure 20.14 Charles Rennie Mackintosh. Glasgow School of Art, Glasgow, Scotland, 1897–1909.

The aspects of the project that most resemble Art Nouveau are the ironwork, railings, and window details. They are loosely based on natural forms. Structurally, the masonry is compression, and the glass and ironwork are tension. This is also figuratively expressed with the contrast of the massive stone piers and the attenuated metalwork.

Mackintosh is one of the designers whose posthumous reputation exceeds anything he enjoyed in his lifetime. Many of his furniture designs are still in production (Figure 20.15). His designs are personal, and they also relate to contemporary developments.

THAILAND

European modernism in the first decades of the twentieth century operated in specific contexts—Paris, Vienna, Weimar, and Amsterdam. When modernism started appearing around the world, the forms functioned as a clarion call for something new and forward-looking. Due to the specifics of the political and cultural context changes were unique to each country. In Thailand, modernism was related to the monarchy and its aftermath, a royal gloss that it lacked in France and Germany.

King Rama V (1853–1910) of Thailand was an

from historical styles and pitting themselves against Art Nouveau. This argument lost some of its currency in this corner of Southeast Asia, where modernism had a different role to play.

The King, who owned several palaces, wanted this one to be in a modern European style. Where other parts of the palace incorporate Baroque and Romanesque elements, and the exterior is mostly Jugendstil, a few of the most innovative rooms, such as the stairwell, are clearly moving in the direction of the Secessionist style that Germany knew because of the buildings in Darmstadt (Figure 20.16). Overall, the building is one in which modernism is not antithetical to historicism, but capable of coexisting with it. The Palace was started in 1910 and finished by the King's equally progressive son, King Rama VI (1881–1925). Thailand thwarted the imperialist policies of England and France, and when members of the royal family looked to hire European architects, they preferred Germans and Italians.

FRANK LLOYD WRIGHT

Frank Lloyd Wright (1867–1959) had a long career. He was prolific, universally acclaimed, and beloved by the masses. Yet his impact on modernism is curiously less than that of Le Corbusier and Mies van der Rohe, even though their austere projects were less likable. Wright is important for two reasons: for his early contribution to modernism, and for his unique contribution to the development of a regional, almost vernacular, American architecture. He is a rare example of an architect, in the top echelon of important architects, who made his career largely by designing houses, and modest ones at that. Wright started out his career working for Adler and Sullivan, and for a time there was stylistic overlap in their work. Particularly with respect to the use of ornament, his early projects bore a similarity to Sullivan's designs.

Figure 20.15 Charles Rennie Mackintosh. Argyle Chair. Glasgow, Scotland.

innovative leader known for his ambitious political and economic reforms. He successfully avoided the colonization attempts of England and France. The King hired a German architect, Karl Döhring, to build a palace for him. Döhring's palace, a modern structure, gestures to the future and affirmed Thailand's place as part of a global culture. So Thailand's brand of vaguely Secessionist-looking architecture derives from the German variant of it. In Vienna, the collective identity of the self-proclaimed Secessionists depended on differentiating themselves

Figure 20.16 Karl Döhring. Phra Ram Ratchaniwet. Bangkok, Thailand.

Houses

He left Sullivan and established his own office, out of his house, in the Chicago suburb of Oak Park, in 1893. Wright's earliest commissions show the influence of Victorian design, Arts and Crafts, and Queen Anne. The Winslow House is at once an inventive house by a prominent architect and one that grows out of the vernacular traditions of American suburbia (Figure 20.17). The Winslow House, River Forest, Illinois, is also one of a few Wright projects that bear a resemblance to Austrian Secessionist works.

The hipped roof is a common feature of American houses, but Wright gives it a strong horizontal profile, so that it reflects the horizontality of the American prairie. He does this by cantilevering the cornice over the façade. By then recessing the second-story windows within a continuous dark band,

he furthers emphasizes the horizon. On later projects, the glazing would be continuous, an American domestic version of Le Corbusier's ribbon window.

The front façade is symmetrical, axial, and grandly formal. A hint of the developments to come is seen in the rear elevation of the Winslow House, in which the internal features push out to the exterior. Wright, like Sullivan, sought to develop a uniquely American, if not Midwestern, type of architecture. Prairie Style, in the realm of residential architecture, had a significant impact. His color palettes derived from indigenous plantings.

The so-called Prairie Style is typically dated from 1900 to World War I. Unlike Arts and Crafts designers, Wright had no instinctual dislike of industry. The family is the cornerstone of family life, and this is symbolically represented in his houses with scrupulous attention to the design of the fire-

Figure 20.17 Frank Lloyd Wright. Winslow House. River Forest, Illinois, 1893.

place, the front door, and the dining room table. These features, in Wright's houses, become icons of the family. The single-family detached house itself became a symbol of the American family. Prairie houses were appealing to clients; appreciating them did not require that one be a member of the avant-garde.

Wright was a believer in crafting a totally designed environment, a belief akin to the Secessionist Gesamtkunstwerk, down to furniture, custom built-ins, and stained-glass windows. Jokes and tales abound about his post-occupancy dealings with clients in which Wright visited completed jobs and set about removing pictures and rearranging furniture.

The *Wasmuth Portfolio*, a 1911 German publication, presented his work to a European audience. The European avant-garde, including Mies van der Rohe, Le Corbusier, and Walter Gropius, embraced Wright. The high-contrast black-and-white photos of the publication made his works look more progressive than they were, as though they were cubist designs by Rietveld. Initially, European audiences knew of his work only through the medium of published photographs. This and subsequent publications, ensured Wright an international prominence that started at an early stage in his career and remained throughout the twentieth century.

Wright's later work was organic, asymmetrical, and grew out of his thinking first about interior volumes. The features that came to be known as the Prairie Style are more pronounced in the Ward Willets House of 1902.

The Winslow House and the Ward Willets House hint at what was to come; with the Robie House, Chicago, Illinois, we see Wright in the middle of producing his Prairie Style houses and in confidant command of his powers.

The defining characteristics of his architec-

Figure 20.18 Frank Lloyd Wright. Robie House, dining room and chairs, Chicago, Illinois, 1908-1910.

ture are also present in his furniture design. The vertical lines of the chairs are formed by a series of simple millwork slats, a detail that Arts and Crafts designer Voysey also employed. The iconic dining room table and chairs of the Robie House make the dining room and its furniture, like the centrally located hearth, a symbol of the family (Figure 20.18). The exaggerated height of the chairs forms an implied space in which the chairs themselves become the boundaries of a transparent "room." While a little unstable for an imbibing diner, the ensemble is visually stunning and at one with its context.

His architectural reification of the nuclear family was perhaps a compensation for his own failings in that direction. His marriage spectacularly fell apart and he left his wife to marry Olgivanna Hinzenberg in 1928. He defaulted on the mortgage of his Wisconsin home and studio, Taliesen. Although often fraught with financial problems himself, Wright was a capitalist, with few of the socialist leanings of his European counterparts.

His primary contribution to modernism is not always visible in his interiors, but is best seen in plan (Figure 20.19). The Martin House has generous living spaces and servants' quarters that wealthy

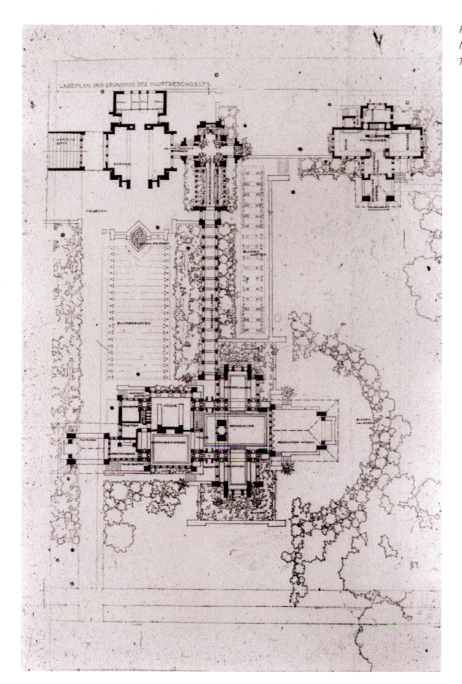

Figure 20.19 Frank Lloyd Wright. Martin House, Buffalo, New York, 1904.

clients demanded. It appeared during the period in which Wright's projects focused heavily on ornamentation.

Cross axes dominated his more expansive floor plans, as they do with the Martin House. The public rooms of the interiors are formed by interconnected but overlapping spaces. Rooms were no longer discrete entities separated by walls and doors but overlapping areas without boundaries; Colin Rowe described this innovation as "transparency" (Rowe 1978). For the Martin House, Wright designed bookcases, tables, upholstered furniture, armchairs and sofas, lamps, rugs, textiles, and stained-glass windows.

In 1905, Wright went to Japan. He admired Japanese architecture and collected Japanese prints.

Figure 20.20 Frank Lloyd Wright. Alice Millard House, exterior wall detail, Pasadena, California.

The decorative period includes one of his largest works, the Imperial Hotel in Tokyo, 1912–1913, for which he also designed the furniture (Meech 2001).

The Museum of Modern Art in New York (MoMA) invited Wright to participate in an exhibition of modern architecture in 1932 (Wojtowicz 2005). The cocurators, Henry-Russell Hitchcock and Philip Johnson, insisted that the design of the exhibition reflect the forward-looking tenor of the projects. Because of the book's title, authored by Johnson and Hitchcock, the exhibition came to be known as "The International Style." The exhibition, the book, and Wright's participation in it are significant moments in the twentieth-century exploration of new ways of designing space. Wright exhibited a large model for an unbuilt house, the House on the Mesa, a project that expressed Wright's belief in the organic expression of nature, landscape, and materials.

In Wright's oeuvre, the relationship between house, material, and landscape achieved its ultimate expression in Falling Water, 1934–1937. This project also illustrates that over the course of his career, his use of glass increased.

Wright visited Rio in the fall of 1931. People around the world did not necessarily copy his forms in Africa, Asia, and Latin America, but his approach to landscape and materials suggested a path for creating a local architecture and not simply importing forms. His midcareer projects display an interest in modularity and grids.

Although known as the preeminent American architect, there is a universalizing aspect to his work. Like other progressive architects of his time, he abhorred the nineteenth-century parade of historical styles, which is not to say that he was categorically opposed to all historical influences, just European ones. He occasionally incorporated elements whose inspiration lay in Aztec, Turkish, or Japanese design history.

In the 1920s, Wright started experimenting with concrete blocks for walls, floors, and ceilings on projects in California, Arizona, and Mexico (Figure 20.20). He called his use of concrete block the "textile-block" system. He experimented with patterns and also used steel reinforcing bars. His work with concrete block drew upon pre-Columbian design for inspiration.

Although primarily a designer of houses, he designed a few unusual skyscrapers. They are particularly innovative in section, relying on a tree-trunk structure, one of which is the Johnson Wax Administration Building. For Johnson Wax, he also designed the open-plan office furniture (Figures 20.21 and 20.22).

Gradually, his work became less decorative and he investigated the possibilities presented by permutations of simple geometries, such as triangular "grids" and round houses.

Wright managed to be modern, local, and universal. He is a key but ambiguous figure in the critical debate surrounding the introduction of European modernism to the United States. Neil Levine says that Wright worked in the European international style yet refocused its energies and made it American. The last structure he completed during his long career affirmed him as a significant modernist, the Solomon Guggenheim Museum in New York.

Figure 20.21 Frank Lloyd Wright. Johnson Wax Administration Building. Chair. Racine, Wisconsin, 1938.

Figure 20.22 Frank Lloyd Wright. Johnson Wax Administration Building. Desk, Racine, Wisconsin, 1938.

CONCLUSION

Chapter 16 examined the reform movements; in Chapters 17 and 18, Africa and Japan faced the technological innovations of the nineteenth century; Chapter 19 presented Art Nouveau. Those chapters and this one, are all answers to the question Where did modernism come from? The rallying point for artists of different movements spread across the globe was their opposition to Victorian historicism, the use of styles, and what they considered to be the degraded state of design. Committed to leaving the nineteenth century behind, artists showed little consensus for how to greet the twentieth, despite more than occasional common interests and points of agreement. Designers were grappling with how to use new materials, like glass and metal, and reconsidering the relationship between decoration and form, and form and function.

With hindsight we see that modernism was percolating across Europe with movements including the Vienna Secession, De Stijl, and Russian Constructivism. In the United States, Frank Lloyd Wright had a different motive for decrying historicism; he sought to create an American architectural vocabulary. Across the globe, pockets of Art Nouveau flourished where the design principles had a different weight—and sometimes were less vigorously maintained. In Thailand and Turkey, an architect could combine forward-looking forms associated with both Art Nouveau and the Secessionists. The proliferation of forerunners to modernism was becoming a global design event.

Even within one design sphere, turn-of-the-century Vienna, there were differing opinions. Loos—the person, his writings, and his designs—were difficult, extreme, and experimental, if truthful. Hoffmann, Klimt, and their artworks, in contrast, were likable, popular, exuberant, if occasionally decadent. Relying on intuition often resulted in designs that appealed to the masses; designing for the masses often resulted in designs that attracted the elite.

The precursors to the modernists were not in lockstep. Yet it would be intellectually lazy to dismiss their collective efforts at change as irreducibly different. The grid and planes had arrived, and with them an industrial aesthetic. Buildings were designed from the inside out, which usually resulted in asymmetry. The status of ornament, history, tradition, and style were all tenuous. This chapter presented the projects, designers, and movements that straddled two centuries, yet there is no doubt that their look was to the future.

Sources

Billcliffe, Roger. *Mackintosh Furniture*. Cambridge: Lutterworth Press, 1984.

Bock, Ralf. *Adolf Loos: Works and Projects*. New York: Rizzoli, 2007.

Boyd, Virginia. *Frank Lloyd Wright and the House Beautiful: Designing an American Way of Living*. Washington, D.C.: International Arts and Artists, 2007.

Carter, Brian. *Johnson Wax Adminstration Building and Research Tower*. London: Phaidon, 1998.

Gravagnuolo, Benedetto. *Adolf Loos: Theory and Works*. New York: Rizzoli, 1982.

Hoever, Peter, ed., *Josef Hoffman Designs*. Munich: Prestel, 1992.

Kaplan, Wendy, ed., *Charles Rennie Mackintosh*. New York: Abbeville, 1996.

Kristan, Marcus. *Adolf Loos: Wohnungen*. Vienna: Album Verlag, 2001.

Meech, Julia. *Frank Lloyd Wright and the Art of Japan: The Architect's Other Passion*. New York: Abrams, 2001.

Pare, Richard, and Jean-Louis Cohen. *Lost Vanguard: Soviet Modernist Architecture, 1922–1932*. New York: Monacelli Press, 2007.

Prat, Nathalie. *Jean Prouvé*. Paris: Galerie Jousse Seguin–Galerie Enrico Navarra, 1998.

Reed, Peter, ed. *The Show to End All Shows: Frank Lloyd Wright and the Museum of Modern Art, 1940*. New York: Museum of Modern Art, 2004.

Rowe, Colin, and Fred Koetter. *Collage City*. Cambridge: MIT Press, 1978.

Safran, Yehuda. Adolf Loos, from *The Dictionary of Art*, vol. 19. New York: Macmillan, 1996: p. 652.

Sarnitz, August. *Adolf Loos, 1870–1933: Architect, Cultural Critic, Dandy*. Cologne: Taschen, 2003.

Shimomura, Junichi. *Art Nouveau Architecture: Residential Masterpieces 1892–1911*. San Francisco: Cadence Books, 1992.

Storner, William. *The Frank Lloyd Wright Companion*. Chicago: University of Chicago Press, 2006.

Topp, Leslie. "Otto Wagner and the Steinhof Psychiatric Hospital: Architecture as Misunderstanding." *Art Bulletin* 87, no. 1 (March 2005): 130–156.

Witt-Dörring, Christian, ed. *Josef Hoffmann: Interiors 1902–1913*. New York: Neue Galerie, 2006.

Wojtowicz, Robert. "A Model House and a House's Model: Reexamining Frank Lloyd Wright's House on the Mesa Project." *Journal of the Society of Architectural Historians* 64, no. 4 (December 2005): 522–551.

DISCUSSION AND REVIEW QUESTIONS

1. How did the Vienna Secessionists formally predict modern trends?
2. How were the forerunners to modernism reacting against Victorian design?
3. In what ways did the Secessionists not live up to their own antidecorative stance?
4. What were some of the materials that they favored, and what does this say about their art?
5. What is meant by transparency in plan?
6. What made Prairie Style local? Why did people around the world admire it?
7. Loos equated the use of ornament to a lower level of societal development. Give evidence for and against this position.
8. What did the Secessionists have in common with Art Nouveau proponents, and how did they differ?

CHAPTER 21

HEROIC MODERNISM
MYTHS AND REALITIES

1919–1931	1929	1938–1941	1939–1940	1939–1945
Bauhaus	Barcelona Chair	Breuer in Britain	Aalto's Finnish Pavilion	WW II

This chapter is subtitled "Myths and Realities" because the self-proclaimed modernists were bent on creating a myth of their endeavors. They were not merely designing but purposely forging a movement. And more so than the leaders of other artistic movements, modernist designers succeeded in constructing a myth, a story complete with gods, lesser gods and goddesses, and shining temples on the hill. Despite decades of scholars who have examined the premises and products of modernism, and debunked many of the myths (that modernist architecture was white, that it developed only in France and Germany), it is astonishing that as much as our knowledge of modernism as a pluralistic phenomenon grows, its status as a simplified iconic entity remains. It's almost as though the more challenges to it, the more resolute it becomes. The hold of modernism on the contemporary consciousness is so strong that the movements and submovements that followed it, such as postmodernism and deconstruction, are defined in relation to modernism. Many architects and designers today describe what they do in relationship to modernism.

Modernism is a slippery term, something French sociologist Bruno Latour addresses in his book *We Have Never Been Modern* (1993). Latour's paradoxical point is that people of most epochs have sought to be current. Many people confuse modern and contemporary because the words are used indiscriminately. Here, "modern" refers to the grand period of the avant-garde, associated first with Germany and France, and later other parts of Europe, of the 1920s and 1930s, and the style associated with it, leaving the word "contemporary" to refer to the current state of affairs.

EARLY MODERNISM

Although it often seems as though modernism arrived out of nowhere, with the wisdom of hindsight we see that many nineteenth-century artistic endeavors—Art Nouveau, the aesthetic movements, and Prairie Style—were exploring specific issues that contributed to the modern movement. In addition, there was the development of skyscrapers, railroad stations, elevators, moving pictures, automobiles, and photography. While many roads led to modernism, in the early 1920s two countries, Germany and France, were particularly important, and especially the individual contributions of three men:

Walter Gropius (1883–1969), Mies van der Rohe (1886–1969), and Le Corbusier (1887–1965).

Modernism is a term used by many professions, although their views of Modernism are not all the same. When considering Modernism in art, music, literature, dance, and theater, certain similarities bridge the disciplinary divides. Proponents of Modernism shared several premises, most important the break with the past and the embrace of the present and future. The machine was a source of aesthetic inspiration, taking the central place once held by nature. *Functionalism* was a term used in many professions to describe the new way of designing.

Most of the modernists presented themselves and their work as a break from the past, and in many respects this was true. They were openly critical of architects whose designs incorporated historic references. An attitude that united the modernist designers was the belief that nineteenth-century Victorian designers, distracted by eclecticism, or the battle of styles, had it wrong. George Kates, a collector of classical Chinese furniture, is one of those who, writing about his experiences in the 1930s, made clear that he was no less than contemptuous of "the general level of taste in our stupid nineteenth century" (Kates 1952).

A corollary to rejecting the past was embracing the present and looking toward the future. Largely because of technological innovations, the modernists felt that the twentieth century was uniquely different from other time periods and required a new approach to design. Interior design historian John Pile writes: "The most important development in early twentieth-century design was the emergence of a design vocabulary appropriate to the modern world of advanced technology and the new patterns of life that it brought about" (Pile 2000, p. 323). Modernism was finally an expression of interior design, architecture, and furniture design that embraced the achievements of the previous century's Industrial Revolution.

The Bauhaus

The Bauhaus is a building, and it was a design school, a movement, a revolution to some, and, arguably, a style. From their base in Dessau, Germany, students and instructors created works that are virtually synonymous with classical modernism. In 1911, the architect Walter Gropius had achieved great success with his innovative design for the Fagus Shoe Factory in Alfeld an der Leine, Germany. Gropius was fresh from working in the Berlin office of Peter Behrens, where, astonishingly, for a brief period in 1910 his coworkers included Charles Edouard Jeanneret, later known as Le Corbusier, and Mies van der Rohe.

The famed city of Weimar, home to Goethe, Schiller, Nietzsche, and Liszt, had two schools related to the arts, a school of fine art and a school of applied art. When Gropius became director, he merged them and bestowed upon the single entity the name "Staatliches Bauhaus," thus indicating the close relationship between art and craft. Simply referred to as "the Bauhaus," the new name signaled Gropius's intention to take the school in a new direction, and with it the future of architecture and design. The mantra of the school was to espouse all the principles we now know as modernism, and Gropius and his colleagues had specific pedagogic methods in mind for how an academic institution could achieve them.

In 1925, the Bauhaus relocated to Dessau, Germany. For that propitious move, Gropius designed several buildings, including, most famously, the Bauhaus (Figure 21.1). Since the time of Gothic cathedrals, architects have sought to create what seemed impossible: a wall of glass. Glass is not a structural material; it can barely support its own weight, and the slightest tensile force causes it to shatter. One of the significant modern achievements is the separation of structure from wall, which has several implications. With the signature building

Figure 21.1 Walter Gropius. Bauhaus, 1925–1926. Dessau, Germany.

of the Bauhaus, the glass sheathing surrounding the design studios is effectively hung from the floor slabs; hence the term "curtain wall." This is the technology that rendered skyscraper façades, or "skins," possible. It also signified new spatial developments on the interior, which was no longer a suite of individual rooms but an open free-plan flooded with natural light. An added benefit is that the Bauhaus building positively glows at night.

Those working inside the Bauhaus forged a new approach to design pedagogy, as well as promoting modern design. Its educational philosophy was an alternative to the Beaux-Arts approach. The Bauhaus curriculum was interdisciplinary and considered the knowledge of craftwork essential to being a designer. It was egalitarian in theory, with a large number of women and foreign students. It promoted

functionalism, which was a code word for modernism. The trajectory of a student's education included a year of general instruction, followed by hands-on experience in a workshop, with a final project.

The interdisciplinarity of the Bauhaus exhibited itself over the years in a variety of specializations. Many workshops devoted to one discipline were taught by artists and professionals who practiced in another. The areas of specialization included architecture, town planning, interior design, furniture design, advertising, exhibition design, stage design, photography, film, dance, textiles, fashion, and the creation of objects in wood, metal, or ceramics. The roster of teachers recruited by Gropius included Paul Klee, Wassily Kandinsky, Josef Albers, László Moholy-Nagy, and Marcel Breuer. Another central tenet of the Bauhaus was that designers, if properly trained, knew how to design in an abstract sense and, with the correct outlook, could design anything. They could put their talents to use on objects of any scale and type, including such diverse objects as cigarette packages, buses, and bus stops.

Walter Gropius

Gropius designed a suite of furniture for the Feder department stores in 1927, an important year for the modern movement (Figure 21.2). Gropius's furniture designs are important in the history of office furniture because of their materials, method of fabrication and installation, design, and function. The pieces were made of plastic laminate, metal tubing, and plywood—all straightforward materials. Because of their modularity and standardized parts, they could be prefabricated and manufactured on an assembly line, which eased their eventual installation. Their rectilinear design was straightforward, there were no superfluous details, and they responded to the need for storage and the actual process of working in an office.

Mies van der Rohe and Lilly Reich

The same year, 1927, Mies, who would be the final director of the Bauhaus, oversaw a project that was a who's who of European modernist architects, the Weissenhofsiedlung in Stuttgart (Joedicke 1990). Mies was responsible for the site plan and one of the buildings of the combination building exhibition and housing project. Other buildings were done by Le Corbusier, Mart Stam, and Walter Gropius. Mies hired a young designer, Lilly Reich, to oversee the exhibition halls in Stuttgart that accompanied the architectural exhibition. Lilly Reich was born in Berlin in 1885. Mies was born in Aachen in 1886 and had moved to Berlin in 1905. After working for Behrens he became vice president of the Deutscher Werkbund, a showcase for German design in Frankfurt.

Reich assumed command of the artistic direction

Figure 21.2 Walter Gropius. Furniture for Feder Stores, 1927.

Figure 21.3 Ludwig Mies van der Rohe. Tugendhat House, Brno, Czechoslovakia, 1928–1930.

of the exhibition halls of the Weissenhofsiedlung, and she personally designed the clean, modern layouts. Reich's career involved a variety of design activities, including store windows, exhibition displays, and fashion design. A talented designer, her contributions have only recently achieved attention, decades after her death. Prior to meeting Mies, Reich had directed the exhibitions at the Werkbund. The entire period of Mies's involvement with furniture is coincident with his personal relationship with Lilly Reich, approximately 1924–1927 (McQuaid 1996).

Gropius resigned as director of the Bauhaus in 1928 and Hannes Meyer took his place, a tenure fraught with tension. In 1930, Mies became director, a position he held until the Nazis shuttered the Bauhaus.

During the time of the van der Rohe/Reich collaborations, Mies designed and completed a sumptuous villa in Brno, Czechoslovakia. One of the most important innovations of the modern movement figured into the house's design: the separation of building from structure. In a view of the dining area of van der Rohe's Tugendhat House (1929), columns stand separate from a curved wooden partition that is crisp and thin (Figure 21.3). The building's structural elements are different entities from

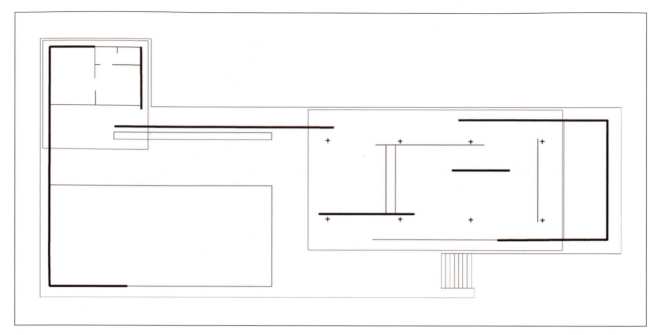

Figure 21.4 Ludwig mies van der Rohe. Barcelona Pavilion, 1928–1929.

those that define spatial regions. The semicircle provides an elegant backdrop for dinner, a modern and open rendition of a formal dining room. Curves are not normally associated with Mies's work, but he occasionally uses them to great effect. The shiny X-shaped stainless-steel columns support the flat plane of the roof. The simple sled-based cantilevered chairs, used as dining chairs, came to be known as Brno chairs. They proved extremely successful in post-WW II office buildings.

The jewel of Mies's early efforts came in 1928 when he received, on short notice, the commission to design the German Pavilion at the International Exhibition at Barcelona, commonly known as the Barcelona Pavilion (Figure 21.4). Other parts of the exhibition featured cavernous halls that contained all sorts of items on display, including furniture, some by Reich, some by Mies, and some collaborations. The Barcelona Pavilion, the highlight of their design efforts, was practically designed overnight and served a specific purpose. A modest-size pavilion, its function was to provide the setting for an inaugural ceremony with the Spanish king and queen,

Alfonso XII and Victoria Eugénie, to sign their names in a golden book (Safran 2005, p. 53).

In the Barcelona Pavilion, X-shaped columns similar to those of the Tugendhat house support the flat roof. A series of vertical planes slip and slide, denoting the various areas where separate functions were to take place. With a clear debt to Frank Lloyd Wright, there are no individual rooms but a series of spaces that are transparent and overlap.

Mies, more so than anyone, employed luxurious materials in his designs, as evidenced by the Barcelona Pavilion, in which expensive wood and marble dominate (Figure 21.5). The initial building was a temporary structure for an exhibition; it was rebuilt in 1986 at great expense. (Safran 2000.) Le Corbusier criticized the use of luxurious materials in his publication on decoration.

The pavilion featured two copies of a chair designed for the opening ceremony: the Barcelona chair (Figure 21.6). It is therefore no less than a modest version of a royal throne. The matching ottoman was also influential, as the detailing of its legs became the basis for a bench and a coffee table (Glaeser 1977,

Figure 21.5 Mies van der Rohe. Barcelona Pavilion.

Figure 21.6 Mies van der Rohe and Lilly Reich. Barcelona Chairs and Ottomons, 1928.

p. 12). One of the most successful chairs of all time, the Barcelona chair had a particularly grand debut. The chair and the building whose name it bears are milestones of twentieth-century design. The deceptively simple piece of furniture is made of stainless-steel bar-stock, with horse-hair cushions covered in pigskin and delineated with welts and buttons.

The original chairs were chrome-plated. Mies came to prefer using stainless steel, as the chrome plating tended to flake. An exquisite piece, it was not initially meant for mass production nor to be particularly comfortable. The original cushions were made out of white kid leather and fastened with straps and buckles. The Barcelona chair came after a period in which Mies and Reich developed a series of utilitarian chairs made of tubular metal. In the nuanced vocabulary of modern furniture, bar-stock is a more elite material than tubing.

The Barcelona chair was designed in 1928 and has been in continuous production since then. George Nelson, an accomplished postwar furniture designer, included Mies's Barcelona chair in his publication of 1953. He wrote: "The chair, like all of his buildings and furniture, has been designed with the most painstaking attention to detail and demands perfect execution" (Nelson 1953, p. 133). The signature work of Mies and Reich, the Barcelona line is successful because of its creators' unwavering attention to detail and quality. Nelson also notes that the Barcelona chair is "One of the most costly pieces in production, it has no substitute where the height of elegance is the aim of the interior designer" (Nelson 1953, p. 133).

The Barcelona chair looks reasonably comfortable, with its raked back, and has pleasing lines. It sits close to the ground, yet it is really not meant for relaxing. It is well suited for the use it usually finds itself in—in the lobbies of contemporary apartment buildings and waiting rooms of corporations.

In the 1930s, after the Barcelona Pavilion and chair, Mies did studies for several chaise longue designs, although they were never built. For the Villa

Figure 21.7 Mies van der Rohe and Lily Reich. MR Chair, 1927. Nickel-plated tubular steel, cane seat.

Tugendhat he designed a chair that is similar to the Barcelona chair, although it is slightly larger and more comfortable (Blaser 1982, pp. 66–72). The Tugendhat chair (1930) seems an improvement over the Barcelona chair, yet it ultimately proved less successful. Several variations of another successful Mies/Reich design, the MR chair, exist, with and without arms, and with a variety of seating materials (Figure 21.7). Steel tubing is not used in a minimalist way but to form elegant curves that are just short of being extravagant. It is another example of the artistic and commercial success of the furniture that resulted from the collaboration of Mies and Reich.

Women in the Bauhaus

The year 1931 saw Mies and Reich collaborate in the Berlin Building Exhibition, which more or less marks the end of his involvement in furniture. Gunta Stölzl (1897–1983), a former student, had been director of the Bauhaus weaving workshop, and the creator, throughout her long career, of many successful textile designs, but she left in 1931 for

Figure 21.8 Lilly Reich. International Exposition Barcelona, German textiles exhibit.

Switzerland. In 1932, Mies hired Lilly Reich to teach at the Bauhaus in Dessau, taking over for Stölzl as director of its weaving and interiors workshops.

The appointments of first Stölzl and then Reich as directors of a workshop highlight the prominence of women in the modern movement, and specifically at the Bauhaus, as both students and instructors. Although in theory the Bauhaus did not treat women differently, revealing the school's aims for social equality, they tended to specialize in "women's crafts," textiles, furniture, ceramics, and industrial design. The 1920s in the United States saw the rise of women as professional decorators. In the same period in Germany, women associated with the Bauhaus made serious inroads toward equality in the design world.

Reich's design for an exhibit promoting German textiles is indicative of the simple layouts she created for a variety of exhibition halls, known for their clarity and straightforward organization (Figure 21.8).

The word most often connected to the early designs of the avant-garde was *functionalism*. This is the word the modernist designers used to describe their work. Their works did not constitute a style, they constantly stressed, but were simple expressions of a logical and rational approach to design. The Frankfurt kitchen is a case of a professional female designer employing her talents on a project to help the plight of women homemakers. A central tenet of the Bauhaus philosophy is that well-trained designers could apply their talents to any task. Grete Schütte-Lihotzky's Frankfurt kitchen is incredibly complex, designed down to the level of detail of where to store salt (Figure 21.9). It had a tremendous impact. It impressed many with its hygienic and efficient appearance.

Figure 21.9 Grete Schütte-Lihotzky. Frankfurt kitchen, 1926.

Occasionally, there were conflicting attitudes toward design and method of creation among the Bauhaus leaders. One example involves the faculty and their approach to craftsmanship. They officially espoused an anti-elitist position and respected the knowledge of those who crafted objects and were familiar with construction techniques. The division of the school into workshops underscores the belief that knowledge of design could only grow out of the experience of making things.

The Weimar Bauhaus had a metal workshop, and students produced a variety of cooking and serving pieces, pots and pans, coffee and tea services, and household items such as electrical lamps. Exhibiting the influence of the Cubist movement on their designs, most products stayed as close to pure

Figure 21.10 Marianne Brandt. Glass and aluminum ceiling lighting fixture. Bauhaus, Dessau, 1926.

geometries as possible, departing only for functional reasons. The most talented student in the workshop was Marianne Brandt, who excelled at making light fixtures. Brandt stayed with the workshop in its move to Dessau, eventually becoming its director. The metal workshop reflected a gradual shift in the school's allegiance to craftsmanship, a shift encouraged by Gropius. To extol the virtues of craft is one thing; to put it into practice is another, especially for a school and a movement committed to industrial production. Bauhaus instructors were ideologically committed to a machine aesthetic, and many of their writings express antipathy for what they saw as the retrograde Arts and Crafts movement. An uneasy truce was realized by a shift in their philosophy. Bauhaus students and teachers were to create models, crafted by hand, that were destined for industrial assembly-line production. Brandt excelled under these guidelines; many of her metal and glass lamps were mass-produced, and some still are.

Marianne Brandt's deceptively simple design for a ceiling light fixture is one of the many examples of Bauhaus-designed products that have become ubiquitous (Figure 21.10).

Graphics, Theater, Dance, and Film

The debate over the role of craftsmanship, meaning work by human hands, and industrial production, meaning work by machine, also occurred when considering the construction of buildings. Even though buildings such as the Villa Tugendhat displayed a machine aesthetic, smooth lines, alternating shiny and honed materials, and planar surfaces, the method of construction remained, as it always had been, accomplished by hand. Mies himself had worked as a bricklayer, a skill he was always proud to demonstrate.

The Bauhaus revolution touched all areas of the arts, including painting, graphics, photography, furniture design, and collages. The modern era that was being forged in the Bauhaus workshops required an adequate graphic representation and found it under the leadership of Moholy-Nagy. In his workshop, students worked in a variety of graphic activities, including wood blocks, lithographs, and typography, a department that would today be considered graphic design and advertising. Moholy-Nagy and others were interested in developing a modern typeface (Kostelanetz 1970, p. 77).

Moholy-Nagy arrived at the Bauhaus in 1923. His work was informed by his knowledge of the work of El Lissitzky, Man Ray, and de Stijl artists Rietveld, Mondrian, and van Doesburg. He believed that the photograph would eventually triumph over painting (Staatliches Bauhaus Weimar 1923, p. 141). He sought to improve the visual effectiveness of graphic layouts, relying on simplicity, legibility, and also a dynamic placement of text and image. The title page designed by him in the year of his arrival is an early step (Figure 21.11). It has vertical type, and the junction of horizontal and vertical indirectly creates a visual flow on the diagonal.

In the Bauhaus tradition of exhibiting competency in several artistic realms, Oscar Schlemmer (1883–1943), polymath to the core, is credited as a painter, sculptor, teacher, choreographer, costume

Figure 21.11 Laszlo Moholy-Nagy. Title page, 1923.

designer, and dancer (Gropius 1960). He taught the introductory course in design at the Bauhaus.

Considering the hard edges and pure forms of Bauhaus buildings, interiors, and furnishings, it is not immediately apparent how that approach would resonate with artists, such as Schlemmer, whose primary subject was the human figure. In Schlemmer's metal sculptures, one sees the connection between his work and that of other Cubist artists (Figure 21.12). Schlemmer reduced the human anatomy to basic forms, and he then formed the human figure as a series of connected geometric shapes.

Cubism as an artistic movement predated the Bauhaus designers. Colin Rowe, among others, feels that the modernist impulse appeared in art before it did in architecture, especially in the paintings of Ozenfant, Le Corbusier, Juan Gris, and Pablo Picasso.

Schlemmer was anxious to carry his novel approach to the human figure to the world of theater, in which he was also active. He conceived and choreographed a ballet, *The Triadic Ballet,* for which he created innovative costumes. The French phrase

"success d'estime" is perfect to describe Schlemmer's ballets that, by all accounts, were more interesting than entertaining. The Bauhaus performances explored Schlemmer's unusual approach to the human figure, an approach opposite the direction of portraiture: There is a disavowal of any features in the direction of particularity or sentiment; he was not interested in a naturalistic portrayal of the body in displaying any anecdote, narrative, or emotion, nor in overtly pleasing a viewer of an artwork or a member of the audience. His works explore movement, color, the relationship of the human body to pure geometries, and the position of geometries in three-dimensional space. His sculpture is similar to the costumes he developed for the ballet. Howard Dearstyne, one of the few American Bauhaus students, saw the mechanical ballet and commented:

Figure 21.12 Oskar Schlemmer. Abstract figure.

I encountered something new when I saw Schlemmer's players on the stage. From one to three persons participated. No word was spoken, no story suggested by sign or gesture, no human emotion communicated to the audience. It was unrelated to any drama I had enjoyed in New York City. The performances consisted solely of bodily movements synchronized with music, a form of dance. The movements were abrupt, staccato, angular—more like mobile geometry than fluid arabesques. The performers appeared only remotely human, as did the mannequins in Schlemmer's paintings, divested of their human identity and wholly of their individuality by being encased in costumes which converted them into assemblages of geometric shapes. (Dearstyne 1986, pp. 174–175)

Schlemmer's interest in mechanical-looking movements and figures, and his mixture of puppets, marionettes, and heavily costumed human figures, all worked together to deemphasize the flesh of the humans.

Bauhaus Furniture

Marcel Breuer (1902–1981), born in Hungary, taught at the Bauhaus in the 1920s and eventually became the head of the school's cabinetmaking shop. He expressed an interest in crafting modern furniture from the start (Hyman 2001). In Breuer's postwar career, his most famous commission was the UNESCO building in Paris. Less well-known as an architect than Mies and Gropius, he was extremely productive and successful with his furniture designs.

Many of the early modernists sought the holy grail of modern furniture design: to make the first modern inexpensive chair out of tubular metal. Mart Stam (1899–1986), a Dutch architect who moved to Berlin in the 1920s, is credited with designing the first cantilevered steel tubular chair, a milestone in furniture design. Stam married Lotte Beese, a former Bauhaus student. His chair attracted the attention of Mies van der Rohe and Marcel Breuer, who followed suit by adopting Stam's ideas in their own designs. This simple idea achieved its most elegant and financially successful iteration with Marcel Breuer's Cesca chair of 1925 (Wilk 1981).

In the 1930s, due to growing pressure and interference from the Nazis, Breuer relocated to London. There, he created several pieces of furniture for the Isokon Company, one of the early producers of modern design in the United Kingdom. His work in London is known for expanding the initially limited palette of modernist building materials. He designed a building that incorporated large expanses of roughly cut stone. For one desk, he used glass as the top (Figure 21.13). His Long Chair was one of many experiments with plywood. Breuer's stay in England was short-lived, and he soon ended up in the United States.

In 1933, the Bauhaus closed.

A position that several designers took up—notably Charlotte Perriand (1903–1999), Le Corbusier, Mies van der Rohe, and Alvar Aalto—was an appreciation of types, the idea that certain industries had produced exquisite examples of design (possibly unknowingly), and that the role of the designer was to pick them out and use them, or, in other words, to be an industrial connoisseur. Sinks, radiators, and Thonet chairs fall into this category.

Michael Thonet (1796–1871) started a company that produced a broad line of products, yet it is famous for two: a bentwood rocking chair and an inexpensive café chair. The firm, Gebrüder Thonet, was successful with their innovative method of bending wood with steam. Millions of their inexpensive chairs were sold, and they are still seen in restaurants and coffeehouses around the world. A detail of Thonet's café chair graces this book's cover.

Figure 21.13 Marcel Breuer. Desk, 1935–1936. Sycamore veneer, chromium-plated tubular metal, glass, linoleum, and rubber fittings. Manufactured by Isokon Furniture Co.

FRANCO MODERNISM

Outside of Germany and Holland, the other major center of early modernist design activity was France. Le Corbusier dominated the scene, although, the so-called School of Paris was diverse in its members and their work.

Le Corbusier

Born in Switzerland, he headed to Berlin and worked for Peter Behrens in 1910 and 1911. In 1917, Le Corbusier decamped to Paris and set up an office with his cousin, Pierre Jeanneret (1896–1967).

At an exhibition of decorative arts in Paris in 1925, Le Corbusier presented his vision for the domestic interior with his furnished Esprit-Nouveau Pavilion. The prototype for a residence was a modular design in several respects. It featured modular storage units and standard pieces of furniture (Marcus 2000). Using pieces that were typical, cheap, and obvious, it was possible to craft a comfortable and sophisticated interior that was an emancipation from Victorian design. The design centers on a

double-height living space, a strategy that Le Corbusier used to great effect later in the Unité d'Habitation, Marseilles, his solution for large-scale public housing. (Curiously, although the Unité became the paradigm for public housing worldwide, it was a privately owned building.) The unit was also an exploration of modularity on a larger scale, because it was his intention that it could be repeated to constitute an entire apartment building. Cubist art decorated the walls in both projects. The Esprit-Nouveau Pavilion was a prototype, the Unité a realized housing project based on it. A built-in storage unit of the latter acted as a space divider between the kitchen and the double-height living space (Figure 21.14).

Le Corbusier was not fond of the term "decorative art," because "decorative art can no longer be considered compatible with the framework of contemporary thought" (Le Corbusier 1925, p. 115). Although he felt that the word "design" was too broad, he preferred it, as it validated the modernist insistence on functionalism: "It seems to incorporate all the theory of rationalism: the use of new techniques,

Figure 21.14 Le Corbusier, Utility kitchen in a duplex apartment in the Unité d'Habitation, a housing complex in Marseilles, 1946–1952.

weightlessness combined with solidity, the juxtaposition of different kinds of materials, and above all the concept of maximum functionalism."

The project Le Corbusier designed for his friend, the artist Amédée Ozenfant, also prominently features a double-height space (Figure 21.15). It includes many details that came to be associated with Le Corbusier and modernism itself. It incorporates ribbon windows, curved ramps and stairways, metal railings, Thonet chairs, and a corner made of glass. In traditional architecture, corners are structurally important because they hold up the roof. So to have glass meet glass at a corner (Frank Lloyd Wright was fond of this) is a bravura move, to proclaim that the rules have changed.

Charlotte Perriand and Furniture

Charlotte Perriand, an associate of Le Corbusier, was born in Paris and studied at the École de l'Union Centrale des Art Décoratifs. After having finished her studies, she contributed to the Salon d'Automne of 1927 (McLeod 2003, p. 15). She intended her project, *le bar sous le toit,* to garner attention and evidently it did (Perriand 2003, p. 13). Le Corbusier and his coworkers were impressed, and Perriand started working in his office; Perriand worked for him from 1927 to 1937. Hired to concentrate on the studio's furniture design and production, she was responsible for their interiors work and promoting their designs in a series of prominent exhibitions (Musée des Arts Décoratifs 1985, p. 18).

Figure 21.15 Le Corbusier. Paris house and studio for Amédée Ozenfant, 1923.

Le Corbusier was already a major force in architecture, having published widely, although his greatest commissions were still to come. When he met Perriand, he was smarting from not receiving the commission for his innovative League of Nations Project (Perriand 2003, p. 55). While working for Le Corbusier, Perriand organized showing their furniture designs at the Salons d'Automne of 1928 and 1929. Perriand's design emphasizes the horizontal, with a modular storage unit on the right literally reflecting the ribbon window on the left. Lounge seating, a chaise-longue, and arm chairs from the Le Corbusier/Perriand/Jeanneret collaboration furnish the space (Figure 21.16).

Perriand and Le Corbusier were well aware of Thonet's bentwood chairs, and their chaise is reminiscent of Thonet's rocking chair of 1860. They frequently used Thonet chairs in their projects, such as the Salvation Army hostel, the Swiss Pavilion resident hall at the Cité Universitaire in Paris, the Esprit Nouveau Pavilion, and Ozenfant's Studio. Many of the pieces designed by Le Corbusier and Perriand shown at the salons were subsequently produced by Thonet.

Their lounge chair made its debut at the Salon d'Automne of 1928 (Figure 21.17). It has double tubing at the sides and an integral prolongation of the chaise acts as the footrest. Despite its formal

Figure 21.16 Charlotte Perriand. Salon d'Automne.

similarity to Thonet's bentwood rocker, the chaise longue is not a rocking chair. The position is decided upon by the sitter before climbing aboard; once sat upon, it remains in a fixed position.

While working together on the chaise, they agonized over the base, eventually deciding on lacquered sheet metal, inspired by products in an aviation catalog. While not intentional, the legs resemble horse hooves. Perriand tracked down pony skin and calfskin from Parisian furriers. The chaise longue, with its use of pony skin, evokes the modernist interest in "the primitive." This is parallel to Picasso's interest in African art, as exemplified by his painting *Les Demoiselles d'Avignon*. Their use of animal hides suggests a desire to find simple materials, a search for the vestigial.

Perriand reiterated Le Corbusier's three-pronged philosophy about furniture, thereby indicating her total agreement with it: A modern furniture piece should strive to be a "standard unit"; it should act as an artificial limb; and it should embrace new technology. Le Corbusier and Perriand reveled in finding common manufactured objects, such as radiators, sinks, and telephones, that they considered "standard units" in which industrial processes responded perfectly to human needs. The use of types was also true of Bauhaus designers, many of whom used Thonet chairs when furnishing their houses at the Weissenhofsiedlung. Le Corbusier and Perriand sought to do the same for the human activities of sitting and reclining, creating pieces that operated in a clearly logical and functional way.

Figure 21.17 Le Corbusier, Pierre Jeanneret, and Charlotte Perriand. Chaise-longue, 1928. Tubular metal frame, H-base, and ponyskin.

Another consistent design goal of their furniture is "that household objects can be regarded as artificial limbs, or decorative art turned orthopedic." In her memoirs, Charlotte Perriand (2003) wrote: "While our chair designs were directly related to the position of the human body, . . . they were also determined by the requirements of architecture, setting, and prestige" (p. 29). With the chaise they were successful. When viewed in profile, it copies the form of the human body, with its round cushion taking the place of the human head. Many have noted that it acts as an armature not only of the body but of the mind. It seems perfectly suited to serve as a Freudian couch, something on many people's minds in those days.

By its appearance, the chaise seems to operate in a functional mode and eschew decoration. Made of tubular metal, it has no extraneous decoration but its decorative aspects, as they may be, derive from and are contiguous with the structure.

Of the many women active in the early days of modernism, our knowledge of Charlotte Perriand's contribution is precise, because her relationship with Le Corbusier was strictly professional, so history is not complicated by the specter of love and marriage. Her career garnered considerable attention later in life when she was able to document her work. Perriand published her memoirs in 1998 (and published them in English in 2003). Unlike the uncertainty that surrounds the contributions of Lilly Reich (and Aino Aalto, see page 504), Perriand's role is clear: "I worked with Pierre Jeanneret at the atelier on full-scale designs during the day, fine tuning them with Corbu in the evenings" (Perriand 2003, p. 30).

Figure 21.18 Le Corbusier, Charlotte Perriand. Gran Confort chair, 1928.

The Le Corbusier/Jeanneret/Perriand chaise longue was not initially successful. Because of its formal severity, for years it was one of the least popular pieces of contemporary design. Germany and France were, initially, the leaders of modernism, and it is curious how the biography of Charlotte Perriand repeats many of the details of the life of Lilly Reich. A woman is born in a European metropolis, studies decorative arts, and forms an alliance with a talented member of the avant-garde who hails from elsewhere. The primary difference is that Reich and Mies were intimately involved, whereas the relationship between Perriand and Le Corbusier was strictly professional.

Le Corbusier's and Perriand's chair, the Gran Confort chair, shown in Figure 21.18, is a frame of steel tubing filled with several removable leather-upholstered cushions. It also came in a two-seater, and was one of their most successful designs.

Housing

Le Corbusier's Maison Domino diagram relates to his interiors work and his urban design (Figure 21.19). Often compared to the Abbé Laugier's eighteenth-century primitive hut, it reduces a building to its barest elements. Colin Rowe, ever the jokester, compared it to a club sandwich complete with toothpicks; he more seriously added that "by returning to origins and first principles, we recover purity" (Rowe 1994, pp. 56–57). This minimal icon of building-as-shelter consists of the structural support of columns, the horizontal planes of the floor slabs, and the stair that vertically connects them. The implication is that space-defining pieces, conspicuously absent, constitute a fourth element. So the architectural features that define space are not structurally operative. This diagram is significant for the development of the modern field of corporate interior design, for essentially what interior designers do when designing a space for a company in a skyscraper is work within the column grid and between the floor slabs, an activity predicted and made essential by the Maison Domino.

Although the modernist era was influential for interiors, furnishings, and kitchens, the key modernist figures, in their writings, reserved their most persuasive and fervent language for urban design. An area of concern was social improvement of societal ills and the belief that modern architecture could solve serious urban problems. The modern movement had a significant impact on the global

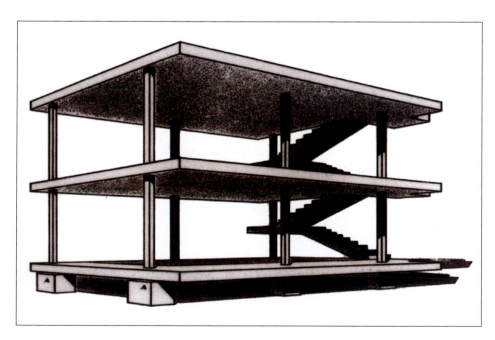

Figure 21.19 Le Corbusier. Maison Domino.

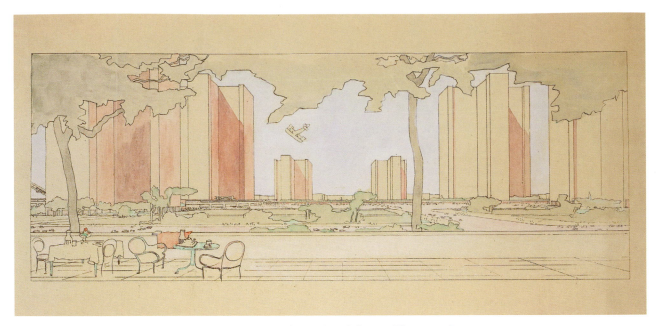

Figure 21.20 Le Corbusier. Contemporary City, 1922, for a city of three million people.

landscape at the urban scale. Many of the modernist impulses—the rupture from tradition, the idealistic utopianism, the pragmatic desire to solve problems, a fetishization of the machine—were mixed up with a naïve but sincere desire to do good on a large scale. This led to a series of planning developments and social engineering initiatives that changed forever the look of cities across the globe.

Urban planners and architects of the 1920s were grappling with the legacy of the nineteenth-century Industrial Revolution and its impact on cities. Cities were crowded, dark, and smelly. Regarding infrastructure, the challenges were enormous. Cities designed for horse-drawn carriages had to be revamped for planes, trains, and automobiles.

Le Corbusier submitted a series of drawings of his urban proposals, a Contemporary City (Ville Contemporaine), at the Salon d'Automne in Paris in 1922 (Figure 21.20). It was the first in a series of urban design proposals that he worked on throughout his career. A pencil drawing shows an al fresco dining area, with Le Corbusier's proposal dominating the background. It is a dramatic alternative to

the historic urban center. The crux of the proposal is a series of twenty-four skyscrapers in a park; this combination was to replace the dense urban fabric of most world cities. By lifting the buildings up on **pilotis**, the verdant ground-plane continued unencumbered, under and through apartment block and office alike. Pilotis are cylindrical columns or piers, but the word was essentially appropriated by Le Corbusier to refer to his projects.

These towers in the park were configured to maximize light and air. The lack of air and light in crowded urban centers had been a big problem for cities. This is an architectural move that, decades later, would be decried for being anti-street, as the buildings no longer line, and therefore define, the street. No traditional streets figure in Le Corbusier's urban design, in the sense of shops lining a street, separated by sidewalks filled with sauntering pedestrians. This building type was influential for the planning of public housing (which exploded in the postwar period) and hospitals, apartments, and universities, especially dormitories.

The Contemporary City proposal addresses infrastructure problems by placing automobiles on one level and airplanes on another. In the sketch, an airplane lingers in the sky, a surprisingly benign element; it languidly hangs there, like a gentle firefly, a little out of place but not really a menace.

All is seen from the perspective of an outdoor dining terrace whose diners have just briefly fled the scene. The departed left their glasses and a water carafe. This being a project for public housing, best not to show wine bottles, a favored motif for Le Corbusier elsewhere. The only historical references are provided by the furniture on the terrace, simple metal chairs and tables.

The challenges facing urban centers before World War II were different from those they would face after the war. The scourge of abandoned urban centers had not yet arrived. The plans for the Contemporary City show another feature of the new way to design cities: to have them grow linearly instead of concentrically. The new city plans developed for Abuja, Nigeria, and Brasília, Brazil, were designed with the knowledge of Le Corbusier's urban vision.

In 1925, Le Corbusier proposed just such a plan for Paris, his Ville Voison, which proposed to replace block after block of Paris's historic center with an immense field of skyscrapers in the park, a direct result of his Ville Contemporaine. William Curtis writes: "Instead of the grimy industrial city, a brave new world of light, greenery, air, cleanliness, and efficiency was to arise" (Curtis 1996, p. 247). Architects of the modern period were particularly interested in housing, with the belief that they could provide comfort, shelter, education, and empowerment through new democratic cultures and mechanization processes which were not available in traditional societies. One of the results of directly tying their architecture to housing is that the perceived success or failure of modernism itself was attached to the coattails of public housing projects.

Mechanical Lyricism

Historian of modernism Kenneth Frampton referred to Eileen Gray's work as possessing a "mechanical lyricism" (Frampton in Riley 1990, p. 15). Expanding the term's usage, it can also refer to other modernist designers whose works do not easily fit into the category of canonical modernism.

Eileen Gray

Eileen Gray (1878–1976) was an architect, interior designer, and furniture designer, several of whose pieces have entered the pantheon of modern furniture classics. Of Scottish and Irish heritage, she saw the Universal Exhibition in Paris in 1900, a visual experience that prompted her to move to Paris in 1902. In 1907, she started learning painstaking finishing techniques from Japanese lacquer artist Seizo Sugawara, a collaboration that lasted forty years. A friend of Gertrude Stein and Natalie Clifford Barney, with fashionably short hair, and dressed in coats and dresses by fashion designer Paul Poiret, she struck a cutting figure on the Parisian scene.

She worked from her apartment and sold her furniture designs from a trendy decorator's shop that she held on to until the 1970s (Constant 2000). Eileen Gray's work presents the opportunity to see what happens when a female decorator takes the reins of modernism. In 1919, she designed apartment interiors for the milliner Suzanne Talbot. The Talbot apartment was a bit of a sales job for Gray, for the client, and for modernism itself. At this early date, it was by no means a foregone conclusion that modernism would prevail, that it would not become an intriguing item on the sidelines of design, like Egyptian revival.

Gray had to be aware that modern architecture was largely a male-dominated profession, so her

Figure 21.21 Eileen Gray. Bibendum chairs flanking side table.

projects seem intent on proving her commitment to modernism. The Talbot apartment is unabashedly modern, with white walls, a gridded glass floor, and frameless pivot doors with invisible hardware (Baudot 1998). Gray's own armchair, the Bibendum, is formed from three leather tubes; some ninety years later, it still looks futuristic (Figure 21.21). The project leaves no doubt that Gray was a committed member of the avant-garde.

But she was also a decorator who catered to wealthy, sophisticated clients. Her project had to operate successfully within the visual idiom of an elite, in-the-know clientele. The Talbot apartment achieves its glamorous air largely through the materials Gray selected: lacquer, leather, and fur. But if the project was really going to be successful, it had to do more, and this is where things get interesting. Part of the allure of the fashion industry, of which both Talbot and Gray, in different capacities, were a part, was to play upon people's values, to tap into the notions that they hold dear. But at the very top rung of the design professions, the strategy is to slightly shift the comfort level of the consumers, to

make them covet items they did not know existed. Gray's Talbot apartment does this brilliantly with its series of African objects, obscure yet erudite items, which were the epitome of taste.

Pointing out the obvious, Talbot's apartment is hardly an ethnographic study of African art and, in fact, part of how it functions, in the middle of Paris, is by decontextualizing the pieces, setting them within a readily understandable context. There is nothing frightening or demanding about the design. It features a very convincing African-looking throne by Pierre Legrain (1889–1929) that looks as though it could be pulled up to a dressing table. Many modernists played this game. The exotic objects or materials add a quality of texture, pattern, and mood to a room that would otherwise be too stark, too white, and too plain.

Gray's fondness for black lacquer was coincident with the current rage for "otherness." This manifested itself in the popularity of African artworks, and especially the popularity of African-American singer Josephine Baker in Paris. Baker had herself photographed, her hair slick and her skin glowing, deliberately looking like an art deco object. Le Corbusier wrote that "it is an excellent thing to keep an element of the savage alive in us" (Le Corbusier 1925, p. 85). Philip Johnson had a boyfriend in Harlem, jazz was everywhere, and the fondness for polished black surfaces was something that modernist designers co-opted from Art Deco.

Gray's architectural projects were few, but one of them, her own house at Roquebrune, was built on the Mediterranean in the period 1926–1929. She lived in the house known as E.1027 for several years with Jean Badovici (1893–1956), a Romanian architect with whom she had a six-year collaboration.

It is now considered one of the landmarks of the modern movement, as is the iconic bedside table from her bedroom, whose height is adjustable with a cable mechanism (Figure 21.22). While her work for Talbot was appropriately luxurious for a fashion designer, her own home was comparatively simple and restrained.

Figure 21.22 Eileen Gray. Bedside table.

Pierre Chareau

Pierre Chareau is another of the French modernists who had a limited architectural career. His modest body of work is so exquisite that his reputation has grown posthumously, largely due to a single project: his remodeling of a doctor's house and office.

Born in 1883, Pierre Chareau first worked as a furniture maker, and his subsequent professional activity doing interiors for elite clients shows in the attention to detail that is a hallmark of his projects. His most famous project, the Maison de Verre (or House of Glass), is a remodeling of an eighteenth-century hotel (Figure 21.23). Commissioned in the 1920s, it is a doctor's office and residential apartment; an existing residential apartment, untouched by Chareau, sits on top. A double-height grand salon is the dominant space. It is a place dedicated to art, with a piano and beautifully designed bookcases along with a rolling ladder made of steel and wood. The face the apartment presents to the courtyard is a giant glass block façade that lets in diffused light during the day. Shiny brass-framed windows illuminate the rooms at the rear of the house. The residence features a juxtaposition of scales, the dramatic double-height space offset with a single-story dining room and bedrooms. Ironworker Louis Dalbet collaborated with Chareau on perforated metal screens that rotate and provide privacy.

Likened to a finely crafted piece of furniture or musical instrument, the house has also been called a gorgeous machine. Its lyricism represents a different strain of French modernism. The Maison de Verre always seemed an alternative to rigid modernism. Critic Nicolai Ourousoff refers to the Maison de Verre as "the high point of classical Modernism" (Ouroussoff 2007, p. 1). Chareau's contemporary and friend Paul Nelson wrote: "This house approaches Surrealist sculpture. The pivoting door suspended in front of the metal staircase is a Surrealist sculpture of absolute beauty."

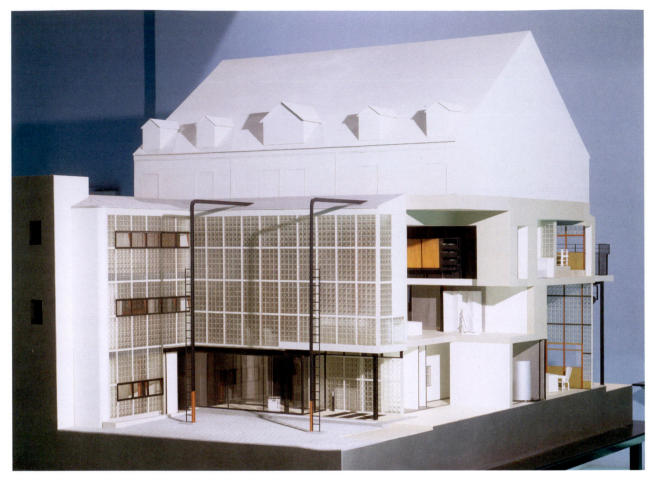

Figure 21.23 Pierre Chareau. Maison de Verre, 1928–1931. Model.

A stool shows the confident hand of Chareau in working with seating (Figure 21.24). It, like the house, is simultaneously delicate and robust. The broad expanse of metal that acts as the base and the rear support is brusque; the front legs are formed by two almost ridiculously delicate metal rods; the smooth edges and wood material of the seat adds warmth, and the seat curves ergonomically.

The talented Chareau was not destined for a long career. He fled France when the Nazis arrived, and he died in the United States, in 1950, in New York, with little money earned from his scant commissions.

Figure 21.24 Pierre Chareau. Stool, 1927.

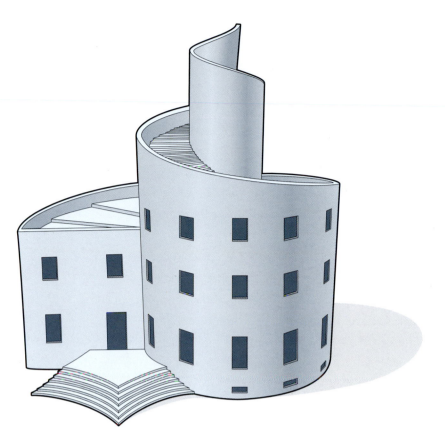

Figure 21.25 Emilio Terry, Maison en colimaçon (Spiral House), 1933

Emilio Terry, Salvador Dalí, and Surrealism

Emilio Terry (1890–1969), a Cuban who emigrated to Paris, is included here to purposely upset the apple cart, and to underscore that not all modernists followed a strict formula. Surrealist painter Salvador Dalí admired Terry's work and painted Terry with a house model in the background. Terry's *"maison en colimaçon,"* or Spiral House of 1933, is a proposal for a house that follows the curves of a seashell (Figure 21.25). It is made of cardboard and painted wood. In an age when the major designers were singing the praises of the machine, both as inspiration and as a means of manufacture, Terry was making a gesture to nature, a provocative move to publicly differentiate his approach to design from that of other designers. Terry's work is related to Dada and surrealism. The other provocation evident in Terry's work is simply the fact that the house's

form represents anything at all. Hard-core functionalists were disinclined to express narrative and subject. Form was to result from a functionalist design process and not be chosen from the outset.

NORDIC MODERNISM

In looking at the furniture designs from the prewar careers of Mies van der Rohe, Le Corbusier, and Alvar Aalto, it is astonishing that so many similarities in the historical circumstances led to their creation, some significant, some merely oddly coincidental. For all three men, despite long careers, their greatest successes with furniture came early, not late. All three overtly expressed an admiration for the work of Michael Thonet. When considering the furniture of Le Corbusier, Mies van der Rohe, and Alvar Aalto, one runs into three women: Charlotte Perriand, Lilly Reich, and Aino Aalto. These women played crucial and parallel roles in collaborating with them on interiors and furniture design. A comment made about Aino Aalto is typical; one source claims that Alvar Aalto often named her as his codesigner even when she was not, and that she was more of a critic than an architect.

Alvar Aalto

Alvar Aalto (1898–1976) represents another strand of modernism, one related to his geographical location, Scandinavia, his favored materials, wood and stone, and to his general approach, which can be considered the softer side of modernism.

He shared many of the central beliefs of the modernists and kept himself abreast of their developments. He visited their buildings, attended their exhibitions, and collected their furniture. He similarly saw the modern movement as a break from the past and saw the importance of responding to the present and thinking about the future. He wrote regularly about functionalism, and several of his projects have a distinctly utopian thrust. His approach to hygiene was wrapped up in providing adequate air and light, and ease of maintenance. Where he follows a different path is that he was less obsessed with furthering a machine aesthetic, and his projects relate to nature and their locality in a way that others do not, stances that render his version of modernism more palatable to a wider public. His works avoided the opprobrium that Gropius and Mies and Le Corbusier sometimes garnered.

Purists scoff at the term "Scandinavian design," which smacks of commercialism and IKEA, but Aalto's work largely avoided being labeled as cold and austere. Aalto's modernism distinguished itself because he "left the barebones of doctrinaire functionalism behind him" (Shand in Museum of Finnish Architecture 1985, p. 72). The popularization of Aalto's approach can be seen in Scandinavian design, which lacks the subtlety and depth of Aalto's works but nonetheless owes something to him for

providing an alternate, and ultimately more broadly appealing, brand of modernism.

Scandinavia was ripe for modernism because of the pioneering work of people like Erik Gunnar Asplund. And Aalto was not alone; another early modernist was Arne Jacobsen, whose staggered low-rise Bellavista housing complex near Copenhagen in 1934 was an early example of modernism. Jacobsen was to go on to become an accomplished designer of furniture, industrial arts, interiors, and architecture.

Alvar Aalto and Aino Aalto, Interiors and Furniture

Alvar Aalto started making furniture in 1919 when he started doing interiors projects. Prior to his success as an architect, he and his wife Aino (1894–1949) enjoyed a lengthy career as furniture designers. Their earlier furniture designs were inspired by historical styles, including the German iteration of Art Nouveau (Jugendstil), Vienna Secession, and several Neoclassical traditions, including Biedermeier. Several of the historical styles they brought to life are clearly influenced by American versions of European furniture pieces, such as their simplified Windsor chairs. These early Aaltos' chairs have a complicated genealogy: They are streamlined Scandinavian versions of American translations of the English eighteenth-century classic. Igor Herler refers to Aalto's early work as "light classicism," an apt term. The Aaltos applied their modernist aesthetic across the historic styles, simplifying line and form and minimizing decoration. Thomas Kellein, who wrote a book about their furniture designs, notes that "prior to 1929 Aalto's furniture was anything but modernist" (Kellein 2005, p. 13).

Aino and Alvar Aalto married in 1924 and moved to Turku, Finland's Baltic port. The circumstances that led to the development of the Aaltos' modernist aesthetic have been well documented and include their travels, which focused on attending modernist conferences and exhibitions. They

Figure 21.26 Alvar and Aino Aalto. Paimio armchair.

took a trip in 1928 to Holland and France, and another in 1929 to attend the Congrès International d'Architecture Moderne (CIAM). They looked at avant-garde buildings and cultivated professional relationships and friendships with like-minded progressive designers. They collected modern furniture pieces themselves, such as Breuer's Cesca and Wassily chairs. Their travels, their friendships, and the pieces they collected were all activities that consolidated their commitment to modernism.

After collaborating with his wife on a variety of interiors projects and furniture designs, Aalto established his modernist credentials in 1929 with a six-story office block for a newspaper company, the Turun Sanomat in Turku, Finland, his first large-scale modern building. With its ribbon windows, tapered pilotis, white walls, and functional layout, the Turun building gave him a reputation to rival those of other European modernists. It was successful at establishing Alvar Aalto's ability to design large-scale buildings.

If he burst onto the European architectural scene with the Turun Sanomat building, his reputation was cemented with the Paimio Sanatarium,

1930–1933, a health and recovery facility for which he and his wife also provided the furnishings.

The Paimio armchair, also known as Armchair 41, made its debut as part of the furnishings of the sanatorium by Aalto that opened in 1932 (Figure 21.26). It is a functionalist piece of furniture that is also sculptural, with a frame in bent laminated birchwood that makes a continuous loop. The loop is the primary supporting mechanism; three solid wooden bars attach to it, act as stabilizers, and support an L-shaped plywood seat that is lacquered. The loop takes the place of legs. The most significant feature of the chair is that all parts are made of wood. The Paimio armchair is specifically designed for the activity of reading, a posture more relaxed than sitting upright in a chair, yet more formal than lounging. As he further developed the Paimio armchair, he revised its width, making it slightly narrower.

Considered one of Aalto's greatest works, the Paimio Sanatorium reinforces modernism's connection to health. It also marks a significant moment, not only for his architecture but for his furniture design, and the relationship of building to furniture. From this point onward, Aalto firmly eschewed

Figure 21.27 Alvar Aalto. Villa Mairea, Noormarkku, Finland.

historical styles. Only once he had firmly embraced modernism would he state that his furniture designs were inextricably linked to the architectural projects they were designed for. The chair was not a part of the original 1929 project, but was developed when the Sanatorium was completed in 1932.

The most obvious difference between this chair and the Bauhaus chairs is that it was made of wood. Kellein (2005) stresses the essential difference between the Aaltos' work and that of other modernists: "Surrounded as they were by Breuer's tubular steel tables and Thonet's bentwood chairs, a love of simple forms and a preponderance of wood had evidently become the chosen style for the Aalto's home by 1929" (p. 123). Initially, the Aaltos mimicked the modern pieces in their personal collection and worked with metal tubing. Over time, they turned increasingly to wood.

The Villa Mairea at Noormarkku, Finland, 1938–1941, is a residence for a wealthy couple, with a Nordic romantic use of local materials and clever detailing (Figure 21.27). John McAndrew, in a

Figure 21.28 Alvar Aalto. Finnish Pavilion, New York World's Fair, 1939–1940.

MOMA catalog, writes, "The national character, closely allied, can be seen in the general Scandinavian trimness, and above all in the use of wood" (McAndrew, MOMA, p. 3). The personal character of the house reveals itself in the inventiveness of the forms and the use of materials, many of them local, and the witty resolution of details and connections. The national character is above all in the use of wood and stone. It is not only a change of material, but the new materials affected the form. And part of the local character is that the birch plywood came from Finland. This is what gave his designs a regional touch.

Aalto's design for the New York World's Fair of 1939 lined a boxlike space with free-flowing curvilinear side walls, made from wooden strips, on which photographs were mounted (Figure 21.28). This project presented him to an American audience and led to his being hired to teach at the Massachusetts Institute of Technology and his most prominent American commission, Baker Hall, a dormitory at MIT, 1947.

From 1934, Aalto's furniture was exhibited and sold in England, Italy, and the Netherlands. His modern achievements with the Turun building and the Paimio Sanatorium might seem like the opening act of a brilliant career designing furniture. Yet within a year of the Paimio opening he turned away from furniture design. Aalto turned to large-scale architecture and urban design. His greatest achievements with the intimate scale of furniture ended in 1933.

BRITISH MODERNISM

The springtime of modern architecture, the early 1920s, was not initially an era of significant developments on the British Isles. Scottish-born Eileen Gray was in Paris, and Mackintosh decamped to southern France, where, with little else to do, he painted. The artistic movements of Cubism, De Stijl, and Futurism had less of an impact in Britain. In contrast, the Beaux-Arts–inspired firm of Mèwes and Davis thrived. Lutyens, a friend of architect Arthur Davis, produced projects that resonated with certain contemporary trends but that were nonetheless related to the vernacular tradition of the British countryside.

By the 1930s, a small but committed coterie of modernists started to produce significant work in Britain, their leading figure being Berthold Lubetkin (1901–1990). Lubetkin, born in Russia, brought with him to Britain a familiarity with the Russian modernist movement, Russian Constructivism, and

Figure 21.29 Berthold Lubetkin. Penguin Pool, London Zoo.

no sentimental ties to the traditions of British architecture. He had studied with Auguste Perret; during his stay in France, he saw Le Corbusier's Esprit-Nouveau pavilion firsthand (Allan 1992). He moved to England in 1930, where he married Margaret Church, a radical architecture student.

For his Penguin Pool at the London Zoo, he collaborated with Ove Arup. (Ove Arup was the prominent engineering firm that later had a contentious working relationship with Danish architect Jorn Utzon while working on the Sydney Opera House.) The Penguin Pool represents another kind of modernism, with its free-flowing curves, reinforced concrete ramps in a double-helix formation, imaginative jumps in scale, and nary a grid in sight (Figure 21.29). Certainly one of the beguiling peculiarities of the modern movement is the temporal coexistence of projects like Mies van der Rohe's Reichsbank (1933), an exercise in rationality, and imaginative flights of fancy such as Lubetkin's Penguin Pool. Henry-Russell Hitchcock touched upon precisely this aspect of modernism's twin impulses in his article "The Architecture of Bureaucracy and the Architecture of Genius" (1947). Following Hitchcock's lead, van der Rohe's work would be an example of the "Architecture of Bureaucracy," while Lubetkin's pool is a prime example of the "Architecture of Genius."

Other modern projects in Britain include Lubetkin and Tecton's High Point Flats at Highgate, and Wells Coates's Isokon Flats in Hampstead. Wells Coates, an understudied figure of British modernism, was a talented furniture designer. Erich Mendelsohn arrived in 1933 and partnered with Serge Chermayeff in the De La Warr Seaside Pavilion. Walter Gropius worked with Maxwell Fry, who after Gropius's departure would embark on a distinguished career with his wife, Jane Drew, in West Africa.

THE LIGHTER SIDE OF MODERNISM

Just as Frampton's phrase "mechanical lyricism" described those with an unusual place in the modernist fold, Gray, Chareau, and Terry, another phrase by Frampton is appropriate to end the chapter. This chapter began by looking at Walter Gropius, Mies van der Rohe, and Le Corbusier—mainstream figures in any history of modernism. But a brief look at someone on the fringes of the design world will deepen and complicate our understanding of modernism. Frampton described Paul Nelson as belonging to the lighter side of modernism.

Paul Nelson

Nelson (1895–1979) worked for Auguste Perret for three years, and one of the notable features of his career is that he repeatedly crossed the Atlantic, traveling between the United States, where he was born, and France, where he became a citizen. He acted as a conduit of architectural information between continents and sectors of the arts. He was well connected in the art world, counting Georges Bracque, Alexander Calder, and Joan Miró as his friends. He was similarly connected to literati: F. Scott Fitzgerald, Ernest Hemingway, and Ezra Pound.

Writing about the School of Paris, the modernists whose activities centered on the Île-de-France, Kenneth Frampton coined the categories of light and heavy to describe two strains of modernist design. About modernism, he emphasized that "far from being monolithic, it was a product of intense cross-fertilization" (Frampton in Riley 1990, p. 10). Le Corbusier, according to Frampton, was a heavy, not because of the ponderousness of his pronouncements (one presumes) but because of the weighty nature of his works in concrete. Looking at Chareau, Gray, and Nelson, in contrast, their works are

Figure 21.30 Paul Nelson. What a Widow!

"light" because of their deft **tectonic** expression and also in their explorations of material translucency.

Frampton made popular the use of the word "tectonic" to describe architecture, particularly modern architecture (Frampton 1995). Tectonic emphasizes construction and materials, and the relationship of a building to its constitutive parts. But it is also an aesthetic and expressive term whose catchphrase is "the poetics of construction." The tectonic approach sees meaning in materials, their texture, and the architectural details that connect them. This allows for variety within the modernist fold, with some emphasizing weighty rough materials (Le Corbusier, late in his career), and others lighter machined materials (Nelson).

The connection between modernism and health was explicit in Nelson's oeuvre. He designed and built hospitals and other medical facilities throughout his career, and focused on unique ways of configuring surgeries and surgery pavilions.

Nelson had an interesting interlude during one of his visits to the United States (1929–1930). His orbit overlapped with that of the actress Gloria Swanson, and at her insistence he was hired as the artistic director of her next film, *What a Widow!* (Figure 21.30). For her he designed a modern backdrop, cubist and pure, that presented her in the au currant realm she desired, and thereby exposed American audiences to European modernism, a good three years before its official debut at the

Museum of Modern Art's exhibition of 1932. Photographic stills from the film look decidedly Corbusian, with horizontal windows, visible columns, and rounded stairways, like an imagined version of his Villa Savoye. Nelson also relied on the repeated modernist strategy of punctuating his modernist backdrop with recognizable types, but Nelson's types are different from Le Corbusier's radiators. Items from another arena lend qualities of elegance when plunked down intact into a new world—in this case, a grand piano, a violin, two men impeccably dressed in tuxedos, and Swanson herself.

CONCLUSION

This chapter introduces modernism as a force to be reckoned with. The chapters that follow grapple with the consequences of modernism.

In twentieth-century architecture and design, many male architects' wives were accomplished and professionally trained designers and architects. This appears a mixed blessing. Many women, certainly, thrived in partnership with their husbands because they were in a personal and professional relationship that respected their abilities and gave them an outlet for their work. Yet it also means that many women had a difficult time making a career in the design field outside of the supportive framework of marriage.

In 1938, Mies emigrated to the United States; Lilly Reich stayed in Berlin and managed his interests (Lambert 2001). After World War II, the Barcelona chair and many of his other pieces were made and sold by Knoll. Walter Gropius taught at Harvard. Marcel Breuer taught there for a while before he established his own firm in New York. Philip Johnson, Paul Rudolph, and Anne Tyng were just three of the students who were a part of the Bauhaus-inspired design milieu at Harvard.

The 1920s and 1930s saw several buildings created that changed the course of twentieth-century architecture. This august group includes the Villa Savoye, the Barcelona Pavilion, and the Paimio Sanatorium. Just as these are landmarks in the history of architecture, the furniture they introduced are landmarks for the history of design. Ironically, those who most clearly sought to make standard pieces, Le Corbusier and Aalto, fashioned handmade luxury pieces that became collector's items. Mies van der Rohe made a chair for a king and achieved the greatest popular success of his furniture career. Likely the two biggest names in twentieth-century architecture, Le Corbusier and Mies van der Rohe, both designed furniture prolifically in the 1920s and 1930s. Despite successful careers that lasted for decades, they were not to repeat that success within the realm of furniture design. After World War II, they turned to large-scale architectural projects and urban design.

In the postwar period, twentieth-century design moved on from classical modernism to more popular references and an increased interest in technology. This started the process of the dissemination of modernism in the 1950s, the subject of the following chapters. Modernism would blossom around the world with new forms and meanings. It would have unintended consequences. Some would recoil from it. Some would superficially latch on to its revolutionary shapes, uninterested in the thoughts that led to them. In the 1970s, subsequent movements expanded the repertory of themes. In the 1980s, modernism would be condemned. In the 1990s, modernism would rise, like Phoenix from the ashes, in a new form.

Sources

Allan, John. *Berthold Lubetkin: Architecture and the Tradition of Progress*. London: RIBA, 1992.

Baudot, François. *Eileen Gray*. London: Thames and Hudson, 1998.

Carter, Peter. *Mies van der Rohe at Work*. New York: Praeger, 1972.

Constant, Caroline. *Eileen Gray*. London: Phaidon, 2000.

Curtis, William. *Modern Architecture Since 1900*. London: Phaidon, 1996.

Dearstyne, Howard. *Inside the Bauhaus*. New York: Rizzoli, 1986.

Di Puolo, Maurizio. *Le Corbusier, Charlotte Perriand, Pierre Jeanneret*. Rome: De Luca Editore, 1976.

Drexler, Arthur. *Ludwig Mies van der Rohe*. New York: G. Braziller, 1960.

Drexler, Arthur. *The Mies van der Rohe Archives*. New York: Garland, 1986.

Frampton, Kenneth. *The Evolution of 20th Century Architecture*. Wien: Springer, 2007.

Frampton, Kenneth. *Studies in Tectonic Culture: the Poetics of Construction in Nineteenth- and Twentieth-Century Architecture*. Cambridge: MIT Press, 1995.

Frampton, Kenneth. *Harry Seidler: Four Decades of Architecture*. London: Thames and Hudson, 1992.

Frampton, Kenneth. *Modern Architecture: A Critical History*. London: Thames and Hudson, 1992.

Frampton, Kenneth, and Michael Moran. *The 20th Century Architecture and Urbanism*. Tokyo: A+U Pub, 1994.

Giedion, Sigfried. *Space, Time, and Architecture*. Cambridge: Harvard University Press, 1982.

Glaeser, Ludwig. *Ludwig Mies van der Rohe: Furniture and Furniture Drawings from the Design Collection and the Mies van der Rohe Archive*. New York: Museum of Modern Art, 1977.

Gropius, Walter, ed. *The Theatre of the Bauhaus*. Middletown: Wesleyan University Press, 1960.

Hyman, Isabelle. *Marcel Breuer, Architect: The Career and the Buildings*. New York: Abrams, 2001.

Joedicke, Jürgen. *Weissenhofsiedlung*. Stuttgart: K. Kramer, 1990.

Kates, George. *The Years That Were Fat*. Cambridge: MIT Press, 1952.

Kellein, Thomas. *Alvar and Aino Aalto: Design*. Ostfildern-Ruit: Hatje Cantz, 2005.

Kostelanetz, Richard, ed. *Moholy-Nagy*. New York: Praeger, 1970.

Lambert, Phyllis. *Mies in America*. New York: Abrams, 2001.

Latour, Bruno. *We Have Never Been Modern*. Cambridge: Harvard University Press, 1993.

Le Corbusier. *L'Art décoratif d'aujourd'hui*. Paris: G. Crès et cie, 1925.

Lupton, Ellen, and Miller, J. Abbott, eds. *The ABCs of Triangle, Square, Circle: The Bauhaus and Design Theory*. Princeton: Princeton Architectural Press, 1991.

McQuaid, Matilda. *Lilly Reich, Designer and Architect*. New York: Abrams, 1996.

Marcus, George. *Le Corbusier: Inside the Machine for Living: Furniture and Interiors*. New York: Monacelli, 2000.

McLeod, ed. Charlotte Perriand: *An Art of Living*. New York: Abrams, 2003.

McQuaid, Matilda. *Lilly Reich, Designer and Architect*. New York: Abrams, 1996.

Musée des Arts Decoratifs. *Charlotte Perriand: un art de vivre*. Paris: Flammarion, 1985.

Museum of Finnish Architecture. *Alvar Aalto Furniture*. Cambridge: MIT University Press, 1985.

Nelson, George. *Chairs*. New York: Whitney Publications, 1953.

Ouroussoff, Nicolai. "The Best House in Paris." *The New York Times*, August 26, 2007, p. 1.

Pallasmaa, Juhani, ed. *Alvar Aalto Through the Eyes of Shigeru Ban*. London: Black Dog Publishing, 2007.

Perriand, Charlotte. *A Life of Creation: An Autobiography*. New York: Monacelli Press, 2003.

Pile, John. *A History of Interior Design*. New York: Wiley, 2000.

Riley, Terence, and Joseph Abram, eds. *The Filter of Reason: Work of Paul Nelson*. New York: Rizzoli, 1990.

Riley, Terence, and Barry Bergdoll, eds. *Mies in Berlin*. New York: Abrams, 2001.

Rowe, Colin. *The Architecture of Good Intentions: Towards a Possible Retrospect*. London: Academy Editions, 1994.

Safran, Yehuda. *Mies van der Rohe*. Lisbon: Blau, 2000.

Schlemmer, Tut, ed. *The Letters and Diaries of Oskar Schlemmer*. Middletown: Wesleyan University Press, 1972.

Staatliches Bauhaus Weimar. *Staatliches Bauhaus Weimar 1919–1923*. Munich: Kraus, 1980 (1923).

Vellay, Marc, and Kenneth Frampton. *Pierre Chareau: Architect and Craftsman, 1883–1950*. New York: Rizzoli, 1985.

Whitford, Frank, ed. *The Bauhaus: Masters and Students by Themselves*. London: Conran Octopus, 1992.

Wilk, Christopher. *Marcel Breuer, Furniture, and Interiors*. New York: Museum of Modern Art, 1981.

DISCUSSION AND REVIEW QUESTIONS

1. Art Nouveau artists clearly were inspired by nature. What inspired or motivated the modernists in their design process?
2. The modernists claimed to be antihistory; when did they ignore their own rule?
3. What role did women play in modernism? Who were some of the major female designers?
4. What does functionalism mean?
5. What specifically did the modernists dislike about Victorian design?
6. Who were the major figures and where did they practice?
7. Specifically in the furniture realm, what were some of the modernist goals?

CHAPTER 22

ART DECO, TRADITIONAL DESIGN, AND THE RISE OF THE DECORATOR

1920s	1925	1925–1939
Art Deco	Exposition Internationale des Arts Décoratifs	Art Moderne

In 1925, a world's fair opened in Paris, L'Exposition Internationale des Arts Décoratifs et Industriels Modernes. It was sponsored by the French government to support French decorative arts; there was some fear that she was losing ground in this vital arena to Germany. The exposition was intended to show the world that France excelled at making well-designed and -crafted objects and interiors. The contributors were ostensibly unified in their collaborative mission to tout the superiority of French design. Yet even in the planning stages, it became apparent that there was a rift, a division into two camps: decorators and functionalists. The decorators included figures such as Emile-Jacques Ruhlmann. The functionalists included Le Corbusier. The functionalist stream was handled in Chapter 21. This chapter covers those who did not feel so strongly modernism's pull, or who felt it but expressed it differently.

What connects the three strands of design considered in this chapter is that they are responses to a similar economic and artistic climate, yet they are responses in three distinct design directions.

ART DECO

The terms we now use to describe the two groups that emerged in Paris are problematic, as they were not in use at the time. "Art Deco" is an abbreviation of "Arts Décoratifs," and while commonly used to describe the design trend that emerged from the exposition, the term has only been in use since the 1960s. As Christopher Long writes, the problematic term "is unusually elastic and imprecise" (Long 2007, p. ix). Most of the exhibitors referred to their designs as "*moderne,*" and if they were to ascribe to a stylistic moniker, they would use "*style moderne.*"

"Art Deco" is a frequently used phrase that has currency in the design field. And, even if imprecise, it does generally indicate a differing attitude between two groups. The functionalists and the decorators were both responding to their time period, the 1920s, but they did so differently. The designs of the functionalists were aimed toward mass production, a wide swath of the marketplace, and considered the social good that design can achieve. The functionalists emphasized the value of engineering and assembly-line construction. The decorators crafted exquisite objects that were labor intensive,

515

aimed at an elite market, and not burdened by a belief in the redemptive obligations of art.

Art Deco designs are intricately related to a decade, the 1920s. The 1920s are also known as the Roaring Twenties, for good reason. In the United States, the aftermath of World War I was a period of economic prosperity, whose end would come with the market crash of October 1929 and the start of the Depression. Technologically, it is related to the increased presence of automobiles, movies, and radio. Culturally, it included such varied manifestations as the Charleston, jazz, and bobbed haircuts for women. F. Scott Fitzgerald's novel *The Great Gatsby* (1925) perfectly captured the tenor of this period as it played out among the social elite.

The speed with which Art Deco traveled from France to the United States, and elsewhere, indicates that it quickly became an international phenomenon. The forms associated with twentieth-century optimism in France and the United States resonated with other groups of people who looked to the future for different reasons. To name two: In Mexico, the Mexican Revolution of 1910–1921 ended, so the 1920s heralded a new postcolonial age. And 1923 was the year that Atatürk founded the modern nation of Turkey, announcing that the smoldering ashes of the Ottoman Empire had gone out and that those living in Anatolia could look forward to a bright, secular, and democratic future. Art Deco forms in both these countries reflected this optimism.

Part of the reason scholars and antiquarians have difficulty with the term Art Deco is that it is used indiscriminately in several ways. This chapter takes its cues from how it is generally used and also recognizes the limits of its usefulness. First, it refers to the period of design immediately following the Exposition of 1925, indicating the French decorative arts aimed at an elite clientele. Then it considers the effect that these forms had in the United States, and specifically their interaction with sky-

scrapers. Finally, it considers the iteration of Art Deco forms around the world.

France

The major figures on the decorative side of the divide, typically classified as the pioneers of French Art Deco, include Paul Follot (1877–1941), Jean-Michel Frank (1895–1951), André Mare (1887–1932), Jacques-Émile Ruhlmann (1879–1933), Michel Roux-Spitz (1888–1957), and Louis Süe (1875–1968). A significant feature of Art Deco (along with Rococo and Art Nouveau) is that it is one of the few styles whose finest works are in interiors, furniture design, and designed objects. There are Art Deco buildings, to be sure, but Art Deco is primarily known for objects, pieces of furniture, lamps, textiles, and jewelry. The ranks of Art Deco artists include Louis Cartier (1875–1942), a jeweler, and Paul Poiret (1879–1944), a fashion designer who himself created interior designs. Jean Dupas (1882–1964) is one of the few painters whose work belongs exclusively to the realm of Art Deco.

Art Deco is related to commercialism and, by extension, capitalism. French department stores supported the designers who exhibited at the Exposition and hired them to do window displays. The major Parisian department stores—Au Printemps, Galeries Lafayette, Au Bon Marché, and Grand Magasins du Louvre—were all supporters of Art Deco. The explicit support by the retail industry is again in contrast with the modernists whose works bear more than a whiff of socialism. Art Deco was more commercial and less highly theorized.

Some works, particularly graphic works, predate the 1920s and clearly indicate tendencies that look forward to what would later be called Art Deco. Many pieces also postdate the 1920s. As with all styles and epochs, the general maxims by which the era is known are sometimes at odds with specific artistic utterances. Looking across the spectrum of Art Deco pieces, one encounters a delightful complexity and occasional incongruity; this is what makes it such an appealing area of study.

The understanding of artistic movements changes over time. Art Deco, once seen as the antithesis of Art Nouveau, is now seen by some as an emanation from it. And although modernists and Art Deco artists were once seen in opposition, there are considerable areas of overlap, including common interests, materials, and finishes. Like modernism, Art Deco has affinities to Cubism, Russian Constructivism, and Italian Futurism.

There is always the case of figures so individually talented that it is difficult to pigeonhole their work. Eileen Gray, often considered an Art Deco decorator, is now more likely considered within the modernist camp. She's Deco because of fine finishes, rich clients, and she worked as a decorator. She's a modernist because of the absence of historical detail in her projects and her adherence to functionalism and Cubism, and Le Corbusier admired her work. Yet other designers seem to perfectly belong to a style, in no small part because our definition of it

comes from their work. Ruhlmann and Frank (discussed below) are Art Deco to the core.

One of the most succinct definitions of Art Deco comes from a writer who spent his career studying it. Alastair Duncan writes: "The term 'Art Deco,' coined in the late 1960s, remains an appropriate way to describe the distinctive decorative arts style which evolved in Europe immediately prior to the First World War, and which remained in fashion in some countries of its adoption until the late 1930s" (Duncan 1988).

Ensembliers

World War I was a tragedy for the Frank family, although it was a tragedy that started the design career of Jean-Michel Frank (1895–1941). Jean-Michel's two brothers were killed in the war and his father, of German-Jewish descent, committed suicide; his mother died in a mental institution. Because of his family's losses, he inherited a sum of money that allowed him to pursue his career of choice, decorator. He participated in the 1925 exhibition as one of the high style decorators.

Figure 22.1 Jean-Michel Frank. Cube armchairs veneered in shagreen.

The French might refer to a decorator as a *"décorateur"*; they more frequently use the word *"ensemblier."* The denotation refers to one who creates an ensemble, chooses objects, combines them, and in so doing, makes aesthetic choices. There is an undercurrent of taste in the usage of this word, whereas the staunch functionalists grounded their design (or so they said) in abstract principles (*Éditions du Centre National de la Recherche Scientifique* 1979, p. 1184).

Frank's projects after the exhibition include decorating the Parisian townhouse of the Vicomte de Noailles, a project that included vellum-clad walls, bronze doors, white lacquer, and sharkskin. His all-white apartment for the fashion designer Elsa Schiaparelli in 1927 was sparsely furnished and made with inexpensive materials and garnered significant attention.

Frank was also involved in the design business as a patron, hiring Alberto and Diego Giacometti, Salvador Dalí, and Emilio Terry. In 1939, he fled Europe for Argentina, where he worked briefly, fulfilling the desire of wealthy Argentines for the latest trends in Parisian design. The year 1941 saw Frank in New York, despondent, and he jumped to his death from a New York high-rise. A distant relative of his, Anne Frank, also gained renown posthumously for her moving Holocaust diary.

Two chairs from the height of Frank's career display several aspects of his attitude toward design (Figure 22.1). Known as cube chairs, they are explorations of accommodating the seated human figure, comfortably, within a shape that is close to a perfect cube. Their decoration is limited to the use of an extravagantly exotic material, known as **shagreen**, the skin of the small spotted dogfish. Shagreen is also called sharkskin. The use of this material on the chairs indicates that decoration should be integral to the material and applied flat, not as an extraneous form.

Jacques-Émile Ruhlmann (1879–1933) was a French furniture designer known for fine craftsmanship. He started exhibiting his designs in 1910.

Figure 22.2 Jacques-Émile Ruhlmann. Elephant chair.

Figure 22.3 Edward Brantwood Maufe. Paris Exposition of 1925.

With his contribution to the Exposition Internationale of 1925, he cemented his reputation as a major figure in design. He had his own pavilion, which also exhibited the works of other designers. The foremost twentieth-century cabinetmaker, he sought to raise French furniture-making to the level it had enjoyed in the eighteenth century.

He specialized in unusual materials, such as ebony, zebrawood, tropical veneers, sharkskin, and ivory, or he employed traditional veneers used in contrasting patterns. He sold several pieces to a famous collector, the Maharaja of Indore. Ruhlmann's work is usually noted for its strict geometries and geometric stylization, yet with his elephant chair he, like other Art Deco designers, explored circular forms to great effect (Figure 22.2). The elephant chairs were exhibited at the Exposition Coloniale.

Britain

Edward Maufe (1883–1974) was an architect who formed part of the English delegation to the 1925 Exposition. His works had stylistic ties to English Arts and Crafts, and he also worked in the English Gothic style. The stylishness of his work, evident in the desk sent to Paris, contrasted with the functionalist strain of modernism (Figure 22.3). He perfected a technique of making silver-lacquered furniture.

This writing desk is made of mahogany. Its appearance at the 1925 Exposition garnered praise. It uses silk tassels for drawer pulls, a feature usually associated with French designs. Art Deco pieces make occasional references to traditional architectural vocabularies, such as classicism, and some innovatively give life to Egyptian and Aztec forms. This is one of the features that set their work apart

Figure 22.4 Owen Williams, Daily Express Building. London, 1932.

Figure 22.5 Denham Maclaren. Armchair. Glass, metal fittings, zebra skin, 1930.

from that of the strict modernists. The Maufe desk makes discreet historical references, with fluted pilasters adorned with subtle bases and capitals. Maufe made less expensive versions of this piece.

Owen Williams (1890–1969) was an engineer and architect and was considered Britain's leading expert on reinforced concrete. Although he moved increasingly toward a functionalist/modernist position, he had little interaction with the major figures of the British modern movement (Maxwell Fry, Jane Drew, Wells Coates, etc.). The lobby of the Daily Express Building in London is an unusual work for Williams (who is more known for his knowledge of straightforward concrete construction, utilized in factories), yet it is one of the seminal works of English Art Deco (Figure 22.4). The design incorporates a variety of metallic finishes, and it is mostly lit by recessed cove lighting, tucked into a series of stepped planes that dramatically finish in zigzags. Metallic reveals offset one expen-

sive material after another, including black glass. A showpiece of its time, it was designed to demonstrate that its client, a newspaper company, was up-to-date (Yeomans 2001, pp. 67–79).

Denham Maclaren's striking chair, shown in Figure 22.5, is highly inventive. Some British furniture designers were interested not in working within boundaries set by others, but in exploring new territory. Glass is a difficult material to use structurally, a feat Maclaren managed successfully. This chair is so innovative that it resists easy classification, but its innovative use of materials and incorporation of animal skins bring it into the Art Deco fold.

Ironies abound in the artistic productions of this period. It is certainly curious that a group of objects that were designed to appeal to an elite appealed to the masses, whereas the modernist projects, which sought to raise the plight of all, were actually very elite.

United States

Art Deco appeared in the United States in ways similar to its use in France—as an appealing design vocabulary with which to outfit a store window or the splashy lobby of an apartment building. Yet it also became associated with the skyscraper, a development not foreseen by the organizers of the Paris exposition. The careers of Raymond Hood (1881–1934) and William Van Alen (1883–1954) were devoted to explorations of how Art Deco forms could be adapted to tall buildings. Donald Deskey (1894–1989) and Paul Frankl (1878–1958) were active in the realm of interiors and furnishings.

Figure 22.6 Reinhard and Hofmeister. Rockefeller Center, New York, 1931–1932.

Urban Design and Architecture

The Chicago School skyscrapers of the 1890s were examples of a logical and inspired response to the economic and technological environment. They expressed the building's structure, which they used as a starting point for a straightforward artistic statement. Yet the glory was short lived, and many architects turned to historic forms to inspire their skyscraper designs, covering steel frames with Greek columns or Gothic arches. Modernists, including Louis Sullivan and Walter Gropius, did not hesitate to point out how ludicrous this was. With the advent of Art Deco, another architectural vocabulary was at hand, appropriate and appealing for the cladding of high-rise buildings. The marriage of Art Deco to skyscrapers seemed preordained. The City of New York also lent its assistance. Many were concerned about the possibility of massive office blocks turning streets into dark, airless canyons, so a 1916 zoning ordinance required that as buildings rose, they had to progressively step back, with the uppermost floors occupying no more than 25 percent of the lot size. This lent a distinctive profile to New York skyscrapers, many of which were tapered by a series of set-backs, often capped off with a spire. This profile was in touch with other aspects of 1920s Art Deco design, including the use of metal, the vertical emphasis, and the favored zigzag motif.

While Art Deco is rightfully considered a decorative style, one of the finest twentieth-century urban designs comes under its tenure, Rockefeller Center (Figure 22.6). Despite Le Corbusier's passionate attention to city planning, the legacy and efficacy of his urban vision remains contentious. Rockefeller Center, born of the grid of New York, is an urban design that incorporates skyscrapers and involves public amenities, statuary, fountains, rooftop gardens, all miraculously nestled into the center of one of the world's most vibrant metropolises. Rockefeller Center unfolds onto three New York City

Figure 22.7 William Van Alen. Chrysler Building, elevator doors, 1928–1930.

blocks, between Fifth and Sixth Avenues (Stern 1982, pp. 13–15). At its center is a T-shaped plaza, with a sunken court and the famous ice-skating rink.

The defining feature of an Art Deco skyscraper is its emphasis on verticality. Vertical piers are continuous, while the horizontal bands, the spandrels above and below windows, are intercepted by the vertical piers. Raymond Hood perfected the design of the middle portion of a skyscraper with his projects for countless tall buildings, including the Chicago Tribune Tower and the Daily News Building.

Yet the epitome of Art Deco skyscraper design came from the hand of William Van Alen (1883–

1954). The name of the Chrysler Building, 1929, reflects the ties of architecture to industry. It has setbacks and the standard emphasis on verticality in its shaft. Yet the design of the spire and the lobby renders it an icon of American Art Deco (Gray 2001, p. 67). At its top, the vertical massing morphs into a series of overlapping curves, sheathed in metal and punctuated with triangle-shaped windows that glow at night.

The lobby elevator doors hint at the form of the spire. A fan shape is part of a similar design of overlapping curves, emphasized with alternating bands of color and separated by bronze. A triangular light functions as the elevator call light, also a hint of the windows that grace the top of the building (Figure 22.7).

Interiors, Stage Design, and Furniture

Two of the leaders of American Art Deco, Paul Frankl and Joseph Urban, were born in Austria. Joseph Urban (1872–1933) was one of a group of Austrian architects who brought to American Art Deco their personal knowledge of the Secessionist movement, and specifically the works of Otto Wagner, Adolph Loos, and Josef Hoffmann. Trained as an architect, Urban was active in Vienna as an architect, interior designer, stage designer, and book illustrator. He first visited the United States as designer of the Austrian pavilion at the St. Louis Exposition in 1904. In 1911, he moved to the United States. Over the course of his career, he created sets for the Boston Opera Company, the Metropolitan Opera, and the Ziegfeld Follies. His work as artistic director of William Randolph Hearst's movie studio led to his commission to design the Hearst Building in New York. Another project, the New School of Social Research, is considered New York's first international-style building (Carter 1992, p. 169). Some of his works still stand, including the most extravagant, Mar-a-Lago, the house of Marjorie Merriweather Post. Urban's professional activity

Figure 22.8 Paul Frankl. Skyscraper writing desk.

in theater and film underscores an oft-noted quality about Art Deco interior design: Even when designed for real buildings, they look theatrical.

Paul Frankl is known for his skyscraper furniture, in which he sought to create a uniquely American style of design by relating to skyscrapers (Long 2007). A stepped writing desk is a typical example of Frankl's brand of Art Deco furniture (Figure 22.8). It incorporates the form inspired by the setbacks of skyscrapers. He was aware of the commercial nature of many of his designs. He opened the Frankl Galleries in New York, where he saw firsthand that modern design could sometimes be a selling point yet could also turn people away. He thought the United States lagged behind Europe in terms of modern design, and he aligned himself with modernists such as Marcel Duchamp, Francis Picabia, and Man Ray.

Donald Deskey (1894–1989) was an American interior and industrial designer. He studied in Paris, where he was exposed to and learned to appreciate the work of French designers. In New York, he developed window displays for Saks Fifth Avenue (Hanks 1987, p. 10). He designed interiors, furniture, lamps, and textiles.

In a period known for the use of novel materials, Deskey's work still manages to stand out: He favored cork, copper, pigskin, linoleum, Bakelite, Formica, brushed aluminum, and macassar ebony. His interiors for Radio City include aluminum wallpaper (Figure 22.9).

Tropical Art Deco

Art Deco undeniably had an international appeal and, like Art Nouveau, an international success. While generally thought of as French, French Art Deco was chronologically followed by American Art Deco which was, in turn, followed by Art Deco across the globe. Art Deco buildings and designed objects appeared everywhere—in Africa, the Americas, Asia, and Australia.

In the 1930s, another kind of Art Deco arrives on the world stage, lightheartedly known as Tropical Art Deco. This represents a third phrase of Art Deco, at the furthest remove from Paris. Places with warm climates, including Miami, Florida, and Havana, Cuba, were two of the centers of this kind of Deco. Purists scoff at the inclusion of such buildings in the Art Deco realm, as they stray too far, they feel, from the French originals. The debate pits 1930s Miami against 1920s Paris and takes us unto the murky area of stylistic names and definitions.

Figure 22.9 Donald Deskey. Radio City Music Hall, lobby. New York, 1932.

Figure 22.10 Henry Hohouser, Cardozo Hotel. Miami, Florida.

Tropical Art Deco is less reliant on expensive materials and more reliant on silhouette and paint. Miami architects used a variety of pastel hues. Art Deco was popular, and an Art Deco exterior announced to passersby that the company housed within was current (Figure 22.10). This was particularly the case with business ventures that relied on bringing in customers—movie theaters, stores, bars, and hotels—or, as with the *Daily Express,* for businesses that simply wanted the architectural image to present them as modern. Suzanne Tise writes: "A highly exaggerated and commercialized version of Art Deco was popular in cinemas and theatres during the late 1920s" (Tise 1996, p. 522).

This popularized version of Art Deco spread remarkably fast, to all corners of the globe, and its diffusion was based on its commercial success and not ponderous theorizing. The term "*art moderne*" is sometimes used to refer to this kind of Art Deco, later in time and divorced in spirit from the Parisian sort. It relies more heavily on mechanical iconography, looking at automobiles and steamships,

items not part of the original French repertory of themes.

The existence of Art Deco buildings all over the world—in the United States, in South Africa, in Brazil, in China—is a sign of each country's wealth. An elevator door, a tall building that emphasizes the vertical, a lobby with cove lighting—all are proof that many places economically prospered in the 1920s.

Eritrea, in the Horn of Africa, was a local center of African modernism. The Bar Zilli relies on a judicious use of stone, an expensive material, offset with fields of plaster, a less expensive material (Figure 22.11). Art Deco arrived in Ethiopia, Somalia, and Eritrea due to Italian colonists, yet it was not received as an Italian tool of repression but as part of an international modern movement that Africans were anxious to join. A recent publication is rare among books in that it addresses African twentieth-century architecture. The editor, Edward Denison, notes: "Far from the motherland, Eritrea provided a perfect environment for innovation and experimentation" (Denison 2003, p. 63).

Figure 22.11 Bar Zilli. Asmara, Eritrea.

Graphics and Fashion

An example of the commercial success of Art Deco is its prevalence in advertising. Typeface and forms associated with Art Deco were perceived by viewers as modern and new. In a period in which photographic printing techniques were increasingly available, Ludwig Hohlwein (1874–1919) was a successful commercial artist in Munich who produced handmade lithography work. This flatter stencil-style of posterwork avoided photographic processes. Although trained as an architect, he is considered a master of modern poster art. Even in a less exalted art form such as an advertisement, Art Deco characteristics are noticeable. The streamlined form is coupled with a high contrast use of colors (Figure 22.12). This belongs to a strain of Art Deco graphic work that invokes classical sculpture. Hohlwein's male figure is almost absurdly heroic for the purpose at hand: selling coffee.

Scholars such as Judith Butler promote the idea that the human body is a social construction, a sign of its time. At first this claim bewilders: Surely the human form cannot biologically change itself every decade to respond to fashion's latest whim. Her theories succeed to the extent that each period has its favored body type, favored body parts, or a "constructed gender" (Butler 1999, p. 48). Certain human figures seem to exemplify an era's aesthetic vision. Nancy Cunard, tall and reed-thin, is one such person, and the knowledge that she was active in the art world, as a publisher, author, and patron, confirms that she was in all respects a woman of the 1920s. Dresses from the period are also evidence of the bodies they so beautifully wrapped.

Voisin of Paris made a dress in 1925 using an expensive material that looks luxurious—silk velvet (Figure 22.13). The design carries few of the encumbrances of the history of the dress, in fact, most

Figure 22.12 Ludwig Hohlwein.

Figure 22.13 Voisin of Paris. Silk velvet evening dress, 1925.

traditional evening dress elements are eliminated. It also pushes the social mores of its day. Its wearer has bare arms, and loose strips of cloth form a short skirt that is meant to fly about when subjected to the sideways kick of the Charleston. With the exception of its belt, all its lines are vertical, like a radiator grille or the shaft of a Deco skyscraper. The 1920s attitude toward the ideal female figure was a dramatic change from what it had been in the late nineteenth century. Then bustles, corsets, and large hats all conspired to render the female figure as curvaceous as possible. The ideal female figure of the Roaring Twenties had a flat chest. Women not so naturally endowed were known to bind themselves. The profile of this dress is similar to the simple lines of Art Deco pilasters and low-relief sculpture.

A study of the silhouettes of Coke bottles reveals that the bottles change over time, corresponding to changing ideals of an idealized female figure. The Voisin dress is completely modern, while

Hohlwein's poster draws upon popular representational techniques. Art Deco pieces were new, but designed in a heavily stylized fashion that made historical forms current.

All eras have their ideal body types, and favored body parts, and animals. The Art Deco artists were fond of chevron shapes, zigzags, stepped profiles, straight hair, bangs, greyhounds, and deer. Some Art Deco themes and interests cross stylistic divides.

Both avowed modernists and the designers now classified as Art Deco had many similar interests. For example, many were fascinated by African art and materials. Yet sometimes the interests of modernists and their more decoratively-inclined comrades diverged. Egyptian motifs were evidently too historical and too decorative to be of use to modernists, yet they were important source materials for Deco designs.

TRADITIONAL DESIGN— A POPULAR CONTINUITY WITH THE PAST

The 1920s produced a large class of wealthy people who desired homes that reflected their status. This includes the "robber barons," a term usually used pejoratively to describe industrialists and businessmen who dominated their industries and amassed great wealth in the late nineteenth and early twentieth centuries. There is more than a hint of questionable business practices among business leaders such as John D. Rockefeller, Cornelius Vanderbilt, John Jacob Astor, Henry Ford, and Andrew Carnegie. Some economists counter that these business leaders were essential to transforming the United States into a world power, and that they, for the most part, operated through fair business practices in the free market. Questions about their complicity aside, there is no doubt that they had great cultural impact. They were patrons of the arts with the houses they commissioned and the artworks and furnishings they bought to fill them. For this endeavor, they needed assistance in selecting traditional furnishings and finishes, and then arranging them.

The posthumous reputations of traditional architects and designers have flowed and ebbed, in opposite relationship to the ascendancy and fall of modernism. As the tenets of modernism took hold in the 1950s and 1960s, the reputations of Julia Morgan, Arthur Davis, and Addison Mizner crashed, while those of Louis Sullivan, Charles Rennie Mackintosh, and Adolf Loos soared. Only in the late 1970s and 1980s, with the coincident rise of postmodernism, were the careers of traditional architects reevaluated. They were rediscovered by scholars, but for the general public they had never lost their appeal. A review of their buildings, interiors, and drawings reveals that many of them were, in fact, talented architects, artists, and designers. Operating as a traditional architect involved two areas of skill: a thorough knowledge of architectural history and an accomplished ability to draw and paint.

Britain

Edwin Lutyens (1869–1944) was England's preeminent architect for half a century. His career provides an alternative trajectory to the development of English modernism, as his work presents a successful integration of traditional architectural languages and the romantic or vernacular. He was raised in the English countryside, in Surrey, and he was familiar with historic agricultural buildings. His early works have much in common with the English Arts and Crafts movements, specifically the houses of Philip Webb and C. F. A. Voysey, in which, despite a romantic assemblage of features associated with agricultural buildings, a clarity in plan and façade emerges that is distinctly modern. Lutyens used traditional building materials and probed the relationship between house and garden. He, along with landscape architect Gertrude Jekyll, combined the formal and the picturesque.

His work exhibited a growing interest in geometry. A feature of his work was an occasional ambiguity and willingness to build in whatever style his clients wanted. He developed a castle style, and some buildings make clear references to Romanesque, Tudor, Neoclassical, Georgian, and Gothic styles. He wanted to land a big, prestigious commission, which he eventually did. He designed some government buildings in South Africa, where he met Herbert Baker. His most prominent commission was to design a scheme of buildings for the new capital in New Delhi, India, an example of monumental classical planning. For this he brought along Baker. In India, Lutyens's most prominent project was the Viceroy's House.

He is less well known for his furniture designs, but they exhibit the qualities evident in his buildings. There is an appreciation of traditional detailing and references to specific styles, but at the same time there is an unmistakable air of inventiveness (Figure 22.14).

Like his friend Arthur Davis, when working on urban buildings, he designed classical stone façades for steel-framed buildings. Knighted in 1918, he was always suspicious of the modern movement. About Lutyens, Pevsner wrote: "The paradox of the revivalist in whose work geometry is more insistent than in any living architect bar Corbusier" (Pevsner 1951, p. 217).

The Alsatian Charles Mèwes (1860–1914) and the Briton Arthur Davis (1878–1951) studied at the École des Beaux-Arts. From their London office, Mèwes and Davis designed Ritz hotels in London, Paris, and Madrid (Binney 1999). The Ritz Piccadilly, in London, 1903–1906, was the first steel-framed building in London, not that this was evident from the inside (Figure 22.15). This successful partnership

Figure 22.14 Edwin Lutyens. Round Table.

developed many of the interiors for early-twentieth-century ocean liners, using an interesting office arrangement: Mèwes did the designs for the German Hapag-Lloyd Line, including the *Imperator*, and Davis did the designs for the Cunard Line, including the *Aquitania* (Zerbe 1999, pp. 106–110). Their projects responded to modern programs, relying on their deep knowledge of eighteenth-century French architecture and furniture, acquired at the Beaux-Arts.

David Watkin sensed the discomfort that Davis felt about the direction that British architecture was taking: "Distressed by the insistence of the directors of the Cunard Line that his interiors for the Queen Mary should be in an art deco style of which he disapproved, Davis suffered a nervous breakdown" (Watkin 2004). The twentieth-century version of the battle of styles was keenly felt by many.

Figure 22.15 Charles Mewes and Arthur Davis. Ritz Hotel—Piccadilly. Lobby.

United States

McKim, Mead, and White was the preeminent American architectural firm of the nineteenth and twentieth centuries. It was modern as a business entity, though committed to a renewal of past forms; over the course of its long practice, the firm created some 900 designs. At one time, McKim, Mead, and White had more than seventy employees (Roth 1983, p. 57). Their architecture was widely accepted and understood by the public, who held the architects in considerable esteem.

Stanford White (1853–1906), the most flamboyant of the firm's three partners, served members of the new wealthy class. White's shooting because of his affair with Evelyn Nesbitt has guaranteed him a dubious place in history that has little to do with the quality of his firm's work. With the houses they lived in, the buildings they designed for clients,

Figure 22.16 David Adler. Mr. and Mrs. Lester Armour House. Lake Bluff, Illinois, 1931.

and the public institutions to which they gave large sums of money, they impacted architecture and interior design. The success of McKim, Mead, and White, and firms like it across the globe, leaves no doubt that creating traditional architecture was big business.

If McKim, Mead, and White is a large-scale example of a thriving firm that specialized in traditional architecture, David Adler is an example of a small firm, in the same stylistic vein, known for accomplished residential work. Most cities around the world had an accomplished architect who met the needs of clients who wanted traditional houses. David Adler (1882–1949) studied at Princeton, the Polytechnikum in Munich, and the École des Beaux-Arts in Paris. In Chicago, he worked for the architect Howard Van Doren Shaw. Important in many of his houses is symmetry, typically focused on a prominent entry sequence. He gave equal attention to both the front and rear elevations of his houses. He often collaborated with his sister on interior designs.

Adler worked skillfully and academically within the rules of a particular historic period. He was not one for upending traditions. Of note with the Armour house is that it has the grandeur and presence that the client desired. The symmetrical façade, surprisingly flat and theatrical (Figure 22.16), looks like a crisp sheet of white paper. The building is Georgian in its massing and federal in its detailing. Adler further emphasizes the flatness with a lawn that strikes the house's rear elevation with little intermediation of extensive terraces, lawn furniture, and plantings. With Adler, American historical architectural styles are up to the task of creating grand country houses for the mid–twentieth century.

California and Florida

Julia Morgan (1872–1957) was born in San Francisco. She pursued an engineering degree before deciding to study architecture. She also studied in Paris, at the École des Beaux-Arts. The imprint of her traditional French training is visible throughout her career.

After returning to San Francisco, Morgan opened her own office in 1904. She did hundreds of buildings over the course of her career—houses, primary and secondary schools, and a number of college buildings. The Julia Morgan School for Girls in Oakland is named after her. In 1919, William Randolph Hearst hired her to design a main building and guesthouses for his property at San Simeon (Kastner 2000, pp. 84–87). Twenty-five years of construction bound Hearst and Morgan together as collaborators on several Hearst projects in California, Arizona, and Mexico.

Early in her career, she was working within the stylistic parameters of the American Arts and Crafts movement. By the late 1920s, she was confidently designing in the Spanish-Moorish-Gothic idiom that became her hallmark and that became synonymous with California. For the Berkeley City Women's Club, 1929–1930, her pool is more straightforward than her flights of fancy for Hearst. Her work was often lavish and theatrical, although on the drafting board of Julia Morgan, the architectural vocabulary of Spanish colonial was absolutely appropriate for a variety of modern functions, such as an up-to-date athletic facility. In the lounge, Venetian Gothic windows, vaulted ceilings, tiled floors, and Spanish Renaissance chairs contribute to creating an atmosphere grounded in centuries-old tradition—although built in the 1920s (Figure 22.17).

The southeast coast also saw a sustained interest

Figure 22.17 Julia Morgan. Berkeley Women's City Club lounge, 1929–1930.

Figure 22.18 Addison Mizner. Casa Nana, George Rasmussen house. Palm Beach, Florida, 1926.

in traditional architecture. The romantic vernacular of many Spanish-inspired buildings in Florida is often quite informal. Yet in designing a home for the industrialist James Deering, F. Burrall Hoffman turned to nothing less than the Italian Renaissance, and any comparison between the Deering family and a Florentine papal family such as the Medicis is purely intentional. Colombian landscape architect Diego Suarez planned the extensive gardens that spread out over ten acres, and Paul Chalfin was the general artistic supervisor for the project, which included furniture, light fixtures, doors, fireplaces, and artwork (Rybczynski 2007, pp. 231–232). Many pieces were purchased by Deering and Chalfin on shopping trips in Europe. The elaborate house took

two years to build. At the height of construction, some one thousand workers toiled away at the Villa Vizcaya.

With its combination of Renaissance planning and Spanish and Moorish detailing, the building was once derided as kitsch, the home of a man with too much money to burn. Its reputation, and consequently that of its designers, has been rehabilitated in recent years. A significant moment in that process was when historian Colin Rowe started talking about the house favorably, stating that it could withstand comparison to actual Renaissance palazzi.

The association of Florida with the architectural tradition of the Spanish Renaissance is largely an invention of men like Hoffman and Addison Mizner. The Spanish left Florida in 1821, and left little in the way of an architectural legacy. Addison Mizner (1872–1933) was a world traveler, a connoisseur of antiques, art, and furnishings. He collaborated in several types of business ventures with his brother, Wilson. His is an American rags-to-riches-to-rags story, as he became a society architect despite having no formal academic training. He apprenticed with Willis Polk in San Francisco, learning architecture on the job, in the period 1893–1897. Like Morgan, he learned by traveling, especially in Central and South America (Curl 1984, pp. 12–15). Fluent in Spanish, he studied briefly at the University of Salamanca, Spain.

The existence of many architects who created buildings in historical styles was driven not just by clients but by the education and experiences of the architects as well. Mizner loved traveling, and purchasing antiques and reproductions, and selling them to clients or using them in the houses he designed for them. He described his trips to Europe, in which he bought furnishings to be resold in the United States, as "raids" (Mizner 1932).

He traveled to China with his brothers. He was fond of Japanese gardens, documented by his many sketches and watercolors. In Hawaii, he befriended ex-Queen Liliuokalani and supported himself painting ivory miniatures. He entered a boxing match in Australia, which he won. He imported Guatemalan coffee and Guatemalan woodworking, which he resold. He traveled to Samoa, Italy, and Morocco.

His town planning for Boca Raton, Florida, reveals his keen eye for business. For example, he innovatively developed the idea of selling houses on the fairways of a golf course. Stanford White also helped him obtain commissions.

Mizner's Casa Nana is more playful than most houses by Adler (Figure 22.18). Mizner was adept at creating houses for moderately wealthy clients, whose more modest riches placed them lower on the social and economic scale than Astors and Vanderbilts.

His houses typically focus on a central dramatic feature. In George Rasmussen's house, a circular stair tower contains the double-height entry hall. He effortlessly drew upon and combined Gothic, Romanesque, Spanish, and Moorish traditions.

THE RISE OF THE DECORATOR

Just as architects David Adler and Julia Morgan responded to the need of a wealthy class of people for houses that reflected tried-and-true notions of status, there was also a growing need for professionals to help with outfitting the interiors of these houses. Interiors historian John Pile refers to the phenomenon as "The Rise of the Decorator" (Pile 2000). Interior decorating, as a profession, interestingly proceeded in different directions from that predicted by the work of architects also involved in producing traditionally styled houses.

Elsie de Wolfe (1865–1950) is well known as the pioneer professional interior decorator. Educated privately in New York and Edinburgh, she started her career as an actress. After redecorating her home to acclaim, she turned her attention to interior decoration and formed her own company in 1901 (she retired entirely from the theater in 1905). De Wolfe was influenced by Sarah Cooper Hewitt, the granddaughter of the industrialist Peter Cooper. Sarah Hewitt and her two sisters founded the museum that developed into the Cooper-Hewitt National Design Museum in New York.

In 1903 de Wolfe, together with Elizabeth Marbury, her manager and companion, bought and restored the Villa Trianon in France (Sparke 2005, p. 301). Known for her social connections, the architect Stanford White helped de Wolfe obtain the project that started her career: the interior of the Colony Club in New York. In 1913, she published her first book, *The House in Good Taste,* likely written with the assistance of a ghostwriter. Her social connections included wealthy people on both sides of the Atlantic. Some of her connections involved Charles Parson, president of the New York School of Fine and Applied Arts. When de Wolfe moved to France, she closely associated with many elite, including the American Van Day Truex, head of the Paris campus of Parson's. In Paris, de Wolfe acted as an art dealer and collector. In 1926, she married Sir Charles Mendl, a British diplomat to France. The new Lady Mendl counted among her friends Diana Vreeland, Elsa Maxwell, Marcel Proust, and Bernard Berenson.

Elsie de Wolfe did not share the academic approach of Arthur Davis and Stanford White, whose knowledge of French architectural styles was extensive. De Wolfe was committed to eighteenth-century French furnishings, but she used them inventively. She lived in a time when there was a general disdain for Victorian design (an attitude she shared with the modernists) yet it was not immediately apparent how the vocabulary of eighteenth-century French interiors and furnishings could be adapted for the twentieth century. De Wolfe, and others after her, showed the way. She was respectful but not fearful of the periods she used. She relied heavily on white paint and did not hesitate to recommend having wood paneling painted. In the dining room of the New York house she shared with Marbury, she brought about a "dramatic transformation" employing Louis XVI chairs, white paint, and mirrors (Sparke 2005, p. 31) (Figure 22.19).

De Wolfe was a professional woman who helped interior design become a separate entity from the architectural profession. Stanford White's support suggests that he saw her not as a competitor for his core business activities but as a valued consultant. The purview of interior design was not an area of work that most architects were either interested in or capable of doing. This had not always been the case. In eighteenth-century England, France, and Germany, most interior design work, meaning wood paneling and ordering furnishings, was done by men. Another important benchmark for the professionalization of interior design was the development of academic programs. The field of interior design would soon have its own schools.

De Wolfe was a pioneer in many respects, and several of the parameters of her individual approach to the interior decorating business came to be representative of the entire profession. In no small part because of de Wolfe, interior design became a field open to women. Less discussed, although by no means a secret, is that it became a field in which gays and lesbians could operate openly. De Wolfe also played a role here. Songwriter Cole Porter, an erudite man with occasionally bawdy tastes, counted de Wolfe among his friends. This did not keep him from writing thinly veiled verses about Lady Mendl:

> Elsie de Wolfe, old and weary
> Might have lived and died a fairy,
> But Sir Charles Mendl she met and wed,
> And *on dit*, they went to bed.

Porter was a master of double entendre, and hinted that the Mendls had a marriage of convenience. Porter was one of the most prominent songwriters of his day, and Mendl's appearance in a Porter song underscores that she had become a figure in American popular culture.

Interior design was a field in which gay men and lesbians could work without their private lives being a disadvantage, and in fact, it sometimes figured positively in their networking across an array of professions, from entertainment to art to furniture design.

Francis Elkins (1888–1953) was David Adler's sister. No doubt inspired by de Wolfe's success, after she married and moved to California in 1918, she ran her own interior design business. She collaborated with her brother on many projects and also worked independently. They worked on several houses on Chicago's North Shore and also in the

Figure 22.19 Elsie de Wolfe, dining room.

San Francisco Bay Area during the 1920s and 1930s. She and Adler traveled together to Europe many times. On one trip, she met Jean-Michel Frank. At first it might seem odd that the modernist Frank should have befriended Adler and Elkins, but he did, and both brother and sister incorporated some of his furniture into their designs. Elkins was, in fact, responsible for introducing Frank's work to the United States. She also used a palm frond table by Emilio Terry to great effect. Her friendship with the French designers was important for her career. Elkins's work, more so than her brother's, blends traditional design with avant-garde elements.

The Kersey Coates Reed House, 1931–1932, is one project that displays her collaboration with her brother and her characteristic mix of traditional fur-

nishings, modern pieces, and Chinese art. For the library, she had the walls covered with tan Hermès goatskin and used a leather sofa and table by Frank (Salny 2005, p. 72). A photograph of the library illustrates precisely what it is that decorators do: combine elements of architecture and art with pieces of furniture to craft a work of interior design. The height of her collaboration with her brother was from 1926 through the late 1930s.

Dorothy Draper (1889–1969) belongs to the second generation of decorators. Like de Wolfe, she relied on her social connections, a factor that served her extremely well during the development of her interior decorating business, Dorothy Draper & Company, which she started in 1925. At the age of twenty-three, Dorothy Tuckerman married Dr.

Figure 22.20 Dorothy Draper. Metropolitan Museum of Art Cafeteria, 1954 (destroyed).

George Draper, with whom she had three children.

As with de Wolfe's clients, Draper's clients wanted interiors to include traditional pieces of furniture, but they did not necessarily want to see them used in traditional ways. Draper showed how twentieth-century designers could use traditional pieces of furniture and be modern. She did a few stylistically modern projects, and in them showed people how to incorporate decorative pieces and patterned textiles. Whereas designs by Mies van der Rohe and Charlotte Perriand seemed austere to some, designs by Draper were fun and appealing.

Draper began creating homes for other society members, in a style that was uniquely her own and a complete departure from the perceived gloom of the Victorian style of decorating. The type of design associated with Draper (and her imitators, which were legion) is sometimes referred to as "modern baroque." She went far afield from strict traditional designs, an approach that was ideal for restaurants, hotels, and stores. While some considered her work gaudy, it is more charitably described as bold. Draper, an innovative American interior decorator of the early- to mid-twentieth century, was the writer of a syndicated newspaper column and also landed on the covers of *Time* and *Life* magazines, leaving no doubt about the extent of her influence.

Draper's contribution to design received official recognition in May 2006 when the Museum of the City of New York held an exhibition of her work.

Freewheeling in her use of historical styles, she sometimes, famously, disfigured original finishes, of furniture or woodworking, to achieve a new look. Her designs drew on many influences, but she was particularly known for dramatic use of black and white on floors, walls, and upholstered pieces, as with her cafeteria for the Metropolitan Museum of Art (Figure 22.20). The style that she created and successfully executed is still influential today.

Billy Baldwin (1903–1983) designed an entrance hall for Cole and Linda Porter's apartment and included it in a book on his design philosophy, illustrated with his projects. One image caption "Country House on the 33rd Floor" refers to Porter's song "Down in the Depths on the 90th Floor" and is also a wry recognition of the incongruity of designing a high-rise apartment to look like a well-appointed French country house.

Baldwin's design for the entrance hall includes the clever design moves he was known for: He upholstered a Louis XV settee in what was clearly a twentieth-century textile. What makes it work as part of an ensemble is that it and the artwork are elements in a consistent brown and eggshell color scheme. Baldwin frequently worked with a restricted color palette.

If Viscaya was for a fabulously wealthy family, Van Day Truex showed that elegance could shape the lives of people of more modest means. He was not a wealthy person, but he decorated his homes with French antiques, proving that with careful placement, elite-style decorating could be affordable. He was not dogmatic, often combining expensive antiques with inexpensive or modern pieces.

The best school for training interior designers was the New York School of Fine and Applied Arts, later the Parsons School of Design. Led by Van Day Truex, it became the foremost training ground for interior decorators.

The quality of admiring historical styles, while simultaneously treating them off-handedly, was characteristic of de Wolfe, Draper, and Baldwin. This attitude toward historical styles, and antiques, was also characteristic of other designers around the world, one of them an eccentric figure in France, Madeleine Castaing (1894–1992). Castaing was a French interior designer and antiques dealer (Liaut 2008). She owned a shop in Paris where she sold antiques and modern works of art. Her favorite periods were neoclassical—empire, second-empire, and Biedermeier. She combined neoclassical furnishings with contemporary textiles, favoring bold stripes and leopard prints. Her own home sported a leopard-print carpet. Examples of her unorthodox views of decorating and fashion were many; she advocated plastic flowers, and in her later years wore a wig with a clearly visible chin strap. She supported the work of the designer Poiret, the artist Modigliani, and counted Yves Saint Laurent among her clients; he admired her penchant for bamboo furnishings. She was photographed wearing a dress that matched the upholstery of the chair she sat in.

CONCLUSION

Architects and designers who operated within recognizable historical styles played important roles throughout the twentieth century. The 1920s is the decade associated with Art Deco, one of the styles, along with Rococo and Art Nouveau, in which the greatest artistic achievements are found in interiors, furnishings, and designed objects. France had been a major center for those artistic periods of the eighteenth and nineteenth centuries, as it was for Art Deco, one of the most significant design developments of the twentieth century. In many respects, Art Deco designs had a lot in common with the modern designs coming out of Germany and France. As with many modernist pieces, Art Deco works display affinities to Cubism, Russian Constructivism, and Italian Futurism. Further evidence of the

Modernism/Art Deco link was the presence of Austrian designers, who were familiar with the Secessionists and who became the big names in American Art Deco.

A lesson learned from the decorators was that the middle class could successfully emulate the lifestyles of the rich. When looking at Art Deco, Modernism, and the ongoing appeal of traditional design, the irony is that fancy designs appealed to the masses while populist designs made of humble materials often found rich fans.

Comparing this chapter to the preceding chapter, significant differences separate Art Deco and modernism. Art Deco designers were less concerned with functionalism and the ability of their products to affect the social good. Art Deco was connected to the fashion world, one example of its ties to elite circles. Stylistic differences were felt deeply by the people involved, and a schism developed between the designers/decorators known as *ensembliers* and the modernists. Some designers overlooked differences and were able to collaborate, such as Frances Elkins and Jean-Michel Frank. For many, the antipathy that they felt toward Modernism could not be overcome.

Important sidebars to the story of design include the growing importance of women in shaping the interior design profession, and the increased visibility of gays and lesbians. In addition to their professional achievements, both groups were instrumental in fostering an academic and professional infrastructure to support the design field, another significant development of the twentieth century. European modernism was anointed with the title "The International Style"; the next chapter addresses the topic of Modernism and the world. Art Deco has just as much right to a global claim, as its spread from France to the United States, and then from both to around the world, demonstrates.

Art Deco works are easily identifiable, with their shiny materials and characteristic zigzag forms. The works were unashamedly decorative. This chapter presented three design strands—Art Deco, traditionalists, and decorators. Looking at all three confirms the ability of designers to offer differing views of what the world should look like and how to go about designing and crafting man-made objects. Differences abound; what all three shared was the activity of contending with how to make history new, adaptable, and relevant.

Sources

Albrecht, Donald, ed. *Paris/New York: Design Fashion Culture, 1925–1940.* New York: Museum of the City of New York, 2008.

Alonso, Alejandro, et al. *Havana Deco.* New York: Norton, 2007.

Benton, Charlotte, ed. *Art Deco 1910–1939.* Boston: Bulfinch, 2003.

Binney, Marcus. *The Ritz Hotel: London.* London: Thames and Hudson, 1999.

Bréon, Emmanuel. *Jacques-Émile Ruhlmann: Furniture.* Paris: Flammarion, 2004.

Bréon, Emmanuel. *Jacques-Émile Ruhlmann: Interior Design.* Paris: Flammarion, 2004.

Bréon, Emmanuel, and Pepall, Rosalind. *Ruhlmann: Genius of Art Deco.* Montreal: Montreal Museum of Fine Arts, 2004.

Butler, Judith. *Gender Trouble: Feminism and the Subversion of Identity.* New York: Routledge, 1999.

Carter, Randolph and Robert Reed Cole. *Joseph Urban: Architecture, Theatre, Opera, Film.* New York: Abbeville Press, 1992.

Curl, Donald. *Mizner's Florida: American Resort Architecture.* Cambridge: MIT Press, 1984.

Denison, Edward. *Asmara: Africa's Secret Modernist City.* London: Merrell, 2003.

Duncan, Alastair. *Art Deco Furniture: The French Designs.* New York: Holt, Rinehart, and Winston, 1984.

Éditions du Centre National de la Recherche Scientifique. *Trésor de la Langue Française,* vol. 7. Paris: Éditions du Centre National de la Recherche Scientifique, 1979.

Fisher, Richard. *Syrie Maugham.* Dallas: Duckworth, 1978.

Gray, Susan, ed. *Architects on Architects.* New York: McGraw-Hill, 2001.

Hanks, David. *Donald Deskey: Decorative Designs and Interiors.* New York: Dutton, 1987.

Kastner, Victoria. *Hearst Castle: The Biography of a Country House*. New York: Abrams, 2000.

Lewis, Adam. *Van Day Truex: The Man Who Defined Twentieth-Century Taste and Style*. New York: Viking Studio, 2001.

Liaut, Jean-Hoël. *Madeleine Castaing*. Paris: Payot, 2008.

Long, Christopher. *Josef Frank: Life and Work*. Chicago: University of Chicago Press, 2002.

Long, Christopher. *Paul T. Frankl and Modern American Design*. New Haven: Yale University Press, 2007.

Mizner, Addison. *The Many Mizners*. New York: Sears Pub., 1932.

Pennoyer, Peter, and Anne Walker. *The Architecture of Delano and Aldrich*. New York: Norton, 2003.

Pevsner, Nikolaus. "Building With Wit: The Architecture of Sir Edwin Lutyens." *Architectural Review* cix (1951): pp. 217–225.

Pile, John. *History of Interior Design*. New York: Wiley, 2000.

Roth, Leland. *McKim, Mead, and White, Architects*. New York: Harper and Row, 1983.

Rybczynski, Witold. *Vizcaya: An American Villa and Its Makers*. Philadelphia: University of Pennsylvania Press, 2007.

Salny, Stephen. *Frances Elkins: Interior Design*. New York: Norton, 2005.

Sparke, Penny. *Elsie de Wolfe: The Birth of Modern Interior Decoration*. New York: Acanthus, 2005.

Stern, Robert. *Raymond Hood*. New York: Rizzoli, 1982.

Thorne, Martha, ed. *David Adler, Architect: the Elements of Style*. New Haven: Yale University Press, 2003.

Tise, Suzanne. "Art Deco" in Jane Turner's *The Dictionary of Art*. New York: Grove, 1996, pp. 519–522.

Tise, Suzanne, and Yvonne Brunhammer. *The Decorative Arts in France, 1900–1942*. New York: Rizzoli, 1990.

Varney, Carleton. *The Draper Touch: The High Life and High Style of Dorothy Draper*. New York: Prentice-Hall, 1988.

Watkin, David. "Davis, Arthur Joseph (1878–1951)." In *Oxford Dictionary of National Biography*. Oxford: OUP, 2004. http://0-www.oxforddnb.com.library.unl.edu:80/view/article/62902 (accessed April 25, 2008).

Yeomans, David, and David Cottam. *Owen Williams*. London: Thomas Telford, 2001.

Zerbe, Peter. *Die Grossen Deutschen Passagierschiffe*. Hamburg: Nautik Historie Verlag, 1999.

DISCUSSION AND REVIEW QUESTIONS

1. What are the characteristics of Art Deco that distinguish it from 1920s and 1920s German and French Modernism?

2. What are some characteristics Art Deco shares with other movements—where it was tapping into broad interests?

3. How has the reputation of some designers changed posthumously?

4. What did decorators do?

5. What does it mean if design is popular—that is, appeals to the masses? What makes Art Deco decorative?

6. What makes a design elite? Give specific examples of either designs or materials used.

7. What did Art Deco designers and modernist designers have in common?

8. How did Art Deco designers and modernist designers differ in their approach?

9. In what ways did Art Deco designers relate to and incorporate history?

10. What are the differing characteristics between the French and American versions of Art Deco?

11. How did traditionally trained architects and designers respond to the twentieth-century condition? Why are traditional designs appealing to many people?

CHAPTER 23

OTHER MODERNISMS

1936	1939–1941	1953–1970
Le Corbusier & Niemeyer, Ministry of Education, Brazil	Charlotte Perriand in Japan	Modern Architecture in Cambodia

Modernism, it is commonly said, started in Germany and France. Then, in a classic case of anthropological diffusion, one scenario explains its spread by the variety of mechanisms that cause cultural trends to traverse the globe. Travel, journals, books, and exhibitions were some of the vehicles that distributed the lessons of modernism. World War II compelled many Bauhaus designers to emigrate to Britain, to the United States, Brazil, Argentina, Kenya, and Japan. Who-worked-for-whom was another mechanism of knowledge diffusion and served as a designer's pedigree. Le Corbusier worked for Peter Behrens and thereby learned from him; many burgeoning architects and designers worked in Le Corbusier's office, learned from him, and took with them their newfound knowledge when they returned to their home countries. Le Corbusier was particularly significant in this regard. Josep Luis Sert, Kiyoshi Ikebe, Rogelio Salmona, Emilio Duhart, Robert Matta, and Oscar Niemeier, to name a few, all worked at one time in his office.

And of course there are the buildings the masters did themselves around the world: Le Corbusier in India, Japan, Argentina, the United States, and Tunisia; Louis Khan in Bangladesh; Frank Lloyd Wright in Japan. Despite several attempts, Mies had less of an impact on international building and most of his works grace American soil.

Scholars from William Curtis to Colin Rowe, whose statements on modernism are still considered sacrosanct, write that modernism was initially an avant-garde, European intellectual movement that spread around the world in the 1950s. And there is more than a kernel of truth to this explanation. But there is another story that explains the rise of modernism around the world, and that is that it flowered, independently, at multiple locations. That is the subject of this chapter.

European and Western architects and designers play a role here, just as Asian, African, and Latin American architects are present in other chapters. And certain figures, such as Antonin Raymond and Geoffrey Bawa, whose identities and allegiances are complicated, can only be described as early citizens of a global design world.

Modernism spread at different paces to different places, and was received sometimes with measured skepticism, sometimes with unbridled enthusiasm. It was initially slow to raise its head in the United States and Britain, yet proved a quick study in Mexico and

Brazil. Modernism was never a monolithic entity or style, and in some arenas it was reflexive and responsive to local conditions. Far from the idea that multiple global modernisms were void, many find that the "foreign" versions are more successful than the European variety, with their sensitivity to materials, history, local traditions, and emotional richness.

It is surprising how early on committed modernists spanned the globe. The standard story for modernism's spread is that it occurred after World War II; yet, as this chapter shows, modernism was percolating across the globe as early as the 1920s and 1930s. After World War II, those areas that had temporarily lagged behind quickly caught up. When examining the rise of modernism around the world, we see that in Brazil, South Africa, Mexico, and Japan, modern ideas and projects were present as early as the 1920s. Clearly, another narrative of cultural genesis is at play. If one considers that modernity is the nebulous entity by which the world lurches forward, and that modernism is the artistic representation of coming to grips with the present and the future, then all regions of the globe experienced modernity and thereby played a part, albeit unequally, in creating "modernism." No region was immune to the technological effects of automobiles, airplane travel, television, radio, telephones, telegraphs, Technicolor movies (and later computers, jets, the Internet, the Walkman, the mobile phone, and the MP3 player). These were experienced as innovations, or as devices whose use became increasingly widespread. All areas of the globe were modern and thereby produced their unique form of modernism.

LATIN AMERICA

In Latin America, one explanation for the multiplicity of forms that modernism took is that different Latin American countries had vastly different histories. Mexico and Peru had ancient cultures. The primarily indigenous groups of Brazil and Argentina were talented in textiles, baskets, and pottery, but did not have monumental architecture. Bolivia was poor; Argentina, befitting its name, was rich.

Mexico

For Mexico, the important contemporary contextual note is that modernism is related to the Mexican Revolution, 1910–1920. The political revolution that ended a thirty-year-long dictatorship was followed by a design revolution. Mexico first built a firm foundation of modernist design with works in the 1920s and 1930s by Luis Barragán, Juan O'Gorman, and others. A constant theme in this chapter is that modernism meant different things in different places. Even in one location, such as Mexico City, it held different meanings for different people. As a broad-brush generalization, early Mexican modernism is viewed in conjunction with the revolution and democracy. Yet the leader of Mexican modernism, Barragán himself, opposed it. The dictatorship had favored the wealthy, and Barragán, something of an elitist, was no fan of the people's revolution.

Known as the first modernist in Mexico, José Villagran Garcia approached new architecture from the perspective of functionalism, architecture's relationship to modern art, and its ability to solve special needs in Mexico, from education to housing. An architect and a teacher, Garcia saw two of his pupils become major figures in the development of Mexican modernism. One was Mario Pani, who counted University City among his achievements; Mexico's flagship university was founded in 1551 but moved to its new campus in 1954. Another architect associated with the university was Juan O'Gorman.

Juan O'Gorman's House and Studio for Diego Rivera and Frida Kahlo (1929–1930) looks to Le Corbusier's Ozenfant studio and also Russian Constructivism. It was built for a compelling couple,

Figure 23.1 Juan O'Gorman. Home and studio of Diego Rivera and Frida Kahlo. Mexico City, Mexico.

two Mexican artists who both had strong personalities. It's a modern work with geometric profiles, metal railings, and curved stairways, but its bold use of colors and palisade of cacti foreshadow that Mexican modernism was to be no pale imitation of European modernism (Figure 23.1).

It is also a beguiling architectural portrait of a couple, two artists each with their own studios on the top floor, his a bit larger, which reflects Rivera's oversized body and ego. The connections between the two almost separate structures are tenuous (like their unconventional marriage), a catwalk on the top floor and a discreet path on the ground. It was also an opportunity for O'Gorman to experiment with a design that could be industrialized, thus addressing Mexico's housing deficit, an interest of the Mexican revolutionary party.

One of the outstanding features of Mexican mod-ernism, inaugurated with O'Gorman's Rivera/Kahlo house, is how thoroughly it became a part of the local architectural vocabulary. Modernism became enmeshed in the domestic realm in a way that did not happen in the United States, where the modern house met resistance. Mexico embraced the modern house. Mexico is doubly important for the history of architecture, because the reconsideration of modernism as a global phenomenon largely starts with the rehabilitation of the career of Luis Barragán.

Barragán

Latin American Modernism has an appealing champion in the figure of Luis Barragán (1902–1988). Keith Eggener succinctly writes that Barragán "endeavored to reconcile modernism with the indigenous architecture of Mexico, in order to express a distinct sense of place" (Eggener in Sennott 2004, pp. 116–117). First among his achievements was his confident relationship to history and tradition; European modernists, in contrast, often seem conflicted about history and uneasy in their approach to tradition. Barragán's projects easily make reference to many traditions, including pre-Columbian, Spanish colonial, and the rural hacienda tradition.

Another successful feature of his architecture is its reliance on a deep understanding of local construction techniques. European modernists developed a crisp aesthetic of white planes that was difficult to achieve and hard to maintain. The problems with Le Corbusier's signature Villa Savoye began shortly after its completion; the roof leaked and the walls grew spotty. Barragán ingeniously worked with local building methods that did not require complicated detailing from outside that tradition.

In the 1940s, one of the projects that display many of the features associated with Barragán's architecture, lightheartedly referred to as Barraganismo, can be seen in his own Barragán House, Mexico City (1947) (Figure 23.2). The stairhall has a concrete stair, a painting by Matthias Goeritz, and an inexpensive wood chair with a straw seat. The Galvez House (1955) is another frequently published work. A recurring motif in his buildings is that certain details make a sophisticated commentary on the grid's relationship to modernity. An all-encompassing grid fills some windows, with the result that the landscape beyond is overlain with an ordered system of lines, breaking the view into little segments (Rispa 2003, pp. 28–29). Other windows feature a simple cross, a decidedly light touch with religious overtones. Barragán was deeply religious and prominently featured the cross in his own house. The cross also renders obvious the glass's presence as a transparent plane. Because of its inherent planarity and rectilinearity, Barragán's work is most often compared to Mies's, yet Bar-

Figure 23.2 Luis Barragan. Barragan House, Mexico City, Mexico, 1947.

ragán himself cites Le Corbusier as the greater influence.

Another room in Barragán's home utilizes a chair that he used on several projects. It was designed in collaboration with Clara Porset, a Cuban designer. Known as the *butaca* or *butaque* chair, it was based on a traditional Mexican chair, although Porset simplified its lines. She created several versions of the chair (Zanco 2001, p. 86 and p. 101).

Just as European artists relate to the works of Picasso and Mondrian, Barragán was active in the art scene in Mexico City and knew personally many of the surrealists and minimalists, including Diego Rivera and Mathias Goeritz, the latter of whom was a frequent collaborator. And the colors! An example of the technical simplicity of his architecture are the dramatic effects Barragán achieved with paint. He favored saturated colors, including pinks, blues, yellows, and reds, that give his buildings a character unlike anything built in Europe.

Barragán's work expresses a confident approach to the landscape. Most architects give lip service to relating to nature, yet Barragán does so in an unusual way, often by not making obvious overtures to the landscape. While his designs frequently make reference to the landscape, he is confident enough to block it out on occasion, with high walls; a typical Barraganesque detail is to have a wisp of tree visible, like a clip of a photograph of a tree, in the distance, floating above a plane. The relationship of Barragán's houses to nature bears resemblance to Mies van der Rohe's collages. Barragán was clever enough to realize that, correctly done, one way to relate to nature is to seemingly ignore it.

Barragán was not a strict functionalist. His buildings have an emotional quality that arises from his use of materials, color, and natural light. He developed a carefully orchestrated sense of surprise and discovery in his houses. His works defy the common criticism of modern buildings, that they are impersonal or cold. His buildings, and photographs of them, evoke a sense of serenity and peace, even when in urban surroundings. But nowhere is the metaphysical aspect of Barragán's work so evident as with his San Cristobal Riding Stables of 1968, Barragán's magnum opus. It is a work of landscape as much as a work of architecture, with Aztec-inspired massive walls, expansive pools, and red walls. It is incredibly photogenic (Eggener 2001, p. 75).

Barragán's international reputation was a long time in coming, but once people started turning their attention to his pink walls there was no turning back. In 1976, the Museum of Modern Art held a retrospective of his work. In 1980, he won the Pritzker Prize. The inclusion of Luis Barragán into the canon of modern masters has been so instrumental that it has resulted in a reevaluation of just what modernism is.

The Breadth of Mexican Modernism

The project for a new university campus in Mexico City, University City, was a monumental collaborative effort that included many architects, including Mario Pani, Juan O'Gorman, and Teodoro González de León. Eschewing American and English academic models, it put Le Corbusier's city-planning principles into action. The complex includes O'Gorman's Library (1950), the most prominent building whose façades are richly covered with mosaics that link modern scientific achievements with Aztec graphic representation also designed by O'Gorman.

Nearby, the sports pavilions designed in 1953 by Espinosa Arai ingeniously echo the massing of low platforms found in pre-Columbian sites such as Mitla. Made of stone, these forms contain the audience seating for the sports venues and the high-dive platform.

In Chapultepec Park, the National Museum of Anthropology in Mexico City by Pedro Ramírez Vásquez (1963–1964) is a stunning building that makes subtle allusions to the pre-Columbian cultures whose artifacts it houses. It is a modern structural marvel with a huge roof that covers the immense courtyard, miraculously supported on a single column that is also a fountain.

Mexico City entered the informal international race to have a major skyscraper with the Torrelatinoamerica (1957), competently designed by Augusto Alvarez, proving that Mexican modernists were capable of mastering tall-building technology. Feliz Candela experimented with concrete thin-shell technology to produce a variety of sculptural forms that housed everything from open-air markets to churches (Faber 1963). The talent pool of Mexican designers was deep, talented, and prolific.

Ricardo Legorreta (b. 1931) is a protégé of Barragán, which is visible in his work that employs forms reminiscent of Aztec and Mayan architecture

Figure 23.3 Ricardo Legorreta. Camino Real Hotel. Cocktail lounge. Mexico City, 1967.

yet is enlivened with a color palette derived from Mexican folk art. The Hotel Camino Réal in Mexico City is sophisticated, pleasing to the public, and looks modern and Mexican (Legorreta 2004, p. 290). Its popular cocktail lounge is filled with modern classic furniture. Harry Bertoia's Diamond Chairs sit on a glass floor under which there is running water (Figure 23.3). Yet Legorreta is not afraid to incorporate Spanish colonial elements, one of his design strategies that results in a moving evocation of locality. Legorreta and his son, Victor Legorreta (b. 1966), practice together and represent the second and third generations of Mexican modernists.

Brazil

The other major center of early Latin American modernism was Brazil. Rio de Janeiro was a South American center of Art Nouveau, with some of the finest projects done by Eliseu Visconti. To the extent that modernism grew out of the modernizing trends inherent in Art Nouveau, a lack of a historically based vocabulary, and the embrace of new materials, Brazil was well-positioned for modernism to flower.

Rio de Janeiro and Brasília

Albertos Santos Dumont (1873–1932) was one of the inventors of the airplane. There is controversy over who had the first airplane flight (the argument stands on how long a plane has to stay aloft to be considered flying). Americans claim that the Wright Brothers achieved the first flight; Brazilians stand by Dumont. The argument over this pivotal modern achievement also plays out in the field of design. And, interestingly enough, Dumont was an innovative creator in many fields. He designed his own house, the Casa Encantada in Pétropolis, a city in the mountains close to Rio, which includes a unique flight of scalloped stairs.

The formal arrival of modernism in Brazil is easily traced to one building, the Ministry of Education in Rio de Janeiro, 1936–1945, in which no less than Le Corbusier was the consulting architect. Hired to act as his assistant was a precocious young Brazilian architect, Oscar Niemeyer (Underwood 1994, p. 20). The Ministry of Education has, like Corbusier's influential apartment block the Unité, pilotis, a roofscape, and brises-soleil. The latter is a porous architectural screen that lets in air and shields the building from direct sunlight. This engaging façade element was particularly well suited for tropical climates and became a favored device for sporting a local decorative motif.

Niemeyer was born in Rio in 1907. In 1930, he went to the National School for the Fine Arts, where Lucio Costa was director. Among the students was the landscape architect Roberto Burle Marx, who would be a future collaborator with Niemeyer and the designer of Rio's Copacabana sidewalks.

Brazil and Oscar Niemeyer were embarking down their modernist road extraordinarily quickly, starting in the 1930s. Some two decades later, Niemeyer was an established architect in his home country. With the house that Niemeyer designed for himself in the Canoas district of Rio, he established his international reputation as a modernist of note (Figures 23.4 and 23.5). Niemeyer's house promoted a sensuous alternative to mechanistic modernism (Underwood 1994, p. 78).

This small house was built in 1953 and is reminiscent of the lightweight concrete structures in Mexico made by Felix Candela. It challenges several modernist conventions. As an iconic work of

Figure 23.4 Oscar Niemeyer. Niemeyer House. Canoas, Rio de Janeiro, 1953.

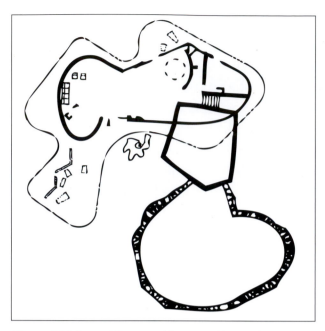

Figure 23.5 Oscar Niemeyer. Niemeyer House. Canoas, Rio de Janeiro, 1953.

domestic architecture, it draws comparison to the Mies's Farnsworth House and Philip Johnson's Glass House. Yet it is a poetic alternative to the hyperrationality of both.

A curvilinear white concrete roof caps the walls, many of which are formed from large panels of plate glass. Its whiplash curves hug the Brazilian landscape, and it opens up to forest, sky, and water. A curvilinear pool perches on top of a large outcropping of rock; Burle Marx did the naturalistic landscaping. It was built, in a timely fashion, just before the organization that Le Corbusier founded, CIAM, met in Brazil in 1954. (The International Congresses of Modern Architecture was a group of like-minded modernists who promoted avant-garde architecture.) It was elegantly furnished with classic modern pieces of furniture, some European, others made in Brazil. "The shapely design was not the first stone thrown at the glass Bauhaus box, but it was the first cast by a prince of the realm" (Hess 2006, p. 31).

Brazil, like many countries in the 1950s, wanted to present itself to the international audience as progressive, and a quick means to do that was through modern architecture. Niemeyer collaborated with his former teacher, Lúcio Costa, in designing a new capital of Brazil, Brasília. This project, controversial and influential, managed to be monumental with a starkly modern vocabulary. Lúcio Costa created a plan in which the grid was absent. It is a plan destined to grow linearly. Because of its large-scale curves, it is compared to a bird or airplane's wings (a subtle nod to Santos Dumont). Niemeyer did an impressive group of major buildings. The long-lived Niemeyer had a prolific career, equaled by few in terms of longevity or quantity and quality of work, including many buildings that formed the core of the capital city of Brasília, 1957–1958.

São Paulo

The rise of Niemeyer presents the activity in the country's artistic and governmental capital, Rio de Janeiro. But Brazil's business center, São Paulo, was home to a lively modern art scene that had been active since the 1920s. São Paulo held a Modern Art Week, Semana 22, in 1922, a seminal moment for the introduction of artistic modernism into Brazil. The industrial city sought to refashion itself as cosmopolitan, international, and more modern than Rio. The goal was to expose Brazilian artists to significant contemporary art trends, to renew avant-garde artistic activities in Brazil, and to lay claim to the legacy of European modernism, especially geometric abstraction. With assistance from Nelson Rockefeller and the Museum of Modern Art in New York, The Museum of Modern Art of São Paulo was founded in 1951. Brazil's place in the contemporary art world was cemented in 1953 when Picasso's *Guernica* put in an appearance at the Bienal (Leite and Burbridge 1995, pp. 197–217). Abstraction offered an alternative to South American stereotypes that frequently portrayed Brazil as exotic and flamboyant, the prime example being the Hollywood movies of Carmen Miranda.

Flavio de Carvalho was an architect and painter who built seventeen modernist houses in São Paulo in the 1930s. Leite and Burbridge describe the designer's own house: "The unusual atmosphere of the farmhouse was created largely by its interior decoration, where Carvalho combined handcraft and feather art made by Brazilian Indians" (Leite and Burbridge 1995, p. 212). Modernism was gaining a stronghold in Brazil in the 1930s, by designers who shared the international sympathies of relating to indigenous cultures.

Into this environment arrived Lina Bo Bardi (1914–1992). Italian-born, she had been the editor of the Italian design magazine *Domus* before moving to Brazil in 1947. In 1949, she founded the Brazilian design journal *Habitat*. She started a company,

Studio d'Arte Palma, that produced modern furniture (Ferraz 1994, pp. 64–67). She taught industrial design and built her own house (Figure 23.6). Her largest building was the Museu de Arte de São Paulo. Of Lina Bo Bardi's many furniture designs, the one to achieve the most international attention is her eponymous masterpiece Bardi's Bowl (1951) (Figure 23.7).

Brazil had a significant cadre of imported modernist architects and designers, including Jorge Zalsupin, Michel Arnoult, Gregori Warchavchik (1896–1972). It also produced a distinguished roster of homegrown modernistas: In addition to Costa and Niemeyer, Paulo Mendes do Rocha, Joâo Batista Villanova Artigas, Rino Levi, Sergio Bernardes, and Joâo Filgueiras Lima all did modern work. Signifi-

Figure 23.6 Lina Bo Bardi. Glass House. Interior. São Paulo, Brazil.

Figure 23.7 Lina Bo Bardi. Bardi's Bowl, 1951.

cantly, Brazil became a thriving center for locally produced modern furniture; many pieces did well on the international market.

Some of the other major furniture designers include João Carlos Cauduro, a Brazilian who studied industrial design in Florence and who ended up doing urban furniture (Leon 2005). Délia Beru, from Argentina, arrived in Brazil and started the firm Casa Teperman, which represented Herman Miller. In 1998, she opened Casa 21, which manufactured the designs of Eileen Gray. In the 1970s, Ernesto Hauner (1931–2002) worked for Bo Bardi's firm Mobilinea.

Argentina

Compared to Mexico and Brazil, modernism took root slowly in Argentina, which is curious because it started out the postwar period wealthier and more technologically advanced than either of those countries. Argentina, like Brazil, is a country whose indigenous people were skilled in textiles and pottery yet not active with monumental architecture.

Argentina also had a large immigrant population. Argentina seemed perfectly enamored of concrete, parabolic vaulting, reinforced concrete shells, and they embraced Brutalism for a while, one of modernism's more extreme offshoots.

Architecture

Amancio Williams (1913–1989) was an architect and urban planner. In 1949, he met Le Corbusier, who hired him to supervise the construction of a house in La Plata, the Currutchet House, not considered one of Le Corbusier's major works.

Williams's own House Over the Brook, 1945, designed for his father, is a distinguished piece of architecture (Figure 23.8). Boasting a dramatic relationship to nature—a brook flows underneath it—it is related to Frank Lloyd Wright's house Falling Water. Yet it also makes a unique architectural statement. Built like a bridge, a parabolic concrete arch holds the building aloft.

Williams later collaborated with Walter Gropius on an unbuilt project, the West German Embassy. Several of his buildings interface with health and hygiene, but Williams is primarily known for his lyrical forms and an aesthetic that brings architecture in concert with minimalism.

Clorindo Testa (b. 1923) was the leader of the rationalist strain of the South American modern movement. Testa freely admitted his ideological debt to Le Corbusier. About the French modernist, he said: "He became my model both in my university years and after graduation" (Glusberg 1984). He is often presented as a textbook example of a Brutalist architect. Brutalism, or New Brutalism, is related to Le Corbusier's later works. Brutalist works were almost always made in concrete, and a signature detail was showing the impressions made by the wooden formwork. Precise detailing was not a feature of Brutalism, the design equivalent of the Art Brut movement. Testa was a painter, and crisply delineated forms are a feature of both his paintings

Figure 23.8 Amancio Williams. House Over the Brook. Mar del Plata, Argentina, 1943–1945.

and buildings. The Bank of London and South America, 1960, was designed as a box within a box. The concrete façade is supported independently from the glazing on the exterior, and the result is a curtain layering effect of glass and large overhanging concrete slabs (Cuadra 2000, pp. 43–51).

Furniture

Jorge Ferrari-Hardoy (1914–1977) belongs to the cadre of architects who turned to furniture design. Born in Buenos Aires, he lived in Paris, where he collaborated with Le Corbusier, and throughout his life he remained active in CIAM. In 1938, he designed a simple chair of canvas stretched over a wooden frame, known as the Hardoy chair. The frame was later made of metal. The chair, used indoors and out, was enormously successful. "The Butterfly Chair," is sometimes known as "The Sling Chair" (Figure 23.9). Knoll and Artek initially manufactured the chair, which John Pile referred to as "handsome, inexpensive, and easy to make" (Pile 1990, p. 114).

Figure 23.9 Jorge Ferrari-Hardoy, Butterfly Chair.

Uruguay

Uruguayan engineer Eladio Dieste (1917–2000) studied in Montevideo and later taught structures. He next turned to producing a series of buildings based on light supporting structures, perfect for the series of bus stations and markets that he designed in the 1950s (Anderson 2004). He focused on local technology, materials, and construction methods to ground his designs in their local context. He is another example of a South American architect whose oeuvre expresses a fondness for thin-shelled vaults and ceramic tile.

He did the Catholic Church of Atlántida in 1958 (Figure 23.10). Interested in natural resources, he produced works that show a great deal of respect for and knowledge of a material's properties. He worked in brick, the most humble of vernacular materials, and also in reinforced brick. Dieste's work with steel-reinforced brick allowed him to create flowing curved interiors in brick; he transferred structural innovations originally explored in concrete.

Venezuela

There is not a single Latin American country that did not embrace modernism. In Venezuela, Carlos Raúl Villanueva (1900–1975) is credited with being the father of Venezuelan modern architecture. Paulina Villanueva (2000) wrote: "Villanueva placed equal, if not greater priority on the commodious design of interior space—the space where man and architecture meet" (p. 18). Mostly active in the 1950s, he designed his own house in 1952, and the Universidad Central de Venezuela, 1950–1959, for which he designed the campus layout and several buildings.

Lessons from Latin America

Pioneers such as Barragán, O'Gorman, and Niemeyer set the foundation for the second generation of Latin American architects, including Ricardo Legorreta. In the 1980s, Legorreta took off where Luis Barragán began. One of his projects was his Renault factory in Monterey, Mexico, 1984.

The modernist insistence on a break with the past had a different gloss in Mexico (and Peru). Styles associated with nineteenth-century eclecticism were frowned upon, but forms and materials related to the countries' heritages could be a valued source of inspiration. Louis XVI was out, but Aztec and Inca were in.

One significant aspect of modernism is that it was ripe for incorporating aspects of indigenous cultures, relying upon artistic and cultural traditions. Modernist designers had always enjoyed the bold shot in the arm of the "primitive" culture, vestigial elements, as part of their aesthetic bag of tricks. Amancio Williams took note of what Eileen Gray and Charlotte Perriand did, so he too threw an animal hide on the floor. But in his case, it was a cow hide, which makes a connection with the Argentine pampas tradition of cowboys and ranching.

Figure 23.10 Eladio Dieste. Catholic Church of Atlántida, Uruguay.

AFRICA

Kwame Anthony Appiah writes that, throughout history, most Africans have defined themselves in terms of bloodlines and local communities, but the idea of a shared African identity, much less a common culture, is a recent phenomenon, dating to the last 100 years. Africa has an enormous diversity: "It would take an eye completely insensitive to the particular to reduce this magnificent miscellany to the expression of the spirit of a singular, coherent, African nature" (Appiah in Phillips 1996, p. 7). Only then is the idea of Africa, in which diversity is a central characteristic of what it means to be African, possible.

A few African countries had some experience with modernism before World War II, but it was in the late 1940s and 1950s that modernism became widespread in Africa. For many Africans, a modernist building was a symbol of a new way of doing things and an optimistic look to the future. In the 1960s and 1970s, many areas experienced a crash course in modernism.

Modernism was called on for highly visible and prestigious projects, such as airports and football stadiums, which operated as instant status symbols. In many cases, countries went from third world to first world seemingly overnight. In countries with significant oil reserves, the important chronological benchmark is neither World War II nor independence, but before and after the discovery of oil, an example of how dating systems vary from place to place. Many African countries had to deal with changing from a rural and agricultural country to an urban industrialized country—quickly.

If there is a constant thread weaving across modern buildings in Africa, it is that, most important, modern architecture in Africa is related to national liberation movements and colonialism's end, occurring in the 1960s. Even if modernism was first introduced under the colonial regimes, modern architecture was associated with a look to a noncolonial future.

Africans had firsthand knowledge of the European masters through the buildings they designed in Africa. Auguste Perret and Jorn Utzon did buildings in Morocco. Le Corbusier visited Algiers in 1933 and 1938, working on urban designs, and a design for a multistoried building, not realized. There were African architecture schools in Khartoum, Kumasi, Nairobi, Addis Ababa, and Johannesburg, places that all played integral roles in circulating information about modernism.

The genesis of modernism is frequently explained by the legacies bequeathed from previous modernizing movements, such as Art Nouveau and Art Deco. It should be noted, therefore, that there are numerous examples of Art Deco in Africa, in South Africa, Tanzania, Senegal, Eritrea, Ethiopia, and elsewhere.

Egypt

Hassan Fathy (1900–1989) was a philosopher and a teacher as much as an architect. Dissatisfied with the international-style buildings that he saw dotting Cairo's urban landscape in the 1950s, he set about proposing an alternative in both words and bricks. He created a system of building that relied upon traditional construction methods. Because of lower labor costs in Egypt, labor-extensive construction methods were possible. He started in the 1940s with New Gourna, a new town built in the shadow of the ancient Mortuary Temple of Queen Hapshepsut. He ingeniously discovered that concrete frame housing had a historical connection with Egypt's native Nubian barrel-vaulted structures. These were made out of mud-brick walls, vaults, and low domes.

Fathy was a critic of non-native architects whose designs required the importation of foreign products not locally available. He introduced his ideas in a book, *Architecture for the Poor, an Experiment in Rural Egypt,* published in 1973. He is therefore known not just for his architecture but for giving an ideological approach to a new method that combines old and new and that added a local flavor to the global architecture. Fathy can be considered an Egyptian kindred spirit of Luis Barragán. Yet a limitation of his work is that it really does not explain how indigenous forms can be interpreted to provide high-rise hotels or airports.

He promoted utilizing local building methods, such as the Nubian earthen-dome, that had existed for millennia. Critical of modernization and industrialization, he was the first overt critic of modern architecture, a trend that was to gain steam. An Egyptian, Fathy sought to return his country to methods that predated Egypt's occupations under both the Ottomans and Europeans, and a way of refocusing contemporary Egyptian society on the vil-

Figure 23.11 Hassan Fathy. Abd al-Razik House. Plan/elevation, gouache.

lage. This was a forceful move to counter the push from rural to urban.

At a time when others publicly broke with the past, he connected with history. A drawing for the Abd-al-Razik House deliberately combines plan and elevation, reminiscent of ancient Egyptian art (Figure 23.11). The Hamid Said House shows the interior of a Nubian barrel vault, a form resolutely applicable to the layout and furnishings of a contemporary Egyptian home (Figure 23.12). The low built-in seating platform is reminiscent of a diwan, and the resulting composition is Nubian, Egyptian, Islamic, African, and modern. For those interested in discovering if there were autonomous African modernisms, the starting point for Africa is the life and works of Hassan Fathy.

South Africa

Two architectural schools of thought came head-to-head in South Africa in the late 1920s and 1930s: the remnants of nineteenth-century eclecticism and international modernism. Unlike elsewhere, this clash erases a larger tragedy—namely, the decimation of the local indigenous groups' traditional architectural practices. The impact of Europeans, chiefly Dutch and English, was so far-reaching in South Africa that precontact traditions in most artistic realms were drastically altered or ceased to exist. For example, the traditional round house no longer exists in South Africa.

Modernism's arrival is coincident with the professionalization of architecture. This process involved the establishment of professional organi-

Figure 23.12 Hassan Fathy. Hamid Said House. Egypt.

zations and educational programs. As Black and Coloured (mixed-race) South Africans were excluded from both, this is a white-on-white story until the end of the twentieth century.

Rex Distin Martienssen (1905–1942) was most responsible for the establishment of modern architecture in South Africa. An architect, theorist, and educator, his position as editor of the *South African Architectural Record* allowed him to publicly advocate for modernist design. This caught the world's attention; Le Corbusier affectionately referred to Martienssen and his like-minded colleagues in South Africa as the Transvaal Group. Martienssen remained friends with Le Corbusier to the end of his life. Highlighting the relationship between modernism and classicism, Martienssen was significantly a respected classicist.

While enthusiasm for the work of Le Corbusier found some supporters, others were not so enamored of the machine-edged purists and felt that Frank Lloyd Wright's brand of modernism, with adjustments, was more adaptable to the exceptional

South African landscape. A means to make architecture locally responsive is to interact with the landscape and use locally available materials, qualities that many admired in the work of Wright. This approach conveniently allowed white South African architects to metaphorically hide in the bush, ignore African indigenous traditions, while nonetheless proclaiming their Africaness.

Modern architecture, it should be pointed out, was not related to the emancipation of locals as it was in other parts of Africa. In South Africa, Blacks and Coloureds found their limited means to express political dissent in contemporary versions of traditional residential dwellings and decoration.

Norman Eaton (1902–1966) was a student in the 1920s, a time when the modern movement was just starting to be recognized and promoted by Martienssen and others. In the trajectory of Norman Eaton's career, some of his buildings, particularly the early ones and the big ones, are clearly modernist. Embracing forms associated with international modernism was not problematic for Eaton. He wanted to be a major architect with large, prestigious projects. He completed several large South African banks in the 1940s. His project for the Ministry of Transport (1944–1948), an unrealized hugely ambitious project, is formally indebted to another unbuilt project, Le Corbusier's League of Nations.

Eaton's sketchbooks indicate that he was eclectic in his tastes and generous in his admiration. A serious traveler, he was fascinated by the Japanese tatami mat as a modular system, and he collected African art. Writing about the kraals of the South African Ndebele people, he admiringly noted that they were "woven out of, and almost wholly dependent upon, the earth and the products of nature from which it drew its material" (Harrop-Allin 1975).

Outside of his large-scale commissions, in his residential projects, Eaton consistently moved away from strict modernism and expressed empathy for the African milieu he grew up in. The houses he designed were mostly in brick, stone, wood, and terra-cotta, and he incorporated rounded forms and patterns based on his studies of local decorative motifs. A door handle of Eaton's Netherlands Bank in Pretoria subtly communicates to visitors entering the bank lobby, lest there be any doubt, that they are, indeed, in Africa (Figure 23.13).

Figure 23.13 Norman Eaton. Netherlands Bank. Pretoria, South Africa, 1946-1953. Door handle detail.

Anglophone Africa

Ernst May (1886–1970) trained in London and was active in Germany in the 1920s. Not formally a member of the Bauhaus, he worked in the international style and was extremely prolific, operating out of his base in Frankfurt. He coped with the rise of National Socialists by going to the USSR in 1930. This seemed a logical move, as he had specialized in publicly funded housing. Once there, however, he had a difficult time seeing his works realized. In 1933, he made an even more dramatic move and relocated to Africa.

Kenya, Uganda, and Tanzania

May used Kenya as his base. He was "interned" (imprisoned) for two years by the English there, having been classified as an enemy. Upon being let out, he produced modern projects in Kenya, Uganda, and Tanzania. Stylistically, these buildings drew upon his German projects of the 1920s. He did not return to Germany until 1953.

One of the odd consequences of colonialism is that it figured into the responses of Africans who were not part of a colonial regime. May was white, a foreigner, a European, and a talented one at that. The reception his works received was in no small part because he had been imprisoned by the English and, moreover, because he was not English.

Ghana, Nigeria, and Togo

Maxwell Fry and Jane Drew were British modernists, trained in Great Britian, who worked in the realms of both architecture and town planning. A married couple, they were professional collaborators throughout their lives. Over the course of their long and productive careers, they worked with Denys Lasdun, Ove Arup, Walter Gropius, and Le Corbusier. They did projects in Britain and elsewhere, but they are mostly known for their projects in British West Africa during the period 1944–1956.

These projects include seventeen schools in Ghana, Nigeria, and Togo.

Rhodri Windsor Liscombe's research brings to light the specifics of how modernism was dispersed to, and grew out of, West Africa (Liscombe 2006). To label the new way of building "the international style" is one thing; to actually build and furnish buildings in Africa is another.

Fry and Drew were committed modernists, concerned with function, modular planning, bold composition, and new materials like reinforced concrete. Yet they also developed an approach, unique to their West African work, referred to by some, wryly, as tropical modernism. During the period of their African constructions, they operated out of both Ghana and Britain and spent years in West Africa, experiences they looked back on with great affection and that had a deep impact on their designs.

They employed several design strategies to give their buildings a local response. They used bold colors and, because they built in a hot and humid climate, ventilation and solar shading were paramount concerns. Most of their buildings were interior volumes placed within a larger envelope of breathable screens. These permeable outer-wall systems allowed air to circulate and cast interior walls in a cooling shadow. This also gave Fry and Drew the opportunity to incorporate a variety of patterns in these outer tracery walls that bear a faint resemblance to local patterns found in basket weaving, textiles, and carving. As Jane Drew wrote, their goal was "to design in a way which, without in any sense copying African detail, gives a response which is African" (Drew in Liscombe 2006). One of these tracery walls contrasts the brilliant sun of the exterior with the shade of the perimeter corridor (Figure 23.14). The University of Ibadan in Nigeria is one of their largest projects.

Their work is tied to the transcultural architectural language of modernism, while simultaneously making local reference to topography, climate, and

Figure 23.14 Maxwell Fry and Jane Drew. University of Ibadan. Sultan Bello Hall. Ibadan, Nigeria.

decorative traditions. Their overall body of work was increasingly attentive to the African subject, as client and worker under their employ. Although they first worked mostly with expatriate architects, over the years African architects played a role as part of Fry and Drew's design team. They collaborated with African artists at several junctures, and their buildings were built by African craftsmen.

Kwame Nkrumah, one of the most significant voices of African independence, felt that modernizing by the British colonialist regime, however well intended and aesthetically successful, still underscored the primary goal: the economic exploitation and political domination of Britain's West African colonies.

Ghana achieved independence from Britian in 1957. The African work of Fry and Drew continues to be admired for their deft ability to create modernism within a local context. One of their employees, T. S. Clark, became the first president of the Ghana Society of Architects.

Nigeria

Oluwole Olumuyiwa (b. 1929) was part of the generation of Nigerian architects who rose to prominence in the 1960s. Olumuyiwa studied in London, then worked in London, Rotterdam, and Zurich. Throughout his career, he did multiple projects for the United Africa Company (Figure 23.15). He helped found the Nigerian Institute of Architects

Figure 23.15 Oluwole Olumuyiwa. Lagos, Nigeria.

(NIA) in 1958, and in 1981 the African Union of Architects.

His later work included projects such as the Eko Hotel, where a built-up gradient allows for breathtaking views of the pool and beach. Lest one presume that an African architect must respect the regionalist approach when designing, Hannah Le Roux noted that Olumuyiwa "represents a transitional figure whose professional background is comparable to that of his colonial predecessors. Somewhat ironically, he stated his resistance to a concept of regionalism in design" (Le Roux 2004, p. 362). He later collaborated with Kenzo Tange on the design of the Central Administrative area of the new Nigerian capital, Abuja.

Francophone Africa

The work of architects in the North African Maghreb represents its own significant strand of African modernism. Because people living in the region were French-speaking, the connections to Le Corbusier were intensified. European architects collaborated with local architects at an early date on projects, and some of these architects went on to have distinguished careers under their own names.

Their works display a familiarity with the French brand of modernism, with adjustments for a hot, dry climate; the influence of Islam is also clear. Balconies and courtyards contain spaces that are prominent, yet shielded from the public eye.

Morocco

French-trained Moroccan architect Jean-François Zevaco (1916–2003) was prolific. His projects are known for their bold forms and a sharp contrast between brilliant white stucco and cyclopean masonry, the large irregular stones associated with Neolithic construction. They are not overly concerned with elaborate swaths of decoration. Many of his projects were for the government, including a house for the president. It was uncompromisingly modern.

One way that African modernism is unique is due to the low cost of labor. Correspondingly, the large-scale use of manufactured products in projects was absent. Zevaco's post office lobby incorporated a large amount of custom millwork, including a lounge seating unit whose individual seats echo the curves of ancient Egyptian stools (Figure 23.16).

The work of Elie Azagury (1922–1979) was closely aligned with De Stijl, foremost his project for the Civic Center at Rabat (1967). Early in his career, Azagury collaborated with George Candilis, an architect known for innovative explorations of multiple-unit housing. The connection might be felicitous, but the Azagury/Candilis collaborations have an affinity with Saharan urban centers such as Timbuktu.

A source of ideological support came from the art scene, where Moroccan artists were similarly dealing with their multiple identities as French-speaking, Arab, African, and Muslim. Moroccan-born Farid Belkahia (1934) was educated at the École des Beaux-Arts in Paris (1954–1959) and then became director of the École des Beaux-Arts in Casablanca. He was a modern painter, at first influenced by George Rouault and Paul Klee. Back in Morocco, he started working with Arabic calligraphy, combining modernism with the ancient art. He also sought to close the gap between art and craft. Ahmed Cherkaoui (1934–1967) and Mohammed Issiakhen were other artists who related the independence struggles of their own countries to the activities of the French avant-garde.

Senegal

In addition to looking at indigenous decorative motifs, colors, and building materials, some African

Figure 23.16 Jean-François Zevaco. Post Office.

architects focused their exploration on the meaning of shapes. Several buildings in Senegal are ruminations on geometric shapes, exploring circles and triangles, seeing in them something inherently African. Even though there are plenty of examples of rectilinear African architecture, when called upon to make a significant architectural statement, many feel that the triangle and the circle best express Africaness. A recent monument on the island of Gorée is formed of circles and slivers of circles. The openings of the monument's tower are evocative of the traditional claustra walls of the Tukulor, one of the Senegalese ethnic groups (Figure 23.17).

Lusophone Africa

Amancio d'Alpoim Guedes (b. 1925) was an innovative architect in Mozambique whose houses were sculptural, innovative spatially, and related to surrealism. Prolific, he spent most of his career in Mozambique, and over the course of twenty-five years

Figure 23.17 Monument on Gorée, Senegal.

designed nearly 500 buildings. In addition to his architectural practice, he was an accomplished painter and sculptor.

Lessons from Africa

With his interest in modern architecture around the globe, historian Udo Kultermann was before his time. He published two books on modern architecture in Africa in the 1960s. Nonetheless, the history of modernism in Africa is a story still waiting to be told. Individual monographs on African architects and designers are rare. And there are fewer materials on interiors and modern furnishings.

Architects and designers working in Africa sought a middle ground between European modernism and local regional architectures, seeking to close the gap between Western forms and local traditions. It some cases, it was difficult to find relevant local traditions that related to the needs of the twentieth-century urban center. A frequent solution was the grafting of the indigenous onto the imported, such as the ubiquitous high-rise hotel with a straw-roofed cocktail lounge sitting grandly at its base. Some modern buildings made their local reference by incorporating local artwork. An examination of a few of the many examples of modern architecture from across the continent reveals a rich body of work that are rarely pale imitations of the original, and that indicate the presence of vibrant autonomous African modernisms.

ASIA AND THE PACIFIC

The canonical narrative of modernism conflates modernism and industrialization, the former being the logical result of the latter. While certainly true in many cases, there remains the necessity of explaining the spread of modernism to the less industrialized parts of the world. Modernism has many sources, and each culture and country had its own methods for interpreting and embracing modernity. Part of "modernism" was the struggle of indigenous cultures to resist domination by their colonizers. There remains the question of how to explain the twentieth-century resurgence of regionalism and vernacular architecture; was it a challenge to the modern movement, or evidence that there were always multiple modernisms?

In Asia, Japan and Korea were reeling from the destruction of World War II. Modernism acted as a salve for these countries eager to look forward, and who also had a pragmatic need to build and furnish massive projects. If there is a common impulse in the modernisms that developed around the world, it is the longing to belong to an increasingly global world and also to explore local roots.

Japan

Japan's engagement with modernity in the nineteenth century had been awkward, for while having wonderful traditions of painting, garden design, and building in timber, these art forms didn't provide a vocabulary that easily lent itself to the large-scale building program of railroad stations, opera houses, world-class museums, and government buildings. It was not immediately clear how a timber tradition, however rich, would lend itself to expression in concrete, steel, and glass.

The challenges facing Japan after World War II were enormous, foremost among them rebuilding their severely damaged country. With the need for so many buildings, the economy took off in the 1950s.

Japan was not a colonial country, yet the desire to develop a modern Japanese architectural style not based on the West was a constant concern. Modernism's association with the West was, from the Japanese perspective, an unattractive alliance, considering the devastation the country had experienced at the hands of Allied forces and the still-visible American military presence. But modernism was not solely an import; Japan was quickly modernizing on its own, moving down the path of industrialization and

urbanization. Regarding the legacy of traditional Japanese architecture, several factors were favorable regarding the ability of Japanese architects and designers to craft a Japanese modernism. The respect for materiality, the modular tatami tradition, the asymmetrical compositions, the exquisiteness of detailing—all were traditional Japanese design values that were sympathetic to modern developments. Put another way, Mies's geometries needed little tweaking to relate to the Japanese system of Shoji screens.

Visiting Japan

Japanese designers had direct knowledge of Western modernism. Frank Lloyd Wright's Imperial Hotel in Tokyo (1916–1922) was filled with inspiring furniture designed especially for it by Wright. Czech-born Antonin Raymond was a figure of growing importance. He arrived in Japan as Wright's assistant and eventually opened his own office.

Charlotte Perriand coped with the threat World War II posed by moving to Japan, where she stayed from 1939 to 1941; during her time in Japan, Perriand lived in the Imperial Hotel. In Japan, she had the chaise longue that she designed with Le Corbusier and Pierre Jeanneret, and other pieces, translated into wood and bamboo (Figure 23.18). She explored the relationship and synthesis between her modern furniture designs and Japanese craftsmanship. The chaise was a design that grew out of an industrial aesthetic. For this exercise in material translation and exploration of local craftwork, she first graphically reduced her furniture pieces to their iconic profiles; the craftsmen she worked with took these shapes and transformed them using the "new" materials. The transformation of this famous chair, and other pieces, into wood and bamboo demonstrates an underlying confidence in indigenous materials. This process revealed a surprising affinity between bamboo and steel, the connection being tensile strength. Perriand and the Japanese craftsmen she collaborated with linked modern forms with centuries-old traditions.

Postwar Modernism

Isamu Noguchi (1904–1988) was foremost an artist, capable of expressing himself in many media, including sculpture, furniture design, stage sets, and gardens. The son of an American mother and a Japanese father, in 1927–1928 he worked in Paris for Brancusi. He created stage designs for the dancer Martha Graham. In 1944, he started creating furniture and lamp designs for Hermann Miller and Knoll, several of which are still in production. His carefully balanced coffee table is now known simply as the Noguchi table and is one of the masterpieces of classic modern furniture (Figure 23.19).

Kunio Mayekawa (1905–1986) worked for Le Corbusier, 1928–1930, in Paris, and then for Antonin Raymond in Tokyo, 1930–1935. His work is known for its integration of international modernism and Japanese traditions based on timber construction. His Harumi Building of 1958, Tokyo, bears the influence of Le Corbusier's Unité d'Habitation, but it is also the building that proved that concrete is a Japanese material.

Kenzo Tange (b. 1913) worked for Mayekawa and was the most important Japanese architect of the 1950s and '60s. His Peace Memorial and Museum at Hiroshima, 1949–1950, proves how adept he was at a variety of modernist means of expression. The memorial itself is a sculptural focal point, with an exquisitely detailed rectangular building acting as a backdrop. Raised on pilotis, it evokes European modernism, but the delicacy of its concrete detailing recalls Japanese residential construction in timber. Tange's most important work came in 1964 with his National Gymnasium, built for the Olympics. With two adjacent steel suspension structures, it is aggressively asymmetrical, curved, and dynamic. It impressed a new generation of Japanese architects, and the roster of architects who studied under Tange includes Arata Isozaki, Kisho Kurokawa, and Fumihiko Maki.

Tange established an office in Tokyo, from which he ran a thriving international practice. In addition to occasional plastic expressions of monumentality such as the Gymnasium, his office produced large numbers of more pedestrian corporate projects. He participated in designing the plan for

Figure 23.19 Isamu Noguchi. Noguchi table, 1944.

Figure 23.20 Kiyonori Kikutake, Skyhouse. Tokyo, Japan, 1957.

Abuja, Nigeria, in 1979. He did projects in the United States, Nigeria, Malaysia, Singapore, Saudi Arabia, and Mexico.

Kiyonori Kikutake (b. 1928) is associated with the utopian movement known as the Metabolists. Yet his individual houses have a sensitivity to detail that was often missing in the aggressive urban plans. Kikutake felt that architecture should have two parts—a permanent part, and a part that could be rejuvenated during periodic reconstructions. This two-pronged approach to design is evident in his own house, Skyhouse, of 1957 (Figure 23.20). Kikutake related the obviously modern structure to the historical Japanese domestic architecture: "The core of the main space of the Skyhouse is a large space that reflected the 16 tatami mat-parlor of my family house" (Kikutake in Vitta 1997, p. 12). The woodwork is evidence of his appreciation of Japanese

timber-frame structures, and the giant concrete piers relate to the Metabolists' desire to build in the air.

Kazuo Shinohari (1925–2006) produced modernized versions of the traditional Japanese house (Schaarschmidt-Richter 1994). His projects often hinge on a single concept that obviously acts as the generator of form. The chaos of the urban realm is reflected in his brash exteriors, which are contrasted by introspective and serene interiors. In reference to an essay he published that year, "Houses Are Art," Shinohari wrote: "Now that rationalism and functionalism, the main force of the time, had collapsed, architecture and design, let alone housing, had become artistic" (Shinohari 1971, p. 48). Two delicate chairs face a table in a corner of the house, where the visual focus is directed toward the exterior (Figure 23.21). The chairs' triangular backrests reflect the triangular windows.

Lessons from Japan

The uncertainty that surrounded Japanese architecture in the immediate post–World War II period seems to have evaporated in the 1970s and 1980s, helped in no small part by Japan's successful economy, but also by a growing confidence in Japan as a distinctive voice that could make a significant contribution to what being modern means. Modernism is the result of the forces of technology, consumerism, capitalism, and urbanism, all of which Japan was experiencing as authentic, not imported, experiences. Japanese designers did not need to look to outsiders for experience with these issues, and could become the model for others, especially with their references to nature, materiality, and spirituality.

India

India became familiar with postwar Le Corbusier when his work was entering a rougher, less pristine phase, embraced by the Brutalists. Louis Kahn was a source of inspiration for Indian and Pakistani architects as well, because of buildings he built in both countries. Many Indian people were already familiar with the work of Antonin Raymond. Though modernism had been halfheartedly introduced by the English, it was definitively a symbol of independence and part of a postcolonial order. The sort of crisis that Fathy faced in Egypt was also faced in India, in which hordes of manual laborers faced competition from mass-produced imported products.

Figure 23.21 Kazuo Shinohari. House in Yokohama, dining area, 1986.

Early Modernism

India became modern via a variety of circuitous paths, few as interesting as the story of the Maharaja of Indore. The Maharaja's full name was Yeshwant Rao Holkar Bahadur (1905–1956). He studied in England and was a familiar fixture of the Paris art scene. He bought sculptures from Constantin Brancusi and collected avant-garde furnishings from Berlin, London, and Paris, including pieces by Marcel Breuer, Le Corbusier, Charlotte Perriand, Eileen Gray, and Emile-Jacques Ruhlmann.

Man Ray is known as both a Dadaist and a surrealist, two artistic movements that fall under the rubric of "modernism." He took a photographic portrait of the Maharaja in 1930, when the young man was twenty-five (Figure 23.22). The Maharaja sits in profile in this photograph, which shows how the human body and photography are equal partners in the history of art and design. The profile renders a prominent nose even more prominent. Other photographers would have minimized its profile; Man Ray glories in its sharp geometries. The Maharaja's shiny black hair has a metallic sheen, which gives it the luster of an elegant material. This portrait is reminiscent of many Bauhaus photographs; an iconic photograph of Eileen Gray similarly captures her in profile. These photographs rely upon the understanding that the human body is also an artistic material and can become a "designed object."

Eckart Muthesius (1904–1989) was also twenty-five when he met the Maharaja. Muthesius had an impeccable modernist pedigree. His father, Hermann Muthesius (1861–1927), founded the Deutscher Werkbund. The Maharaja hired the younger Muthesius to design the family house in India. The enormous house that Muthesius designed, called Manik Bagh (Jewel Gardens), with interiors and furnishings also by Muthesius, was a tour de force of modern design. The house was widely published, revealing the similarities between Muthesius's work and that of his Bauhaus contemporaries. Reto Niggl writes

Figure 23.22 Man Ray. Photographic portrait of Prince Yeshwant, the Maharaja of Indore, 1930.

that "modernism as typified by Muthesius and his client, stands in contrast to the representative, decorative style of the 1920s" (Niggl 1996, p. 21).

Muthesius did many projects for the Maharaja, also designing a railway car, a houseboat (not realized), a meditation temple (not realized), a hotel, hospital, and airplane interiors.

These chairs are either by Muthesius or were commissioned by him (Figure 23.23). The Maharaja's house was filled with custom-designed pieces whose cumulative effect is to confirm that a machine-aesthetic could result in luxurious pieces of furniture.

Antonin Raymond (1888–1976), of Czech birth, became an American citizen and worked in Japan and India. In school in Czechoslovakia, he had admired the work of Frank Lloyd Wright. It was a dream come true for him when, after he moved to the United States, he ended up working for Wright.

Wright sent Raymond to Japan to oversee the construction of the Imperial Hotel in Tokyo. Initially, his work was derivative of Wright's work; then he progressed into a strictly modernist phase, in touch with the 1920s and 1930s. The year 1937 found him working on an ashram, in Pondicherry, India, when his work was less austere (Figure 23.24). He collaborated with the Japanese-American architecture and furniture designer George Nakashima (1905–1990). The modernist underpinnings are present in Pondicherry, but his explorations of the spiritual qualities possible within a modernist vocabulary are clear (Helfrich 2006, p. 170). Adding to the cosmopolitan character of his life and work is the fact that Pondicherry is a French-speaking enclave in India. So a Czech-born American citizen worked in the French-speaking area of India after a stint in Japan. In 1948, Raymond returned to work in Japan with the Reader's Digest Building in Tokyo (1950); Isamu Noguchi designed the garden.

Post-Independence Modernism

Charles Correa (b. 1930) lived and worked in Bombay. He studied in the United States, first at the University of Michigan and then at MIT, where he studied under Buckminster Fuller. He was interested in relating modernism to climate and living patterns, particularly village life. These interests naturally led him to public housing, and he also worked on tourist hotels. One of his highly lauded projects was the Gandhi Memorial Centre in Ahmadabad (1958–1963).

Balkrishna Doshi (b. 1927) studied in Bombay and London. From 1951 to 1955 he worked for Le Corbusier, who hired him to supervise the projects he was building in Chandigarh and Ahmadabad. Doshi then set up his own practice in Ahmadabad. He played a crucial role in arranging for Louis Kahn to build in India. Initially, Doshi's work was similar to the work of Le Corbusier; later in life, he found his own distinctive architectural voice.

Sri Lanka

Contemporary Malaysian architect Ken Yeang (b. 1948) refers to Geoffrey Bawa (1919–2003) as "our first hero and guru" (Yeang in Robson 2002, p. 12). Bawa's ethnic heritage reflects the marvelously

Figure 23.23 Eckart Muthesius. Chairs, 1930–1933.

Figure 23.24 Antonin Raymond and George Nakashima. Ashram, Pondicherry, India, 1935–1942.

complicated heritage of Sri Lanka. (The etymology is complicated, too: In the colonial era, the island was known as Ceylon. The major ethnic group, and their language, is Sinhalese.) He belonged to the ethnic group commonly described as "Eurasian," which, in Bawa's case, meant that he was a combination of Scottish, German, and Sinhalese. Bawa was raised by three women: his mother and his father's two sisters. He worked in Colombo as a lawyer before he turned to architecture.

Bawa traveled extensively. In 1951, he started working as an architect. In 1952, he went to Cambridge, England, where he studied civil engineering and structures. He went to the Architectural Association School. He eventually ended up teaching there, following the path of a classmate of his, the modernist Peter Smithson. There he learned about international modernism.

Bawa's career and his designs relate to two aspects of his identity, both personal and professional. On the one hand he was a trained modernist, familiar with Britain's modern structures, and he knew many of the prominent modernists personally. He returned to Ceylon (as it was then known) and started working for the nation's largest and most prestigious architecture firm, ERB. He outlived the partners and took it over. Under his leadership, the firm proceeded from large-scale traditional buildings to modern corporate offices, tourist hotels, and, ultimately, the firm's and Bawa's most significant commission, the Parliament. Under Bawa's leadership, the firm became internationally known, on a par with the American firm Skidmore, Owings, and Merrill of Chicago. The firm was skilled at receiving both governmental and commercial commissions.

As the firm's projects were increasingly reflecting the nation's indigenous character, so too were the ranks of locals sitting at the drafting desks. Initially, the staff was entirely English, but under Bawa's stewardship it became increasingly Ceylonese. Bawa's office included Sinhalese Buddhists, Tamil Hindus, and Muslims, Catholics, and Anglicans. Many of the architects who initially worked for Bawa had successful careers on their own.

There's a parallel story, which author David Robson calls the Brideshead side of Bawa (Robson 2002, p. 19). Robson wrote the most complete book on Bawa to date (Robson 2002). He referred to Evelyn Waugh's story of a gay elite group at Oxford, under the sway of lead character Sebastian Flyte. Bawa, at Cambridge, acted something like Waugh's lead character. Robson wrote: "Handsome and exceptionally tall, Geoffrey would stride around town in a long black cloak with a gold-handled cane. He had always felt something of an outsider in Colombo, but his eccentricities were welcomed in Cambridge" (p. 20). Bawa belonged to a cosmopolitan group of worldly aesthetes, and he thrived in their company. Throughout his life, he continued to hobnob with wealthy women, designing their houses and gardens, and advising them on antiques and art (Robson 2002, pp. 50–51). He did a house for Minette de Silva, with whom he was close friends. De Silva was the first Asian woman who became a member of the Royal Institute of British Architects. At the end of his life, it was commonly known that he was gay, another aspect of his character that spoke of his ability to operate successfully in several worlds.

Bawa received the most important commission of his life when the Sri Lankan government chose him to design the new Sri Lankan Parliament Building in 1981. Bawa was a good choice, not only because his own family heritage reflected the multi-

Figure 23.25 Geoffrey Bawa. Country home of the late Geoffrey Bawa, now a boutique hotel. Lunuganga, Sri Lanka.

caste and -creed matrix of Sri Lanka. At this point in his career, he was moving away from flat roofs and incorporated pitched roofs into his designs. He was particularly skilled at making the vernacular monumental. Bawa's Parliament looks like an Asian shrine, and it houses a complicated program for a modern government, modeled in part on the Houses of Parliament in London.

Some compare his later work to the "tropical modernism." On the one hand, some of his designs look oddly similar to Scandinavian modernism, but as Maxwell Fry and Jane Drew had proven, modernism could be quite applicable to tropical climates. Bawa had worked for a time with Fry and Drew.

Bawa increasingly relied upon and incorporated traditional forms, such as pitched roofs, into his projects. His walls were not crisp white, but achieved a weathered patina. His residential projects drew upon many influences, such as medieval manor houses, Dutch courtyard houses, and Muslim row-houses. He regularly combined classic modern pieces of furniture with Ceylonese antiques (Figure 23.25).

Thailand and Cambodia

The situation in Thailand is emblematic of how modernism arose in the 1930s in a non-European country, and how it spoke to and responded to a particular political situation. While India and Ceylon experienced colonialism to the hilt, it was a nonissue in Thailand, a country that successfully resisted English and French attempts to colonize it. In Thailand, modernism played a role akin to the role of nineteenth-century Neoclassicism in France, in which it was the style of the new post-royal regime and a means by which the new political system stylistically differentiated itself from the ancient regime.

The 1932 revolution in Thailand ended more than a thousand years of royal absolutist rule and signaled the end to royal and state patronage of Western architects. This was a system that promoted the use of historically based styles—essentially guaranteeing that the nineteenth century would continue into the twentieth. Thai architects who had been educated abroad started to replace the old generation, and they increasingly reflected the new era with a prevalence for modern architecture. Noobanjong writes that Thai architects established an architecture school and that several of them started their careers there (Noobanjong 2003). In 1932, the architecture department at Chulalongkorn University started. The year 1934 saw the establishment of the Association of Siamese Architects (ASA). Modern architecture in Thailand became the symbol of the new order, of building a new nation, and an alternative to the ancient royalist regime.

Princess Rudivoravan, a granddaughter of Thailand's King Mongkut, thought about her parents in conjunction with their furniture: "My mother's quarters in the palace were attractive. As I remember them, the furnishings were Western, but this touch may have been added after I returned from England. It was customary to provide wives whose children had been educated in Europe with more modern furnishings than the traditional Thai. A few years later my people would be sitting on chairs at desks, but at that time the floor served as desk stool. I can still see my father's low writing bench and table, and the bowls of pens with which he wrote" (Rudivoravan 1957, p. 59). In the Princess' recollection, a chair and (tall) desk have multiple associations. They relate to the West, and to Thais like herself with experience living in the West; she was educated in England as a child. She describes the furniture as modern, and items of her generation—not her parents. She remembers her father, whom she writes of fondly, as nobly sitting on the floor in front of his writing bench. A parallel development in Thailand, alongside the preference for modern projects, was the career of Jim Thompson, an American heir who developed a successful silk industry in

Figure 23.26 Vann Molyvann. Institute of Foreign Languages. Staircase. Phnom Penh, Cambodia.

Bangkok. With his own house as an example, he is credited with reviving a fashion for wealthy Thai families to construct lavish houses, filled with Chinese antiques and Khmer sculptures, based on Thai vernacular traditions, and often incorporating actual carpentry from houses dismantled in the countryside and brought to Bangkok by boat. He contributed to the revival of Thai indigenous forms.

The small Southeast Asian nation of Cambodia has one of the world's richest traditions of ancient architecture and sculpture. It was not predestined that Cambodia would experience a second period of architectural achievement in the twentieth century, yet that is what occurred in the period 1953–1970. Helen Grant Ross and Darryl Leon Collins focused on the

cadre of talented architects who produced a limited but highly competent body of work (Ross and Collins 2006). Firmly committed to modernism, as a collective corpus their buildings effortlessly achieve what so many non-Western architects sought to achieve, yet which proved so difficult. Their works related to the international movement yet responded to their own context. They grew out of Cambodia's architectural tradition without being derivative.

Sadly, Cambodia's experience with modernism is more associated with the events that precipitated the end of modernism. Vann Molyvann (b. 1926) studied in Paris, after which he returned to Cambodia. He did a series of projects for Prince Norodom Sihanouk in the 1960s that reveal his French modernist training, but they also refer to Cambodia's grand history of architecture, the monumental temples of Angkor. Sihanouk was a former king turned political leader.

Molyvann's works forged a grand new style of Khmer architecture. The significant characteristic of Cambodian modernism is the evocation of tradition, yet in decidedly modern structures. Some of the buildings are profusely decorated, some feature locally made brick, and many feature steeply pitched roofs. Modernism in many parts of the world was initially dependent on imported talent, but in Cambodia it was mostly a Cambodian affair. The leading figures include Vann Molyvann, Lu Ban Hap, and Mam Sophana. Molyvann's many projects include the Front du Bassac Housing Complex, the Institute of Foreign Languages (Figure 23.26), and Preah Suramarit Theatre. His grandest project, the National Sports Complex, was built in 1963–1964.

The painstaking research of Darryl Leon Collins and Helen Grant Ross is invaluable because it recovers the activities of Cambodians in this period, a task made infinitely more difficult with the scourge of the Khmer Rouge. The Cambodian modernists forged a body of work that is remarkably in concert with international modernism yet expressive of a distinct Khmer sensibility. They operated within a modernist idiom on projects large and small.

Australia

Two architects represent two strands of the architectural scene in Australia, Harry Seidler and Glenn Murcutt. Harry Seidler (1923–2006) was born in Austria and studied in England, Canada, and then the United States. At Harvard, he studied under Walter Gropius, and I. M. Pei was a classmate. His work experience included stints with Marcel Breuer in New York and Oscar Niemeyer in Rio de Janeiro.

International Modernism

Seidler is one of the architects who, like Bawa, worked within the modernist framework as a sign of his connection to an international elite. The sophistication of this style was emphasized in one of his early works, the Rose Seidler House of 1950, which was widely admired (Figure 23.27).

If architects around the world needed a strategy for incorporating local art into their modern buildings, Philip Johnson and Henry-Russell Hitchcock articulated it for them. Their book, *The International Style*, and the exhibition it accompanied, is one of the many mechanisms, in addition to Le Corbusier's publications, that spread knowledge of modernism around the world. They wrote: how "to decorate contemporary buildings without degenerating into mere applied ornament. Mural painting should not break the wall surface unnecessarily. Yet it should remain an independent entity without the addition of borders or paneling to fuse it with the architecture. . . . there is no reason why painting less abstract should not find its place quite as satisfactorily on the walls of contemporary buildings. It is most important that mural painting should be intrinsically excellent; otherwise a plain wall is better. It need not be related, except in scale and shape, to the wall on which it is placed." Sculpture, they wrote, "should retain its own character quite separate from that of its background."

Seidler's primary focus was the integration of geometry with structure, which served him well when his firm started specializing in large-scale complexes that included skyscrapers. These projects included Australia Square, 1961–1967; Grosvenor Place, Sydney, 1982–1988; and Capita Centre, Sydney, 1984–1989 (Frampton and Drew 1992, p. 282).

Some critics thought Seidler's work—and he was a very successful architect—was too foreign. His work, which barely took notice of the Australian landscape, left an opening for an Australian architect who could temper the modern ethos by

Figure 23.27 Harry Seidler. Rose Seidler House. Turramurra, Australia.

incorporating elements drawn from the vernacular and the local landscape.

Regional Modernism

Glenn Murcutt approached architecture differently than Seidler, in both end results and in office practices. He largely works by himself, with his wife as his partner, and built mostly single-family houses. He was raised in Papua, New Guinea, and his work reflects his knowledge of a rough, if not primitive, landscape. He studied at the Sydney Technical College.

His houses draw upon vernacular agricultural buildings, such as toolsheds and woolsheds. His buildings respond to the rural built environment and the Australian landscape. The Marie Short House is one of his early houses, built in 1975

(Fromonet 2003, p. 96). About a house that mixes the vernacular with modernism, Jim Lewis writes: "It was simple, it was light and nimble, and it seemed autochthonous" (*New York Times,* p. 94). Murcutt is also like Aalto in this respect, as he took modern forms and softened them with his use of materials. He won the Pritzker Prize.

Lessons from Asia

Columbia University architectural historian Kenneth Frampton writes: "With all the acuteness that is characteristic of the creative mind at its most sensitive, the so-called pioneers of the modern movement began in various ways to qualify the modern project, either by reinterpreting the vernacular in terms of modern technology in order to create an architecture that was socially more accessible and hence capable of embodying local values while still being engaged in modernization or, alternatively, reverting in some measure, to the stereometric regularity of classicism in order to represent the authority of the State" (Frampton 2007, p. 87). Looking at multiple examples of twentieth-century design in Asia makes clear that there were many responses to the challenge of embracing modernism while remaining rooted in tradition.

CONCLUSION

Modernism was not always imported, but often created locally. The concept of an indigenous modernity that charts its own course is the subject of this chapter. The movement was international, not in the sense proscribed by European theorists, but because it interacted with local cultures from the beginning. Considering the origins of modernism, and specifically its early florescence in Mexico and Brazil, confirms that it was simultaneously imported and it developed in multiple locations.

Mies's professional activities were run from his home base in Chicago. Although he had a number of foreign students at IIT, being in the United States, he was working within a large architectural market. Le Corbusier, based in France, did not have the same wealth of corporate opportunities close at hand. He was, in effect, forced to be more global. Yet it cannot be coincidental that so many African, Asian, and American students worked for Le Corbusier, were inspired by him, and had lifelong professional relationships with him.

The situation of Antonin Raymond is one that was increasingly common as the twentieth century marched toward the twenty-first. A person of one nationality works in another on projects across the globe. The firms of Geoffrey Bawa, Harry Seidler, and Kenzo Tange were the order of the day, as the architecture and design profession extended its global reach.

Regarding the critical reception of modernism, a reassessment of modernism took place. Luis Barragán and Hassan Fathy were the first figures to receive international attention, and it looks as though Vann Molyvann's career is in for a similar reassessment.

Sources

Anderson, Stanford, ed. *Eladio Dieste: Innovation in Structural Art*. New York: Princeton Architectural Press, 2004.

Cuadra, Manuel. *Clorindo Testa, Architect*. Rotterdam: NAI Publishers, 2000.

Denison, Edward, Guang Yu Ren, and Naigzy Gebremedhin. *Asmara: Africa's Secret Modernist City*. London: Merrell, 2003.

Eggener, Keith. *Luis Barragán's Gardens of El Pedregal*. New York: Princeton Architectural Press, 2001.

Eggener, Keith. "Luis Barragán," in Stephen Sennott's *Encyclopedia of 20th-Century Architecture*. New York: Fitzroy Dearborn, 2004.

Faber, Colin. *Candela: The Shell Builder*. New York: Reinhold, 1963.

Ferraz, Marcelo Carvalho. *Lina Bo Bardi*. Milan: Edizioni Charta, 1994.

Frampton, Kenneth. *The Evolution of 20th Century Architecture: A Synoptic Account*. Vienna: Springer-Verlag, 2007.

Frampton, Kenneth, and Philip Drew. *Harry Seidler: Four Decades of Architecture*. New York: Thames and Hudson, 1992.

Fromonet, Françoise. *Glenn Murcutt: Buildings and Projects 1962–2003*. New York: Thames and Hudson, 2003.

Glusberg, Jorge. *Global Architecture: Sepra y Clorindo Testa*. Tokyo: A.D.A. Edita, 1984.

Guillén, Mauro. "Modernism Without Modernity: The Rise of Modernist Architecture in Mexico, Brazil, and Argentina, 1890–1940." *Latin American Research Review* 39: no. 2 (2004): 6–34.

Harrop-Allin, Clinton. *Norman Eaton: Architect*. Cape Town: C. Struik, 1975.

Helfrich, Kurt, and William Whitaker. *Crafting a Modern World: The Architecture and Design of Antonin and Noémi Raymond*. New York: Princeton Architectural Press, 2006.

Hess, Alan. *Oscar Niemeyer Houses*. New York: Rizzoli, 2006.

Johnson, Philip, and Henry-Russell Hitchcock. *The International Style*. New York: Museum of Modern Art, 1932.

Le Roux, Hannah. "Modern Architecture in Post Colonial Ghana and Nigeria." *Architectural History* 47 (2004): 361–392.

Leite, Rui Moreira, and Izabel Murat Burbridge. "Flavio de Carvalho: Modernism and the Avant-garde in São Paulo, 1927–1939." *The Journal of Decorative and Propaganda Arts* 21 (1995): 197–217.

Leon, Ethel. *Design Brasileiro: quem fez, quem faz*. Rio de Janeiro: Viana e Mosley, 2005.

Liscombe, Rhodri Windsor. "Modernism in Late Imperial British West Africa: The Work of Maxwell Fry and Jane Drew, 1946–1956." *Journal of the Society of Architectural Historians* 65, no. 2 (June 2006): 188–215.

McQuaid, Matilda. *Shigeru Ban*. London: Phaidon, 2003.

Nakahari, Mari, et al. *Crafting a Modern World: The Architecture and Design of Antonin and Noémi Raymond*. Princeton: Princeton Architectural Press, 2006.

Niggl, Reto. *Eckart Muthesius: The Majaraja's Palace in Indore*. Stuttgart: Arnoldsche, 1996.

Noobanjong, Koompong. *Power, Identity, and the Rise of Modern Architecture From Siam to Thailand*. diss. University of Colorado at Denver, 2003.

Paul, Andreas, and Ingeborg Flagge, eds. *Oscar Niemeyer: A Legend of Modernism*. Basel: Birkhäuser, 2003.

Phillips, Tom, ed. *Africa: The Art of a Continent*. New York: Guggenheim Museum, 1996.

Pile, John. *Dictionary of 20th-Century Design*. New York: Roundtable, 1990.

Posch, Katarina, Bonnie Rycklak, and Tetsu Matsumoto. *Design: Isamu Noguchi and Isamu Kenmochi*. New York: Five Ties Publishing, 2008.

Raymond, Antonin. *Antonin Raymond: An Autobiography*. Rutland: Charles E. Tuttle, 1973.

Rispa, Raúl. *Barragán: The Complete Works*. New York: Princeton Architectural Press, 2003.

Robson, David. *Geoffrey Bawa: The Complete Works*. London: Thames and Hudson, 2002.

Ross, Helen Grant, and Darryl Leon Collins. *Building Cambodia: New Khmer Architecture: 1953–1970*. Bangkok: The Key Publisher Company, 2006.

Rudivoravan, Princess. *The Treasured One*. New York: Dutton, 1957.

Schaarschmidt-Richter, Irmstraud. *Kazuo Shinohara: Philosopher of Architecture*. Berlin: Ernst and Sohn, 1994.

Taylor, Brian Brace. *Geoffrey Bawa*. Singapore: Mimar, 1986.

Underwood, David. *Oscar Niemeyer and the Architecture of Brazil*. New York: Rizzoli, 1994.

Villanueva, Paulina. *Carlos Raúl Villanueva*. New York: Princeton Architectural Press, 2000.

Vitta, Maurizio. *Kiyonori Kikutake: From Tradition to Utopia*. Milan: l'Arca Edizioni, 1997.

Zanco, Federica. *Luis Barragán: The Quiet Revolution*. Milan: Skira, 2001.

DISCUSSION AND REVIEW QUESTIONS

1. What is an example of how knowledge of design circulated to a particular place around the world?

2. What is an example of a certain thread of knowledge being traced from Europe to another country?

3. Give an example of a modern development in Asia, Africa, or the Americas that was an independent development.

4. Identify a characteristic or circumstance of a non-European modernism that has a quality, form, or material that renders it unique.

5. Name some local variants of modernism and mention some of the key features of each.

6. What were some of the design strategies by which modernists around the world made their designs respond to the local context?

CHAPTER 24

AFTER MODERNISM
MODERNISM CONTINUED,
POSTMODERNISM, AND DECONSTRUCTION

1950s	**1960s**	**1980s**	**1990s**
Modernism continued	**Counter-cultural revolution**	**Postmodernism**	**Deconstruction**

World War II left no one untouched. The rise of National Socialism in Germany led to the closing of the Bauhaus and was the mechanism that drove many Bauhaus designers to the United States. Mies van der Rohe moved to Chicago, where he built a new campus for the Illinois Institute of Technology. After a stint in Britain, where he produced several distinguished furniture pieces, Marcel Breuer emigrated to the United States. Walter Gropius headed to Massachusetts to direct the Department of Architecture at Harvard. Born in Finland, the young Eero Saarinen, had moved to the United States in the 1920s when his father, Eliel Saarinen was developing the design academy Cranbrook, in Michigan. Eero eventually taught there as well.

For those who remained in Europe, it was a fallow period. For Le Corbusier, Pierre Jeanneret, and Aino and Alvar Aalto, the exciting period of prewar modernism was over and they scrambled for commissions. Charlotte Perriand coped with the war by traveling to Japan and Indonesia. A Berliner all her life, Lilly Reich stayed in Berlin until war's end. Her career evaporated and she was destitute.

Anne Tyng went to school with Philip Johnson and was a part of the Bauhaus-inspired design milieu at Harvard. Tyng also knew the architect Edward Durrell Stone.

Along with others who fled Nazi Germany, Hans Knoll moved to New York and started a furniture company. Hans's father, Walter Knoll, had produced Bauhaus furniture. Once in the United States, Hans Knoll founded his eponymous company in 1938.

Florence Schust studied at Cranbrook and then started working at Knoll. Eventually, Florence married Hans. The company they built together played a significant role in continuing to manufacture and market the Bauhaus furniture designs that came to be known as classic modern pieces. Knoll, along with Herman Miller, produced the iconic works of Mies, Reich, Perriand, Le Corbusier, and the Aaltos. These companies also developed new modern office products and promoted new designers.

MODERNISM CONTINUED

The 1950s constitutes a second phase of modernism. If prewar modernism was utopian and theoretical, postwar modernism was practical and applied. The avant-garde movement had progressed from scarcely hidden socialism to full-blown capitalism. The 1950s saw a continuation and exploration of modernist principles and forms, and technological innovations played an important role. Increasingly, the furniture and design business became international.

Architects and Furniture

Mies van der Rohe

Mies van der Rohe moved to the United States in 1937 to escape the Nazis. From 1938 to 1958, he was head of the architecture department at the Illinois Institute of Technology, for whom he would later design a new campus. The central structure of the campus was Crown Hall, built in 1952. One of the most important buildings of the post–World War II period, it was based on the idea of a factory with vast, uninterrupted space. Mies later realized his dream of glass skyscrapers with the Lake Shore Drive apartments in Chicago, 1950, and the Seagram Building in New York, 1957.

One of his most famous buildings is the Farnsworth House, outside of Chicago. Built in 1944, it is a transparent box framed by eight steel columns and is one of the most fundamentally minimalist houses

Figure 24.1 Mies van der Rohe, Farnsworth House. Plano, IL.

ever designed (Figure 24.1). Mies no longer designed furniture, but the pieces he designed in the 1920s and 1930s in collaboration with Lilly Reich continued to sell well. Several of their pieces were specified for the Farnsworth House including the Mies couch and Tugendhat chairs. His office buildings and their imitations created a demand for furniture appropriate to their clean steel-and-glass spaces.

Le Corbusier

The postwar projects of Le Corbusier (1887–1965) signaled a new direction. Three projects—the Maison Jaoul, 1951–1954; Chapel of Notre Dame du Haut, Ronchamp, 1950–1954; and the Dominican Monastery of La Tourette, 1953–1957—displayed a new means of dealing with concrete that would be admired by a new movement of architects.

Brutalism describes a group of like-minded architects of the 1950s and 1960s. The movement started in Britain and soon spread around the world. It was related to the art movement Art Brut, whose chief figure was the artist Jean Dubuffet. The Brutalists built in concrete and idolized the postwar projects of Le Corbusier.

His projects for a new capital city at Chandigarh gave him the opportunity to complete a large-scale governmental complex. For Chandigarh, he designed the Governor's Palace (unbuilt), 1952, the High Court, 1951–1955, and the Parliament Building, 1951–1963. His swan song was built at Harvard University, the Carpenter Center for the Visual Arts, 1959–1963. Although his prewar furniture designed with Charlotte Perriand continued to sell well, he completed no new furniture designs.

Louis Kahn and Anne Tyng

Louis Kahn, one of the most influential architects of the twentieth century, infused the International Style of architecture with a poetic use of light. Although he did only a few projects, he was renowned for his massive concrete buildings architecture that

Figure 24.2 Anne Tyng, Modified Morris Chair.

responded to the human scale and their sites. Kahn and his collaborator Anne Tyng maintained a personal relationship for seven years. In 1953, she traveled to Rome, where their daughter was born. During this time, Kahn and Tyng wrote fifty-three letters whose subjects range from their intense relationship to their individual projects.

Tyng designed a chair that was a modern take on the Arts and Crafts classic the Morris Chair (Figure 24.2).

Eero Saarinen

Eero Saarinen, the son of Eliel Saarinen, was born in 1910. He studied in Paris and at Yale. After a year in art school, he decided to become an architect. He became a United States citizen in 1940 and shortly thereafter embarked on designing furniture with Charles and Ray Eames. They produced an array of furniture products that centered on organic shapes and modern materials. Two of his most famous furniture designs are the Womb Chair and the Tulip Chair (Figure 24.3). Saarinen and his wife named their son Eames, after his collaborator

Figure 24.3 Eero Saarinen. Tulip Chair, 1957.

Charles Eames. Eero's first major work was a project completed with his father, the General Motors Technical Center in Warren, Michigan.

In the 1950s, he received commissions from American universities for campus designs and individual buildings; these include the Noyes dormitory at Vassar, and dormitories, an ice rink, and an auditorium at Yale University. His firm was located in Bloomfield Hills, Michigan until 1961, when he moved the practice to Connecticut. Under Eero Saarinen, the firm carried out many of his most important works, including the Jefferson National Expansion Memorial in St. Louis, Missouri.

Although he's famous for his furniture designs, Eero Saarinen's postwar architecture included some iconic modern masterpieces, such as the TWA terminal in New York (Figure 24.4). Made out of rein- forced steel covered in concrete, it consists of four vaulted domes supported on Y-shaped columns. The domes form an umbrella-like shell that curves 50 feet high and 315 feet long, and which is inspired by the excitement of flight.

Philip Johnson's career remarkably reflects all the major phases of post WWII architecture and design. A quick look at the stages in his career is a trip through twentieth-century design.

Modernism

Philip Johnson designed his own residence, the Glass House, in 1949. It is one of eleven buildings on his forty-seven-acre estate. It employs his masterful knowledge of geometry, proportion, minimal structure, and the effects of reflection and transparency. It was inspired by Mies's Farnsworth House. In this instance Mies did not consider imitation as the sincerest form of flattery and was publicly displeased with Johnson's homage to him.

The Seagram Building was designed by Mies van der Rohe in New York City in 1954. It is known for its elegant proportions and use of luxurious materials. Bronze I-beams were applied from bottom to top, making it the first bronze skyscraper and one of the best examples of the International Style. Johnson was commissioned for the interior of the skyscraper and designed the Four Season restaurant. Both building and restaurant were made official landmarks in 1989.

Classical Modernism

Johnson designed the Sheldon Art Gallery, Lincoln, Nebraska, in 1963. It is an example of a group of modernist structures that achieved monumentality with their resemblance to the classical proportions of Greek temples. One of the most famous of this type of architecture was Lincoln Center in New York City, a civic arena for the performing arts modeled on Michelangelo's Campidoglio.

Figure 24.4 Eero Saarinen, TWA Terminal, New York.

Brutalism

Johnson's addition to the Boston Public Library opened in 1973. Two important stipulations were that the roofline be maintained with that of the original structure, and that a complementary material be used for the exterior would.

1970s

Johnson designed Pennzoil Place with his business partner, John Burgee, in 1976. The complex in Houston, Texas, consists of two thirty-six-story trapezoid-shaped towers covered in bronze-tinted glass (Figure 24.5). It has the detailing of the Seagram Building, but the forms, with dramatic angles in plan and elevation, are unlike anything Mies would have designed.

Postmodernism

Designed in 1986, the skyscraper at 90 South LaSalle in Chicago consists of a faux gabled roof and stone

Figure 24.5 Philip Johnson.
Pennzoil Place. Houston, Texas.

exterior that emphasizes the building's verticality. It looks like a very tall chateau, with arched windows and small rose windows in its gables.

Deconstruction

One of Johnson's Final Projects was a collaboration with Frank Gehry for a pavilion of the grounds of his house in New Canaan, Connecticut.

Designers and Furniture

Arne Jacobsen

Arne Jacobsen (1902–1971) was born in Copenhagen, Denmark. He graduated from the Academy of Arts in Copenhagen in 1928. Jacobsen was interested in the idea of total design, designing furniture for the majority of his projects. In 1930, he started his own design office, which he headed until his death in 1971. He worked independently as an architect and as an interior, furniture, textile, and ceramics designer. In 1956, he became a professor at the Royal Academy of Arts in Copenhagen.

His architecture includes a considerable number of buildings in Denmark, Germany, and Great Britain. The Royal Hotel, 1956–1961, situated in Copenhagen, is his architecturally most accomplished structure. It is credited with having introduced modern architecture to Denmark. His furniture designs include the Ant Chair, 1952, the Swan Chair, 1958, and the Egg Chair, 1958.

Osvaldo Borsani

Osvaldo Borsani (1911–1985) was the son of a craftsman, and an artistic streak ran in the family. His father ran a furniture company that he had started in the 1930s. Osvaldo trained as an architect and eventually took over the family business. With his brother, he founded the design firm Tecno in 1953. Tecno creates high-end furniture for offices. *Abitare,* the Italian architecture and interior design magazine, referred to the extraordinary mechanical inventiveness of his work, typical of the 1950s.

Borsani had a distinguished career and was widely lauded as one of the masters of Italian postwar modernism, although his reputation was greater in Italy than abroad. He was proficient in both the corporate and the residential world. Tecno's furniture pieces focused on the high end of the office furniture market. They also designed tables with laminate tops and varnished steel bases.

What intrigued Borsani was the challenge to create a chaise with an infinite number of positions—a chair that could be incrementally adjusted. Such pieces helped meet the growing need for well-designed office furniture. He was known for tasteful interiors that often combined his own pieces with the works of others, setting them, cheek by jowl, next to antiques and other pieces produced by Tecno.

Figure 24.6 Harry Bertoia. Diamond Chair, 1952.

Harry Bertoia

Born in San Lorenzo, Pordenone, Italy, in 1915, Harry Bertoia came to the United States at the age of fifteen to visit his brother and decided to stay. He began his career as a jewelry maker and later worked for Charles and Ray Eames. In 1950, he opened his own studio and designed a collection for Knoll, eventually called the Bertoia Collection. Famous for their sculptural forms and molded latticework of welded steel, the Diamond Chair and the smaller Bertoia Chair are still in production (Figure 24.6). They are available with leather and fabric pads.

Charles and Ray Eames

Charles and Ray Eames dedicated their careers to the need for high-quality and affordable furniture for home and office. One of their ideas was to create a shell that would be comfortable without padding and could be easily mass-produced. Made alternately of molded plywood, wire mesh, cast aluminum, and fiberglass, many of their designs are still being reproduced. The plywood Eames chair was a long time in production, and the result was successful and widely copied (Figure 24.7). The ESU 400 Series was a line of modular storage units made

Figure 24.7 Charles and Ray Eames. Eames chair, 1946.

from metal and plywood (Figure 24.8). Their upscale lounge chair and ottoman were conceived to be appropriate for home and office.

There has been much thoughtful work on the careers of Charles and Ray Eames, yet one aspect of their work and careers is still understudied: their decades-long interest in India (Mathur 2007). From 1958 onward, the Eameses had commissions in India, traveled there for months at a time, and bought souvenirs that they took back to their iconic case study house in Los Angeles; India was never far from their minds. The Eameses are the Americans par excellence, but looking at their two decades of involvement with the Indian subcontinent casts modernism in a new light. It raises the issue of the role of modernism for those who designed objects in a preindustrial state. It raises the question about the relationship between nationalism and design. The Eames' work in India suggests that our understanding of modernism should be recast as part of a global design culture. In India, Europe, and the United States their work constituted a bridge between modernism and craft communities.

REVOLUTION: THE 1960S

The 1960s was nothing less than a revolution, and although it made its mark upon politics, the military, and economics, its most powerful weapons were cultural. Anne Bony writes: "The decade from 1960 to 1970 was a turbulent one: nothing was certain, everything was called into question. Through the mass media, television in particular, new ideas and new aspirations reached a wide audience. Consumer society was in the ascendant" (Bony, 2004, p. 9).

At the dawn of the third millennium, the 1960s is temporally distant enough to achieve mythic status, and despite the anxiety it once engendered, it is now mostly viewed through Janis Joplin's rose-tinted glasses. To see the 1960s as a stint of halcyon days requires considerable mental editing, overlooking the Vietnam War and the inequities that led to the civil rights movement. Looking across the artistic spectrum of the 1960s, what is consistent was a sense of a new spirit, a sense of naïveté, and a broad-based antiestablishment position.

The most vivid expression of change was rock music, and the defining moment in the history of popular music was the Woodstock Festival of 1969. Jean-Luc Goddard ushered in the decade with a film whose plotline evoked irreverence and informality, and whose choppy and fragmented editing heralded a new era in filmmaking. *Breathless* was released in 1960 and featured two extremely attractive leading actors in its story of criminals on the run. Other films of the 1960s include *Barbarella* (1967) and *2001: A Space Odyssey* (1968). One popular kitsch, the other a classic, both looked to the future and came to define the 1960s. The decade had a reasonably strong economy, and what is historically significant is that advertising and consumerism moved to center stage of the cultural arena.

Figure 24.8 Charles and Ray Eames. ESU 400 Series Cabinet.

Designers

Of the design professions, the most ephemeral are-nas, fashion and advertising, were at the center of the 1960s cultural revolution; while the architecture profession was slow to respond, interiors, furnish-ings, textiles, and wallpapers were not. Their creators were more keenly tuned to nuance, and admittedly not fearful of being inconsistent, they could reflect major cultural shifts. Terence Conran's success with his Habitat store marked an era in which high-qual-ity design was aimed squarely at the middle class. Yet this frenetic vitality barely made a mark, at first, on the field of architecture. While many aspects of life were being turned upside down in the 1960s, Skidmore, Owings, and Merrill was consolidating

its status as the go-to firm for the ultimate corporate symbol, a Miesian-inspired office building.

Critic Reyner Banham summed up the era when he wrote: "The aesthetics of Pop depend on a mas-sive initial impact and small sustaining power and are therefore at their poppiest in products whose sole object is to be consumed" (Banham 1981, p. 96).

Many designers in the 1960s such as Verner Panton and Pierre Paulin, were interested in creat-ing polyfoam furniture for the mass market. Their pieces were informal, inexpensive, and easy to rear-range. In the furniture realm, there was a great deal of experimentation with new materials, such as Plexiglas and plastic, often in bright colors. Several designers experimented with inflatable furniture.

Roberto Matta

Roberto Matta (1911–2002) is an unlikely candidate to create an iconic piece of furniture, for while he once collaborated with Le Corbusier, he is widely known as an accomplished Surrealist painter. The 1960s, the decade in which Matta's Malitte seating unit arrived, was a time period known for confounding expectations. Matta alternately worked as an architect, painter, sculptor, and furniture designer.

Matta was born in Santiago, Chile, in 1911 to a Basque, Spanish, and French family. Though in a Spanish-speaking country, Matta was schooled in French. After high school, he studied architecture and moved to France, where he worked for Le Corbusier. Ultimately, poetry became more appealing to him than the orderly forms of architecture, and Matta met the poets Federico Garcia Lorca and Pablo Neruda. He visited London, where he met with Walter Gropius and Laszlo Moholy-Nagy (en route to the United States), and also with Surrealist artist Rene Magritte.

Through Lorca, Matta met Salvador Dalí, a leader of the Surrealist movement. Matta joined the movement and turned to painting. He returned to Chile in 1954 and became politically active by endorsing the candidacy of Salvador Allende. After the president's death, Matta resettled in Europe, where he turned to sculpture in the late 1950s. His furniture design is an extension of his sculpture and stems from this period. Chairs of the Malitta unit are simply made of polyurethane foam covered with fabric. The Malitte line was frequently photographed with its five pieces piled together, presenting itself as a blocky contemporary art piece.

Joe Colombo

Joe Colombo was born in 1930 in Italy. He was an active painter and sculptor in the abstract expressionist movement. In 1949, Colombo went to school in Milan, first studying painting, then architecture. In 1962, he opened his own office. Colombo de-

Figure 24.9 Joe Colombo. Chair. Made by Kartell, 1965.

signed furniture, lamps, glass, doorknobs, pipes, alarm clocks, and wristwatches. Some of his greatest works were items like the all-in-one baby trolley, and the universale and elda chairs. He also created flexible, modular living spaces that he called machines for living. Colombo designed products for O-Luce, Kartell, Bieffe, Alessi, Flexform, and Boffi (Figure 24.9). His early works were made of plywood lacquered to resemble plastic, and he eventually created all plastic pieces.

EXPERIMENTATION: THE 1970S

History rarely gives us precise dates for the end of an era, but modernism ended on March 16, 1972, at 3:00 P.M., when the Pruitt-Igoe housing project in St. Louis was demolished (Figure 24.10). Critic Charles Jencks anointed this event as the end of modernism. The destruction of Pruitt-Igoe was seen as an iconic blow to the primacy of modern architecture.

Figure 24.10 Pruitt-Igoe, 1957, demolished, 1972. St. Louis, Missouri.

For a twenty-first-century observer, if the 1960s has become the distant past, the 1970s is still too close, and designers are uncomfortable with much that was created. Many consider the 1970s to be the nadir of taste. It had neither the gloss of pristine modernism nor the shock of the 1960s, but instead was—to its detractors—a sea of brown vinyl, shag carpet, smoked glass, and shiny brass railings. Plastic Tiffany knockoffs and a jungle of potted ferns were all too common. John Portman, a highly successful architect and developer, remains a divisive figure of ridicule among many architects. Although British interior designer David Hicks was able to pull off upholstering Louis XVI chairs in punchy geometric textiles, the works of his less astute imitators have not stood up well to the test of time.

Architecture

John Portman

John Portman was a successful architect who created hotels, many of them for the Hyatt Corporation, in the 1960s, 1970s, and 1980s. These include the Embarcadero Center, San Francisco, 1961–1988; the Hyatt Regency, San Francisco, 1973; the Peachtree Center, Atlanta, 1968–1981; and the Renaissance Center, Detroit. Portman created exciting hotel lobbies with sparkling lights and glass elevators (Figure 24.11). Disdained by critics, they were popular with the public and commercially successful.

Designers

Bruce Hannah and Andrew Morrison

Bruce Hannah (b. 1941) and Andrew Morrison (b. 1939) both studied at and later taught at Pratt Institute in New York. A collaborative design of theirs, the Hannah-Morrison chair, was manufactured and sold by Knoll from 1972 to 1977. With a cast-aluminum base, aluminum extruded stretchers, and fabric upholstery reinforced with fiberglass vinyl, this lounge chair won several design awards.

Hannah and Morrison collaborated on several pieces for Knoll, and Morrison is known as the designer of Knoll's workstation system Knoll Morrison. Long considered the Cadillac of office furniture

Figure 24.11 John Portman, Atlanta Marriott. Atlanta, GA.

systems, Knoll Morrison was beautifully detailed. The Hannah-Morrison line was the seating line that included the Lounge Chair 2011. It was designed to fill the need for several types of lounge seating, with and without headrests, and with an upright version for offices. It therefore filled the role of "easy chair."

Florence Knoll and Ettore Sottsass

Knoll's products in the 1960s and 1970s presented one option of how to respond to the increasingly fractured societal design aesthetic: retreat to the Bauhaus ideal. Optimal solutions were always to be found in good design—which also meant good engineering. Modernists who came from schools like

Pratt and Cooper-Hewitt created the works that established Knoll's design philosophy. For a period with little consensus about anything, Knoll's products suggested an answer: an inward focus on good design. Florence Knoll herself was superb at this; no one could detail a sofa as elegantly and economically as Florence Knoll.

Ettore Sottsass (1917–2007) was a leader of the progressive postmodern design group the Memphis Group. He trained and worked as an architect, but he was mostly known for his designs of office furniture, lamps, ice buckets, silverware, and a revolutionary Olivetti typewriter. It was a portable red typewriter, with a carrying case and a carriage at the same height as the keyboard. He studied in Turin and opened his studio in Milan in 1947. For Alessi he designed soup plates and coasters, for Baccarat a decanter, for Knoll a chair, and for Namastre a carpet. The Memphis Group was known for brightly colored furniture, lighting, and ceramics. Their colorful pieces were made of acrylic, aluminum, and tropical woods. Sottsass' forms looked like things: A bookcase took the form of a lightning bolt; his Tahiti lamp looked like a tropical bird with a long yellow neck and red beak. His work was quirky, sometimes irreverent. Other designers he was associated with included Joe Colombo and Gae Aulenti.

The Rise of the Big Firm

The 1970s saw the rise of the big firm, with Skidmore, Owings, and Merrill as the prime example. One of its principal designers was Gordon Bunshaft, whose projects included Lever House, New York, 1951–1952, and the Banque Lambert, Brussels, 1965. One of its most prominent projects from the 1970s was the John Hancock Building in Chicago, designed by Bruce Graham with engineering by Fazlur Khan, 1968–1970.

Firms around the world modeled themselves on SOM, including Hugh Stubbins, Boston; HDR, Omaha; Gantt Huberman, Charlotte; Kenzo Tange, Tokyo; Norman Foster, London; and Smith, Hinchman, and Grylls, Detroit.

POSTMODERNISM

Post modernism refers to developments in art and architecture from the 1960s onward. These activities challenged the precepts of modernism, first in architecture, then everywhere. In architecture, buildings integrated elements of classicism and other historical traditions. In other arenas—such as literary criticism, music, and painting—postmodernism provided a biting critique of cultural values and reinforced a growing pluralism.

Initially, postmodern architecture was related to Pop Art, particularly in the works of Robert Stern, Charles Moore, and Michael Graves. Architects whose works can be described as postmodern are found across the globe, including Hans Hollein in Austria, Ricardo Bofill in France, and Sumet Jumsai in Thailand. Postmodernism is associated with the decade of the 1980s.

Robert Venturi and Denise Scott Brown

Robert Venturi wrote two books that were the bibles for the antimodernist movement, *Complexity and Contradiction in Architecture* (1966) and *Learning from Las Vegas* (1972). The projects he completed with his wife and business partner, Denise Scott Brown, include the Vanna Venturi House, 1963; Guild House, 1962–1966; and their most prominent project to date, the Sainsbury Wing, National Gallery of Art, London, 1989.

Figure 24.12 Robert Venturi and Denise Scott Brown. Queen Anne Chair with Grandmother Pattern.

Figure 24.13 Stanley Tigerman. "The Titanic", photo-collage.

Robert Venturi and Denise Scott Brown, are among the most influential architects of the twentieth century. Venturi received the Pritzker Prize in Architecture in 1991 and has held multiple teaching positions. He coined the phrase "Less is a bore," a wry response to Mies's famous "Less is more." Venturi and Brown's Queen Anne chair is an ironic look at a classic chair (Figure 24.12).

Stanley Tigerman, Margaret McCurry, and Eva Maddox

Stanley Tigerman is a Chicago architect who was initially associated with postmodernism. An engaging personality, his sense of humor is evident in his lectures and in his designs. Tigerman's wife, Margaret McCurry, began her career in the late 1960s. A photo collage that he used as a Christmas card in 1978 is another iconic image that signaled the demise of modernism (Figure 24.13). The collage, titled "The Titanic," shows Mies's Crown Hall the signature building of his modernist campus, the Illinois Institute of Technology, sinking like the doomed ocean liner.

In 1982, Margaret McCurry merged her firm with her husband's to form Tigerman McCurry Architects. In 1994, Tigerman founded a nonprofit organization in Chicago called Archeworks with fellow designer Eva Maddox. It is a multidisciplinary alternative design school that allows students to team up with nonprofit partners. The groups focus on design solutions to contemporary social concerns.

Aldo Rossi

Aldo Rossi is an Italian architect who was associated with the postmodern movement. Rossi's book *L'architettura della città* had a similar effect in Europe as Venturi's books did in the United States. His major projects include the Modena Cemetery, 1972; the Elementary School, Fagnano, Italy, 1976; the Teatro del Mondo, Venice Biennale, 1979; and an apartment block on the Rauchstrasse, Berlin, 1985.

Michael Graves

A group called the New York 5 included Peter Eisenman, Richard Meier, Charles Gwathmey, John

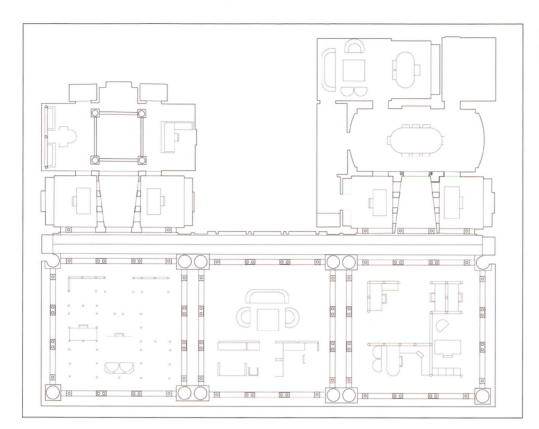

Figure 24.14 Michael Graves. Sunar Showroom, Houston, 1976.

Hejduk, and Michael Graves. Michael Graves was one of the most prominent postmodern designers. He conceptualized a variety of showrooms for the Sunar Fabric Company in Chicago, Dallas, and Houston that were widely published (Figure 24.14). His later projects include large office buildings for Disney, Team Disney, in Burbank, California, 1990, and the Swan Hotel, in Orlando Florida, 1990. He also created several successful furniture designs, including the Oculus Chair (Figure 24.15).

Two buildings built around the same time signaled the ascendancy of postmodernism in the corporate and administrative world. One was Graves's Portland Office Building, Portland, Oregon, 1980–1983, a commission he received by winning a competition. The other was Johnson and Burgee's American Telephone and Telegraph Building, New York, 1979. It was nicknamed the Chippendale Skyscraper because of its recognizable roofline, echoing the outline of a Georgian chest (Figure 24.16).

Figure 24.15 Michael Graves. Oculus chair.

Figure 24.16 Philip Johnson and John Burgee. AT & T Building, New York.

Charles Moore

Charles Moore's Piazza d'Italia, New Orleans, 1975–1979, was one of the first built postmodern projects (Figure 24.17). The Rodes House was for a wealthy family in Brentwood, California, 1976–1979. He also designed an apartment building for Tegel Harbor, in 1980, that was part of an urban redesign of West Berlin. The building exhibition, the Internazionale Bananstellung (IBA), featured many architects' projects, including Steven Eisenman, Arata Isozaki, Aldo Rossi, and Stanley Tigerman.

Traditional Design and Classicism

A group of architects and interior designers, successful in the 1980s, were not postmodern but premodern. They created well-designed projects that met the needs of clients who wanted traditionally designed spaces. The Prince of Wales admired Quinlan Terry, especially his Richmond Riverside Development, 1985–1987. Alan Greenberg is a staunch classicist; one of his larger commissions was the News Building in Atlanta, Georgia, 1988–1992. Mark Hampton is an interior decorator who specializes in traditional residential work. He worked for President and Mrs. Reagan, and created a suite of rooms for the United States State Department. For the patrician philanthropist Carter Burden's New York apartment, he created a neoclassical room befitting a man active in the arts (Figure 24.18).

New Urbanism

At the urban scale, Andres Duany and Elizabeth Plater-Zyberk planned a town that took a nostalgic look at traditional American small towns in the South—Seaside, Florida. The brothers Leon and Robert Krier furthered a similar outlook, operating out of Luxembourg.

Figure 24.17 Charles Moore. Piazza d'Italia, New Orleans Louisiana.

Figure 24.18 Mark Hampton. Carter Burden Apartment, New York.

DECONSTRUCTION

Deconstruction was a widespread phenomenon that is notoriously difficult to define. Fields outside of design explored several themes, such as multiple identities, multiculturalism, and the breakdown between high and low, or between elite and popular culture. A central tenet of most academic fields, after experiencing the work of French philosopher Jacques Derrida, is that meaning is not fixed but contextually created. There is no central agreement as to what deconstruction is or means, but what most proponents could agree on is that they saw it as a movement that countered the stylistic trappings of postmodernism.

Deconstruction was a highly popular and contentious means of interpreting texts, such as great works of literature, and later, anything and every-

thing. It took construction as a metaphoric starting point for literary analysis. Because a text was constructed, the author's intentions were not important, nor the literal meaning of words. Critics revealed the deeper underlying meaning by exposing biases, ripping open seams, and applying preasure. According to deconstruction's promotors, no meaning was fixed, the point was to expose how context was everything. Everything was constructed. At no other point in world history has a philosophy about fundamental truth been so closely related to how one material is designed to join another.

Deconstruction was like postmodernism in multiple respects. It is also called deconstructivism, shortened to "de-con," and was formally related to Russian Constructivism. As a literary movement, its overt influence started in the 1980s, coincident with architectural postmodernism. By the 1990s, postmodernism as an obvious design form was in decline, and deconstruction entered the mainstream. It was no longer the domain of outsiders. The large corporate architecture and interior design firms, S.O.M., Kohn, Pederson and Fox (KPF), and everyone else, started producing designs whose ideological origins lay in what had been an obscure French literary theory.

SITE

James Wines (b. 1932) led a firm, SITE, that in the 1970s unleashed several provocative projects, including the Tilt Showroom and a series of Best Product Showrooms (Figure 24.19). Their roster of provocative projects included some of the most obvious examples of what it meant to deconstruct a building.

Frank Gehry and the Brothers Campana

Frank Gehry's projects include his own house in Santa Monica, Santa Monica Place, 1980; the Schnabel House for the artist Julian Schnabel, 1990; the Fishdance Restaurant, Kobe, Japan, 1986; the American Center in Paris, 1993; and Millenium Park, Chicago, 1999–2005. He has made several furniture designs for Knoll (Figure 24.20).

Related furniture designs were done by the Brothers Campana, the Irmãos Campana, Fernando (b. 1961) and Humberto (b. 1953) Campana, 1991 (Figure 24.21). The Cadeira Favela, or "Slum Chair," was made from recycled found materials. Modernists from the Bauhaus forward had investigated modest materials, but designers associated with deconstruction took this interest to new levels. They worked with the most common, if not debased materials, such as chain-link fencing, cardboard, particle board, and corrugated metal.

1990S

The state of design in the 1990s shows that there was still considerable life to be had in modernism, although with a more pronounced futuristic technological twist. Major figures of this period who are active in both the design and architectural arenas include Rem Koolhaas, Philippe Starck, Andrée

Figure 24.19 James Wines. Best Showroom, Houston, Texas.

Figure 24.20 Frank Gehry.

Figure 24.21 Irmãos Campana (Fernando and Humberto Campana).

Putnam, and Zaha Hadid. In many ways, their designs show a return to the aesthetics that predated the 1980s, when form was related to function and abstraction, and in which purely historical forms had no place.

Philippe Starck, Andrée Putnam, David Adjaye, and Ron Arad

Philippe Starck is France's preeminent designer. Born in France in 1949, he started his first design firm in 1968 after dropping out of school. His career soared after he designed the interiors of two nightclubs that won the attention of the French president François Mitterand, who asked Starck to refurbish his private apartments in the Elysée Palace. Two years later, Starck designed the interior of the Café Costas, Paris, and was on his way to becoming a design celebrity. His edgy redesign of the Paramount Hotel in New York set a new direction for hotel design (Figure 24.22). Prior to Starck, most upper-end hotels were traditionally furnished, with a few classically modern exceptions. He initiated the phenomenon of modern "boutique" hotel design, that drew upon the strengths of both traditional and modern design. His work is more modern and less traditional than postmodernists, yet many of his designs can only be explained with a knowledge of formal meaning, and a sense of humor. He has also designed chairs, lamps, motorbikes, boats, and a line of housewares.

Andrée Putnam is a French designer known for her hotel interiors and minimalist, avant-garde furnishings. She was born and schooled in Paris. She studied piano at the Paris Conservatory before she turned to interior design.

David Adjaye is one of the leading contemporary architects in the United Kingdom. Born in Dar Es Salaam, Tanzania, to Ghanaian parents, he studied

Figure 24.22 Philippe Starck. Paramount Hotel, New York.

architecture at the Royal College of Art; he currently practices in London. Adjaye has won important commissions in the United Kingdom, the United States, and across Europe. His projects are known for his ingenious use of materials and ability to sculpt light.

Ron Arad is an architect, artist, and industrial designer. Born in Tel Aviv, Israel, in 1951, he studied at the Jerusalem Academy of Art from 1971 to 1973, after which he moved to London. He established Ron Arad Associates with Caroline Thormon in both London and Italy. He is currently a professor of industrial and furniture design in London. He has worked for Flos and Vitra (Figure 24.23).

Tadao Ando was born in Osaka, Japan, in 1941 and has since become an admired and influential architect. In 1995, he was awarded the Pritzker Prize. Inspired early on by the works of Le Corbusier, Ando's projects consist primarily of reinforced concrete and attempts to define space in ways

that allow for changing patters of light. In his hands, a common material, concrete, becomes an expressive and beautiful material, as with his Church of the Light (Figure 24.24). One focus of designers who do not align themselves with modernism, post-

Figure 24.23 Ron Arad. MT3 Chair.

Figure 24.24 Tadao Ando. Church of the Light.

modernism, or deconstruction, is the spiritual, reflective qualities of design. Ignoring this vital aspect of life, many feel, was a shortcoming of the modernist approach. Spiritual is not meant in a religious sense but rather how it feels to be in a space, and how one interacts with the world, through technology, light, and materials. This is something Ando does exceptionally well.

Zaha Hadid and Shigeru Ban

Zaha Hadid was born in Baghdad and later studied at the American University of Beirut, where she received a degree in mathematics, and at the Architectural Association School of Architecture in London. Upon graduation she worked for Rem Koolhaas at his Office for Metropolitan Architecture (OMA), where she became a partner in 1977.

Figure 24.25 Zaha Hadid. Designed furniture at Cathcart Road.

She is the first female to win the Pritzker Architecture Prize, and the Guggenheim Museum honored her in 2006 with a retrospective of her work. Her well-known projects include the Rosenthal Center for Contemporary Art (1998), Cincinnati, Ohio; and the Vitra Fire Station (1994), Weil am Rhein, Germany. Throughout her career, she also developed several furniture lines (Figure 24.25). Hadid was one of the first users of computer-aided-drafting (CAD), and her forms are a result of being conceived virtually.

Shigeru Ban works with paper, paper tubes, and cargo containers. Operating out of Paris and New York and Tokyo, he has worked on a variety of small-scale but high-profile projects. He studied at Cooper Union and previously worked for Arata Isozaki.

Diller Scofidio + Renfro

The firm Diller Scofidio + Renfro designs architecture and urban design, but it was a group of unusual projects that garnered them considerable attention. Their innovative projects include the Blur Building, a structure on Switzerland's Lake Neuchâtel that is enshrouded in mist. They redeveloped the support areas of Lincoln Center in New York. One

Figure 24.26 Dilsler Scofidio + Renfro.

of their larger architectural projects to date was the Institute of Contemporary Arts, Boston, 2006. What is significant about their work is that their projects are advanced technologically, yet they are interested in technology not as an end in itself but as a means to an end (Figure 24.26).

The computer room of the museum hangs precariously underneath the part of the museum that cantilevers over Boston Harbor. Structurally impressive, the poetics of the room are the equal of its physics. The entire front wall is glazed and looks down to the water. With the proportions of a computer screen, it looks like the projected destop of an idle computer whose screen saver is on. It's also like the missing fourth wall of a theatre. Computer users who raise their eyes from their keyboards face water, the primordial sea where life began.

CONCLUSION

It is difficult and impossible to predict where things are headed. One can, however, point out some of the current concerns that strike a serious cord, and that rise about the level of fad. An aspect of twentieth- and twenty-first-century design that differs from that of previous centuries is that the means of its creation and dissemination has changed—that is, television and computers. Most people get their information about interior design and furnishings from television, other popular media, and commercial sources. Technologies will continue to affect design's creation and reception.

Julia Child and Bob Vila politely pioneered domestic-improvement television on PBS. The respective hosts of *The French Chef* (1962) and *This Old House* (1979) offered informative alternatives to mainstream escapist programming. In 1991,

Martha Stewart became the reigning queen of domestic television with *Martha Stewart Living,* offering a range of advice, including cooking, decorating, crafting, and floral arranging ideas. Stewart, in innumerable ways, has taken the unofficial mantle of popular American interior designer once held by Elsie de Wolfe. Although in different forms, viewers tuned in to these three shows because they could apply the hosts' ideas to their own lives, or at least be inspired by them. Following in Stewart's footsteps, cable television proved itself as the perfect outlet for lifestyle programming, with several channels focusing some or all of their programming on the home, including Home and Garden Television, and the Discovery Channel. The variety of these shows speaks to practically every aspect of lifestyle.

Recently, the home-improvement sphere was shaken up with a show that initially seemed shocking, Bravo's *Queer Eye for the Straight Guy* (2003). Historically speaking, what was novel about *Queer Eye* is that it made explicit what had long been an interior design secret: that a gay designer is somehow in command of the multiple sensitivities and skills necessary to produce a successfully designed and furnished space. Around the same time, TLC's *Trading Spaces* (2000) and *Extreme Makeover: Home Edition* became popular. Some attribute the success of home shows to both post-9/11 cocooning and the rise in popularity of reality shows.

Critics contend that many shows portray home improvement unrealistically, making it seem as though the process of designing and executing such projects requires only a few days and a modest budget. In addition, on-screen designers often have little formal design training. The entertainment factor is imperative to these shows' success, and they include humor, human interest, aspirational ideals, and elements of surprise.

Looking at the history of design history, and pondering its future, this book presents several subject areas that I hope will continue to be the subjects of individual study. For one, to continue to research and herald the design contributions of women. Secondly, the global reassessment of twentieth-century modernism that began with Luis Barragán and Hassan Fathy should continue. All countries produced interesting modern work, and exploring the lives and words of the designers involved—through detailed studies—is greatly needed. With the exception of Europe, North America, and China, books on the furniture of all regions need to be written. While it is clear that television and film are integral to reflecting and shaping design tastes, researching and writing serious books about these subjects proves difficult. Often the work is not fully credited and the documentation not preserved. In touching on these, and other issues, this book has endeavored to show how design participated in major movements and, just as importantly, design and designed objects suggested alternate paths. My position is that there are multiple characteristics of the field of design (including interior design, designed objects, and furniture), where it differs from art and architecture. One is a lack of ideological purity that ultimately results in more conceptually nuanced compositions. And two, that designers' activities force them to engage with the details of daily life, real and imagined.

In touch with immediate needs and wants, designs of a human scale avoid the single-mindedness of some works of art and architecture. That is their strength, and the subject of this book.

Sources

Adjaye, David. *David Adjaye: Houses, Recycling, Reconfiguring, Rebuilding.* New York: Thames and Hudson, 2005.

Ando, Tadao. *Tadao Ando: Light and Water.* New York: Monacelli Press, 2003.

Banham, Reyner. *A Critic Writes.* Berkeley: University of California Press, 1996.

Banham, Reyner. *Design By Choice.* New York: Rizzoli, 1981.

Boissière, Olivier. *Philippe Starck*. Cologne: Taschen, 1991.

Bony, Anne. *Furniture and Interiors of the 1960s*. Paris: Flammarion, 2004.

Bony, Anne. *Furniture and Interiors of the 1970s*. Paris: Flammarion, 2005.

Diller, Elizabeth, and Ricardo Scofidio. *Blur: The Making of Nothing*. New York: Abrams, 2002.

Eidelberg, Martin, et al. *The Eames Lounge Chair: An Icon of Modern Design*. London: Merrell, 2006.

Frampton, Kenneth. *Le Corbusier: Architect of the Twentieth Century*. New York: Abrams, 2002.

Irvine, Keith, and Chippy Irvine. *Keith Irvine: A Life in Decoration*. New York: Monacelli Press, 2005.

Jodidio, Philip. *New Forms: Architecture in the 1990s*. Cologne: Taschen, 1997.

Mathur, Saloni. *India by Design: Colonial History and Cultural Display*. Berkeley: University of California Press, 2007.

Sparke, Penny. *Twentieth Century Design: Furniture*. London: Bell and Hyman, 1986.

Sudjic, Deyan, and Ron Arad. *Restless Furniture*. New York: Rizzoli, 1989.

Tyng, Anne, and Louis Kahn. *Louis Kahn to Anne Tyng: The Rome Letters, 1953–1954*. New York: Rizzoli, 1997.

DISCUSSION AND REVIEW QUESTIONS

1. The terms *modernism, postmodernism, deconstruction,* and *contemporary* are often used inconsistently. What are some examples, from any field, in which you have heard these terms used? Are there any underlying consistencies in their use?
2. How do people who sell furniture use these terms?
3. How do people in literature departments and other fields use these terms?
4. Who were some of the prewar modernists who had successful careers after World War II?
5. What was appealing about John Portman's hotels?
6. What are the characteristics of design of the 1970s?
7. What first comes to mind when you hear "the 1960s"? How did this impact the world of design?
8. What movement is associated with the 1980s?
9. What movement is associated with the 1990s?

GLOSSARY

Chapter 1: Prehistory

corbel: or false arch, masonry technique in which each layer of construction cantilevers over the preceding layer

dolmen: a megalithic structure consisting of two or more upright stones supporting a horizontal capstone

henge: Neolithic monument in a circular form, created with banks, ditches, and stone or timber construction

lintel: a horizontal member that spans an opening, such as a door or window, and supports the load above it

lithic: using stone

megalith: a prehistoric monument comprising large, undressed blocks of stone

menhir: a large single upright stone

Mesolithic: "Middle Stone Age" period, from the seventh to eighth centuries B.C.E.

Neolithic: "New Stone Age" period, from the fourth to sixth centuries B.C.E., characterized by the use of refined stone implements and extensive use of pottery

Paleolithic: "Old Stone Age" period, before the eighth century B.C.E., characterized by the first development of stone implements

post and lintel: the simplest form of construction, in which vertical members (columns) support horizontal members (beams or lintels)

trabeated: construction method based on the post-and-lintel method

Chapter 2: Ancient Civilizations

ankh: an ancient Egyptian hieroglyphic symbolizing life and prosperity

Assyrian: one of the ancient Mesopotamian cultures in the region fed by the Tigris and Euphrates Rivers

batter: the inclination of the face of a wall

booty: items seized during warfare

canopic: in ancient Egypt, a term relating to the preservation of body parts in preparation for burial

couch: a long piece of furniture for sitting or reclining, without a back support

dado: the lower portion of an interior wall of a room, distinguished from the upper portion

ergonomics: the science of designing furniture pieces to respond to the human form

hieroglyphs: an ancient Egyptian system of writing that used symbols for words or sounds

hypostyle hall: a space with many rows of columns supporting a flat roof

joist: horizontal member that spans a structure's walls

mastaba: an ancient mud-brick tomb with a flat roof and sloping sides

mud brick: building material consisting of wet earth compacted and dried in the sun

necropolis: a large ancient burial ground

polychrome: multicolored

pylon: a truncated pyramidal tower flanking the entrance to an ancient Egyptian temple

pyramid: an Egyptian royal tomb

relief: ornamentation that projects from a flat surface

spathe: the leafy part of a plant that encloses a flower

stretcher: a horizontal furniture element that structurally connects the vertical supports

volute: a spiral scroll, especially of a capital

X-frame chair: a transportable folding chair

ziggurat: a large stepped pyramid temple, common in ancient Mesopotamia

Chapter 3: Classical Civilizations

agora: the large open public space at the center of a Greek city

amphora: a tall Greek vase with a narrow neck and two handles

andron: the area of an ancient Greek house reserved exclusively for men

architrave: the lowest horizontal portion of an entablature or lintel

atrium: the inner courtyard of a building, open to the sky

attic: made in Athens

barrel chair: a circular seat made of timber of straw

barrel vault: a continuous semicircular arch

caldarium: the room with hot water in an ancient Roman bath

capital: the upper element of a column

caryatid: a sculptured female figure used in place of a column

cathedra: an ancient Roman chair with curved back and flared legs; formally similar to the Greek Klismos chair

cella: the central enclosed chamber of an ancient Greek temple

citadel: a hilltop fortress

coffer: a sunken ornamental panel in a ceiling or dome; a chest used to store valuables

Composite: the classical order that combines Ionic and Corinthian elements

Corinthian: the third and most elaborate of the Classical Greek and Roman orders of architecture, characterized by carvings of acanthus leaves on the capital

cornice: the uppermost portion of an entablature; any projecting portion at the top of a wall or building

cyclopean masonry: an elemental type of construction with large irregular blocks of stone

domus: an ancient Roman house for a wealthy or middle-class family

Doric: the earliest and simplest of the three orders of Classical Greek architecture

dromos: a long passageway leading to an ancient underground chamber

entasis: in classical architecture, the slight convexity or swelling of the shaft of a column

forum: the large open public space at the center of an ancient Roman city

frieze: the decorated middle portion of an entablature, between the architrave and the cornice

fulcrum: a Roman headrest for leaning on

horror vacui: fear or dislike of undecorated space

hydria: a wide-body Greek vase with broad flat shoulders, frequently used for black-figure vase painting

hypocaust: a plenum under the floor of an ancient Roman building, used to distribute the heat from a furnace

impluvium: the cistern or pool in the atrium of an ancient Roman house, used to collect rainwater

in antis: columns between the projecting side walls of a building

insula: an ancient Roman apartment block, occupied by the lower and middle class

Ionic: the second of the three orders of Classical Greek architecture, characterized by the use of volutes

klismos: a Classical Greek chair with curved legs, splayed at the front and back, and a concave curved back

kylix: a shallow Greek drinking cup with two handles

loggia: a gallery or pillared room open on one side

lyre: a classical stringed instrument, strummed like a harp

megaron: the archaic Greek structure consisting of a single room with a central hearth and four columns; also used for the large central hall of Minoan and Mycenaean palaces

metope: square spaces between triglyphs in a classical frieze, often sculpted

mezzanine: an interstitial story between principal stories

mosaic: small pieces of glass, stone, or tile composed and set in mortar; either geometric or representational, on floors, walls, or ceilings

oculus: a circular opening in a wall or top of a dome

order: one of the established modes of designing a column and entablature in Classical Greek and Roman architecture, the primary three being Doric, Ionic, and Corinthian

palestra: in ancient Greece and Rome, a public exercise facility for the training of athletes

pediment: in Classical architecture, the low-pitched gable above a portico; also found above doors and windows

peristyle: a colonnade surrounding a building or enclosing a court

pilaster: a rectangular pier or column engaged in a wall

polis: the Greek city-state

portico: a covered porch, supported by columns, forming the entrance to a building

rotunda: a circular, domed room or building—for example, the Pantheon

Satyrs: human figures with goat legs, ears, horns, and tail

sella curulis: an ancient Roman X-shaped folding chair used by officials and dignitaries

stelae: upright flat stone panels used as monuments

stoa: a covered colonnaded porch

stylobate: a structure's base, the platform that supports columns

symposium: an all-male dining and drinking social event

tabernae: an ancient Roman shop within an indoor market, often covered by a barrel vault

tablinum: the main living room of an ancient Roman house, with one side open to the atrium

tessera: a square piece of glass, stone, or tile used in mosaics

triclinium: the dining room of an ancient Roman house

triglyph: rectangular blocks that separate metopes in a frieze, characterized by three vertical elements formed from two grooves

trompe l'oeil: literally, to trick the eye; a painting technique that imitates another material or creates the illusion of a three-dimensional scene

Tuscan: a Roman variation of the Doric order, typically without a fluted shaft

tympanum: the triangular area bounded within a pediment, often carved; also, the semicircular sculpted relief above a door

wainscot: a panel, applied or integral, of the lower portion of an interior wall

Chapter 4: Early Christian and Byzantine

aisle: circulation spaces at the sides or center of a church

apse: the semicircular or polygonal projection at the end of a church

arcade: a series of arches supported by piers or columns

baptistery: a room or building for the Christian rite of baptism; often round or octagonal

basilica: an ancient Roman colonnaded room for public use; term adapted to describe rectangular early Christian churches

clerestory: windows or openings in the upper portion of a wall

cupola: a small dome crowning a roof

entablature: the horizontal upper portion of a Classical order, supported by columns and consisting of an architrave, frieze, and cornice

gallery: an upper story over an aisle, open to the nave

Greek cross: a centralized church plan based on a cross with four equal arms

illumination: image used to adorn and illustrate a medieval manuscript

Latin cross: a church plan with three equal arms and one longer one

monoxylous: made of one piece of a material

nave: the central space of a church, usually flanked by side aisles

pendentive: a triangular element that transitions from the base of a dome to a wall, pier, or column

sanctuary: the most sacred area of a church, typically surrounding the high altar

tesserae: small cubes of stone, glass, or tile used to create mosaics

transept: the transverse arms of a cross-shaped church that intersect the nave

Chapter 5: Romanesque and Islamic

ablutions fountain: a fountain outside of a mosque for ritual cleansing

ambulatory: semicircular space on the perimeter of a choir

aqueduct: an elevated channel (often arcaded) for carrying water

bahut: a leather envelope for protecting a chest during travel

Carolingian: the French and German Romanesque style of the eighth to tenth centuries; literally refers to the reign of Charlemagne (768–814)

chip carving: a technique in which a knife and hammer remove material from a single piece of wood

chevet: the end of a church, opposite the entry, consisting of the choir and ambulatory, often with chapels

choir: an area of the church reserved for clergy; part of the *chancel* behind the transept

crenellated: referring to repeated square indentations on the top of a wall

diwan: an Islamic reception chamber with raised platforms for seating; furnished with carpets and cushions

half-timber: a construction technique in which horizontal and vertical timbers are exposed and infilled with plaster

hutch: a type of storage chest with upright ends that constitute the legs and the sides; not used for travel

Islamic arch: a semicircular pointed arch, often expanding further than 180 degrees; also known as horseshoe arch; in Spain, also known as Moorish arch

maksura: in an Islamic mosque, a sanctuary area with a perforated enclosure

Merovingian: a period of French architecture that predates Romanesque

mihrab: a niche in the qibla wall of a mosque indicating the direction toward Mecca

minaret: a tower adjacent to a mosque, used for call to prayer

minbar: a pulpit in a mosque from where the sermon is delivered

mosque: an Islamic place of worship

Mughal: Islamic dynastic rule of Northern India, sixteenth to nineteenth centuries, known for the splendor of its decoration, and whose finest monument is the Taj Mahal

narthex: the entry chamber or vestibule of a church, directionally transverse to the nave

Norman: English Romanesque style of the eleventh and twelfth centuries

plank construction: construction in which the original wooden materials remain visible

prayer hall: the central space of a mosque, often with many columns

qibla: the wall in a mosque that points toward Mecca and contains the mihrab

Romanesque arch: a semicircular arch, similar to the ancient Roman arch

roshan: in Islamic domestic architecture, a protruding window with open screens, allowing for air to circulate but preventing visual access

sillón frailero: Renaissance chair with hung leather seat, sometimes hinged

strapwork: ornament consisting of interlacing bands, representative of leather

toron: in West African Islamic architecture, the permanent wooden structure that projects from walls, used as scaffolding

vargueño: a Spanish Renaissance drop-fronted desk

voussoir: a wedge-shaped stone used to form an arch

wattle and daub: construction technique in which interwoven twigs (wattle) are plastered with mud (daub)

Chapter 6: Gothic

abbey: a Christian monastery or convent

bastide: in France, a small fort; also, a fortified new town laid out according to a regularized plan

dais: a raised platform in a room

fan vault: a vault with ribs of the same curve and spacing, resembling a fan. Popular in late English Gothic architecture

finial: a formal ornament at the top of an element

flamboyant: literally, "flaming"; late Gothic style with elaborate tracery

flying buttress: a structural element, separated from the walls, that counteracts the thrust of an internal vault

Gothic arch: a semicircular pointed arch

hammer beam: horizontal brackets that extend from the top of a wall to support vertical posts that support the roof

High Gothic: medieval Gothic architectural period

linenfold: Gothic ornamental panel carved to appear as folded linen

quatrefoil: a four-lobed ornament

Rayonnant: French Gothic architecture of the thirteenth century, characterized by complex tracery

ribbed vault: a vault supported by (or decorated with) diagonal ribs, dividing the surface into webs

tongue and groove: same as mortice and tenon, in which a protruding element fits into a groove

tracery: ornamental interlacing pattern, typical in Gothic detailing and emphasizing decoration over structure

trefoil: a three-lobed ornament

triforium: in a Gothic church, an arcaded gallery above the nave and below the clerestory

triptych: an artwork divided into three panels

truss: a rigid frame used as a structural element, especially for roofs

Chapter 7: The Americas

ball court: a pre-Columbian large horizontal masonry structure, flanked with sloped walls at either side, used to play Mesoamerican ball games

Chac-mool: pre-Columbian Mesoamerican stone statue depicting a human figure lying down with a tray or bowl on its stomach

hacha: squat element used in Mesoamerican ball games attached to a yoke around the waist

iconoclasm: the purposeful destruction of art or architecture, often in the name of religion

Mesoamerican: North American and Central American region

metates: stone-grinding platforms, possibly used as seats or sacrificial altars

palma: tall thin element used in Mesoamerican ball games, attached to a yoke around the waist

Pre-Columbian: the Americas prior to the arrival of European explorers

spolia: a synonym for booty, items seized in warfare used to commemorate victory

tablero: a framed stone panel, typical in pre-Columbian Mesoamerican architecture

talud: a base, frequently sloped, that supported an upper framed panel

zoomorphic: designed elements related to animals or animal parts

Chapter 8: From Stupa to Pagoda and from Mat to Chair

chattri: a stone parasol or finial that crowns a stupa

howdah: an ornate carriage used to ride an elephant; also spelled houdah

Jian: the central room of the main hall in a traditional Chinese courtyard house

kang table: kang historically meant heated platform; a low table placed on top of the platform, resembling a modern coffee table

Khmer: an ethnic designation that refers to the ancient Cambodian empire that reached its peak in the ninth to twelfth centuries

mandala: a Buddhist geometric pattern, diagrammatic of the cosmos

pagoda: a Buddhist tower-shaped religious building

palanquin: a boxlike platform attached to horizontal poles, carried on the shoulders of four bearers

quincunx: a geometric arrangement of five objects,

with four at the corners of a square and one in the middle

Sinicize: to make Chinese in character

spandrel: in architecture or furniture, the horizontal element that spans between vertical risers

splat: the central part of a chair's backrest, independent of the vertical supports

stupa: a Buddhist dome-shaped earthen monument

zhuo table: a rectangular table with legs at the corners (not inset)

Chapter 9: Renaissance

asceticism: the practice of rigorous self-denial for religious purposes; associated with restraint and simplicity in design

cabinet: an upright storage unit with shelves and doors or drawers

cassapanca: an Italian Renaissance chest/bench with arms and a back, used both for storage and seating

cassone: an Italian Renaissance large, highly ornamented chest, originally used to store the belongings of a bride

chest: a rectangular volume with a lid, utilized for storage or transport

credenza: a storage unit used for display, taller than a chest, shorter than a cabinet

Dante chair: an Italian Renaissance folding chair based on the X-frame chair

dovetail joint: a strong mortise joint formed by interlocking trapezoidal pieces of wood

eclectic: representative of different sources or styles

gilded: covered in a thin layer of gold leaf

humanism: a mode of thought that rejects religion and focuses on innate human value

inlay: method of ornamentation in which precious materials are set into a contrasting ground material

intarsia: an elaborate composition using multiple wood types, in veneer and inlay, to construct a picture

one-point perspective (linear perspective): the mathematical system developed during the Italian Renaissance for representing three-dimensional space on a two-dimensional surface, with all lines converging on a single vanishing point

palazzo: an Italian large public building or residence

piano nobile: the principal public floor of an Italian Renaissance palazzo, typically the first floor above the ground floor

putti: cupids, common decorative figures in Italian Renaissance art

refectory table: a long, narrow dining table with upright panel supports at either end

rusticated: the use of rough-cut masonry, usually on a lower floor, to create a deep texture; also, manipulated stucco that resembles rough masonry

sacristy: a room or area of a church for storing sacred vestments and vessels

Savonarola chair: a simple, austere X-frame chair, standardized during the Italian Renaissance

sedia: an Italian Renaissance armchair with blocky legs and leather-covered seat and back

sgabello: an Italian Renaissance side chair or stool, with a small seat

stanze: in Italian, literally "rooms"; also refers to a suite of rooms or an interiors project—for example, Raphael's *stanze*

string course: a prominent horizontal element in a façade

terrazzo: a hard floor made of pieces of stone set in a mortar

trestle table: a table supported by two uprights at either end and a stabilizing cross-piece

turned construction: indicating construction with wood pieces that are carved while being rotated

villa: an Italian or Roman large countryside residence

Chapter 10: Baroque

armoire: a large wardrobe

Aubusson: tapestry and textile region of southern France

Baroque: characteristically extravagant or elaborate in style; seventeenth-century style

Baroque armchair: an armchair with straight back and legs, and curved stretchers

Boulle work: the veneered furniture of André-Charles Boulle, his workshop, sons, and imitators, of the late Baroque and Regency periods, characterized by elaborate marquetry

cabochon: an oval convex ornament

canapé: a French sofa, or settee, with back

chaise longue: a long lounging seat with an extended portion for feet, and one raised end

chateau: a large French country house

commode: a low, upright chest of drawers or shelves

console: a small table designed to be placed against a wall

desornamentado: design of Spain and the Spanish colonies in the sixteenth and seventeenth centuries, more austere than Plateresco

drop-leaf: a table with hinged leaves, supported by hinged legs or brackets

ébéniste: a French carpenter who specialized in veneering

ensemble: a complementary furniture set popular in the Baroque period

fluting: shallow concave vertical grooves found on classical columns

girandole: an elaborate wall bracket for candles

japanning: European simulation of Asian style of lacquering furniture

lit en bateau: a sleigh bed, with two ends of equal height, sometimes scrolled

mansard: roofs with all four sides sloping, covering a habitable space, sometimes with dormers

mannerism: an exaggerated or distorted stylistic tendency

marquetry: ornamental veneer work utilizing diverse woods to form scenes or represent objects

mudéjar: Spanish medieval style, of the twelfth to fifteenth centuries, incorporating Islamic motifs

obelisk: a tall rectangular stone pillar tapering to a point at the top

ormolu: gilded bronze ornaments and hardware added to furniture

parquetry: ornamental veneer work utilizing diverse woods to form geometric shapes and nonrepresentational patterns

piazza: an Italian open public square

Regency armchair: a chair with cross-stretchers, curved back, and slightly curved legs

salon: a large formal room used for receiving and entertaining guests

Savonnerie carpet: French carpet manufacturer supported by Louis XIV and specializing in high-pile wool rugs

settée: a seat with back and arms for two or more people

torchère: a candle stand

travertine: a light-color limestone

Chapter 11: Rococo

apron: a shaped piece below a seat rail or tabletop

baldaquin: a fabric canopy

bergère: a comfortable upholstered armchair with a deep seat, separate seat cushion, and closed continuous arms

boiserie: French woodwork of the seventeenth and eighteenth centuries, often painted white

bombé: case furniture with an outward swell

buffet: a side or serving table with open shelves and closed storage

bureau: a piece of furniture with a writing surface, often hinged and concealed

bureau à cylinder: a roll-top desk with a concealed writing surface and storage

cabriole: a leg with a graceful S-curve, used in Ming, Rococo, and Queen Anne furniture

cartoon: a sketch or mock-up of a design to be realized in another medium

cartouche: a French decorative oval tablet with curled edges

causeuse: a synonym for marquise chair

chiffonnier: a short cupboard with closed shelving and doors

Chinoiserie: European art loosely inspired by China

confidante: an upholstered settée with seats at both ends and vertical divisions

dormeuse: a type of chaise longue resembling an upholstered deck chair

duchesse brissée: an upholstered daybed in two or three pieces

encoignure: a corner cupboard

enfilade: a suite of rooms designed with direct visual access between them

fauteuil: an armchair, especially Louis XV and XVI

gondole: an upholstered armchair with a concave, semicircular arched back; tub chair

hôtel: a French town house, public or private

kneehole: a recessed space in a desk for a user's legs

marquise: a broad chair with upholstered seat, back, and arms; synonym: causeuse

méridienne: a small French empire sofa, with one end lower than the other

provincial: sixteenth-, seventeenth-, and eighteenth-century, French country furniture inspired by formal pieces

Regency: a transitional style between Baroque and Rococo

secretary: synonym: escritoire, a small writing desk

sideboard: a table of the medieval period and after, for display or serving, with open or closed storage

singerie: a strain of exoticism with monkey motifs or monkeys dressed as humans

torchère: a candle stand

voyeuse: a low armchair with a padded upper back and used as an armrest for a standing figure, in English, a conversation chair

Chapter 12: England

ball turning: also known as sausage motif, a twisted-looking stretcher made on a lathe, popular in the Jacobean period; also, a feature of continental Baroque design

bartizan: small castle-like turrets that protrude from a wall; initially defensive

bespoke: a commercial transaction predating manufacturing, of individually commissioning furniture

bow-back: a type of Windsor chair with a continuous bent top rail

Caroleon: an English Baroque transitional style between Jacobean and William and Mary

chest on chest or chest on stand: a tall dresser with two sections and multiple drawers

chintz: printed and glazed cotton cloth

comb-back: a type of Windsor chair with a straight top rail

Cromwellian: related to the tenure of Arthur Cromwell, in design a continuation of Jacobean forms with a subtle nod toward simplification

cup-and-cover: the signature design motif of the Elizabethan era, a melon-shaped bulbous form on vertical supports

dais: a raised platform at one end of the great hall where nobles dined

Elizabethan: 1558–1603; one of the great epochs of world history, with design characterized by medieval forms, a profusion of decoration, and the beginnings of the English Renaissance

Fachwerk: German term referring to timber-frame construction, similar to English Tudor

Farthingale chair: a boxy chair with an upholstered seat and back, and no arms, also known as back chair

gate-leg table: a table with a folding top supported by a swinging framed leg

Georgian: the classical style of the reigns of the three English King Georges, important for both architecture and furniture, visually heavier than Queen Anne

great hall: a central feature of English castles and country houses, a rectangular-shaped communal dining hall

Jacobean: during the reign of James I, both the introduction of continental Renaissance forms and the continuation of Elizabethan trends; lighter in visual weight than Elizabethan

Mortlake Tapestry Industry: the principal manufacturer of tapestries and textiles in Restoration England

Queen Anne: a distinct period of furniture, if not architecture, of the early eighteenth century Simple, elegant, curvilinear pieces with light profiles

ribband or ribbon-back: a type of chair decoration in which the wood of the back is carved to resemble curling ribbons; popularized by Chippendale

Restoration: the reestablishment of the English monarchy after Cromwell, related to continental baroque and the grandeur of Louis XIV

scalloping: a decorative motif reminiscent of shells and featuring incised curves

screen: a wall with openings, of wood or stone, that provided a passageway through the English great hall

settle chair: a box-shaped Tudor chair similar to the Italian Renaissance sedia

sleeping chair: an upholstered English armchair with wings

stick-back: another name for the Windsor chair

strapwork: an ornament based on interlaced bands and popular in many media, particularly plasterwork in the Elizabethan and Jacbobean periods

Stuart: stylistically related to English restoration, a Baroque transition style between Jacobean and William and Mary

tester: a bed's architectural canopy

Tudor: 1500–1558, relating to the Tudor monarchs and the end of English medievalism; architecture characterized by timber framing, leaded glass, and Gothic arches, in furniture, a continuation of medieval forms

turned chair: a Jacobean chair based on a medieval triangular stool yet rendered elaborate with numerous turned vertical supports

wainscot chair: a boxy chair, similar to the Italian Renaissance sedia, with turned vertical legs and a carved back

wattle and daub: construction method in which there is a lath, or framework, of lightweight timber filled in with a matrix of mud or plaster. A forerunner to timber-frame construction

William and Mary: characterized by Dutch, Flemish, and French influences, curvilinear and ornate, a submovement of English Baroque, moving in the direction of lighter profiles

Windsor chair: a rustic chair made during the Queen Anne period and utilizing turned legs, stretchers, and vertical supports, with a continuous top rail

Chapter 13: In the Colonies

Afrikaans: a Dutch-based dialect spoken in South Africa

Banisterback chair: a colonial wooden chair with a backrest formed of vertical rails

Batavia: historical Dutch name for Jakarta, Indonesia

bombé: an eighteenth-century casework with a curved body (in contrast to curved externals, such as feet)

camel-back sofa: a Georgian sofa with a rounded back

Churrigueresque: late–Spanish Baroque design, chronologically following Platesque and characterized by elaborate ornamentation

Colonial: related to a colony or colonies; in the United States, of or related to the thirteen British colonies

Coloured: mixed-race ethnic group in South Africa

Concha: shell motif in Spanish or Latin-American art, related to scalloping

escutcheons: a metal plate that acts as a base for hardware, such as a doorknob or drawer pull, attached to a door or drawer

Habitants: a French word for a West African mixed-race ethnic group

Hadley chest: a colonial chest above a drawer or drawers; from the Hadley area of Massachusetts

highboy: a tall chest of drawers

humpback sofa: a Georgian sofa with a rounded back

Kraal: South African indigenous communal enclosure with a stockade at the perimeter

ladderback chair: a colonial wooden chair with a backrest formed of horizontal rails

Lemoenhout: South African furniture made from citrus wood

lowboy: a short chest with one or two drawers; used as a dressing table

Mestiço: Portuguese mixed-race, or Creole, ethnic group; also Mestizo

Mulatto: African mixed-race, or Creole, ethnic group

Pennsylvania Dutch: descendants of German immigrants; from German "Deutsch"

Plateresque: in Spanish, Plateresco; highly ornamented Spanish design of the sixteenth century, related to Baroque

Puritans: a persecuted religious group from England and English colonies who sought to simplify the Church of England and free it of outside influences

Saint-Dominique: French historical name for Haiti

Shakers: early-nineteenth-century New England religious group that related moral piety to aesthetic simplicity

Signares: West African word of Portuguese derivation for mixed-race women of the *habitant* ethnic group

stinkwood: wood native to South Africa that emits an odor after felling

Transitional Tulbagh chair: simplified wooden version of the Tulbagh chair

Tulbagh chair: a caned chair unique to South Africa and based on a Queen Anne chair and a Dutch box-chair, with a vase-shaped splat and box stretchers

Yellowwood: light-colored wood native to South Africa

Chapter 14: Neoclassical

Adamsesque: English Neoclassical design that resembles the work of the Adams brothers

Beaux-Arts: literally, the fine arts—painting, sculpture, and architecture; also refers to the Parisian school École des Beaux Arts

Biedermeier: Neoclassical vernacular design in Germany

City Beautiful movement: nineteenth- and twentieth-century movement to improve urban infrastructure and associated with classical design

classical: authoritative, traditional, of or relating to a form or system felt to be of first significance before modern times, specifically refers to the art and design of ancient Greece and Rome

Directoire: a French Neoclassical style, similar to Empire, related to the government of the Directory

Directory: the representative French government that followed the revolution, 1795–99

Empire: the French government of Napoleon, 1804–15, and the Neoclassical style associated with it

Federal: Neoclassicism in the United States

gout grec: the initial name for the fashion for ancient Greek artifacts, prior to Neoclassicism

Hitchcock chair: classically inspired wooden chair made by American furniture maker Lambert Hitchcock

Jeffersonian: Neoclassical and Federal design in the United States that resembles the works of Thomas Jefferson

laurel wreath: a crown made of laurel leaves, from the classical period, and a popular Neoclassical motif

lyre: a classical musical instrument, a popular Neoclassical motif

Récamier: a settée, named after David's painting of Juliette Récamier

Regency: English Neoclassical period

Restoration: nineteenth century restoration of the French Bourbon monarchy

Chapter 15: Victorian and Historical Revivals

cast iron: iron alloy formed in a mold

Folly: whimsical picturesque garden pavilion

Janissary: Turkish or Turkish-inspired music

Japonisme: the European cult of Japanese-inspired artworks

polychromy: something of multiple colors

Richardsonian Romanesque: Romanesque revival style associated with Henry Hobson Richardson that was as much forward- as backward-looking

Romanticism: a nineteenth-century literary and arts movement that emphasized emotion

Saracenic: Islamic architecture and design; also, Turkish design

whatnot: Victorian open shelving unit

Chapter 16: Reform Movements

Anglo-Japanese: furniture and decorative arts pieces by English designers inspired by Japan; related to Japonisme

Chicago School: referring to the late-nineteenth-century architects and engineers who pioneered the skyscraper

Hudson River Valley School: a group of New York landscape painters associated with Romanticism

Muckrackers: nineteenth-century journalists who investigated harmful business practices

Prairie Style: midwestern American architecture movement whose leader was Frank Lloyd Wright

Pre-Raphaelites: art movement, related to Romanticism and Arts and Crafts, whose members sought inspiration in medieval art

vernacular: a term, derived from linguistics, referring to indigenous or humble architecture or furniture not consciously designed

Chapter 17: Africa

bedstead: a framework of wood or metal that supports a mattress

bou-bou: African traditional dress

elbow-chair: name for a European armchair in Ghana

Kente cloth: African strip cloth

sunsum: Ashanti (Ghanaian) spiritual principle of a seat's user

Chapter 18: Japan and Japanisme

biombo: Baroque Mexican screens based on Japanese prototypes

Shinto: indigenous pre-Buddhist religion of Japan

shogunate: a military political entity

shoji: partitions made of wood and paper

tansu: chests and cabinetry

tatami: modular straw mats

Chapter 19: Art Nouveau

aedicule: a small single-roomed structure used as a shrine

Art Nouveau: a nineteenth-century style characterized by stylized natural forms; important for decorative arts

azulejos: glazed tiles

curtain wall: a modern glass façade that is hung from a building's structure and is not self-supporting

Jugendstil: German variant of Art Nouveau

Modernisme: Spanish variant of Art Nouveau

Stile Liberty: Italian variant of Art Nouveau

Chapter 20: Protomodernism

avant-garde: culturally progressive, vanguard

Cubism: a modern art movement that emphasized geometric forms

Dada: a nihilistic art movement committed to formless expression and nonrepresentational form

De Stijl: twentieth-century Dutch art and architecture movement influenced by Cubism

Deutscher Werkbund: a German association of architects and designers beholden to functionalism; a harbinger of the Bauhaus

Expressionism: a modern art movement characterized by stylization, related to Cubism, and committed to representing inner experience

functionalism: a modernist design theory based on a building's or object's use

Futurism: an Italian movement inspired by technology and a Utopian urban view

Gesamtkunstwerk: unity of the arts—a nonhierarchical philosophy of the arts in which all arenas are equally valid and that supports collaboration across professional lines

Kunstwollen: "will to form," art historian Alois Riegl's concept of artistic volition

Ringstrasse: Vienna's nineteenth-century urban-renewal project

Russian Constructivism: a post-revolutionary Russian avant-garde movement, a utilitarian and technological form of modernism

Secessionists: a group of Viennese artists who sought to unite the arts and who were opposed to Art Nouveau and nineteenth-century historicism

Wiener Werkstätte: Viennese workshops, a business-oriented confederation whose intent was to foster the business prospects of the Secessionists

Chapter 21: Heroic Modernism

Bauhaus: the 1920s modern movement in Germany; also, a design school and a building of that school

brises-soleil: a porous façade screen that lets in air and casts the building in shadow

modernism: twentieth-century avant-garde movements that embraced functionalism and rejected ornamental and historic styles

pilotis: cylindrical free-standing columns associated with modernism and Le Corbusier

Surrealism: a modern movement inspired by dreams and the subconscious

Chapter 22: Art Deco, Traditional Design, and the Rise of the Decorator

Art Moderne: a term that often refers to a later phase of Art Deco, characterized by mechanical iconography (cars, trains, and buses)

Bakelite: synthetic rubber

Cubism: a modern art movement that emphasized geometric forms

ensemblier: a French term for one who creates an ensemble as an aesthetic action

linoleum: hard, washable flooring material made from cork and linseed oil on a canvas backing

Modern Baroque: a whimsical term for efflorescent modernist designs

robber barons: a pejorative term for nineteenth- and twentieth-century American industrialists

shagreen: the rough skin of a shark or dogfish, popular in the Art Deco period

vellum: translucent paper used as wallpaper in the Art Deco period

Chapter 23: Other Modernisms

Brutalism: name taken from a French word for raw concrete, *"beton brut"* and related to the art movement Art Brut. A strain of modernism that emphasized not perfection but materiality, especially that of concrete

International Style: a broad term for modernism that includes European and American works

minimalism: not a defined movement, but an artistic attitude that sought spirituality in the qualities of materials and sparsely designed space

Chapter 24: After Modernism

deconstruction or deconstructivism: an architectural movement of the late 1980s and 1990s, in tandem with a method of literary interpretation; with frequent references to popular culture, technology, common materials, and revealing structure, with formal similarities to Russian Constructivism

fiberglass: materials, including textiles, made from glass filaments

New Urbanism: the urban design strain of postmodernism that rejected urban modernism and sought to reshape town planning by relying on traditional civic planning

Pop Art: an art movement that recognized commerce and popular culture and the incorporation of found objects

postmodernism: a rejection of modernism, and a return to historically inspired forms, of the late 1970s and 1980s; related to a philosophy in which truths are not inherent but socially constructed

INDEX

Illustration Credits

Frontispiece: The Bridgeman Art Library/Getty Images
Preface Opener: © Klaus Leidorf/zefa/Corbis
Ch. 1 Opener: © Hitendra Sinkar Photography/Alamy
1.1: Photo © Michael Cope 2004 Hand axe from McGregor Museum, Kimberley, South Africa
1.2: The Bridgeman Art Library/Getty Images
1.3: Joe Cornish/Getty Images
1.4: c.istockphoto-katy15pints
1.5: c.istockphoto-fotoVoyager
1.6: © Les Gibbon/Alamy
1.8: © Diego Lezama Orezzoli/CORBIS
Ch. 2 Opener: Erich Lessing/Art Resource, NY
2.2: Courtesy of the author
2.3: The Art Archive/Dagli Orti
2.4: Werner Forman/Art Resource, NY
2.5: © The Art Archive/Corbis
2.6: © Roger Wood/CORBIS
2.7: © Andrea Jemolo/CORBIS
2.8: dbimages/Alamy
2.9: © Roger Wood/CORBIS
2.11: Photo © Boltin Picture Library/The Bridgeman Art Library
2.12: Michael Jacobs-Woodfin Camp
2.13: Robert Harding Picture Library Ltd/Alamy
2.14: Werner Forman/Art Resource, NY
2.15: University of Nebraska-Lincoln Libraries
2.16: University of Nebraska-Lincoln Libraries
2.17: Egyptian National Museum, Cairo, Egypt/The Bridgeman Art Library
2.18: Imagebroker/Alamy
2.19: Statue of King Senkamanisken; Nubian, Napatan Period, reign of Senkamanisken, 643–623 B.C.; Findspot: Nubia (Sudan), Gebel Barkal, B 500 Trench A; B 800 room 904; Granite gneiss; Height x width: 147.8 x 50.1 cm ($58\frac{3}{16}$ x $19\frac{3}{4}$ in.); Museum of Fine Arts, Boston; Harvard University—Boston Museum of Fine Arts Expedition, 23.731
2.20: Folding stool (reconstruction); Nubian, Meroitic Period, 1st century A.D.; Object Place: Sudan, Nubia, Meroe; Findspot: Sudan, Nubia, Meroe (Beg.), Tomb W 415; Wood, bronze and silver; Height: 39.5 cm ($15\frac{9}{16}$ in.); Museum of Fine Arts, Boston; Harvard University—Boston Museum of Fine Arts Expedition, 23.152
2.21: Conical eggshell-ware bowl; Nubian, Terminal A-Group, 3100–3000 B.C.; Findspot: Nubia (Egypt); Pottery; Height x rim diameter: 15.5 x 16.2 cm ($6\frac{1}{8}$ x $6\frac{3}{8}$ in.); Museum of Fine Arts, Boston; Gift of Dr. George A. Reisner, 19.1548
Ch. 3 Opener: Sites & Photos/Art Resource, NY
3.1: The Art Archive/Dagli Orti
3.2: Imagebroker/Alamy
3.3: Courtesy of the author
3.4: Art and Architecture Collection, Miriam and Ira D. Wallach Division of Art, Prints and Photographs, The New York Public Library, Astor lenox and Tilden Foundations.
3.5: © Lee Snider/Photo Images/CORBIS
3.6: Courtesy of the author
3.7: The Metropolitan Museum of Art, Gift of Norbert Schimmel Trust 1989 (1989.281.71) Image © The Metropolitan Museum of Art
3.8: Bildarchiv Preussischer Kulturbesitz/Art Resource, NY
3.9: Saridis S.A.
3.10: Bildarchiv Preussischer Kulturbesitz/Art Resource, NY
3.11: Saridis S.A.
3.12: Bildarchiv Preussischer Kulturbesitz/Art Resource, NY
3.13: Musee Municipal Antoine Vivenel, Compiegne, France/Lauros/Giraudon/The Bridgeman Art Library International
3.14: Musee Municipal, Laon, France/Lauros/Giraudon/The Bridgeman Art Library
3.15: © Ashmolean Museum, University of Oxford, UK/The Bridgeman Art Library International
3.17: the Gallatin Painter *Water jar (hydria)* (detail) Greek Late Archaic Period, about 490 BC Place of manufacture: Greece, Attica,Athens; Ceramic, Red figure; Height: 41.7 cm diameter 27cm; Photograph c. 2009, Museum Fine Arts Boston; Francis Bartlett Donation of 1912
3.18: © Italy Alan King/Alamy
3.19: © Roger Wood/CORBIS
3.20: Courtesy of the author
3.21: Vanni/Art Resource, NY
3.22: University of Nebraska-Lincoln Libraries
3.23: The Art Archive/Dagli Orti
3.24: © Cuchi White/CORBIS
3.25: Werner Forman/Art Resource, NY
3.26: Alinari/The Bridgeman Art Library
3.27: The Art Archive/Bibliothèque des Arts Décoratifs Paris/Dagli Orti
3.28: Bildarchiv Preussischer Kulturbesitz/Art Resource, NY
3.29: Image copyright © The Metropolitan Museum of Art/Art Resource, NY
Ch. 4 Opener: Scala/Art Resource, NY
4.1: © Atlantide Phototravel/Corbis
4.2: Courtesy of the author
4.3: CuboImages srl/Alamy
4.4: Bildarchiv Monheim GmbH/Alamy
4.5: The Art Archive/San Apollonaire Nuovo Ravenna/Dagli Orti
4.6: The Art Archive/San Vitale Ravenna Italy/Dagli Orti
4.7: Haghia Sophia, Istanbul, Turkey/The Bridgeman Art Library
4.8: Scala/Art Resource, NY
4.9: Alan King Cyprus/Alamy
4.10: The Art Archive/Archbishops Palace Ravenna Italy/Dagli Orti
4.11: Biblioteca Medicea-Laurenziana, Florence, Italy/The Bridgeman Art Library
4.12: © 2008 The British Library
4.13: University of Nebraska-Lincoln Libraries
4.14: University of Nebraska-Lincoln Libraries
4.15: Photo: Kojan & Krogvold/Universitetets Kulturhistoriske Museum, Oslo
Ch. 5 Opener: © nagelestock.com/Alamy
5.1: Bibliotheque Nationale, Paris, France/Giraudon/The Bridgeman Art Library
5.2: Erich Lessing/Art Resource, NY
5.3: Bildarchiv Monheim GmbH/Alamy
5.4: © Vanni Archive/CORBIS
5.5: Michael Busselle/Corbis
5.6: Courtesy of the author
5.7: © Jon Hicks/Corbis
5.8: Courtesy of the author
5.10: Courtesy of the author
5.11: © V&A Images, Victoria and Albert Museum
5.12: Erich Lessing/Art Resource, NY
5.13: © Musees cantonaux du Valais. Heinz Preisig, Sion
5.16: © Sandro Vannini/CORBIS
5.17: © Bruno Morandi/Robert Harding World Imagery/Corbis
5.18: © Murat Taner/zefa/Corbis
5.19: ©Topham/The Image Works
5.20: Réunion des Musées Nationaux/Art Resource, NY
5.21: Blaine Harrington/Dinodia Photo Library
5.22: Reproduced courtesy of; The Sudan Archaeological Research Society, London
5.23: © Roger Wood/CORBIS
5.24a: Popperfoto/Getty Images
5.24b: Reproduced courtesy of; The Sudan Archaeological Research Society, London
5.25: The Art Archive/Manuel Cohen
5.26: Coleccion Museo Franz Mayer, fotografo Jorge Vertiz
Ch. 6 Opener: © Interphoto Pressebildagentur/Alamy
6.1: © Richard Glover/CORBIS
6.2: Courtesy of the author
6.2: Bildarchiv Monheim GmbH/Alamy
6.3: © Massimo Listri/CORBIS
6.4: Erich Lessing/Art Resource, NY
6.5: © Mimmo Jodice/CORBIS
6.6: © Adam Woolfitt/CORBIS
6.7: Courtesy of the author
6.8: Réunion des Musées Nationaux/Art Resource, NY
6.9: Chris Hammond/Alamy
6.10: HIP/Art Resource, NY
6.11: Bridgeman-Giraudon/Art Resource, NY
6.12: Réunion des Musées Nationaux/Art Resource, NY
6.13: Linenfold paneled room; English, Tudor style, 16th century and later; Object Place: Europe, England; Oak, glass, stained glass; Museum of Fine Arts, Boston; Gift of Mrs. Edward Foote Dwight in memory of her father and mother George Parsons and Sarah Elizabeth; Eddy Parsons, 23.604.1-4
6.14: © age fotostock/SuperStock
6.15: Collection Rijksmuseum Amsterdam
6.17: Westminster Abbey, London, UK/The Bridgeman Art Library
6.18: The Print Collector/Alamy
6.19: Coleccion Museo Franz Mayer, Photograph by Michal Zabe'
Ch. 7 Opener: DEA/M.Borchi/Getty Images
7.1: Bildarchiv Steffens/Henri Stierlin/The Bridgeman Art Library
7.2: © age fotostock/SuperStock
7.3: Peter M. Wilson/Alamy
7.4: ©Werner Foreman/Topham/The Image Works
7.5: Courtesy of the author
7.6: Peter Horree/Alamy
7.7: © Macduff Everton/CORBIS
7.8: Macduff Everton/Getty Images
7.9: ©Rick Strange/AA World Travel/Topfoto/The Image Works
7.10: David Cole/Alamy
7.11: The Art Archive/Dagli Orti
7.12: The Art Archive/Museo del Templo Mayor Mexico/Dagli Orti
7.14: The Art Archive/Dagli Orti
7.15: © V&A Images, Victoria and Albert Museum
7.16: Craig Lovell/Eagle Visions Photography/Alamy
7.17a: Bildarchiv Steffens/Henri Stierlin/The Bridgeman Art Library
7.17b: mediacolor's/Alamy
7.18: © 2002 The Field Museum, A114206d, Object number 6.2832
7.19: Benson Latin American Collection-Univ. of Texas at Austin
7.20: Coleccion Museo Franz Mayer, Photograph by Jorge Vertiz
7.21: © Kelly-Mooney Photography/Corbis
Ch 8 Opener: © Roger Coulam/Alamy
8.1: © David Cumming; Eye Ubiquitous/CORBIS
8.2: © Christophe Boisvieux/Corbis
8.3: Ajanta, Maharashtra, India/The Bridgeman Art Library
8.4: © V&A Images, Victoria and Albert Museum
8.5: China Images/Alamy
8.6: Martin Puddy/Getty Images
8.7: IPN_John Martinotti/StockShop
8.8: Courtesy of the author
8.9: Tim Hall/Getty
8.10: Photo Mark Hinchman
8.11: Photo Mark Hinchman
8.12: © Luca Tettoni/Corbis
8.13: Arcaid/Alamy
8.15: Dennis Cox/Alamy
8.18: Victoria & Albert Museum, London/Art Resource, NY
8.19: Minneapolis Institute of Art/Gift of Ruth and Bruce Dayton
8.20: Minneapolis Institute of Art/Gift of Ruth and Bruce Dayton
8.21: © V&A Images, Victoria and Albert Museum
8.22: © V&A Images, Victoria and Albert Museum
8.23: Victoria & Albert Museum, London/Art Resource, NY
8.24: Minneapolis Institute of Art/Gift of Ruth and Bruce Dayton
8.25: Minneapolis Institute of Art/Gift of Ruth and Bruce Dayton
8.26: Minneapolis Institute of Art/Gift of Ruth and Bruce Dayton
8.27: © V&A Images, Victoria and Albert Museum
8.28: Clothes Cupboard Philadelphia Museum of Art: Gift of A.W. Bahr, 1939
Ch 9 Opener: DeA Picture Library/Art Resource, NY
9.1: ©The Print Collector/HIP/The Image Works
9.2: ©The Print Collector/HIP/The Image Works
9.3: © Massimo Listri/CORBIS
9.4: © Christie's Images/CORBIS
9.5: Courtesy of the author
9.6: © Guido Baviera/Grand Tour/Corbis
9.7: Erich Lessing/Art Resource, NY
9.8: Holmes Garden Photos/Alamy
9.9: bpk/RMN/René-Gabriel Ojéda/Art Resource, NY
9.10: © V&A Images, Victoria and Albert Museum
9.11: DeA Picture Library/Art Resource, NY
9.12: Private Collection/Joanna Booth/The Bridgeman Art Library
9.13: Erich Lessing/Art Resource, NY
9.14: Bildarchiv Monheim GmbH/Alamy
9.16: Collection Rijksmuseum Amsterdam
9.18: Scala/Art Resource, NY
9.19: Collection Rijksmuseum Amsterdam
9.20: The Metropolitan Museum of Art, Gift of George Blumenthal, 1941; (41.100.324-.327) Image © The Metropolitan Museum of Art
Ch 10 Opener: © Arcaid/Alamy
10.1: Vladimir Khirman/Alamy
10.2: Courtesy of the author
10.3: Courtesy of the author
10.4: Scala/Ministero per i Beni e le Attività culturali/Art Resource, NY
10.5: © Bob Krist/Corbis
10.6: Imagno/Getty Images
10.7: Erich Lessing/Art Resource, NY
10.8: © Georges Schneider/epa/Corbis
10.9: © Adam Woolfitt/CORBIS
10.10: Bildarchiv Monheim GmbH/Alamy
10.11: Erich Lessing/Art Resource, NY
10.12: Réunion des Musées Nationaux/Art Resource, NY
10.13: Andrzej Gorzkowski/Alamy
10.14: Réunion des Musées Nationaux/Art Resource, NY
10.15: Réunion des Musées Nationaux/Art Resource, NY
10.16: Réunion des Musées Nationaux/Art Resource, NY
10.18: National Trust/Photo: V&A Images/Victoria and Albert Museum
10.19: Private Collection/© Partridge Fine Arts, London, UK/The Bridgeman Art Library International
10.20: © V&A Images, Victoria and Albert Museum
10.21: © Partridge Fine Arts, London, UK/The Bridgeman Art Library
10.22: © RMN/Daniel Arnaudet/Art Resource, NY
10.23: © RMN/Droits réservés/Art Resource, NY
Ch 11 Opener: Erich Lessing/Art Resource, NY
11.1: Réunion des Musées Nationaux/Art Resource, NY
11.2: Image copyright © The Metropolitan Museum of Art/Art Resource, NY
11.3: DeA Picture Library/Art Resource, NY
11.4: The Art Archive/National Gallery of Scotland
11.5: Courtesy of the author
11.6: Scala/Art Resource, NY
11.7: Erich Lessing/Art Resource, NY
11.8: Bildarchiv Monheim GmbH/Alamy
11.9: © NTPL/Andreas von Einsiedel
11.10: DeA Picture Library/Art Resource, NY
11.11: Réunion des Musées Nationaux/Art Resource, NY
11.12: DeA Picture Library/Art Resource, NY
11.13: Mary Evans Picture Library/Alamy
11.14: Art Resource, NY
11.15: © V&A Images, Victoria and Albert Museum
11.16: Foto: Museum for Applied Art Frankfurt.
11.17: Foto: Museum for Applied Art Frankfurt.
11.18: Musee Conde, Chantilly, France/The Bridgeman Art Library International
11.19: © V&A Images, Victoria and Albert Museum
11.20: Art Resource, NY
11.21: © V&A Images, Victoria and Albert Museum
11.22: © V&A Images, Victoria and Albert Museum
11.23: © V&A Images, Victoria and Albert Museum
Ch 12 Opener: © Sandro Vannini/CORBIS
12.1: Tim Graham/Alamy
12.2: ©NTPL/J. Whitaker
12.3: © V&A Images, Victoria and Albert Museum
12.4: © V&A Images, Victoria and Albert Museum
12.5: © V&A Images, Victoria and Albert Museum
12.6: ©NTPL/Andreas von Einsiedel
12.7: ©NTPL/Andreas von Einsiedel
12.8: © V&A Images, Victoria and Albert Museum
12.9: University of Nebraska-Lincoln Libraries
12.10: Side chair about 1650–1700; Object Place: Boston, Massachusetts, United States; Maple, oak; 82.23 x 38.42 x 38.42 cm ($32\frac{3}{8}$ x $15\frac{1}{8}$ x $15\frac{1}{8}$ in.); Museum of Fine Arts, Boston; William E. Nickerson Fund, 1977.496
12.11: © V&A Images, Victoria and Albert Museum
12.12: High chest of drawers 1700–25; Object Place: Massachusetts, United States; Curly maple, mahogany inlay, modern brasses; Overall: 162.9 cm ($64\frac{1}{8}$ in.); Museum of Fine Arts, Boston; Bequest of Charles Hitchcock Tyler, 32.255
12.13: Dressing Table Philadelphia Museum of Art: Bequest of R. Wistar Harvey, 1940
12.14: Tea Table Philadelphia Museum of Art: Gift of John F. Haley, Jr. and Anne Rogers Haley in Memory of Fred F. Rogers, Jr., 1994
12.15: Side Chair Philadelphia Museum of Art: Gift of Daniel Blain Jr., 1997
12.16: Windsor bow-back arm chair 1797–1808; Object Place: United States; Benjamin Frothingham, American, 1734–1809; Ash, pine, maple Overall: 98.1 x 43.8 x 44.5 cm ($38\frac{5}{8}$ x $17\frac{1}{4}$ x $17\frac{1}{2}$ in.) Randall 199; Museum of Fine Arts, Boston; Annie A. Hawley Bequest Fund, 60.7
12.17: Chest on Chest Philadelphia Museum of Art: Gift of the heirs of Helen Cuyler Morris, who inherited the chest from her mother, Francis Lewis Cuyler, 1994
12.18: Art Resource, NY
12.19: DeA Picture Library/Art Resource, NY
12.20: Adrian Sherratt/Alamy
12.21: The London Art Archive/Alamy
12.22: The Metropolitan Museum of Art, Friends of the American Wing Fund, 1962 (62.16) Image © The Metropolitan Museum of Art
12.23: © Bonhams, London, UK/The Bridgeman Art Library
12.24: The Metropolitan Museum of Art, Gift of Charles K. Davis, 1946 (46.171.1a,b) Image © The Metropolitan Museum of Art
Ch. 13 Opener: © Peter Harholdt/CORBIS
13.1: Winterthur Museum, Bequest of… Photo by Lazlo Bodo
13.2: The Metropolitan Museum of Art, Gift of Mrs. J. Insley Blair, 1948 (48.1158.9) Image © The Metropolitan Museum of Art
13.3: The Metropolitan Museum of Art, Gift of Mrs. Russel Sage, 1909 (910.125.709) Image © The Metropolitan Museum of Art
13.4: Collection of the New-York Historical Society, USA/The Bridgeman Art Library